Mark Lightbody Mark was born and grew up in Montreal. Educated there and in London, Ontario, he holds an honours degree in journalism and among a variety of occupations, worked for a while in radio news. He has travelled in nearly 50 countries, visiting every continent but Antarctica. His first foray across Canada was made at age four. Since then he has repeated the trip numerous times using plane, train, car and thumb.

Aside from writing the Lonely Planet guide to Canada, Mark has worked for us on *Papua New Guinea – a travel survival kit*, *Australia – a travel survival kit*, *Malaysia, Singapore & Brunei* and *South-East Asia on a shoestring*.

He now lives in Toronto.

Acknowledgements

For this edition, thank yous to Jill and Konrad Sieciechowicz for their information from each end of the country, Michael Abraham, the next best thing to a Newfoundlander, and to Vince Duobaitis, my west coast guide extraordinaire.

Also warm thanks to those who sent letters, many of whom will see that their information was not neglected. And appreciation is due the travellers that I met across the country for their ideas and help, in particular Verena Hofer and Anita Gunzinger for their rides and picnics.

Lonely Planet Credits

Editor	Debbie Lustig
Designer, maps & colour	Peter Flavelle
Design & illustrations	Glenn Beanland
Additional maps	Graham Imeson
Typesetting	Ann Jeffree

Thanks also to the LP editors who helped proof-read, correct, index and *kvetch*: Jon Murray, Debbie Rossdale, Sue Mitra, Peter Turner, Katie Cody, Tom Smallman, Michelle de Kretser, James Lyon and Mr Everist.

This Edition

This edition, a major overhauling of the book, was a lot of work but a lot of fun. All the country's major cities and towns were re-visited and their sections re-written, and many smaller towns and rural areas were researched for the first time. New regions were added to every province and the chapters expanded. I travelled coast to coast and as always, got a few surprises. Some highlights included:

Sailing off the coast of Newfoundland in search of icebergs and whales. But the only thing I saw in the water was my breakfast when I lost it over the side. I wasn't the only one turning green.

Indicative of the increasing cosmopolitan developments in cities across Canada, I discovered not one but two new Vietnamese restaurants in Halifax, Nova Scotia. Over on Prince Edward Island, I circled nearly the entire province by car giving several beaches my personal attention.

On a quiet September night in a northern Quebec park, the wolves howling around the tent seemed so close I kept looking over my shoulder as I heaped wood on the fire to keep it good and bright.

Back home in Ontario, Ottawa celebrated the opening of the grand, new national art gallery. Some of the province's huge northland was visited, from gold-mining Timmins, with its welcoming October blizzard, to the great ports of Lake Superior, where I bumped into my old next door neighbor in a museum.

Crossing the prairies during a heatwave, it was so hot even the sky was sunburned. I left Edmonton for British Columbia one morning and at dinner learned that the city's first ever tornado had hit at noon, wiping out houses and tossing cars like confetti. Gotta keep movin'. In convivial Banff surrounded by mountains, people from all over the world, Texas to Tokyo, Stockholm to Sydney were met, and as usual, trails or dinner tables shared.

Fishing off Victoria in the Pacific Ocean for the first time I reeled in after getting a couple of good tugs on the line and nearly freaked to find a flippin' shark.

It's a huge country, there's always more to find.

Acknowledgements

Gun Andreasson (Sweden); Rob Atkins (UK); Mrs L J Cull (UK); Peter Duncan (Canada); Ruth Ennals (UK); Bob Finkelsteing (Canada); Mark Fisher (Australia); Vincent Foderg (Canada); D Hart (Australia); James Hitselberger (USA); Philip A Humphrey (Australia); Malka Kaufman (Canada); Ann Logan (Australia); Ruth Machachland (Canada); Rod Martin (UK); Jeff Mills; Stephen Mortimer (UK); Jennifer Munns (Canada); Lynn Owen (Canada); Jan T Pollack (Canada); Janice Ruhl (USA); J Schiebelbeing (Canada); Laura Schisgall; Audrey Walsh (Australia); William Wang (USA); Brian Waters (Canada).

A Warning & a Request

Things change – prices go up, schedules change, good places go bad and bad places go bankrupt – nothing stays the same. So if you find things better or worse, recently opened or long since closed, please write and tell us and help make the next edition better! All information is greatly appreciated and the best letters will receive a free copy of the next edition, or any other Lonely Planet book of your choice.

Extracts from the best letters are also included in the *Lonely Planet Update*. The *Update* helps us make useful information available to you as soon as possible – it's like reading an up-to-date notice board or postcards from a friend. Each edition contains hundreds of useful tips, and advice from the best possible source of information – other travellers. The *Lonely Planet Update* is published quarterly in paperback and is available from bookshops and by subscription. Turn to the back pages of this book for more details.

Contents

Introduction

Canada is big, spacious, rugged, uncluttered and tremendously varied. You can stand in isolated places where perhaps nobody else has ever stood, yet the cities are large and modern, offering art and culture as a balance.

From the Atlantic Ocean it's over 7000 km to the Pacific coast. In between, you can have a coffee and a croissant at a sidewalk café or canoe on a silent northern lake. You can peer down from the world's tallest building or over the walls of a centuries-old fort. You can hike amid snow-capped peaks or watch the sunset where it's an unobstructed 30 km view to the horizon.

The four very different seasons can bring the winters Canada is known for, but also sweltering hot summer days and a beautiful range from one to the other.

It's said that the national personality was shaped by life in a northern frontier; people constantly came from the wild to the settled areas and back again. Because the country is so young, a modern identity is still forming. But it's there, distinctly different from Canada's neighbours' to the south. The cultural mosaic is made up of English, French and many other peoples, from Europeans to Far Easterners.

Inflation has dropped to 5% or below in the past few years, so prices haven't been rising dramatically. The Canadian dollar remains low compared with the US greenback, making exchange rates excellent for Americans while holding steady for many other currencies. For Canadians, this is another good reason to see the homeland.

With its history, people, land and nature, Canada has a lot to offer the traveller.

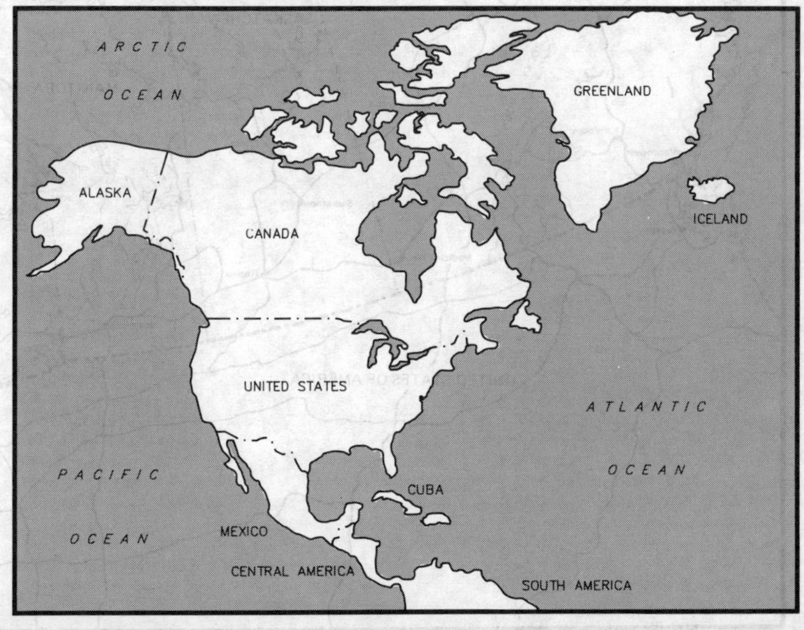

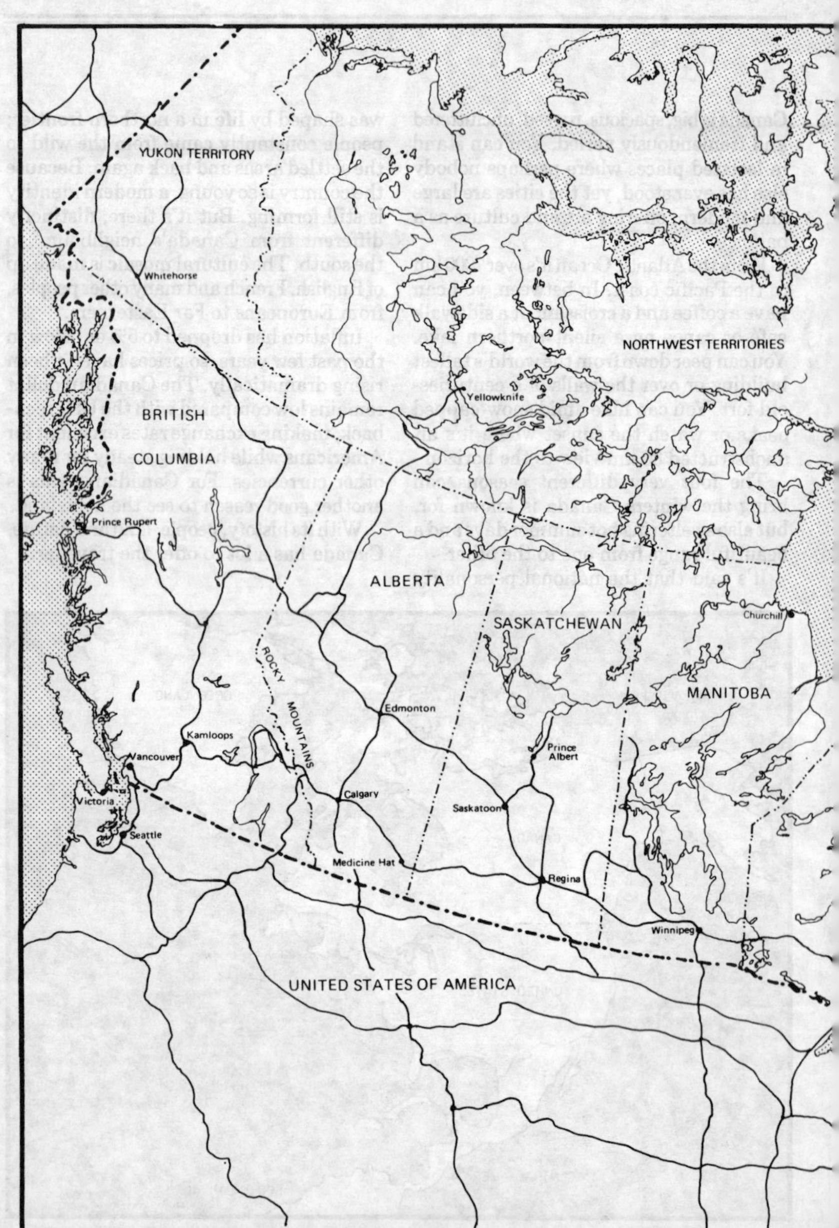
YUKON TERRITORY
Whitehorse
NORTHWEST TERRITORIES
Yellowknife
BRITISH
COLUMBIA
Prince Rupert
ALBERTA
SASKATCHEWAN
Churchill
MANITOBA
ROCKY
MOUNTAINS
Edmonton
Kamloops
Vancouver
Prince Albert
Calgary
Victoria
Saskatoon
Seattle
Medicine Hat
Regina
Winnipeg
UNITED STATES OF AMERICA

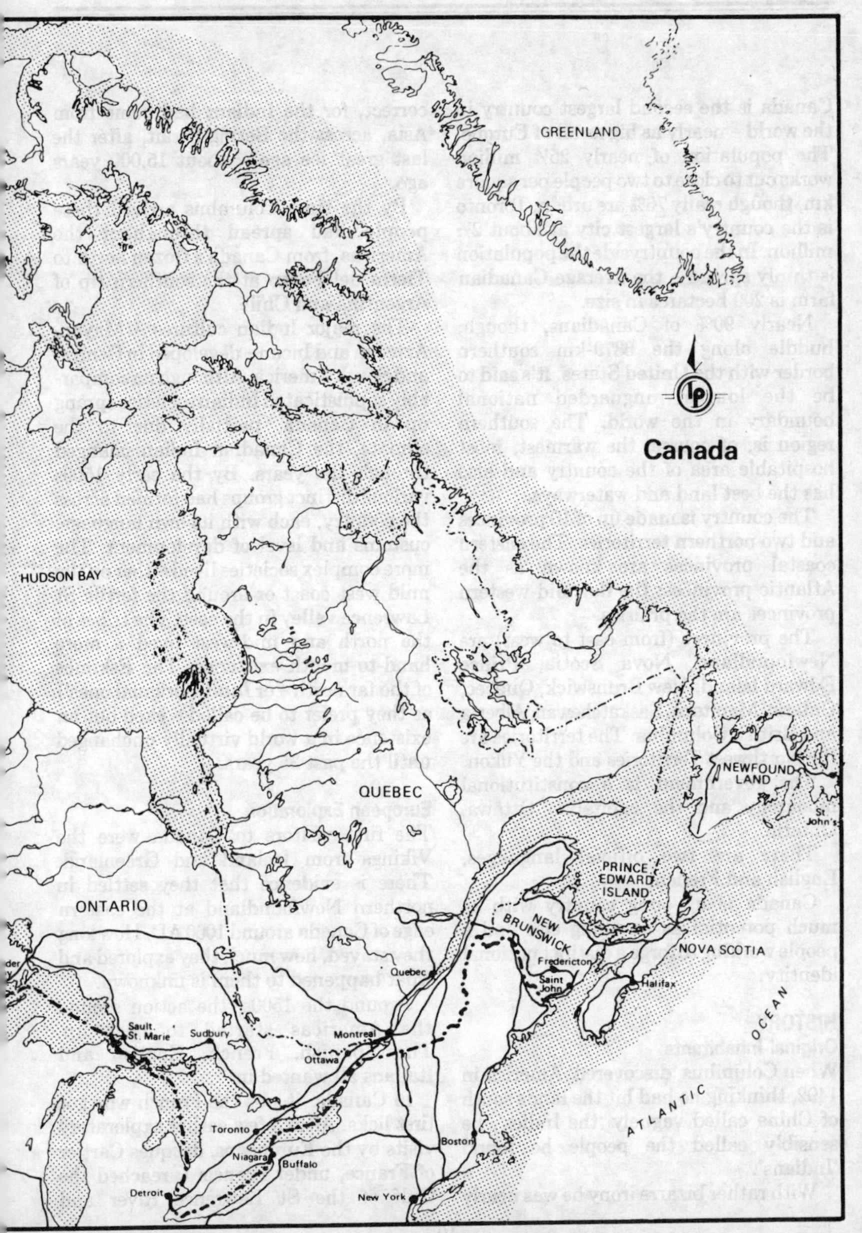
GREENLAND
Canada
HUDSON BAY
QUEBEC
ONTARIO
NEWFOUND-
LAND
St John's
PRINCE
EDWARD
ISLAND
NEW
BRUNSWICK
NOVA SCOTIA
Fredericton
Saint
John
Halifax
ATLANTIC
OCEAN
Quebec
Montreal
Ottawa
Sault
St. Marie
Sudbury
Toronto
Niagara
Buffalo
Boston
Detroit
New York

Facts about the Country

Canada is the second largest country in the world – nearly as big as all of Europe. The population of nearly 25½ million works out to close to two people per square km, though really 76% are urban. Toronto is the country's largest city at about 2½ million. In the countryside the population is thinly spread – the average Canadian farm is 200 hectares in size.

Nearly 90% of Canadians, though, huddle along the 6379-km southern border with the United States. It's said to be the longest unguarded national boundary in the world. The southern region is, of course, the warmest, most hospitable area of the country and also has the best land and waterways.

The country is made up of 10 provinces and two northern territories. The eastern coastal provinces are known as the Atlantic provinces; the flat mid-western provinces are the prairies.

The provinces (from east to west) are Newfoundland, Nova Scotia, Prince Edward Island, New Brunswick, Quebec, Ontario, Manitoba, Saskatchewan, Alberta and British Columbia. The territories are the Northwest Territories and the Yukon.

The government is a constitutional monarchy and the capital is Ottawa, Ontario.

There are two official languages, English and French.

Canada is a young country with as much potential as anything else and a people working to forge a distinct national identity.

HISTORY

Original Inhabitants

When Columbus 'discovered' America in 1492, thinking he had hit the lands south of China called vaguely 'the Indies', he sensibly called the people he found 'Indians'.

With rather bizarre irony he was nearly correct, for the Indians had come from Asia, across the Bering Strait, after the last great ice age – about 15,000 years ago.

By the time Columbus arrived these people had spread throughout the Americas, from Canada's frozen north to Tierra del Fuego at the southern tip of Argentina and Chile.

The major Indian cultures – Mayan, Aztecan and Incan – developed in Central and South America. Although no comparably sophisticated Indian societies sprang up in Canada, partially due to the climate, the Canadian Indian changed through the years. By the early 1500s various distinct groups had formed across the country, each with its own language, customs and level of development. The more complex societies lived either on the mild west coast or around the fertile St Lawrence valley in the east. The tribes of the north and mid-west lived a more hand-to-mouth existence. The Eskimos of the far north – or *Inuit* ('original ones') as they prefer to be called – eked out an existence in a world virtually unchanged until the past 35 years.

European Exploration

The first visitors to Canada were the Vikings from Iceland and Greenland. There is evidence that they settled in northern Newfoundland at the eastern edge of Canada around 1000 AD. How long they stayed, how much they explored and what happened to them is unknown.

Around the 1500s, the action around the Americas started to heat up. The Spanish, French, English and Italians all wanted in.

In Canada, it was the French who got first licks. After a few earlier exploratory visits by the Europeans, Jacques Cartier of France, under Francis I, reached the Gulf of the St Lawrence River and claimed all the surrounding area for France. The year was 1534. It was probably from Cartier that Canada got its name. Originally Kanata, a Huron-Iroquois word for village or small community, its derivative showed up in Cartier's journal. The name became used for the St Lawrence area and eventually became the official name of the new country.

The French didn't bother much with this new colony throughout the 1500s, but the economic development pattern which began then has continued through Canada's past to the present. This is, put bluntly and simply, the selling of its resources to whomever is buying, thus enabling the country to pay for everything else it needs. The first commodities prized by the French were the fish of the east coast and furs for the fashion-conscious of France.

Samuel de Champlain, another Frenchman, began further explorations in the early 1600s. He settled Quebec City, and Montreal was founded soon after in 1642 as a missionary outpost. Throughout the 17th century fur-trading companies dominated this new world. In 1663 Canada became a province of France. There were about 60,000 French settlers by then – they are the ancestors of a good percentage of today's French Canadians.

Throughout the 1600s the French fought the Indians, who soon realised that they were getting a raw deal in land development and the fur trade. The French kept busy, too, with further explorations. They built a long chain of forts down to Louisiana in the southern US – another major settlement. In the 1730s another of the major explorers, Pierre Gaultier de Varennes, Sieur de la Verendrye, was responsible for another series of forts. This one stretched across the south of what are now the provinces of Ontario, Manitoba and Saskatchewan.

The Struggle for Power

Of course, the British weren't just sipping pints through all this. Though concentrating on the lands of the US east coast, the Hudson's Bay Company (still one of Canada's main department-store chains) had moved into the Hudson Bay area in northern Ontario around 1670.

The British soon muscled into settlements on the Canadian east coast. By 1713 they had control over much of Nova Scotia and Newfoundland. And then, for a while, there was peace.

In 1745 a British army from New England, America, moved north and captured a French fort in Nova Scotia. The struggle for control of the new land was on. What is known as the Seven Years' War began in 1754. The French held the upper hand for the first four years. In one of Canada's most famous battles, the English defeated the French at Quebec City in 1759. Both General Wolfe, leader of the English, and the Marquis de Montcalm, who led the French, were killed in battle. After this major victory, the British turned the tide. At the Treaty of Paris in 1763, France handed Canada over to the British.

The British, however, didn't quite know how to manage the newly acquired territory. The population was nearly exclusively French. At the time in Britain, Roman Catholics had very few rights. They couldn't vote or hold office. In 1774 the Quebec Act gave the French Canadians the right to their religion, the use of French civil law in court and the possibility of assuming political office. The British, however, maintained positions of power and influence in politics and business. It was during this period that the seeds of the Quebec separatist movement were sown.

During the American Revolution against Britain, 1775-1783, about 50,000 settlers – termed 'Loyalists' due to their loyalty to Britain – shifted north to Canada. They settled mainly in the Atlantic provinces and Ontario.

This migration helped to balance the number of French and English in Canada.

Soon after, Quebec and Ontario were formed with their own governors. Throughout the late 1700s and into the 1800s Canada's frontiers were pushed further and further afield. Sir Arthur Mackenzie explored the north (Mackenzie River) and much of British Columbia. Simon Fraser followed the river named after him to the Pacific Ocean. David Thompson travelled the Columbia River, also in British Columbia. In 1812, Lord Selkirk formed a settlement of Scottish immigrants around the Red River Valley near Winnipeg, Manitoba.

Also in 1812, the last war between Canada and America began. Its causes were numerous, but the American attempt to take over its northern neighbour was only part of the campaign against Britain. Each side won a few battles, and in 1814 a draw was declared.

The Dominion Period

With the American threat ended and the resulting confidence in themselves, many of the colonists became fed up with some aspects of British rule. Others spoke out for independence. In both Upper (Ontario) and Lower (Quebec) Canada, brief rebellions broke out. In 1840 both areas became united with one government, but by now the population in Upper (English, mainly) outnumbered that in Lower Canada (French) and wanted more than a half say. The government bogged down, with Britain attempting to work out something new. Again you can see the historical disputes between the British and French.

Britain, of course, didn't want to lose Canada completely as it had the United States, so it stepped lightly and decided on a confederation giving a central government some powers and the individual colonies others.

In 1867 the British North American Act (BNA Act) was passed by the British government. This established the Dominion of Canada and included Ontario, Quebec, Nova Scotia and New Brunswick. The BNA Act became Canada's equivalent to a constitution, though far less detailed and all-inclusive. John A Macdonald became Canada's first prime minister. The total population was 3½ million, nearly all living in the east and mostly on farms. It had been decided at the Act's signing in 1867 that other parts of the country should be included in the Dominion whenever possible.

The completion of the Canadian Pacific Railway – one of Canada's great historical sagas – joined the west coast with the east, literally linking those areas with the Dominion. By 1912 all provinces had become part of the central government except Newfoundland, which finally joined in 1949.

In the last few years of the 19th century Canada received large numbers of immigrants, mainly from Europe.

The government continued to grapple with French and English differences. These reached a peak during WW I, which Canada had entered immediately on Britain's behalf. In 1917, despite bitter French opposition in Quebec, the Canadian government began a military draft.

The Modern Era

After the war Canada slowly grew in stature and prosperity, and in 1931 became a voluntary member of the Commonwealth.

With the onset of WW II, Canada again supported Britain, but this time also began defence agreements with the US, and after Pearl Harbor, declared war on Japan.

After the war Canada experienced another huge wave of European immigration. The post-war period saw economic expansion and prosperity right across North America.

The 1960s brought social upheaval and social welfare programmes with their ideals and liberalism. Canada's first Bill of Rights was signed in 1960. Nuclear-power generators and American nuclear warheads in Canada became major issues. The Quebec separatist movement attracted more attention. A small group used terrorism to press its point for an independent Quebec. In 1976 the Parti Quebecois, advocating separatism, won the provincial election. Since that time, though, sentiments have changed and separation is pretty much a forgotten if not dead issue. In 1980, a Quebec referendum found most Quebecers against independence. Topics of most concern now seem to be based on economics, not ideology.

In 1967 the country celebrated its 100th anniversary with the World's Fair in Montreal – Expo – as one of the highlights.

The 1988 World Economic Summit of the world's seven major industrial nations was held in Toronto and the winter Olympics were hosted in Calgary, each bringing increased prestige and favourable attention to our somewhat fragile international self-image.

GEOGRAPHY

Canada is about 7730 km across yet still its only neighbour is the US, which includes Alaska in the north-west. With such size the country can boast a tremendous variety of topography. Though much of the land is lake and river-filled forest, there are mountains, plains and even a small desert. Canada has (or shares with the Americans) seven of the world's largest lakes and also contains three of the globe's longest 20 rivers. The country is blessed with the most fresh water of any country. About 25% of the country is covered in forest. Canada's highest mountain, Mt Logan at 5950 metres, is found in the south-west Yukon.

There are five main regions, plus the vast Arctic region.

The far eastern area includes Newfoundland, Prince Edward Island, New Brunswick, Nova Scotia and part of Quebec. The land is mainly hilly and wooded.

The St Lawrence-Great Lakes Lowland is the area between Quebec City and Windsor, Ontario, and includes most of the large towns, cities and industry. In all, about half of Canada's people live here. The land, once all used for farming, is generally flat.

Most of the north is taken up by the Canadian Shield, also known as the Precambrian Shield, formed 2.5 billion years ago. This geographic area covers all of northern Manitoba, Ontario and Quebec and stretches further east and west from there. It's an enormous, ancient, rocky, glacially sanded region of typically Canadian river and lake-filled timberland. It is rugged, cool and little developed, with mining and logging the two primary ingredients in human settlement.

Through Manitoba, Saskatchewan and parts of Alberta are the plains – a huge, flat region responsible for Canada's abundant wheat crop.

The fifth area is the Mountain Region covering most of British Columbia, parts of Alberta and the Yukon. The Rocky Mountains form the eastern edge of the region. They rise from 2000 to 4000 metres. Along the western coast is another range of mountains. In between lies a long, narrow valley called the Rocky Mountain Trench. The interior of BC consists of valleys, plateaux, hills and basins. The province is by far the most scenic in the country.

CLIMATE

Seasons

Summer: June-August
Fall: September-October
Winter: November-March
Spring: April-May

As you can see, the winters are long. In more than two-thirds of the country the average January temperature is -18°C (below zero Fahrenheit). The warmest areas of the country are the BC coast and southern Ontario and Niagara, with the longest summers and shortest winters.

The west and east coasts are very wet with 2500 mm of precipitation a year. The prairies are fairly dry, and south-eastern Canada is humid. Outside the main cities, nights are cool all year round.

Along the US border, summer temperatures are usually in the mid and upper 20s Celsius (75-85°F). Each year there are a few days in the 30s Celsius (86-100°F).

WILDLIFE

Canada, with so much land, much of it relatively remote, is abundant in wildlife yet conservation is an ongoing necessity. Campers and hikers, with any luck at all, can see a number of different animals in the wild. The following are some of the most interesting and/or most common.

Bears

These are Canada's largest and most dangerous animals. They are widely distributed, and as there are four types, most of the country is populated with at least one kind. For detailed information on the hazards of bears, see the Dangers & Annoyances section in the Facts for the Visitor chapter.

Grizzly Bear This is the most notorious. It is found on the higher slopes of the Rocky and Selkirk Mountains of British Columbia, Alberta and the Yukon. The grizzly is big – standing up to 275 cm high. It can be recognised by the white ends of its brownish hair and the hump on the back behind its neck. It can't see well but makes up for that with its excellent senses of smell and hearing. To make matters worse, it's a very fast animal. The best thing about a grizzly is that it can't climb trees. Like other bears, it is normally afraid of people but can be unpredictable and is easily provoked.

Black Bear This bear is found all across Canada and is the one most likely to be spotted. The black bear often mooches around campgrounds, cottages and garbage dumps. It is usually less than 150 cm long and 90 kg in weight. It's active during the day and unfortunately can climb trees.

Brown Bear Actually a black bear but brown in colour, the nocturnal brown bear is found mainly in BC, Alberta and the Yukon.

Polar Bear The polar bear is very large – up to 680 kg – with thick, whitish fur. It is found only in the extreme north but can be viewed in zoos. A majestic animal, it is graceful in the water despite its size and apparent awkwardness. Due to hunting, it is now a protected animal.

Beaver
One of Canada's symbols, the beaver is an animal known for its industriousness, hence the expression 'busy as a beaver'. Found all across Canada, it is usually seen in the early morning or early evening paddling across a stream or lake, its head just above water. It chews down trees for food and for material with which to build its home. This home looks like a rounded pile of mud and sticks and is located in streams and ponds dammed off by the beaver.

Buffalo
The buffalo exists only in government parks. It is a huge, mean-looking animal but is really little more than a cow. Its near extinction has become symbolic of Europeans' effect on North American Indians and their environment. Technically, Canadian buffalo are bison, not buffalo.

Wolf
The wolf looks like a large, silver-grey dog. Its ferocious reputation is more myth than fact. Hunting has pretty well banished it to the northland but you may hear the wolf's howl late at night if you're in the bush. It usually hunts in packs and rarely harms humans.

Coyote
More widespread than the wolf, the coyote is smaller and more timid, with an eerie howl used for communicating. It is now more scavenger than hunter and is often the victim of massive poison-bait campaigns by western ranchers and farmers.

Deer
Various types are plentiful in the woodlands of Canada, ranging across the entire width of the country. They are very quiet and timid and the object of much hunting.

Moose
This is one of the largest animals and a popular target for hunters. The moose is found in woods and forests all across Canada, particularly around swamps. Moose are for the most part a more northerly ranging animal than deer. They have large, thick antlers and are brown. The moose is very reclusive, generally solitary and may be seen swimming to escape biting bugs. The male bellows in October and November hunting for a mate. At this time, their behaviour can be erratic and the normally timid moose can become aggressive.

Rocky Mountain Goat
This goat is as close as you can get to an all-Canadian animal. Found in BC and the Yukon, it is white, hairy, has horns and looks like an old man. Around populated areas it is quite tame. Generally though, it prefers the higher, more remote mountain regions. One of its food staples is clay, and you may see one pawing at the ground and gobbling up clumps of earth. Strange but true.

Lynx
Another nearly exclusively Canadian animal, the lynx is a grey cat about 900 mm long and is found all across Canada. It has furry trim around its face and sharp pointed ears. The mainly nocturnal cat eats small animals. Humans are its main enemy.

Skunk
The skunk resembles a large black cat but has a white stripe down its back and a big, bushy tail. It is seen everywhere – in woods, around garbage, in larger city parks, even in residential suburbs. It's dangerous only in that its defence mechanism is the spraying-out of the foulest, longest-lasting, clothes-clingingest

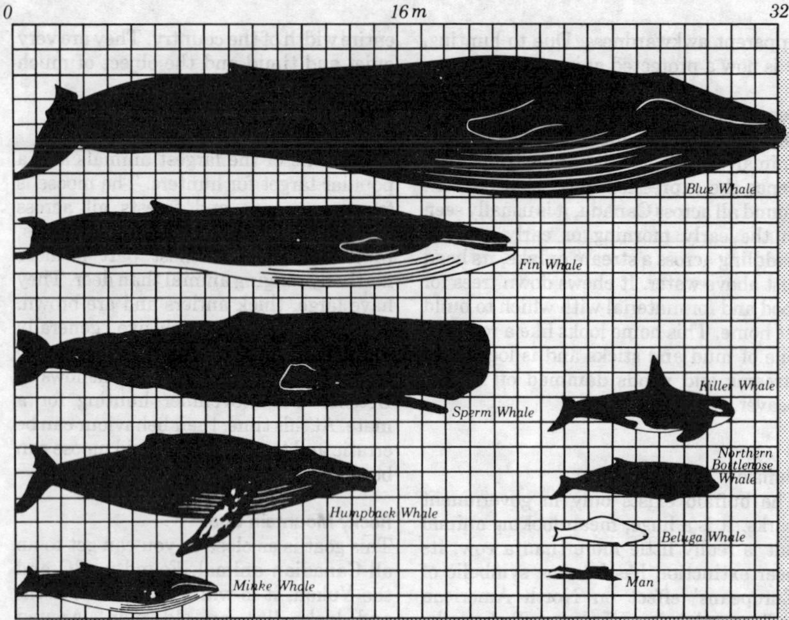

smell you can imagine. The cure is a bath in tomato juice. Watch out!

Porcupine
A very curious animal about 900 mm long, the porcupine weighs 18 kg. It is grey, lives in the woods across Canada and feeds mainly on bark and tree buds. Its protection from abuse is its hollow, barbed quills which project from its body like long hair. They are very easily dislodged, as many a dog will remember.

Caribou or Reindeer
These animals live in herds in the far north and are still used by some Inuit for food and for their hides. Their numbers are now carefully monitored, as over-hunting and radioactive fallout have affected them. A full herd on its seasonal migration is said to be a wondrous sight.

Birds
Five hundred species have been spotted in Canada but many of them are quite rare. Some of the more notable among our feathered residents are the loon, a water bird, with a mournful yet beautiful call which is often heard on the quieter lakes across the country in early morning or evening. It is most abundant in northern Ontario.

Canada geese are seen across the country, especially during spring and fall migration when their large V-shaped formations are a not unusual sight in the sky. Big, black and grey, these so called honkers can be aggressive.

There are many varieties of duck, the mallard being most common. The whiskey jack, found mainly in the Rockies, is a fluffy, friendly and very commonly seen bird that will eat out of your hand. Owls may be seen or heard in wooded areas across the country. Sparrows of countless, but practically indistinguishable, species are the most common garden songbirds.

Whales & Seals

Whale-watching has become so popular it is now a successful commercial enterprise (a point for the conservationists). A number of different species can be seen off the coast in BC, in the St Lawrence River in Quebec, and in the Atlantic Ocean off the country's east coast.

In the Atlantic provinces the bloody, annual seal hunt (for pelts, boots, coats, etc) has finally diminished following the European Common Market ban on imports (another point for animal welfare).

Fish

Northern pike, bass and trout are the most common freshwater fish. Salmon is found on the west coast and a highly sought after freshwater version lives in the Atlantic provinces. Arctic Char, found only in the far north (and some southern menus), is very fine eating.

GOVERNMENT

Pierre Elliot Trudeau, a liberal, became Canada's prime minister in 1968 and, except for a brief period in 1979, held power until his retirement in 1984. Despite great initial support and international recognition, Trudeau was, to be kind, not a popular man at the end of his stay. During his leadership, however, he was largely responsible for the formation of a Canadian Constitution, the last step in full independence from Britain. It came into being in 1982.

The 1984 election saw the Progressive Conservatives, led by Brian Mulroney, sweep into power with a tremendous nationwide majority, slamming the door on the Trudeau era.

Following the customary pattern, this government, too, has now fallen from grace with a large thump. Major issues of late have been Mulroney's very controversial attempts to establish free trade with the United States and overhauling the distinctions between provincial and federal powers, rights and jurisdictions. The colossal national debt is another concern. As far as I can tell there is no political saviour waiting in the wings to sweep the country off its feet.

Canada's Rhinoceros Party has begun its charge up to the next federal election.

While the Conservatives, Liberals and New Democrats go on about interest rates, trade, defence and taxation, the Rhinos, who won almost 100,000 out of 12.5 million votes in each of the past two elections, want to:

- pay off the national debt with credit cards.
- use bubble gum as currency that they can inflate and deflate at will.
- sell seats in the Senate for $10.
- move the Rocky Mountains to improve the view.
- press for an abortion policy that is retroactive for politicians.
- draw a 200-mile offshore limit in watercolor so that fish will see it and stay within Canadian waters.
- repeal the law of gravity.

The Flag

Canada's current flag was proclaimed in 1965 after 2000 public design entries were hotly debated in parliament. The side bars represent the ocean boundaries and are not blue because an important reason for the entire procedure was to fly independence from England and France. Before the new flag, the Red Ensign, which included a Union Jack, rippled over the country from 1924.

PEOPLE

About 45 of every 100 Canadians are of British stock. French descendants of the original pioneers make up about 30% of the population. Most people of French descent live in Quebec but there are large numbers in New Brunswick, Ontario and Manitoba.

The English-speaking population has

grown mainly by immigration from the Old Country and the US. Over 3½ million Canadians are of Scottish or Irish ancestry.

Generally speaking, the French are Catholic, the English Protestant, but religion does not play a large part in Canadian life.

Early European settlers went to the prairies but can now be found everywhere, particularly in the large cities. Canada's third largest ethnic group is German. Other major groups are Italian, Ukrainian, Dutch, Greek, Polish and Scandinavian. Recently, Asians and to lesser degrees, Latin Americans and Blacks from the Caribbean have been immigrating in larger numbers.

The native Indians now number about 300,000 and the Inuit about 20,000, totalling about a third more than before Europeans arrived. Inuit is the general name for the Eskimo peoples in Canada. This is their preferred name, as it distinguishes them from the Eskimo of Asia or the Aleuts.

Since the early pioneering days the Indians' lot has led to sadness, even tragedy. At first their numbers dropped dramatically with the influx of European diseases. Then, they lost not only their power and traditions but also their land and eventually, in many cases, their self-respect.

About 72% of the Indians now live on government reservations, most in poverty. In the cities, with little education and few modern skills, many end up on skid row.

Indian leaders have recently become more political, making stands on constitutional matters, land claims and mineral rights. It is through these channels, however slow-moving, that the native voice will be heard in the future.

Canadian Inventions

Canadians can lay claim to quite an assortment of the products of human ingenuity. The Indians have given the world snowshoes and the birchbark canoe;

The Canadian coat of arms includes elements from English, Irish, Scottish and French heraldry, as well as Canada's own maple leaf.

the Inuit developed the winter parka and accompanying boots known as *mukluks*. More recent inventions include the electron microscope and the clothes zipper (a mixed blessing!).

Canadians have been active in the food arena, too. Important research developed strains of wheat suitable to a variety of world climates. Pablum, baby cereal, was created in Canada and perhaps even more significant was the development of instant mashed potatoes.

Other firsts include the paint roller (a simple yet great little device), the telephone, the friction match and the snowmobile.

Canada also developed the manipulable space arm used on the US space shuttle craft.

Insulin was discovered by Banting and Best in 1921.

ACTIVITIES

Canada's greatest attribute is its natural environment. This, for the most part, is what it has to offer visitors, what makes it unique. Much of Canada's appeal lies in the range of physical activities possible. Camping, hiking, canoeing, fishing and observing flora and fauna quickly come to mind. There are wilderness trips of all types, organised or self-directed. Long-distance cycling has become more popular recently. There is downhill skiing in many parts of the country – slopes in the Rockies are excellent and higher than any in the European Alps. Hang-gliding is always gaining converts. People even surf off the west coast. And if you want to try your luck, you can pan for gold.

Provincial tourist offices have information on activities in their regions, and also details on private businesses offering adventure tours and trips. Many provinces have booklets and maps on canoeing and hiking. All have information on national and provincial parks, many of which can be highlights of a trip to Canada.

But also enticing are the clean, safe and vital cities where you can find arts and cultural activities if the outdoors starts to wear you down.

Entering the various lotteries is a favourite Canadian pastime.

National Parks

Canada has over 30 national parks, ranging from coast to coast and from the US border to the far north. Each has been developed to protect, preserve and make accessible a unique, special or otherwise interesting and significant environment. The network continues to expand with a few new ones currently in the works. All of them are well worth visiting. Parks Canada produces a good little booklet, *National Parks of Canada*, which outlines the features and facilities of the parks. Most have camping. Several are close to major population centres and are heavily used, others are more remote and offer good wilderness opportunities. Many manage to combine both characteristics. Among the most popular are Fundy National Park in Nova Scotia and all of the ones in the western Rocky Mountains.

Some parks rent canoes and/or rowboats. In parks with numerous lakes and rivers, a canoe is ideal; you can portage to different lakes. Doing this a few times may be hard work but you'll be rewarded with peace and solitude.

Entrance fees to national parks are $2, or $10 for a year.

In addition to national parks, the system contains over 70 National Historic Parks and sites. These are for 'day use only' and present various aspects of Canadian history, from forts to pioneer homesteads to early Viking settlements. Most include interpretation centres, some with costumed workers, which offer an accurate glimpse of life during an earlier era. Many have picnic areas.

For more information on the national and provincial parks, see under 'Camping' in the Accommodation section of the Facts for the Visitor chapter.

World Heritage Sites
Canada has nine sites designated by the World Heritage Convention of the United Nations. Six of these are natural and all are either national or provincial parks. They are: Nahanni National Park, Kluane National Park, the Rocky Mountain Parks, Wood Buffalo National Park, Dinosaur Provincial Park and Head-Smashed-In Bison Jump, Alberta. The remaining three involve human endeavour: Anthony Island Provincial Park in British Columbia, an old Haida Indian settlement; L'Anse Aux Meadows in Newfoundland, a 1000-year-old Viking camp; and Quebec City, a European-like gem.

Sports
Canada's official national sport is lacrosse, an old Indian game similar to soccer but played with a small ball and sticks. Each stick has a woven leather basket in which the ball is caught and carried.

The sport that really creates passion, however, is ice hockey. To play professionally is the Canadian little boy's dream. This is especially true in Quebec, home of the Montreal Canadiens, a hockey legend and one of the most consistently successful professional sports teams anywhere. If you're in Canada in winter, a game between good teams is recommended.

American-style football, though with some modifications, is also very popular, and American baseball has gained a good following now that there are teams in Montreal and Toronto.

Skating on frozen rivers and outdoor ice rinks is a common, pleasant way to exercise. Joggers are now a familiar sight, too.

Events
Major events are listed under the city or town where they occur. There are many others.

Tourism Canada, the federal information office, publishes a small booklet each year called *Events & Attractions*. It doesn't cover all events and offers little description.

Provincial tourist departments print up more detailed and extensive lists of their own, which include cultural and sporting exhibitions and happenings of all kinds. Military and historic celebrations, ethnic festivals and music shows are all included. Some provinces produce separate booklets for summer and winter activities and events.

Major provincial and national holidays are usually cause for some celebration, especially in summer when events often wrap up with a fireworks display.

HOLIDAYS & FESTIVALS

National Holidays

New Year's Day
  1 January
Easter
  Good Friday, Easter Monday
Victoria Day
  Mid-May
Canada Day
  1 July
Labour Day
  First Monday in September
Thanksgiving
  Second Monday in October
Remembrance Day
  11 November (banks & government)
Christmas Day
  25 December

Provincial Holidays

Newfoundland
  St Patrick's Day, mid-March; St George's Day, end of April; Discovery Day, end of June; Memorial Day, beginning of July; Orangeman's Day, mid-July
Quebec
  St Jean Baptiste Day, 24 June
Yukon
  Discovery Day, second week in August
All other provinces
  1 August (or close to it)

LANGUAGE

English and French are the two official

languages of Canada. You will notice both on highway signs, maps, tourist brochures and cereal boxes. The French spoken in Canada is not the language of France. At times it can be nearly unintelligible to a Parisian. It also varies from region to region. The native tongue of Quebec is known as Quebecois or *joual*, but variations occur around the province.

Many immigrants use their mother tongue, as do the Indians and the Inuit. Few white Canadians speak any Indian or Inuit language but some words such as igloo, parka and kayak are commonly used. The Inuit language is interesting for its specialisation and use of many words for what appears to be the same thing; eg, the word for 'seal' depends on whether it's old or young, in or out of the water. There are 20 or so words for 'snow', depending on its consistency and texture.

French for the Traveller

Following is a short guide to some French words and phrases for the traveller. In the third column, the combination 'ohn' should sound very nasal. The 'n' shouldn't be pronounced. Quebec French employs a lot of English words although with unique pronunciations, so this may make understanding and speaking easier.

English	French	Pronunciation
yes	*oui*	wee
no	*non*	nohn
please	*s'il vous plaît*	seel voo pleh
thank you	*merci*	mehr-see
you're welcome	*je vous en prie*	zhe vooz ohn pri
hello (day)	*bonjour*	bohn joor
hello (evening)	*bonsoir*	bohn swar
hello, how are you?	*comment ça va?*	common sa vah?
I'm fine	*ça va bien*	sa vah bee-ahn
excuse me	*pardon*	par-dohn
big	*grand*	grond
small	*petit*	peh-tee
cheap	*bon marché*	bohn mar-shay
expensive	*cher*	share
here	*ici*	ee-see
there	*là*	lah
much, many	*beaucoup*	boh-coo
before	*avant*	ah-vonh
after	*après*	ah-preh
tomorrow	*demain*	de-mahn
yesterday	*hier*	yeah
welcome here	*bienvenue*	bee-ahn ven-oo
toilet	*toilette*	twah-leht
bank	*banque*	bohnk
travellers' cheque	*un cheque voyage*	shek vwoy-yazh
the bill	*l'addition*	la-dis-yohn
store	*magasin*	mag-a-zahn
a match	*un feu*	un feuh
museum	*musée*	mew-zay
gas	*gaz*	gaz
lead-free (gas)	*sans plomb*	sohn plom
self-serve	*service libre*	sairvees lee-br'

Questions

where/where is . . .?	*où?/où est . . .?*	oo/oo ehh . . .?
what?	*comment?*	commonh?
huh? (slang)	*quoi?*	kwah?
how much?	*combien?*	kom-bee-ahn?

Signs

entrance	*entrée*	on-tray
exit	*sortie*	sor-tee
platforms	*quai*	kay
information	*renseign-ments*	ron-sayn-mohn
no camping	*interdiction de camper*	an-ter-dic-shion de campay
no parking	*statione-ment interdit*	stas-iohn-mohn ahn-ter-dee
tourist office	*bureau de tourisme*	bew-ro de too-rism

Accommodation

hotel	*hôtel*	o-tell
youth hostel	*auberge de jeunesse*	o-bairzh de zheuness
room	*chambre*	shombr

Travel

bus	*autobus*	auto-boos
train	*le train*	le trahn
ticket	*billet*	bee-yay
plane	*avion*	a-vee-ohn
return ticket	*aller et retour*	alay eh reh-tour
train station	*la gare*	lah gahr
bus station	*la station d'autobus*	la stas-ion d'auto-boos
left	*à gauche*	a go-shh
right	*à droit*	a drwat
straight ahead	*tout droit*	too drwa

Food

restaurant	*restaurant*	res-ta-ronh
snack bar	*casse croute*	kass krewt
eggs	*oeufs*	er
French fries (chips)	*patates frites*	pa-tat frit
bread	*pain*	pahn
cheese	*fromage*	fro-majh
vegetable	*legume*	lay-goom
fruit	*fruit*	frwee

Drinks

water	*de l'eau*	de low
milk	*du lait*	doo leh
beer	*bière*	bee air
wine	*vin*	vahn

Some Useful Phrases

I am a tourist
je suis touriste
zhe swee toureest

Do you speak English?
parlez-vouz anglais?
parlay vooz anglay?

I don't speak French
je ne parle pas francais
zhe neh parl pah fronh-say

I understand
je comprends
zhe com-prohn

I don't understand
je ne comprends pas
zhe ne com-prohn pah

Do you want to sleep with me?
voulez-vous coucher avec moi?
voolay voo cooshay avek mwah?

Get lost! Beat It!
allez-vous-en
alay vooz ohn

Numbers

1	*un*	uhn
2	*deux*	der
3	*trois*	twah
4	*quatre*	cat
5	*cinq*	sank
6	*six*	cease
7	*sept*	set
8	*huit*	weet
9	*neuf*	neuf
10	*dix*	dees
20	*vingt*	vahn
21	*vingt et un*	vahnt-eh-un
22	*vingt-deux*	vahn der
25	*vingt-cinq*	vahn sank
30	*trente*	tronht
40	*quarante*	car-ohnt
50	*cinquante*	sank-ohnt
60	*soixante*	swa-sohnt
70	*soixante-dix*	swa-sohnt dees
80	*quatre-vingt*	cat-tr' vahn
90	*quatre-vingt-dix*	cat-tr' vahn dees
100	*cent*	sohn
500	*cinq cents*	sank sohn
1000	*mille*	meel

Facts for the Visitor

VISAS

Visitors from all countries except the United States need a passport. Americans do need identification; a birth certificate or driver's licence is best. Visitors from most western countries don't need a visa. People from Asia, Third World and developing countries and communist nations definitely need one. Visa requirements change frequently and they must be obtained before arrival in Canada, so check before you leave – Europeans included. Visas are issued free by Canadian consulates in these and other cities:

Australia
  Canberra, Sydney, Melbourne, Perth
UK
  London, Manchester, Birmingham, Glasgow, Belfast
USA
  Most large cities

A visa does not guarantee entry. Admission is up to the discretion of the immigration officer at the border. This depends on a number of factors, some of which you control. An exit ticket is not officially required, nor a show of money, but you may be asked to present either. It's mostly common sense. If you turn up looking shabby with $20 for a six-month stay, forget it. Have a reasonable amount of money and an estimation of your daily expenses ready. If you have friends or relatives where you can stay, mention it. If you have a Hostel Card, show it. Visitors from western countries should have little difficulty.

The normal stay granted is three months. This is renewable, though a quick trip out of the country, to the US, may be required.

If you are refused entry but have a visa you have the right of appeal at the Immigration Appeal Board at the port of entry. Those under 18 should have a letter from a parent or guardian.

Studying or Working

Student and work authorisations must be obtained outside Canada and mav take six months to obtain. A work permit is valid for one specific job and time, for one specific employer. If you want to study here, get the information and apply in your own country.

It is difficult to get a work permit; opportunities go first to Canadians. However, employers hiring casual, temporary, construction, farm or forestry workers often don't ask for the permit. Visitors working here legally have Social Insurance numbers beginning with '9'. If you don't have this, and get caught, you'll probably be told to leave the country.

Many young European women come to Canada as nannies. Many countries have agencies where details on these arrangements can be found.

SWAP Of particular interest to Australian students may be SWAP (Student Work Abroad Programme). Organised by the Canadian Federation of Students (CFS) and Student Services Australia, the programme allows Australian students to spend a year in Canada on a working holiday.

After an orientation programme in Vancouver (which includes a copy of this Lonely Planet book!) you find your own job, with help from CFS. Most jobs are in the service area – waiters, bar attendants, cleaners and maids, particularly in the snowfields over winter – although SWAP participants have worked in other fields ranging from farm hands to bell-hops. You are issued with a one-year, non-renewable visa which allows you to work anywhere in the country. SWAP participants must be

Australian citizens and pass a medical check-up.

Student Travel Australia arranges group departures at reduced fares leaving from all Australian capital cities around November-December each year, which includes a stopover in Honolulu. For full details contact Student Services Australia (tel (03) 348 1777), PO Box 399, Carlton South, Victoria, 3053.

CUSTOMS

Don't get caught bringing drugs into Canada. The sentence is seven years minimum. It doesn't matter if you're a nice person; the judge has no choice by law. This includes marijuana and hashish, as they are termed narcotics in Canada.

If you're 19 or over you can bring in 1.1 litres (40 oz) of liquor (it's cheaper in the US) as well as 200 cigarettes, 50 cigars and one kg of tobacco. You can bring in gifts up to $40 value.

If you have a dog it will need proof of a rabies shot in the past 12 months.

Firearms need a permit. Registering excessive or expensive sporting goods, cameras, etc, might save you some hassle when you leave, especially if you'll be crossing the Canada-US border a number of times.

If you've rented a car in the US and are driving it into Canada, bring a copy of the rental agreement to save any possible aggravation by border officials.

MONEY

Approximate exchange rates are:

US$1	=	C$1.20
£1	=	C$2.03
A$1	=	C$0.94
DM1	=	C$0.64

American Express and Thomas Cook are the best travellers' cheques to use in either American or Canadian dollars. Some smaller places don't know exchange rates, so you'll have to pay for a call to find the rate as well as the mailing charges. Some

banks now charge a couple of bucks to cash travellers' cheques, so ask first; if a charge is levied, cash several, as generally the charge remains the same whether it's one cheque or five. Despite this service charge, banks usually offer better rates than hotels, restaurants and visitor attractions, etc. The difference can be a few percentage points.

Canadian banks also slap a C$5 surcharge for cashing each travellers' cheque denominated in non-Canadian currency, so it's best to buy travellers' cheques in Canadian dollars.

If you buy something that will be taken out of the province where you bought it within 30 days, you don't have to pay sales tax. Call a provincial government office to obtain the forms for reimbursement – it's worth the trouble on a tent, camera or similar purchase.

All prices and figures quoted in this book are in Canadian dollars, unless stated otherwise.

COSTS

Finding places to sleep and eat isn't much different here than it is in Europe or the US. The Canadian lifestyle, like the Canadian personality, is a little bit British, a little bit American and somehow different from both. There are no formal social classes, but widely different incomes, and therefore a range in housing, eating and entertainment prices. For most visitors, the biggest expense will be accommodation costs. There are, however, alternatives to the standard hotels which can make a bed nothing to lose sleep over.

Food prices are lower than in much of western Europe but higher than those of the US and about parallel to those of Australia.

TIPPING

Normal tipping is 10% to 20% of the bill. Tips are usually given to cabbies, waitresses and waiters. Tipping helps for service in a bar too, especially if a fat tip is given on the first order. After that you won't go thirsty all night.

TOURIST INFORMATION

Canadian Tourist Offices

In Canada each province has a governmental ministry responsible for tourism and the major cities generally have an office for distributing provincial information. In addition, most cities and towns have at least a seasonal local information office. Many of these are mentioned in the text. Tourism Canada can supply basic information booklets for visitors and within these are the addresses of all the provincial and territorial head offices.

CUTS For budget, young or student travellers, the Canadian University Travel Service Ltd (CUTS) offers a wealth of information. This is Canada's student travel bureau with offices in Halifax, Ottawa, Toronto, Saskatoon, Edmonton and Vancouver, usually on the University campus.

For student discounts you must have an International card (ISIC) available at these outlets. You must have proper ID though; this isn't Athens or Bangkok.

CUTS deal mostly in ways to get you out of Canada cheaply. They also sell European train passes, arrange working holidays and set up language courses.

Within Canada, CUTS can arrange tours and canoe trips and help with domestic flights. They have a 'Discount Handbook' which lists over 1000 stores and service establishments offering bargains to ISIC card holders.

IYHA Canada is a member of the International Youth Hostelling Association and besides offering beds, some of the hostels run field trips, operate travel agencies or have stores selling outdoor supplies and guide books. The hostels are also great sources of information through the guests, staff and bulletin boards. For more information on them, see the Accommodation section.

Overseas Offices
There are Canadian tourist information offices, called Tourism Canada, in many countries, usually in the major city or cities. If you want information beforehand and can't find an office, try calling the embassy, consulate or high commission.

England
- Canada House, Trafalgar Square, London SW1 5BJ

France
- Office du Tourism du Canada, 37 Ave Monta, 5 75008 Paris

West Germany
- Kanadisches Fremdeverkehrsampt, 6 Frankfurt, Biebergasse 6-10

Australia
- Canadian Government Department of Tourism, 8th floor, AMP Centre, 50 Bridge St, Sydney 2000

Japan
- 5th floor, Yamakatsu Pearl Building, 5-32 Akasaki, 8-chome Minato-ku, Tokyo 107

USA
- Most states have an office in the major city

Canada
- Tourism Canada, 235 Queen St, Ottawa, Ontario K1A 0H6.

GENERAL INFORMATION

Post

Letters Mail service is neither quick nor cheap but basically reliable. First class mail is possible up to 500 grams. These are the rates for 1st class mail:

Letter or postcard in Canada (up to 30 grams): 37c
Letter or postcard to USA (up to 30 grams): 42c
Letter or postcard to other countries (up to 30 grams): 74c

Aerogrammes are the same price as letters or postcards. Over 500 grams, mail goes parcel post, which can be air, surface or a combination. Over 10 kg, mail goes surface only. This is slow.

Packages There is registered mail, special delivery, surface and air mail for packages. Check at the post office.

Some countries require a customs declaration on incoming parcels. Check at the post office whether you must fill one of these out when sending packages.

Telephones

Blue or red telephone booths can be found on street corners and in hotel lobbies, bars and public buildings. You can dial long-distance direct if you know the area code. Long-distance rates drop one-third after 6 pm, two-thirds after 11 pm. On Saturday from noon to 11 pm, you get two-thirds off. On Sunday, the rates are cheapest: two-thirds off most of the day, half from 6 pm to 11 pm.

Time

Canada spans six of the world's 24 time zones. As shown on the map, the eastern zone in Newfoundland is unusual in that it's only ½ hour different from the adjacent zone. The time difference coast to coast is 4½ hours.

Canada uses Daylight Saving Time during summer. It begins on the last Sunday in April and ends the last Sunday in October. It is one hour later than Standard Time, meaning a seemingly longer summer day.

Eastern Saskatchewan uses Standard Time all year round. Why, I don't know.

Business Hours

Banks Most banks are open Monday to Thursday from 10 am to 3 pm, and from 10 am to 5 or 6 pm on Fridays. Trust companies are usually open Saturday; the whole lot are always closed on holidays.

Stores Opening hours are 9 am to 5 or 6 pm. Many (in cities, department stores and plazas) remain open until at least 9 pm on Thursdays and Fridays.

Bars Hours vary according to the province. Most open at noon and close around 2 am. In Quebec laws are more liberal; bars stay open until 3 or 4 am.

HEALTH

Normally no vaccinations are required and nothing is recommended for protection here. You need shots for cholera and yellow fever if you're arriving here from an endemic area or have been in contact with these diseases.

If you're going to do a lot of camping, particularly in the back country and woods of Alberta or British Columbia, you may need to take precautions against an intestinal parasite known as 'Beaver Fever'. See the Dangers & Annoyances section for more information.

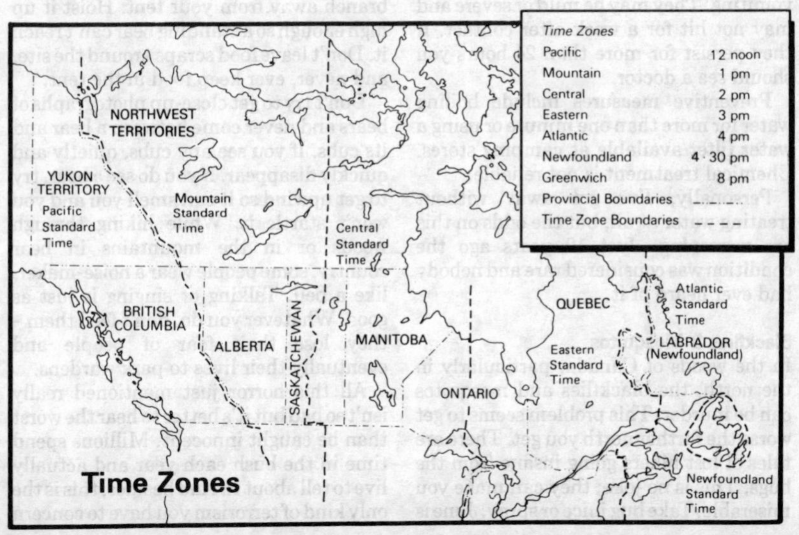

Travel Insurance

Check to see if your health insurance covers you during a visit to Canada. Medical, hospital and dental care is expensive. The standard rate for a bed in a city hospital is at least $500 a day.

The Blue Cross in Canada has an insurance policy for visitors. It's called 'emergency coverage' and costs $3 a day single, $6 a day family, for a maximum of two months. It doesn't cover any expenses arising from a condition you had prior to arrival or due to pregnancy. The insurance can be purchased upon arrival or at home before leaving. For information write the head office at 150 Ferrand Drive, Toronto, Ontario, M3C 1H6.

DANGERS & ANNOYANCES

Beaver Fever

In the past few years an intestinal parasite called *Giardia lamblia*, also known as Beaver Fever, has been causing more and more back country hikers a lot of discomfort. The organism inhabits streams, lakes and rivers, and is spread through human and animal faeces. Symptoms include diarrhoea, gassiness, cramps and vomiting. They may be mild or severe and may not hit for a week after contact. If they persist for more than 24 hours you should see a doctor.

Preventive measures include boiling water for more than one minute or using a water filter available at camping stores. Chemical treatment is not reliable.

Personally, I've got away without treating water at all, but the odds on this are worsening. Just 10 years ago the condition was considered rare and nobody had ever heard of it.

Blackflies & Mosquitos

In the woods of Canada, particularly in the north, the blackflies and mosquitos can be murder. This problem seems to get worse the further north you get. There are tales of lost hikers going insane from the bugs. This is no joke; they can make you miserable. Take bug juice or spray. June is the worst month, and as the summer wears on or if things are dry, the bugs disappear. Some years this is not much of a problem; other years it's very bad, depending on weather and other conditions.

The bugs are at their worst deep in the woods. In clearings, along shorelines or anywhere there's a breeze you'll be safe, except for the buzzing horseflies, which are basically teeth with wings.

Mosquitos come out around sunset; building a fire will help keep them away. Try to have a tent with a zippered screen.

If you do get lost and are being eaten, submerge your body if there's water around. This will enable you to think clearly about where you are and what to do. Lemon or orange peel rubbed on your skin will help if you're out of repellent.

Bears

Another problem encountered camping in the woods is the animals – most importantly bears – who are always looking for an easy snack. Keep your food in nylon bags; a sleeping bag sack is good. Tie the sack to a rope and sling it over a branch away from your tent. Hoist it up high enough so a standing bear can't reach it. Don't leave food scraps around the site, and never, ever keep food in the tent.

Don't try to get close-up photographs of bears and never come between a bear and its cubs. If you see any cubs, quietly and quickly disappear. If you do see a bear, try to get upwind so it can smell you and you won't startle it. While hiking through woods or in the mountains in bear country, some people wear a noise-maker, like a bell. Talking or singing is just as good. Whatever you do, don't feed them – they lose their fear of people and eventually their lives to park wardens.

All this horror just mentioned really isn't so bad but it's better to hear the worst than be caught innocent. Millions spend time in the bush each year and actually live to tell about it. And besides, this is the only kind of terrorism you have to concern yourself with in Canada – bugs are better than bombs, if you ask me.

ACCOMMODATION

Hotels

Good, inexpensive hotels are not a Canadian strong point. Though there is a wide range of hotel types, the word usually means one of two things to a Canadian – a rather expensive place to stay or a cheap place to drink. Canada is too young to have developed a large network of good family-run hostelries.

Most new hotels are part of international chains and are designed for either the luxury market or for business people.

Canadian liquor laws have been historically linked to renting beds, so the older, cheap hotels are often principally bars, and quite often low-class bars at that. This type is found all over the country. For the impecunious who don't mind some noise and a somewhat worn room they can come in handy. Prices are usually about $15 to $20 but rooms are often taken by more permanent guests.

Between the very new and the very old hotels, there are places to be found in the smallish band in between. In the larger cities in particular, good, older, small hotels whose main function is renting rooms can still be found. Prices vary with amenities and location and range from about $25 to $70 for singles or doubles.

Overall in Canada, Quebec excepted, there are few of the quaint, charming old hotels you come across in European cities. The alternatives available are motels, bed & breakfasts, tourist homes, and various types of hostels.

Motels

In Canada, like the US (land of the automobile), motels are ubiquitous and until recently represented the only form of moderately priced accommodation. For the most part they are simple and clean, if somewhat nondescript. They can be found in number, dotting the areas along highways and clustered in strips on both sides of larger towns and cities. They usually range from $22 to $60 for singles or doubles.

Outside the cities, prices drop so motels can be a bargain, especially if there are two or more of you. Before entering a big city it's a good idea to get off the main route and onto one of the smaller, older roads. This is where you'll find them as cheap as they come.

Prices tend to go up in summer or when a special event is on. Off-season bargaining is definitely worthwhile. This needn't be haggling as in a Moroccan market; just a simple counter-offer will sometimes work. Unlike many hotels, motels are still pretty much 'mom and pop' operations and so retain more flexibility and often reflect more of the character of the owners.

Bed & Breakfasts

Bed & breakfasts have caught on in Canada only in the past few years, but they are springing up quickly, offering a decent alternative to the top and bottom end hotels. Many cities have associations which manage local member houses; others are listed directly with tourist offices. Several guides which deal exclusively with this type of lodging can be found in all provinces and, both in towns and in the countryside, have appeared on bookstore shelves. Prices of bed & breakfasts vary quite a bit, ranging roughly from $20 single to $60 double with the average being $30 to $35 for two people. Rooms are almost always in the owner's home and are clean and well kept.

Tourist Homes

Another alternative is the simple tourist room. These may be an extra room in someone's home but are more commonly commercial lodging houses. They are found mainly in places with a large tourist trade such as Niagara, Banff, Victoria and Quebec. In Quebec's principal centres they are popular and plentiful, and usually the best places to stay.

Rooms come in a range of sizes and with varying amenities. Some include private bathrooms. The standard cost is about $30 to $35 a double, but could be a bit lower or a lot higher.

Some so-called tourist rooms are really rooming houses rented more often by the week or longer. They usually have shared kitchens. These places are normally used by local people but can be good for long stays. Rates are lower for long-term rentals.

Youth Hostels

Youth Hostels, operated by the Canadian Hostelling Association in conjunction with the international hostelling organisation, are the cheapest places to stay and are where you'll probably meet the most travellers. There are about 50 in Canada costing from $4 to $12.

Most of the main cities have a hostel and some provinces have quite a few scattered around more or less randomly. There are fortunately quite a few in and around the Rocky Mountain national parks. The province of British Columbia also has an informal network of privately-run hostels which charge about the same rates as the official ones.

Hostel members are entitled to lower overnight costs but non-members are welcomed at all hostels. In addition, members can often take advantage of discounts offered by various businesses, including outdoor equipment sold at one of half a dozen hostel shops. Local hostels should have a list of where the various bargains can be had.

Membership costs $15 and is valid for a year all around the world. This is the American Express Card of budget travel: don't leave home without it. It's usually cheaper and more convenient to get a membership in your own country. The handbook will give you the hostels' addresses, dates and rules. Many Canadian hostels are closed in winter. Don't rely solely on the information in the handbook; it's often incorrect.

The national office is in a suburb of Ottawa. One-year memberships are available through this office or at the various provincial offices. The address is:

Tower A, 3rd floor
333 River Rd
Vanier, Ontario
K1L 8H9.

YM-YWCA

The familiar YM-YWCAs still offer good accommodation in a style between those of a hostel and a hotel, but prices have been creeping up. In YM-YWCAs where complete renovations have occurred, costs can now be as high as those of a cheap hotel, especially if there are two of you. However, some permit couples and doubles are pretty fair value. YM-YWCAs are very clean and quiet and often have swimming pools and cheap cafeterias. The average price for men is $20 to $24 a single, and usually a bit more for women. For a complete list and information write to:

YMCA National Council
2160 Yonge St
Toronto, Ontario
M4S 2A1.

Universities

Many universities rent out beds in their residence dormitories during the summer months. The 'season' runs roughly from May to some time in August with possible closures for large academic conferences, etc. Prices average about $20 a day, and at many, students are offered a further reduction.

A membership card, the Travel Canada card, is available for $15 to $30 to families, students, seniors and singles. Cardholders are entitled to 20% off the usual campus prices. A directory is available, and memberships can be purchased through any Travel Cuts travel agency, an outfit associated with universities across the country. There are offices in Montreal (Voyages CUTS), Toronto and several other cities.

Reservations are accepted but aren't necessary. Breakfasts are sometimes included in the price but if not, there is generally a cafeteria which cooks up low-priced meals. The other campus facilities such as swimming pools are available to guests.

Camping

There are campgrounds (that's camping grounds, Australians) all over Canada; they're federal, provincial and privately owned. Government sites are always better and cheaper and not surprisingly, fill up the quickest.

Canada has 31 National Parks, with more being added slowly but regularly. Some are now in the preparatory stages. In national parks, the fees range from $8 to $10 for an unserviced site, to as high as $14 for sites with services like electricity.

A couple of natural hazards – bears, mosquitos and a rare intestinal parasite – may make camping less than pleasant on occasion. For information on these, see the Dangers & Annoyances section in this chapter.

For information on the national parks, try Parks Canada, the National & Provincial Parks Association of Canada, or the Canadian Government Office of Tourism.

Parks Canada puts out a free booklet, *National Parks of Canada*. Write to:

Parks Canada
Ottawa, Ontario
K1A 1G2.

The National & Provincial Parks Association of Canada (tel 366-3494) provides information on where to camp, what's good for solitude, where are the best fishing spots, etc:

National & Provincial Parks Association of Canada
69 Sherbourne Avenue
Toronto, Ontario.

The Canadian Government Office of Tourism publishes three guides on camping across Canada:

Canadian Government Office of Tourism
150 Kent St
Ottawa, Ontario.

There are also entrance fees to national parks of $2 or $10 for a year.

Provincial park camping rates vary with each province but range from $7.50 to $12. Interior camping is always less, about $4. Commercial campgrounds are generally several dollars more expensive.

KOA (Kampgrounds of America) is the name of a chain of campgrounds, found mainly in the USA but with quite a few locations across Canada.

Government parks are usually more scenic, have more trees, are quieter and have less services and entertainments. Tenters generally prefer them.

Government parks start closing in early September for the winter. Dates vary according to the location. Some remain open for maintenance even when camping is finished. Sometimes they let you in at a reduced rate; maybe the showers or something are turned off. Others, late in fall or early in spring, are free. The gate is open and there is not a soul around. Still others block the road and you just can't enter the grounds. So, out of the main summer season you have to investigate. It can save you a fair bit of money.

There are also campgrounds every 150 km or so along the Trans-Canada Highway.

Lastly, many people travel around the country camping and never pay a dime. For those with cars or vans, using roadside rest areas and picnic spots is recommended. I've done this many times. If there are signs indicating no overnight camping, don't do something like set up a tent; but if you're asleep in the car and a cop happens to wake you, just say you were driving, got tired, pulled over for a quick rest, and fell asleep: *'What time is it, anyway?'* For less chance of interruption, little side roads and logging roads off the highway are quiet and private.

For cyclists and hitch-hikers, just walking off into the woods or fields from the roadside and rolling out the sleeping bag is good enough. It's done all over the country. This is a bit of hassle on the prairies where there's not much to disappear behind, but it can be done.

Farm Vacations

Each province has a farm vacation programme enabling visitors to stay on working farms for a day, a week or longer. The size and type of farm vary considerably, as do the activities you can take part in. There are usually chores you can help out with. Rates range from $20 to $30 per adult depending on meals taken; there are also family rates and reductions for children.

Salvation Army

If you're a man and you're desperate or are looking for some 'edge', you can likely find a place at Salvation Army hostels for a couple of nights. It's free and they throw in meals, too, but remember that they're not operated for travelling youth. The Salvation Army (Sally Ann) is mainly populated by unemployed men – often alcoholics – and the environment isn't particularly pleasant.

FOOD

Canadian gastronomy was long based on the English 'bland is beautiful' tradition (although it never quite reached the unimaginative depths of English food). While there are still no distinctive national dishes or unique culinary delights, good food is certainly plentiful. The large numbers of varying ethnic groups spread across the country have had a large hand in recent epicurean improvements. In addition, specialty shops, increased sophistication and knowledge (often through travel) and the natural and health-food movements have all cut into the mainstream and taken business from the ever-present and internationally familiar giant fast food outlets.

In most cities it's not difficult to find a Greek, Italian, Indian or Chinese meal. Fairly recently small bistro-type places, often with lots of plants, have appeared across the country with menus emphasising freshness, spicing and the latest trends. They tend to fill the gap between the greasy spoons and the priciest restaurants. The former are found throughout Canada with names like *George's* or *Linda's Place*. Little changed since the 1930s, these small, basic places are the working class restaurants. Some are excellent, some bad news, but they're always cheap. There's usually a breakfast special until 11 am for about $3, followed by a couple of lunch specials. A fairly balanced if functional meal goes for $4 to $5.

Canadian bread, as a rule, is pathetic. Several travellers have pointed this out to me but it wasn't news. For some improvement from the packaged stuff go to a baker, delicatessen or health-food store.

Lastly, one truly Canadian creation must be mentioned: the butter tart. This delectable little sweet can best be described as . . . well, just get on the outside of one and you'll see.

Prices

The variety and quality of meals available across the country has risen appreciably since the first edition of this book. Of course prices have gone up, too, but are not out of line compared with what you'd pay elsewhere. As with most things, food here is costlier than in America. If you're from Europe, though, or are travelling with a strong currency, you'll find prices reasonable.

Generally for dinner call under $8 cheap, $8 to $15 moderate, $15 to $25 getting up there, and expensive anything higher than that. Lunches are a lot less. Most of the places mentioned in this book fit into the first two categories.

French Food

Most of the country's few semi-original

repasts come from the French of Quebec. French pea soup is thick, filling and delicious. The *tourtieres* (meat pies) are worth sampling. Quebec is also the world's largest producer of maple syrup, made in the spring when the sap is running, and it's great on pancakes or ice cream. The French fries (chips) in Quebec, especially those bought at the small roadside chipwagons are unbeatable. The world's best.

Canadian Indian Food

Native Indian foods based on wild game such as deer (venison) and pheasant are something to sample if the opportunity presents itself. Buffalo meat, just beginning to be sold commercially in a few places, turns up on menus occasionally. It's lean and has more protein and less cholesterol than beef.

The fiddlehead is a distinctive green only edible in springtime. It's primarily picked from the woodlands of the Maritime provinces. Wild rice, with its black husks and almost nutty flavour is very tasty and often accompanies Indian-style meals. Most of it is picked by hand around the Ontario and Manitoba borders but it's widely available in natural food shops.

Markets

Many cities have markets where fresh produce can be bought at good prices. Fruit, in summer, is a good Canadian bargain and the apples, peaches, cherries, etc, are superb. In June watch for strawberries, in August, blueberries. Farmer's stands are often seen along highways and secondary roads.

On both coasts, seafood is plentiful and affordable. On the west coast the salmon is a real treat, and on the east coast try the lobster. In the far north Arctic char is a specialty.

DRINKS

Canadian Club and VO rye whiskey are Canada's most famous drinks. Good stuff.

Liquor must be bought at government stores, usually closed at night and on Sundays. In Quebec, beer and wine can be bought in grocery stores.

The closing hour for bars is generally 1 or 2 am. In Quebec it's 3 or 4 am. Some bars in the large cities remain open later but cannot serve booze past the 'closing hour'.

Beer

Canadian beer, in general, is good, not great. It's tastier and stronger than American brands and is always served cold. The two big companies are Molson and Labatts, with the most popular beers being Molson Export Ale and Canadian Lager, or Labatts 50 Ale and Blue Lager.

A very welcome new trend is the advent of small breweries producing real or natural beers and pubs brewing their own for consumption on the premises.

In a bar, a pint (340 ml) ranges from $1.75 to $3.50. Draught beer, sold only in bars, is the cheapest way to drink; a 170 ml glass can get as low as 85c. Prices usually go up after the night's entertainment arrives. Retail, beer in cases goes for about a dollar a bottle.

Wine

Canadian wine is generally the cheapest available and often tastes like it, although there has been considerable improvement in the domestics over the past few years. The main vineyards are in Ontario's Niagara region and British Columbia's Okanagan Valley. Import duties keep foreign wine prices up but you can still get a pretty low-priced bottle of French wine.

Other Drinks

The fruit growing areas of Quebec, Ontario and British Columbia produce excellent apple and cherry ciders, some with alcohol, some without. In Quebec and the Atlantic provinces, visitors may want to sample a local non-alcoholic brew called spruce beer. It's produced in small batches by individuals and doesn't have a large commercial base but is sold in some local stores. It varies quite a bit and you can never be too sure what will happen when the cap comes off, but some people love the stuff.

Canadian mineral and spring waters have recently become quite popular and are now readily available.

Getting There

AIR

Probably the most common way to enter Canada is to come up from its well-known neighbour to the south, the good ol' USA. Most cheap flights to North America go to the States, with New York, San Francisco and Los Angeles being major destinations. You can then either fly to a major Canadian city, such as Montreal or Vancouver, or catch a bus.

Shopping for airfares is another story. The airline business in and out of Canada is the same as in most places – largely a mystery. Things change and prices go up and down by the day, even by the phone call. Nothing is consistent; deals come and go. As always, persistence, ingenuity and luck will get you everywhere.

My advice is to ask a lot of questions; international routes and prices change continually. If it's possible, shop in a city that has a high number of budget travellers passing through. The most famous of these are London, Athens and Bangkok. In such cities the best bargains can be found. If these departure points are not feasible, shop around the travel agents at home. There are often travel agencies which specialise in trips to North America and which will know of organised charters or good deals.

One of the difficulties in air travel is that most airlines, particularly the larger ones (including the Canadian companies flying internationally), provide the greatest discount on return tickets rather than on one-way fares. You may be able to get around this by buying a return ticket, using it to get to Canada, then selling the unused portion though naturally, this is highly illegal.

From the UK & Europe

The British Airways direct flight to Montreal is £334, C$724. There are no standby or youth fares available, but there are a number of budget and charter deals available from large travel agents and bucket shops.

Budget Airlines Every couple of years a small upstart airline arrives on the scene and creates a sensation with fares that undercut everybody else's on the cross-Atlantic route. Unfortunately they don't seem to have any staying power. They usually fly into and out of New York from a western European city. Laker lasted quite a while and was followed briefly by Highland Express. More recently, there has been Virgin Atlantic (still operating) and the classic People Express which has also flown into history. If you are lucky, one will spring up just before you leave.

More stable and worth looking into is Sabena Airlines, which may have a deal between Brussels and Montreal.

Charters If you are returning to Europe you might investigate these. Air Canada runs charters from London, Paris and Frankfurt to Toronto. The cheapest are from London with a maximum stay of six months. Fares vary a lot depending on the time of year, with the summer months and Christmas being the most expensive season. In any case an advance booking of 21 days is required. One-way fares are expensive and there are not any deals to be had on them. Return fares range from £344 to £452 from London. One-way fares are £373 to £466 (yes, more than returns). These are all to Toronto. Many people sell the other half of their return ticket when they get to Canada.

Canadian Airlines also runs charters from London and Amsterdam for about the same price.

Wardair, a Canadian company big in the charter business, has probably the best return fares to and from Europe and to Florida in the USA. Departure points include London, Paris, Amsterdam, Dusseldorf and Glasgow.

There are probably good charters from France to the province of Quebec. Travel agents or student offices there could help you out.

To the USA British Airways offers some one-way fares to the new world. From the UK to John F Kennedy Airport, New York, the one-way, mid-week fare is £334 or C$724.

A good alternative is Icelandic Air. They fly between Luxemburg and New York via Reykjavik. These flights have always been among the cheapest across the Atlantic.

From New York, it's an eight-hour bus ride (US$68), or a 9¼-hour train ride (US$66) to Montreal.

From Australia & NZ

Qantas offers standard economy fares from Australia to Canada. A one-way ticket to Vancouver is A$1042 all year. A return ticket in high season is A$2016; mid-season A$1820; low season, A$1448.

For those coming from Australia, New Zealand or Asia, landing in the US is often cheaper than flying to Canada direct. After arriving in Los Angeles, San Francisco or possibly Seattle, Washington on the west coast, a train or bus will take you to Vancouver. Qantas and Air New Zealand flights from Australia to US cities (California), are lower by up to A$150 or so. In addition, they often include many stopovers in the Pacific, like New Zealand, Fiji, Raratonga, Honolulu and even Tahiti.

The fares given are only the airlines' official fares. You will find the best deals by shopping around among travel agents.

From Asia

Singapore Airlines and Korean Airlines run cheap flights around the Pacific, ending on America's west coast.

Check in Singapore and in travel agencies in Bangkok. One-way fares from these centres to the west coast of America, with up to five stops, could probably be had for under US$700.

From Hong Kong, one-way fares to Los Angeles – or, for a few dollars more, Vancouver – are also decent and much cheaper than going the other way.

Round-the-World Tickets

If you are covering a lot of distance, a round-the-world ticket could be worthwhile. A good ticket can include a lot of stops in places all over the world, with a maximum ticket validity of 12 months. Check out the huge variety of round-the-world tickets available. Air Canada and Singapore Airlines offer a round-the-world fare of C$2667 for unlimited stopovers (their destinations only), going in one direction over a period of not more than six months.

Departure/Airport Tax

There is a departure/airport tax of $19 levied on all international flights out of Canada, other than those to US destinations.

Most tickets purchased in Canada for international flights out of Canada include this tax; but tickets out of Canada, purchased in another country, usually don't include it. If you did buy your ticket in another country and it didn't include departure tax, you will be asked for this tax after you pass through customs and immigration. When changing money, consider saving enough to cover it.

ALTERNATIVE TRANSPORT

Yacht

Many flights from Australasia stop off in Hawaii; with a bit of persistence and luck it might be possible to find someone with a yacht who needs a hand. Hawaii is a favourite vacation spot with western Canadians, but don't count on hitting the jackpot.

If you're coming from the Caribbean you might also find a yacht there (it's been done). Most head for Florida; from there, some edge up the east coast. Experienced sailors and females have the best chance at getting a place on board.

Bus

If you're in the US, a Greyhound Pass for eight or 15 days is available. With this you can travel nearly to the Canadian border and then get another bus across.

Freighter

This type of cheap, adventurous, romantic travel is pretty well extinct. What with government regulations and Seafarers Unions, etc, most ships' captains won't even want to bother telling you to forget it. Regular passenger-carrying cruises and the freighters which make a point of taking passengers are now usually more expensive than flying. Most people will tell you it's boring anyway.

If you're really interested, Norwegian Shipping Lines is said to be more flexible about hiring and taking travellers on board. Check around northern Europe for a ship on its way to Montreal or New York.

Ford's International Cruise Guide is a quarterly guide listing all freighters with dates and ports of call. It costs about US$6 for a single copy, US$22 for the year. Write to Box 505, 22151 Clarendon St, Woodland Hills, California 91365.

Travel agents may also be of help.

Getting Around

Within Canada, land travel is cheaper and much more interesting than flying. Fortunately, transportation costs have remained remarkably stable over the past several years. The bus and train lines offer good, unlimited-use tickets as well as a variety of return and excursion specials. Driving costs are reasonable, with gasoline prices considerably lower than those in Europe although quite a bit higher than those in the US.

Still, it's a big country and if you really want to get around quickly, your wallet will be thinned. Air fares are expensive, but for those with a little extra money and not much time, the odd flight may be useful. Flying in Canada actually works out a few cents cheaper per km than owning and operating a car. And an open eye and ear can often turn up one of the ever-changing specials or seat sales.

AIR

Unlike the US market, the airline business in Canada is very regulated and this keeps prices high. There is talk of opening things up but when or how or by how much, nobody knows.

The country has three major airlines: the government-owned Air Canada (although the Conservatives are talking of dumping it), Canadian Airlines (formerly CP Air, Pacific Western, Eastern Provincial and several secondary carriers) and Wardair, a private airline with an emphasis on charters. There are also numerous regional and local airlines, ranging from the fairly extensive Quebecair to tiny northern charter companies. Companies serving specific areas include Air Gaspe in eastern Quebec, Great Lakes in the central region and Norcanair in the north. Altogether, these airlines cover most small cities and towns across the country.

The prices and schedules of flights change and fluctuate incredibly often. Phone an airline one week, and the next week they'll tell you something quite different. This is especially true of the main airlines, and often works to the buyer's advantage. The best thing to do is shop around – directly with the airline or through a travel agent – and be as flexible as you can. Waiting a day or two or avoiding a weekend flight could save you a lot.

Air Canada may be cheap for one flight, Canadian for another, although the big three keep pretty well abreast of one another. Each offers some discounts through student fares, standby or excursion rates.

Both airlines offer youth fares to passengers between 12 and 21. On Air Canada, these are valid all year. On Canadian the youth fare is valid from mid-June to mid-September, excluding weekends. Both of these youth fares are standby and can mean reductions of about 30% or more. Standby policies come and go, so ask around.

The best bargains are excursion fares – a return flight with minimum and maximum stays. These normally need to be booked two weeks or a month in advance.

Occasionally, there are short-term specials for promotion of a certain flight. These can be very cheap but are irregular. Canadian Airlines occasionally offer 'seat sales' which are sort of last-minute ticket price reductions.

Wardair runs economical charters between various Canadian cities; highest prices are in July and August and around Christmas. There's a varying minimum stay and a maximum of one year. No student or youth fares on this one.

For students under the age of 26 with ISIC (International Student Identity Card) cards, Quebecair and possibly still Nordair (now part of Canadian) have reductions of between 35% and 45%.

Another thing to consider is getting a ticket for points A to B and stopping off in the middle. This can often be done for little more than the straight-through fare.

Canadian Airlines and Air Canada sometimes offer fly-drive packages which cover airfares and car rentals. Only available on return flights, the packages sometimes include accommodation. Other possibilities include reductions on cars, hotels and bus tours. Hotels used, however, are of the expensive variety. Air Canada has had – and may still have – a plan with reduced rates at university dorms as well. You just have to ask about the latest gimmicks and offers.

Canada's package tour companies sometimes organise charter trips across or around the country using such exclusively charter airlines as Nationair. These trips can be very inexpensive. For information on these possibilities inquire at a travel agency; they handle all such packages.

Many economy one-way and youth fares are listed in the various Getting There & Away sections through the book. Excursion and charter fares are lower than these, but advance notice is needed and there may be other restrictions. Prices also vary depending on the season; they are high in summer and around Christmas.

For cheap tickets to cities around the country, check the classified ads in newspapers and city entertainment papers under 'Travel' or 'Business Personals'. These are often the unneeded return half of a two-way ticket, as return tickets are often the same price or even cheaper than one-ways. Another place to look for these offers is on university and hostel noticeboards. This is not strictly legal as tickets are non-transferable, but it's done a lot and rarely checked. You do have to be the same sex as the purchaser or questions may be asked!

The cost of airfares usually includes tax, but when you're buying plane tickets, it's worthwhile asking. Sales tax can roughly calculated as 10% of the fare plus $4, to a maximum of $50 extra. Remember to budget for this if tax wasn't paid on your tickets. Airfares quoted in this book should be a rough guide.

TRAIN

There are two main rail companies: the government-run Canadian National (CN), and privately owned Canadian Pacific (CP) Rail. Yes, this is the same CP that used to have the airline and still is into trucking, shipping, hotels, mining, etc. It is one of Canada's biggest, most pervasive companies.

Except for some commuter lines, the passenger services of these railroads are now operated by VIA Rail, a government agency and our version of America's Amtrak system. VIA uses CP and CN trains and lines but is responsible for the service independently. Generally, train travel is more expensive than taking the bus and reservations are much more important especially on weekends and holidays. Snack-bar food is usually lousy but the bar car, when there is one, can be fun. From my experience, the trains are not as reliable as the buses and are very often late. Still, you can get up and walk around.

VIA offers several types of cars and different sleeping-room arrangements ranging from the basic seat to private rooms. If you're going long distances you may want to take some of your own food. Train meals can be expensive and, as mentioned, the snack food is not particularly good.

'Across Canada' is a pamphlet showing all the VIA routes in Canada. If you're using one of the rail passes, this will help in planning.

The best-known trains in Canada are those that travel across country, formerly the Canadian (CP) and the Continental (CN), sometimes still called by those names. The trip, taking approximately five days, takes in nearly all of Canada's provinces and vastly different scenery, some of it spectacular. It can be a very pleasant, relaxing way to go, particularly if you have your own room. During the summer months this trip is booked solid, particularly the southern route (the CP line) through Banff and the Rocky Mountains. There are a variety of sleeping arrangements from simply staying put in your seat, to upper and lower pull-out berths to roomettes of varying sizes.

Rail Passes

One-way fares are the costliest way to go but there are various ways of getting prices down. One is with a Canrailpass, valid for varying lengths of time. Here are some passes available, along with the prices for standard economy seats:

	high season	*low season*
Entire System		
22 days	$529	$399
30 days	$579	$439
Winnipeg & East		
15 days	$249	$209
22 days	$279	$239
Winnipeg & West		
15 days	$319	$269
22 days	$359	$299
Quebec City to Windsor, Ontario		
8 days	$169 (same all year)	
15 days	$199 (same all year)	

There is also a new Youth Canrailpass for ages 12-24:

	high season	*low season*
Entire System		
22 days	$389	$299
30 days	$429	$329
Winnipeg & East		
15 days	$179	$149
22 days	$209	$179
Winnipeg & West		
15 days	$239	$199
22 days	$269	$219
Quebec City to Windsor, Ontario		
8 days	$119 (same all year)	
15 days	$149 (same all year)	

High season is from 15 June to 15 September, from 15 December to 4 January, and Easter. Low season is the rest of the year.

All these passes are good for any number of trips and stopovers. Note that the 22-day ones are not much more expensive than the 15-day ones. The youth fares are a good reduction, and children under the age of 11 and senior citizens also get reduced fares.

The pass is also good on some connecting buses; on the Nova Scotia to Prince Edward Island ferry; and presentation of it gets you $2 a day off Tilden Rent-A-Car. You can buy the Canrailpass here or in Europe at a VIA office; there's no difference in cost.

Continental Saver Fares

These fares are meant to lower the price of travel between relatively long distances and cannot be used on short hop trips. They are offered from October to May excluding the Christmas season. Reservations are a must and tickets must be bought seven days before leaving. The return portion must be used within six months. If all these criteria are met, the Continental Savers mean 40-50% off regular ticket prices. The same rate of reduction can be applied to extra optional sleeping arrangement charges. Note, though, stopovers are not permitted and there is a 10% penalty charged for changes or refunds.

Excursion Fares

These fares are geared to shorter trips with destinations less than a day away. The reduced fares can be applied to one, five and 10-day return trips and offer about 15-30% off. Fridays cannot be used as departure days and stopovers are not permitted.

Other

VIA also organises a variety of package tours including hotels, sightseeing and bus trips. Some are long, others weekend jaunts. In addition, they offer activity trips which include white-water rafting and whale-watching in Quebec. These are not especially cheap and can be done on your own for less.

Amtrak is the American equivalent of VIA. Information on them is available at many Canadian train stations. They also sell good-value passes. The two systems are connected at a couple of points by trains or buses.

BUS

Buses go nearly everywhere and are normally cheaper than trains. They are usually clean, safe and comfortable. The two biggies are Voyageur Colonial in Quebec, Ontario and New Brunswick, and Greyhound all over the west. There are also Gray Coach in Ontario, SMT in New Brunswick and Acadia Lines in Nova Scotia, as well as many local lines.

Reservations are not normally needed, although buses between adjacent major cities and towns are very busy on weekends and holidays; a reservation may be useful.

On long trips the journey can be broken any number of times. A one-way ticket is usually good for 30 days, a return for 60.

The bus companies in larger towns offer sightseeing tours ranging from one day to several weeks. Some include accommodation, meals and fees to sights. These can be good value; check prices and exactly what you get carefully. Reservations for these types of trips are necessary.

Bus Passes

Like the trains, bus lines offer passes much like the Eurail pass. The Canada-Ameripass is good for anywhere in Canada and the USA with participating bus lines, which means just about everywhere is connected. In Canadian dollars these passes are: seven days $228, 15 days $301, 30 days $422. These prices vary with the exchange rate.

The Across Canada Ticket is the same thing but can only be used in Canada, coast to coast. Any number of stops are allowed. The cost is seven days $189, 15 days $249, 30 days $349 – all of which are less than the train passes with the exception of low-season youth passes.

There is also an Across Canada Ticket, one-way only, which is a fair bit cheaper still. With this you can only stop at points directly on your one-way route. From Vancouver to Toronto or Montreal (or the other way) it's $99. If you want to include destinations east of Toronto, to the Atlantic provinces for example, the one-way pass goes up to $149.

There is also a pass offered by Voyageur called Tourpass Voyageur which is good for 10 days' unlimited travel in Quebec and Ontario only. The cost for this one is $99 with extra days possible at $10 extra per day.

Visitors from outside Canada can buy the International Canadian Pass which is not available in Canada or to Canadian citizens, at travel agencies in their own country. Prices for these seven, 15 and 30 day passes are even cheaper than the Canada-Ameripass or Across Canada Tickets. A good buy.

Most lines offer various specials. One is a vastly reduced return fare if you go and come within five days and don't depart on a Friday. There are other return excursion fares with varying time requirements.

There are no student or youth fares on buses, but for students there is a 14-trip booklet of tickets that gives you a reduction.

Tips

In summer, the air-conditioners on buses can be far too effective. Bring a sweater on board.

Take your own picnic whenever possible.

Long-distance buses stop at highway gas station restaurants where you pay an awful lot for plastic food.

All buses use the same central bus stations in Canadian cities so you can change bus lines or make connections at the same place.

Watch out for pickpockets in the stations.

DRIVING

In many ways, driving is the best way to travel. You can go where and when you want, use secondary highways and roads and get off the beaten path. It's particularly good in summer when you can camp or even sleep in the car. The cars with reclining seats are great for this – surprisingly comfortable with a sleeping bag.

Canada's roads are good and well marked. There aren't many tolls. The Trans-Canada Highway runs from St John's, Newfoundland across 7000-plus km to Victoria, British Columbia. There are campgrounds and picnic stops all along the route, often within 100 to 150 km of each other. Rural routes are among the smallest road designations. They're found in rural Canada and are marked RR1, RR7, etc.

Sleeping at roadside parks, picnic spots or other areas on the highways is OK. Just don't set up a tent.

A valid driver's licence from any country is good in Canada for three months. An International Driving Permit, available in your home country, is cheap and good for one year almost anywhere in the world.

You can't drive in Canada without insurance. Your home insurance may not cover you in a foreign land.

City rush hours – especially around 5 pm and on Fridays – can be bad, especially in Montreal, Toronto and Vancouver. In fact I recommend avoiding city driving as much as possible, regardless of the time. Taking the bus or walking can be cheaper, with today's hefty parking fees. It's a lot less wearing on your nerves, too.

Gasoline

The price of gas varies quite a bit around the country, with the highest prices being found in the far north and on the east coast. Alberta's prices, with less tax, are relatively low. Fill up there before hitting BC, fill up in the US before crossing the border, fill up in Ontario before rolling into Quebec. Generally, city prices are lower than country prices, and gas stations along major highways always charge more to their semi-captive customers than do the off-highway stations. On average a litre of gas is about 50c, or about $2.25 per imperial gallon. The Canadian (imperial) gallon is one-fifth larger than the American gallon.

Credit cards are usually accepted at gas stations. Many are now self-serve and will not accept large bills at night. The large cities have some stations that are open 24 hours but you may have to search around. On the highways, truck stops have the longest hours and some have showers you can use.

Road Safety

Canadians drive on the right, as in the US, but they now use the metric system; 100 km per hour = 60 mph, 50 km per hour = 30 mph. The speed limit on highways is usually 100 km, in towns 50 km or less.

The use of seat belts is compulsory except in Prince Edward Island, Alberta, the Yukon and the Northwest Territories. In provinces with a seat belt law, like Quebec and Ontario, fines for not wearing them are heavy. All traffic violations in money-short Quebec will cost you plenty, so take it easy there. Most provinces require motorcyclists and passengers to wear helmets and to drive with the lights on.

Driving in Quebec and other areas of heavy snow can be a thrill you're best off without. It also means buying snow tyres. If you get stuck, don't stay in the car with the engine going. Every year people die of carbon monoxide suffocation during big storms.

Traffic in both directions must stop when school buses are stopped with red lights flashing. This means kids are getting off and on. In cities with pedestrian crosswalks like Toronto, cars must stop.

Car Rentals

You can save a lot of hassle renting a car with a credit card. Last time I tried to rent a car, cash was no good. They didn't want it! If you don't have a credit card, let the company have a few days (at least) to check you out. If you're not working they can be sticky. Bring a letter from an employer or banker if you can, and lots of good identification. You may also need to lay down a deposit, sometimes as much as $250 per day. Some companies require you to be over 21, others over 26. You may be asked to buy extra insurance depending on your age, but this isn't much.

The main big companies are Hertz, Avis, Budget and Tilden. Rent-A-Wreck is a well-known used-car rental place. It's best to shop around; rates vary. Some have a daily rate of about $20 plus a km fee. Others offer a flat rate which is nearly always better if you're going far. It costs quite a bit extra to drop a car off in places other than where you got it, but this can be readily done. Weekly rates are generally 10% less than daily rates, and many companies offer special weekend rates. Book early for weekend use and to get a small, more economical car.

Drive-Aways

One of the best driving deals is the uniquely North American Drive-Away system. Basically you're driving someone's car for them to a specific destination. Usually the car belongs to someone who has been transferred and had to fly, or doesn't have the time, patience or ability to drive a long distance. You put down a deposit and are given a certain number of days to deliver the car. If you don't show up, the law is called in. Most outlets suggest a route to take and may give you a very rough km guideline.

You are not charged a fee, but you pay the gas. Sometimes a gas allowance is included, covering part of this expense. If you're really lucky, on a rush job all the gas might be paid. With two or more people, this can be a great deal. Don't tell them you'll have a crowd though, because they'll need to know how many drivers there will be.

Requirements are good identification, the deposit and a couple of photos. Look for Drive-Away companies under transportation or business personals in the newspaper classifieds or in the yellow pages of the phone book. Most big cities have at least one outlet. They exist all through the US too. Some trips will take you across the border; Montreal to Florida is a common route. About eight days is normal for an east-to-west-coast trip. Try to get a smaller, newer car: they're less comfortable but cheaper on gas.

In summer when demand is highest, cars may not be as numerous and a payment could be asked. Occasionally you hear of a Jaguar or something similar available. Class on a shoestring.

Buying a Car

Older cars can be bought quite cheaply in North America. Look in the newspaper or the *Buy & Sell Bargain Hunter Press*. Private deals are nearly always best. Most of the cheaper cars now are the big gas-guzzlers people are trying to get rid of. For a few months' driving, this can be an excellent investment, especially if there are two of you. You can usually sell the car for nearly what you paid for it. An old bomber can probably be had for $1000. West coast cars last longer because salt doesn't have to be used on the roads in winter and the cars rust less quickly. I once bought a clunky old 1958 station wagon for $50 and got 19,000 km out of it in one summer before the transmission gave up, the wiring burnt out and the floor fell out.

BICYCLE

This method of getting around long-distance is becoming more and more popular in Canada. Obviously you'd need a lot of time to cover much of Canada. You can't really consider traversing vast regions; it's best to concentrate on one area. Two of the most popular are the areas around the Gaspe Peninsula in Quebec and all around the Atlantic provinces, excluding Newfoundland. The Gaspe is very hilly, Prince Edward Island is flat, and New Brunswick and Nova Scotia offer a fair bit of variety and are small, with towns pretty close together. You get a good mix of country and city. All these areas have good scenery.

The other major cycling area is around the Rocky Mountains and through British Columbia. The weather here in summer is pretty reliable and again there's grand and varied scenery.

Between these eastern and western sections of the country, cycling would be more a chore than anything else and the landscape is similar for long stretches.

VIA Rail allows passengers to take bicycles for free on trains that have baggage cars. This would mean pretty well any train going a fair way. Local and commuter trains wouldn't be included. You don't have to pack the bike up or disassemble it, but then it may not be covered by insurance. For full coverage I think bicycles must be boxed.

The provincial highway maps have more detail and secondary roads than the usual gas-station maps. Pick them up at tourist offices. Bookshops may also have cycling guides, and cycling magazines might contain useful information.

Some cities, such as Vancouver and Ottawa, have routes marked around town for bikes only.

Cycling Associations

Members of the Canadian Cycling Association receive national and provincial newsletters, a million dollars' worth of liability insurance and information and discounts on events and activities. You join through an associated provincial organisation and the cost is $15 a year. Various local associations link up through the provincial associations for tours and races. They also often have group tours combining cycling and camping.

In Ontario, the Ontario Cycling Association (tel 495-4141) is at 1220 Sheppard Avenue East, Toronto, M2K 2X1. They have maps of cycle routes around the province. Associations in other provinces have similar guides. Check the yellow pages phone books in other cities for cycling associations.

HITCHING

I've always found hitching good here. It's not England, which is a hitch-hiker's dream, but thumbing a ride is still very worthwhile. Two people, one of each gender, is ideal. Three or more – I'd forget it. Ditto for single women.

If you feel you've waited a long time to be picked up, remember that the ride you get may take you over 1500 km.

Out of the big cities, stay on the main highways. Traffic can be very light on the smaller roads. Always get off where there's a gas station or restaurant and not at a side road or farmer's gate.

Around towns and cities, pick your spots carefully. Stand where you can be seen and where a car can easily stop. A foreign T-shirt, like one with 'University of Stockholm', might be useful.

If you're going into a large city, make sure the ride is going all the way. If it's not, get dropped where you can catch a city bus, especially after dark. When leaving, it's best to take a bus out a little way.

You must stay off inter-city expressways, though the feeder ramps are OK. In Toronto and Vancouver particularly, the police will stop you on the expressway.

It's illegal to hitch in downtown Calgary; fines can be steep. Generally, the scruffier you look, the more ID and documents you should have.

Around the large cities, there will be

heavy traffic leaving on Friday and returning on Sunday. Despite the volume I find hitching difficult then because most cars are full with families. Best are weekdays, when you get salespeople and truckers. Many companies forbid truck drivers to pick up people, though some do anyway.

If you're in a hurry, Toronto to Vancouver shouldn't take longer than five days; I've done it in three.

One last tip: if you don't want to spend time in Northern Ontario, get a ride straight through from Sault Ste Marie to Thunder Bay. The same in reverse. Wawa, a small town between the two, is a notorious waiting spot. Its reputation as a tough, anti-hitch-hiker, mining and drinking town is pretty outdated, but it's still a small, cold, nothing-to-do place to try to get a lift out of. I once heard of a guy who waited so long he finally got a job then married and settled in Wawa.

TOURS

Organised group tours are best arranged through the train and bus companies or travel agencies. The larger transportation companies are reliable and your best bet if you must have an organised tour.

Always make sure you know exactly what sort of tour you're getting and how much it will cost. If you have any doubts about the agency or the company it may be dealing with, pay your money into what is called the 'tour operators escrow account'. The law requires that this account number appear on tourist brochures. (You may have to look a while.) Doing this protects you and your money, should the trip fall through for any reason. It's a good idea to pay by cheque because cash is always harder to get back; write the details of the tour, with destination and dates, on the front of the cheque. On the back write 'for deposit only'.

VIA Rail and the bus companies offer trips of varying lengths, including transportation and accommodation. Some offer sightseeing as well.

Goway Travel is a small private company which runs tours throughout the Americas for 18 to 35-year-olds. These are expedition and camping-type trips. They offer tours which cross Canada one way and return through the States. Most of the trips are two to five weeks long and are 'city & sights' oriented. Others are more slanted toward outdoor activities, with everything included but sleeping bags. Participants must help with the chores and cooking. An example is an eight-day canoe trip in Ontario's Algonquin Park. For information contact Goway Travel (tel 863-0799), 40 Wellington St East, Toronto, Ontario.

The Canadian Outward Bound Wilderness School, with offices in Vancouver and Toronto, runs good, rigorous outdoor adventure trips which are more like courses than holidays. Ranging from seven to 24 days, they take place in various rugged parts of the country; many programmes include a solo portion.

The Canadian Universities Travel Service Ltd (CUTS), mentioned in the Facts for the Visitor chapter, runs various trips and outings that include activities like hiking, cycling and canoeing.

The Association of Students' Councils offers six summer canoe trips varying from eight to 17 days, everything included, sometimes even a flight. Most of these are backpacking wilderness trips, portaging canoes or something similar. For information contact CUTS (tel 977-3703), 171 College St, Toronto.

The Youth Hostels Association also runs some tours and special-event trips featuring hiking, cross-country skiing, etc. Check at any hostel for its organised activities.

There are many small companies across the country offering a variety of adventure trips of different lengths and difficulty. Good camping stores often carry pamphlets Information about them is available from good camping stores, hostels and Tourist Offices. The costs for most tours start at around $325 per week.

Newfoundland

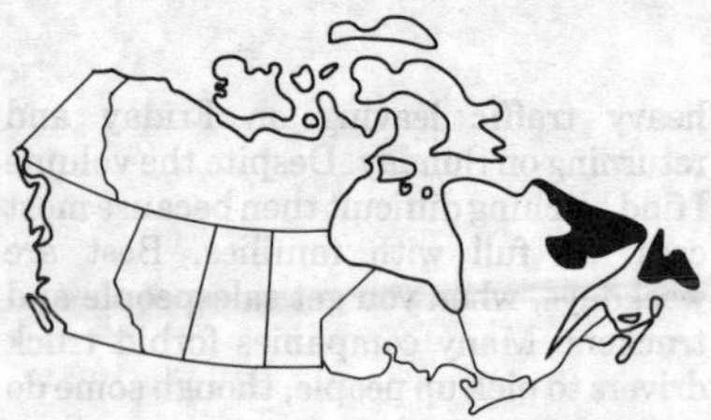

Entered Confederation: 31 March 1949
Area: 404,520 square km
Population: 568,000; second smallest province

Newfoundland has a character unlike that found anywhere else, and even a brief encounter with it is gratifying. This is a rugged, weather-beaten land at the edge of Canada, presided over by the sea and the conditions of the not-too-distant far north.

The people, of mainly British descent, have developed a culture that is, if not entirely their own, considerably different than that of other Canadians. This is apparent in various ways but perhaps most noticeably in the language, with its strong lilting inflections, unique slang and colourful idiomatic expressions. A look at the map reveals villages with names like Nick's Nose Cove, Come-by-Chance and Blow-Me-Down. To the rest of the country the residents here are known light-heartedly as Newfies, and though they are often the butt of Canadian humour there is no real malice felt.

Other peoples have played prominent roles in the development of this land. The Vikings landed and established a settlement in 1000 AD. Inuit and Indian bands were calling the area home long before that. Today, Labrador, the northern mainland portion of the province, is still inhabited mainly by these native people.

All of Labrador and the northern portions of the island are part of the Laurentian Shield, one of the earliest geological formations on earth – possibly the only area unchanged from times predating the appearance of animals on the planet.

Across the province, the interior is mostly forested wilderness with a lot of peat bogs. Almost all the people live along the coast, with its many fiords. From the often-foggy shore, fishermen head to waters legendary for cod, salmon and dozens of other kinds of fish. On the Grand Banks lying south-east off the most populated region (the Avalon Peninsula), fishing boats gather from around the world as they have done before Columbus even saw the new land. In spring, what's left of the controversial seal hunt begins to supply the fashion business with furs. Other industries in this economically depressed province include mining, hydro power, pulp & paper and food processing. Unemployment has been very high for many years.

The discovery of off-shore oil around the province, particularly the huge Hibernia field in the south, has not yet lived up to expectations, due partially to low international prices and the tragic loss of an 'indestructible' oil rig. If and when the wells become operational, a boom of sorts is expected. Unfortunately this will also hasten the change in the traditional way of life and perhaps spell absorption for a large segment of a distinct culture. See it while you can.

Getting around the province presents its own peculiarities. Public road transportation is minimal – the ever-growing road network, while connecting most major towns, remains sketchy in many areas. There is, however, a good ferry system that links together isolated outports, and also the province to the rest of Canada. The intra-provincial routes are quite reasonably priced, too.

The 905-km Trans-Canada Highway is the only road linking St John's to Port Aux

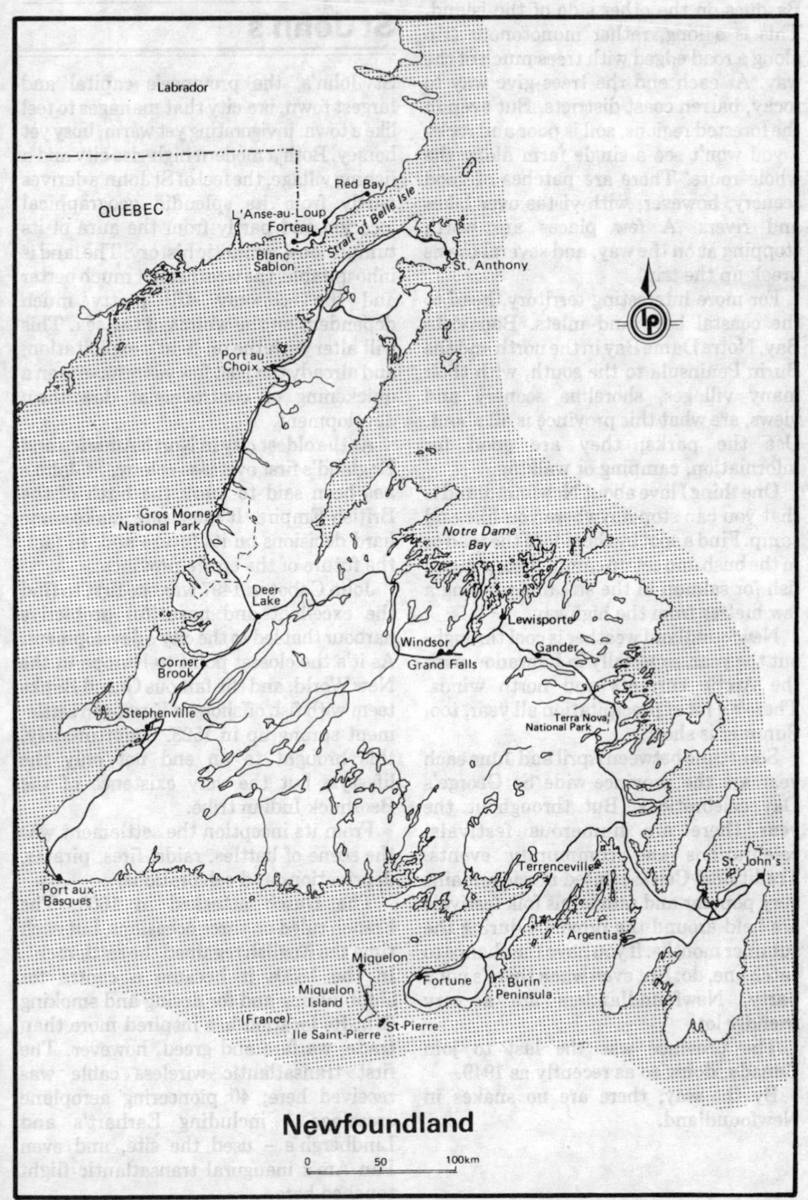
Labrador
QUEBEC
Red Bay
L'Anse-au-Loup
Forteau
Strait of Belle Isle
Blanc Sablon
St. Anthony
Port au Choix
Gros Morne National Park
Notre Dame Bay
Deer Lake
Lewisporte
Windsor
Grand Falls
Gander
Corner Brook
Stephenville
Terra Nova National Park
Port aux Basques
Terrenceville
St. John's
Argentia
Miquelon
Miquelon Island
(France)
Ile Saint-Pierre
St-Pierre
Fortune
Burin Peninsula
Newfoundland
0
50
100km

Basques on the other side of the island. This is a long, rather monotonous trip along a road edged with trees much of the way. At each end the trees give way to rocky, barren coast districts. But even in the forested regions, soil is poor and rocky – you won't see a single farm along the whole route. There are patches of good scenery, however, with vistas over lakes and rivers. A few places are worth stopping at on the way, and several towns break up the trip.

For more interesting territory, head to the coastal bays and inlets. Bonavista Bay, Notre Dame Bay in the north and the Burin Peninsula to the south, with their many villages, shoreline scenery and views, are what this province is all about. Use the parks; they are good for information, camping or walking.

One thing I love about Newfoundland is that you can stop anywhere you like and camp. Find a spot by the side of the road or in the bush and set up camp. Also, you can fish for salmon in the streams running a few metres from the highway.

Newfoundland weather is cool throughout the year, especially in Labrador, with the Arctic currents and north winds. There's a lot of precipitation all year, too. Summer is short.

Sometime between April and June each year are the province-wide St George's Day celebrations. But throughout the year there are numerous festivals, celebrations and community events. Traditional Celtic-related music remains very popular and numerous folk festivals are held around the province during the summer months. If you have the chance to catch one, do. But even when there's not a party, Newfoundlanders are a very friendly lot.

The province was the last to join Canada, doing so as recently as 1949.

By the way, there are no snakes in Newfoundland.

St John's

St John's, the province's capital and largest town, is a city that manages to feel like a town: invigorating yet warm, busy yet homey. Both a modern high-rise city and a fishing village, the feel of St John's derives partly from its splendid geographical location and partly from the aura of its tumultuous, romantic history. The land is inhospitable, the weather not much better and the economy still pretty much dependent on the whims of the sea. This will alter with the oil field's exploitation, and already the past few years have seen a quickening of controversial downtown development.

As the oldest city in North America and England's first overseas colony, St John's has been said to mark the birth of the British Empire. It must now make some hard decisions on its future and, in fact, the future of the entire province.

John Cabot in 1497 was the first to find the excellent and beautiful protective harbour that led to the city's development. As it's the closest point to Europe in the New World, and the famous Grand Banks teem with fish offshore, a European settlement sprang up in 1528. Unfortunately, this brought to an end not only the lifestyle but the very existence of the Beothuck Indian tribe.

From its inception the settlement was the scene of battles, raids, fires, pirates, deprivations and celebrations.

The Dutch attacked in 1665. The French ruled on three occasions, but each time the English regained the settlement. In the 1880s it became a centre for shipbuilding and for drying and smoking fish. Its location has inspired more than trade, warfare and greed, however. The first transatlantic wireless cable was received here; 40 pioneering aeroplane crossings – including Earhart's and Lindbergh's – used the site, and even Pan Am's inaugural transatlantic flight touched here.

Top Left: Marmot (JL)
Middle Left: Mountain Goats
Bottom Left: Hedgehog

Top Right: Big Horn Sheep
Middle Right: Squirrel
Bottom Right: Elk

Top: The Battery, an old section of St John's, Newfoundland (ML)
Bottom: Typical small fishing village near St John's, Newfoundland (ML)

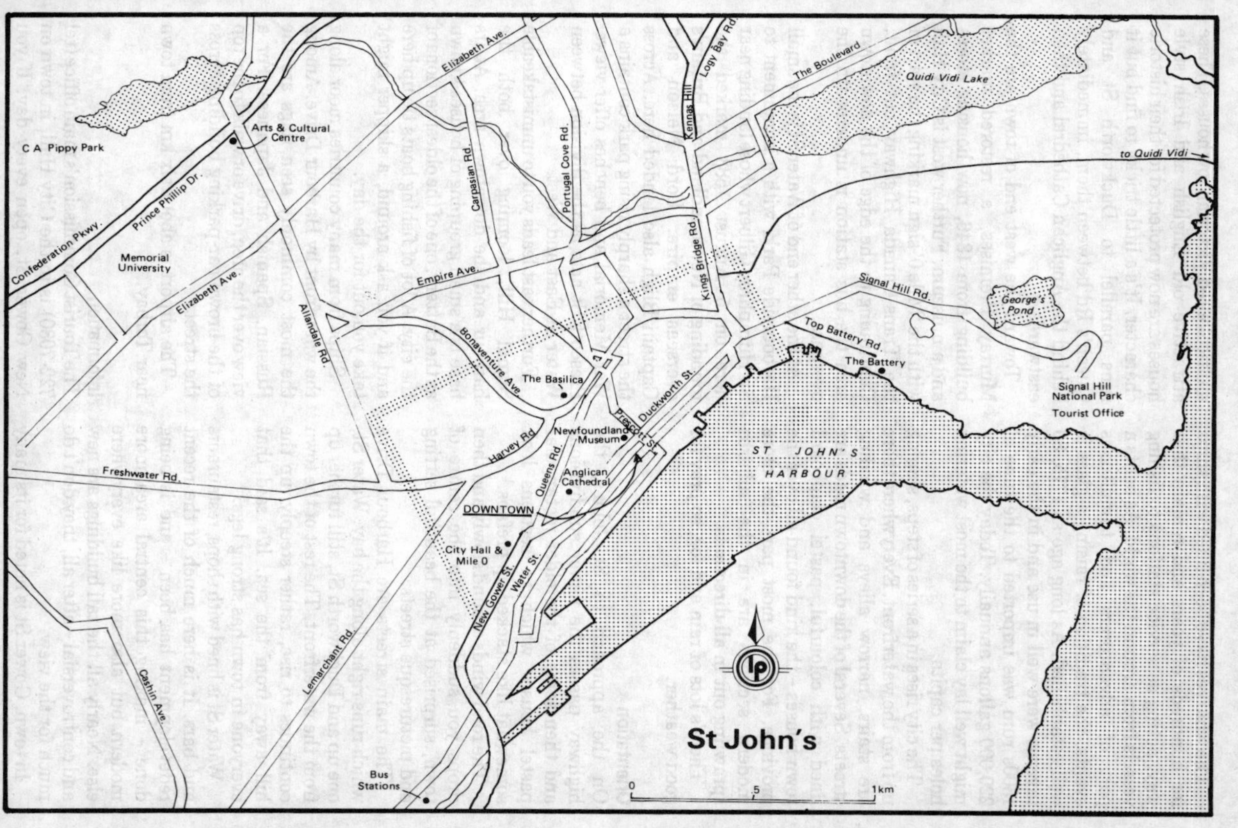
St John's
ST JOHN'S HARBOUR
Signal Hill National Park
Tourist Office
to Quidi Vidi
George's Pond
Quidi Vidi Lake
The Boulevard
Signal Hill Rd.
Top Battery Rd.
The Battery
Logy Bay Rd.
Kennas Hill
Kings Bridge Rd.
Duckworth St.
Prescott St.
Newfoundland Museum
Anglican Cathedral
Queens Rd.
Water St.
New Gower St.
The Basilica
Portugal Cove Rd.
Bonaventure Ave.
Harvey Rd
DOWNTOWN
City Hall & Mile 0
Carpasian Rd.
Empire Ave.
Elizabeth Ave.
Allandale Rd.
Arts & Cultural Centre
Prince Phillip Dr.
Memorial University
C A Pippy Park
Confederation Pkwy.
Freshwater Rd.
Lemarchant Rd.
Bus Stations
Cashin Ave.
0
.5
1km

The wharves have been lined with ships for hundreds of years and remain that way, acting as service stations to fishing vessels from around the world. As befits a port of adventurers and tumultuous events, the tradition of raising a glass is well established. As long ago as 1775, 80 taverns were well in use and in the early 1800s rum was imported to the tune of 220,000 gallons annually. Today the city might well lay claim to the most watering holes per capita.

The city rises in a series of steps, sloping up from the waterfront. Everywhere there are stairs, narrow alleys and winding streets. Several of the downtown roads are lined with colourful, pastel clapboard town houses – the kind found all over the province. For the most part the more modern sections are in the suburbs sprawling out in all directions.

There's lots of rain and fog, so pray for good weather.

Orientation

On the approach to St John's, the highway passes the newer subdivisions and then some of the older rectangular pastel houses which in sections look somewhat like stacked up prefabs.

The road winds around slowly and then drops you suddenly into the centre of town, surprised at the beautiful setting and picturesque streets.

The main streets are Harbour Drive which runs right along the bay, Water St, one up and Duckworth St, still further up from the waterfront. The rest of the town continues to rise, rather steeply, up the hill away from the sea. It's said that everyone in town has strong legs.

Water St is lined with shops, restaurants and bars. It is here much of the recent redevelopment has been – and is being done – making this central area more modern but also more like everywhere else. Nearly all the tall buildings are new and controversial – after all, they don't do much for the view.

In town, Gower St is noted for its many multicoloured Victorian row houses. These attractive old English and Irish style houses are now protected for their historic character. It's a little tricky to find but it runs parallel to Duckworth St and Queen's Rd between them, immediately behind the Anglican Cathedral and then eastwards.

Toward the west end of town are the Murray Premises, a restored market building from 1846, now housing stores and a museum. Further west is City Hall with the 'Mile 0' sign marking the start of the Trans-Canada Highway out front. Continuing to the edge of the downtown area the bus station is underneath the overpass.

At the other end of Water St is the small Harbourside Park, with a monument to Sir Humphrey Gilbert whose landing near here on 5 August 1583 marked the founding of Newfoundland and Britain's overseas empire. Lord Nelson and Captain Bligh also landed here. Across the street a sharply rising park contains a War Memorial and benches offer views. Prescott St acts as the division between Water St East and West.

Further east leads you to unmistakeable Signal Hill, looming over both the harbour and the downtown area. At its base is a small grouping of houses known as the Battery, one of the oldest sections of the city. A lot of fishing boats tie up here and if you ask around, a skipper might take you out for the day.

Ships from many countries moor along the waterfront by Harbour Drive. Among the most commonly seen flags are the Russian, Spanish and Japanese. For a view over the area, drive or walk to the top of the brown car-parking building across the street.

The airport is about six km from town near Torbay.

Information

The Tourist Commission's main office (tel 722-7080) is in the City Hall, in town on New Gower St, open every day. If you start to chat you'll find them very friendly, helpful and knowledgeable. Here, you can get a booklet suggesting a self-guided walk of the downtown area, taking in many of the older buildings and supplying some historical background. Halfway up Signal Hill by road, east of town, there is another information office in the parks building.

There is also an Information Chalet 16 km west of the city on the main highway.

The book department in Bowrings Department Store, Water St has a large and excellent selection of books on the city and Newfoundland.

Newfoundland Museum
Though small, the displays here are good and interesting. There are a few relics and a skeleton – the only remains anywhere of the extinct Beothuck Indian tribe that once lived here. Also on display are exhibits on the Vikings and the history of St John's. Open every day and Thursday evenings, free. It's at 285 Duckworth St.

Incidentally, a fine attraction nearby is the now nearly extinct Canadian traffic cop gesticulating his commands at the corner of Prescott and Duckworth Sts.

Murray Premises Museum
Within this restored market building on west Water St are some shops, a pub and the second branch of the Newfoundland Museum. It's larger than the original on Duckworth St and has exhibits stretched over four floors. Topics covered include the marine, military and naval history of the province. There's some interesting information on the Basques who came to the area in the early 1500s to whale. The entrance is marked by a fine example of the huge Newfoundland dog. Same hours as the Duckworth location and also free.

Courthouse
By the Duckworth museum, the courthouse dates from 1904 and has recently had a major exterior clean-up.

City Hall
Five blocks east of the courthouse is the new City Hall and Mile 0 sign, from where the Trans-Canada Highway starts westwards 7775 km across Canada to Victoria, British Columbia.

Masonic Temple
Up the hill from the Museum you'll see the striking, newly renovated temple, a private men's club.

Anglican Cathedral
Across the street is the Anglican Cathedral of St John the Baptist, dating from 1816. Inside, note the stone walls, wooden ceilings and long, thin stained-glass windows. To enter, go to the side facing the harbour and into the doorway by the toilet. Ring the bell and someone will probably come to let you in.

Basilica of St John the Baptist
Further north up Church St to Garrison Hill, and then right on Military Rd is this Roman Catholic church. Built in 1855, it's considerably more impressive from the outside than the cathedral and, in fact, the Gothic facade dominates the cityscape. Inside, however, it's rather plain although the ceiling is interesting and the pipe organ is a beaut.

There are good views out over the bay from the front steps. Within walking distance are about half a dozen other churches.

Signal Hill National Historic Park
A must if only for the view. Located east of town along Duckworth St, this park rises up the hill forming the cliff edge along the channel into St John's Harbour. The view of the town and out to sea is superb night and day. Watch the many types of fishing vessels move in and out of the port. Halfway up the road from the end of Duckworth is the Visitors' Centre, with a small museum where you can get information about the park or the city in general. During the Battle of Signal Hill

in 1762 the English took St John's and pretty much ended French control of North America. Queens Battery further up has some cannons and the remains of the British battery of the late 1700s. Cabot Tower at the top of the hill honours John Cabot's arrival in 1497. Built in 1900, this tower was where Marconi received the first transatlantic message in 1901 – the wireless broadcast was sent from Cornwall, England. There are guides and displays in the tower. It's free and open daily in summer until 5 pm. Near the tower is Ladies Lookout, which at 175 metres, is the highest point in the park and offers views over what seems like half the province.

Highly recommended in either direction is the 1.7 km walking trail connecting Cabot Tower to the Battery section of town down in the harbour. Going up the trip takes about 90 minutes. The Tourist Office has a map of the park.

Fort Amherst
Across the narrows you can see the remains of this fort. With the Battery and the fort to face, enemy ships wouldn't have had an easy time getting into the bay. On the point, on the fort side, the lighthouse dates from 1813. You're about as close to Europe here as you can be without getting wet.

There are several other historical sites around town:

Commissariat House on Kings Bridge Rd near Gower St, is one of the most complete. Built in 1818, the late Georgian mansion was used by the supplies officer of the British military. When British forces left in 1870, the building was used as a church rectory, nursing home and children's hospital. It is now restored to the 1850 period with many period pieces inside. Open daily in summer and by appointment at other times, free. There's an interpretive centre.

Colonial Building nearby on Military Rd, was the seat of the provincial legislature from 1850 to 1960. It's built of stone from Ireland which was used as ships' ballast, and contains many of the province's old records. Open in summer Monday to Friday from 9 am to 5 pm, free.

Government House is beside Bannerman Park, Military Rd, close to the two sites above. Built in 1830, it was the official residence of the governor of Newfoundland until it became part of Canada and since then, the Lieutenant Governors have called it home.

Quidi Vidi
Over Signal Hill, away from town, is the tiny, picturesque village of Quidi Vidi. This little fishing port has one of the oldest houses in North America, dating from the early 1700s. You can walk to the village from Signal Hill in about 20 minutes or go around by road from St John's. Take Forest Rd, which runs along the lake and then turns into Quidi Vidi Village Rd.

French Battery
Built in 1762, the battery is up the hill from the village, guarding the bay. It's free to look around.

Quidi Village Lake
Inland from the village is this lake, site of the St John's Regatta, which is held the first Wednesday in August. Records show the event started in 1818 and it's probably the oldest competition in North America. Pleasantville, now a suburb at the end of the lake, was an American military base until the 1950s or '60s when they packed up and gave it to Newfoundland.

The Rennies River flowing out of the lake is an excellent trout stream. A conservation group is developing the area and a walking trail, from the lake along the river to Long Pond, has been set up, with others planned. Trout can be seen leaping in the autumn as they ready for spawning. The tourist office has a pamphlet with a map of the river system.

Arts & Cultural Centre
Here you'll find the art gallery – with displays of Canadian painting and sculpture, open Tuesday to Sunday, free – and a theatre. The complex is located about two km from the downtown area at the corner of Allandale Rd and Prince Phillip Drive, near the university. For theatre information call 726-5978.

Confederation Building
Nearby, just off Confederation Parkway, east of the arts centre, is the new home of the provincial government. You can visit the building and the small military museum inside for free. Closed on weekends.

C A Pippy Park
Aside from the Arts & Cultural Centre and Confederation Building, this huge park on the city's northern edge also contains Memorial University. Much of the park is natural with walking trails, picnic areas and a botanical section; there's also a campground.

Bowring Park
West of the downtown area off Pitts Memorial Drive, this is another popular city park and it's big, too. A couple of streams and walkways meander through the park.

Events
The Newfoundland & Labrador Folk Festival is held annually around 27, 28, 29 June in C A Pippy Park, 1 to 10 pm daily. There's camping and the music is great. The festival is held indoors if the weather is bad.

For other festivals – there are several during summer – ask at the Tourist Office.

The Quidi Vidi Regatta is held the first Wednesday in August.

The Signal Hill Tattoo takes place 17 July to 17 August on Tuesday and Thursday evenings; it's very colourful.

Places to Stay
Accommodation in Newfoundland is generally expensive. Most hotels are new and designed primarily for businesspeople, and motels for tourists are also pricey. But St John's has a few older places and throughout the province are tourist homes, some of which are very reasonable.

Hostels The hostel situation in Newfoundland is very changeable and usually minimal. In town here, however, a *Youth Hostel* (tel 737-7590) is set up on the university campus in Hatcher House from May to mid-August. There are buses to town but it's walkable in less than half an hour, even if the roads are not direct. From the campus Newtown Rd leads to downtown.

Other than the hostel, the university offers no rooms and the YM-YWCA has no accommodation either.

Tourist Homes Scattered about the province are 'Hospitality Homes', as they are called here. Some are like small rooming houses, some pretty much like small hotels and still others are just an extra room in a family house. The tourist office should have a list, and in small towns a pub manager will likely be able to give you a few names. These vary quite a bit but are usually friendly, cheap places to stay. In St John's, people call the tourist office through the day to say if they have a room open for the night, so if things are busy give them a second call.

The *Sea Flow Tourist Home* (tel 753-2425, 781-2448) is at 53-55 William St. Mrs Hutchens has four rooms at single $20, double $22 to $25. The cheapest room has no bath, and one room has kitchen facilities.

A second choice is the inexpensive *Mrs Newhook's* (tel 722-3833) at 16 1st Avenue. First St is north from town up Portugal Cove Rd, on the left.

Prescott Inn is a very good bed & breakfast at 19 Military Rd, centrally situated on the eastern side of the central area. It's a well-kept old house with balconies looking out over the harbour. Singles/doubles cost $36/49. The same people run *Prescott House* at 30 Prescott St right in town. Here there are basically two large apartments, both with cooking facilities, one with a fireplace and one with two bedrooms, pretty reasonably priced.

Out of the town centre there's *Mariece Wall's Fireside Guest House* at 28 Wicklow St near the Avalon Mall Shopping Centre. Call 726-4869 for directions. With breakfast, rates are single $25, double $30 and you can use the indoor swimming pool, which is a short walk from the house.

Farther out of town is *Werner's Hospitality Home* (tel 368-3220), at the junction of Routes 1 and 60 just east of the Crossroads Motel. Just two rooms but singles only $20, doubles $25.

Lastly, there is a place over on Bell Island in Conception Bay, across the peninsula from St John's. Chris Petrie runs *The Rock* (tel 488-3104) where singles cost $23, doubles $34. Take the ferry from Portugal Cove at the end of Highway 40 from the city.

If you find these places full, try the Tourist Office. They should have an up-to-date local list. There are usually others not mentioned in provincial guides and pamphlets.

Hotels There are still some pretty good, inexpensive places around town among the more costly.

Parkview Inn (tel 753-2671) is the big, green, barn-like house with white trim at 118 Military Rd, corner of King's Rd. Very central. Singles range from $25 to $35, doubles $30 to $45 and triples are good value at $45. Weekly rates are less 10%. If you're trying to cut corners make sure to ask for the simplest room.

Old Inn (tel 772-1171 or 576-9409), run by Amon Rosato, is a lodge of 14 rooms from singles $20, doubles $28 to $35 and good weekly rates. It's at 157 LeMarchant Rd, the black and white place built in 1892. It's a long walk but the bus goes along LeMarchant Rd.

Bonaventure House (tel 753-3359) at 34 Bonaventure Avenue, not far from the Basilica, is similar but smaller. There are five rooms; singles are $28, doubles $36, including breakfast. Free parking.

Moving up-scale a bit is the *Lester Hotel* (tel 579-2141) at 12 Blackmarsh Rd. Singles in the $55 range and doubles a few dollars more. More central is the *Battery Hotel*, the new-looking place halfway up the hill at 100 Signal Hill. They have all the facilities and a wide range of rooms, some less and some more than the Lester. The top hotel in town is *Hotel Newfoundland* on Cavendish Square at the east end of Duckworth; expensive.

Motels Motels are priced in the middle range or higher. *1st City Motel* (tel 772-5400) is at 479 Kenmount Rd, about six km from the city centre. Prices are $40 to $50 for a single and $5 more for the double.

Greenwood Lodge & Motel (tel 364-5300) is toward Mount Pearl, off Route 60, close to town. Singles are $40, doubles $42. They've got colour TV and a games room, and housekeeping units are available.

The *Crossroads Motel* is at the junction of Routes 1 and 60. Rates are single $35, double $39; complete facilities.

Camping You can camp in *C A Pippy Park* near the university, right in the city. They charge $5 for tenting, $10 unserviced, $12 serviced.

Places to Eat

At 183 Duckworth St is the *Duckworth Lunch*, a small café popular with the artsy and student crowds. They serve good health food at reasonable prices and there are lots of newspapers to read.

In Bowring's Department Store on Water St, the *Captain's Cabin* cafeteria has a good selection of inexpensive meals from breakfast to dinner, and has fine views of the harbour as well. Recommended.

Also cheap and busy is the *Ports of Food*, a food booth assortment in the Atlantic Place Mall on Water St. It's only fast food – Chinese, soup and salads, doughnuts, etc, but it's open every day. *Woolworths* cafeteria is also very low-priced.

Up on George St around the corner from Water St, the *Continental Cafe* is a small, dark place specialising in very good salads. They also serve burritos, felafels, desserts and coffees.

The *Fishing Admiral Pub* is a good place for a drink at night but also serves up a good-value lunch. There's a selection of seafood platters, chowders and fish & chips. Most meals are about $5; it's more expensive at dinner.

St John's has the best fish & chips in the world, and quite a few places to prove it to yourself. Locals tend to have their favourites and competitions are held to determine popularity, but to me they were all top-rate. Try *King Cod* at 122 Duckworth St, *Caram's* in the middle of Water St near McBrides Hill or the ever-popular *Ches's* at both 5 and 9 Freshwater Rd, a short walk from the centre. Unless you're really hungry don't order the large serves, because you *really* get a piece of fish. There are others to try, just ask around.

Upstairs at the King Cod, the *Upper Flat*, a less casual dining room, offers other seafood like salmon, scallops and a local dish called *brewis*. The latter is a blend of fish, onion and a bread-like mix that's soaked overnight. Another local specialty is cod tongues which are really closer to cheeks. They're often served deep-fried with very unimpressive results, but if you can, try them pan-fried too.

Casa Grande is a nicely decorated Mexican restaurant at 108 Duckworth St. It holds about 10 small wooden tables encircled by wicker chairs and has dishes from $6. Open daily, but no lunches on Sundays.

At 223 Duckworth St is the St John's version of the *Spaghetti Factory* chain, with good-value Italian dishes. And at 106 Water St (the door is around the side), the *Curry House* serves Indian food.

Lastly, you may want to check out the Fish Market at the end of Harbour Drive at the west end of town.

Nightlife

St John's at night is a lot of fun. You won't have to search too long in this town if you're thirsty because per capita, there must be more watering holes here than anywhere.

George St is pretty crazy with crowds and line-ups at a variety of bars. The *Corner Stone* has videos and live rock, *Weekenders* has new wave music and others cater to different age groups and musical preferences. All are cheap or free to get in.

The *Graduate House*, known as the Grad, at 112 Military Rd has a free movie night on Wednesday or Thursday and often has very popular weekend parties.

The *Ship Inn* down the steps beside the Arts Council, 267 Duckworth St, is good with live music. *Kibbitzer's*, down one of the narrow alleys off Water St, is like being in someone's living room and offers various games like chess to play. Friendly and open very late.

There are several pubs along Water St and one in the Murray Premises. The LSPU Hall, up the stairs from Duckworth St near the Arts Council, often has plays, concerts, comedy nights, etc. Worth checking out as it's the centre for the very active arts community.

Try to seek out some live Newfie music, an excellent folk music with Celtic origins, usually based on the fiddle. You may also want to sample Screech, a particularly strong rum once available only here, but now widely available and still tasty.

Apart from these suggestions, you can drink in the quiet lounges of the better hotels or attend a theatre or dance performance at the Arts & Culture Centre on Confederation Parkway.

Getting There & Away

Air Air Canada to Halifax costs $189, youth fare $95, and the fares to Montreal are $266, youth $133.

Canadian Airlines flies to Charlottetown for $211, youth $106.

Bus The station (tel 737-5911) is located at the far west end of town on Water St, underneath the overpass. It's about a 15 to 20-minute walk from town. Terra Nova operates the Road Cruiser buses on these, the main bus lines:

Port Aux Basques: two daily at 8 am, one direct, one slow – $58 one-way

Grand Falls: 5.30 pm daily, 12.30 pm Friday, Saturday and Sunday – $33.

There are several small, local lines around the province as well: Newhook's Bus Line runs to Argentia; and Fleetline Buses (with an office on George St) have a daily service to the Conception Bay area.

Train The last trains in the province died in late 1984, leaving bus transport the only possible transportation. It was the end of an era when the narrow-gauge trains, with each car heated by its own oil stove, finally succumbed to economics. Now only the bus runs up to Carbonear and down to Argentia, where the ferry to Nova Scotia docks. There is one exception and that is basically a freight-carrying line run by Terra Nova, the bus company, which also takes passengers between Corner Brook and Bishop's Falls.

Ferry The Marine Atlantic ferry for North Sydney, Nova Scotia, docks at Argentia on the west coast of the Avalon Peninsula. Newhook's Bus Lines runs a minibus between Argentia and St John's. The fare is about $8 one-way and they have an office in downtown St John's.

The ferry goes in each direction three times a week in summer only. It departs Argentia Tuesday, Thursday and Saturday, and the crossing time is 18 hours. A ticket is $33, car $80, bicycle $10. Rooms and beds are extra. In July or August reservations are a good idea: telephone 227-2311, or in Sydney phone (902) 794-7203.

If you're in a car, you'll get a free car wash as you board the ferry back to the Canadian mainland. This is to get rid of two bugs found only in Newfoundland and harmful to potatoes.

Getting Around

Airport Transport There is no city bus to the airport; taxi is the only way. The airport is about six km north of town out Route 40 towards Torbay.

Bus There are a few bus routes in and around town and together they cover most areas. Route 1 does the central area. By transferring from this one to an adjoining loop, say the No 12 going west, you can get a pretty good tour for under $2. For information phone 722-9400.

Car Rentals There are several agencies in town. Among the chains there is Budget (tel 726-1707) at 51 LeMarchant Rd. For a local outfit try Hickman Motors (tel 726-6990) on Kenmount Rd. Gas (petrol) is expensive in Newfoundland – the costliest in Canada. Also, if you drive a car one-way between St John's and Port Aux Basques, you'll have to pay a return charge of about $100. Basically though, the rates are about the same here as anywhere else.

Tours For a relatively small city, the number and variety of tours available is noteworthy. The Newfoundland Historic Trust offers walking tours of the old city twice daily in summer leaving from the Hotel Newfoundland. In addition, some years the city does much the same tour from mid-June to mid-September, leaving from City Hall and free. Call the Tourist Office for times.

McCarthy's Party (tel 834-5705) offer four different excursions. The three-hour tour of the city at $10 is good, but really doesn't provide too much you can't do yourself for free. The other ones are more worthwhile and include a trip along Marine Drive, one to Cape Spear and another day-long spin around Conception Bay. Lots of interesting historical tidbits and humour is woven into the commentary.

Fleetline (tel 722-2608) offers trips ranging from a half day around town to a full week around the province. Another goes to St Pierre et Miquelon. They have an office on George St.

Other tours are done by boat. Harbour Charters, for example, runs a trip from the waterfront out to sea in search of whales and icebergs. The 2½-hour trip costs $20. Try to pick a calm day as it allows the boat to travel further and also permits a little cod jigging. There are great views along the coastline, but it can get rough (this is the North Atlantic, after all – no reason to mention how I lost my breakfast overboard!) and cold, so take warm clothes – it may be balmy in the protected harbour but it's quite a different story once outside the narrows.

Bird Island Charters (tel 753-4850) is similar but visits the Sea Bird Sanctuary Islands which include the largest puffin colony on the east coast of America. Daily departures from Bay Bulls, south of town. There's a shuttle service to get you to the dock.

The Tourist Office will have information on other tour possibilities.

AROUND ST JOHN'S

Marine Drive, north of St John's up towards Torbay, goes past nice coastal scenery. There are rocky beaches but it's good for a walk or picnic at both Middle Cove and Outer Cove. Offshore around Torbay is a good whale-watching area. Puffins live and feed here also. Marine Drive ends at Pouch Cove but a gravel road continues to Cape St Francis. Good views. West of town, head to Topsail for a great view of Conception Bay and some of its islands.

South of St John's, the road goes to Cape Spear (about 13 km) and Witless Bay, good areas for viewing sea birds. Off Witless Bay are some island bird sanctuaries; the best months for visiting are June and July. You may be lucky enough to go out to the islands with local fishermen.

At Cape Spear there is a National Historic Park centred around the lighthouse, which dates from 1835. A guide will show you around and offer all sorts of information, like how many coats of paint layer the inside walls (you won't believe it). Cape Spear is the most easterly point in North America: next stop, Ireland.

Around the Island

AVALON PENINSULA

The peninsula – more like an island hanging onto the rest of the province by a thin strip of land – is the most densely populated area of Newfoundland, with nearly half the population. Conception Bay is lined with scores of small communities but all around the coast you'll find fishing villages. In the southern central section is a large wilderness area with a growing herd of caribou. The Tourist Office can suggest driving and camping tours around the peninsula.

Harbour Grace, on Conception Bay 100 km from St John's, was first settled in 1583 and was once a pirates' haunt. It has an airstrip designated an historic site. Fish processing is the main economic activity.

Northern Bay Sands, past Carbonear on Conception Bay, has beautiful beaches. On the inland side is a spot for freshwater swimming. The water is too cold in the ocean.

At the bottom of Trinity Bay, Dildo (when you stop sniggering) is a good spot for whale-watching. Pothead whales come in by the school; humpbacks, a larger species, can also be seen in summer. Both can be viewed even from the shore.

North up the coast a few of the towns

have absolutely lovely names: how about 'Heart's Delight' and 'Heart's Content'? In Heart's Content an historic site tells the story of the cable station here, where the first transatlantic cable was laid.

Both towns mentioned have a hospitality home (appropriately, Heart's Desire doesn't!) In the town of the same name, *Heart's Delight* (tel 588-2577) is run by Mrs Gertie Legges, who charges $18 for singles, $22 for doubles and a little more for breakfast. *Noseworthy's* (tel 583-2035) in Heart's Content is $20/22 for singles/doubles. If this place is no longer operating there is a motel in town, though it is considerably more costly.

Salmonier National Park is in the centre of the Peninsula on Highway 90, 12 km south of the junction with No 1. Here you can see many animals found in the province, enclosed in the park's natural settings. A marked trail through the woods takes you past the animals – moose, caribou, beaver, etc. Open daily from June to September. Small admission fee.

The south-west portion of the peninsula is known primarily for Argentia with the large ferry terminal for boats to Nova Scotia. Nearby in Placentia, settled in 1662, you'll find the remains of a French fort at Historic Castle Hill, with a visitors centre and fine views. The old graveyard by the Anglican Church offers more history. There is a hotel in town.

In the southern area from Holyrood Bay to St Mary's Bay, your chances are excellent for seeing whales, particularly the humpback which feed close to shore. The best times are between mid-June and mid-July. Fishermen may offer closer looks at other whales in the area, including the fin, blue, sperm and minke.

BONAVISTA PENINSULA

Trinity

Halfway up Bonavista Bay (turn off the Trans-Canada at Clarenville), Trinity is one of the oldest settlements in the province. First discovered in 1500, the village has a fascinating history which includes the first court in North America – convened in 1615. Many buildings along the town's narrow streets have been restored or renovated. Visit the museum and the fort remains.

Also in town is Ocean Contact, a whale-watching and research organisation. They offer day expeditions, short holidays and all-inclusive, expensive week-long trips that take in other wildlife and local geographic and historic attractions. Ocean Contact works out of the *Village Inn* (tel 464-3269), a good place to stay with rooms from $38 to $45. They have films and slides on whales and other sea-life.

Alternately, there is the *Crossroads Guest House* (tel 464-3555). Single $20, double $24 and breakfast $3.50, with other meals available. The owners speak French and German as well as English.

A third place to stay is *Trinity Cabins* (tel 464-3657), with cabins in the $26 to $36 range. There's a beach nearby but they have a pool as well.

Bonavista

This largish town of 5000 at the end of the peninsula, is where John Cabot landed on 24 June 1497 and first saw the 'new found land'. (The King of England rewarded him with £10 and he later drifted down to the St John's harbour and stopped there.) It took until the 1600s for Bonavista to become a permanent village. From then through the 1700s, like other settlements along the coast, it was battled over by the English and French. You can visit the lighthouse that dates from 1843 and is now a provincial historic site. You can also watch whales in early summer.

For accommodation, there is *Whiffen's Hospitality Home* (tel 468-7361) with singles at $25, doubles $30 with breakfast. It's the white two-storey house opposite the Royal Canadian Legion Hall.

Returning down the peninsula, take the No 235 for some good coastal scenery.

Along the beaches here and around the Avalon Peninsula in late June and early July, millions of caplin – a small silver fish – get washed up on shore by the tides. I think this is partially due to spawning and partially due to being chased by hungry cod. Anyway, the shore is alive with the fish, and people go down with buckets and bags to scoop up a free meal.

Terra Nova National Park

This east coast park, split by the Trans-Canada, typifies the regional geography. The rocky, jagged coastline on beautiful Bonavista Bay gives way to long bays, inland lakes, ponds, bogs and hilly woods. There's canoeing, fishing, hiking, camping, sandy beaches, even swimming in Sandy Pond. You can rent bicycles in the park – a good way to get around. You'll see lots of wildlife – moose, bear, beaver and otter – and from May to August, icebergs are commonly seen off the coast.

BURIN PENINSULA

Jutting south into the Atlantic Ocean, the peninsula has been the base for European fisherman since the 1500s. The Grand Banks off the peninsula (part of the continental shelf) teem with fish. The wooded northern area supplied timber for building and ships; the southern end is mostly barren, glacier-stripped rock.

If you've come here on your way to St Pierre et Miquelon, the ferry leaves from Fortune on the south-west coast. It's possible to stay either here or nearby in Grand Bank. In Fortune, the *Seaview Motel* has singles for $38 and doubles for $40; closer to Grand Bank, the *Townview Drive Inn* has housekeeping cabins at $27/30 for singles/doubles, and in Grand Bank, the big old *Thorndyke* house offers rooms at a good price, or you can just stop for afternoon tea.

Terrenceville

Terrenceville is the eastern port for the southern coast Marine Atlantic ferry which skips along the bottom of the province from Port Aux Basques. This is one of the province's unique adventures and with new roads always being built, will likely be history in 10 years. The ferry serves about 10 communities, most of them otherwise isolated. It carries the sick to the doctor – and later the bill in the mailbag. Each trip is somewhat different as the stops made varies; if all the stops are made, the trip is four days long. It's possible to break the journey and although none of the stops have official hotels, it's not uncommon to find someone to take you in for the night. The ferry charge is very low, for full details call Marine Atlantic at 695-2124.

In Terrenceville there is, unfortunately, no place to stay but the ferry arrives the night before the morning departure, so you can sleep on board. Buses run from St John's to Argentia but they don't stop at Terrenceville on the way, although the driver may pick you up if he's in the right mood. If he's not, you'll have to hitch from where the road branches off. You could also catch a taxi; Slaney's Taxi (tel 753-3287) has an office in St John's and runs a daily service to and from the Burin Peninsula.

ST PIERRE ET MIQUELON

This is probably the oddest side-trip in Canada. Once called the 'Islands of 11,000 Virgins', these two dabs of land, lying 16 km west off Newfoundland's Burin Peninsula, belong to France. The tiny islands represent the only French holdings left in North America. The 6000 residents drink French wine, eat baguettes and pay for it in francs.

First claimed by France in the 1500s, the islands were ceded to France by England in 1783 with the Treaty of Paris.

As always, the main livelihoods are fishing and supplying fishing boats, but today, tourism brings in extra money. There are about half a dozen hotels and even more guest houses, some of which are quite reasonably priced. Accommodation can be tight in high season so you may want to check before you go. The food is said to be very good. *Chez Dutin* has been recommended.

A few days make a good visit – exploring, relaxing, enjoying a different culture. There's a museum and cemetery to visit and bicycles are available for hire. From mid-July to the end of August, folk dances are held in the town square. August and September are best for weather.

A ferry connects St Pierre to Miquelon, a much less visited and less developed island 45 km away. Miquelon's people are largely of Acadian background while St Pierre's are French and Basque.

Getting There & Away

Canadians don't need passports to visit St Pierre and Miquelon. There's a daily ferry from Fortune, on Highway 210 on the Burin Peninsula, which costs about $30 (no vehicles taken). Gander Aviation flies from Gander for $140. SPM Tours from St John's offer one to five-night packages, including transport and accommodation.

GANDER

A town of about 12,000, Gander is known for its airport, which served the first regular transatlantic flights and then was a major link for planes in WW II on their way to Europe. The Gander airport was chosen because it is close to Europe and yet inland far enough to be free of the coastal fog. The airport is now known for being the site of thousands of defections from Russia, Cuba and Eastern Bloc countries. The plane touches down and passengers ask for political asylum.

There's actually nothing special to do here. For eating, try the *Highlight Restaurant* at the corner of Elizabeth and Fraser Drives, which serves simple Chinese dishes and cheap combination lunches; or south from Fraser Drive on Bennet Drive is the *Bread Shoppe*, a good bakery with a wide selection of breads and pastries.

There are numerous motels. Cheapest is the *Airport Inn* (tel 256-3535) on the highway, which has singles for $30, doubles $36. Or there are campgrounds 16 km north of town at Jonathan's Pond and at Square Pond 34 km east of Gander.

There's a tourist info chalet on the Trans-Canada Highway.

NOTRE DAME BAY & AREA

This coastal area north of Gander is typically rugged and scenic though relatively populated. About 80 little villages are found around the bay nestled in small coves or clinging to the rocky shoreline. From Gander there are two road loops – one through Lewisporte, the other eastward to Wesleyville – that make good circular tours. A few of the towns have small museums dealing with various aspects of local history.

Offshore is a large cluster of islands, including New World, Fogo and Twillingate. New World you can drive to; to get to Fogo you take a ferry. Twillingate is said to be good for whale-watching and viewing icebergs – take a boat tour here, or try and catch the Twillingate Fish, Fun & Folk Festival, a major annual event. The latter two islands have hospitality homes: *Payne's* (tel 266-2359) on Fogo, and *Pelley's* (tel 884-2437) on Twillingate. Tread carefully on Fogo; the president of the Canadian Flat Earth Society has stated that Fogo is at the edge of the world!

Lewisporte, about 60 km from Gander, is a major ferry terminal for trips north and to Labrador. For ferry information and reservations call 535-6876. You can camp in town at *Municipal Park* ($4 to $5) or at *Notre Dame Provincial Park*, about 11 km from town. *Chaulk's Hospitality Home* (tel 535-6305) is on Main St.

West of Lewisporte, the bay becomes less populated and, as the road network declines, less accessible.

GRAND FALLS & WINDSOR

These two small towns sit in pulp-and-paper country. Grand Falls has the Mary March Museum on Cromer Avenue, which outlines the life of the extinct Beothuck Indians. They lived in much of the province before Europeans arrived, but the clash of cultures spelled the end for this tribe; the last two women died in the early 1800s and supplied much of the information used in the museum.

There are restaurants and motels in both towns. The *Town & Country Inn* (tel 489-9602) at 6 Church Rd in Grand Falls has nine rooms at $25/30 for singles/doubles. It has a lounge, a restaurant and a TV/games room.

Just out of town is Beothuck Provincial Park, where an exhibit re-creates a turn-of-the-century logging camp. There's also a reconstructed Beothuck Indian village on an island in Exploits River, which runs along the highway.

From nearby Bishop's Falls there is train service to Corner Brook.

NORTHERN PENINSULA

This long arm of the island extends northward from Deer Lake. There is only one road, the 430, which ends at St Anthony on the north-east tip. If you're driving you've got to come back the same way. The road, known as the Viking Trail, edges along the western shoreline through Gros Morne National Park all the way up to Labrador.

Gros Morne National Park

This is an area of mountains, lakes, fiords and barren highland tundra, much of it difficult to get at. Some of the mountains here, making up part of the Long Range mountain chain, are snow-capped all year round and caribou and moose can be found in the park, too. There are some well-marked trails or you can follow some of the old hunting tracks. For a good view, try the James Callahan Trail to the top of Gros Morne Mountain. For information about lengthier trips, ask at the information office.

The scenery from the highway is good along the East Arm, a fiord. There are sandy beaches at Challow Bay and Western Brook, though the water never gets above 15°C. At Western Brook Pond there's a six km trail into the woods, and at the trail's end is a small lake with cliffs of nearly 700 metres. Boat tours on the lake are available; they take about two hours and cost about $50 for up to four people.

Supplies are available from Rocky Harbour, the main village, and you'll find several campgrounds in the park. A ferry goes across the bay continually all day, connecting the park roads.

Port au Choix

Lying halfway between Gros Morne and the northern tip is this National Historic Park with excavations from the province's very early history. You'll see artefacts from the Maritime Archaic People, inhabitants of 4000 years ago, and some from the later Dorset Eskimos.

L'anse aux Meadows National Historic Park

At this National Historic Park on the most northerly tip of the Northern Peninsula are Viking remains from 1000 AD. They were the first known European community in the western hemisphere, 500 years before the arrival of Columbus. It's not known how long they stayed or why they left, but the Norse people left eight dwellings, a few tools and bits of jewellery. Articles of similar style have been found in Iceland, Greenland and Scandinavia. Restoration still goes on and you can see the remains of the buildings and visit the interpretive centre for more information.

There are motels along Highway 430 and camping is possible, too. Nearby, St Anthony has a population of 2500. *Decker's Boarding House* (tel 454-2312) is here, with singles for $18, doubles for $36 including all meals. *Howell's Tourist*

Home (tel 454-2536), has nine rooms at $20/25 for singles/doubles and breakfast is $2.50, with other meals available.

The Grenfell Mission runs a handicraft centre where hand-embroidered parkas can be bought.

CORNER BROOK

This is Newfoundland's second largest town with 30,000 people. An all-pervading smell will tell you the focus of the town is the huge pulp & paper mill. There are free tours of the mill daily. Another important industry is herring. There are very good views on the road through town and beyond along Humber Arm. You can see the big log booms out in the bay. Also, from Corner Brook there are boat and fishing trips; ask at the Tourist Office.

At 33 Main St you'll find *Power's Tourist Home* (tel 634-2048), where there are two rooms at single $18, double $20. Also in town is the *Delightful Guest Home* (tel 634-2165) at 1 Elswick Rd, with singles/doubles for $25/30 with a light breakfast. There are quite a few other tourist homes, all inexpensive, as well as a motel and hotel. (Strange, considering the dearth in Port Aux Basques.)

A good short side trip is along Humber Arm past Blow-Me-Down, with camping at the tip of the peninsula at Bottle Cove.

Pope's Bed & Breakfast is 25 km east in Pasadena. It's close to a beach and very reasonable at $20 a single and $25 a double, including breakfast. *Hickey's Hospitality Home* (which may have closed) is recommended with Newfoundland meals available.

The province's only remaining train service is from Corner Brook to Bishop's Falls in the centre. It's both a freight and passenger line run by Terra Nova and the schedule is variable, so verify times. Also note that Canrail passes are not valid.

STEPHENVILLE

This town of 10,000 is on St George's Bay between Corner Brook and Port Aux Basques. It's in the centre of Newfoundland's French-speaking communities.

The Stephenville Festival is a two-week English theatre event, usually held in late July with local and internationally known participants. The festival offers a range from Shakespeare to modern Newfoundlanders' plays. Good student reduction on tickets.

During lobster season (April to July), the tasty devils are sold in the streets from trucks and trailers at good prices.

Aquaterra Tours (tel 643-4978) runs trips around the area from 15 June to 15 September. There are six organised tours ranging from two hours in town to a four-hour trip around Port au Port Peninsula, $4 to $8. The guides will also help you plan your own activities as well as hiking, cod jigging and boat tours.

The road out to Port au Port Bay was once called the French Shore and was used by the French for fishing from the early 1700s to the early 1900s. Red Island was at one time France's most important fishing base in the new world.

PORT AUX BASQUES

For many visitors this is the first glimpse of Newfoundland. On the approach by ferry from Nova Scotia, the rocky, barren, treeless landscape looks a little forbidding but appealing in a rough, undeveloped way. For the many people heading to the province for its ruggedness, this uncommercialised port is a welcome sight.

Port Aux Basques, named by Basque fishermen in the 16th century, has also been a fishing station for the French and Portuguese.

Today, it's the principal terminal for the Marine Atlantic ferry, which links the island to the Canadian mainland. They are now the largest employer in town, though there is also freight-handling and fish-packing.

Orientation

The ferry pulls into a small but well-protected bay. The town is to the left of the landing and back the way you came in. It consists of narrow, hilly streets overlooking the sea. They're lined with the brightly coloured wooden houses so common in the province.

To get to the old section of town, cross the bridge after leaving the ferry and turn left.

For the new area of town turn right along the Trans-Canada. Go past a number of gas stations and turn left at the Motel Port Aux Basques. This will take you to the shopping mall, centre of the new district. If you have time to kill before the ferry, there's a movie theatre in the mall.

Also in the shopping plaza parking lot is the town pool in the white metal building. It's open for public swimming at certain hours.

Information

The Tourist Office is on the Trans-Canada a few km out of town on the way to St John's. It's on the right-hand side.

Places to Stay

Not much to report here – the only choice is between two expensive motels. The *Grand Bay Motel* (tel 695-2105) near the shopping mall, is the cheapest motel with singles/doubles for $50/55. It has a bar and restaurant and modern, well-equipped rooms. *Hotel Port Aux Basques* is even more.

Ask at the Tourist Office about hospitality homes. The one I heard about seemed to have given it up; perhaps another has opened.

For more reasonable prices you'll have to hit the highway. *Tompkins Hotel & Tourist Home* in Doyles, 34 km away, is a start.

Places to Eat

There's an *A & W Restaurant* in the new mall specialising in hamburgers and root beer.

On the main street in the old town, a *Pizza Delight* and a Chinese place offer what choice there is.

Getting There & Away

Ferry There are daily Marine National (tel 1-800-563-7701 – free call) ferries between Port Aux Basques and North Sydney, Nova Scotia all year. In summer there are three or four a day, but get your ticket early or make a reservation. Early morning or late-night trips are less crowded. If you're walking or have a bicycle you shouldn't have any trouble. Fares are $12 per person, $5 per bicycle, $37 per car and it takes six hours for the crossing. There's a restaurant, sometimes with a good breakfast special.

The night ferry saves you the cost of a night's bed, because on board you can sleep anywhere – the floor of the TV room is popular. If you get between two rows of seats it's like being in a tent. With a sleeping bag you can also sleep out on the deck; look for the area that is walled in with perspex. There are a few benches where you can stretch out. When you get up in the morning, the bodies lying everywhere make you wonder if the food was poisoned! You don't miss anything going at night – there's nothing to see.

Ferries also go along the south coast to Terrenceville from Port Aux Basques (see the sections in this book on Outports and Terrenceville).

Bus The Roadcruiser bus service leaves twice daily from the ferry dock for the 904 km to St John's. The trip takes about 14 hours and costs $58 one-way. You can stop at any of the towns along the way.

Train There are no passenger trains in Newfoundland.

Other Attractions

If you travel early in the morning, odds rise that you'll see some of the abundant provincial wildlife. Coming off the ferry at 6 am within an hour of Port Aux Basques, I saw half a dozen long-haired horses on the road, a rabbit and a cow moose with her calf.

At John Cheeseman Provincial Park, not far from town, is a good sandy beach where you can camp. There are also beaches and camping at Mummichog Park, 24 km from town and at Grand Codroy Park, 34 km out.

OUTPORTS

'Outport' is the name given to the tiny coastal fishing villages accessible only by boat. Some are on the ferry lines, others are not. These little communities represent some of the most remote settlements in North America. Change is coming but for the moment these outports harbour the rough Newfoundland life at its most traditional. Many have no TV or outside contact, and some have adult residents who have never seen a car. These villages are the best places to see the unique culture of the Newfoundland people born in Canada of European blood.

Of course, getting to and from them is not all that easy. Marine Atlantic ferries service the Northern Peninsula and connect Newfoundland to the mainland. (See the Labrador section for more details.) Along the southern coast, the provincial government runs three different routes with the main ports Port Aux Basques, Terrenceville, St Pierre, Fortune and Argentia. In between, stops are made at the smaller outports. They cover a lot of northern islands, too. These ferries charge on a per-km basis and the fares are very low. In contrast, the Marine Atlantic routes, which are the more major links, are fairly costly. With either service, there are restaurants on board and sleeping cabins at extra charges. The Port Aux Basques-Terrenceville ferry runs just once a week; others are more frequent.

For full details pick up the pamphlets listing all routes, times and prices. On the provincial lines examples are: Ramea to Burgeo to Grey River on the southern shore (a one-hour 20-minute trip) – $2 a person, $15 per car one-way. Gaultois to Hermitage, $1.25.

On the northern coast of the island, Lewisporte is the main ferry terminal. A provincial map will show you the ferry routes, including those in Labrador. There is one Marine Atlantic trip weekly from Lewisporte to Goose Bay, Labrador, with over 30 ports of call. The fares are $55, $80 for a car.

For places to stay, ask around ahead of time or just take a chance on arrival. You can stay on the ferry if you're continuing on without a stopover. This can be tiring if you're doing it on the cheap; sleeping on the floor or in a chair can be uncomfortable after a few days, especially if the sea is rough. There are cabins and the prices are quite fair.

LABRADOR

Labrador is the part of the province – three times the size of the island – that is sectioned into the Quebec mainland. The Strait of Belle Isle separates Labrador from the Newfoundland island. This vast, rugged land is one of the last incompletely-explored areas in Canada. The geological base of Labrador is the ancient Laurentian Shield – possibly the oldest unchanged region on earth. It's thought the land looks the same as it did before life on the planet began.

Until very recently, small numbers of Eskimos and Indians known as 'liveyers' were the only residents. They lived in little villages dotted along the rocky coasts as they had done for centuries, eking out an existence fishing and hunting. The interior was virgin wilderness.

Today a new people, with a completely different outlook and lifestyle, have arrived. The whites have been lured by the natural resources and potential they see.

And so, not far away from the traditional way of life, lie some of the world's most sophisticated industrial complexes. Most of the development has been far inland, near the border of Quebec. Labrador City and Wabush, with the latest technology, are two new towns that produce half of

Canada's iron ore. Churchill Falls is the site of an enormous hydro-electric plant that supplies power to the eastern USA.

Happy Valley-Goose Bay is an older settlement first established as an Air Force base in WW II. It's now mainly a supply centre and is accessible from Lewisporte, Newfoundland by ferry.

Labrador doesn't get a lot of visitors. The industrial sites are more or less for workers only. Due to the bountiful fish and game though, hunters and fishermen are being attracted. They are catered for with fly-in camps, etc, which are not cheap. So that leaves the east coast, which in some ways is the most interesting. Tiny villages are accessible by ferry from Newfoundland proper and by supply ferries running up the coast. Though not easy to organise, and with a lot of chance involved, a trip like this could be excellent.

In the past few years, an excavation team has found three Basque whaling galleons from the mid-1700s on the sea bed just off Red Bay. The ice-cold waters have kept them well preserved and they will stay where they are, making the area an underwater museum.

Places to Stay

There are expensive sports camps and hotels catering to the new developments. But in several towns clustered near Blanc Sablon there are small guest houses that are very fairly priced. They change very quickly so I haven't listed any particular ones. Get an updated list at the Tourist Office or ask on arrival. But note that often the lists are not complete.

In Charlottetown the *Charlottetown Inn* is $40/55 for singles/doubles. In Goose Bay there is the *Golden Eagle Inn* (tel 896-5595) at 3 Spruce Avenue, singles/doubles cost $30/35 with a light breakfast.

Camping is possible but is recommended only in a van. Remember this is a cold, wet and windy place. Other than that, you're on your own. You can sleep on the ferries, or you could ask around in the towns and villages and might be offered a bed.

Getting There & Away

Air The most common way to reach Labrador is to fly. Canadian Airlines has daily flights from around the Atlantic region; Labrador Airways services the Labrador coastal communities and Quebecair flies to Blanc Sablon from Montreal, Quebec and Sept Isles.

Train A train line links western Labrador, including Labrador City, to Sept Isles, Quebec, on the St Lawrence River.

Boat The Strait of Belle Isle ferry joins St Barbe, on the Newfoundland island Northern peninsula, to Blanc Sablon, Quebec, at the Labrador border. The ferry runs from 1 May to 30 November. There are two round trips per day until October; from then there's just one daily. It's $8 or for car and driver, $22. During the 80-minute crossing, you may see ice floes drifting southward to the melting warmer waters. Shrimps grow like crazy here.

The Marine Atlantic ferries also link Blanc Sablon with Rimouski and Sept Iles, Quebec.

Another main departure point from Newfoundland island is Lewisporte on the north coast. This ferry stops along the Northern Peninsula and then heads for Goose Bay, Labrador. There are roughly two sailings a week.

Getting Around

Within Labrador a local ferry service goes north up the coast as far as Nain, sailing about once a week with meals and cabin space available on the boat. There are about five villages on this route. These trips are really the only way to see anything of Labrador and its changing older settlements.

The only road in eastern Labrador is an 80-km stretch of gravel from Blanc Sablon up the coast to Red Bay.

Nova Scotia

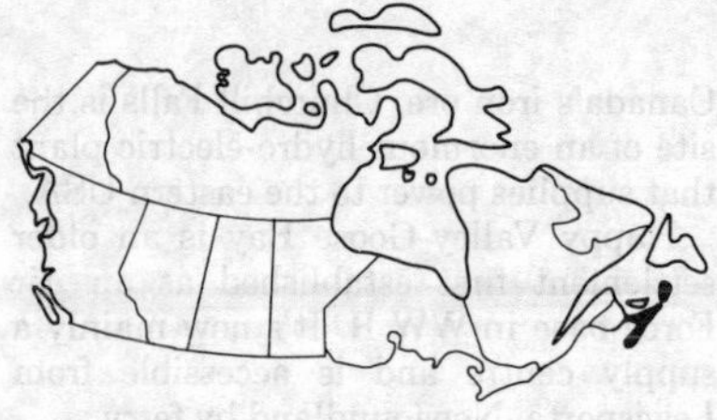

Entered Confederation: 1 July 1867
Area: 55,491 square km
Population: 847,442

You're never more than 56 km from the sea in Nova Scotia. This feature has greatly influenced the history and character of the province; for generations the rugged coastline, with countless bays and inlets, has provided shelter for small fishing villages, especially along the southern shores. The ocean's tides, most notably in the Bay of Fundy, are the highest in the world. As a consequence, the rivers carry brackish waters far inland to connect with the 400 or so lakes. Due to the vast amount of waterways, canoeing in the province is excellent. Diving all around the coast is also good.

Inland, much of the province is covered with forest, while low hills roll across in the north. The Annapolis Valley, famous for its apples, is gentle, scenic farm country, beautiful in springtime with pink and white blossoms. Cape Breton Island is more rugged, providing yet another side of the varied topography.

The people are of English, French and Scottish ancestry. The Highland Scots landed here in 1773 and thousands followed to settle Nova Scotia, which means 'New Scotland'. In some areas you can still hear Gaelic spoken. The locals are sometimes known as bluenoses, evidently after the bluenose potato (though I've never heard the term). The boat on the Canadian 10c coin (dime) was made here and is also called the Bluenose.

A visitor wouldn't notice it, but manufacturing is the most important industry, along with shipbuilding, dairy goods and paper. Fishing, of course, is also a major business – the catch includes cod, lobster and scallops.

The sea keeps the weather moderate; the Atlantic coast is coldest. Summer and autumn are usually sunny, though the eastern areas and Cape Breton are often windy. Rain is heaviest on the east coast.

The Nova Scotia Tourist Office has designed nine different road routes through the province which best show the scenery and sights. The tourist routes are generally on the older, smaller roads, not the main highways. Each route is marked with symbols. A booklet detailing all the routes is available free; it's worth having.

Tourists who spend three or more days in the province may become members of The Order of the Good Time. This social organisation was founded at Port Royal (now called Annapolis Royal) in 1606 by the French explorer Samuel de Champlain. Ask about it at information offices. They can also tell you about the provincial farm vacation programmes.

AMHERST

Amherst is the geographical centre of the Maritimes and a travel junction. There's not much to do or see, but it's a pleasant town with many old buildings. Some are a century old and restored; most are on the main street of town, Church St. Check out the *Kim Lam Chinese Restaurant*, looking rather out of place with its elaborate facade.

The Amherst Point Migratory Bird Sanctuary is not far from town along the marshy coast of Cumberland Basin, part of the Bay of Fundy. Much of the area is a National Wildlife area but it's really only

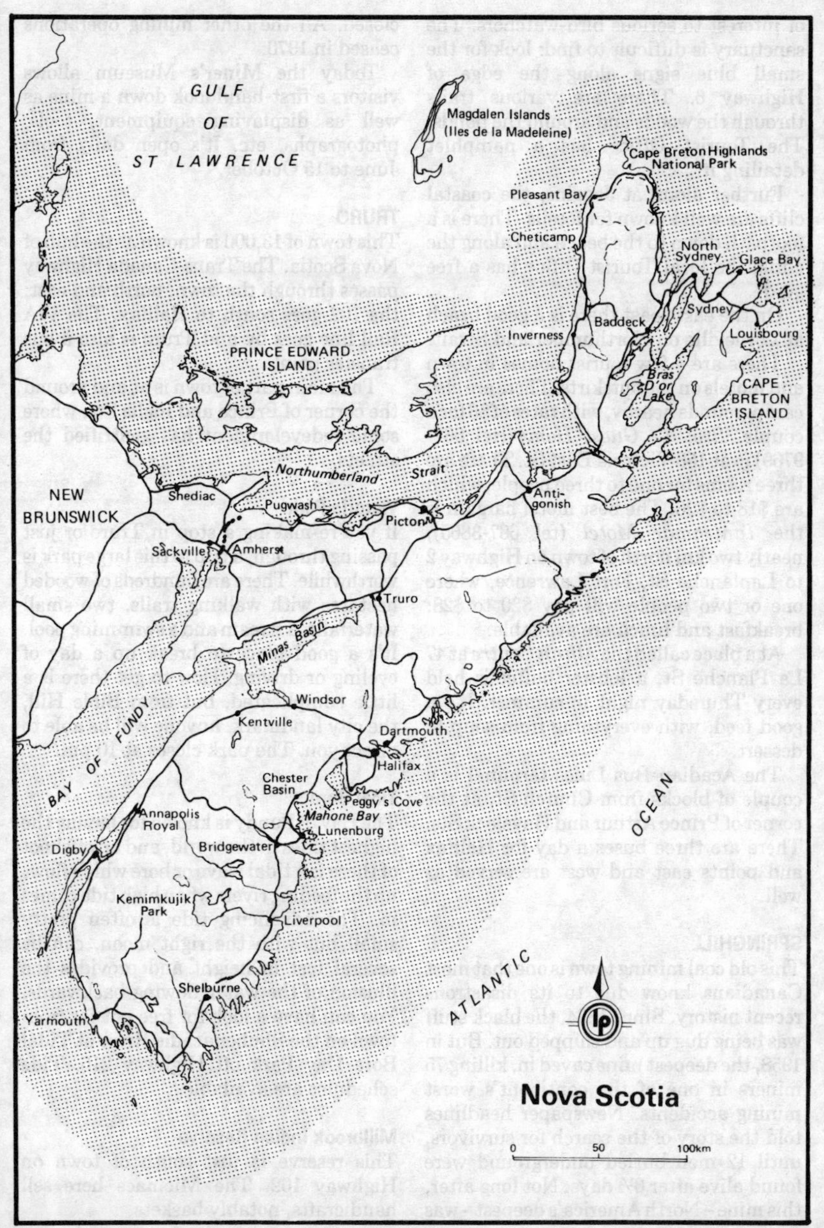
GULF OF ST LAWRENCE
Magdalen Islands
(Iles de la Madeleine)
Cape Breton Highlands National Park
Pleasant Bay
Cheticamp
North Sydney
Glace Bay
Sydney
Baddeck
Inverness
Louisbourg
Bras D'or Lake
CAPE BRETON ISLAND
PRINCE EDWARD ISLAND
Northumberland Strait
NEW BRUNSWICK
Shediac
Pugwash
Picton
Antigonish
Sackville
Amherst
Truro
Minas Basin
Windsor
Kentville
Dartmouth
Halifax
BAY OF FUNDY
Chester Basin
Peggy's Cove
Mahone Bay
Lunenburg
Annapolis Royal
Digby
Bridgewater
Kemimkujik Park
Liverpool
Shelburne
Yarmouth
ATLANTIC OCEAN
Nova Scotia
0
50
100km

of interest to serious bird-watchers. The sanctuary is difficult to find: look for the small blue signs along the edge of Highway 6. There are various trails through the woods and around the ponds. The Tourist Office has a pamphlet detailing it.

Further along at Joggins, the coastal cliffs are well known for fossils. There is a footpath down to the beach and along the cliffs; the local Tourist Office has a free guide.

On the east coast there is a good beach at Lorneville on Northumberland Strait.

There are a few tourist homes in town and motels on the outskirts. There are also campgrounds nearby, with rates of $6 for a couple. *Brown's Guest Home* (tel 667-9769) is at 158 Victoria East St. There are three rooms for one to three people, which are $18 to $26. The best motel bargain is the *Tantramar Motel* (tel 667-3865), nearly two km north of town on Highway 2 to Laplanche St, Fort Lawrence, where one or two people will pay $20 to $28; breakfast and lunch are available.

At a place called the *Alfran Centre* at 47 La Planche St, a lobster buffet is held every Thursday night in summer. It's a good feed, with everything from soup to dessert.

The Acadian Bus Lines terminal is a couple of blocks from Church St, at the corner of Prince Arthur and Havelock Sts. There are three buses a day for Halifax and points east and west are served as well.

SPRINGHILL

This old coal mining town is one that most Canadians know due to its disastrous recent history. Since 1834, the black stuff was being dug up and shipped out. But in 1958, the deepest mine caved in, killing 75 miners in one of the continent's worst mining accidents. Newspaper headlines told the story of the search for survivors, until 12 men buried underground were found alive after 6½ days. Not long after, this mine – North America's deepest – was closed. All the other mining operations ceased in 1970.

Today the Miner's Museum allows visitors a first-hand look down a mine as well as displaying equipment, tools, photographs, etc. It's open daily from June to 15 October.

TRURO

This town of 13,000 is known as the hub of Nova Scotia. The Trans-Canada Highway passes through the town, north and east; the 102 goes south to Halifax. The VIA Rail line goes by and Truro is also a bus transfer point.

The main part of town is at and around the corner of Prince and Inglis Sts, where some redevelopment has gentrified the streets.

Victoria Park

If you're making a stop in Truro or just passing through, a trip to this large park is worthwhile. There are hundreds of wooded hectares with walking trails, two small waterfalls, a stream and a swimming pool. It's a good place to break up a day of cycling or driving. How to get there is a little complicated, but from Bible Hill, the city landmark, anyone will be able to direct you. The park closes at 10 pm.

Tidal Bore

The Bay of Fundy is known for having the highest tides in the world, and an offshoot of these is a tidal wave or bore which flows up the feeding rivers when high tide comes in. The advancing tide is often pretty small but with the right moon, can be several feet in height and provides the illusion of the water flowing backwards. You can have a look for free not far from town on the Shubenacadie River at Tidal Bore Day Park off Highway 215. Tide schedules are available.

Millbrook Indian Reserve

This reserve is just south of town on Highway 102. The Micmacs here sell handicrafts, notably baskets.

Shubenacadie Wildlife Park

This provincial park contains examples of Nova Scotia wildlife, including birds, waterfowl, foxes and deer in large enclosures. It's off Highway 102 at Exit 10, 38 km south of Truro, and opens every day during daylight hours, mid-May to mid-October. Free.

Stewiack

At this little town south of Truro, you're half-way between the north pole and the equator.

Events

Nova Scotia's largest provincial exhibition and agricultural and amusement fair is held here in August.

Places to Stay

There are several bed & breakfasts in Truro, but the YMCA in town has no rooms to rent and the nearest hostel is near Wentworth, on the way to Amherst. There are a few other places to stay several km out of town.

As you come into Truro via Bible Hill you'll see *Foothill Motel & Cabins*, seven km east of town. It's a good place to stay, with cabins with cooking facilities at $32 for two people. Open from 1 May to 31 October. Nearby is a bakery with home-made treats.

The *Blue House* (tel 895-4150) at 43 Dominion St, is one of several bed & breakfasts that have opened recently to improve the variety. It's central, has three rooms and is good value at $21/32 for singles/doubles, including a full breakfast.

Cheapest of a costly bunch of motels is the *Sunrise* at singles $30, doubles $34. It's 11 km south of town on Route 2.

The *Youth Hostel* (tel 548-2379) is not quite halfway to Amherst near Wentworth on Valley Rd. It's open all year and costs $5 for members, $6.50 for non-members. The bus stop is three km away; good hiking nearby.

Places to Eat

At 517 Prince St in town, the *Iron Kettle* is a friendly, inexpensive restaurant in a building dating from 1875. Also on Prince St but leading out of town, the *Rainbow Motel* has an all-you-can-eat lobster buffet in summer. Further out on Robie St toward the Trans-Canada Highway, there are numerous eating places.

For light meals, the *Mirage Cafe* is beside the train station.

Getting There & Away

Bus The station (tel 895-3833) is at 280 Willow St. It's near the hospital along the motel strip – you'll see the blue & white Acadian Bus Terminal sign.

Halifax: six buses a day – $6.75

Sydney: two buses a day, each taking a different route – $21

Saint John, New Brunswick: one morning and one evening bus daily – $27.

Train The station (tel 1-800-561-3952) is in town on Esplanade St, near the corner of Inglis St. Connections to Montreal can be arranged here; some other schedules and fares follow:

Halifax: four a day during the week and one on Saturday and Sunday – $8.10

Sydney: twice daily – $27

Saint John, New Brunswick: one daily, two on Friday and Saturday – $29.

Halifax

With a population of about 120,000 and over twice that number in the metropolitan area, Halifax, the capital of Nova Scotia, is the largest city in the Maritimes. The city was the home of Canada's first representative government, first Protestant church and first newspaper. Residents are known as Haligonians.

The port here is the busiest on the east coast, due to its being a year-round harbour (while most have to close in winter due to ice). Canada's largest naval base is here.

Compared to the backgrounds of other Canadian cities, the interesting history of Halifax is a very long one. The area was first settled by Micmac Indians. Halifax itself was founded in 1749 as a British stronghold with the arrival of 2500 people. The town was actually to act as a military base counterbalancing the French fort at Louisbourg on Nova Scotia's south-east tip.

The harbour was used as a British naval base during the American Revolution (1775-1783) and the War of 1812. During both world wars, Halifax was used as a distribution centre by supply ships heading for Europe. This function brought many people to the city.

In 1917 a French munitions ship carrying an enormous cargo of TNT collided with another foreign ship in the harbour. The result was the biggest man-made explosion ever, prior to the A-bombs dropped on Japan in 1945. Half the city was flattened, 2000 people in town were killed and windows were broken as far away as Truro, Nova Scotia.

Today the military still lends much to the economy, with six bases nearby. Other major industries are oil refining, manufacturing and food processing.

The city lies on a peninsula between the harbour and an inlet called the North West Arm. The downtown area is hilly and the city in general as green as any I've seen. There are parks everywhere, best seen from Citadel Hill, which provides views of the town and waterfront.

Recently, restoration and renovation have improved the city, particularly down along the water in the Historic Properties. This is now a lively people place with restaurants and bars in and amongst Halifax's original buildings. The city may often be lost in fog, but its strengths are in this blending of the old and the new and its attractive natural setting. It's a pleasant and worthwhile place to visit.

Dartmouth, a twin city, lies west across the harbour and has business and residential districts of its own.

Orientation

Halifax sits by a very large natural harbour at mid-point on Nova Scotia's south shore.

The downtown area, dating from the earliest settlement until today, extends from Lower Water St on the waterfront and west up to the Citadel, a star-shaped fort on the hill. Cogswell St to the north and Spring Garden St to the south mark the other boundaries of the capital core.

From this central area the city spreads in three directions. At the extreme east end of the downtown area is the water and the area known as the Historic Properties. This is the original commercial centre of town, now restored and containing offices, shops, restaurants, the Tourist Office, etc. It's a busy, visitor-oriented place, good for getting a feel of the city. Up from the Historic Properties there's an interesting mix of new and old buildings. The streets are wide and there are plenty of trees. At the end of Granville St, Duke St is a small but pleasant pedestrian mall, lined with fine old buildings in Italianate style from about 1860.

Main streets leading up from the shoreline are Sackville St and Spring Garden Rd. The latter is lined with shops, including grocery stores. At the corner of South Park St and Spring Garden Rd are the large Public Gardens, a nice city park diagonally opposite Citadel Hill.

South of town at the end of the peninsula and adjacent to North West Arm is Point Pleasant Park, the city's largest park, which is pleasant indeed with woods and beaches. South Park St, which becomes Young Avenue, will take you there from the downtown area, past the very large houses of the city's wealthy district.

The airport is 40 km north-west of town on the No 102.

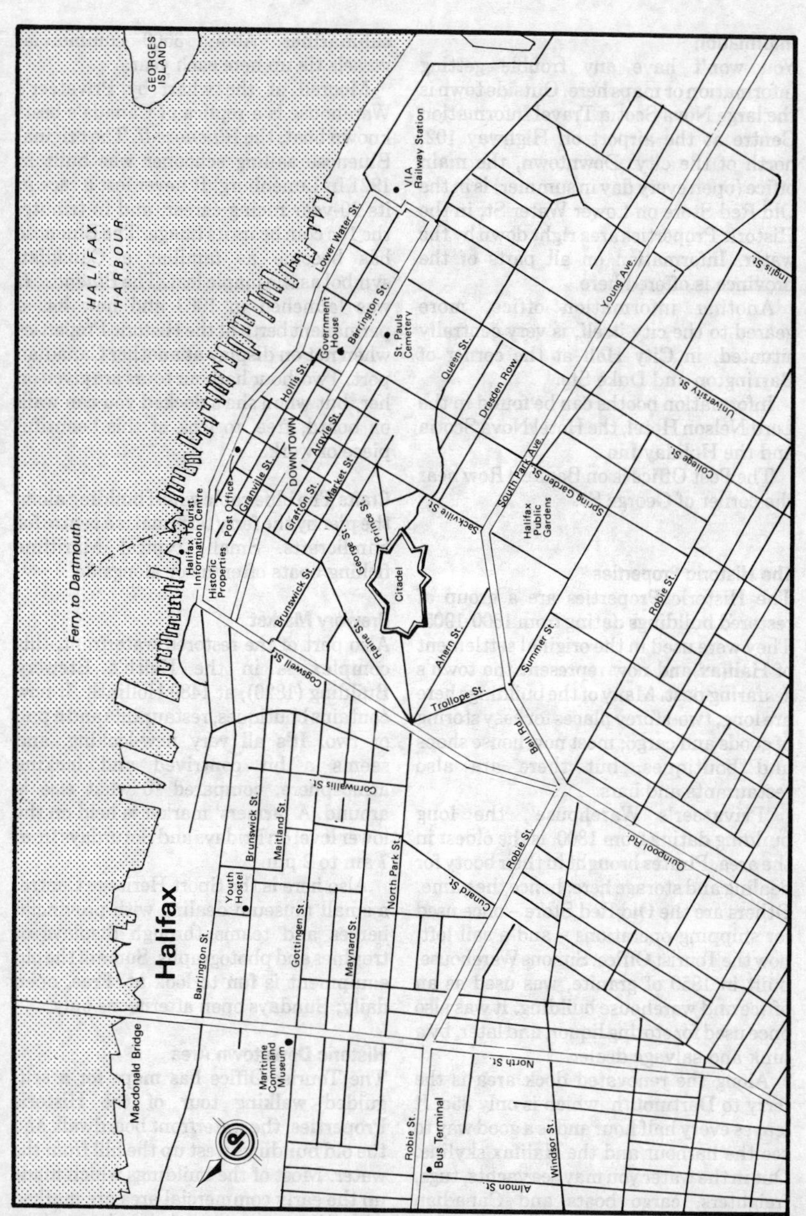
Halifax
HALIFAX HARBOUR
GEORGES ISLAND
Ferry to Dartmouth
VIA Railway Station
Lower Water St.
Barrington St.
Government House
St. Pauls Cemetery
Hollis St.
Argyle St.
DOWNTOWN
Granville St.
Post Office
Halifax Tourist Information Centre
Historic Properties
Grafton St.
Market St.
Prince St.
George St.
Brunswick St.
Citadel
Rainie St.
Cogswell St.
Ahern St.
Trollope St.
Sackville St.
South Park Ave.
Spring Garden Rd.
Halifax Public Gardens
College St.
University Ave.
Dresden Row
Queen St.
Young Ave.
Inglis St.
Robie St.
Summer St.
Bell Rd.
Quinpool Rd.
Cunard St.
North St.
Almon St.
Windsor St.
Bus Terminal
Maynard St.
North Park St.
Cornwallis St.
Gottingen St.
Maitland St.
Youth Hostel
Barrington St.
Macdonald Bridge
Maritime Command Museum

Information

You won't have any trouble getting information or maps here. Outside town is the large Nova Scotia Travel Information Centre at the airport on Highway 102, north of the city. Downtown, the main office (open every day in summer) is in the Old Red Store on Lower Water St, in the Historic Properties area right down by the water. Information on all parts of the province is offered here.

Another information office, more geared to the city itself, is very centrally situated, in City Hall at the corner of Barrington and Duke Sts.

Information booths can be found in the Lord Nelson Hotel, the Hotel Nova Scotia and the Holiday Inn.

The Post Office is on Bedford Row near the corner of George St.

The Historic Properties

The Historic Properties are a group of restored buildings dating from 1800-1905. They were used in the original settlement of Halifax and now represent the town's seafaring past. Many of the buildings here are long, two-storey places for easy storing of goods and cargo; most now house shops and boutiques, but there are also restaurants and bars.

'Privateer's Warehouse', the long building dating from 1800, is the oldest in the area. Pirates brought in their booty for dealing and storage here, hence the name. Others are the Old Red Store – once used for shipping operations – and a sail loft, now the Tourist Office. Simons Warehouse, built in 1850 of granite, was used as an office and warehouse building. It was also once used for storing liquor, and later, by a junk and salvage dealer.

Along the renovated dock area is the ferry to Dartmouth, which is only 35c. It leaves every half hour and is a good way to see the harbour and the Halifax skyline. Out in the water you may see yachts, tugs, freighters, cargo boats and Canadian military vessels such as destroyers or submarines. About 3500 commercial vessels tie up here each year.

Moored at the wharf by Privateer's Warehouse is a replica of Canada's best-known boat, the *Bluenose II*. The original Bluenose sailing schooner was built in 1921 in Lunenburg. It never lost a race in its 20-year racing career, and in tribute, the 10c coin bears its image. The Bluenose has become as familiar a Canadian symbol as the maple leaf. The *Bluenose II* was launched in 1963 and now has a permanent berth at the Historic Properties when not on display at another Canadian port. Two-hour harbour tours are given on her, but when she's docked you can walk on board, free, to look at this beautiful piece of work.

Crafts The blue cable wharf building along the pier by the ferry terminal is a centre for handicrafts. Small, typical Maritime fishing boats often moor alongside.

Brewery Market

Also part of the restored waterfront, this complex is in the Keith's Brewery Building (1820), at 1489 Hollis St. It now contains boutiques, restaurants and a pub or two. It's all very new-looking, and seems a bit contrived and lacking atmosphere, compared to what else is around. A farmers' market is held on the lower level on Fridays and Saturdays from 7 am to 2 pm.

Also here is the Sport Heritage Centre, a small museum dealing with provincial heroes and teams through displays of trophies and photographs. Some of the old equipment is fun to look at. Free, open daily; Sundays open afternoons only.

Historic Downtown Area

The Tourist Office has maps for a self-guided walking tour of the Historic Properties, the waterfront boardwalk and the old buildings west up the hill from the water. Most of the buildings which made up the early commercial area are marked with plaques giving a brief history. The brochure adds a few details and makes them easier to find. Using the map, you'll take about an hour to do the circuit. Some of the best spots are:

Province House On Hollis St near Prince St, this fine example of Georgian architecture has been the home of the Provincial Legislature since 1819. There are free guided tours Monday to Friday, 9 am to 5 pm.

Government House This is between Hollis and Barrington Sts, near the corner of Bishop St. Since 1807, it's been the residence of the provincial Lieutenant-Governor. It was built by Governor John Wentworth.

St Paul's Cemetery Across the street from Government House on Barrington St, this cemetery, first used in 1749 has graves of people from all faiths, many of them having died young. Numerous soldiers, sailors and stories lie buried here.

St Paul's Church This is on Barrington near Prince. It was the first Protestant Church in Canada (1749) and the first Church of British origin in the new land. It's open to visitors Monday to Friday 9 am to 5 pm, with guided tours after 1 pm. The tour includes some interesting tidbits about the church; you'll hear about the silhouette cast by a certain hole in the stained glass.

City Hall This is at the opposite end of the sunken courtyard from St Paul's Church. Built in 1890, it's a gem of Victorian architecture.

The Citadel

This is a huge, oddly-angled fort atop Halifax's big hill, and has always been the city's towering landmark.

In the mid-1750s, the English realised that the crunch was coming with France over possession of the new land. Halifax was a good location for English purposes; it could be used as a centre of rule over Nova Scotia, and more importantly, it could be used as a military base from which to deal with the French, who were in Louisbourg and Quebec City with forts of their own. In 1749, with the founding of Halifax, construction of a citadel began.

The fort visible today, built from 1828 to 1861, is actually the fourth one on the site. It is open daily from 9 am to 8 pm in summer, and 9 am to 5 pm from early September to 14 June. Admission is $2 in summer, free the rest of the year. I recommend the guided tours, which include theatrical presentations; the movie is also worthwhile. The guide will explain the fort's shape and how, despite appearances, the fort was not very well designed or constructed. There are excellent views in all directions – of the city, Dartmouth and waterfront areas.

Citadel Hill is a good park in itself and a popular sun-bathing spot. Halfway down toward the Historic Properties, or up from George St, is the Old Town Clock, built in London but erected here in 1803. It was designed by the Duke of Kent while he was Commander of the Citadel.

Also in the compound are the Centennial Art Gallery, with changing exhibitions of modern Canadian painting and sculpture, and the Museum of Nova Scotia, which is a branch of the provincial museum, contained in the old barracks. You can view some early Nova Scotia furniture, Micmac artefacts and handicrafts, along with details of the Great Halifax Explosion of 1917.

Nova Scotia Museum

The main part of the provincial museum (tel 429-4610) is at 1747 Summer St, near the corner of Sackville St, south-west of the Citadel. History, wildlife, geology, people and industry are all covered. The three-dimensional animal exhibits are excellent – you feel you can reach out and touch the display; the fish of Nova Scotia are also presented well. The history section is good, with an old stagecoach and a working model of a late-1800s sawmill. Also worth noting is the excellent mushroom display. Open 9.30 am to 5.30 pm, Wednesdays to 8 pm and Sundays just 1 pm to 5 pm. Free.

Maritime Museum of the Atlantic

This large museum is a must for boat buffs but also has enough interesting displays to warrant a peek from anyone. It's very spacious and contains full-scale examples of many regional vessels, with plenty of models, photographs and historical data as well. The lens from a Halifax lighthouse is impressive but I particularly liked the painted figureheads taken from various ships, many of them wrecks. Also very good is the portion of a boat you can enter which sways as though out on the sea.

Outside at the dock you can explore the CSS Acadia, a retired survey vessel from England. The museum is open 9.30 am to 5.30 pm daily, but Sunday 1 to 5.30 pm only. It's at 1675 Lower Water St.

Maritime Command Museum

This is on the Canadian Forces Base, off Gottingen St between North and Russell Sts near Macdonald Bridge. It's in the fine-looking stone building on large grounds protected by numerous cannons. You'll see mementoes like uniforms, medals, etc, from the military past of the Maritimes. Open Monday to Friday from 9.30 am to 3.30 pm, Saturday and Sunday 1 to 5 pm.

Art Gallery of Nova Scotia

This gallery is housed in the old Post Office, a Heritage building dating from the mid-1800s. It's very central at 6152 Coburg Rd near the harbour. Provincial and other Canadian works make up much of the large collection.

Halifax Public Gardens

A small but well-kept and pleasant formal city park at the corner of South Park St and Spring Garden Rd. There are occasional band concerts in the gazebo.

Point Pleasant Park

Highly recommended. This is a 75-hectare wooded park with walking trails, picnic spots, a restaurant, a beach, and an old Martello Tower – a round defence structure. There are lots of joggers and sunbathers, good views all the way around the perimeter, and no cars allowed.

The park is at the far south end of town at the tip of the peninsula. The No 9 bus goes to and from it from the downtown Scotia Centre or you can drive to the park's edge. Whichever way you come, check out the size of the houses along Young St.

At the city edge of the park is the Port of Halifax, a very busy terminal with containers piled high and ships from everywhere steadily coming and going. Walk out to the lighthouse by the port for great views and a peek at the shipping activity; kids'll be tossing in lines hoping for the big catch.

York Redoubt

This 200-year-old fort overlooks the harbour from a bluff just south of the North West Arm (south of downtown). Aside from the view, there are mounted guns and historical information and displays. The grounds are open all year but the buildings just daily, in summer.

McNab's Island

Out in the harbour, easily seen from York Redoubt, this small island makes a good break from the busy and/or hot city, with guided walks, beaches, picnic tables and hiking. There's also a teahouse for basic snacks or seafood. Ferries depart for the island through the day from the dock area, and tickets ($6.75) can be bought at the little office by Cable Wharf Market.

Hemlock Ravine

A system of linked walking trails winds through this large wooded estate once called home by Edward, the Duke of Kent, Queen Victoria's dad. It includes a view of Bedford Basin and amidst the gardens some very impressive 30 metre-tall trees. To get there, drive along the Bedford Highway past Birch Cove and then look for the signs. It's not far and once there, feels a long way from a city.

Events

The Nova Scotia Tattoo is held in Halifax from 6 to 9 July, or around that time every year. It's called the province's 'greatest entertainment extravaganza'.

The city also hosts schooner races in July.

Activities

Canoeing To rent a canoe in Halifax for exploring nearby waterways, try the Trail Shop (tel 423-8736), or Camper's World (tel 463-2709). They can also give you some tips on good spots to go. The Tourist Office has information on canoeing, too. Recently the city's Recreation Department has offered rentals on the North West Arm, along which you can paddle.

Diving There are about 50 wrecks at the mouth of Halifax harbour and good diving along the coast. For info and equipment rentals, try Northern Shore Diving Centre (tel 429-8263) at 5233 Prince St, the Dive Shoppe, which may still be at 1869 Upper Water St, or Aqua Dive Shop (tel 469-6948) at 211 Pleasant St in Dartmouth.

Beaches Try Black Rock Beach in Point Pleasant Park; Crystal Beach, 20 km west of town; or Queensland Beach, 35 km west of town.

Ask at the Tourist Office for activities on the lakes within the Dartmouth city borders.

Places to Stay

Hostels The *Youth Hostel* (tel 422-3863) is in a big, old building at 2445 Brunswick St. There's room for 50, and cooking facilities as well. Prices are $8 members, $11 non-members and the rates go down if you stay more than one night. Open from 6 pm to midnight. It's one block from Macdonald Bridge, west of the Historic Properties, and 10 to 15 minutes' walk from downtown. This is not the best area of town; late at night, women may want company coming or going.

The *YMCA* (tel 422-6437) is in an excellent location at 1565 South Park St, across from the Public Gardens and very near Citadel Hill. Single rooms for men and women are $20 and rooms for couples go for $30. It was renovated during the summer of 1984. There's a small, cheap cafeteria and use of facilities like the gym and swimming pool. Open all year.

The *YWCA* (tel 423-6162), for women only, is at 1239 Barrington St, between the downtown centre and the VIA Rail Station. There are 30 rooms; singles are $18, doubles $30 and they have good weekly rates.

Halifax has the highest ratio of educational facilities to population on the continent; this is good for the traveller, as they offer rooms in their dorms during the summer months.

At *Dalhousie University*, rooms are available from mid-May to mid-August in the Howe and Sherref Hall residences. Contact Room 210 in the Dalhousie Student Union Building (tel 424-8840) at 6136 University Avenue. Both are on the campus: Howe residence is at Coburg Rd and LeMarchant St; Sherref Hall is at South St and Oxford St. Reservations are required. Singles cost $24 to $27, doubles $32 to $38, with breakfast. For students with ID a single is $14, double $18, no breakfast. All three meals are available very inexpensively.

Rooms are also available mid-May to mid-August at *Fenwick Place*, an off-campus high-rise residence at 5599 Fenwick St. Call the Accommodation Office (tel 424-2075) in the building for information. It's central and close to the university, with rooms for $10 or about $15 if you haven't brought your own bed linen.

The *Technical University of Nova Scotia* (tel 429-8300) also has rooms from mid-May to the end of August which are $16/28 for singles/doubles; students pay $14/22. It's off Barrington St at Bishop St, a 10-minute walk east from the central core.

Mount Saint Vincent University rents from 15 May to 15 August; contact the Conference Officer (tel 443-4450) at 166 Bedford Highway on the campus. Student rates are single $12, double $18. Others pay single $18, double $24. They offer excellent weekly and monthly rates, especially for students. Meals are available and there is a coin laundry. The university is a 15-minute drive west of town on the Bedford Highway (also called Highway 2), and overlooks the Bedford Basin.

Yet another university with accommodation is St Mary's University (tel 420-5486), which is also cheap and not far from the centre.

Bed & Breakfasts, Tourist Homes & Hotels
There are many bed & breakfasts in town and over in Dartmouth as well. Some fine ones – though more costly – are found in heritage houses and mansions. The *Halifax Bed & Breakfast Organization* (tel 429-7685) connects visitors to residents in the programme. They'll help out if you're stuck or have some special preference.

The *Fountain View Guest House* (tel 422-4169) is the bright blue place with white trim at 2138 Robie St, between Compton Avenue and Williams, across from the park and west of Citadel Hill. Open all year. The seven rooms, all with TV, go for $18 to $22 for singles, $22 to $30 doubles plus tax; each extra person is $3. It's popular, so try in the morning. There are also rooms to rent next door (though there is no sign); ask at the Fountain View.

The *Waken 'n' Eggs* bed & breakfast (tel 422-4737) is within walking distance of downtown sites at 2114 Windsor St. It's in a restored house. Costs are $25 single, $30 double with shared bath, or $5 more for private facilities. All prices include breakfast.

Hartley House (tel 422-5859) at 2177 Windsor St, is another nearby possibility.

Mrs Daisy Andrews (tel 455-6591) at 3614 Robie St has one double room which is $18 a single, $28 for two. Also on Robie St at No 1756 is the *Apple Basket* bed & breakfast (tel 429-3019), across the street from the Camp Hill Hospital. Rates are $35 singles or $40 doubles. Non-smoking adults only.

Cheaper is the *Birdland Bed & Breakfast* (tel 443-1055) at 14 Bluejay St. Prices of $25 singles, $35 doubles or triples include breakfast and afternoon tea. Open June to October. Cyclists, children and pets are all welcome. The host, Diana, also knows the area's attractions.

There are also a couple of places to check on MacAra St, running off Gottingen St a few blocks north of North St. *Jean Walsh* (tel 455-2215) at No 5671 has one housekeeping room at $30 a night but just $80 a week. A couple of blocks away at No 5685 is *Mrs Blakeney's* (tel 454-8914), with one room at $30 single or double.

Better is the *Running Lights Inn* (tel 423-9873) at 2060 Oxford St, with rooms furnished with antiques and nautical bric-a-brac. Singles/doubles are $25/30 and it's very central.

Winnie's Lodge (tel 423-8974) at 5492 Inglis St near the park, has rooms at single $25, double $30 and very good weekly rates, but on the singles only. There's a kitchen for guests.

The following places are in the $30 or more category.

Heritage House (tel 423-4435) is a bed & breakfast at 1253 Barrington St, next to the YWCA. Rooms are $32 to $35 for singles, $38 to $45 doubles. Free afternoon tea. Excellent location.

For hotels try the *Gerrard* (tel 423-8614) at 1234 Barrington St. It's a small place in a good location, and the building is an historic residence built in 1860. There are nine rooms at singles $30, doubles $40. Free coffee and parking.

The *Queen St Inn* (tel 422-9828) is at 1266 Queen St near Morris St. It's also an old house dating from about 1860, with six tastefully decorated rooms, all different. Singles are $30, doubles $40.

Similar is the *Haliburton House Inn* (tel 420-0658) at 5184 Morris St, built in 1820 and recently renovated with antiques, library and garden. Each of the 40 rooms has private bath; $40 to $55 for singles, $50 to $65 doubles.

Lastly, there's the *Sterling* (tel 423-9346) at 1266 Barrington St (near the Gerrard). Rooms are $38/43 for singles/doubles and they have a dining room. Not particularly friendly.

Motels Motels here tend to be a little expensive and are clustered along the No 2, Bedford Highway, north-west of town along the bay called Bedford Basin. They offer good views of the bay and cool breezes; bus Nos 80 or 81 go into town – a 15-minute drive away.

The *Travellers Motel* (tel 835-3394), open year-round, is right at the city limits. The small cottages (rather than the motel units) are the best buy at $38 for two people with shower, TV and pool.

The *Sea King* (tel 443-0303) is the big brown place at 560 Bedford Highway and has 33 fully equipped rooms at $42/47 for singles/doubles. Breakfast is available, and there's a pool.

A third choice is the *Bluenose* (tel 835-3388) at No 636 on the highway. Rooms are single $40, double $42 to $44. Breakfasts from 7 to 11 am. Off-season rates are available from 1 October to 15 May. It's away from the road and quiet.

Further out is *Stardust Motel* (tel 835-3316), 1067 Bedford Highway, which is bigger, with 51 rooms, 31 with kitchenette. Singles and doubles cost $40 to $42.

Camping *Smith's Camping Ground* (tel 835-3713) is 11 km west from Halifax. It's on Route 2 which runs off Highway 102. Take the Bedford exit and it's about two km along, at traffic lights. There are only 15 places at $7 each. Open from 1 June.

Haverstock's Campgrounds are 15 km from town on the Highway 213, six km from Bedford Exit 3, five km west of the 102.

Along the 103 and 333 are three campgrounds within 25 km of town: *Seaside Camping, Safari Camps Wayside Park* and *King Neptune Campground*.

There are also a couple of campgrounds on Route 102, south and west of town.

Places to Eat

Halifax has a good selection of restaurants offering a variety of foods in all price ranges, and generally the quality is high.

For breakfast, the *Athens*, corner of Barrington and Blowers Sts, offers the works for $1.99; or try *Smitty's* across from the Public Gardens, corner of Spring Garden Rd and Summer St, for inexpensive pancake breakfasts and limitless coffee refills.

For lunch or just a snack try the excellent *Khyber Cafe* at 1288 Barrington St, which has fresh baked goods, sandwiches and salads. It's very comfortable and the walls are decorated with beautiful Eastern rugs. Open every day.

Not far away, *Christopher's* at 1711 Barrington St offers a wide variety of sandwiches, inexpensive meals and desserts in a European-like setting. Chairs right by the sidewalk allow you to watch the human traffic as you munch.

At *Juicy Jane's*, 1576 Argyle St, they sell good sandwiches to take out.

The *Midtown Tavern* at the corner of Prince and Grafton Sts is highly recommended – a good example of the Canadian working persons' tavern. It's packed with locals at lunch and is noisy, friendly and cheap. Excellent sirloin steaks with vegetables, French fries and cole slaw are under $4. Draught beer is $1.25.

Halifax is well-blessed with other pubs

and many are good for a meal. The *Thirsty Duck* is at 5470 Spring Garden Rd; go through the store and up the stairs. They've got burgers, fish & chips, etc, at low prices and draught beer to wash it down. There's an outdoor patio, too.

Several other pubs can be found in the mall area of Granville St at Duke St. Both the *Split Crow* and the *Peddlar's Pub* have outdoor sections and the latter has live music on Saturday afternoons.

Nearby there are numerous places to console the inner self along Argyle St, including the popular *Applause*.

Also for lunch or dinner, *Satisfaction Feast* is a well-established vegetarian restaurant. It's at 1581 Grafton St in the pale blue building, open 11 am to 9 pm. Recommended.

Lawrence of Oregano has a spaghetti special that's hard to beat if you're economising: from 4 to 8 pm, dinner with garlic bread is just $3. Other Italian dishes are about $6. It's at 1712 Argyle St opposite the park. The *Old Spaghetti Factory* on Prince St is similar.

For Mexican food, try *Mariano's* on the corner of Grafton and Blowers Sts – it's the one with the 1950s American diner look; wide selection, open late and inexpensive.

There are two places for Indian food. The *Guru* at 1665 Argyle St is good and about $7 for main dishes. Closed Sunday. Cheaper is the *Chicken Tandoor*, open for dinners only with dishes for $5. It's downstairs at 1264 Barrington St, closed Tuesday.

There are two good Vietnamese places in town. The *Tu-do* (meaning 'freedom') at 2085 Gottingen St, two blocks from Cogswell St is recommended. They serve very reasonably priced curry dishes, some with vermicelli noodles and some with my favourite south-east Asian ingredient, lemon grass. Open every day until quite late, especially Friday and Saturday nights. The alternative is the slightly more casual *King Spring Roll* on Barrington St out toward the train station. Also busy and good with a more extensive and cheaper menu. Good value.

And there is seafood here, of course. *Pepe's Café & Grill*, on Spring Garden Rd near South Park St, is a pub type of place with meals for about $8, chowder $2 to $3. The *Silver Spoon* at 1865 Hollis St, primarily a seafood house, is more pricey, but prepares meals with interesting sauces and spicing. *McKelvie's*, on the corner of Prince St and Bedford Row, and the *Five Fishermen*, 1740 Argyle St, are also established seafood places with meals from $12 up.

Cogswell St and its continuation, Quinpool Rd, are commercial streets with plenty of eating spots. The *Anchor Restaurant* is one of the most noteworthy. It's a simple inexpensive place that does what it does very well. The menu has about half a dozen Greek entrees and the remainder is mainly seafood. Popular.

For do-it-yourself ocean fare, go to *Fisherman's Market* in the white building beside the ferry terminal. Boiled lobster is $6.49 a pound – a one-pounder being the usual meal and as small as they can legally catch them (also available live). And all over town you'll see chipwagons, always good for a quick snack of decent French fries.

The *Tiny Tea Room* at 1479 Dresden Row serves afternoon cream teas.

Lastly, the *Cave* at 5244 Blowers St, tucked in the little doorway, is open to 4.30 am on weekends. Down in the basement, this small bistro offers good desserts and is particularly well known for its cheesecake.

Nightlife

Halifax is lively at night and there is a very active pub and music scene.

Ginger's on Hollis St near the train station has varying types of bands – folk, blues, bluegrass. Amateur night on Tuesday; free; lots of traditional Maritime music and the pub's own beer.

Scoundrels at 1786 Granville St is a

very popular pub-like spot. No cover charge.

Privateer's Warehouse in the Historic Properties (near the Bluenose's docking area on the waterfront) has two bars and a restaurant. The *Middle Deck* presents rock and blues bands, cover charge $2. The *Lower Deck* has lesser names and is cheaper. It often presents Maritime folk music – good stuff. The long wooden tables are like those in an old-style beer house.

Pepe's at 5680 Spring Garden Rd has live jazz.

Secretary's on Sackville St near Granville St is definitely not highbrow, with lots of contests and hijinks for young drinkers.

The *Misty Moon* (tel 422-5871) at the corner of Barrington and Sackville Sts is one of the best-known rock bars. Sometimes it stages well-known bands from across Canada, and nearly always good ones. Open seven days a week until 3 am. Admission varies, but can be high.

The *Palace* (tel 423-7154) at 1721 Brunswick St, across from the Citadel, brings in name acts of every type. Performances are jazz or rock – usually just one-night stands.

There are several pubs with no admission fees in the downtown old Properties section – along and around Hollis and Granville Sts. *Cayside Lounge* in the Clipper Cay in the Historic Properties is a quiet spot for a drink. It offers good views and newspapers from around the world.

The *Youth Hostel* runs a coffee house the second and fourth Friday nights of the month. Cost is $2. Folk and traditional music.

Cinema For films there's *Wormwood's Dog & Monkey Cinema* (tel 422-3700) in the National Film Board at 1588 Barrington St. Frequently changing films, $2 each. The *National Film Board* at 1671 Argyle St is similar but many showings are free.

Getting There & Away

Air Air Canada (tel 429-7111) to:

Montreal – $188, student $94

Toronto – $247, student $124.

Canadian Airlines (tel 861-3860) to:

St John's, Newfoundland – $195, student $98.

Bus The Nova Scotian bus line is the Acadian line; it connects with the New Brunswick SMT Lines. The Acadian Bus Station (tel 454-9321) is at 6040 Almon St, which runs south off Robie St, west of the Citadel. The No 3 city bus on Robie St goes from the station into town and back. Following are the one-way fares to several destinations:

North Sydney: (one express daily, other milk runs) – $26.50

Yarmouth: $23.25

Amherst: $15.50

Saint John, New Brunswick: (several daily) – $33.25

Fredericton: $38.50.

MacKenzie Bus Line serves the south shore between Halifax, Bridgewater and Yarmouth, leaving Halifax from the VIA Rail station. Buses from Lunenburg also use this line.

Train The train station (tel 429-8421) is an easy walk from the downtown area out Hollis St. It's at Terminal Rd by the big old CN Hotel Nova Scotian. Some services are:

Sydney: 2 pm – $35

Yarmouth: 5.30 pm, Sunday 7 pm – tickets a bit less than Sydney

Saint John, New Brunswick: 8.10 am – $36

Montreal: 12.30 pm – $94 (this train arrives the next morning, about 20 hours later).

Very cheap return fares are available except if you leave on a Friday.

Getting Around

Airport Transport There are no city buses to the airport. It's a long way out on Highway 102, north toward Truro.

An airport bus leaves frequently from the major hotels like the Lord Nelson. The trip takes about 45 minutes for the 33-km ride and is no bargain at $8. Allow 90 minutes before flight time.

An alternative is Share-A-Taxi (tel 429-8888). Call at least three hours before flight time and they'll find other passengers and pick you up. Price is about the same as the bus.

Bus City bus fares here are quite reasonable. For bus route information call 426-6600. The No 1 goes from Halifax Shopping Centre, through town and along Bedford Highway where the motels are. Nos 7 and 80 leave from town for the bus station.

Ferry A ticket over to Dartmouth is 35c one-way or three for $1, and the ride makes a nice, short mini-tour of the harbour. Ferries run every 15 minutes to 6 pm, then every 30 minutes. The last one is at 11.30 pm. On Sundays they run from noon to 5.30 pm.

Car Rentals Autohost (tel 425-3774) is at 1240 Hollis St. They charge $33 a day or $200 a week plus insurance. You must be 25 years old.

Byways (tel 429-0092) at 2156 Barrington St, charges $32 per day with the first 250 km free. The weekly rental rate is $180.

Rent-A-Wreck (tel 865-0074) charges $14.95 per day in town, $8.95 out of town; insurance $6 a day. The rates are cheaper by the week.

Other car rentals in town are Budget (tel 454-8501) at 6194 Young St, and Avis (tel 423-6303) at Scotia Square. Both have offices at the airport.

There's a slew of car rental places at the airport.

Bicycle Velo Halifax (tel 423-4697) is a local bicycle club which organises trips around the province as well as Wednesday-evening rides around Halifax.

The Trail Shop (tel 423-8736) at 6260 Quinpool Rd, rents bikes at $10 a day.

Rickshaws Halifax is the only place in the country where I've seen real old-style Asian rickshaws; powered by muscular young men.

Tours A wide selection of tours by bus, boat or foot are available here. For a complete list see the Tourist Office, but here are some of the more established and interesting.

T I P Tours (tel 479-1379) offer a personal tour using a car and up to four people at a time. A three-hour Halifax trip is $12, but best are the longer trips including visits all over the province, some overnight. A Peggy's Cove trip for four hours is $18; full-day trips are about $40.

Gray Line (tel 454-9321), a tour bus company seen across Canada, also has tours in and around town and they will pick you up from your hotel. Always competitive fares and reliable. The 2½-hour town tour is $10 and takes in many of the essential sites. There is also a double-decker bus tour (tel 420-1155), which leaves from the Historic Properties several times a day; also $10.

Atlantic Tours (tel 423-6243) and Cabana Tours (tel 423-6066) offer trips around the province and can supply guides.

Halifax Water Tours (tel 423-1271), from Privateer's Wharf at the Historic Properties, have boat tours of the Halifax harbour. The two-hour, narrated trip goes past both new and old city landmarks and costs $9.75. From 13 June to 6 September there are four runs daily; out of the peak season there are two; in winter they close down completely. The boat carries 200 people and has both open and closed decks, a snack bar and bar.

The *Bluenose II*, perhaps the country's best known boat, also goes out on two-hour harbour cruises but is slightly more

Top: The rugged coast of the Cape Breton Highlands National Park, Nova Scotia (RE)
Bottom: Nova Scotian boat sheds (RE)

Top: Unusual beach formations, Rocks Provincial Park, New Brunswick (ML)
Bottom: New Brunswick's longest covered bridge, Hartford (ML)

expensive at $11. Usually the sails are not unfurled until the boat is at the outer reaches of the harbour.

The *Mar II* does tours around the harbour as well.

A number of private entrepreneurs offer tours of the harbour or charters on their yachts, especially on weekends and holidays (in summer). Shop around the boats tied along the wharf area. The *Polaris* has moonlight sailings for $12. The *Harbour Cruises* trip includes an historical commentary.

Helicopter trips to Devil's Island (reputed to have ghosts) and above the city are also offered.

Some summers the Waterfront Development Corp (tel 422-6591) plans free guided walking tours of the historic water's edge.

AROUND HALIFAX

Dartmouth

Dartmouth is Halifax's twin city, northwest across the Halifax Harbour. It's a city of 70,000 and has 23 lakes within its boundaries. The lakes are stocked with fish and are good for swimming; seven have supervised beaches.

The city was founded in 1750, one year after Halifax, when Governor Cornwallis sent troops over to get wood for construction and fuel.

Today the two are connected by passenger ferry and two bridges – the 'old' Macdonald Bridge and, farther inland, the 'new' MacKay Bridge.

The ferry from Halifax lands you at the centre of things in Dartmouth. Portland St is the main street; it's quite an attractive tree-lined and pebbled road with wide sidewalks. Along here you'll find numerous restaurants, both cheap and not so cheap, as well as several antique/junk shops. Beside the ferry terminal is a small park with good views.

There are a number of historic sites near the waterfront or neighbouring downtown area. You can pick up a walking tour guide at a Tourist Office in either city. Buildings in old Dartmouth are primarily of wood rather than of brick or stone as in Halifax.

There are places to stay on this side of the bay as well. The *Tudor Lodge* (tel 435-5947) is at the entrance to Portland Estates. It's an English-style cottage with two rooms and a suite with varying luxuries for the visitor. Good value from $35 with breakfast in bed.

One restaurant to try is the *New Scotland Chowder House* down a small lane off Portland St, with several chowders as well as the usual light meals. There are a couple of take-out places up Portland St, and the park next to the ferry terminal is not a bad spot for a sandwich at noon.

The *Moosehead Brewery* at 656 Windmill Rd offers tours through the summer months.

Activities The city's lakes are used for fishing, swimming and boating.

The Shubenacadie Canal connects Dartmouth with the Minas Basin in the Bay of Fundy. The Micmacs once used it as a route across the province; it's now interrupted in places but is a fine canoe route with some portages needed. According to Indian legend, Lake William contains a great rattlesnake.

Events These include: the Pipe & Drum Festival in mid to late July; an Old Time Fiddlers' Contest in early July; the Dartmouth Natal Day Celebration in early August; and the Winter Carnival, 10 days in early February. A three-day Multicultural Festival is held in June along the waterfront and features ethnic foods and arts.

Peggy's Cove

Canada's best-known fishing village lies 43 km west of Halifax on Highway 333. It's a very pretty place with fishing boats, nets, lobster traps and old pastel houses, making it picturesque to outsiders.

Peggy's Cove is not unlike numerous other fishing villages, but because it's close to the capital it gets a lot of attention. During peak tourist season it gets very busy and there really isn't a lot to see. The village, dating from 1811, has just 50 residents and most of them are fishermen.

The large granite boulders littered all over the landscape add an odd touch; they are 415 million years old.

Pioneer Village Hostel
This rustic *Youth Hostel* is on a wilderness lake just 30 km south-west of Halifax. Its three cabins are accessible only by an eight-km hike. There are 12 beds; for information ask at the Halifax hostel. Open all year.

The South Shore

This refers to an area south and west of Halifax to Yarmouth. The tourist route through here, on older, smaller roads, is called the 'Lighthouse Route'. Several museums and points of interest are found along the route, which was named for the many lighthouses along the shore. There's lots of lobster and other seafoods.

The South Shore contains many small fishing villages and several small cities. The coastal scenery is good, typically rocky, jagged and foggy. The latter qualities have made the coast as much a favourite with modern day smugglers, transporting illegal drugs, as it once was to rum runners.

CHESTER

This is a village of 1000 overlooking Mahone Bay, once the haunt of pirates and prohibition bathtub gin smugglers. It's now a small summer resort and home of an adult puppet theatre. The tourist booth has a good brochure on local history and what to see in town. Nearby are one government and one private campground.

New Ross
Here, 26 km north, is a living agriculture museum set up like a working 19th-century farm. Also in New Ross is a Youth Hostel.

Gold River
Here, not far west of Chester, the salmon fishing is excellent.

Oak Island
This small island is said to be where the infamous Captain Kidd buried his treasure. Despite nearly 200 years of digging, it's still up for grabs and has become one of the country's biggest ongoing mysteries. Three farmboys stumbled upon a deep shaft in 1795, and since then six lives and millions of dollars have been lost on the world's longest-running and most costly treasure hunt. The search – now using a lot of sophisticated equipment – goes on.

To get there, turn off Highway 3 at Oak Island Rd and then you can get a boat for a nominal fee.

LUNENBURG

This very attractive town of 3000 is known as the fishing town that built the *Bluenose* sailing schooner. Lunenburg is surprisingly quiet and free of tourists on the residential streets. There are many nice wooden houses, some made in the old shingle style. Some are brightly painted, others are raw, the wood turned grey from the coastal weather.

The town has the largest fish-processing plant in North America, employing 1000. It produces the Highliner supermarket seafood products.

At the end of town, up the hill on Lincoln St to Blockhouse Hill Rd, is the Tourist Office and a great view of the area.

The Lunenburg Fisheries Museum is down at the water. It has one building and three ships to inspect: a dragger, a rum-runner and a fishing schooner. In the building are exhibits on fishing and fish processing, and a 25-minute film on marine life. There's also an aquarium. Open daily from mid-May to September. Admission is $2.

Check out the old Electric Building across the street from the museum; there's also a golf course across the water from the museum.

Near the Post Office, Earl Bailly has a studio displaying historical relics and an odds and sods collection of curios from the world's ports, brought back by sailors.

In July, a craft festival is held and a month later, the Folk Harbour Festival is a weekend of traditional music and dance.

Places to Stay

There are a few camping spots right at the Tourist Office, for $5.50 a tent. Others are not far from town. There are also a couple of guest houses and bed & breakfasts in town and several motels in the area; rooms in motels are about $30/40 for singles/doubles.

Bluenose Lodge, (tel 634-8851) at 10 Falkland St, has rooms for $25 singles or doubles, with meals available.

BRIDGEWATER

Bridgewater is an industrial town with a couple of things to see. The Des Brisay Museum has a small collection of goods of the early, mainly German, settlers; free. The Wile Carding Mill on Victoria Rd is an authentic water-wheel mill from 1860, also free (carding is the straightening and untangling of wool fibres in preparation for spinning).

LIVERPOOL

Liverpool is on the Mersey River, near four sandy beaches: Beach Meadows, White Point, Hunt's Point and Summerville. All are within 11 km of town; there are others further west. You'll find motels in the area, as you will all along the coast. There is a *Hostel* here (tel 354-5868) on Main St in Trinity Parish Hall, by the Kinsmen Service Centre. Beds are $4 to $6.

SHELBURNE

This shipbuilding town of 2500 is known as the birthplace of yachts. As well as prize-winning yachts, the town produces several other types of boats. It sits on a slight hill overlooking a good harbour.

Shelburne, like many Fundy region towns, was founded by Loyalists and in 1783 had a population of 10,000, making it the largest community in British North America. Many of its inhabitants were former members of the New York aristocracy. Some of the Loyalist houses still stand.

Ross-Thompson House, built in 1784, is the only original store left and now acts as a small Loyalist museum. Furniture, paintings, artefacts and goods may be viewed in the stores of the time. It's free and open daily. Nearby is a place where they still make wooden barrels the old way.

The Shelburne County Museum is in a Loyalist House of 1787, along with relics of the Loyalist settlement. It's at the corner of Dock St and Maiden Lane, very close to Ross-Thompson House.

For eating, the *Tea Cup* (in an old house), is recommended. They serve a full English afternoon tea, including biscuits, Devon cream and home-made jams. Light lunches are also offered.

There's a good government campground just west of Shelburne. Tent sites, $6.

Activities

Maritime Canoe Outfitters (tel 875-3055) rent and sell equipment and supplies for those canoeing and camping in this wilder area of the province. Everything you need for a canoe trip can be rented for $25 to $30 per day. They're in Lower Ohio, eight km inland on the Roseway River. Maritime also run various sorts of guided nature trips. An extended, six-day guided wilderness tour is offered with food included in the price. You can expect to see lots of wildlife (in the wild).

Yarmouth to Windsor

ANNAPOLIS VALLEY

This region of Nova Scotia stretches from Yarmouth along the north Bay of Fundy shore to Windsor and the Minas Basin. One of the first European-settled areas in Canada, the district formed part of 'Acadia', the French name for this new land. The 'Acadian Shore' and its history are still evidenced today.

The region is best known, though, for the very scenic valley of the Annapolis River. It's famous for apples and in springtime the blossoming valley is at its best. The Evangaline Trail tourist route passes through this area.

The Tourist Office has a pamphlet listing country inns and bed & breakfast places, many in small towns between Yarmouth and Wolfville.

YARMOUTH

With its population of nearly 10,000, Yarmouth is the largest town in western Nova Scotia. A rather drab-looking place, it's a transportation centre of sorts where the ferries from Portland and Bar Harbour, Maine, land. Yarmouth is also the centre of the French-speaking community along this bit of coast.

There's a large Tourist Office down at the ferry docks and a more locally oriented one at 404 Main St in Frost Park, opposite the Court House.

The Runic Stone

At the door of the Isaac Walton Killam Memorial on Main St, the stone has writings on it believed to be by Vikings who landed here about 1000 years ago.

Yarmouth County Museum

This museum is at 22 Collins St, in the grey stone building. Most of the exhibits are to do with the sea - ship models, paintings, etc. There are also some rooms done in various period styles. It's open 9 am to 5 pm daily in summer, Sunday 1.30 to 5 pm; shorter hours in the off season, closed Mondays. Admission is $1.

Fireman's Museum

This museum on Main St has a collection of beautiful fire engines dating from the 1930s. They look like the kind in children's stories that have personalities and abused emotions. Admission $1; open 9 am to 9 pm, to 5 pm on Sundays.

Places to Stay

For a fairly small town there is no shortage of accommodation here and there's a choice of some pretty good places. There's half a dozen bed & breakfasts, a couple of guest houses and plenty of motels. The town's going rate is not bad at all at about $20/35 for singles/doubles, give or take $5.

A Youth Hostel can be found in the *YMCA* (tel 742-7181) on Main St. It's a huge place with room for 100 and yet is still low-priced.

Collins St Bed & Breakfast (tel 742-3713) at No 11 charges $20/35 for singles/doubles.

Sophie's Guest House (tel 742-7447) is at 504 Main St. It has just three rooms which are single $20, double $25, including continental breakfast. The *Sunset Guest House* (tel 742-2080) is more costly with singles or doubles $30; open 1 June to 1 October, it is at 109 Brunswick St in the large white house. Another guest house is *The Gables* at 55 William St.

At 216 Main St, near the ferry terminal, is the *Ferry Inn & Motel*. The rooms in the hotel section are $30 for one or two people, extra guests $3 each. The units are more costly.

Places to Eat

The *Kitchen Garden*, 350 Main St, offers good value with home-made foods buffet-style. It opens early for breakfasts. Not far away in the big gabled place at 577 Main St, *Captain Kelly's Kitchen* specialises in fish and beef. *Harris' Quick 'n' Tasty*, a few km from town, is a good, reasonably-priced seafood spot. There are both more expensive and cheaper places in town, including a *Kentucky Fried Chicken*.

Getting There & Away

Ferry The Marine Atlantic (tel 742-3515) ferry to Bar Harbour, Maine, 160 km away, takes about six hours. It leaves at 4.30 pm daily during the summer months and less frequently the rest of the year. The fare is $31 per adult, $60 per car and $7.50 per bicycle. The prices go down quite a bit from October to May.

Another ferry run by Prince of Fundy Cruises sails back and forth to Portland. The trip to Portland, Maine is 320 km, therefore more expensive and takes about twice the time, but you could make back the fare in the casino! Either way, call in as reservations will probably be required.

In Portland there is a Nova Scotia Tourist Office in the Portland Pier area, across from the old Thomas Block Building.

Bus Acadian Lines (tel 742-5131) has a twice-daily service to Digby for $7.50 and also runs two buses a day to Halifax, which costs $23.25.

MacKenzie Lines also go to Halifax twice daily. The depot is in the VIA Rail Station at the south end of town on Main St.

Train VIA goes to Halifax once a day via Kentville. The train makes a lot of stops and the trip takes about 5½ hours; it costs $29 one-way.

Getting Around

The Texaco Station at the far south end of town rents cars.

DIGBY

A town of 2500, Digby is in the Annapolis Basin, an inlet of the Bay of Fundy. This is the ferry terminal for the *Princess of Acadia* which plies the waters between Digby and Saint John, New Brunswick. The town is well known for its 'Digby Chicken' or smoked herring, and for being one of the country's prime scallop-fishing ports.

From the top of the hill by the high school there is a good view of the area.

For a place to sleep, try *Salvia House* (tel 245-2247), 115 Montague Row opposite the Digby Bandstand. Singles are $20 to $24, doubles $22 to $24, triples $27. Most rooms are equipped with at least a sink and some have TV. It's open all year and there's a picnic table and barbecue you can use.

Westway House (tel 245-5071) is a bed & breakfast place at 6 Carlton St. Singles are $20, doubles $27, including continental breakfast; for a couple of bucks a full breakfast will be provided.

Lovett Lodge (tel 467-3917) is another bed & breakfast, also good value. Singles/doubles cost $23/26, with full breakfast. It's eight km east on Highway 101.

Wingberry House (tel 834-2516) at Sandy Cove is $30 per couple, with breakfast and dinner available and swimming nearby. To get there, take Highway 217 west from Digby. Turn left at the bottom of the first long hill in Sandy Cove, and go to the end of the road. Turn right and it's at the end of the street.

There are also a few private campgrounds around Digby.

Old Acadia

Fifty km up the coast from the Digby County line, along St Mary's Bay, Old Acadia is where the province's largest, mainly French-speaking Acadian population lives. Summer festivals are held in the small villages. The history and sights of the area are detailed in a booklet titled *The Acadian Shore*, available from the Tourist Office.

Getting There & Away

In summer there are three ferry trips from Digby to Saint John, New Brunswick, daily; the crossing takes about 2½ hours. Prices are steep at $13 per passenger and $40 per car, with bicycles $5. Reservations are a good idea; call Marine Atlantic at 1-800-565-9470, toll-free.

You can drive around in a small car for less in petrol money but it takes longer, as you must go right around the bay and up through Moncton, New Brunswick.

ANNAPOLIS ROYAL

This little town is near the site of Canada's first permanent European settlement and was founded by Samuel de Champlain in 1604. As the English and French battled over the years for the valley and land at the mouth of the Annapolis River, the settlement often changed hands. In 1710, the English, with a decisive victory, changed the town's name from Port Royal to Annapolis Royal in honour of Queen Anne.

A farmers' market is held every Saturday morning in summer.

In late summer, there should be some jobs available picking apples. Check before the season starts or all the hiring will have been done. Check in any of the valley towns, too – Bridgetown, Laurencetown, Middleton.

Lower St George St

This street in town contains many historic buildings with three different centuries represented. The Farmer's Hotel, which possibly dates from as early as 1730, is the oldest building in English Canada. The O'Dell Inn Museum and Robertson-McNamara House both provide historic displays, the former on the Victorian era, the latter on local history. Admission to both is free.

Runciman House, from 1817 and furnished in Regency style, is run by Heritage Canada and also offers glimpses of former years.

Fort Anne National Historic Park

Right in the centre of town, this park preserves the memory of the early Acadian settlement plus the remains of the 1635 French fort. On the grounds is the museum with replicas of various period rooms, artefacts, uniforms and weapons; the Acadian room was transferred from an old homestead.

Historic Gardens

Five different garden types are set out here, including Acadian and Victorian. Admission is charged. The gardens are also in the centre of town.

Tidal Power Project

This offers visitors the chance to see a hydroelectric prototype harnessing power from the Bay of Fundy tides. There's also an interpretive centre that explains how it works. Free and open every day in summer.

Port Royal Habitat National Historic Park

Fifteen km from Annapolis Royal, this is the actual site of the first European settlement north of Florida. It has a replica of Champlain's habitation, constructed in the original manner. Free; open daily.

Places to Stay

All budget classes are well represented here from inns to motels to cabins by the sea. There are a good half dozen bed & breakfasts in or near town and a couple of motels along the primary routes.

Right in town at 82 Victoria St is the *Bread & Roses Bed & Breakfast* (tel 532-5727) in a restored house built in 1882. Singles are $44, doubles $48.

About one km east of town on Highway 201, RR1, are *Helen's Cabins* (tel 532-5207), which are $12/15 for singles/doubles, with hot plates for quick cooking. Open 1 May to 1 October.

The *Shining Tides* (tel 532-2770) is a few km from the Habitation National Park in Port Royal. There are three rooms, with singles $23, doubles $25, and that includes a light breakfast.

At Victoria Beach, 26 km from Annapolis Royal, are the *Fundy View House & Cabins* (tel 532-5015) with rooms in the house or in cabins with kitchens. Singles are $22 to $25, doubles $27 to $33.

Open from 15 June to 15 September. There's swimming and fishing here.

About 25 km from Annapolis Royal is a *Youth Hostel* (tel 532-2497), in South Milford on Highway 8. It's open mid-May to mid-October and there are nine beds, members $4, non-members $6. The hostel is in the Beachside Park Campground; to get there, turn west in South Milford onto Clementvale-Virginia Rd.

KEJIMKUJIK NATIONAL PARK

This park contains some of the province's least-touched wilderness. It's an area of glacial lakes, good for canoeing, and evergreen forests, where the hiking is easy on the gentle, rolling hills. Some portage routes are marked; many were used by the Micmac Indians. Lots of frogs and reptiles inhabit the many bogs. Deer also abound in the park.

There are primitive campsites along the trails and the main campground for the park at Jeremy's Bay. Access north or south is by Highway 8. Canoes are available for rent.

KENTVILLE

This town of 5000 marks the east end of the Annapolis Valley and acts as a focal point to a couple of nearby places of interest.

There are several motels here and two bed & breakfasts conveniently located right on Main St. The *Apple Blossom* is at No 148 and the *Wildrose* is at No 160. Both charge $30 single, $35 double. Not far away, the *Country Squire* is on Main St in Port William and is a similar sort of place which includes the morning meal.

Cape Blomidon

North of Kentville, this spit of land juts into Fundy Bay at the Minas Basin. It has good scenery, a viewpoint near Blomidon called the Lookoff and fine camping at the government site. There are also beaches.

WOLFVILLE

This is a small, green, university town. Main St has a little museum dealing with the early Loyalists and New England planters. Painter Alex Colville lives in town and over on the Acadia campus some of his work is hung in the Beveridge Art Centre.

There are two up-market inns in town where you won't go without and a *Youth Hostel* (tel 542-9028) on Crowell Avenue near University St.

Grand Pre National Historic Park

This park is a memorial to the Acadians, who had a settlement here from 1675-1755. 'Grand Pre' means 'Great Meadow' and refers to the lands the Acadians dyked along the shoreline.

In 1755 the Acadians were expelled from their lands by the British, who were locked in battle with France over Nova Scotia and paranoid over the Acadians' loyalties. About 14,000 Acadians were forced out of this and nearby areas. The sad, bitter departure was the theme for Longfellow's narrative poem, 'Evangeline'. Many Acadians headed for Louisiana and New Orleans, where their name became Anglicised to 'Cajun' (often heard in songs and seen on restaurant menus). Others went to various Maritime points and north-eastern America; some hid out and remained. In later years many of those deported returned.

A museum in the park has a section on Longfellow and a collection of artefacts. Also on the grounds are a church and gardens. The park is five km east of Wolfville and opens daily from June to September; free admission.

WINDSOR

Windsor is a small town on the Avon River, at one time the only English stronghold in this district of French power and Acadian farmers. There's an old blockhouse still intact amid portions of the British Fort Edward of 1750.

Another site is Haliburton House, once the home of Judge Thomas Chandler Haliburton, one of the founders of written

American humour. He created the 'Sam Slick' character in Mark Twain-type stories. Although these aren't read much now, many Haliburton expressions are often used today, like 'quick as a wink' and 'city slicker'. Haliburton's large estate is free and open to visitors from mid-July to mid-September. It's just north of Lake Pesaquid, in the eastern section of town.

The Northumberland Shore

This is the north coastal district of the province from the New Brunswick border to Cape Breton Island. The Northumberland Strait is between this shore and Prince Edward Island and has some of the warmest waters north of the American Carolinas. Highway 6, also called the Sunrise Trail Tourist Route, runs along this strip of small towns, beaches and Scottish history.

On Highway 104 right at the New Brunswick border is a large Tourist Office with maps and overviews of the driving trails around Nova Scotia.

PUGWASH

On the coast along the Sunrise Trail from Amherst is this small port, with good beaches nearby. The water along this coast averages slightly warmer than 20°C in summer. The town has become well known for the International Thinker's Conferences held here, organised by Cyrus Eaton, a Nova Scotian and one of America's top financiers. A colourful 'Gathering of the Clans' also takes place here, each year on 1 July.

PICTOU

This was where the Highland Scots first landed in 1773; thousands followed to settle 'New Scotland'. They spread from the Northumberland Shore through Cape Breton, reminded of home by the landscape and weather. In town are several buildings and historic sites relating to the early Scottish pioneers.

There's a farmers' market every Saturday from April to December in the Community Centre, Front St, where you'll find baked goods and farm produce. In mid-July is the Lobster Carnival, a two-day festival, and two km east of town is a small Micmac museum.

The ferry to PEI leaves from near here at Caribou. For details see the Getting There & Away section of Charlottetown, in the Prince Edward Island chapter.

Places to Stay

Fraser's Tourist Home (tel 485-4294), 12 High St, is recommended. There are three rooms in the 100-year-old house, with singles $15, doubles $30, breakfast included.

Birchwood Cabins (tel 485-6948) is at Lyons Brook, four km from Picton Rotary (roundabout) on Highway 376. They have two cabins at $15 for singles, $18 for doubles.

NEW GLASGOW

This town might be of some use as a stopping point if you're coming or going on the ferry to PEI. Otherwise it's not worth a visit. There are several well-kept churches which struck me as the only attractive buildings in town.

The *Hazeldean Tourist Home* (tel 992-2628) is 11 km east of town across from the Irving Garage off Highway 104. Singles are $23, doubles $25, and it's open from mid-June to the end of September.

ANTIGONISH

If you're coming from New Brunswick or PEI, this is the place to spend the night or even a couple of days. Antigonish is also a good stop between Sydney and Halifax. A pleasant, small town with a few things to see, it has a good hostel, places to eat and the beach nearby. It's a university and residential town with no industry.

The name is pronounced with the accent on 'nish'.

Information
Ask the owner of the Youth Hostel and *Whidden's Trailer Court*. He's a wealth of information about the town, area and local history.

The Tourist Office itself is just off the highway at the west entrance to Antigonish, coming from New Glasgow.

St Ninian's Cathedral
This is the seat of the Catholic diocese for the adjoining three counties and all of Cape Breton. It was begun in 1868 and is built of blue limestone and granite from local quarries. Work in the interior comes from a variety of sources including Quebec, New Hampshire and Europe. St Ninian was an obscure priest from Ireland who travelled and taught in the Scottish Highlands in the fourth century.

St Francis Xavier University
The attractive campus of this 120-year-old university is behind the Cathedral near the centre of town. It's a nice place to walk around just for a look-see.

County Courthouse
In 1984 this 129-year-old building was designated a National Historic Site. Restored in 1970 although it was in good repair, it still serves as the county's judicial centre. The design by Alexander Macdonald is typical of many of the province's courthouses from the mid-19th century.

Beaches
There are some good sandy beaches on the coast east or north from town. For the eastern ones take Bay St out of town.

Monastery
East of town, the old Monastery is now home to the Augustine Order of monks. It was originally a Trappist monastery established by French monks in 1825. Visitors are welcome; you get a tour of the buildings and grounds.

Events
Antigonish is known for its annual Highland Games held in mid-July. These Scottish games have been going on for 120 years. You'll see pipe bands, drum regiments, dancers and athletes from far and wide; there are competitions, performances, singing, dancing, fiddling and a Pipe Band Tattoo. The events last a week. For information or tickets, see the Antigonish Highland Society at 274 Main St. The International Gathering of the Clans took place here in the summer of 1983.

Places to Stay
The *Youth Hostel* in *Whidden's Tent & Trailer Court* (tel 836-3736) is good. This camping ground is right in town at the corner of Main and Hawthorne Sts, and is open from early June to late August. Rates are $6.50, a bit more for non-members. There is a kitchen and 30 beds, or you can tent. Also at the site are two rooms rented out in the house for $15 the single, $30 the double. There are weekly rates on these, the apartments and the trailers. The owner/operator is a friendly, interesting old man who knows nearly everything about the town. He'll recommend restaurants, too.

For rooms at the *University* from mid-May to mid-August, call the Residence Manager (tel 867-3970 or 867-2258). It has a dining room, laundromat and pool and is centrally located. Singles are $16, doubles $25 and good weekly rates are available. Tax is extra.

There are also numerous inns, motels, cottages and a couple of bed & breakfasts. *Hillside Housekeeping Cottages* (tel 232-2888), 19 km east of town at Tracadie, are a better bargain than motels in the area. Basic cottages are $24/28 for singles/doubles, or with cooking facilities, $28/32. The cottages are 10 minutes from the beach.

Places to Eat

A stroll down Main St and around the town will turn up several places for a bite. At the *Bonnie Brae Inn*, there's decent food and prices and they'll give you an extra helping if you're staying at the youth hostel.

Farmer Brown's in the big red barn by the CN Station has very cheap breakfasts and good buys on clams. *Wong's* is friendly and provides the local Chinese option with the standard moderate prices. The *Venice* has a good lunch salad bar.

For more of a real dinner out, the *China Cup Tea Room* at 95 College St behind the town hall offers various creatures from the sea; closed Sundays.

Getting There & Away

Bus The station (tel 863-6900) is on the Trans-Canada Highway at the turn-off for James St into town, on the west side of the city. Like the train station, it's within walking distance of the downtown area. The destinations and prices include:

Halifax: three in the afternoon – $15

Sydney: also three afternoon trips – $13.50

Charlottetown: 1.15 pm daily – $22 (includes ferry).

Train Follow Main St east through town, veer right at the red barn-like restaurant and you'll see the station.

Halifax: 9.59 am, 2.50 pm – $19

Sydney: 5.14 pm, 8.50 pm – $17

Charlottetown: 9.59 am – $26.

Tours Several driving tours of the area can be done with a descriptive pamphlet available from the Tourist Office. They're no more than 80 km each. Good scenery, Acadian villages and points of historical note are principal attractions.

The Eastern Shore

This designation refers to the area east from Dartmouth to Canso at the extreme eastern tip of the mainland. It's one of the least-visited regions of the province; there are no large towns, little industry and a slow, narrow road almost as convoluted as the rugged shoreline it follows. As in most of the province, the population is clustered in many small coastal villages. Marine Drive is the marked scenic route through this area. Along the way you'll find plenty of beaches, campgrounds and some interesting attractions as well.

Jedore Oyster Pond

Quite the name for a town. See the small museum here – it's a model of a typical 1900s fishing family's house.

Clam Harbour

The beach here has an annual sand-sculpting contest held in mid-August.

Tangier

A visit to Willy Krauch's smokehouse is worthwhile. Salmon, eels and mackerel are smoked. He'll tell you all about them, and more.

Taylor Head Provincial Park

Just east of the village of Spray Harbour, the park contains good examples of Krummholz vegetation – trees and plants stunted and twisted from the poor conditions here: fog, wind, salty air. There's also a sandy beach. East from here the fishing is good, with trout and salmon amongst the catch.

Liscomb Park Game Sanctuary

North of Sheet Harbour lies this large (518-square-km) preserve. There's lots of wildlife, and the park offers good canoeing. Near Liscomb Mills beyond the sanctuary is *Rumley's Lodge & Cabins* (tel 779-2607), a cheaper place to stay than the average motels in the area. A cabin or a room in the house is just $15 single or double, with private bath but no TV (big deal). Breakfast is offered.

Sherbrooke Village

This pioneer village is just out of Sherbrooke on the way up to Antigonish. It re-creates life of 100 years ago through buildings, demonstrations and costumed workers. Open daily from 15 May to 15 October.

Something else to look for here is *The Bright House* restaurant in town. Situated in an inn from 1850, it specialises in roast beef and fresh seafood and does them well.

Canso

With a population of just 1200, this town at the edge of the mainland is probably the largest on the whole eastern shoreline. From as early as the first attempted settlement in 1518, Canso has seen it all: Indian battles, English and French landings and captures, pirates and the ever-present difficulties of life ruled by the sea.

Cape Breton Island

The island, known across the country for its rugged beauty, is actually several islands clustered around the large Bras d'Or Lake. This part of the province drew many Scottish immigrants because of its resemblance to the Highlands. The coast is rocky and jagged, the land a blend of mountains, valleys, rivers and small lakes, and the words most often used to describe the weather are windy, wet, foggy and cool. Summer, however, can be warm and sunny.

Cape Breton Island has always conjured up notions of remote isolation. Except for Sydney and Glace Bay, two large industrial cities, most towns are small enough to be considered villages and in some places, Gaelic is still spoken. But as from its founding, life is hard here and unemployment very high. Fishing and mining are the main industries.

For the visitor it is a very appealing, undeveloped area with a national park in the Cape Breton highlands and a top historic site in Louisbourg.

Information

There is a bed & breakfast programme in Cape Breton with prices at about $20/26 for singles/doubles. Ask at the many Tourist Offices for their complete list. There are also campgrounds and, usually, a few hostels scattered around the island. Check up on these, too, as their locations change annually.

As you cross the Strait of Canso onto the island you'll be hit for $1.50 for using the causeway. (It's free on the way back – they say that's why the locals who leave never come back.) A big Tourist Office sits on the east side of the causeway.

The Cabot Trail, the scenic 184-mile highway route around the northern cape, can be busy and crowded in July and August. Try to visit the smaller places.

North Sydney is the terminal for ferries to Newfoundland.

INVERNESS

This is the first town of any size on the northern shore on the Ceilidh Trail (Highway 19). There's miles of beach with some nice secluded spots and very few people, though the water's too cold for most humans. There are campgrounds north of town.

CHETICAMP

Just before the Cape Breton Highlands National Park is this town, centre of the local Acadian community. The *Musee Acadien* is a combination restaurant and craft shop. Downstairs is a small, neat café tended by women in traditional Acadian dress, where you can try *rapure*, a tasty old specialty, or potato pancakes, both under $3. You can also sample gingerbread, codfish and chowders. (Here, as in Newfoundland, 'fish' means cod; others are called by their names.) Upstairs is a crafts store – one of the many in town – where you can see women weaving or buy some of the local handicrafts. Most of the stuff is pretty trashy; some textiles are OK.

St Peter's Church is the focus for religious activity in the area.

Whale-watching cruises are run three times daily in July and August, leaving from the Government Wharf on the harbour opposite the church. Aside from (maybe) seeing whales, there are good views of the coastline on the three-hour trip. The boat operates in June, September and October as well but not as frequently.

From Cheticamp, the Cabot Trail becomes more interesting, with good views and lots of hills and turns as you climb to the highest point just before Pleasant Bay.

Places to Stay

There's camping nearby at the park boundary. Just before the park is *Cabines LeBlanc* (tel 224-2822) with six cabins, singles or doubles $24 to $26. Open June-October.

In Petit Etang are *Ann's Cottages* (tel 224-3444), of various sizes, some with cooking facilities. The rates are roughly $34 for four people.

There are many motels in the area.

CAPE BRETON HIGHLANDS NATIONAL PARK

In the middle of the highlands, this park not only has some of the most impressive terrain in the area, it is one of the most scenic in Canada.

The Cabot Trail is at its best along the northern shore and then down to Pleasant Bay. The road winds right along the shoreline between mountains, across barren plains and valleys up to French Mountain, the highest point at 459 metres. Along the way are lookout points, the best of which is at the summit. Save the trip for a sunny day when you can see down the coastline.

From French Mountain the road zigzags through switchbacks and descends to Pleasant Bay, just outside the park. If you're driving, make sure your brakes are good and can afford to burn off a little lining. I saw lots of cyclists in the area and they were working pretty hard. I certainly wouldn't take my inaugural bicycle trip here.

Hiking trails abound and are, of course, the best way to see the park and maybe glimpse some of the wildlife. Black bears, lynx, fox, otter and moose are some of the animals you might see, along with 185 species of birds. Most of the trails are short and near the road. For longer, overnight camping hikes, ask for advice at the information office.

There are eight campgrounds in the park, some for tenters only. These tend to be small, with space for 10 to 20 people. Camping is $7.50 for a tent with any number of people. In the campgrounds, pick a site and set up. A warden will come around, probably in the evening, to collect the money. Park entry is $2.

At the eastern entrance to the park are Igonish and Igonish Beach. Some of the best scenery is from here to Cape Smoky. The park's recreational facilities are here and it's a good place to get supplies. There are several campgrounds, a park information office and motels here, too.

Eight km north of the park entrance near Igonish is *Driftwood Lodge* (tel 285-2558), run by Mrs Kulig. Rooms in the older building are cheapest and start at $24 for doubles without bath; if you want the view you'll pay more. Off-season rates apply in early June and September-October. Breakfast is served, and a German-Polish lunches and dinners are available.

NORTH SYDNEY

This small town is important as the Marine Atlantic terminal for ferries to either Port Aux Basques or Argentia, Newfoundland.

There isn't much in town but it makes a convenient place to put up if you're using the ferry. Tourist information is available at the Tourist Office at the ferry landing;

you can also call the Board of Trade on 564-6543.

Sydney Mines

This is a town not far east of North Sydney. You can get a bus that goes about three-quarters of the way from North Sydney to the Princess Mine Museum, a coal mine and the principal attraction in Sydney Mines.

A trip down the coal mine is worthwhile if only to see the conditions workers must face. You can take a good tour for $5 which includes going down a 250-metre shaft and seeing some of the gear and equipment needed, as well as viewing some of the surface buildings. At one time operations were carried out eight km from shore, below the sea floor. But ask at the Tourist Office for bus information and opening hours and days of the mine before you go. It was closed with equipment problems when I was there and doesn't seem to have reopened.

Places to Stay

Right in town is *Paul's Hotel* (tel 562-5747) at 10 Pitt St with 24 rooms, some with shared facilities and the more expensive ones with private bath, which range from $20 to $26.

Kawaja Tourist Lodge (tel 794-4876) is two km west of the ferry terminal with a view over the water. It's at 88 Queen St, which is called Commercial St in town. This is a nice place, open year-round with singles for $18 to $20, doubles $20 to $22. Another is *Macleod's Lodge & Cottage* at 620 George St.

There are at least half a dozen motels nearby.

Twenty minutes from the ferry, *Sally & Murray Edmunds* have a bed & breakfast place (tel 794-4155) on RR4, Balls Creek. With breakfast, singles are $20, doubles $30.

There are also several privately-owned campgrounds just north of town off the Trans-Canada Highway.

Places to Eat

You'll find a few basic restaurants in town – the *Harbour Deli* for submarine sandwiches, *Napoli's* for pizza. Around the corner from Commercial St near the landing is *Robert's Home-Style Bakery*, where you can pick up a few things for the ferry trip. *Lick-a-Chick* – that's the name – is a chicken take-out chain with franchises in the area.

Getting There & Away

Ferry For detailed information on ferry crossings, see the St John's and Port Aux Basques sections in the Newfoundland chapter. Reservations may be required; the phone number for Marine Atlantic in North Sydney is 794-7203.

Bus There is no real bus station in North Sydney; the station is in Sydney. But at the Texaco station on the Trans-Canada Highway just out of town, a Halifax bus leaves at 9.39 am and 11.24 am. The latter makes fewer stops on the way; both are $25.25.

A green & white bus runs along Queen St regularly between North Sydney and Sydney, to the south.

Train The station is north up Archibald St off Commercial St, going away from the water. There are two departures to Halifax: 6.55 and 11.46 am – $32. These trains also go to Antigonish.

SYDNEY

Sydney is the second largest city in the province and a hard-drinking, drab, rather grim industrial centre specialising in steel and coal. It has the largest self-contained steel plant in North America and secondary industries of pulp and paper, machine works and foundries. There is little reason for the tourist to visit, with the ferry terminal in North Sydney and the area's main attraction in Louisbourg.

The difficulties of Cape Bretoners are reflected here. Sydney has a long, bitter history of hard work – when there is any – with low pay and poor conditions. One of the highest unemployment rates in the country is regularly tallied here and work-related illness is high. The hardships, however, have resulted in a people able to smile at misfortune and generally friendly to strangers.

Nearby Glace Bay is much the same, a town whose life depends on the coal miners. The mining museum and village replica burned down in 1980; the Tourist Office will know if they have been replaced.

Places to Stay

The *Cleifden House Hotel* (tel 564-6311) is the bright yellow place on the corner at the bus station. Singles/doubles are $22/26 with a sink and TV.

Better and still reasonably priced is *MacLeod's Lodge & Cottage* at 620 George St. In the lodge, singles start at $15, doubles at $24.

Edna & Eric Smith have a bed & breakfast (tel 562-6560) with singles at $22, doubles $27. There are good views. It's three km from town toward South Bar. Phone for directions.

Again, there are plenty of motels.

Getting There & Away

Bus The Acadian Lines station (tel 564-5533) is at the corner of Wentworth and Bentinck Sts. There are three buses a day to Halifax ($28), and one to Charlottetown, PEI, which leaves at 9 am daily, arriving at 5.45 pm ($32).

Train The station is at the bottom of Pitt St.

Halifax: one daily which goes on to Montreal – $35

Truro, Halifax, Moncton, Saint John: 11.20 am – $45 (to Saint John)

Amherst: 6.30 am – $32

Charlottetown: 6.30 am (arrives at 7.55 pm) – $38.

LOUISBOURG NATIONAL PARK

This excellent historic fort site is about 50 km south of Sydney on the south-east tip of Cape Breton Island. There is no bus to it but hitching is pretty easy. There are campsites on the way. The park is open daily in summer and admission is $4.

After the Treaty of Utrecht in 1713, the French lost their bases in Newfoundland. This left them Prince Edward Island, St Pierre & Miquelon and Cape Breton, which became the centre for exporting cod to France. It was also chosen as the spot to build a new military base. Louisbourg, a massive walled fort and village complex, was worked on continually from 1719 to about 1745. It looked daunting but was poorly designed, and the English took it in 46 days in 1745 when it was barely finished. It was returned to the French under the terms of another treaty, only to fall under the English siege of 1758. In 1760, Wolfe (who had led the Louisbourg onslaught) took Quebec City and the walls of the fort were all destroyed. It was abandoned and with no commercial use, began to decay.

In 1961, with the closing of many Cape Breton coal mines, the federal government formed a make-work project: the largest historical reconstruction in Canada. Today the site depicts French life here in the 1700s with remarkable detail. All the workers, in period dress, have taken on the lives of typical fort inhabitants. Ask them anything – what the winters were like, what they ate, what that tool is for, how this was made, who they had an affair with – and they'll tell you. There are many buildings of interest with appropriate contents. The restaurant serves food typical of the time. Definitely go to the bakery and buy a one-kg loaf of soldiers' bread. It's delicious; one piece with cheese makes a full meal. (But take a plastic bag; they won't give you one as they didn't have plastic in 1750.)

You'll need a lot of time to see it properly: plan about half a day at the site. The best times to visit are in the morning –

when there's more happening and fewer tourists – and during June or September. Take in the movie in the interpretive centre first. Outside the peak months of July and August, you can talk with the workers and they are not harried by hordes of people. Even in peak time a visit is worthwhile, though.

The weather here is very changeable and usually bad. Take a sweater and raincoat even if it's sunny when you start out.

AROUND BRAS D'OR LAKE

Baddeck

An old resort town in a pastoral setting, Baddeck is on the north shore of the lake, halfway between Sydney and the Canso Causeway. In this area as well as other parts of Victoria County, you may still hear Gaelic spoken.

Alexander Graham Bell Museum Alexander Graham Bell, the inventor of the telephone, had a summer place in Baddeck. This large museum is dedicated to him and his work. It's a National Historic Park that covers all aspects of this incredible man's inventions and innovations; written explanations, models, photographs and objects detail his varied works. On display are medical and electrical devices, telegraphs, telephones, kites and seaplanes. You'll need a few hours if you want to see it all. Admission is free; open daily until 9 pm in summer.

There's a good view of the bay and part of the saltwater Bras d'Or Lake from the roof.

Place to Stay About 30 km from Nyanza where the Cabot Trail begins, is the *Normaway Inn* (tel (902) 248-2987). Dating from 1928 and sitting on 200 acres, it has nine rooms, four two-bedroom cabins and a very good dining room. Prices are fair with doubles starting at $45; the two-bedroom cabins are $75. They have bicycles and there are walking trails on the property; there's also fishing for salmon or trout at the nearby Maregaree River. A good spot to treat yourself.

Iona

This is a small village south of Baddeck, on the south side of the peninsula by Barra Strait in Bras d'Or Lake (on Highway 223). Iona is a bit out of the way, but may appeal for that reason. The Highland Village Museum shows examples of Scottish homes, the first pioneer houses in the new land, and later ones in which new skills and materials were employed. A Highland festival is held on the first Saturday in August. You must take the ferry over for a small charge.

SOUTH OF BRAS D'OR LAKE

This is a little-visited area where many of the roads have not been paved. There are several small communities here and along the coast; a tour of them could be very interesting.

Sable Island

Lying south of Cape Breton about 150 km from the mainland is the 'graveyard of the Atlantic'. Countless ships from the 1500s to the present have gone down around the island, with its rough seas and hidden sandbars. The island, 32 km long by 1½ km wide, is little more than a sandbar itself with no trees, nor even shrubs. But there are about a dozen people, a small herd of tough, wild ponies and lots of cranberries. The people maintain the two lighthouses, a meteorological station and a few other installations. The ponies are believed to have survived a shipwreck in the 1500s.

Prince Edward Island

Entered Confederation: 1 July 1873
Area: 5657 square km
Population: 123,000 (the smallest province)

The Micmac Indians say Glooscap, a god, painted all the beautiful places on earth. Then he dipped the brush in all the colours and created this, Abegweit, his favourite island.

Now known as The Island, or PEI, Prince Edward Island is the smallest and surprisingly, most densely populated province. You'd never guess this though, as the island is very pastoral and peaceful and the towns aren't big at all. Laws against billboards further add to the slightly old country flavour of the island.

Prince Edward Island is mainly a farming community with potatoes, which are sold all over the country, the main crop. The rich, red soil is the secret, they say. Fishing is also important, particularly lobsters, oysters and herring. The lobster suppers held throughout the province, tasty and reasonably priced, have become synonymous with the island.

There is little manufacturing, as transportation costs are prohibitive. Industry hasn't been helped either by the lack of energy sources.

The quiet, gently rolling hills edged with good beaches have made tourism a reliable money-maker. Because of warm ocean currents the province has a milder climate than most of Canada. July and August are the driest months in a fairly damp year.

Very recently there has been political talk of connecting the province to the mainland via some sort of causeway/bridge, but at this point it hasn't even been determined if it's wanted, so the notion is purely theoretical so far.

Charlottetown

Charlottetown is an old, quiet country town that also happens to be the historic provincial capital. Its slow-paced and tree-lined colonial and Victorian streets make it the perfect urban centre for this gentle, bucolic island.

The population is 45,000 in this, Canada's smallest capital, so the downtown area is compact and everything is within walking distance.

When the first Europeans arrived in the early 1700s, they found the area had already been settled by the Micmac Indians. Charlottetown was established named after Charlotte of Mecklenburg-Strelitz, who became King George III of England's Queen.

It was here in 1864 that discussions to unite Canada were first held. An agreement was finally reached in 1867, when the Dominion of Canada was born. Though times are much less heady these days, many of the town's people are employed by the various levels of government.

Today, the city is the focal point of the large tourist trade as well as the business and shopping centre for the province. In July and August the streets are busy with tourists, but out of season things are pretty quiet.

Orientation

Highway 1 becomes University Avenue, the town's main street. At the corner of University Avenue and Grafton St is the

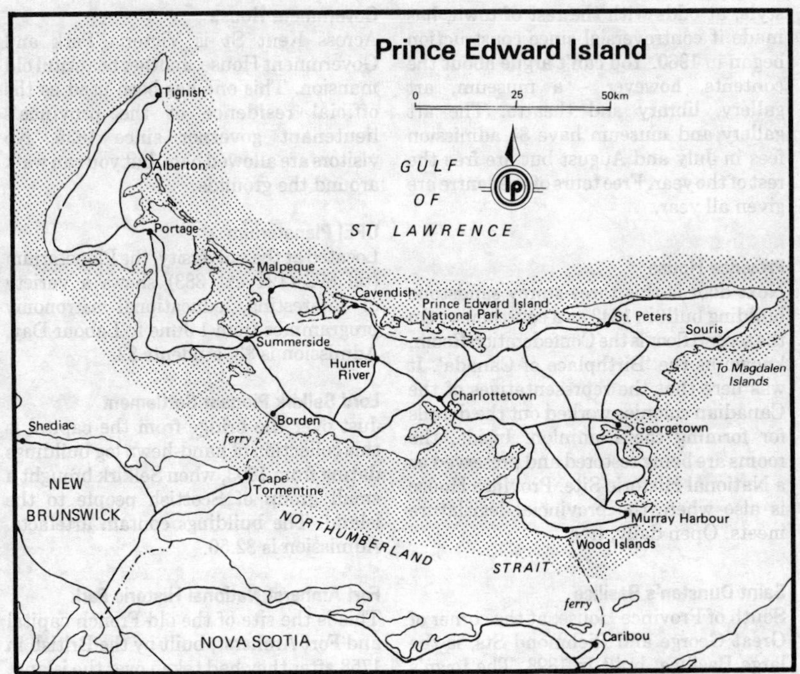

large, modern, arts centre complex. South a few blocks is the city harbour.

On Water St at the harbour are the new law courts and the yacht club.

Another main street is Queen St, parallel and one street to the west of University Avenue. From the harbour, up a few blocks on and around Queen St, is old Charlottetown. A number of buildings have been renovated and are now often used as government offices, restaurants and shops. Many of the buildings have plaques giving a bit of the history and the date; some are over 100 years old. The farmers' market is held in this area on Saturday mornings.

West of town is the large Victoria Park, with a road running along its edge and the bay.

The streets just out of town are pleasant to stroll, looking almost as though they belong in a different era. Lots of trees and flowers front the large, old, well-kept wooden houses.

Information

The Tourist Office for Charlottetown and the main office for the whole island (tel 368-4444) is on the corner of University Avenue and Summer St. Coming into town from Borden, you'll find it on the right in a shopping centre, about two km from the downtown area. They're open all year.

There are about 12 offices around the island, including some at the ferry terminals. Each has a two-way radio and can arrange accommodation anywhere on the island within an hour.

Confederation Centre of the Arts

This is the large modern structure at the foot of University Avenue. Its architectural style, at odds with the rest of town, has made it controversial since construction began in 1960. You can't argue about the contents, however – a museum, art gallery, library and theatre. The art gallery and museum have $1 admission fees in July and August but are free the rest of the year. Free tours of the centre are given all year.

Province House

Next door is this three-storey sandstone building built in 1843 as a courthouse. On the second floor is the Confederation Room, known as the 'Birthplace of Canada'. It was here that the representatives of the Canadian colonies worked out the details for forming the Dominion. Inside, the rooms are being restored and preserved as a National Historic Site. Province House is also where the provincial legislature meets. Open daily, free.

Saint Dunstan's Basilica

South of Province House, at the corner of Great George and Richmond Sts, is the large Basilica, built in 1898. The town's Catholic church is surprisingly ornate inside. It's painted in an unusual style, with a lot of green trim which blends well with the green and blue tints in the marble.

St Paul's

On Church St, east of Province House, is this red sandstone building, the oldest Protestant church on the island. It dates from 1747.

Beaconsfield House

This beautiful yellow Victorian mansion, at 2 Kent St, was built in 1877. It is now the headquarters of the PEI Heritage Foundation. The rooms on the first floor are used for exhibits relating to local history. There is also a bookstore specialising in books about PEI. Open during the week, free.

Government House

Across Kent St is Victoria Park and Government House, another beautiful old mansion. This one has been used as the official residence of the province's lieutenant governor since 1835. No visitors are allowed here, but you can walk around the grounds.

UPEI Planetarium

Located at the university, the Planetarium (tel 892-4121 ext 383) shows a variety of interesting, educational astronomy programmes from 1 June to Labour Day. Admission is $3, students $2.

Lord Selkirk Pioneer Settlement

Just over the bridge from the capital is this collection of hand-hewn log buildings dating from 1803, when Selkirk brought a small group of Scottish people to the island. The buildings contain artefacts. Admission is $2.50.

Fort Amherst National Historic Park

This is the site of the old French capital and Fort Amherst, built by the British in 1758 after they had taken over the island. There isn't really anything left to see, but in the Interpretive Centre are exhibits and an audio visual show. Free admission.

Skate Country

Five km from town on Route 236, Lower Malpeque Rd, is this modern roller skating rink with music and lights. Skates are available at just $1, admission is $4. Good fun if you're in the right mood.

Sailing Charters

A 12-metre yacht moored at the foot of Pownal St in the Yacht Club runs charter tours for a maximum of 10 people. The rate is $35 an hour, $93 for three hours and $205 for seven. You go where the group decides.

Events

The Charlottetown Festival is held each year from mid-June to mid-September.

This is a theatrical event with dramas and musicals, and each year, *Anne of Green Gables*, a story written in PEI, is performed. It's a family show, famous as 'Canada's favourite musical'. Tickets to any of the plays are available at the Arts Centre and range from $10 to $20.

Recently, some newer, more modern plays have been added, including one about Elvis Presley which stirred some controversy due to its colourful language. There are also summer theatre and dance programmes both in town and around the province.

A new tradition seems to be developing: the annual Blue Grass Music Festival held in July. It's a two-day, camping event held at a park or campground. Tickets are not costly.

Places to Stay

Hostels The *Canadian Youth Hostel* (tel 894-9696) at 153 Mount Edward Rd is good, close to town and friendly. There's room for about 65 people in this barn-like building very close to the university. There's a kitchen available and the rates are $6, $8 non-members. It's about three km from downtown. To get there, follow University Avenue west from town toward Borden. Turn right at Belvedere Avenue. The hostel is near Mount St Mary's Convent.

The university itself has rooms from mid-May to the end of August. Reservations are a good idea. Single or double $40.

Charlottetown has a YM-YWCA and a Salvation Army but neither of them rent rooms.

Tourist Homes Fortunately the city, like the entire island, has an abundance of guest houses. The quality is high and the prices excellent. PEI guest houses and tourist homes are some of the best accommodation deals in Canada. A double room can cost as low as $15 and rarely more than $25, and sometimes that includes breakfast. Many are located in beautiful old east-coast-style wooden homes. The Tourist Office has a complete list of these places. In town, there are quite a few. Here are several to try.

Gateway House, (tel 894-9761) at 206 Fitzroy St, has three rooms, two with double beds. Open mid-May to mid-September. Single or double, $14 to $15.

Flack's Tourist Home, 202 Hillsborough St, is in a big old house at the corner of Fitzroy St. They have three rooms with double and single beds. Open 1 May to 1 October, the home is very close to town. The rate is $20 or for two double beds, $28.

Gillis' Overnight Guests (tel 894-3522) is at 237 Pownal St, very centrally located. The owner has one single room and one with two single beds and charges $25 for the double. Open June to September.

There are a couple of places on Edward St on the east side of town, close to the race track. Houses here are smaller and older, and still not a long walk to the city centre. *Cameron's Tourist Home* (tel 894-8174) is at 95 Edward St. There are three rooms with a choice of single, twin or double beds. This one is open all year; cheaper out of season. Singles/doubles are $16/18, weekly rates $105 to $115.

A couple of people on York Lane also rent rooms in the same price range.

There are also bed & breakfast places where a morning feed costs $2 to $3. Many of these are on farms just out of main towns. In Charlottetown itself you could try *Baker's Lodging* (tel 892-4662), 51 Hutchinson Court, about three km from the town centre. Single $19, double $28. Here the morning meal is included as well as an evening snack. Weekly rates. Another is the *Almost Retired Tourist Home* (tel 566-1285), $20 single or double. It's about five km from town.

Motels There are motels along Highway 1 west of Charlottetown towards Borden. Also on this commercial strip are drive-in movies, restaurants and petrol stations. Motels here are usually at least $35. Some

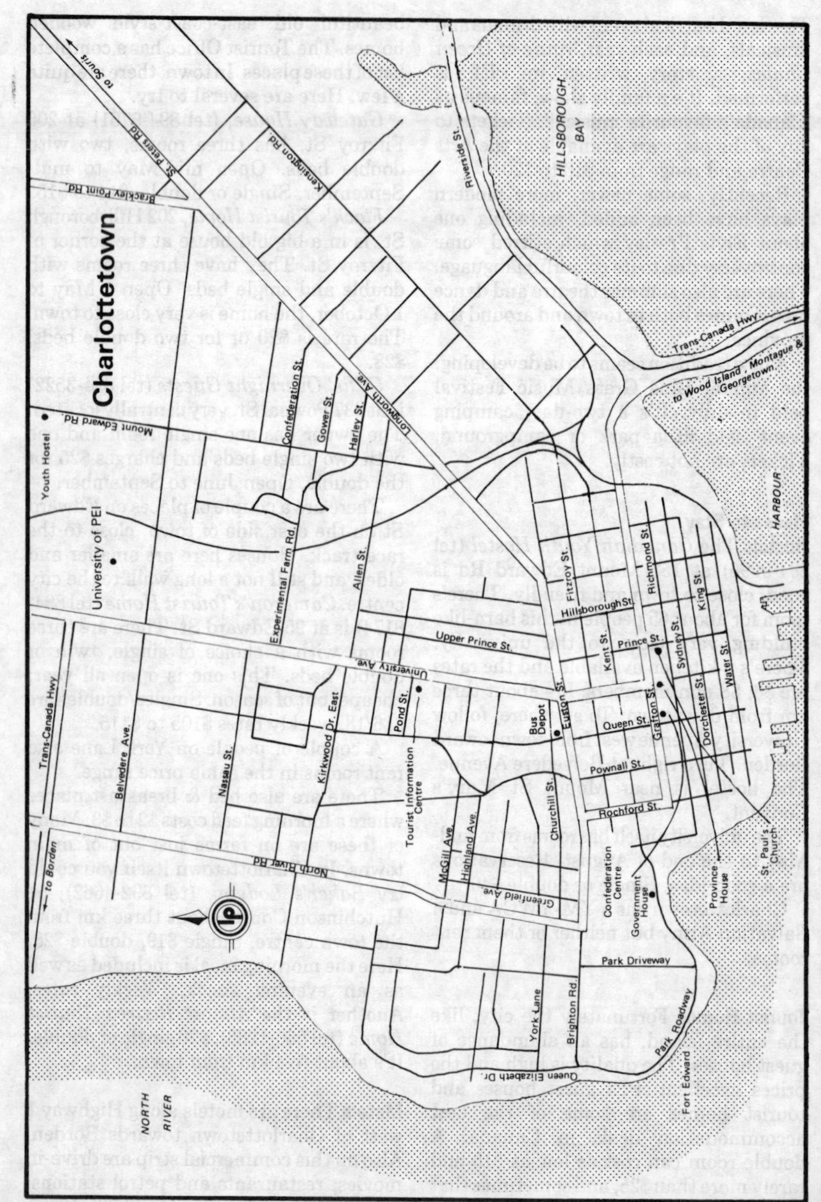
Charlottetown
to Souris
St. Peters Rd
Kensington Rd.
Brackley Point Rd.
Mount Edward Rd.
Youth Hostel
University of PEI
Trans-Canada Hwy
to Borden
Belvedere Ave.
Nassau St.
Experimental Farm Rd
Kirkwood Dr. East
Confederation St.
Gower St.
Harley St.
Allen St.
Longworth Ave.
University Ave.
Pond St.
Tourist Information Centre
North River Rd
McGill Ave.
Highland Ave.
Greenfield Ave.
Upper Prince St.
Bus Depot
Euston St.
Churchill St.
Fitzroy St.
Kent St.
Hillsborough St
Richmond St.
Prince St.
Grafton St.
Queen St.
Sydney St.
King St.
Dorchester St.
Water St.
Pownall St.
Rochford St.
Confederation Centre
Government House
Province House
St. Paul's Church
Park Driveway
Park Roadway
York Lane
Brighton Rd.
Queen Elizabeth Dr.
Fort Edward
Riverside St.
HILLSBOROUGH BAY
Trans-Canada Hwy.
to Wood Island, Montague & Georgetown.
HARBOUR
NORTH RIVER

further from town are a little more modest.

Close to town on the south side is the *Garden Province Motel*. It's small and well off the highway but, like many of the motels, expensive. Single or double $58.

Three km from town on the Trans-Canada is the *Queen's Arms Motel* (tel 368-1110), with a heated pool. About $55 for two people. Also housekeeping units available.

Further out, near the Highway 2 junction, is the brown *Zenith Motel*. Doubles are $43, up to four people $55. There is a laundromat.

Camping The island is covered with campgrounds – private, provincial and one national. Provincial parks are $8 for an unserviced site. Privately owned places charge more but accept reservations. Government parks operate on a first-come, first-served basis, are usually better and often full. The Tourist Office can give you vacancy reports. The only campground near Charlottetown is *Southport Trailer Park*, at 20 Stratford Rd overlooking the Hillsborough River, which charges $10. Weekly rates are lower.

Places to Eat

There isn't a vast selection of restaurants here but with all the fresh seafood, things aren't too bad. The larger hotels all have their own conventional dining rooms.

Cedar's Eatery, open every day and right in the middle of town on University Avenue, is a fine little place. At the chunky wooden tables the specialty is Lebanese, ranging from felafels to more expensive kebabs. There is also the standard Canadian fare: soups, salads, sandwiches, steaks, and Old Abbey, a local beer. Open very late.

For a simple meal or snack, the cheap and unpretentious *Lunch Bar* at 34 University Avenue fills the bill. It's been here forever.

The *Old Dublin Pub* is at 127 Sydney St with pub meals and live entertainment at night.

There are a couple of Chinese places around town; my choice would be the *King's Palace* on Queen St near Grafton St. Good value lunches.

In Confederation Court Mall at the corner of Kent and Queen Sts, the second floor has a menagerie of cheap fast food outlets. Pizza, chicken, burgers, etc.

The *Rose & Grey* on Richmond St behind the Confederation Arts Building is highly regarded and they have a nice bar section as well. Tasty lunch specials change daily. At night features include pastas and steaks.

Among the seafood spots in town are *Samuel's* in The Inn on the Hill, and the *Claddagh* in the old historic area at 129 Sydney St. Down at Charlottetown's waterfront on the Prince St wharf is *Mackinnon's* where you can buy fresh mussels, clams, and oysters, as well as live or cooked lobster.

Out at the university, you can get an inexpensive feed in the cafeteria on the ground floor of the Steeles Building. Open Monday to Friday from 7.30 am to 6 pm, Saturday and Sunday 10 am to 6 pm. Full course meals are served. It's near the youth hostel across the field off University Avenue.

For a splurge there's *Dalvay-by-the-Sea*, a Victorian seaside lodge offering a varied menu, lobster bisque to *coq au vin*. Reservations required.

Back in town, along Sydney St or around the big Arts Building you'll always be able to find a café for a cappuccino.

Cows on Queen St near Grafton is very small but they turn out good home-made ice cream.

Nightlife

Charlottetown may be the capital, but it's really a country town and therefore doesn't have much action at night.

The *Avenue Bar* on Kent St off University Avenue is the most popular spot and serves up loud rock music.

Further down Kent St is the *Tradewinds*, a much spiffier dancing spot. Open until 1 am.

A third spot is the *Silverados* at 36 Grafton St for country music. They have a huge, sunken dance floor. Local Schooner and other beer is $2 a pint.

Getting There & Away

Air Charlottetown has a small airport, north of the city. Air Canada and Canadian Airlines connect PEI with the major Canadian cities and some New England American points like Boston.

Air Canada one-way to:

Toronto – $247, youth $124 (you must also pay tax for these fares).

Canadian Airlines to:

St John's, Newfoundland – $211, youth $106

Montreal – $182, less on night flights and ones with stopovers

Halifax – for the cheapest fares take the slower 40-seater airplanes.

Ferry Most people get to PEI by ferry, either from New Brunswick or Nova Scotia. There are two ferries linking the island with the mainland, taking cars, buses, bicycles and pedestrians.

One joins Cape Tormentine, New Brunswick, with Borden in west Prince Edward Island. This trip is 14 km, takes 45 minutes and is run by Marine Atlantic, a government ferry system. The fare is $2.30 per person, $6 per car and $1 per bicycle. There are nearly 20 crossings a day between June and September, slightly fewer the rest of the year.

In peak season, arrive before 10 am or after 6 pm to avoid long delays. A reservation may help but isn't necessary. In Borden, telephone (902) 855-2010. In Cape Tormentine, (506) 538-2278. There's also a long distance number; get it at Tourist Offices in New Brunswick or Nova Scotia and call toll-free.

Charlottetown is about 60 km from Borden and the drive takes about 35 minutes.

The other route, run by Northumberland Ferries, joins Wood Islands, PEI in the eastern section of the province to Caribou, Nova Scotia. This trip is 22 km and takes 1½ hours. Fares are $3 per person, $9.60 per car, and $1.50 per bicycle. In summer there are 20 runs in each direction daily. This route, too, is very busy; during peak season you may have a one or two-ferry wait. There's a cafeteria on board. The head office is in Charlottetown at 54 Queen St, or for telephone reservations call 1-800-565-0201, no charge.

Bus You can take the once-daily bus to or from PEI. A ticket includes the ferry. The price to New Glasgow in Nova Scotia is $14.50. From there there are connections to points around the Maritimes. You may have to change again in Amherst, however.

The station, in the VIA building, is on Queen St at Eusten St. This is also the home of Island Transit, the provincial bus service.

Train There is no passenger train service to, from or on the island, but you can still buy a rail ticket to Charlottetown. The VIA train system will get you to Amherst, Nova Scotia. From here you use the ferry and bus, all included in the same ticket. There are two trips from Amherst daily.

Getting Around

Airport Transport A bus leaves the airport for the downtown area after each flight arrival, also to meet departures. The airport limo is $5. Otherwise take a taxi, but it's only a few km to the airport so a cab isn't costly.

Bus Island Transit in the VIA bus station (tel 892-6167), 308 Queen St, runs the limited bus service around the province. There are two summer routes and one year-round run.

In summer, route 1 goes between Charlottetown, Wood Islands and New Glasgow, Nova Scotia. Route 2 runs between Charlottetown, Souris and the ferry for the Magdalen Islands. Each run has many daily trips.

The year-round run goes from Charlottetown to Tignish and back, and stops everywhere along the way. There are no buses on national holidays, Wednesdays or Sundays. On Saturday the bus goes east only, not returning until the following Monday.

One-way fares: Wood Islands $6.25, Souris $7, Summerside $5.50.

There is no real bus line to the north coast beaches but see under 'Tours' for how to get there.

Bicycle The island is criss-crossed with narrow roads running through the peaceful, unhurried countryside. The landscape is gently rolling but offers no major hardship for cyclists. It's here you see the island at its most natural with few or no tourists.

At the Bike Shop in Charlottetown they rent bikes and have touring supplies. Rentals are also available in Stanhope at the Stanhope Beach Lodge.

Rentabike is at the junction of Routes 6 and 13, at Cavendish village, near the beach and has hourly and daily rates; open every day in summer. There's some good riding in the area, like along the Gulf Shore Parkway.

Car Rentals A car, for better or worse, is the best and sometimes only way to see much of the island. There are several outlets in the capital.

Avis Rent-A-Car is on University Avenue. Their cars range from $30 to $40 per day depending on the size, with unlimited mileage. Without a credit card, you'll have to pay in advance and put a deposit on top of that.

Hitching Thumbing around the island is common and accepted, and is often done by residents. The island is almost free of violence and it is generally considered a safe place to hitch.

Tours Abegweit Sightseeing Tours (tel 894-9966) at 157 Nassau St, Charlottetown, offer double-decker bus trips around the island. They have three trips: the north shore, the south shore and Charlottetown itself.

Each takes in some of the commercial attractions of the area. The north shore trip is about six hours long and costs $17; it's all inclusive. The city tour is just an hour and costs $4. And there's a south shore trip with a stop at Fort Amherst National Historic Park.

If you just want to go to the beach for the day, you can take the North Shore Tour Bus. They'll pick you up on the way back. The cost is $5 one-way, $7.50 return.

Around the Island

The island is small and easy to get around. In one day it's possible to drive from Charlottetown up to the beaches for a swim, along the north coast all the way up to North Cape, then back along the western shoreline, over to Summerside and down to Borden to catch the evening ferry. And you're not even rushing!

The island offers a wide variety of attractions, oddities, local museums, historical sites and many children-oriented activities. You can get a list at the information offices or just check them out as you come across them.

Three equal sized counties make up the island: Prince, in the west, Queen's, in the middle and King's to the east. Each county has a scenic road network mapped out by the tourist bureau. Though far from the only routes, these ones do take in the better known attractions, and the historical and geographical points of note.

Places to Stay

Tourist homes are found in towns and on farms all over the province and are generally very reasonably priced. Get details at the Tourist Offices. There are 15 provincial parks with campgrounds and these charge $8 for unserviced sites, $10 to $11 for trailers. There are plenty of privately owned campgrounds too. These often offer more commercial extras. Prices are up to $11 unserviced (but usually less), and $7 to $14 for hookups.

Places to Eat

There are nearly 40 outlets around the island for buying fresh seafood – good if you're camping and can cook your own food. Some guest houses offer cooking facilities or use of barbecues.

Also look for the famous lobster suppers held in church basements or community halls – these are usually buffet-style and good value. Perhaps not as much fun, many restaurants now also offer lobster suppers on a regular basis.

NORTH OF CHARLOTTETOWN

PEI National Park

Just 24 km north of the capital, this is one of Canada's smallest national parks but it has 40 km of coastline and includes some of the country's best beaches.

Sand dunes and red sandstone cliffs give way to wide beaches (widest at Cavendish) and the warmest waters around the island. The Gulf Stream does a little loop around the island, causing water temperatures higher than those found even further south along the east coast. This is not bathwater however.

There are several beaches along the park. Cavendish at the west end is the most popular and gets very crowded in peak season. Brackley and the areas at the extreme ends of the park are more popular with young people. Brackley Beach is very wide and has sand dunes. Watch out for riptides. A couple of short hiking trails begin in the Dalvay Beach area. One called Long Pond is quite good with a small graveyard, some remnants of old stone dyke walls and a spring for a cool drink. A day park permit is $3.

Windsurfing Rentals and lessons are available at the Stanhope Beach Lodge. The rate is $10 an hour for a board, less by the day. Canoes and sailboats are also for rent. On Thursday nights surfboard races are held, with prizes.

Places to Stay Among the campgrounds in the park, the one at Rustico is good and treed but the beach isn't so good: a bit rocky. The campgrounds offer the only shade around. Outside the park are many private campgrounds. *Forest Hill* and *Marco Polo* are popular with young people.

There are also many tourist homes, but without a car it's difficult to get around. Many visitors rent a cottage for a week or two and there are many of these to choose from in the area.

Places to Eat For munchies there is very little within the park, just a couple of snack bars. In Stanhope, at the eastern edge of the park there's a bar and a little nightlife at the *Stanhope Lodge*. Basic facilities are located here as well.

Cavendish

More or less just a crossroads at the junction of Routes 6 and 13 south of the park, this little town is the area's commercial centre. You're there when you see the gas station, Cavendish Arms Pub and the church and cemetery.

Just east of town is a restaurant complex all done in cedar shakes. It contains a few fast food places including one for breakfasts. *Thirsty's*, across the street, is a bar. Nearby is a grocery store and bicycle rental outfit. There are two of the best known lobster supper houses nearby, one in New London eight km west and one in New Glasgow, about the same distance on Route 13. Lobster plus all you can eat chowder, salads, breads and desserts. And you may get some live music to help it down, too. *Fiddles 'n' Vittles* three km west of town on Route 6 has been described as a fun place to eat, the food is good and they have a half price kids' menu.

East of Cavendish is a water-slide, golf course, and other diversions including, for some reason, a life-size replica of the space shuttle. At Stanley Bridge the Marine Aquarium is not worth the $5 admission. North Rustico Harbour is a tiny fishing community with a lighthouse.

House of Green Gables This house near Cavendish is known as the place where Anne, the heroine of Lucy Montgomery's books, lived. It's free and worth a visit for the period furniture and the feeling it gives of life here in the late 1800s.

WEST OF CHARLOTTETOWN

Lady Slipper Drive

This is the marked tourist route around this area of the island. The northern section of Prince county is, like so much of the province, pretty farm country but the southern portion is rather flat, less scenic and possibly the least visited area on the island.

Summerside

The second largest city in the province, Summerside is a town of 10,000. Residents from the capital used to move to this side of the island in the hot weather months.

The approach along Highway 1A is much like that of Charlottetown, with motels and hamburger joints, but also a few campgrounds.

There isn't much in town; everything is on the one main street, Water St. It's a quiet village with nice old homes on streets trimmed with big trees.

South of Summerside, Borden is the terminal for ferries to Cape Tormentine, New Brunswick.

Places to Stay For accommodation, *Faye & Eric's* (tel 436-6847) is at 380 MacEwan Rd. They have three rooms with one double bed in each plus a deluxe suite with all the extras, including a whirlpool bath. The price of $25 to $35 includes a light continental breakfast. The suite is $65 a day.

The *Summerside Inn* (tel 436-5208) is in an 1800s house three blocks from the centre of town at 98 Summer St. Six rooms are available, ranging from $25 to $45 double. Continental breakfast included. There are several others, such as the *Whitehouse* on Fitzroy St and *Morrison's* at 253 Maple Avenue.

Places to Eat Of the several restaurants, *Anne's Place* is recommended. It offers a good selection and reasonable prices. Chicken and lobster plates from $5 to $8 are good value. You can also try *rapure*, an old island dish. It looks like green cake but is a tasty pork & spice concoction. On the east side of town, *Seafoods Delight* is reasonably priced.

Each year in mid-July for a week, the lobster festival is held. This entails nightly feasts, contests, and games.

Acadian Museum

The museum is in Miscouche and has a small collection of early Acadian memorabilia. Most of the descendants of these early French settlers live in this section of the province. Six thousand of them still speak French as a first language. Admission to the museum is $2 and it's open every day in summer.

Pioneer Acadian Village

A replica of one of the settlements of the early 1800s, the village has a school, store and church. Admission is $2 and it's open daily. The village is near Mont Carmel on the south coast.

Malpeque Bay

North of Summerside, this bay produces the world-famous oysters of the same name.

Lennox Island

A band of about 40 Micmac families live on this island reservation in Malpeque Bay. The scenery is nice and there's a museum dealing with the history of the tribe, along with an Indian craft shop.

Around Prince County
Tyne Valley is worth a visit if you're in this vicinity. Stop at the *Crafts & Tea Shop* for some home-baked goodies out on the little sun porch. There are a few craft dealers here including a pottery.

If you're near Tignish at mealtime, drop in at the Royal Canadian Legion. Cheap, and you're bound to find conversation.

Up at the northern tip, North Cape is a wind-blown promontory with a lighthouse beaming out to sea. There's a weather station here and along the east side in particular are some pretty high cliffs.

Cedar Dunes Provincial Park at the south-east tip has a lighthouse, restaurant and beach.

EAST OF CHARLOTTETOWN
King's is a district covering the eastern third of the province.

The King's Byway
This sight-seeing route around the area is peopled by ancestors of the Scottish settlers, rather than the French.

Souris
On the north-east point of the island is where the ferry for the Magdalen Islands in Quebec docks. The 134-km trip takes five hours.

Fishing Along the north coast there is a lot of fishing – you could try a charter in search of tuna. North Lake is a well known fishing port.

Camping The best provincial park in this section of the province is Campbell's Cove. At East Point there are cliffs and another lighthouse to climb. At Brudwell Park the campground is just a bare field, but there's a lodge and a golf course for those not roughing it. Good beach, swimming and picnicking at Panmure Island Park.

New Brunswick

Entered Confederation: 1 July 1867
Area: 73,437 square km
Population: 696,403

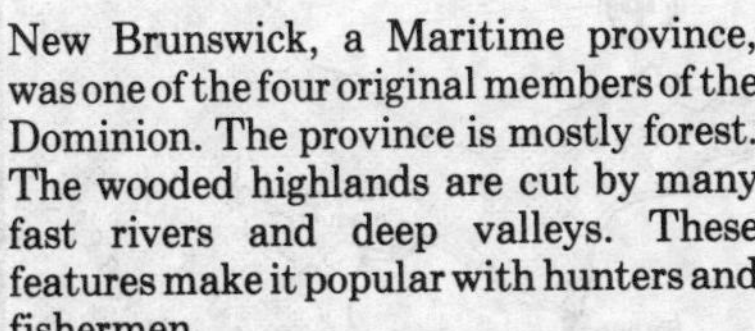

New Brunswick, a Maritime province, was one of the four original members of the Dominion. The province is mostly forest. The wooded highlands are cut by many fast rivers and deep valleys. These features make it popular with hunters and fishermen.

Lumber and pulp & paper operations are two of the main industries. Manufacturing and minerals are also important. The Saint John River Valley is a scenic farming area.

The eastern side of the province is coastal lowland. There are beaches along the Bay of Fundy and the Gulf of St Lawrence.

Roughly six out of 10 people live in urban areas. You may be surprised at how much French you hear in the province. About 37% of the population have French ancestors and even today 16% speak French only. New Brunswick is Canada's only officially bilingual province.

Summers are usually not very hot and winters are cold. Generally there is more rain in the south. The driest month is August.

There are lots of camping spots and the province has a 'Stay on a Farm' programme if you are interested.

In 1984 New Brunswick celebrated its 200th birthday.

Southern New Brunswick

ST ANDREWS-BY-THE-SEA

As its name suggests, this is a summer resort of some tradition and gentility. Together with the fine climate and picturesque beauty, St Andrews has a long, charming and often visible history – it's one of the oldest towns in the province and has long been on equal terms with Saint John. Today the wealthy and the less fortunate provincial residents, and visitors alike, have made a St Andrews summer both popular and well known.

The aboriginal Indians were the Passamaquoddies, a very few of whom still live in the area.

White settlement began in 1783 after the American Revolution. Many British pioneers, wanting to remain loyal, deserted their new towns and set up in the British territory around the fort in Castine Maine – a very pretty area. The British-American border was changed with the war's end and these people once again found themselves on American soil. The tip of the bay across the water was scouted and agreed upon as a place of equal beauty. So the pioneers loaded up ships and headed out, some even dragging their houses on rafts behind them, and St Andrews was founded in 1784.

Prosperity came first with shipbuilding, and when that was dying, continued with tourism. In the early part of the century, Canadian Pacific built the Algonquin Hotel, which more or less started St

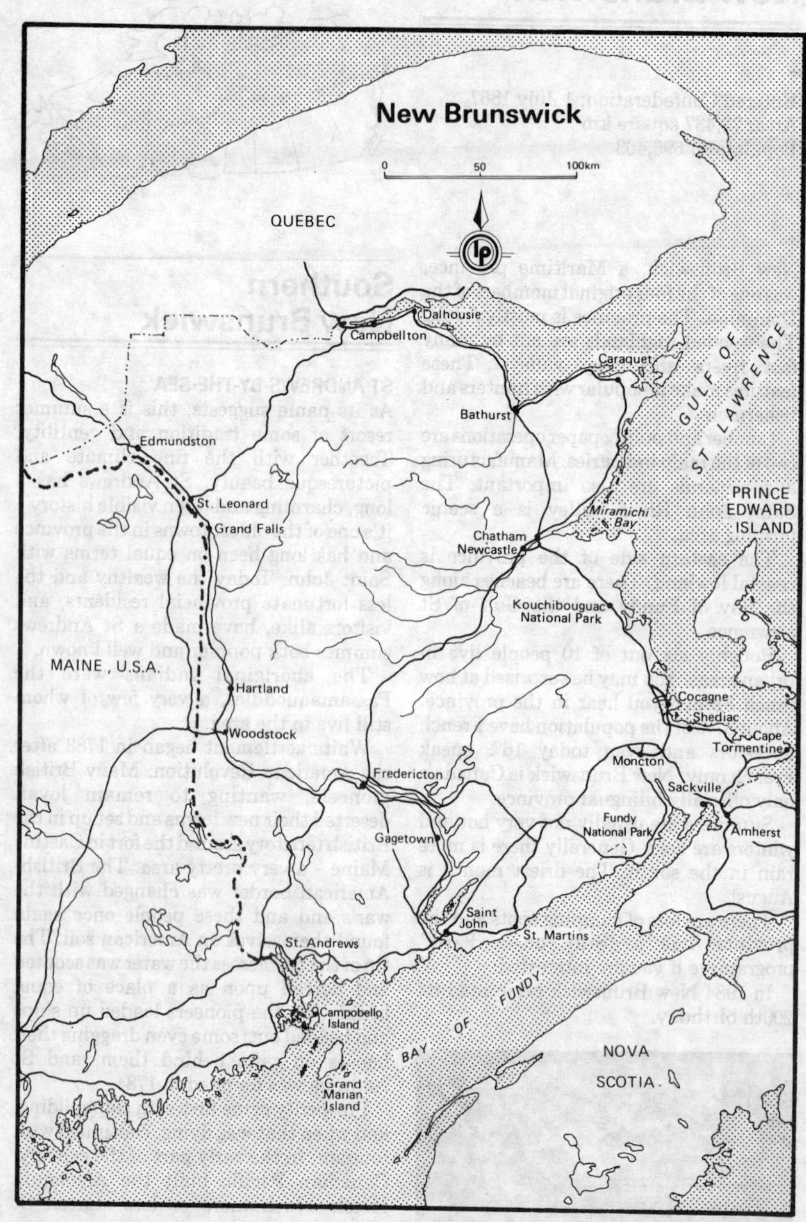
New Brunswick
0
50
100km
QUEBEC
Dalhousie
Campbellton
Caraquet
GULF OF
ST LAWRENCE
Bathurst
Edmundston
St. Leonard
Grand Falls
PRINCE
EDWARD
ISLAND
Miramichi
Bay
Chatham
Newcastle
Kouchibouguac
National Park
MAINE, U.S.A.
Hartland
Woodstock
Cocagne
Shediac
Cape
Tormentine
Moncton
Fredericton
Sackville
Fundy
National Park
Amherst
Gagetown
Saint
John
St. Martins
St. Andrews
BAY OF FUNDY
Campobello
Island
Grand
Manan
Island
NOVA
SCOTIA

Andrews as a retreat. Soon moneyed Canadians and Americans were building luxurious summer cottages alongside the 19th-century mansions of the lumber, trade and ship-building barons. Nearly a hundred of the beautiful houses first built or brought here from Maine are still used and maintained in excellent condition. Though many well-known families keep houses here, the casual visitor is now also important to the town's affairs.

Walking Tour of St Andrews
There are over 200 houses more than 100-years-old in town, many marked with plaques. A lot of them are real gems. Pick up the walking guide from the Tourist Office – it gives a map and brief description of 35 particularly interesting places. Even without the guide, walking around the residential streets is worthwhile.

Blockhouse Historic Site
The restored wooden guardhouse is the only one left of several that were built for protection in the war of 1812. As it turned out, they weren't needed. Made of hand-hewn timber, structures like this were easy to make, practical to live in, and strong enough to withstand most attacks. Down toward the shore is a battery of three cannons. Open daily in summer, free. The park is at the north-west end of Water St.

Sunbury Shores Arts & Nature Centre
This is a non-profit educational and cultural centre. They offer instruction in painting, weaving, pottery and other crafts in summer, as well as natural science courses.

Huntsman Marine Laboratory
The lab is part of the Federal Fisheries Research Centre – St Andrew's most important business. Some of Canada's leading marine biologists work here supplying knowledge to international markets.

At the Huntsman Lab there's an aquarium open to the public as well as a small museum. The aquarium displays most specimens found in the local waters. Open daily from June to mid-September, $1.50. It's west of town on Brandy Cove Rd.

Katy's Cove
Just north of town, this sheltered bay is good for swimming.

Ministers Island
An island accessible at low tide, even by car, when you can go on the hard-packed sea floor. A few hours later the route is under three metres of water.

St George
This town, not far from St Andrews towards Saint John, boasts the best drinking water in Canada. The secret, they say, is the source – deep artesian wells. I didn't hear this until I'd left, so I didn't sample the water and can offer no opinion. What do you think?

Places to Stay
There is a wide range of places and prices here.

Merrill's Cabins (tel 529-3200) are at 160 Reed Avenue. There are only four cabins but they go for only $20 single, $22 double. Reed Avenue turns into the 127 to Saint John.

In town, the *Gleason Arms* (tel 529-3532) is at 159 Water St. Three rooms, $25 single, $35 double.

The *Heritage Guest House* (tel 529-3875) at 100 Queen St, has singles ranging from $20 to $24 and doubles for $25 to $28.

Moving slightly up-market is the *Seaside Inn*, 340 Water St. Rates are $25 single, $36 double. The nearby *Seaside Beach Resort* is about $10 more.

The classic Canadian Pacific *Algonquin Hotel* has rooms starting at $82. Gardens, dining rooms, the works.

Camping There are several places to choose from. At the far east end of town on Indian Point is *Kiwanis Passamaquaddy Park* for tents and trailers.

Near St Andrews are two provincial parks with beaches. *Oak Bay* is eight km east of St Stephen, north of St Andrews. Further afield is *New River Beach*, a little more than halfway to Saint John. They have 115 camping spots.

CAMPOBELLO ISLAND

Like many wealthy families, the Roosevelts bought property in this peaceful coastal area at the end of the 1800s. Today you can see the 34-room 'cottage' where Franklin D Roosevelt grew up (1905-1921) and which he visited periodically throughout his presidency in the US. The 1200-hectare Roosevelt Campobello International Park is the site of the house, and preserves the flora and fauna; a reception centre has more information. Open late May to mid-October, daily.

You can camp at the Herring Cove Provincial Park, where there is a sandy beach.

Campobello and Deer Islands together provide a link between New Brunswick and Lubec, Maine. To get to Campobello, catch the government ferry from Back Bay on the New Brunswick mainland, to Deer Island. The ferry is free and operates continually from 1 am to 9 pm. Then from Deer Island to Campobello Island, catch another ferry. This one operates from late June to early September, making seven trips in each direction daily, ending at 6.30 pm. It leaves about every 1½ hours and takes 45 minutes; fees are $7 for car and driver, $2 per passenger.

Campobello Island is connected by bridge to Lubec, Maine.

There are a couple of places to stay in Welshpool as well as some cabins for rent at Wilson's Beach. Things tend to be pricier here than on the mainland: the area has always catered to those who needn't account for every shekel.

Deer Island

Cline Marine Charters (tel 747-2023) in Richardson on Deer Island offer whale-watching tours for $10 an hour. There's a minimum of three hours, which is standard. The ferry from the mainland to Deer Island is free.

GRAND MANAN ISLAND

South of Campobello is this larger, quiet, interesting island. On one side are ancient rock formations estimated to be six billion years old. On the other, due to an underwater volcano, are volcanic deposits 'only' 16 million years old. These phenomena draw many geologists.

In 1831, James Audubon first documented the many birds which frequented the island. About 312 species live or pass by each year, including puffins and Arctic terns. Don't miss the puffins' fishing act.

Offshore it's not uncommon to see whales feeding on the abundant herring and mackerel. Species include the humpback, finback (rorqual), minke and pothead. Fishermen will take you for a closer look or to see the fishing operations.

Back on land, there are various short walking trails around the 20 by eight-km island. Most popular are those of North Head, particularly the one to 'Hole in the Wall', an unusual rock formation. It begins at the lovely old Marathon Inn.

The museum in Grand Harbour has examples of the birds seen on the island, explanations of the geology and some reminders of the Loyalist days. Open in the afternoons only.

Roger's Van Tours is a good service offering van trips around the island which depart right from the ferry terminal and take in many of the island's points of interest. It's a five hour tour, so taken with the ferry crossing time it makes for a complete day. Tours are given from June to the beginning of September, excluding Sundays.

Machias Seal Island

Sixteen km south-west of Grand Manan is this small island bird sanctuary. Unlike in others, visitors are permitted, but are limited to 25 per day. The feathered residents include terns, puffins and a few others in lesser numbers. Trips can be arranged from Seal Cove on Grand Manan Island if the seas aren't too rough.

Places to Stay

The *Cross Tree Guest House* (tel 662-8263) in Seal Cove has just three rooms and charges from $25 for singles and $35 doubles. Also in Seal Cove are the *Spray Kist Cottages* (tel 662-8640), run by Mrs M Laffoley. Her four units are from $35 per day or $150 per week. Or try *Cherry Nook Cottage* (662-3321), at $25 single or double.

There are several places at North Head. *Fundy Folly* (tel 662-8433) is reasonable at $20 single, $30 double, with breakfast for $2. The beach is within walking distance.

Lastly, at Grand Harbour Mr & Mrs Hobbs run the *Grand Harbour Inn* (tel 662-8681), $32 single or $38 double. The fee includes a continental breakfast.

There are many others on the island, most very reasonably priced.

Getting There & Away

The ferry is from Blacks Harbour, south of St George on the mainland. In summer, there are six trips on weekdays and four on Sundays, though there are usually queues if you have a car anyway. There are fewer trips outside the summer months. The trip takes about two hours and costs $18 for a car, $6 per adult.

Saint John

Saint John is the province's largest city and leading industrial centre. Sitting at the mouth of the Saint John River, on the bay, it is also a major port able to remain open all year.

In recent years the city has undergone considerable refurbishing (a process still continuing) and the downtown area is much improved.

As well as the recent renovations, Saint John has a proud past. Known as 'The Loyalist City', it is the oldest incorporated city in the country. There is evidence of this Loyalist background everywhere, as you'll see. The town museum dating from 1842 is Canada's oldest.

The Maliseet Indians were here when the British and French began squabbling about furs. Samuel de Champlain had landed in 1604. Soon a fort was built and was changing hands between the two Old World enemies. However, the area remained pretty much a wilderness until 1755, when about 4000 British, loyal to the homeland and fleeing revolutionary America, arrived. They built up and incorporated the city in 1785. It was soon a prosperous ship-building centre. Though now utilising iron and steel rather than wood, shipbuilding is still a major industry in town. The dry dock is one of the world's largest. Fishing is also important.

The city is very often blanketed in fog, particularly in the mornings. This helps to keep the area cool, even when the rest of the province is sweating it out in mid-summer.

The name, Saint John, is always spelled out in full, never abbreviated, to avoid confusion with St John's, Newfoundland.

Orientation

The city sits on the waterfront at the mouth of the Saint John River. The central downtown area lies on a square peninsula jutting into the bay east of the river.

King Square, a small, pleasant park, marks the centre of town. Its pathways are placed to duplicate the pattern of the Union Jack flag. To the east of the square,

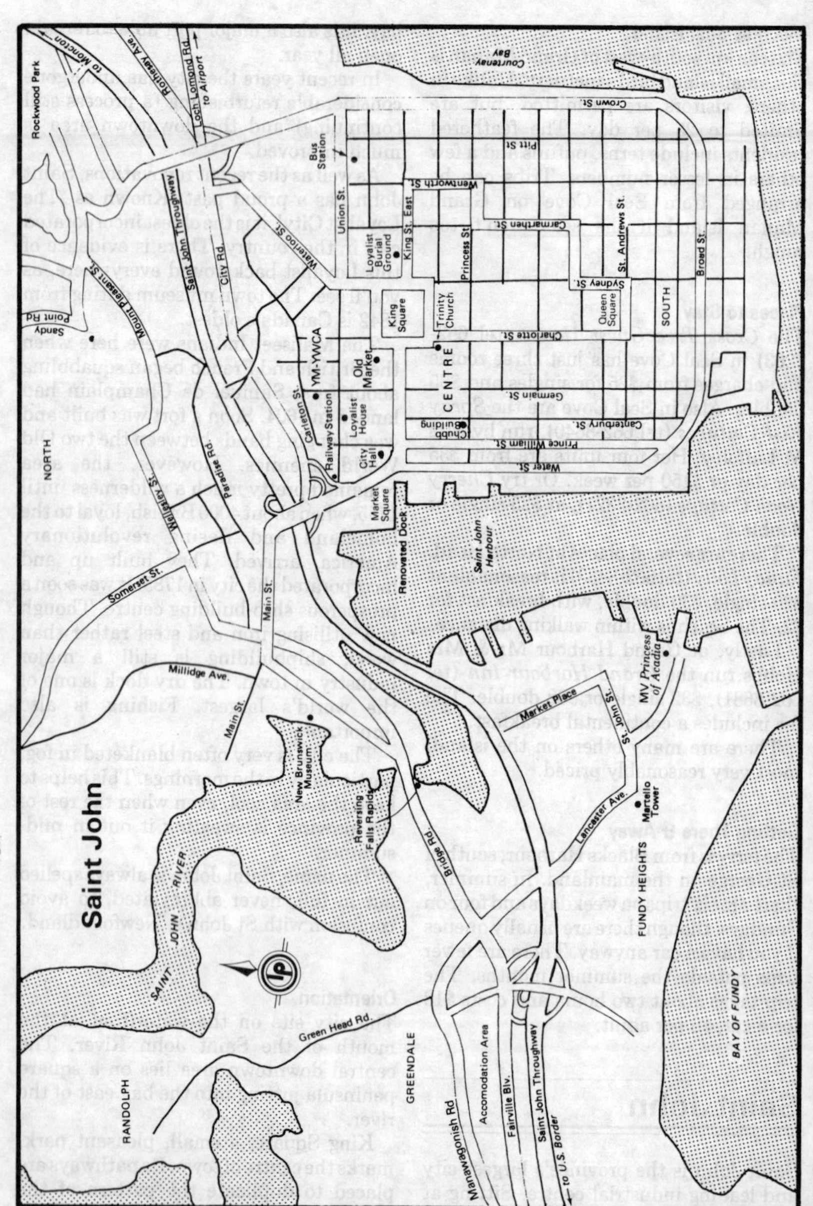
Saint John
NORTH
CENTRE
SOUTH
GREENDALE
RANDOLPH
FUNDY HEIGHTS
BAY OF FUNDY
Saint John Harbour
Courtenay Bay
SAINT JOHN RIVER
Rockwood Park
to Moncton
Rothesay Ave
Loch Lomond Rd.
to Airport
Bus Station
Union St.
Waterloo St.
Saint John Throughway
City Rd
Mount Pleasant St.
Sandy Point Rd
Crown St.
Pitt St
Wentworth St
King St. East
Loyalist Burial Ground
Carmarthen St
Princess St
St. Andrews St
Sydney St.
Broad St.
Queen Square
Charlotte St.
King Square
Trinity Church
Old Market
YM-YWCA
Germain St.
Carleton St.
Loyalist House
Canterbury St.
Chubb Building
Prince William St.
City Hall
Railway Station
Water St.
Market Square
Paradise Rd.
Wellesley St.
Renovated Dock
Somerset St.
Main St.
Millidge Ave.
New Brunswick Museum
Reversing Falls Rapids
Market Place
St. John St.
MV Princess of Acadia
Lancaster Ave.
Martello Tower
Bridge Rd.
Green Head Rd.
Manawagonish Rd
Accomodation Area
Fairville Blv.
to U.S. Border

across the street, is the Loyalist burial ground with graves dating from 1784.

West of the square are the principal downtown streets – Germain, Canterbury and Prince William – running south off King St. One block further west is the Saint John Harbour. Here is the newly developed waterfront area and market square, with shops, restaurants and the Trade and Convention Centre. Across the street is City Hall. Across the inlet are container terminals and the ferry landing for Digby, Nova Scotia.

South from King Square a few blocks is Queen Square, laid out in the same fashion. To the west four blocks is Courtenay Bay, the dry dock and the shipbuilding yards.

North of town is the large Rockwood Park, a sports and recreation area with a campground.

The famous reversing falls are west of town where the river flows into the harbour, under the bridge on Highway 100.

Further west leading out of town is a mostly residential and industrial district built on rolling hills overlooking the river and the Bay of Fundy.

Information

The Visitor & Convention Bureau (tel 658-2814), on the 11th floor of City Hall at the foot of King St, has an information area. Open all year.

Down at the waterfront in summer there's the unique and more convenient Tourist Office in an old tugboat.

There is another complete information office at the Reversing Falls Visitor Centre (tel 635-1238), at the falls. It's in Saint John West on Route 100, and is open mid-May to mid-October. A fourth alternative for information is on Route 1 at Island View Heights in Saint John West (tel 672-6990). It's handy if you're coming from St Stephen or Fredericton. Open from June 1 to early September.

The post office is on Prince William St.

Reversing Falls

The falls are the biggest attraction in the city and one of the best-known sites in the province. When the high Bay of Fundy tides rise, the current in the river reverses, causing the water flow to go upstream. When the tides go down, the water flows the normal way. Whoopee! In my opinion they're a joke; by no stretch of the imagination could this trickle be termed falls. It's incredible to see so many people crowding to look at this non-attraction. Since you'll probably go anyway, at least it's free and the Tourist Office here is good and helpful.

Loyalist Trail

The British Loyalists were really the founders of this town, turning a fort site into Canada's first legal city. Some of the early landmarks are still visible and interesting. From the Tourist Office get a Loyalist Trail Walking Tour pamphlet. This has a map and details of the best historical spots in the downtown area. Many of the places mentioned are no longer there; you just see the site of such and such – which is sort of useless unless you have a very active imagination – but some remain to visit.

Also, following the route is a good excuse to look at the many fine old buildings around the city, which contrast well with the modern ones. A good number of old buildings are now being restored.

Loyalist House

At the corner of Union and Germain Sts, this is the city's oldest unchanged building. It dates from 1810. The Georgian-style place is now a museum of the Loyalist period and contains some fine carpentry. Open every day in mid-summer, weekdays only in June and September, 10 am to 5 pm. Admission $2.

Loyalist Burial Ground

These interesting grounds are just off King Square, in a park-like setting. Here you can see tombstones from as early as

1784 slowly eroding and falling to the earth.

Old Courthouse

The County Court of 1829 is noted for its spiralling stone staircase, rising three storeys without any support.

Prince William Walk

This self guided walk around town details the heritage commercial architecture of the downtown area and includes many of those fine buildings strolled by on the Loyalist Trail.

By the mid-19th century, Saint John was a prosperous industrial town headed by its wooden ship-building enterprises – the third largest in the world. In 1877 two-thirds of the city, including most of the mercantile district, was reduced to ashes by fire.

The replacements, primarily of brick and stone, are now considered some of the country's best examples of 19th century commercial architecture. This walk takes in much of a preserved 20-block area. Pick up a pamphlet at the Tourist Office.

Trinity Church

On Charlotte St near King Square, the church was built in 1880.

Old Market

On Market St south of King Square is the interesting market that's been held in the same building since 1876. Inside the door is a guest book to sign, a pamphlet with historical information and a tape-recorded commentary. Check out the heavy old roof beams with the ship-building design influences. Unfortunately, the 100-plus years have taken their toll, and major work is required on the roof to keep the market continuing. The weight of winter's snow is the main problem.

Inside, the atmosphere is friendly but busy. Aside from fresh produce stalls, most active on Fridays and Saturdays when local farmers come in, there are several good eating spots, a deli and some antiques for sale.

New Brunswick Museum

Located west of town at 277 Douglas Avenue, near the Reversing Falls, this is an eclectic place with an odd collection of things, some good, some not. There's a very good section on marine wildlife, including some aquariums and information on lobsters (you may as well know about what you'll probably be eating). There's a collection of stuffed animals and birds, mostly from New Brunswick. The displays on the marine history of Saint John are good, with many excellent models of old sailing ships.

In the other half of the museum is an art gallery which includes local, contemporary work. Museum hours are 10 am to 5 pm daily from May to September, closed Mondays the rest of the year. Admission is $1.50, students 50c.

Market Square

At the foot of King St is the recently redeveloped waterfront area known as Market Square. It offers views over the working dockyards and container terminals along the river. In summer there is an information booth here.

In the adjacent complex is a major hotel, a convention centre and a new shopping and restaurant centre. The indoor mall is one of the best designed I've seen and is actually pleasant to be in. Someone told me there are 35 restaurants in here, and that count must be close. There is also a library, art gallery, craft shop and benches just for sitting. An enclosed walkway connects City Hall across the street.

Many of the restaurants are along the outside wall and have patios under umbrellas in summer.

Barbour's General Store

This is a renovated old general store situated in the square area. Inside it's packed with merchandise sold 100 years ago, including old stoves, drugs, hardware and candy. Most items are not for sale. Beside it the Old School shows a typical early one-room school with original desks.

City Hall

At King St near Prince William St in the modern section of town is the new City Hall. On the top floor is an observation deck for a good view (on fog-free days) of the city and harbour.

Carleton Martello Tower

This National Historic Site is just off Lancaster Avenue, which leads to the Digby ferry terminal. Look for the signs at street intersections. A Martello tower is a circular, two-storey, stone coastal fortification. They were built in England and Ireland at the beginning of the 19th century. In North America the British built 16 of these during the early 1800s. You can see others in Halifax and Quebec City. There are guides to show you around, answer questions, and give you some background information. Go when there's no fog because the view from the high promontory is good. Open daily from 1 June to 31 September; free.

Chubb Building

Back in town at the corner of Prince William and Princess Sts is this building erected in the late 1800s. Chubb, the owner, had likenesses of all his children and half the town's politicians placed on the facade in little rosettes. Chubb himself is immortalised as a grinning gargoyle.

Cherry Brook Zoo

The zoo has about 25 species of animals, including many endangered species. It's situated at the far northern edge of Rockwood Park in the north of the city and opens every day 10 am to dusk. Admission $3, students $2.

Telephone Pioneers Museum

This museum, located in the lobby of 1 Brunswick Square, has a collection of telephone equipment from early models to the latest technology. Open Monday to Friday, free.

Rockwood Park

800 hectares of recreational facilities, picnic spots, paths through the woods and small lakes.

Events

Loyalist Days, a five-day event held the third week of July each year, celebrates the city's Loyalist background. Featured are a re-creation of the first arrival, period costumes, parades, arts and crafts, music recitals, lots of food and performances. It all ends with fireworks, as do many Canadian events, on the last night of the festival.

In 1985 the city marked its 200th birthday as Canada's first incorporated city and also hosted the Canada Games – a sort of mini-Olympics involving young Canadian athletes. A new swimming pool complex – the Aquatic Centre – was completed near City Hall for the Games.

Places to Stay

Hostels The *Youth Hostel* in Saint John (tel 657-6366) is located in the YM-YWCA at 27 Wellington Row. Open in summer only, there is room for 20. Members pay $6.50, non-members a few dollars more.

For women, there's the *Salvation Army Evangeline Home* (tel 634-1950) at 260 Prince St. They charge $10 a night, $5 for students.

The *YMCA* (tel 634-7720), for men only, is at 19-25 Hagen Avenue. It has a central location and clean, private single rooms at $17.50 or $55 per week. They offer use of facilities like the pool, common room and snack bar with cheap food. There are 30 rooms; you get your own room key and the lobby is always open.

Tourist Homes Manawagonish Rd seems to be accommodation street in Saint John. Along this road are guest houses, cabins and motels of varying prices, although most are reasonable. It's located west of the downtown area, parallel to and north of Highways 1 and 100. City buses go into town from Manawagonish Rd.

At No 968 is *Fundy View Guests* with just four rooms. Rates are $12 singles, $2 each extra person.

Johnson's Tourist Home (tel 672-8135) is at 888 Manawagonish Rd. Three rooms here, at $14 single, $16 double.

Not too far away at 238 Charlotte St is the *Five Chimneys Bed and Breakfast* (tel 635-1888), which charges from $20 single, $30 double.

Motels There are also many motels along Manawagonish Rd.

Fundy Ayre Motel (tel 672-1125) is at No 1711. The place is quite small with only 11 units at just $30 single or double with one bed. As with other motels, it's more if two people use two beds.

Further out is the *Anchor Light Motel* (tel 672-9972). Singles $20, doubles $22 to $24.

Further along still westward, the road becomes Ocean West Way. Here at No 2121 you'll find the *Regent Motel* (tel 672-8273). They have 10 rooms for $28, single or double.

Others in the area range up to $40 with many about $30. These offer more extras and may be newer.

On the other side of town is a strip of motels along Rothesay Avenue on Highway 100, which leads out to Moncton. It's north-east of the downtown centre but a little closer than Manawagonish Rd. Most of the places here are more expensive.

The small *Bonanza Motel* (tel 633-1710), 594 Rothesay Avenue, is OK at $22 single, $24 double.

Hotels There are actually few hotels in town and they tend to be in the upper price brackets. The *Hilton* is right in the centre of things in Market Square. The *Holiday Inn* is also central at 350 Haymarket Square and is about $20 cheaper at $65 single. *Keddy's Fort Howe* is more reasonable and really quite good. It's located at the corner of Main and Portland.

Camping Just north of Rothesay Avenue, north of the downtown area, is the huge *Rockwood Park* with its small lakes, picnic area, golf course and part of the University of New Brunswick campus. Near the southern entrance to the park is a campsite, conveniently close to downtown and the main roads out of the city. Rate is $8 with a tent.

Places to Eat

The eating situation in this town has changed tremendously since my initial visit (perhaps it was my comments in the first edition that did it, ha! ha!). Taking most of the credit is Market Square, which single-handedly has added more than two dozen places to munch at. So we'll start there.

The *Woodshed Steak House* has good value lunches at $3.99 for steak or fish. At night, fish dinners are $7 to $9; others are up to $14. They have, as do many others, an outdoor area. *Diggers* has inexpensive seafood and an oyster bar. *Grannan's* is not strictly budget but is not expensive either. On the main level, *Baldy's* is good for lunches and snacks. They serve burgers, fish & chips and the like.

Upstairs on the second level, *Mother's* is mainly a pizza place but has some other Italian dishes. This is a countrywide chain now, but their pizza is very good. Meals run to $5 to $7.

In the *Food Hall* at one corner of the main floor is a slew of fast-food places with shared tables. They offer cheap food including chicken, donairs to doughnuts and submarine sandwiches. A plate of rice with vegetables and chicken from the Chinese place is $3.50, including green tea.

Reggie's Restaurant at 69 Germain St, near Loyalist House, specialises in smoked meat from *Ben's*, a famous Montreal deli. Also on the menu are lobster rolls – a local favourite – and chowders at $2.50. It's a good, casual place open at 6 am for breakfast specials. *Reggie's II* is a smaller outlet located in the YMCA.

The *Parrtown II Tavern* has set up on Prince William St near the corner of Church after having to move for the waterfront restoration. Though new, it still attracts the working crowd and offers cheap steaks, tavern meals and draught beer. Good value.

Woolworths, beside the market, offers cheap, basic meals from $2.50. *Diana*, across from the park between Union and King Sts, is your basic restaurant, offering $5 specials.

The market is a good place to be when hunger strikes. Aside from the produce there's *Lambert's Coffee Corner*, the funky yellow place that's mostly stools at the counter in the south corner of the building. This tiny spot is a local institution and very busy. A specialty here is the tasty lobster roll at $3.90, and people come just for the home fries, which are excellent (but ask for just quarter order – their portions are enormous). Also in the market is *Jeremiah's*, a deli and sandwich bar; on its east side is a salad-to-go booth. Lots of cheeses here too.

Incredible Edibles, at 42 Princess St in the Brodie Building, is a nice spot for a bit of a splurge, with pastas, curries, omelettes and local desserts such as blueberry cobbler – a fruit-based dessert with a crispy cakey crust, usually topped with milk or cream. Yummy!

For Italian food there's *Vito's* on Hazen Avenue at the corner of Union St. A bit pricey at $10 to $12, but Monday nights are all-you-can-eat spaghetti for $3.50.

Lastly, the *Bamboo East* at 136 Princess St offers Chinese food. Weekday buffet is $5.95, weekend dinner buffet $8.95 and there's *Dim sum* at noon, Sundays. A la carte is available, but not cheap.

Nightlife

Market Square also has a number of nightspots. *Baldy's* has rock 'n' roll with dancing. *Lighthouse* is a pub-like spot. The *Grapevine* offers over 100 types of wine and hors d'oeuvres for late snacking.

The biggest rock club in town is *The Switch* at 115 Prince William St. No cover charge. The *1880* at 134 Sydney St is dressier and offers a variety of good live music.

Getting There & Away

Air Air Canada (tel 693-1231) to Montreal costs $136, youth standby $78, both plus tax. Canadian (tel 657-3860) flies to St John's, Newfoundland for $216, youth $108, plus tax.

Bus SMT Bus Lines is the provincial carrier. It connects with Voyageur Lines in Edmundston and Acadia Lines in Nova Scotia. The station (tel 693-6500) is at 300 Union St, a five-minute walk from the town centre.

Quebec City: 9.30 am, 5 pm – $49
Fredericton: three times a day – $9.75
Moncton: $13.25.

For Cape Tormentine (Prince Edward Island), you take a VIA Rail bus from the train station.

Train The VIA station (tel 642-2916 or 1-800-361-7773 after 5 pm), is a 10-minute walk from downtown, north-west of King Square near Loyalist House. Fares listed here are one-way:

Quebec City: one daily – $86
Fredericton: one daily – $9
Truro, Nova Scotia: 8.45 am, 4.15 pm – $29
Montreal: 5.05 pm (through Maine) – $68.

Ferry The Marine Atlantic ferry, *The Princess of Acadia*, sails between Saint John and Digby, Nova Scotia, across the bay. Depending on where you're going, this can cut off a lot of km driving around through Moncton and then Amherst, Nova Scotia, but the ferry is a rip-off. For the distance covered it's much more expensive than other ferries. This is heavily used by tourists, which is one explanation. Fares are $13 per person one-way and $40 per car. Bicycles are $5.

Crossing time is about 2½ hours. In summer there are three daily, one in the morning, one in the afternoon and one at night. Arrive early or call ahead for reservations, as the ferry is very busy in July and August. Walk-ons should be OK. There's a restaurant on board. To make reservations in New Brunswick, Nova Scotia or PEI, call 1-800-565-9470 toll-free.

Getting Around

Airport Transport The airport is east of town out along Highway 111. There is an airport bus costing $5.50 that leaves approximately 1½ hours before all flights, from top hotels like the Hilton at Market Square and the Delta Brunswick. For a share-taxi call *Vets* at 634-1554.

Bus For information on routes and times call 635-1986 or ask at the Tourist Office.

Car Rentals Delta (tel 634-1125) at 374 Rothesay Avenue, is open seven days. They charge $26.95 with 250 free km, then 12c per km. The weekly price is $159 with 1800 freebies. Rent-A-Wreck (tel 632-8889) is at 390 Rothesay Avenue. They charge $8.95 a day and up, plus 8c per km.

Driving West of the centre of town the Trans-Canada Highway (the No 1) crosses over the Saint John River. There's a toll bridge (25c). Further out connections can be made to Highway 7 for Fredericton.

Tours There are harbour boat tours at 2 pm and 7.30 pm daily through the summer. Tickets are available at the info office on Market Square.

A pleasant day's outing is to take the boat over to Partridge Island, a National Historic Site, where there are guided tours. The boat leaves from Market Square during the summer.

The Saint John Transit Commission offers 2½-hour bus tours around town during the summer months. Departures and tickets from Barbour's General Store at Market Place; one daily early in the afternoon. In September and October there are fall foliage tours up the valley, lunch included. This area of New Brunswick is one of the best in the country for the colours of its changing leaves.

NORTH OF SAINT JOHN

This is a beautifully scenic area of deeply indented bays, rivers and islands, eventually leading to Grand Lake and Fredericton. It's prime New Brunswick cottage country. The Saint John River flows south through here to its mouth at the Bay of Fundy and the ferries connecting roads in the area are all free. The Kingston Peninsula, not far from Saint John, is typical of the river valley landscapes. It's beautiful in the fall when the leaves change colour, and Crystal Beach is a popular spot for camping and swimming. If you're driving to Fredericton, don't take the dull Highway 7. Choose the 102, which winds along the riverside through small communities. At Gagetown is a huge Canadian Forces Base.

St Martins

A 2½-hour drive east of Saint John will take you to St Martins, one of the province's historic towns, situated on the Bay of Fundy. This was once a centre of the wooden ship-building trade. There's a good beach here and you can explore caves cut into the shoreline cliffs. There is camping at the Seaside Park.

Fundy National Park

The park is 129 km east of Saint John,

about halfway to Moncton, accessed by Highway 114. Next to Banff, this is Canada's most popular National Park. Situated on the Bay of Fundy – with the world's highest tides – the park has five campgrounds, about 80 km of hiking trails and some dirt roads for touring around in your car. There's also an arts and crafts school amongst the more developed attractions. Irregularly eroded sandstone cliffs and the wide beach at low tide make a walk along the shore interesting. There's lots of small marine life to observe and debris to pick over. There's also a fair bit of wildlife in the park: on one visit I nearly drove into a deer, and it was high noon! The ocean is pretty cool here, so there is a saltwater swimming pool not far from the eastern entrance where you can have a dip, but you must pay for the privilege.

Camping with a tent is $7. Aside from the campgrounds, there are sites along the back-packing trails. In addition, there are motel-style rooms and chalets at the *Caledonia Highlands Inn* within the park. The chalets come with cooking facilities and are very comfortable.

At the small town of Alma just east of the park on Highway 114, you absolutely *must* stop at *The Home of the Sticky Bun* and buy a trunkful.

Cape Enrage Heading east to Moncton take the smaller road, the 915, as it detours closer to the coast and offers some fine views. At Cape Enrage out on the cliffs at the end of the peninsula, the power of the elements is often in strong and stimulating evidence. Further along near Harvey is the Mary's Point Bird Sanctuary.

MONCTON

Moncton, with a population of 60,000, is the third city of the province and a major transportation and distribution centre for the Atlantic Provinces. The ferry for Prince Edward Island is nearby, and the train to Nova Scotia goes through. It is small and nondescript, but a much needed face-lift has improved the central area. And due to a couple of odd attractions – Magnetic Hill and a tidal bore – it's worth a brief stop on the way by.

The area was first settled by the Germans from Pennsylvania. Initially the town was called 'The Bend' after the turn in the Petitcodiac River, and specialised in shipbuilding. There's now a fairly large French population here and many people are bilingual; the Universite de Moncton is the only French university outside Quebec.

Orientation

The small downtown area runs north and south off Main St. The river lies just to the south; the Trans-Canada goes east north of town. Between Duke St and Foundry St, the sidewalks have been gentrified and many of the old buildings now contain restaurants and nightspots.

Information

There are several Tourist Offices. The central area bureau is at City Hall, 774 Main St, next to the large Hotel Beausejour. There's another on the western side of town on St George St by Centennial Park. A third office is located right beside Magnetic Hill where Mountain Rd meets the Trans-Canada, north-west of the downtown area.

Magnetic Hill

This is the best-known attraction in the area and is worth a visit. Gravity here seems to work in reverse: start at the bottom of the hill in a car or bike and you'll drift upward. Go as many times as you like; maybe you can figure it out. The hill is at the corner of Mountain Rd (126) and the Trans-Canada; it's free and the kids will like it. There's also a small zoo next door.

The Tidal Bore

This is a twice-daily incoming wave caused by the tides of the Petitcodiac

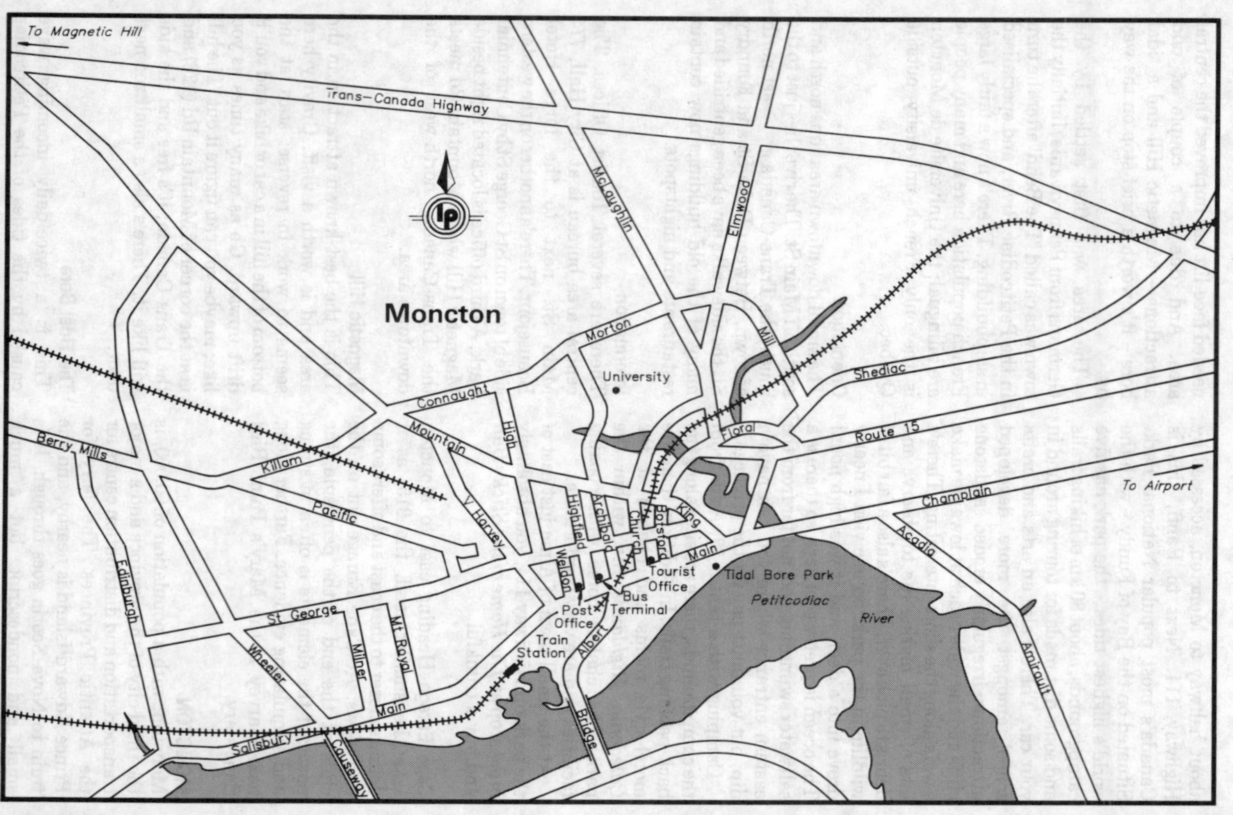
To Magnetic Hill
Trans-Canada Highway
Moncton
McLaughlin
Elmwood
Morton
Mill
University
Shediac
Connaught
High
Mountain
Floral
Route 15
Berry Mills
Killam
To Airport
Champlain
Pacific
V Harvey
Highfield
Archibald
Church
Botsford
King
Acadia
Main
Tidal Bore Park
Weldon
Tourist Office
Petitcodiac
River
Bus Terminal
Post Office
Edinburgh
St George
Mt Royal
Milner
Albert
Train Station
Amirault
Wheeler
Main
Bridge
Salisbury
Causeway

River, which are in turn related to the tides in the Bay of Fundy – known as the world's highest. The bore rushes upstream and sometimes raises the water level in the river by six metres in a few minutes. The wave itself varies from a few cm to over 30 cm high.

A good place to watch for it is in Bore Park at the east end of Main St. The pleasant park is filled with old men sitting on the benches. It also has on display a bore timetable. Don't expect anything spectacular; most times the wave is not at all impressive. The bore is best in spring and fall, if it's raining or if the moon is right.

Moncton Museum

Located at 20 Mountain Rd near Belleview St, the museum has a collection of memorabilia covering the town's history, from the time of the Micmac Indians and early settlers to the present. Displays show the influence of shipbuilding and the railway on the area and an old-style street has been re-created. It's free and open daily in summer, closed Monday the rest of the year. Next door is the oldest building in town, the Free Meeting House of 1821, used by numerous religious congregations through the years.

Acadian Museum

On the university campus, this museum has a collection of artefacts of the Acadian people, the first French settlers of the Atlantic region. The displays chronicle every aspect of the day-to-day life of these people, who were driven out of Nova Scotia to New Brunswick by British troops. Free and open daily, weekends open afternoons only.

Thomas Williams House

Built in 1883, this 12-room Victorian Gothic house remained in the family as a home until 1983, when it was bequeathed to the city as a Heritage House. Much of the fine original work remains intact both inside and out and the furnishings add to the overall effect. The tea room on the verandah is fun. Open June to September except for Mondays, it's at 103 Park St in the central area.

Events

In mid-August is the Acadian Handicraft Festival at the College Notre Dame d'Acadie on Archibald St; in early May there's the Acadian Art Festival, and in July a bluegrass and old-time fiddle music festival is held.

Places to Stay

Hostels There was once a hostel here but it was torn down due to hefty heating expenses. There hasn't been another since.

The *YWCA* (tel 855-4349) is near the train station in a nice old stone place at the corner of Highfield and Campbell. They have a very cheap cafeteria. For women only, it's $17.

The *Université de Moncton* (contact Housing Services, tel 858-4008) rents rooms during summer in two of the residences. They have shared washrooms and there is a cafeteria. Singles $17, doubles $22; for students and seniors, singles are $12, doubles $16; very good weekly rates.

Hotels The *Sunset Hotel* (tel 382-1163) at 162 Queen St is central, well kept and the least expensive spot. Rooms are $22 single, $26 double. There's a TV in the lobby and free parking.

At 46 Archibald St is the yellow, wooden *Hotel Canadiana* (tel 382-1054). It's a beautiful place – like a step back in time – with wood everywhere and hanging lamps; it's now over 100 years old. Singles or doubles cost $35 to $45. It's centrally located, near Main St.

The *Hotel Beausejour* on Main St is the largest and most expensive place in town and is primarily for business clientele.

Tourist Homes The lack of hotels is partially offset by quite a few guest houses and bed & breakfast places. *Mountain View Tourist Home* (tel 384-0290) is at 2166 Mountain Rd. They have three rooms at very reasonable prices: singles/doubles cost $18/22. It's a simple place but good.

Within walking distance of the downtown area is *Victoria Bed & Breakfast* (tel 382-1649) at 50 Park St. It's in an old stone house. Rates of $29 single, $35 double include a good health-food breakfast. No smoking.

Wilbur Bed & Breakfast (tel 382-0406) at 613 McLaughlin Drive is cheaper but not so central. It costs $20/25 for singles/doubles.

Out of town off Highway 2 on RR1 is *Lutes Bed & Breakfast* (tel 384-7974) with singles/doubles for $22/30. Ring them up and they'll give you directions.

Motels There's no shortage of motels, and a fair range of prices.

Not far from town is the *Beacon Light Motel* (tel 384-1734) at 1062 Mountain Rd, accessed by Highway 126. It's decent and costs $34 for doubles.

On Highway 2 near Magnetic Hill are numerous motels. The *Atlantic* (tel 384-2509), charges $30 single, $34 double. The *Restwell* (tel 384-6400) in the other direction (east) is $30 single or double.

The *Brentwood Motor Court* (tel 388-5391) is at 1751 Main St. It's reasonable at single $26, double $30 and up. There are several others strung out along RR1, towards and at River Glade.

Right in the central area is the *Midtown* at 61 Weldon St, but it's pricier at $45 singles or doubles.

Places to Eat

At 700 Main St, *Crackers* is a nice place for sandwiches, salads, ribs or Italian food. At night it becomes a sort of club and is open very late on weekends. Across the street is *Spanky's*, a cleaned up tavern with inexpensive food and beer, and late afternoon happy hours. *Len's* at 840 Main St is a classic workingman's restaurant, open every day, packed for lunch.

In summer, a couple of take-out booths pop up in the little mall area at Main and Robinson Sts in the centre of town, where there are benches to sit at. *The Metropolitan* store has the lowest prices in town.

Probably the best known restaurant is *Cy's*, a very well established seafood place on East Main St. It is not cheap and, from what I hear, a little over-rated, but certainly all right.

Mountain Rd has quite a number of eating spots, including *Ming Garden* for Chinese food at No 797, *Ponderosa* for good value steak dinners at No 956 and *Kelsey's* at No 938, a loud, casual something-for-everyone establishment. For pizza, spaghetti, etc, try *Vito's* at 726 Mountain Rd.

Nightlife

The *Urban Corral*, 333 St George St, has live country and western music from 9 pm to 1 am, except Sunday. *Ziggy's* on Main St attracts the young with a different diversion each night. The *Coliseum* is home to major shows, concerts and sporting events.

Getting There & Away

Train The station (tel 382-7892) is located south-west of the downtown area by Cameron St off Main St. Look for it behind the building at 1234 Main St. The prices below are for one-way fares:

Halifax: three daily – $25
Montreal: two daily – $77
Saint John: one daily – $14
Campbellton: one daily
Edmundston: one daily.

To Montreal, one train goes through Maine, the other through Quebec; most departures are in the late afternoon. If you take the US route, you must have proper ID and comply with US immigration requirements.

Bus The station for SMT Lines is at 961 Main St (tel 857-2980), between town and the train station. Some schedules are given below, together with one-way ticket prices:

Fredericton: 9 am, 2.30, 5.20, 8 pm daily – $16.75

Saint John: 9 am, 2.30, 5.30, 7.45 pm daily – $13

Halifax: 10.45 am, 3.15, 5.50 pm daily – $22

Newcastle: 11.15 am, Thursdays only 5.30 pm – $12.75.

Other fares (one-way) to: Edmundston – $32, Montreal – $64.

AROUND MONCTON

Covered Bridges

Within 100 km of Moncton, 27 of the province's historic covered bridges can be seen. They were known as 'kissing bridges', because you and yours could tuck the old horse and buggy in there away from curious eyes. Two driving trips south of Moncton, called the Scenic Trail and the Covered Bridge Trail, take in many of these bridges.

Dobson Trail

Just south of Moncton at Riverview, this 60-km hiking trail leads you through the Albert County Hills and its maple forests down to Fundy National Park.

St Joseph

Here, 24 km south of town, a National Historic Site tells the story of the Acadians, the early French settlers of the Maritime region. Crafts, photographs, maps and guides reveal the difficult history of these pioneers.

Hillsborough

Hillsborough, situated a short distance south of Moncton, is a small town overlooking the Petitcodiac River. From here a restored steam engine pulls antique coaches along the river to Salem, about eight km away. It takes an hour for the return trip. The fare is $5, less for kids and half price on rainy days. Through July and August there are four trips daily. There is also a longer trip with dinner served on board.

The Rocks Provincial Park

Continuing south from Hillsborough, you'll encounter the park at Hopewell Cape, the point at which the river meets the Fundy waters in Shepody Bay. The 'rocks' are unusual erosion formations known as 'flowerpots'. The shore is lined with these irregular geological forms, caves and tunnels created by erosion from the great tides. An exploratory walk along the beach at low tide is well worthwhile: check the tide tables at any Tourist Office. You can't hit the beach at high tide but the rock towers are visible from the trails above. Camping is not allowed but there are picnic areas and a restaurant.

SACKVILLE

Sackville is a small, staid university town. There really is nothing to see but you may want to quickly drop in as you're going by. The park on the university grounds makes a good leg stretch and the art gallery on campus displays the work of students.

Outside Sackville are the Tantramar Marshes, an expanse of a couple of thousand acres of wetlands, home to great numbers of waterfowl. The Tintamarre National Wildlife reserve is within the area. Biologists at the Wildlife Service in Sackville will offer information for those wishing to know or see more.

Mount Allison University (tel 364-2251), right in the centre of town, opens rooms to visitors from May to August. They cost $20 single, $32 double, a few dollars less for students. They also serve inexpensive meals.

There's a good bed & breakfast place at 146 West Main St called *The Different Drummer* (tel 536-1291). It's a fine old Victorian house; each of the four rooms is furnished with antiques and comes with bath. Breakfasts include home-made muffins and bread. Singles are $28 and doubles $34.

At the *Marsland's Inn* on Bridge St,

you can get a very good dinner whether you're spending the night or not. Ask about the chef's special. Not cheap but good value. *Borden's Motel*, which you can see from the highway, offers good cheap meals and the lobster rolls have been recommended. On York St, across from the university, the little *Vienna Coffee House* is the place for a coffee and snack.

On the road south from town all the antennae are part of the CBC's international short-wave broadcast equipment.

Fort Beausejour National Historic Park
Right by the Nova Scotia border at the shoreline, the park preserves the remains of a French fort built in 1751 to hold the British back. It didn't work. Led by Colonel Monckton, the fort was taken over before it was even finished. Later it was used as a stronghold during the American Revolution and the War of 1812. There are some pretty good displays within the fort and some evocative pictures set in the surroundings. A museum provides more details and guides will answer questions. Free, open daily. The views over the marshy end of the Bay of Fundy alone make a trip out here recommended. Picnic tables are provided.

PEI Ferry
East of Sackville on the coast is Cape Tormentine, the terminal for the ferry to Borden, PEI.

Just north of Bayfield is a very long, almost empty beach with the remains of an old wreck at one end.

SHEDIAC
This summer resort town on the coast, 22 km north-east of Moncton, is home to the annual lobster festival in July. The beaches along Northumberland Strait are blessed with warm waters, especially here because of sand bars and shallow water. Most popular are Parlee Beach (east of Shediac) and Pointe du Chere, with water temperatures of 20°C all summer.

There are other beaches on the small coastal roads and north and south of Shediac, and lots of camping places. Though none are great, the best is probably *Parlee Beach Park*, beside the provincial beach where it's $7 for one person with tent.

There is little in town itself, but the big, white *Hotel Shediac* is prominent and the dining room offers both seafood and steaks.

East of town is a strip of eateries and take-out joints. You'll find clams and lobsters, cooked or fresh, dead or alive. *Fisherman's Paradise* packs 'em in with fair prices, but that doesn't mean cheap. *Shediac Pizza* is good and inexpensive; try the pizza burger. Also along the strip are a couple of motels, a bar or two and a new water-slide complex.

Lobsters can be bought at various outlets and at the wharves. Boil them in ocean water, and with a bottle of wine and some French bread you've got a cheap deluxe meal. Dig for clams and mussels, too.

Cocagne
North up the coast from Shediac, Cocagne hosts a hydroplane regatta around the second week of August.

Eastern New Brunswick

North of Fredericton and Moncton lie the province's vast forests. Nearly all the towns are either along the east coast or in the west, by the Saint John River running beside the border of Maine, USA. The interior of northern New Brunswick is nearly inaccessible, rocky, river-filled timberland.

Inland, highways in this area can be quite monotonous, as thick forest lines both sides of the very straight roads. It's like driving down unending corridors, on these routes in particular: south of Campbellton to St Leonard, from Bathurst to Chatham and from there to Moncton. Coastal routes are more interesting.

KOUCHIBOUGUAC NATIONAL PARK

The highlights of this park are the beaches with offshore sand dunes stretching for 25 km. The sands are good for beachcombing and digging clams; seals are often seen offshore. The water is warm but difficult to swim in because it's very shallow.

Inland there is canoeing (with rentals), hiking trails both short and long, and quiet roads for cycling. There's freshwater fishing for a variety of fish, and the park also has moose, deer, black bears and smaller mammals.

Camping is from May to October, at a large site with firewood supplied. There are also campsites for backpackers and canoeists.

The park is very popular and busy throughout July and August, particularly on weekends. Get there early in the day to obtain a campsite, about $8. The park is 100 km north of Moncton.

NEWCASTLE

Though the site of another huge paper mill, Newcastle is a pleasant little town – a good place to break up the trip north or south. Around the nice, central square are some fine old wooden buildings and shops, some unpainted and ancient-looking. In the central park is a statue to Lord Beaverbrook, one of the most powerful press barons in British history and a statesman and philanthropist of no small reputation. Beaverbrook was born Max Aitken in 1879 and spent most of his growing years in Newcastle. Among the many gifts he lavished on the province are the 17th-century English benches and the Italian gazebo located in the square here. His ashes lie under the statue presented as a memorial to him by the town.

Each summer the Miramichi Folksong Festival, now over 30 years old and the oldest in North America, is held. Through traditional song, local history and culture are preserved. Good fun, and worth catching.

Just off the park at the corner of Castle and Pleasant Sts is an odd-looking but excellent place to stay. It's called *Castle Lodge* (tel 622-2442). Inside the old, vine-covered, red-and-green wooden house are five rooms rented out by – yes – an old lady. Singles $14, doubles $17; you share the one bathroom. An alternative is *Governor's Mansion* (tel 622-3036), across the river in Nelson-Miramichi. They have five rooms at $20 single, $26 double.

South of town off Highway 8 is another of Beaverbrook's gifts – a forest park called 'The Enclosure', now part of a provincial park. If you just want to look around The Enclosure, tell them at the gate and you won't have to pay the park fee. From 19 June to 15 September there is camping in the park.

AROUND NEWCASTLE

The Miramichi

South-west of Newcastle, the South-west Miramichi River extends beyond Doaktown, about halfway to Fredericton. The area, in particular the main river, is renowned for Atlantic salmon fishing. Together with the Restigouche and Saint John Rivers it has gained the province an international reputation amongst serious anglers. Even Prince Charles has fished the Miramichi! Both residents and visitors need licences and there are special regulations for non-residents. Check at the Tourist Office or the Forest Service of the Department of Natural Resources.

Doaktown has become more or less the unofficial fishing centre for the region. There are numerous fishing lodges and outfitters in and around town as well as motels and bed & breakfasts.

Also in town is the Salmon Museum, which is actually pretty interesting and includes pools of live salmon ('king of the fresh water game fish') on the 3½-acre grounds.

Other points of interest include the

Glendella Mansion (a rather unexpected sight), Doak Historic Park, concerning local history, and a nearby 1870s covered bridge, one of the province's oldest. And, oh yeah, don't miss the moose on the east side of town.

Miramichi Bay

Around the bay and along the road south towards Richibucto are many beaches. The water in Northumberland Strait from Miramichi to Shediac is warmed by spin-off currents of the Gulf Stream. Folks here, like those in northern PEI, claim the waters are the warmest north of Virginia in the USA.

Chatham

This was a prosperous town when it was the centre of wooden shipbuilding, but the development of steel ships put an end to that. There's now nothing to recommend it but a small, idiosyncratic museum, which is open mid-June to the end of August.

There is quite an Irish history here and to commemorate this, an Irish festival is held annually, usually in July: music, dance, food, film, crafts, a parade and even genealogy experts to help trace your Irish roots. There are a few bed & breakfast places in and around town.

BATHURST

Bathurst, yet another industrial town based on pulp and paper, is on the bleak side. It looks large on the provincial map but is really quite small, with about 17,000 people.

North of town in Petit Rocher on the coast is the New Brunswick Mining and Mineral Interpretation Centre, a mining museum with varying exhibits on the mining industry. There's also an observation tower offering views to the Gaspe and along the Acadian shoreline.

South from here is the Acadian Coast, populated in the main by descendants of Canada's earliest French settlers. Many of their traditions live on in music, food and language; it's a different French from that spoken in Quebec.

GRAND-ANSE

This small town boasts the popular Pope's Museum, which houses reproductions of 264 popes from St Peter to the present, as well as various religious articles.

CARAQUET

The oldest of the Acadian villages, Caraquet was founded in 1757. It has one of the oldest churches in the province, St Anne du Bocage. Also in town is the Acadian Museum, with relics and photographs. It's open daily in summer, closed Sundays in the off season.

Fourteen km west of town is Village Historique Acadien, a museum set up like a village of old, with 17 buildings and workers in period costumes of the years 1780-1880. The museum depicts daily life in such a village; open daily. It's located on Route 11 towards Grande-Anse.

Further south are many small fishing towns, both English and French, as well as a number of beaches.

CAMPBELLTON

This most northerly town in the province, population 10,000, is situated on the Baie des Chaleurs. If you're travelling from Quebec you'll probably pass through. Across the border is Matapedia and Highway 132 leading to Mont Joli, 148 km into Quebec.

The last navy battle of the Seven Years' War with America was fought in the waters just off the coast here in 1760.

Nearby Sugarloaf Mountain has excellent views of the town and part of the Restigouche River. It rises nearly 400 metres above sea level. There's camping in Sugarloaf Park and skiing in winter. About 10 km west of town is Morrisey Rock, another place for a good view of the scenic river area.

The Restigouche River, named by the Micmacs, is excellent for salmon fishing. It runs south-west from Campbellton. All along the river there are fishing camps, clubs, supply stores and some pools open to the public.

Access to Mt Carleton Provincial Park, with the most wilderness in the province, is from Five Fingers, a town south-west of Campbellton along the Restigouche. The park is roughly 130 km south of Campbellton.

There is little to see or do in town and no reason to stay. But if you need accommodation, ask around about the *Youth Hostel*. Campbellton has had one but it may not be there now. *Idlewilde Cabins* (tel 753-4665) at 417 Mountain Rd, are simple but reasonable at $30 double. There are several other places to stay; check Roseberry St.

DALHOUSIE

The town's main industry is newsprint, but Dalhousie has some other attractions. From here there are boat cruises up the Restigouche or deep sea fishing charters available. There's good views and scenery all along the Baie des Chaleurs, as well as lots of camping spots and motels.

You can take a ferry going to Miguasa, Quebec here, which cuts about 70 km off the driving trip around the bay. It runs every half hour between 7.30 am and 7.30 pm, from the end of June to sometime in September. The trip takes 15 minutes and costs $7.50 with a car – good if you're heading for the Gaspe Peninsula.

The many small towns seem to have their own festivals in July or August. If you hit it right, you can go from one to the other. Ask at the Tourist Office for the list of summer events.

MT CARLETON PROVINCIAL PARK

The park, surrounded by a large tract of unspoiled land used only by loggers, encloses Mt Carleton, 820 metres high and one of Atlantic Canada's highest mountains. There is little development in the park and gas and groceries are not available, but there are maintained hiking trails and camping areas. Canoe rentals are available at Riley Brook and Nictau.

Fredericton to Edmundston

FREDERICTON

Fredericton is the queen of New Brunswick's towns. Unlike most, it is non-industrial and a very pretty, genteel, quiet place.

Three hundred years ago, the Maliseet and Micmac Indians lived and fished in the area. In 1762 the British founded a town over the abandoned French settlement. They named it in honour of Prince Fred, the second son of King George III. When the American Revolutionary War ended in 1783, about 6000 people arrived in town. It was made the capital of the newly formed province, separated from Nova Scotia in 1785.

Long ago the town produced Canada's first English-speaking poet, Loyalist Jonathan Odell. Later, Lord Beaverbrook, who was to rise to international prominence, was born here. Today, Fredericton still presides over high society as home of the province's lieutenant governor, the legislature and the university dons.

About a fifth of the 45,000 people work for the government, this being the capital. Of the light industry here, food processing, woodworking and leather goods are the most important.

There are many old buildings and beautiful houses remaining; the river runs gently by and the streets are tree-lined, prompting the title 'City of Stately Elms'. There's not a lot to do, but Fredericton makes a nice spot to relax for a day or two.

Orientation

The city is on a small, rounded peninsula that resembles a slight hump of land jutting into the Saint John River.

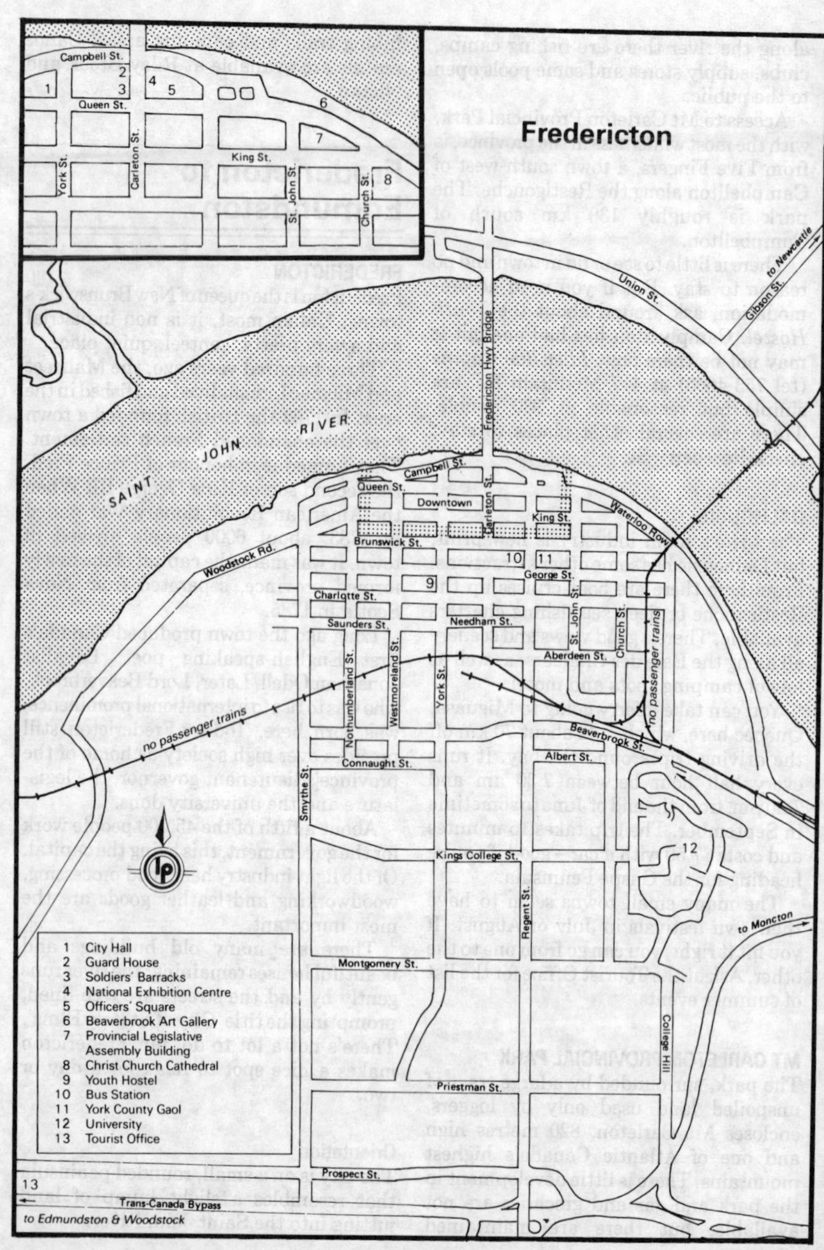

Fredericton
Campbell St.
Queen St.
King St.
York St.
Carleton St.
St. John St.
Church St.
1
2
3
4
5
6
7
8
SAINT JOHN RIVER
Fredericton Hwy Bridge
Union St.
Gibson St.
to Newcastle
Campbell St.
Queen St.
Downtown
Carleton St.
King St.
Waterloo Row
Woodstock Rd.
Brunswick St.
10
11
George St.
9
Charlotte St.
Saunders St.
Needham St.
St. John St.
Church St.
no passenger trains
Aberdeen St.
York St.
Westmoreland St.
Northumberland St.
Smythe St.
no passenger trains
Beaverbrook St.
Albert St.
Connaught St.
Kings College St.
12
Regent St.
to Moncton
Montgomery St.
College Hill
Priestman St.
Prospect St.
13
Trans-Canada Bypass
to Edmundston & Woodstock
1 City Hall
2 Guard House
3 Soldiers' Barracks
4 National Exhibition Centre
5 Officers' Square
6 Beaverbrook Art Gallery
7 Provincial Legislative Assembly Building
8 Christ Church Cathedral
9 Youth Hostel
10 Bus Station
11 York County Gaol
12 University
13 Tourist Office

There are three bridges – two for cars and the middle one for trains only.

The Westmorland St Bridge connects the downtown area to the north shore. Further east, the Princess Margaret Bridge links the Trans-Canada segments across the river. Across the river, which isn't far, are the green woods and farmlands like those found along much of the river valley. From the Westmorland St Bridge you can see some fine big houses and a couple of church spires on the side away from town.

Coming into town from the Trans-Canada, take Exit 292B (Regent St). Regent will take you straight down to the centre of town.

In town, King and the parallel Queen St are the main streets, just a block up from the river. Northumberland and Saint John Sts are the west and east edges of the small downtown area. The park at the corner of Queen and Regent Sts, called Officers' Square, is pretty much the centre of things.

As you head east from Queen St, out of the downtown area, there's a small strip of park between the road and the river. This is known as The Green and extends eastwards for many blocks. Near the Art Gallery is a statue of Scottish poet Robbie Burns. There are good views along the river here and big shade trees to relax under. Several points of interest lie in The Green.

As you go further east, Queen St becomes Waterloo Row. Here it's the houses on the other side of the street that deserve your attention. Each is different from its neighbour and all are large and well maintained, some with grand balconies, turrets and bizarre shapes. Nos 50, 82 and 146 particularly impressed me. The lieutenant governor's residence is here; look for the coat of arms. There aren't too many streets in the country like this one.

Back on The Green you'll pass the Loyalist Memorial beside Waterloo Row, commemorating the British founders. Nearby is the old Loyalist Cemetery, similar to the one in Saint John. The tombstones show many were born in England, Ireland or other countries, and died young. Strangely, the inscriptions make the pioneers and their hardships come alive.

Church and Brunswick Sts, branching out from the corner where Christ Church Cathedral sits, also have numerous large brick or wooden houses. The grey one at 767 Brunswick St was 200 years old in 1984.

Information

The Visitors' Information Centre (tel 455-9500) is in City Hall on Queen St. It's open Monday to Friday year-round, 8.30 am to 5 pm, but keeps later hours during the summer.

You can also get information at the Legislative Assembly (tel 453-2527) on Queen St. Open weekdays all year, with longer hours in summer. From 15 June to 15 September it is also open Saturday, Sunday and holidays from 10 am to 9 pm.

There's a tourist bureau (tel 455-3092) on the Trans-Canada Highway near Hanwell Rd, Exit 289. Open daily from early June to late September, 9 am to evening.

Tourism New Brunswick (tel 1-800-442-4442) will also help with information about most places in the province.

Downtown, the post office is on Queen St not far from Regent St. A good thing to know if you're driving is that there is free parking behind the Legislature on Queen St. Just tell the attendant you're a visitor from out of town.

Officers' Square

This is the city's central park – on Queen St between Carleton and Regent Sts. The square was once the military parade ground and still sits amongst several military buildings.

At 10 am Monday to Friday, from mid-July to the third week in August, you can see the 'Changing of the Guard' ceremony in full uniform. At 2 pm the troops go through a brief tattoo with a rifle salute.

Also in the park, on summer Tuesday evenings at 7.30 pm, free band concerts are given, attracting crowds. It might be a marching, military or pipe band; sometimes classical music is played, too. If it rains, the performance is switched to Thursday night.

In the park is a statue of Lord Beaverbrook, the press baron and the province's most illustrious native son.

On the west side of the square are the former Officers' Barracks built between 1839 and 1851. The older section, closest to the water, has thicker walls of masonry and hand-hewn timbers. The other, newer end is made of sawn timber.

York-Sunbury Historical Museum

This museum is housed in the old officers' quarters off the park, a building typical of those designed by the Royal Architects during the colonial period. The museum has a collection from the city's past: military pieces used by local regiments and by British and German armies from the Boer and both world wars; furniture from a Loyalist sitting room and Victorian bedroom; Indian and Acadian artefacts and archaeological finds.

The highlight of the museum is a stuffed 19-kg frog. It was the pet of a local innkeeper. Nineteen kg! Perhaps he fed it the patrons who were incapable of walking home. Hours in summer are Monday, Friday, Saturday 10 am to 6 pm; Tuesday, Wednesday, Thursday 10 am to 8 pm; Sunday 12 to 6 pm. During other seasons it's open Monday, Wednesday and Friday afternoons. Fee $2.

Soldiers' Barracks

At the corner of Carleton and Queen Sts in the Military Compound you can see where the common soldier lived in the 1820s. Also in the compound is the Guard House (1828) where the naughty ones were sent. It now contains military memorabilia. A well-written, interesting history of the Guard House is available at no charge. Likewise, visits to this National Historic Site are free.

Legislative Assembly

Built in 1882, this government building stands on Queen St near Saint John St, east of Officers' Square.

Guides will show you around pointing out things of particular merit, like the wooden Speaker's Chair and the spiral staircase. When in session, visitors are welcome to listen to the proceedings. Open daily, free.

Beaverbrook Art Gallery

Another of Lord Beaverbrook's gifts to the town is this gallery, right opposite the legislature on Queen St. There's a collection of British paintings including works by Gainsborough, Turner and Constable. They also have a Dali as well as Canadian and provincial works. Open Tuesday to Saturday 10 am to 5 pm, Sunday and Monday 12 to 5 pm. Fee $1.50.

Christ Church Cathedral

Built in 1853, this is a fine early example of the 19th-century revival of decorated Gothic architecture. The cathedral is interesting because it's very compact – short for the height yet with balance and proportion that make the interior seem both normal and spacious.

You'll see good stained glass, especially around the altar, where the walls are painted above the choir. Free tours are offered. The church is just off Queen St at Church St, by the river, east of town.

National Exhibition Centre

On the corner of Queen and Carleton Sts in town, this building dates from 1881 and has been used as a post office, customs house and library. The exhibition centre on the first floor displays travelling exhibits which vary dramatically. Newfoundland folk art, hooked mats, art photographs from the National Gallery and Japanese kites are some examples. Usually good, always free.

Upstairs is the Provincial Sports Hall of Fame with tidbits from local sportsmen of achievement.

Boyce Farmers' Market

This market is on George St between Regent and Saint John Sts. It's open Saturdays only, from 7 am to noon. There are nearly 150 stalls selling fresh fruit, vegetables, meat and cheese, and also handicrafts, home-made desserts and flowers. *Goofy Roofy's Restaurant* is here, too.

Conserver House

Located at the corner of Brunswick St and Saint John St is this house from 1890, now used as a model of, and information centre on energy conservation. Tours and advice are free. Closed Saturday afternoons and Sundays.

Walking Tour

A walking tour of some of the above plus other historical sites is outlined on the map of Fredericton, available at the Tourist Office. A booklet gives descriptions of the various sites. The walking tour takes in 21 spots in the historic downtown area, starting from city hall.

Parks

In addition to the riverfront park and several smaller city parks, you can visit the following two. Odell Park, south-west of the downtown centre off Smythe St, is a 160 hectare area that contains primeval provincial forest. There are picnic tables, a kids' zoo and walking paths. Killarney Lake Park is about five km from town over the Westmorland St Bridge. A spring-fed lake is used for swimming and fishing.

Activities

Rent a canoe for drifting along the river. One place they're available is Woolastock campground, 29 km west of Fredericton. Another is McGivney Boat and Canoe (tel 472-1655), Lower St Mary's, five km east of Howard Johnson's on the Trans-Canada.

Sailboards are for rent from Atlantic Boardsailing (tel 455-2220), Queen St, at $8 an hour, $35 per day. Windsport Fredericton (tel 472-2503), 71 Riverside Drive, offers kayak instruction and white-water trips.

There are free swimming pools at Henry Park and Queen Square. At the YM-YWCA, 28 Saunders St, there is a small admission fee.

Events

The annual New Brunswick Day Canoe Race is held near the beginning of August in the Mactaquac Headpond.

A free provincial handicrafts show is held at Mactaquac Park on the weekend before Labour Day. All types of handicrafts are exhibited and sold. Fredericton is a centre of the old craft of pewtersmithing.

The Fredericton Exhibition is an annual six-day affair starting on Labour Day (the first Monday in September). It's held at the exhibition grounds, at the corner of Smythe and Saunders St. The exhibition includes a farm show, a carnival, harness racing and stage shows.

From May to September each Saturday night at the Playhouse theatre, various country music artists from Atlantic Canada perform.

South of town, Oromocto holds a two-day Scottish Highland Games festival each summer with music, dancing, and contests.

Places to Stay

Hostels Fredericton has a member *Youth Hostel* (tel 454-1233) and it's a good one. It's centrally situated in a big, old schoolhouse at 193 York at the corner of George St, by the church. Rates are $6.50 members, $8 non-members. Breakfasts cost $2 and dinners are available. The hostel opens at 4.30 pm and the people there are friendly. It's open early June to

September – the exact dates are uncertain. And it has the strangest toilets I've yet seen.

There's no accommodation in the YM-YWCA building here.

The *University of New Brunswick* rents single and double rooms in the dorms, available from mid-May to mid-August. For tourists, singles are $18, doubles $26, and for students the price drops to $9 and $16. Contact the Director of Housing on 453-4891. Facilities include a pool. The campus is within walking distance of the downtown area in a south-east direction. It runs south of Beaverbrook St about five blocks from Regent St.

Hotels & Tourist Homes There isn't a vast selection of budget places in town but the ones that exist are good.

The *Elms Tourist Home* (tel 454-3410) is the nice yellow-and-black house at 269 Saunders St. This is a tree-lined residential street two blocks south of Brunswick St. Rates are $25 singles, one bed (two people) $30, two beds (two people) $35 and kitchen facilities are available.

The *Back Porch Bed & Breakfast* (tel 454-6875) is central at 266 Northumberland St, with two rooms priced the same as above and good breakfasts on the back porch. It's open all year.

The *Carriage House Bed & Breakfast* (tel 454-6090) is over at 230 University Avenue, also central. For $30 single, $35 double the morning meal is included. There's a shared TV room.

Moving up-scale, the venerable *Lord Beaverbrook* (tel 455-3371) at 659 Queen is relatively moderate at $60 single and $64 double for a place of its class. They have 165 rooms with all the amenities.

Motels The bulk of the city's accommodation is in motels around the edges of town. On the west side of town on RR6, which is the Trans-Canada West, there are a couple of places.

Country Host Motel (tel 459-3464, has rooms for $29 single, $32 double.

The *Roadside Motel* (tel 455-8593 is much bigger but the prices are only slightly more at singles/doubles for $30/32.

On the east side of town on RR8 (also known as the No 2 or Trans-Canada for Moncton) is the *Norfolk Motel* (tel 472-3278). Single rooms are only $21 here, doubles $24.

Just off the highway before Princess Margaret Bridge, east of the university, is Forest Hill Rd. At No 502 is the *Fredericton Skyline Motel* (tel 455-6683), which charges $30 for singles, $32 to $34 for doubles. To get there, head for the highway over the bridge toward Moncton; Forest Hill Rd runs east of the highway. A taxi fare here from the centre of town costs $4.25. The *Journey's End Motel* has large, clean rooms for $38 singles, $45 doubles. Part of a Canadian chain, here it's located at 255 Prospect St, one north of the Trans-Canada toward town off Regent St.

Camping The best place nearby is *Mactaquac Provincial Park* (tel 363-3011), 20 km west off the Trans-Canada Highway on the 105, on the north side of the river. A tent is $7. There's swimming and a grocery store. Another provincial park is just south of King's Landing on Lake George.

There are several camping places closer to Fredericton though not as nice as the parks. They're OK for stopping overnight or short stays. There are three privately owned sites on the Trans-Canada before you reach Hanwell Rd.

Another place that's a little quieter is toward town from the highway, *Kelly's Camping & Trailer Court* (tel 455-6827). Head for the downtown area on Hanwell Rd from the Trans-Canada. Turn left at Colonial Heights and then left again at Golf Club Rd. The campground is on your left.

South-east 30 km from town is the *Sunbury Oromocto* campground at French Lake, off Highway 7.

Places to Eat
The M&T Deli, a small but comfortable and casual delicatessen, sits at the bottom of Regent St at No 62. It serves all the standards, including smoked meat from Montreal's *Ben's*. Various sandwiches, bagels and cheeses are served at the stools. About $3 and up. Closed Sunday.

The *Greenhouse Restaurant* is in the new enclosed shopping mall at the corner of Brunswick and York Sts. They serve good breakfasts, including health blender drinks for $1.99, lunches with 10 different salads, soups and sandwiches. At dinner there are one or two specials.

Also in the mall is *Krispins* with lunches at $3 to $5 and the *Fundy Fish Market* for cheap cold plates, sandwiches, shrimp, crab, tuna, etc.

For your basic Canadian standard there's *Gallagher's* at 74 York St. They serve burgers. Opposite the Justice Building on Queen St is *Zellers*, a Woolworths-type store and cheap cafeteria. Lunch is about $3. They serve all the usual stuff but also shrimps, seafood and even lobster sandwiches.

On Queen St is a place for Chinese food: the *Capital Garden*, by the post office. From 11.30 am to 2.30 pm, Monday to Friday is an all-you-can-eat buffet for $6.25. It includes ribs, chicken balls, egg rolls and rice. On Saturday and Sunday nights dinner is $8.25.

Mei's at 74 Regent St is better and offers some Sichuan-style dishes but dinner for two is $20 to $25.

Goofy Roofy's is a small place set up in the Saturday market, open only Saturday mornings for breakfast and lunch. Prices range from $3 to $4.50. The 'goofy' is the boisterous, brash, notorious woman-cum-celebrity who runs the place. Get your quips ready.

At 594 Queen St on the corner of Regent St, is *La Vie en Rose Café*, a snazzy little place for desserts and coffee.

Lastly, for more expensive fare there's *Martha's* at 626 King St, specialising in Hungarian dishes, and the *Victoria & Albert* at 642 Queen St, a good seafood-and-steak restaurant.

Nightlife
The *Rollin' Keg* is a rock music bar on King St between Regent and Carleton Sts. Young, jeans crowd.

Next door is the *Club Cosmopolitan* with a fairly expensive restaurant, a lounge and the local singles disco.

The University of New Brunswick often has concerts and folk performers. Films are also shown at the university for $2 at the Tilley Hall Auditorium.

Getting There & Away
Air Fredericton is a small city, but as the provincial capital it does get a fair bit of air traffic. Many flights in and out are stopovers between various other points. Air Canada serves the city and has one non-stop flight daily from Toronto.

Bus The SMT bus station (tel 455-3303) is at the corner of Regent and Brunswick Sts. Schedules and fares to some destinations include:

Moncton: 12.15, 4.30, 5.15 pm daily – $16.75 one-way
Quebec City: 12.30, 6 pm – $49
Halifax: 12.15 am, 4.30 pm – $38.50
Amherst, Nova Scotia: $23.25
Campbellton, New Brunswick: $31.25.

You can get the special Canada Fare here, which is good on all connecting bus lines. Anywhere in Canada costs $95 one-way.

Train There is no longer any passenger train service into or from Fredericton. But there is a bus service which connects to trains at Fredericton Junction about 40 km south of town. For information and tickets, there are several agents in town: Blaine Thomas, 99 York St, and Maritime Travel, 498 Queen St are two. Buses leave from the Beaverbrook Hotel and from the Student Union Building at the university, so you could enquire at these points as well.

Road Distances in the Atlantic region are small; a few hours of driving will take you across any of the provinces. Cape Tormentine is 300 km via Trans-Canada Highway, Routes 16 and 2. To Halifax, 415 km, take the 102, 104 and then the Trans-Canada. To Quebec City, 576 km, take the Trans-Canada (2).

Getting Around

Airport Transport The airport is 16 km south-east of town. There's an airport bus from the Lord Beaverbrook Hotel before and after flights. It leaves 45 to 60 minutes before flight time and costs $4.50. Generally no service on Sundays and holidays though. A taxi to the airport runs to about $13.

Bus The city has a good system and the fare includes free transfers. For information, ring 474-0212.

The university is a 15-minute walk from the downtown area; if you want to take the bus, take No 9 south on Regent St. It runs about every 20 minutes.

For hitching on the Trans-Canada, you want the Fredericton Mall bus, the No 10 from town. If you get off up near the Mall, off the Trans-Canada Highway, take the No 2 for downtown.

Car Rentals Budget (tel 452-1107) is at 407 Regent St. Their rate is $31 a day with 150 free km. By the week it's $180 with 1050 free km, then 12c per km.

Delta, at 304 King St, is more reasonable at $20 a day with 150 free km, then 12c per km. Weekend rates are $40 with the first 400 km free.

Rent-A-Wreck (tel 453-1234), across the street at 119 Westmorland St, has cars starting at still less. Tilden on Prospect St is a fourth possibility.

Driving Free tourist parking passes are available from the Visitor's Centre, City Hall, which enable you to park in lots and at meters free.

Tours Throughout July and August, an actors' group leads a free walking tour around town. Ask at the Tourist Office.

Trius Tours offer inexpensive car tours around town; for larger groups a van is used. Trius is primarily a taxi company.

Some years bus tours are offered on summer afternoons from the Tourist Office. A replica of an old paddle-wheeler which docks at the Regent St wharf provides river cruises, some with dinner.

AROUND FREDERICTON

King's Landing Historical Settlement

The settlement is located 37 km west of Fredericton, on the way to Woodstock. Take Exit 259. Here you can get a glimpse of (and taste) pioneer life in the Maritimes. A community of 100 costumed staff inhabits 11 houses, a school, church, store and sawmill typical of those used a century ago. The staff will answer questions about their chores, the tools, or life in general in such a village. The *Kings' Head Inn* serves traditional foods and beverages.

The settlement is open 6 June to 26 June and 8 September to 12 October from 10 am to 5 pm, and 27 June to 7 September, 10 am to 6 pm. Admission $4.

On weekends in July and August and on Sundays only in June, there's a bus from the SMT terminal in Fredericton. It leaves for King's Landing at 10 am and 1 pm and costs $5.50 return. With the bus ticket, admission to the site is only $3.

Mactaquac Provincial Park

Twenty-two km west of town is the province's biggest provincial park. It runs along the 100-km-long pond formed by the Mactaquac Power Dam. The park offers swimming, fishing, picnic sites, camping and boat rentals. There's also a golf course where you can rent all equipment.

Mactaquac Power Dam

The dam across the park is responsible for the small lake and therefore the park's location. The 400,000 kW output makes it the largest in the Maritime provinces. Free tours, lasting about 45 minutes, include a look at the turbines and an explanation of how they work.

Woolastock Wildlife Park

Just a few km west of Mactaquac park, Woolastock (tel 363-2352) is open daily 9 am to sunset. The park has a collection of Canadian animals, many typical of this region. You'll see moose, bear, wolves, coyotes, foxes, caribou, hawks, owls and more. There are also some water slides, picnic areas and camping. If you camp, the wildlife section is free.

Up the river around here are several campgrounds and many touristy attractions. There's horse riding, craft shops and small museums.

Gagetown

Gagetown refers to both a small town and the largest military base in the Commonwealth. This is the source of all the military vehicles you've probably seen on the highways. Both are located down the Saint John River a short distance from Fredericton. At Camp Gagetown, the base, you can visit the military museum with articles from both world wars, the South African War and the Korean War. Admission is free. Along the way from Fredericton are farmers' markets and roadside stalls offering fresh produce.

Gagetown itself, on the river, has numerous crafts outlets and good examples of earlier architecture, some dating from the 1700s.

East Towards Moncton

From Highway 2, along the river east of town, the eye absorbs beautiful farmland and eventually the dairy centre of Sussex. Other than the views though, there is very little along the way.

Grand Lake, the province's largest, is a summer resort area with lots of cottages and a couple of provincial campgrounds. At Cambridge Narrows on nearby Washademoak Lake is *The Lake Resort*, a well-known R&R spot with saunas and spas in a European style. *Cafe Mozart* here is a very good restaurant and the German tortes have quite a reputation.

Sussex is a small town with one of the streets, Queen, somewhat redone and reminiscent of earlier decades. It's off Main St opposite the VIA station. Here you'll find the *Broadway Cafe*, a little sanctuary from the standard small town greasy spoons. Recorded music, inexpensive lunch specials and licensed.

On towards Moncton, look for the old potato storage houses and barns half buried in the ground.

St Croix Waterway Recreation Area

This area of 800 square km is situated south-west of Fredericton near the Maine border. The town of McAdam is pretty much the commercial centre of this little-developed territory of woods and lakes. In McAdam itself, check out the Canadian Pacific Rail Station dating from 1900, one of the finest in Canada and made a National Historic Site in 1983. Sixteen km from McAdam is Spednic Provincial Park, with rustic camping and access to some of the Chiputneticook chain of lakes. The St Croix River is good for white-water canoeing. Other canoe routes connect lakes, and about 100 km of hiking trails wind through the area. Another campground is found at Wauklehegan.

SAINT JOHN RIVER

The Saint John River, beginning in Maine, USA, flows south for over 700 km before entering the Bay of Fundy at Saint John.

Known as the 'Rhine of America', it winds along the western border of the province past forests and beautiful lush farmland, through Fredericton between tree-lined banks, and then around rolling hills to the bay. The valley that protects it is the most scenic land in the province. It's particularly picturesque and gentle from just north of Saint John to about Woodstock.

There are bridges and ferries across the river at various points. The Trans-Canada Highway Route 2 follows the river up to Edmundston and then crosses into Quebec. In earlier days the river was the highway for the Indians of the area.

Some of the small towns along the route have a bed & breakfast spot or two. Expect to pay about $22/28 for singles/doubles; see the provincial accommodation guide for more information. There are also campgrounds along the way.

Woodstock

A small town set in a rich farming area, Woodstock acts as a tourist cross-road; the Trans-Canada goes through here, as does the road to Maine in the US. The No 95 to Bangor, Maine, and then the No 2 is an alternative and shorter route to Montreal.

Main St through town has some fine, old, large Maritime houses. On the north side of town is *The Hometown* (you can't miss it), a good spot for a meal.

There is a bluegrass music festival held in town in summer.

Hartland

Hartland itself is an attractive little town with a nice setting – though not much to see – but it does have the grand-daddy of New Brunswick's many wooden covered bridges, now things of the past. The bridge here, at 400 metres, is the longest in the world. There are 74 of these dotted around the province; the Tourist Office has a complete listing if you're interested. The bridges were covered to protect the timber beams used in the construction. With such protection from rain and sun, a bridge lasts about 80 years. They are generally high and wide because cartloads of hay pulled by horses had to pass through. Nearly all the bridges left are on secondary or smaller roads.

Halfway between here and Grand Falls is a provincial park at Kilburn.

Grand Falls

A town of 7000, Grand Falls consists of one main street and the falls. Located in a park in town, the falls drop about 25 metres and have carved out a gorge with walls as high as 70 metres. Entrance is 50c.

The town celebrates its primary resource, the potato, in a festival each year around 1 July.

Highway 108, the Plaster Rock Highway, cuts across the province to the east coast. The highway cuts through forest – animals such as deer and moose are commonly seen on or beside the road. There are some camping spots along the way.

St Leonard

As the name suggests, St Leonard is primarily a French town, as are many in this region. Some are old Acadian settlements.

In St Leonard is the Madawaska Weavers group, who use hand looms to make material for ponchos and scarves.

From here, Highway 17 runs north-east through the dense forests of northern New Brunswick. Near St Quentin, Highway 180 branches off eastwards and leads to the province's largest park, Mt Carleton Provincial Park.

EDMUNDSTON

If you're coming from Quebec there's a good chance this'll be the first town in the Maritimes you get a look at, as the border is only about 20 km away. At the border is a large, helpful Tourist Office. From here it is three hours' driving to Fredericton.

Edmundston is an industrial pulp & paper centre with numerous mills in and around town. The population of about 13,000 is 85% French-speaking. Nearly all of them, like most of New Brunswick's French, speak English.

Of course, where there are French people there are impressive churches and cathedrals, and Edmundston is no exception. Their cathedral here is the Roman Catholic Cathedral of the

Immaculate Conception, located on a hill off Rue Laporte, west of the downtown area.

The main centre of town is Church St (Eglise) and around the city hall, a few blocks from Church St. There are numerous restaurants and shops here plus a new indoor shopping mall. Victoria is also a busy commercial street. One of the nicest looking places for a bite is *The White Tulip*, a bistro on Hill St just off Church St.

At 195 Herbert Boulevard is the Madawaska Museum, which outlines the human history of the area from the original Malecite Indians through the colonialists to the present. It also has displays on local industries such as the timber trade. The museum is on the corner of the Trans-Canada Highway. Open daily in summer, closed Monday the rest of the year. Nominal charge.

There is no inner-city bus service so you'll have to do some walking here, but the distances are not great. The train station is not far from the bridge on St Francois.

Events

Each year on the nine days preceding the first Monday in August is the 'Foires' Festival, which celebrates the physically non-existent republic of Madawaska. The people of the area from various national ancestries term themselves 'Brayons', the inhabitants of Madawaska. There are cultural, social and sporting activities as well as some good traditional Brayon cooking to sample.

Places to Stay

On Power Rd (Rue de Pouvoir) in the north-west section of the city, just off Highway 2, are a couple of cheap tourist homes.

The *Modern Tourist Home* (tel 739-7438), 224 Power Rd, charges just single $12, double $14. *City View* (tel 739-9058) at No 226, next door, has five rooms, singles/doubles $20/22.

There are also plenty of motels. The *Lawrence* at 33 17th St is $24. Others are more expensive.

There are a couple of provincial parks within 15 km of town.

Getting There & Away

Bus The station is in the Lynn Motel on Church St, at the bridge over the Madawaska River. You can catch buses here for numerous destinations, including Quebec City, Halifax and Moncton, and Maine and Boston, USA.

There are three buses daily to Quebec City, $30 on Voyageur Lines. To Halifax and Moncton there are two daily on SMT Lines, which serves New Brunswick; $57 for Halifax and $32 to Moncton.

Train The station is on St Francois, which runs along the Saint John River, south of the central area.

Montreal: 7.30 am (arrives 7 am the next day) – $72

Moncton: 7.30 am – $36

Saint John: 7.30 am (arrives 6.45 pm) – $47.

Note that the train to Montreal is not direct. It goes to Moncton first, so the trip is ridiculously long. In fact, most trains go to Moncton and you must transfer once there.

For Montreal, you're much better off getting to Rivière-du-Loup, Quebec, by any means possible – it's only 120-odd km – and then getting a train from there. From Rivière-du-Loup to Montreal the fare is $40 and there are two trains a day, one early in the morning and one very late at night.

Quebec

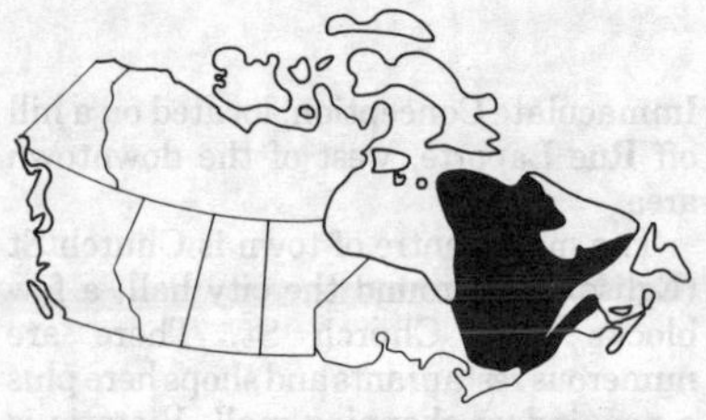

Entered Confederation: 1 July 1867
Area: 1,540,687 square km
Population: 6,438,403

'Kebec', an Algonkian Indian word meaning 'where the river narrows', is, as the world knows, the heart of French Canada. Explorer Samuel de Champlain of France first heard and recorded the word when he founded Quebec City in 1608. Jacques Cartier, another explorer, had landed here in 1534 when the settlement was known as Stadacone (the 450th anniversary of Cartier's landing was celebrated in 1984).

The province is Canada's biggest, and the largely French population makes it quite different from other parts of North America. This is reflected in various aspects of life here: architecture, music, food and religion. About 90% of the population is Roman Catholic, although the Church's influence has declined sharply in recent decades.

Quebec is often at odds with the rest of English-speaking Canada, particularly in its politics. Most people are familiar with the movement to separate Quebec from the rest of Canada. This desire was formally channelled into the elected Parti Quebecois, a provincial party led by the late René Levesque, a colourful, charismatic man. To the hard-liners' dismay, their goal of an independent Quebec has lost favour among the inhabitants and most now feel it is not realistic or practical. In the late 1980s, however, some Quebec politicians are attempting to renew the issue.

This recent twist is in part due to the rebounding Quebec economy which was in the doldrums for a number of years. Quebec's wealth has long been potential rather than actual. Despite abundant natural resources, manufacturing is the prime industry. There are vast amounts of hydroelectric power and the province is the No 1 paper producer in North America. Other important industries are aluminium, minerals, timber, apples and a local specialty, maple syrup.

Roughly half the province is forest; north of Montreal and Quebec City are the Laurentian Mountains. The area south of Montreal contains much of the provincial farmland.

The St Lawrence River provides a link between the Great Lakes and the Atlantic ocean, serving major Canadian and American ports.

Along the St Lawrence River, where most visitors will be, summers can be hot and winters are always cold. Snow can be many metres deep. Generally, the farther you go east, the colder it gets.

Montreal

Some cities take a bit of getting used to – you need time to know and appreciate them. In Montreal, it ain't so. This city has an atmosphere all its own. It's a friendly, romantic place where couples kiss on the street and you can talk to strangers.

Montreal is an interesting and lively blend of things English and French, flavoured by the Canadian setting. There are about three million people in Greater Montreal – it's the second largest city after Toronto – and about 12% of all Canadians and 40% of Quebec's people live here. Two-thirds of the population are

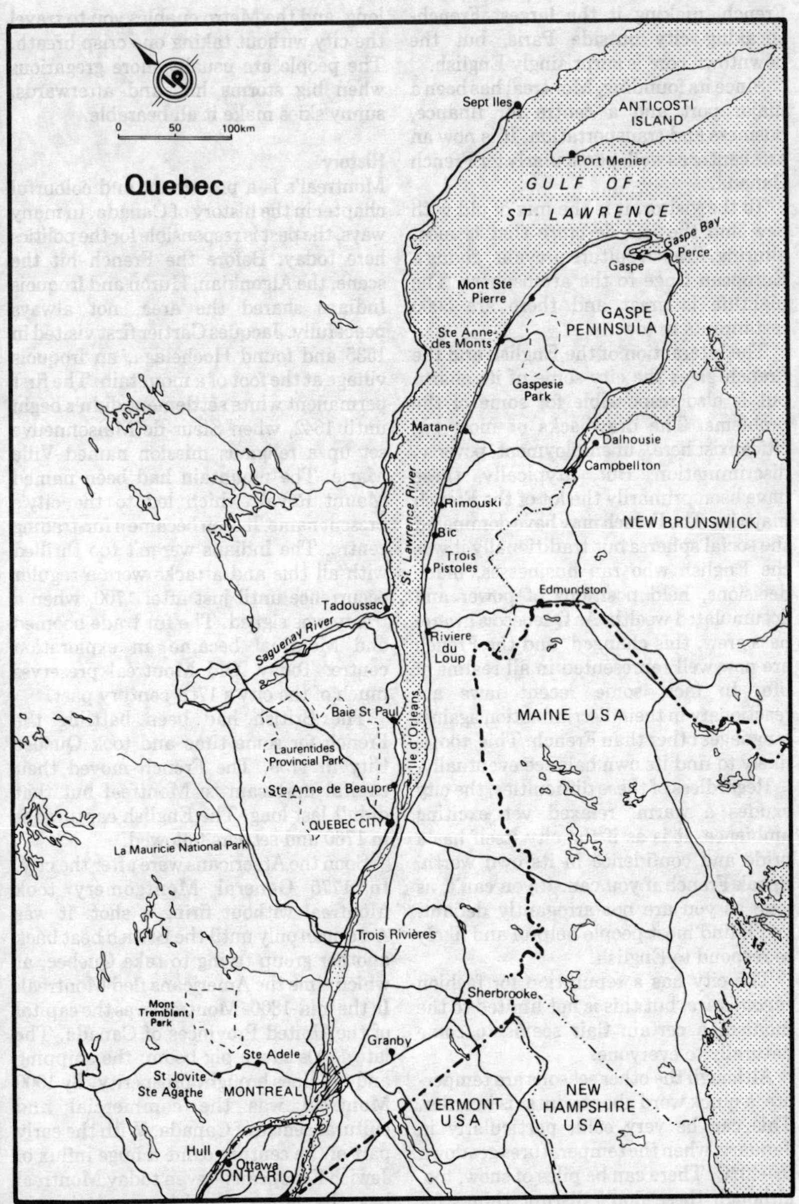
Quebec
0 50 100km
Sept Iles
ANTICOSTI ISLAND
Port Menier
GULF OF ST LAWRENCE
Gaspe Bay
Perce
Gaspe
Mont Ste Pierre
GASPE PENINSULA
Ste Anne des Monts
Gaspesie Park
Matane
Dalhousie
Campbellton
Rimouski
NEW BRUNSWICK
Bic
Trois Pistoles
St. Lawrence River
Edmundston
Tadoussac
Saguenay River
Riviere du Loup
Baie St Paul
MAINE USA
Ile d'Orleans
Laurentides Provincial Park
Ste Anne de Beaupre
QUEBEC CITY
La Mauricie National Park
Trois Rivières
Sherbrooke
Mont Tremblant Park
Granby
Ste Adele
St Jovite
Ste Agathe
MONTREAL
VERMONT USA
NEW HAMPSHIRE USA
Hull
Ottawa
ONTARIO

French, making it the largest French-speaking city outside Paris, but the downtown core is surprisingly English.

Since its founding, Montreal has been a major port and a centre for finance, business and transportation. It is now an arts centre as well, particularly for French Canada.

To the visitor, it is the mix of old with new and the *joie de vivre* that is most alluring. French culture prevails, giving a European tinge to the atmosphere. The nightlife is great and there are 5000 restaurants in town.

The interaction of the English and the French gives the city some of its charm but is also responsible for some of the problems. The drawbacks of most big cities exist here – unemployment, poverty, discrimination. But, atypically, these have been primarily the lot of the French majority. The French may have dominated the social spheres but traditionally it was the English who ran businesses, made decisions, held positions of power and accumulated wealth. As Quebecois awareness grew, this changed, and the French are now well represented in all realms of life. In fact, some recent laws are reactionary in their discrimination against languages other than French. This, too, is likely to find its own balance eventually.

Regardless of these difficulties, the city exudes a warm, relaxed yet exciting ambience. It is as if the city itself has a pride and confidence in its own worth. Speak French if you can. If you can't, as long as you are not arrogantly defiant, you'll find most people helpful and likely to respond to English.

The city has a reputation for fashion *savoir-faire*, but this is not limited to the monied; a certain flair seems to come naturally to everyone.

Although the other seasons are temperate, a quick word about winter is in order. This can be very cold, particularly in January, when the temperatures get down to -40°C. There can be piles of snow, too, although these don't disrupt things for long, and the Metro enables you to travel the city without taking one crisp breath. The people are usually more gregarious when big storms hit, and afterwards, sunny skies make it all bearable.

History

Montreal's is a prominent and colourful chapter in the history of Canada. In many ways, the past is responsible for the politics here today. Before the French hit the scene, the Algonkian, Huron and Iroquois Indians shared the area, not always peacefully. Jacques Cartier first visited in 1535 and found Hochelaga, an Iroquois village at the foot of a mountain. The first permanent white settlement didn't begin until 1642, when Sieur de Maisonneuve set up a religious mission named Ville Marie. The mountain had been named Mount Royal, which led to the city's present name. It soon became a fur-trading centre. The Indians weren't too thrilled with all this and attacks were a regular occurrence until just after 1700, when a treaty was signed. The fur trade boomed and Montreal became an exploration centre. Today, Old Montreal preserves much of the city's 17th-century past.

The British had been battling the French for some time and took Quebec City in 1759. The French moved their capital upstream to Montreal but that didn't last long. The English captured it in 1760 and settlers followed.

Soon the Americans were after the city. In 1775 General Montgomery took Montreal without firing a shot. It was American only until the British beat back another group trying to take Quebec, at which time the Americans fled Montreal. In the mid-1800s Montreal was the capital of the United Provinces of Canada. The late 1800s saw a big boom; the shipping and rail lines brought prosperity. By 1900 Montreal was the commercial and cultural centre of Canada. With the early part of the century came a huge influx of Jewish Europeans – even today Montreal has the largest Jewish population in

Canada. After both wars, immigrants of many nationalities arrived.

From the 1920s to the '40s, Montreal gained a reputation as Sin City. This was due partially to Prohibition in the USA, partially to Latin temperament. Brothels, gambling houses and gangsters thrived and the nightlife was known far and wide. Politicians and law-enforcers are said to have turned a blind eye. All this changed with the arrival of Jean Drapeau, who was elected mayor in 1954 and, except for a five-year period in the early '60s, was mayor right into the mid-80s. He cleaned up the city, encouraged redevelopment, brought the World's Fair in 1967 and the Olympics in 1976. Still, he was touched by scandal and many dubbed him 'Emperor' for his megalomania. But Drapeau was immensely popular and he certainly helped develop Montreal's international reputation.

Orientation

The city sits on an island roughly 40 km long by 15 km wide where the Ottawa River flows into the St Lawrence. There are bridges connecting all sides to the mainland, which reinforce the impression of really not being on an island at all. Despite the size of the city and the island, it's both easy to orient yourself and to get around Montreal. In the middle of the island is Mount Royal, a 233-metre-high extinct volcano. The core of the city, which is actually quite small, is below this, in the south central section of the island.

The downtown area is bounded by Rue Sherbrooke to the north, Avenue Atwater to the west, Rue St-Antoine to the south and Boulevard St Laurent to the east. This is the busy area of skyscrapers, shops, restaurants, offices and luxury hotels.

The small park, Dominion Square, marks the centre of the downtown district. It's a peaceful spot surrounded by some new and many old buildings; the green roofs around are oxidised copper. On the south-west corner is Windsor Station, the venerable CP rail terminal. To the south is the CP hotel, Chateau Champlain, where you won't be staying. On the east side is the permanent-looking, stone Sun Life Insurance building.

The Cathedral of Montreal (Marie-Reine-du-Monde, or Mary Queen of the World Cathedral) with its pastel, gilt-trimmed interior, is to the south-east.

Just to the east is the Queen Elizabeth Hotel, below which is the CN-VIA train station where most passenger trains now leave. South, down the hill from the park on Rue Peel, is the main post office.

North a block up Rue Peel from the park is Rue Ste Catherine, the main east-west artery. This is the main shopping street where the department stores are and also many cinemas. If you're driving, it's one-way only, eastbound.

Above Rue Ste Catherine is Boulevard de Maisonneuve and then Rue Sherbrooke, the two other main east-west streets. All three run a long way in each direction.

If you keep walking uphill on Rue Peel for a number of blocks you'll finally come to Avenue des Pins, across which is the edge of Mount Royal Park. You'll see some steps. At the top is an excellent view of the city, the river and the surroundings to the south: great day or night. This is the city's largest park, pleasant to stroll in on a warm day. The Cross on top, lit at night, is a city symbol.

Another place for a good view of the downtown area and to get your bearings, is the Observation Tower of the Canadian Imperial Bank of Commerce (CIBC) at 1155 Boulevard Dorchester Ouest, corner of Rue Peel. It's open from April to October, 10 am to 10 pm daily.

The area downtown and west to Loyola Campus on Rue Sherbrooke is pretty much English and residential. Westmount at the foot of the mountain is one of the city's wealthiest and most prestigious districts.

Running north and south of Rue Ste Catherine west of Rue Peel are Rue Bishop,

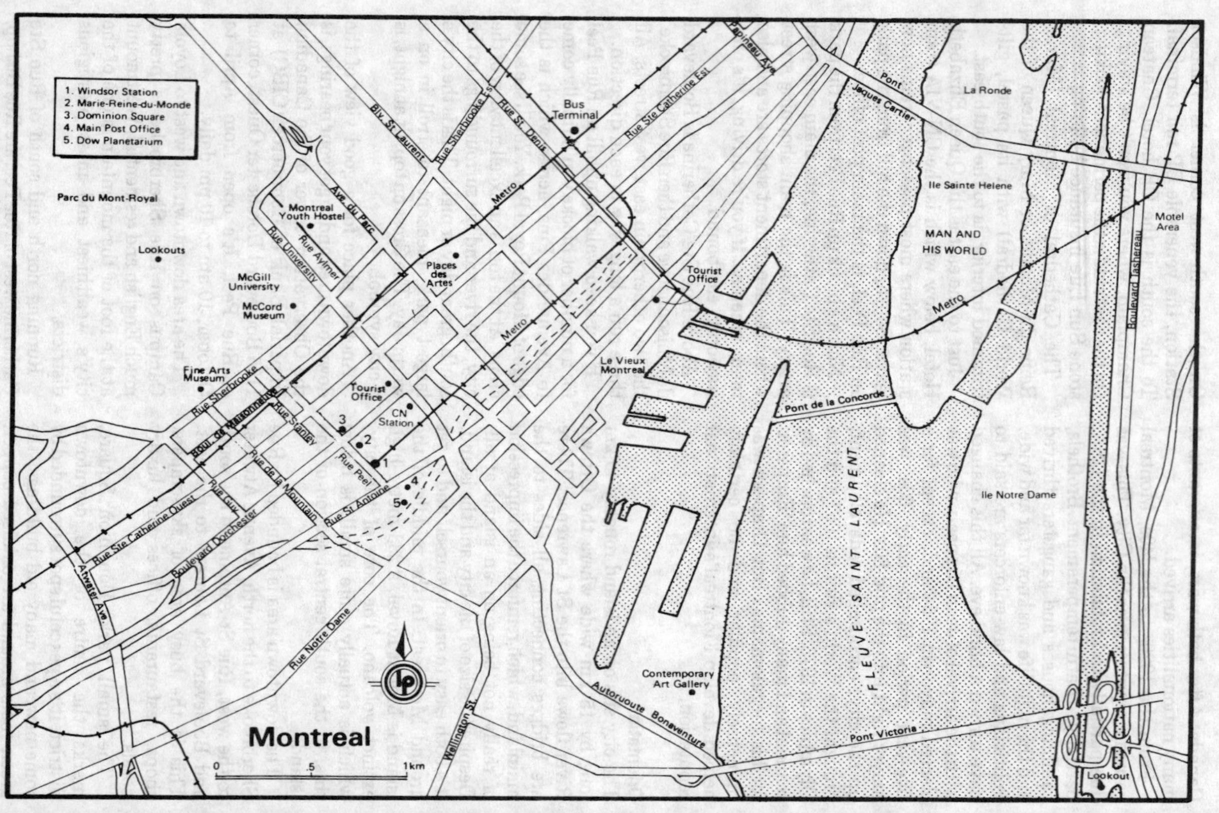
1. Windsor Station
2. Marie-Reine-du-Monde
3. Dominion Square
4. Main Post Office
5. Dow Planetarium
Parc du Mont-Royal
Lookouts
McGill University
McCord Museum
Fine Arts Museum
Montreal Youth Hostel
Rue Aylmer
Rue University
Ave. du Parc
Blv. St Laurent
Rue Sherbrooke E
Rue St. Denis
Bus Terminal
Rue Ste Catherine Est
Papineau Ave
Metro
Places des Artes
Tourist Office
CN Station
Le Vieux Montreal
Tourist Office
Rue Sherbrooke
Boul. de Maisonneuve
Rue Stanley
Rue Peel
Rue de la Mountain
Rue Guy
Rue Ste Catherine Ouest
Boulevard Dorchester
Rue St Antoine
Atwater Ave.
Rue Notre Dame
Wellington St.
Autoruoute Bonaventure
Contemporary Art Gallery
Pont Jacques Cartier
La Ronde
Ile Sainte Helene
MAN AND HIS WORLD
Motel Area
Boulevard Tashereau
Pont de la Concorde
Ile Notre Dame
FLEUVE SAINT LAURENT
Pont Victoria
Lookout
Montreal
0
.5
1km

Rue Crescent and Rue de la Mountain – the centre of one of the nightlife areas. There are many restaurants, cafés and discos here. The two big cafés on Boulevard de Maisonneuve between Mountain and Crescent are a good place to get a feel of the area. The statue at the corner of Sherbrooke and Bishop was designed for Toronto, but the moral babysitters there wouldn't have it, so Montreal, with a smile, accepted it.

Below and parallel to Rue Ste Catherine is Boulevard Dorchester, a wide street known for its high buildings. The Place Ville Marie at the corner of Rue University, in the shape of a cross, is another landmark.

East along Rue Ste Catherine you'll see Phillips Square, a meeting place where guitarists and bums busk and bask. Further east, just past de Bleury, is Place des Arts, a complex for the performing arts. A few more blocks east is Boulevard St Laurent (St Lawrence Boulevard), known as The Main. This is one of the city's best-known streets, with an interesting history and ethnic make-up, and lots of inexpensive restaurants.

To the east of The Main, Rue Ste Catherine Ouest becomes Rue Ste Catherine Est and arbitrarily separates east from west Montreal; east of here is predominantly French. About 10 blocks east (you can get a bus) is St Denis, which has been transformed into a Paris-like café district. St Denis was originally an all-student area, but more expensive establishments are moving in. However, there is still something for everyone. Little bars, some with jazz, abound. French is the tongue here but don't let that deter you – it's a good chance to practise.

Two blocks further east is Rue Berri. Terminus Voyageur, the bus station with American and Canadian destinations is a block north on Berri at Boulevard de Maisoneuve.

Old Montreal is south-east of downtown; both Boulevard St Laurent and Rue St Denis lead into it.

There is a small but determined Chinese community clustered along Rue de Lagauchetiere between Rue St Urbain and Rue Clark. Rue de Lagauchetiere runs east-west past the train stations.

The streets of east-end Montreal and some parts of the northern section are lined with two or three-storey apartments with outside staircases. Such housing, peculiar to Montreal, was built in the '20s and '30s. The stairs were put outside to save space inside.

Street Names Although Montreal is a bilingual rather than a French city, and most of the streets were actually named by the English, most of the city's streets use the French labels, 'Rue' (street), 'Chemin' (road), etc. A street with east and west sections is referred to by its French name, too. *Est* means East and *Ouest* means West. Hence, the east part of Rue Ste Catherine is known as Rue Ste Catherine Est and the west part, Rue Ste Catherine Ouest.

In addition, most squares, parks, stations and bridges are known by their French names, so it's Place Royale (Royal Square), Parc de l'Esplanade (Esplanade Park), etc.

A street which was recently renamed is Boulevard Dorchester. It is now known as Boulevard Rene Levesque, in honour of the Quebecois leader. The two names will probably be in use for the next few years, after which it will officially be known as Boulevard Rene Levesque. Whether Montrealers take to this renaming of a very old street to honour a deceased politician remains to be seen. In this book, it is referred to throughout as Boulevard Dorchester.

Information

There are several Tourist Offices around town. In the downtown area, across Boulevard Dorchester from the Queen Elizabeth Hotel, is Place Ville Marie, one of the city's best-known buildings. It's sometimes referred to as the PVM.

Outside, around the corner at University and Cathcart, is the central Tourist Office (tel 873-2015). It faces the square by the Royal Bank. Open Monday to Friday 9 am to 5 pm.

In Old Montreal you'll find another one at 174 Rue Notre Dame Est (tel 871-1595), not far from Place Jacques Cartier. It's busy but helpful, open 9 am to 5 pm daily in season, 9 am to 5 pm weekdays only the rest of the year.

A new Tourist Office is being set up in Dominion Square near the corner of Peel and Dorchester. Both train stations are nearby and Ste Catherine is just a short walk.

The Convention & Tourist Bureau (tel 871-1129) is in the Place Bonaventure building, right in town, by the VIA Rail train station.

The office for provincial tourist information (tel 873-2015) is in Place Ville Marie on the Terrace level, corner of University and Cathcart.

The city also has an information kiosk at the airport.

There are several government historic parks and old forts within about 50 km of the city. Details are included in Tourist Office attractions guides.

All Montreal's museums are closed on Mondays.

Warning Pedestrians, beware in Montreal. Might is right and drivers take full advantage of this. The careless may not get a second chance.

Old Montreal (Vieux Montreal)

This is the oldest section of the city, dating mainly from the 1700s. Place (Square) Royale, sits where Ville Marie, Maisonneuve's first small fort-town, was built, when fighting with the Iroquois was both lengthy and fierce.

The narrow, cobblestoned streets divide old stone houses and buildings, a good number of them now housing intimate little restaurants and clubs. Scattered through the area are squares and churches and the waterfront is never far away. Old Montreal is a must for romantics, though unfortunately a bit crowded in peak season. With all the activity and history, it's a perfect area for just wandering where your feet take you. But do yourself a favour and don't bring your car down here – it's too busy and you won't find a parking spot.

The main streets are Rue Notre Dame and Rue St Paul. The area is bounded by Rue McGill on the west, Rue Berri on the east, Rue St-Antoine on the north and the river on the south, with Boulevard St Laurent dividing the area east from west. The Metro stops in Old Montreal are Place d'Armes or Champs-de-Mars.

Near City Hall and the Tourist Office is the square Place Jacques Cartier, the centre of the area which, in summer, is filled with visitors, vendors, horse-drawn carriages and musicians. At the Tourist Office nearby, there's an 'Old Montreal Walking Tour' booklet available, which is free and has all sorts of interesting historical tidbits, and points out the most noteworthy spots.

Many buildings are themselves marked with informative plaques. Highlights are:

Place d'Armes, the other major square in the area. A monument to Maisonneuve stands in the middle. On the square is **Notre Dame Cathedral**, which you shouldn't miss. Built in 1829 and big enough to hold 5000, the church has a magnificently rich interior. There's a small museum at the back.

The **Church of Notre Dame de Bonsecours** is on St Paul. It's known as the Sailors' Church and has several models of wooden ships hanging from the ceiling. From the tower in the church there's a good view. The miniature vignettes in the small museum are also quite good.

Calvet House is across from the church. The house, from 1725, has been restored and is now a museum showing the furnishings of that time. Closed Monday; free.

On Rue Notre Dame, across from City Hall, is the **Chateau de Ramezay**. This was the home of the city's French governors for about 40 years in the early 1700s. The building housed a great variety of things since, but is now a museum with a collection of artefacts, tools and miscellanea from early Quebec. Closed Sunday mornings and all day Mondays. Admission is $1, students 50c.

Also in Old Montreal is the the **Montreal History Centre** in the old fire hall on Place d'Youville. Audio-visuals and displays outline some of the history of the city, with tours running every 20 minutes. It's closed Mondays; inexpensive.

Not far away is the **Musee Marc Aurele Fortin** at 118 Rue St Pierre, which is less a museum than a gallery dedicated to this Quebec landscape painter (1888-1970). Other painters are also represented in the changing exhibitions. Closed Mondays; admission $2.

The **Sir George-Etienne Cartier National Historic Park** consists of two historic houses owned by the Cartier family. One details the life of the prominent 19th century lawyer and politician and the changes in society in his lifetime, and the other offers a glimpse of a middle-class home during the Victorian era. It's at 458 Notre Dame Est. Free and open every day in summer, Wednesday to Sunday the rest of the year.

Quai Jacques Cartier is a waterfront redevelopment, south of Place Jacques Cartier, and still under construction. It includes an art gallery, restaurants, a large open flea market (*marche aux puces*) and a handicraft centre. At the eastern edge is the old port of Montreal with its Sailor's Memorial Clock Tower now used as an observation tower open to the public. Boat tours of the river depart nearby. Music, dance and mime performances take place here through the summer. The Esplanade de la Commune is a wide promenade along the river from Rue Berri west to McGill . A hovercraft runs from here over to Man & His World and a ferry goes over to Parc de la Cite du Havre, where there's a restaurant and some picnic tables.

Jacques Cartier

Rue St Denis

This street, east of St Laurent between de Maisonneuve and Sherbrooke, has recently become the centre of a café, bistro and bar district with lots of open-air places and music. Snoop round on the side streets, too. Some places are cheap, so many students still frequent the area. It's very lively at night.

Going south on St Denis will lead you into Old Montreal. North up St Denis toward Sherbrooke, you'll see Place St Louis, a small park surrounded by old houses. East of the square is Rue Prince Arthur – with good, varied, ethnic eating places.

Mount Royal

Known as 'the mountain', this is the city's best and biggest park. It was designed by the same man who did New York's Central Park. The Chalet Lookout has great views of the city: you can walk up to it from downtown (see Orientation section), or drive most of the way through the park and walk the rest. East of the Lookout is the huge steel cross, lit up at night and visible from all over the city. Within the park is Beaver Lake, a depression-era 'make work' project. The park has lots of trees and is used in summer for walking, picnicking, horseback riding and frisbee-throwing. In winter there is skating and skiing. There are some nice trails with views.

In the middle of the park is the Mount Royal Art Centre, with paintings on display and a sculpture garden surrounding the building.

If you're driving here, take Guy from the downtown area to Cote des Neiges and then look for signs. To the left is another small park called Parc Summit. There is another good lookout here, this one out to the western residential districts.

St Joseph's Oratory

This impressive, modern-style basilica, completed in 1960 on and around a 1916 church, is in honour of St Joseph, patron of healers, and Brother Andre, a monk said to have the power to cure illness. Piles of crutches testify to the strength of this belief. Brother Andre's heart, which is on view here – a display ranking with the weirdest – was stolen a few years ago but finally returned intact. You can see the dome of the Oratory from anywhere in the south-west of the city. From it, the view of that part of the city is good. Open daily; free. There is a small museum dedicated to Brother Andre. On Sundays there are free organ concerts at 3.30 pm.

The Oratory is at 3800 Chemin Queen Mary, off the western slope of Mount Royal. From downtown, take the Metro to Guy, then transfer to the No 65 bus.

Canadian Historical Museum

This wax museum (tel 738-5959) is across the street from St Joseph's Oratory. It contains about 200 international historic figures, many in period or geographical settings. It's nothing too special. Open daily in summer to 9.30 pm, in winter to 5.30 pm.

Man & His World

This is an exhibition ground made up of holdovers from the greatly successful World Expo of 1967. The site is on two islands: Ile Ste Helene, much expanded by landfill, and Ile Notre Dame, a completely man-made island. The islands lie north-east from the downtown area and can be reached by taking the Metro to the Ile Ste Helene stop.

Originally totalling 83, there are now 30 pavilions and display centres housing cultural and technological exhibits. Some of the architecture is still futuristic and impressive. There are also exhibitions held on Ile Notre Dame in the Palais de la Civilisation. Much of the grounds are parkland, which you can stroll around for free. The grounds are open to midnight, the pavilions 11 am to 8 pm. Open 23 June to 29 August. Admission to the site – except La Ronde – was free last time I went, but the admission policy is always changing.

La Ronde is a large amusement park with restaurants and bars as well as rides and games, at the extreme north end of Ile Ste Helene. 'The Monster' is a roller coaster, ranked as one of the world's best – hold on to your stomach. Also at the site is the Aquarium in the Alcan Pavilion, with 100 species of marine life including trained dolphins, and a good beer garden. Full admission, including all the rides and the aquarium, is $15. With only some rides, it's $8. But like Man & His World, every time I turn around the policy is different, so these prices may change. Open 10 am to midnight, an hour later on weekends, 21 June to 29 August plus weekends in June and Labour Day weekend.

Both Man & His World and La Ronde stage events through the summer; get a schedule.

There are also some portions of an old fort near La Ronde. Inside the remaining stone ramparts is the David M Stewart Museum (tel 861-6701) with artefacts and tools from Canada's past. There are demonstrations by uniformed soldiers and others in period dress and military parades are held daily in summer by the museum. Admission is $2.50.

Incidentally, it's worthwhile taking the subway to the Ile Ste Helene stop rather than driving, as they hit you pretty hard for parking.

Underground City
To alleviate congestion and to escape winter's harshness, Montreal created a huge underground city beneath the city centre. Though much of it is actually underground, the term really covers anything connected by underground passageways. Thus you can go to the train stations, find a hotel, see a movie, eat out, go dancing or shopping, all without taking a step outside. The notion is very functional and innovative, but there's really not much to see. The shops are all modern and most of the system looks no different from a contemporary shopping mall, the differences being this is bigger and has the Metro going through. Major building complexes like Place Ville Marie, Place Bonaventure and Place du Canada are all connected and within easy walking distance. Others, like Place des Arts and Complexe Desjardins, are a Metro ride away. The Tourist Office has a good map of the entire system; it's a good place to go on rainy or snowy days.

Musee des Beaux Arts (Fine Arts Museum)
This is the city's main art gallery (tel 285-1600), with both modern and pre-Columbian works. Europe, Africa, the Middle East and other areas are covered. There's also a display of Eskimo art and special shows from time to time. Like all Montreal museums, this one is closed Monday, open 11 am to 5 pm other days. It's at 1379 Sherbrooke Ouest at Crescent. Admission is $2, students 75c.

Contemporary Art Gallery
This gallery (tel 873-2878) is on Cite du Havre, which is south of the downtown area on the waterfront near Victoria Bridge. The times I've been there, at least half of it has been closed off, everything was disorganised and the shows were nothing to write home about. It's free but not worth it. I'm told they may soon be moving to a downtown location – perhaps this will improve things.

McCord Museum
At 690 Sherbrooke Ouest is this small museum dealing with Canada's early history, mostly before the arrival of Europeans. The collection includes Indian and Inuit works, early Canadian costume, folk art and 700,000 photographs! Open Wednesday to Sunday 11 am to 5 pm; free.

Saidye Bronfman Museum
This museum, at 5170 Rue Ste Catherine, on the west side of Mount Royal, has a collection of contemporary art. It's free and open Sunday to Thursday.

Midget's Palace
This is one for the novelty lovers. It's both a home and a museum for midgets (tel 527-1121) where everything is scaled down to size. I lived in Montreal for years but just recently found this place, and it's been open since 1913. Open 10 am to 10 pm, it's on Rachel near St Hubert on the north side, close to the bus station. If you've never felt 10 feet tall, now's your chance.

Marie-Reine-du-Monde (Cathedral of Mary, Queen of the World)
Also known as the Cathedral of Montreal, this church is a smaller version of St Peter's Basilica in the Vatican, built in 1870. You'll find it just off Dominion Square near the Queen Elizabeth Hotel. Note the unusual canopy over the altar.

George Stephen House
This Renaissance-style mansion dating from 1880 was built for the man who gave it his name, the first president of the Canadian Pacific Railway. The 15 rooms

inside are rich with quality materials and craftsmanship; the woodwork is tremendous. Long the home of the private Mount Stephens Club, it is now open to the public from Thursday to Sunday, noon to 4 pm in July and August only. It's at 1440 Drummond.

Saint James United Church

This church, at 463 Ste Catherine Ouest, is unusual in that the portals open onto the street but have stores and offices built in beside them. The church is actually behind the street.

Olympic Sports Complex

Ask any Montrealer and you'll find that the scandal, indignation and tales of corruption and government incompetence surrounding these buildings are as great as the structures themselves. Nevertheless, the complex, created at enormous cost for the 1976 Olympics, is magnificent.

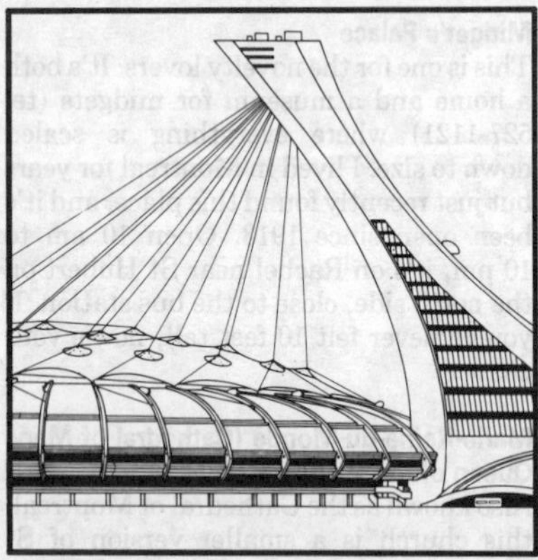

Showpiece is the multi-purpose Olympic Stadium, able to hold 80,000 spectators. Though not complete – the roof arrived from Paris, France only in late 1981, but there is no money to put it up – it certainly is grand. Also on the grounds is the Velodrome, another boldly designed stadium built for cycling and now used for roller-skating and skating as well. During summer, professional football and baseball are played here.

The swimming complex, also impressive, has six full-size pools including a 20-metre-deep scuba pool. Public swimming costs $1.

Also in the complex is Olympic Village, the housing sector with apartments and restaurants.

Guided tours of the site in French and English (tel 252-4737) leave from the lobby of the Swimming Complex every day. The fee of $4.40 (students $3.30) chisels away at the local citizens' debt. It's worth it, however, if you're interested in architecture or sports.

The entire site is in Parc Maisonneuve on the extreme eastern side of the city, off Sherbrooke at Pie IX. The Metro stop is Viau.

Botanical Gardens

These 81-hectare gardens are the third largest in the world after those in London and Berlin. You'll see 26,000 types of plants in 30 garden settings and various climate-controlled greenhouses. The collection of 700 orchid species is particularly impressive, as are the Japanese bonsai and Chinese *penjing* with plants up to 100 years old. Displays change with the seasons. Open every day; free. To view the greenhouses costs $2. The gardens are next to the Olympic Buildings in Parc Maisonneuve. The Metro stop is Pie IX.

Chateau Dufresne

This museum displays decorative art and handicrafts. It's a fine building dating from 1916-18, each room furnished with objets d'art and finery. Open Friday to Sunday only, noon to 5 pm; admission $2. It's in front of the Botanical Gardens at the corner of Boulevard Pie IX (pronounced 'Pee Neuf').

McGill University

At the corner of University and Sherbrooke, this is one of Canada's most prestigious universities. The campus is rather nice to stroll around, since it sits at the foot of the mountain. The Redpath Museum houses McGill's natural history collection, which includes animals and birds.

Place des Arts
This is a modern centre for the performing arts. There are three main theatres in the newish complex on Ste Catherine at Jeanne Mance. Free tours lasting about 45 minutes are given on Tuesdays and Thursdays at 1, 2, 3 and 4 pm. There's not that much to see.

Complex Desjardins
This is the newest of the city's connected underground building complexes. It's a modern, multi-use structure with offices, shops and a hotel (the Meridien) covering several storeys, with a large open space in the centre for walking, watching and putting on shows. You can keep an eye on things from the Hotel Meridien's café on the top floor. The mall is open 24 hours a day and has lots of benches and places to sit. It is linked to Place des Arts across the street and the subway system underground. **Alexis Nihon Plaza** at Ste Catherine and Atwater is much the same.

St Lawrence Seaway
This system of locks, canals and dams opened in 1959, enabling ocean-going vessels to sail 3200 km inland via the Great Lakes. Across Victoria Bridge from the city is an observation tower over the first locks of the system, the St Lambert Locks, where ships are raised 15 metres. Explanatory displays show how it works. Open from April to December, 9 am to 9.30 pm; free. In January, February and March the locks are closed – they're frozen like the river itself, until the spring thaw.

Dow Planetarium
This is at 1000 St Jacques Ouest (tel 872-4530), near Windsor Station. It offers laser shows as well as regular star and solar system programmes; the shows are usually good and interesting. Entry costs $3, laser shows $5.

Canadian Railway Museum
This museum (tel 632-2410) is at 122A St Pierre in St Constant, a district on the south shore near Chateauguay. The museum, with Canada's largest collection, has examples of early locomotives, steam engines and passenger cars. Admission is $3 and it's open from May to early September. To get there, take Champlain Bridge from town to Route 15, then 137 at the Chateauguay cut-off to 209.

Lafontaine Park
This is a large city park which also has a children's zoo. It's off Sherbrooke Est between the street of the same name and Papineau, a few blocks east of St Denis.

Markets
Two fairly central markets are the Atwater Market, south on Atwater at the Lachine Canal and the Marche de Maisonneuve, between Rue Ontario and Letournea. They're open daily except Sunday; Saturdays are best.

Montreal Exchange
Another market to visit is the stock market, where tours are given for a nominal fee, daily during July and August. For details and times, ring 871-2424. The Exchange is on the 4th floor, 800 Victoria Square.

Jetboating
A couple of companies offer boat trips through the nearby Lachine Rapids. Lachine Rapids Tours (tel 284-9607) at 105 Commune Ouest, have 90-minute trips leaving from Old Montreal, costing $30. They also have trips using rubber rafts, which cost about $20. Another company running rubber raft trips is Voyageur Lachine (tel 637-3566).

Lachine
Out in Lachine, a suburban town west of

Montreal is a government historic park called The Fur Trade in Lachine (tel 283-6054). It's at 1255 Boulevard St Joseph, at 12th Avenue. The museum tells the story of the fur trade in Canada, which was so critical to the development of the country. By public transit, take the Metro to Lionel Groulx and then the No 191 bus west. Admission is free. Not very far from downtown or well known, it's been recommended by a reader.

Nearby on Boulevard St Joseph but down at 7th Avenue, free walking tours are given along the Lachine Canal, which was built to connect Montreal for trade purposes. Wednesday to Sunday only.

Caughnawaga (cog-na-wah-ga) Indian Reserve

South of Lachine over the bridge on to the south shore, this Iroquois reserve can be visited. There's a museum and fort as well as mission buildings from the ealy 1700s. Visits are free and can be made daily from 10 am to noon and from 1 to 5 pm. It's about 18 km from central Montreal.

Events

The Montreal Jazz Festival is held at the end of June or the beginning of July; the Montreal World Film Festival is held in mid to late August.

Places to Stay

Montreal, like Quebec, is very popular with tourists in summer, so rooms can be hard to find and cost slightly more than during the rest of the year.

Hostels The most permanent downtown *CYHA Hostel* is at 3541 Aylmer, with 108 beds. Members pay $9, non-members $12. It's open all year, 8 am to 2 am. Aylmer runs off Sherbrooke, just to the east of McGill University; get off at the McGill Metro stop.

There may be other summer hostels – ask at the Aylmer one.

The *YMCA* (tel 849-5331) is at 1450 Stanley. It's central too and huge, with 350 beds. Singles are $27 for men, $28.50 for women and $42 for couples (married only). The cheap cafeteria is open 7 am to 3 pm.

The *YWCA* (tel 866-9941), for women only, is at 1355 Boulevard Dorchester Ouest. Singles are $28 and up and doubles range from $42 to $49. There's a cafeteria and a pool.

McGill University, at the corner of Sherbrooke and University, opens its residences from 15 May to 15 August. The accommodation office is at 3935 University (tel 392-4224 or 392-4982). Singles are $25, or $19 for students. They have cafeterias, laundry rooms, etc. Some residences include breakfast but are more expensive.

Very central Concordia University, at 7141 Sherbrooke Ouest, is even cheaper. At *College Francais* (tel 495-2581), 185 Fairmont Ouest, dorms are just $6.50 and a double room is $25.50.

Lastly, the French *Universitaire de Montreal* (tel 343-5431), 2350 Edouard-Monpetit, offers rooms at $22 or $14 for students. Another to try is *College Jean de Brebeuf* at 5625 Decelles.

Tourist Homes & Small Hotels Most standard hotels in the city are costly. Tourist homes are the alternative and there is a good, central assortment of them. Nearly all are in older houses and buildings with 10 to 20 rooms. Quality ranges from the plain and functional to old-world-charm comfortable. Price is the best indicator but sometimes just a few dollars can make quite a difference. All are OK, though.

My first choice would be the St Denis-bus station area. There are quite a few places here and the location is convenient. *A l'Americain* (tel 849-0616), a small European-style hotel at 1042 St Denis, between the café district and Old Montreal, is good. They have 20 rooms at singles $25 to $45 and doubles $5 more. The rooms on the top floor are very reminiscent of French movie tryst scenes.

You'll find plain, cheaper rooms nearby and across the street at *J D Hotel*. Another is the *Maison de Touristes de la Couronne* at No 1029. A little nicer is *Hotel St Denis* at No 1254.

Further north up St Denis there's the *Castel St Denis* (tel 842-9719) at No 2099, up the hill, just south of Sherbrooke. It's close to the bus station and good value. Singles are $25 to $35, doubles $30 to $40.

East of St Denis is *Le Breton* (tel 524-7273), in an excellent location on a pleasant street. It's at 1609 St Hubert, beside the bus station. Singles cost $25 to $32, doubles $28 to $40; some rooms come with shower or bath, TV, etc. Further south, at 1001 St Hubert on the corner of Avenue Viger, is *Hotel Viger Centre Ville* (tel 845-6058). They have a wide variety of rooms from $15 for singles, $18 for doubles. Near Ste Catherine at No 1216 St Hubert is *Maison Kent*, with singles from $26 to $39, doubles $29 to $42. If you don't need your own bathroom, you'll save quite a bit.

West of St Denis there are a couple of places to stay on Rue Ontario. At No 305, *Maison de Tourist Villard* has good rooms with singles for $20, doubles $30. Next door is *Karukera Tourist Rooms*.

On Rue Sherbrooke Est at Hotel de Ville, between St Laurent and St Denis, are three tourist homes next door to each other, all in old houses. *Hotel Tourist Pierre* is at No 169, *Hotel Manoir Shangri La* is at No 157. The *Armor Tourist House* on the corner is a large place, lined with natural wood inside. It's friendly but busy. Rooms range from $22 singles, $25 doubles, up to $48 depending on size, private bath, etc. You'll find more or less the same prices as next door.

At 258 Sherbrooke Ouest, west of Rue Jeanne Mance, is the yellow-and-green *Maison Casa Bella* (tel 849-2777). Singles are $20 to $32, doubles $22 to $38. Central.

There are also places scattered about the downtown centre. Several can be found along Ste Catherine near St Laurent, where the men and painted ladies appear about 6 pm at night. They're *not* selling insurance (!) but the area is not really tough. *Villa de France* (tel 849-5043) at 57 Ste Catherine Est, is a well-kept, friendly place with a pair of antlers on the lobby wall. The woman at the desk speaks French and English. Without bath, singles/doubles cost $17/22; with bath, add $5. There is another fairly well-kept place at 17 Ste Catherine Ouest, with prices about the same.

At 9 Ste Catherine Ouest is the *Hebergement l'Abri du Voyageur*, which is nothing fancy. The rooms are simple but clean, and if you're really on a budget, they're quite OK. Rates are $20/30 for singles/doubles.

Going west, the *Ambrose* (tel 844-0342) at 3422 Rue Stanley, is nicer and in a better location but it costs more, of course, with singles $30 to $60, doubles $55 to $70. Compared to the sterile international hotels, it's still a bargain. They have 22 rooms. One street over at 1208 Rue Drummond is *The Vines*, which has nine rooms costing $21 for singles, $25 doubles. The rooms are simple, but it's very central.

Lastly, there are a couple on MacKay south of Dorchester. The *Aux Berges* at 1070 MacKay limits itself to serving male homosexual visitors. Nearby, *Chateau Paris* at No 1480 Overdale, in the small painted brick building, had a more traditional clientele, last time I checked. Both are on central but quiet streets and have rooms in the $25 to $35 range.

Bed & Breakfasts Another alternative to the high-priced hotels are the bed & breakfasts. These have caught on so much it's hard to keep up with all the various associations which organise the rentals. *Downtown Bed & Breakfast Network* is an agency run by Bob Finkelstein. He has checked over 50 private homes for quality, hospitality and uniqueness beyond minimum requirements. Hosts range from students to lawyers, the places from mansions with fireplaces in the bedrooms, to Victorian homes, to apartments filled with antiques. Rates are quite reasonable at $25 to $30 for singles, $35 to $45 doubles. For info and reservations, call 289-9749 or write to 3458 Laval Avenue, Montreal, H2X 3C8.

Montreal Bed & Breakfast (tel 738-9410) is a similar organisation but with some higher-priced homes which offer something special. There are half a dozen others; the Tourist Office will have a complete list. Prices are generally quite moderate.

Hotels & Efficiencies If you really like hotels, the *Europa* (tel 866-6492) at 1240 Drummond near Ste Catherine, will fill the bill at a price as reasonable as you're likely to find: single/doubles for $65 to $80.

The *Crescent Hotel* (tel 878-2711) at 1214 Crescent has rooms with complete cooking facilities for $75 a night for two. If you stay for six nights, you get the seventh free. All kitchen supplies are included, as are air-con and TV.

Others include: *Hotel Montreal Crescent* (tel 878-9797), 1366 Boulevard Dorchester, with prices from $70 to $90, and *Ramada Inn* (tel 256-9011) at 5500 Sherbrooke Est, $85 to $95.

Motels There are two main motel districts in Montreal, with others scattered. All motels charge less in the off-season (ie not in summer); the rates here are summer ones. The area closest to town is conveniently situated along Rue St Jacques. It's west of downtown, south and parallel to de Maisonneuve. Look around where Cavendish runs into St Jacques from Sherbrooke. This area is about 10 minutes' driving from the centre. Coming from the west, ie Dorval, Highways 2 and 20 flow into St Jacques.

The Colibri (tel 486-1167) at 6960 St Jacques charges $24/28 for singles/doubles. It's behind Harvey's hamburger place and is white with purple polka dots.

The Aubin (tel 484-5198), 6125 St Jacques, has singles for $30 to $32, doubles $35 to $40. It's small, with only 20 rooms.

The *Cavalier* at No 6951 charges $25 to $30 for singles, $33 to $40, doubles. Nearby *Motel Rapheal* (tel 485-3344), is good value at $42.50 for doubles, with swimming pool and restaurant.

The second district for motels is on Boulevard Tashereau on the south shore, across the river on the mainland. The street is also known as Highway 134 and stretches out of the city in both directions. Many of the motels are at the bridges – check at Jacques Cartier Bridge (Old Montreal) and Champlain Bridge in the west end. Victoria Bridge is between the two.

At 1277 Boulevard Tashereau is *La Parisienne* (tel 674-6291). Singles or doubles cost $55.

The *Falcon Motel* (tel 676-0215) is at 6225 Tashereau, with singles $38 to $47, doubles $40 to $47. Ask for the rooms with no extras.

The *Florence* at 5791 Boulevard Tashereau has 32 rooms at $37 to $55.

A couple of places on Sherbrooke are *Le Paysan* at 12400 Sherbrooke Est, $45 to $85, and *Le Marquis* at No 6720, similarly priced. Others in the area are more costly.

A good bargain is *Hotel Metro* (tel 381-2577) at 9925 Lajeunesse, where singles/doubles are $25/35, TVs and city maps included. From the Metropolitan East Highway take exit 73 St Hubert; go to Sauve; then you'll see Lajeunesse. Or get off at the Sauve Metro station.

Lastly, you may want to try *Auberge Chomedy Inn* (tel 681-9251) at 590 Boulevard Labelle – adult movies, water beds and mirrors on the ceiling. Reduced prices on – oh my God – Sundays.

Top End The following hotels are in the 'expensive' category.

Le Chateau Champlain (tel 878-9000), Place du Canada, $150 to $210.

Bonaventure Inn (tel 878-2332), Place Bonaventure, $200 to $275.

Ritz Carlton (tel 842-4212), 1228 Sherbrooke Ouest, $200 to $250. The penthouse suite here is the most expensive place to stay in Canada (and probably not too shabby either).

Camping There's not too much camping close to town here. It's best to check on Highway 134, on the south shore on the mainland (Boulevard Tashereau). The highway leads east-west from town and has some small lots for spending the night. They're mainly designed for trailers; farther out it's a bit better for tents. There are also some places (including a Kampground of America) as you come from the west, before you actually get on the island of Montreal. They're just off the highway around Dorion. The same goes for the Quebec City side.

Places to Eat

The French have long been responsible for Montreal's excellent restaurant reputation, which various immigrant groups have only added to over the years. There is no shortage of restaurants here, and you'll find good food in all price ranges. Many places have lunch specials – always the best bargains – and at dinner, a table d'hôte fixed price complete dinner.

In Montreal women used to be barred from all taverns, nowadays however, there are few men-only taverns left. Tavern-style places that admit men and women are called brasseries.

If you want to bring your own wine for a meal, you can get it in a *depanneur* (convenience store). In Quebec you can pick up a bottle of French wine, bottled in the province, for $5 to $6 at the liquor outlets, or from grocery stores where the price goes up about 50c.

Central *Ben's*, at the corner of de Maisonneuve and Metcalfe, is an institution. Montreal is known far and wide for its smoked meat and Ben's is known across the country. It's a very informal deli, full of office workers at lunch time. Sandwiches are served lean or fatty – you can ask for your preference – and they're $2.75 or $3-something with French fries, pickle and coffee.

Moulin a Café is one of many good standard places on Mountain and Crescent. This is at 2046 Mountain and is one of the cheaper spots. They have about 20 daily lunch specials, most $6.25 to $7.50. Dinner doesn't cost much more and the choice includes goulash, rice and vegetable dishes and several German items.

Aida's at 2020 Crescent at Maissonneuve has felafels and other cheap light meals.

The *Bar B Barn* at 1201 Guy is too small – it's usually packed with a line-up out front to boot – but they serve the best and biggest spare-ribs you've ever had. It's a comfortable, attractive place as well. The only other thing on the menu is chicken. Good value, $10 to $15. There's parking around the back.

On Ste Catherine Ouest at 1631 is *Chalet Lucerne*, a famous local barbecue chicken spot. A quarter chicken is $5.50, half $6.95 with extras.

Further east on Ste Catherine on the third floor of the complex next to Eaton's department store, is the *Magic Pan Creperie*, with crepes from $5.50 to $6.25.

The busy *Tramway* is in the centre of town at 1122 Ste-Catherine Ouest. It's basically a brasserie although spiffier, with standard meals and steaks.

The *Rymark Tavern*, around the corner and south of Peel toward Windsor Station, is an old gem that's been around a long time. They serve cheap beer with inexpensive, standard tavern fare; the speciality is ham boiled in beer with baked beans, and it makes a decent lunch. Check out the wood panelling. The tavern is popular with area office men.

O Blitz at 1189 Mountain is one of several good brasseries in the area. They're busy at noon because of the cheap beer and meals, $4.25.

For a splurge there is *Chez Pauze*, another old-time place (it began in 1862) with a good name. It's on the north side of Ste Catherine Ouest at 1657, toward the Forum at Atwater. Seafood is their specialty. Meals range from $10 to $20.

On Metcalfe up from Ste Catherine are two well-known, long-established steak houses – *Joe's* and *Curly Joe's*, with similar menus and prices. At *Curly Joe's*, good steak dinners range from $8 to $15; the meal includes a baked potato or French fries and an excellent all-you-can-eat salad bar. Salad bar only, $5. Good value.

Dunn's, at 892 Ste Catherine Ouest near Peel, is a deli open (and usually pretty busy) 24 hours a day. Good for a late night snack or early morning breakfast.

There are several Indian restaurants in this central area. At 1241 Guy is the *Woodland Indian Restaurant* with a very extensive vegetarian menu. Next door the *Pattaya* is a fancier place offering Thai food, and next to that, *The Curry House* has dinner for three for about $40 and some very interesting dishes available. There is also *Pique Assiete* at 2053 Ste Catherine Ouest, one of the city's oldest Indian restaurants. Dinner for two costs under $25. This was the first of the international Bombay Palace chain of Indian restaurants.

For lingering over a coffee, there are numerous cafés in the Crescent and Mountain area. There are a couple of Parisian-style ones on de Maisonneuve here. Less ostentatious is *Cafe Drummond* at 2005 Drummond.

For making up your own meal, try shopping around *Le Fauberg* at 1616 Ste Catherine Ouest. The basement of this new Parisienne-style mall is devoted to food and is a sort of market, which includes a bakery and liquor store.

Old Montreal is a fine place to splurge. Menus with prices are posted outside. For good French seafood, try *Auberge la Belle Poule*, at the corner of St Paul and St Sulpice, with dishes at $14 to $17. The Dover sole is good with lobster soup and *escargot* from the Prix Fixe menu. If you need help with the French menu, the waiters will explain. The only drawback is the price of the wine. Also good is *La Sauvagine* at 115 St Paul on the corner of St Vincent. Lunch prices range from $5 to $8, dinners $13 to $18. Both restaurants are comfortable and friendly.

Another fine but more expensive place is *Les Filles du Roy* at 415 Rue Bonsecours. The dining room here is softly lit by a skylight until dark. They serve French food and offer a bountiful lunch buffet for $14.50.

There are inexpensive places here, too. *A la Bonne Bouffe* at 250 St Paul, corner of Place Jacques Cartier, is a real bargain. Lunches run from $3.50, everything included. The food is good and this is a dining room, not a greasy spoon. At 273 St Paul Est is *L'Usine de Spaghetti Parisienne* with meals at $6 to $10, including all the bread and salad you can eat.

On the east side of St Francois Xavier at No 447 is a small student-type Tunisian place specialising in North African meals, including various couscous and lamb dishes. Prices range from $3.50 to $6.50. This is a pleasant café mostly frequented by young people. Bring your own wine.

The very informal *Brasserie Lambert Closse*, on Rue St Vincent near Rue Therese, is also cheap. It's not far from Notre Dame and the Tourist Office – around the back, down the alley. Tables are available outside in summer. They serve various lunch specials at $3.75 to $5, also cheap mugs of beer. Dinners are similar. A brasserie for very cheap breakfasts and lunches is at the corner of St Paul and St Laurent.

Chez Delmo, 211 Notre Dame Ouest, is slightly away from the heavily touristed area and relies on locals for business. It's very busy at lunch serving its inexpensive seafood specialties; the daily specials are cheapest. They're open for lunch until 3 pm, then later for dinner. Lunches run to about $7 to $8 and are served at the long counters on both walls – a strange set-up. Dinners are $13 to $16 for a main dish. Recommended in *Where to Eat in Canada*. Closed weekends.

There are lots of cafés set up around Place Jacques Cartier, with outside tables in summer. They're great for sipping a coffee, resting the feet or contemplating life's mysteries. The *Restaurant des Gouverneurs* is cheapest although they all charge more for the outdoor tables. The small café at 143 St Paul Ouest, away from the crowds, is reasonable with light lunches for $4. They serve croissants and espresso, too.

Prince Arthur & Area Prince Arthur is a small street recently turned into a very pleasant eating area. The restaurant area of Prince Arthur runs west from Place St Louis on St Denis (just north of Sherbrooke) to a block west of St Laurent. Many small, mostly ethnic restaurants line the 'pedestrians only' street. Greek and Vietnamese restaurants are most prominent but there are French and Polish among others. Most of the restaurants here have a 'bring your own wine' policy. For Vietnamese food, try *Xuan* at 26 Prince Arthur Ouest. Meals range from $6 to $11 and they serve very good food.

An excellent Greek dinner can be had at *La Casa Greque* at 200 Prince Arthur, for about $20 for two. Very good value. I've also had a good lunch at *La Cabane*, another Greek place. Brochettes – more or less shish-kebab – are a hot item in the city with many eateries offering them, as you've probably noticed.

The *Croissanterie* on the east side of St Denis, downstairs just south of Ontario, is a great place for breakfasts. *Café au lait* and one or two of the fresh sweet buns or croissants will hold you for a few hours.

On Ontario just west of St Denis, in the 300 block, there are several cheap cafés for light meals, mostly patronised by students and arty types. *Le Petit Peu* serves vegetarian dishes and health foods.

Le Calife at 1633 St Hubert is a small, unpretentious place with offerings like vegetables with couscous and mint tea or coffee for $3.50. You can select other Tunisian meals as well.

The Main & Avenue Duluth St Laurent, the major north-south street which divides the city streets east from west has long had a reputation for its characters, varied ethnic groups, their businesses and restaurants. It's affectionately known as The Main.

Just south of Ste Catherine are several of the city's best known French fries/hot dog palaces. Memorably good. The dogs are known as 'steamies' for the way they're cooked. If you ask for 'all dress', everyone will understand and you'll get the full Quebec treatment, complete with chopped cabbage.

Just north of de Maisonneuve at 1600 St Laurent, is the very cheap *Restaurant Shaheen* for Pakistani curries. Much further north is a must: *Schwartz's* at No 3895. It's a small, very casual, friendly deli that's practically never closed, is always packed and has absolutely the best smoked meat in town. They make it right on the premises and age it naturally without chemicals.

Duluth runs east-west off St Laurent at about the 4000 block. Much like Prince Arthur it's a narrow old street, once a red light district, that has been redone as a restaurant centre. From just east of St Laurent, running east to St Denis and beyond, there are numerous Greek, Italian and Vietnamese eateries. Near St Laurent at 65 Duluth Est, *Le Camelia* is a moderately-priced Vietnamese place. At No 450 try *La Maison Greque*, which is very busy but large, with an outdoor area for good value brochette dinners. There's a *depanneur* (convenience store) nearby to grab a bottle of wine. Further east near St Hubert, there are a couple of more expensive French restaurants.

Chinatown in Montreal is small but well entrenched. Though its restaurants can't compare to those in Toronto's or Vancouver's Chinatowns, there are quite a few. As always, it's best to go with three or more people so you can sample more dishes. The district is centred on Lagauchetiere Ouest between St Urbain and St Laurent, east of Dominion Square, north of Old Montreal. The food is mainly Cantonese; many places offer lunch specials from $5.

The *Jasmine Café* at 62 Lagauchetiere is open every day. The full-course meals are a very good deal, averaging $5. Bring your own wine. The *Restaurant Hunan* at 1092 St Laurent, is more expensive but has some spicy Sichuan dishes.

On St Laurent, the *Cristal de Saigon* has very cheap but plain Vietnamese food, and the *Fung Lam* is the same but has Cantonese. *Lung Fung* at 81 Lagauchetiere is a bigger, more modern place said to have excellent spring rolls.

Avenue Parc Avenue Parc, running north up beyond the mountain has numerous Greek restaurants.

Things to Buy

At *La Vieille Erabliere*, 401 St Vincent in Old Montreal, you can taste pure maple syrup, a Quebec specialty. The province produces about two-thirds of the world's output and the centre explains how it is made and lets you sample and buy some. It comes as syrup, sugar or candy – good stuff, great on ice cream. The centre may have moved recently, so check at the Tourist Office. Many grocery stores stock maple syrup too, if you want to buy some for a present.

The Canadian Guild of Crafts at 2025 Peel has a small and rather expensive collection of the work of Quebec artisans and other Canadiana, as well as Eskimo prints and carvings. Free to look.

Nightlife

Montreal nightlife is good, varied and comes in two languages. Clubs serve alcohol until 3 am: that's civilisation. Many don't get going until around 10 pm or later. Films, plays and shows are not censored here as in more puerile places, eg Ontario.

Live Music & Disco *The Rising Sun*, (tel 861-0657) at 286 Ste Catherine Ouest, brings in established blues, jazz and reggae acts – good but admission can be hefty.

The Moustache, at 1445 Closse downtown, is a very popular, head-bangin' rock 'n' roll place; cheap.

The Limelight is on Stanley in the busy nightclub area just off Ste Catherine. It's a giant disco with a light-and-sound extravaganza. The busy Limelight is constantly changing, but seems to draw all sexual persuasions. Admission is $4.

Crescent and Mountain Sts are lively at night, with mostly disco-type places (no jeans allowed). *L'Esprit* at 1234 Mountain below Ste Catherine, is in a former funeral parlour. They're slightly dressy, and admission is $5 on weekends. *Thursdays* on Crescent is a singles-style spot. Nearby there are several pubs over on Bishop . It's fun just to wander around this area at night, maybe have a beer and people-watch.

The *Metropolis* at 59 Ste Catherine Est is the largest dance club in town, with bars spread over three floors and impressive sound and lighting systems. Open Thursday to Sunday.

The *Old Munich* is in the large, square building on St Denis at the corner of Dorchester. Inside it's a vast, cavernous, pub-like place that's often full of people of all sorts and ages. The place has a real party atmosphere. In the centre, amidst the smoke and noise, a band encourages a break from drinking with a dance to

German Oktoberfest-type music. No cover charge.

The Yellow Door Coffee House (tel 392-6743) at 3625 Aylmer is a survivor of the '60s, where American draft dodgers found refuge. It still presents folk music in a casual ambience.

Le Blue Note, at 40 St Paul in Old Montreal, has blues, big band and soul music, with dancing as well. Admission is a few dollars. Nearby at 104 St Paul, *Aux Deux Pierrots* is a huge, two-storey spot with local French singers and a casual atmosphere; free.

The *St Vincent* is at the corner of St Vincent and St Paul in Old Montreal. This is a large, inexpensive French-style pub offering good entertainment. Highly recommended on Friday or Saturday night for a real hootenanny.

New wave music can be heard at *Les Foufounes*, 97 Ste Catherine Est. Cheap.

There are several good spots for jazz in town. *L'Air du Temps* (tel 842-2002) is in Old Montreal at 191 St Paul Ouest at the corner of Francois Xavier. They have nice decor and atmosphere. Solo music starts at 5 pm, groups after 9.30 pm; performers are mostly local musicians. No cover charge.

At *Biddles* (tel 842-8656) at 2060 Aylmer, you might get a standard trio, a swing band or a vocalist. You can eat here, too; no cover charge. *The Grand Café* at 1720 St Denis presents live jazz at a modest price. Not far away on Ontario, local musicians play at *Café Theleme*, also no cover charge. Lastly, there is *La Boheme*, 3781 St Laurent, $2.50 admission.

Strip Clubs Montrealers enjoy clubs where people take their clothes off. There are plenty around. For men (although couples are seen), there is *Chez Parée*, a loud, no-holds-barred busy spot at 1258 Stanley. *Les Filles d'Eve*, 1192 Ste Catherine Ouest, 11 am to 3 am, is similar. These clubs are free to get in, but the beer is expensive. Tip the doorman for your choice of seat. Another place with a similar set-up is *L'Axe*, open seven days, at 1755 St Denis on the corner of Ontario. Men and couples occasionally dance here as well.

Women can find much the same thing in several places where men take it all off. One to try is *Club 281* at 281 Ste Catherine Est at the corner of Sanguinet.

Other For a view of the city, try the rooftop bar in the luxury *Chateau Champlain* on Dominion Square. Drinks are costly but the view is fine.

The *Bali Hi* in the Alexis Nehon Plaza, corner Ste Catherine Ouest and Atwater, serves bubbling, smoking, exotic cocktails in a simulated Pacific Island environment. Quiet.

The Comedy Nest at 1234 Bishop presents stand-up comics, usually several in a night. Admission is charged. For theatre, the *Centaur Theatre* (tel 288-3161) at 453 St Francois Xavier, generally has the best in English presentations. *Les Ballet Jazz*, a Montreal modern dance troupe, has a very good reputation and often performs in town. *Place des Arts* presents an array of concerts, the symphony, and dance.

Cinema There are several English repertory film theatres around town, usually offering double bills and midnight movies on weekends. These theatres are always cheaper than the chains showing first runs.

The *Seville* (tel 932-1139) is at 2155 Ste Catherine Ouest, one block east of the Atwater Metro stop. They charge $2.99 per movie – American and European.

Cinema V (tel 489-5559), 5560 Sherbrooke Ouest, is much the same. It's near the corner of Girouard (pronounced 'jeer ward').

The McGill and Loyola campuses often run film series.

Getting There & Away

Air There are two airports. Dorval, 20 km west of the centre of town, is used for domestic and North American flights. Mirabel Airport is just over 50 km northwest of the town's centre and handles all other international flights. Many airlines serve Montreal, including the major Canadian ones. Quebecair also serves the province of Quebec. A selection of fares includes:

Air Canada (tel 393-3333) to: Halifax ($177; $89 under 22, standby); Toronto ($144; $72 under 22); Winnipeg ($298; $149 under 22). Canadian Airlines (tel 931-2233) has the same prices as Air Canada. Quebecair (tel 636-3890) has flights to Toronto ($113; $61 youth).

Bus The terminal is at the corner of Boulevard de Maisonneuve and Rue Berri, near St Denis; it's very central. The nearest Metro stop is Berri de Montigny. The station serves Voyageur Lines (tel 842-2281) and Greyhound from the US, and also Vermont Transit, which runs between here and Boston, about seven hours away. Voyageur destinations include:

Ottawa: every hour – $15.50

Toronto: about five a day, more on weekends – $35.70

Quebec: $24.95.

Murray Hill (tel 937-5311) at 1380 Rue Barre, runs ski bus expresses in season. They make two runs into the Laurentians and two to Vermont spots. Most runs start at a major downtown hotel.

Train There are two train stations right near each other in the central area. You can walk underground from one to the other in 10 minutes.

The CN Station, below the Queen Elizabeth Hotel at the corner of Dorchester and Mansfield, gets most VIA Rail (tel 871-1331) passengers. Use the Bonaventure Metro station.

Windsor Station, the CP Terminal, is at Peel and Lagauchetiere, a few blocks from the CN. Use the same Metro stop. It's

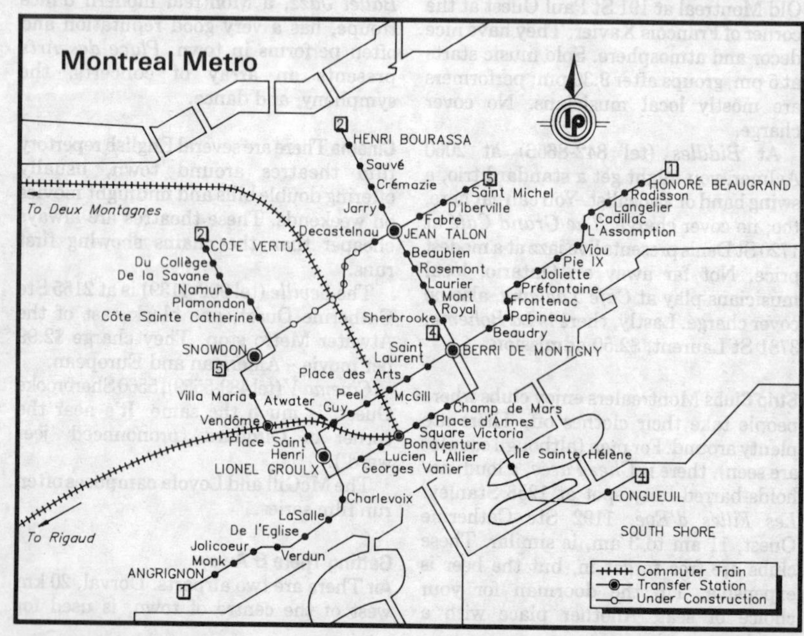

mainly local commuter trains which use this venerable old station now.

There are four or five trains a day to Ottawa, and five a day to Toronto, starting at 7.30 am.

Fares: Ottawa $19, Toronto $49, Quebec City $27.

For information on American destinations call Amtrak, 1-800-426-8725, at no charge. Amtrak to New York costs $63 one-way, with very cheap returns available.

Road The Trans-Canada Highway runs right through the city. Highway 15 leads south to US 87 for New York.

Highway 401 joins Montreal to Toronto and beyond.

Car Sharing Allo Stop (tel 282-0121) at 4319 Rue St Denis, is an agency that gets drivers and passengers together. Call a day ahead and tell them where you want to go. Prices are good – $12 to Quebec City, for example. They also go to Toronto, New York and other cities. You must pay a $2 membership fee.

Getting Around

Airport Transport The cheapest way to Dorval Airport is to take the Metro to Cremazie, then catch the No 100 bus west toward the airport and ask the driver to let you off for the No 209, which will take you right in. Total cost: $1.

There is also the Aerocar bus (tel 379-9999) to Dorval airport for $6, leaving every 20 minutes from the Queen Elizabeth Hotel. The Aerocar bus to Mirabel costs $9 and runs every 30 to 60 minutes.

Murray Hill (tel 937-5311) runs a limo service to either airport; they'll pick you up anywhere.

Bus & Metro There is a Metro (train subway) bus system. The Metro runs to 1.30 am and some buses run even later. One ticket can get you anywhere in the city as it entitles you to a transfer to any connecting bus or train. On the Metro, you get a transfer from the driver. A book of tickets is $5 for six or $1 each.

Metro routes are shown on the tourist map and stops are indicated above ground by large blue signs with a white arrow pointing down. The system runs basically east-west with a north-south line intersecting at Berri-de-Montigny. It runs on rubber tyres and is safe, clean, fast and quiet. For information, call 288-6287.

Car Rentals Renting is expensive in Montreal. Rent-A-Wreck (tel 871-1166) at 1444 Dorchester Ouest, charges $16.95 plus 10c per km, and $7.95 insurance.

Budget (tel 879-1414) on Metcalfe below Ste Catherine, charges $48 per day with 100 free km, 10c per km over that. Tax is extra.

Tilden (tel 878-2771) at 1200 Stanley has exactly the same rates as Budget.

Driving In town, most streets are one-way and the drivers are very aggressive. Watch the action at yellow lights. Pedestrians are fair game; pedestrian crossings mean little.

Bicycle Montreal is continuing to improve as a biking city. The city publishes a map of routes and trails which is available from city libraries, police stations and tourist offices. One route leads from the edge of Old Montreal, west all the way to Lachine along the old canal. Parks Canada (tel 283-6054) runs guided historical trips along this bike path.

At Parc des Iles-de-Boucherville, there are 22 km of trails, connected to the islands by bridges and ferries. The main entrance, on Ile Ste Margeurite, is served by city buses. Bikes can be rented at the park. A ferry connects Quai de Boucherville to l'Ile Grosbois from Thursdays to Sundays, 10 am to 4 pm for $1. Most of the country routes here offer views of the city.

Le Monde a Bicyclette is a cycling association which runs free trips through various parts of the city. They meet on Sunday mornings at a downtown location and start from there. Their office (tel 844-2713) is at 3700 Rue St Dominique.

For rentals, try Cycle Peel (tel 486-1148) at 6665 St Jacques Ouest.

Caleche The horse-drawn carriages seen mainly around Dominion Square, Old Montreal or on the mountain charge $20 to $25 an hour. Four or five people can ride at a time. In winter, sleighs are used for trips up and around Mount Royal.

Tours Gray Line (tel 280-5327) at 1241 Peel on Dominion Square, operates eight sightseeing tours. The basic city orientation tour takes 2½ hours and costs $12.25. You'll take in some of the sights and residential districts. The full-day trip is 7½ hours for $23.75. Other bus trips are to the Laurentians north of Montreal and a sunset tour.

The other major tour company is Murray Hill (tel 937-5311), 1380 Rue Barre, which also operates from all major downtown hotels. They have six tours, some in town, others around the outskirts. Like Gray Line, Murray is a reputable company with more or less the same prices.

There is a train tour to the coastal district Charlevoix, which makes a good day trip, travelling along the river as far as Pointe-au-Pic. For more details, see the Pointe-au-Pic section in this chapter.

Montrealistes Walking Tours (tel 744-3009), offers walking tours in the popular areas of town such as Chinatown and Old Montreal, and also some in other, less-visited, interesting areas of town. History, galleries, museums and cafés may be included. The cost is about $5; more with a meal.

Montreal Harbour Cruises Ltd (tel 842-3871) have boat tours from Victoria Pier at the foot of Berri in Old Montreal. The 1½-hour trips around the port are $9.50. Sunset trips are also available and are a couple of dollars less. They also offer disco-dancing trips taking three hours, with drinks available.

Around Montreal

OKA

This is a small town about 60 km north-west of Montreal, where the Ottawa River meets the St Lawrence. It's on the north mainland shore, north of Dorion on the edge of Lac des Deux Montagnes, a bulge in the river. The place is well known for the Trappist monastery, now 100 years old, and the cheeses it produces. The cheese-producing was taken over by business people, and the monastery of 70 monks has been opened to visitors. There are religious artworks, a mountain with the stages of the Cross and several old stone buildings.

ROUGE RIVER

Not far north-west of Montreal near the Ontario border, the Rouge River is well known for white-water rafting. Several companies offer day or weekend trips. One to try is New World River Expeditions, which has an office in Montreal. They have a lodge with pool and bar, so you're not roughing it in the bush the whole time.

THE LAURENTIANS

Between 80 and 150 km north of Montreal, this section of the ancient Laurentian Shield is a mountainous, rolling, lake-sprinkled playground. The land proved a dismal failure for lumber and mining, but when skiing caught on, so did this area as a resort-land. The district today is used not only for the best in eastern skiing but for camping, fishing and swimming in summer. The many picturesque French towns dominated by their church spires and the good scenery make it popular for just lazing and relaxing as well. Plentiful accommodation and restaurants provide a wide range of services, from elegant inns with fine dining rooms to modest motels.

The Laurentian Autoroute, also known as Highway 15 (with tolls), is the fastest route up from Montreal and the way the buses go. The old Highway 117 north is slower but more pleasant. A second major route goes north-east of Montreal to Joliette and then smaller roads continue further north.

The better-known towns and resorts are all clustered near the highways. Cottage country spreads out a little further east and west. In general terms the busy area ends at Mont Tremblant Provincial Park. The smaller villages on the upper areas of Highway 117 are quiet and typically 'Laurentian'.

To find less developed areas or to camp, you pretty much have to head for the big parks, as most of the region is privately owned. Many of the towns have Tourist Offices so you can ask about things as you go. Outside the parks, campgrounds are generally privately owned too, and tend to be small and busy. Motels are next up the economic scale; the lodges are generally (but not always) quite pricey. There is usually a hostel somewhere in the area, but locations change often, so ask in Montreal.

The busiest times in the Laurentians are July, August, around Christmas, February and March. At other times, prices tend to go down, as do the crowds. Autumn is a good time, the hills are very colourful and the cooler air is ideal for walking. The whole area – in all seasons – has a festive, relaxed atmosphere.

In ski season, special buses operate between Dorval Airport and various hills. They're a little more expensive than the usual bus; return tickets are cheapest.

Mont Gabriel

This is the first stop-off, a summer-winter recreation centre with very good skiing. One of the area's numerous water-slides is here, too. The *Auberge Mont Gabriel* atop the mountain is one of the larger, more expensive lodges in the Laurentians.

Ste Adele

Ste Adele is one of the nicer-looking of the highway towns, with a popular recreation area, Lac Rond.

At 151 Rue Lesage, there's a place to stay called *Pension Ste Agathe*. It's in an old house and has five rooms for rent (with breakfast included) at moderate rates; dinner is available.

Ste Agathe

With about 7000 people, this is the largest town in the Laurentians and a busy resort centre. With numerous bars, cafés and restaurants, as well as shops for replenishing supplies, there is always plenty of activity. The local bakery, on Rue Ste Agathe, is known far and wide.

At the edge of Lac des Sables, more or less in town, there is room for a picnic and cruises of the lake depart from the wharf. Around the lake are beaches and places to camp.

Bed & breakfasts, inns (auberges) and motels all tend to be quite busy, especially on weekends, so planning ahead is advisable. At the end of July, watch for the annual music and dance festival.

St Jovite

This smaller town further north is by Mont Tremblant, which lies just outside the park of the same name. The mountain, at 960 metres, is the highest peak in the Laurentians. With over 20 runs, it's the most popular skiing spot, and marks the northernmost point of the easily accessible Laurentian destinations. St Jovite is the supply centre for the Tremblant area with its many surrounding lakes.

At the foot of the mountain, 146 km from Montreal, is Mont Tremblant Village, an accommodation centre which has a chair lift to the peak in summer and winter.

In Weir, not far south of St Jovite, is the Laurentides Satellite Earth Station, an international telecommunications installation. Free guided tours of the facilities and 10-storey-high antennae are available, as well as slide presentations. It's open daily from mid-June to Labour Day. Follow the signs from Weir.

St Donat

North-east of Ste Agathe, this little lakeside town is the supply centre for the main entrance to Mont Tremblant Provincial Park which lies just to the north.

There are beaches on Lac Archambeault and 90-minute cruises around the lake offered throughout the summer.

Accommodation of all types can be found in and around town. Bars and cafés along the main streets are lively at night.

Mont Tremblant Provincial Park

Opened as early as 1894, this is a huge area – over 1500 square km – of lakes, rivers, hills and woods. There are many campsites in the park – some with amenities but most very simple and basic. The most developed area is north of St Donat. Roads are paved, canoes can be rented, and the campgrounds have showers, etc. Not too far from the entrance there are a couple of good walking paths with views and a little further in, a fair-sized waterfall with picnic tables.

Towards the interior, some campsites are accessible only by foot, canoe or unsurfaced roads, some of them rough old logging routes. The more off-the-track areas abound in wildlife. In the far eastern section one September, we had whole lakes to ourselves, saw moose and heard nearby wolves howling as we sat around the fire. Nights were very cold so be prepared.

Lanaudiere

This refers to the region north-east of Montreal and though it is essentially still 'up north' or 'the Laurentians', it has cultivated its own identity.

Joliette is a principal town and centre of the local tobacco-growing industry. You may notice that in some areas, the farmland is divided into long strips. These are known as 'rangs' and were a traditional way of divvying up the land not seen outside the province.

There is also a lot of maple syrup production in the area. In spring, many farmers allow visitors to the 'sugar shacks' for a look-see and a taste. Or you can see how it's done all year at Chez Madelaine in Mascouche, where they provide information and sell various maple goodies. I don't want to rush you, but it's said that acid rain could well wipe out this traditional industry.

Rawdon, the other main town, has Moore Canadiana Village, a re-created 1800s town, complete with workers in costume. Most of the buildings are authentic. The schoolhouse, for example, is from 1835.

There are numerous lakes in the region, many with inns, resorts or campgrounds.

THE EASTERN TOWNSHIPS (Les Cantons de L'Est)

The 'Garden of Quebec', generally known as 'Estrie' by the French and extending from Granby to the New Hampshire border, is appreciated for its rolling hills, green farmland, woods and lakes. It's a very popular resort area, with fishing and swimming in the numerous lakes in summer and excellent skiing in winter. The area abounds in cottages, chalets and inns, both private and commercial. The region also has a reputation for its many fine but expensive dining rooms.

In spring, 'sugaring off' – the tapping of trees for maple syrup, and then the boiling and preparation of it – takes place throughout the region. In autumn, a good time to visit, colours are beautiful as the leaves change, and apple harvesting takes place with the attendant cider production.

The townships have a long history and, as evidenced by the place names, were until quite recently predominantly English.

Granby

This town is known far and wide for its zoo, even though it's not particularly good. I swear everybody in Quebec knows of it, if in fact they haven't been there at one time or another. It seems it has been there forever. The insectarium contains 100,000 little creatures.

Granby is also well endowed with highly respected restaurants and hosts a gastronomical festival every autumn.

Sherbrooke

Sherbrooke is the principal commercial centre of the region and a fair-sized city in its own right. It's a bilingual town with several small museums, a wide selection of restaurants including *Au Petit Sabot* and *l'Elite* – two well-established four star eateries – and a pleasant centre lying between the Magog and St Francois Rivers. The Sherbrooke Visitors & Convention Bureau (tel 562-4744) is at 220 Rue Marchant.

On the outskirts are Bishops University, and the Shrine of Beauvoir, dating from 1920, a site of religious pilgrimages with good views over the city and area.

Places to Stay The *Youth Hostel* (tel 567-9717) is at 154 Boulevard Queen North; they charge $8. In summer, rooms are also available at low rates at the university.

There are other places to stay in and around town, including the *Sherbrooke Bed & Breakfast Association* (tel 565-7780) at 1464 Vermont St, with singles/doubles for $20/25.

Getting There & Away There's a VIA Rail station in town and frequent bus services to Montreal.

South of town, Highway 55 leads to Rock Island, a small town which is the major entry point into the USA, close to the states of New York, Vermont and New Hampshire.

Magog

This is an attractive town of 15,000 sitting right at the northern tip of large Lake Memphremagog. The main street, Principale, has a resort flavour with its numerous cafeś, bars, bistros and restaurants.

On this same street but just west of town, the Tourist Office can help with information about the area. Daily boat cruises are offered around the lake in summer, lasting a little over two hours.

There are several places to stay in and around town. Right in the centre of things is *Hotel Union* with very low rates; others, including motels, are rather pricey.

Lake Memphremagog

This is the largest and best-known lake in the Eastern Townships. Most of the lakefront properties are privately owned.

Halfway down the lake at St Benoit-du-Lac is a Benedictine monastery where monks continue the tradition of singing the ancient Gregorian chant. Visitors can attend services and there's a hostel for men and one for women if you want to stay. One of Quebec's cheeses – l'Ermite, a blue – is made and sold here.

Rock Island, the busy border crossing to the USA, is at the southern end of the lake and contains four of the Townships' best French restaurants.

Mont Orford Provincial Park

Just out of Magog, this is a good but relatively small park (though the largest in the Townships). Dominated by Mont Orford at 792 metres, the park is a skiing centre in winter but fills up quickly with campers in summer as well. You can swim here, use the walking trails, and the chair lift operates through the summer.

Each summer, the Orford Art Centre presents the *Jeunesses Musicales du Canada* music and art festival.

Knowlton

Nearby, south of Highway 10 on 243, is Knowlton which is on Lac Brome, with a good history museum which includes a tearoom. A favourite meal in this area is Brome Lake Duck.

Sutton Junction

Near this village on Rural Route 4 sits the farm of Madame Benoit, Canada's best-known cook. For many years she has appeared on national television and she's authored a couple of dozen cookbooks. Well, this is home – a 125-year-old farmhouse. You can't get a meal but a shop sells the books and various sheepskin products that are made locally. The property is indicated simply with a mailbox marked 'Bernard Benoit'.

Sutton

Further south, Sutton is synonymous with its important ski hill, one of the area's highest.

Lake Champlain

Although essentially an American lake which divides Vermont from New York, it does protrude up into Quebec as well. Steeped in history, the area is now very popular with Canadians and Americans as a summer vacation and cottage spot. The lake is good for swimming and fishing and in places is very scenic. At Plattsburgh, New York there is a very good and very busy beach, where any weekend you'll find plenty of Quebeckers.

MONTREAL TO QUEBEC CITY

Along the river, on Highway 138 east of Montreal, you begin to get a sense of small-town Quebec. Stone houses with light blue trim and tin roofs, silver-spired churches, ubiquitous chip wagons called *cantines* and main streets with shops built right to the road, are some characteristics. The best section is from Trois Rivieres onwards.

A much quicker route is the recently completed Highway 40, a four-lane expressway that can get you from Montreal to Quebec City in 2½ to three hours. There are not too many services along this route, so watch your gas levels.

There is also one fast and one slow route along the south shore to Quebec and beyond. The old Highway 132 edges along the river but isn't as nice as its north side counterpart (Highway 138), and the No 20 – the Trans-Canada Highway – is fast but boring until at least Quebec City, where it's a little closer to the water. At Trois Rivieres the river can be traversed.

Saint-Antoine-de-Padoue Church is on the north side of the river in Louiseville. It would be hard to miss, but take a peek inside, too; it's one of Canada's grandest churches and is very impressive. Next door is a helpful tourist booth.

La Domaine Joly de Lotbiniere is a stately museum on the south shore of the St Lawrence, between Lotbiniere and Ste

Croix. It was built for Henri Gustave Joly de Lotbiniere (1849-1908), once the prime minister of Quebec. Not only is this one of the most impressive manors built during the seigneurial period of Quebec, it remains nearly as it was in the mid-1800s. It's now a government-operated museum containing period furniture and furnishings, and the grounds and outbuildings are a treat in themselves. Lunch and teas are served.

Trois Rivieres

Trois Rivieres, 350 years old, is the largest town between Quebec's two main cities. The old town, with its reminders of a long history, is small but good for a stroll. Just north of town is the **Saint Maurice Ironworks National Park**, which was the first major iron-ore operation in North America. Along with several motels, there is a youth hostel here: *La Flotille* (tel 378-8010) at 497 Rue Radisson. Rooms are $7 to $8.

Beyond the city, the road becomes very hilly with gradients of up to 17%. There's lots of camping along the way as well as stands offering fruit, cider and wood sculpture – an old Quebec folk art. The old-style double wooden swings on many a front lawn are popular in Quebec but rarely seen in the rest of Canada.

Grand Mere & Shawinigan

These medium-sized towns on the St Maurice River are rather grim, with little to hold the visitor. Both are industrial; pulp & paper has long been the backbone of the area. At Shawinigan, there is also a large hydroelectric power station that can be visited. If you're heading for any of the northerly parks, stock up here because the food and supply selection doesn't get any better further north.

Between here and La Mauricie National Park, there isn't much in the way of accommodation, so you're pretty much stuck with one of the few ordinary motels in Grand Mere or Shawinigan. The small town of Ste Flore, however, between Shawinigan North and the entrance to the National Park, has four restaurants of note, all on its main street. One has crepes, two seafood and steak, and the most expensive serves French.

La Mauricie National Park

North from Trois Rivieres, up past Shawinigan and Grand-Mere, this is the only national park among the many very large provincial wilderness parks north of the St Lawrence River.

The park consists of 550 square kms, straddling northern evergreen forests and the more southerly hardwoods of the St Lawrence River Valley. The low, rounded Laurentian Mountains, probably the world's oldest, are part of the Canadian Shield that covers much of the province. Between these hills are many small lakes and valleys. Within the park, mammals include moose, fox, bear and beaver. There's also fishing for trout and bass.

The park is excellent for canoeing. There are maps of five canoe routes, ranging in length from 14 to 84 km, for beginners to experts. Canoes can be rented for about $10 a day at Lake Wapizagonke, itself very scenic with sandy beaches, steep rocky cliffs and waterfalls.

Hiking trails, guided nature walks and an interpretive centre are offered. Some of the trails go along or offer views of the St Maurice River, which is one of the last rivers in the province where logging companies still float down their timber to the mills. Along the edges you can see the strays that get collected periodically.

There are serviced campgrounds available, at $6 a night, with free firewood.

Interior camping is free but you do need to pre-plan your route and register. On holiday weekends in summer, calling ahead to check on availability is a good idea; phone (819) 532-2414. No fires are permitted so take a stove. Supplies are available in Grand-Mere, but the selection is minimal; it's better to bring most stuff with you.

The park is 220 km north-east of Montreal. There is no longer a bus from Montreal up here nor even to Shawinigan, so driving is the only transport.

Two adjacent provincial parks also offer wilderness camping; one is to the north, one to the west, but road access is more difficult.

English is at a premium up here, so be prepared to communicate in French.

Quebec City

Quebec City, rich in history, culture and beauty, is the heart of French Canada. If you're anywhere in the eastern part of the country, make the effort to visit.

The town is unique in several ways, most noticeably in its European appearance and atmosphere. It has the charm of an Old World city. Montreal has this feel to some degree, as does the French Quarter in New Orleans, but nowhere in North America is the picture as complete. The entire old section of town, essentially a living museum, has been designated by UNESCO as a World Heritage Site.

As the seat of the Provincial Parliament Buildings and Laval University, this is the centre of Quebecois consciousness, in both its moderate and extreme manifestations. Quebec City has been the centre of French nationalist thought for hundreds of years and many of today's intellectuals and politicians still speak of independence.

Although many people are bilingual and there is a small English minority, the overwhelming majority are French-speaking and 94% have French ancestors. But this is a tourist town, ranking with Banff and Victoria among the country's most visited, so English is spoken around the attractions and in shops. However, if you can, speak the language: this will make you more friends. It will also enable you to feel more comfortable away from the busiest areas. Quebec is a year-round tourist centre, though July and August get very crowded.

Quebec is also an important port, lying where the St Charles River meets the St Lawrence. It sits on top of and around a cliff, an excellent setting with views over the St Lawrence River and the town of Levis (pronounced not as in jeans but 'lev-ee') across the river.

Much of Quebec's past is still visible – the many churches, old stone houses and narrow streets make it an architectural gem, and the old port of Quebec remains the only walled city in North America.

The climate in Quebec must be mentioned as this is a city with both summer and winter attractions. Summers are much like those of Montreal or southern Ontario, though generally not as hot and always a bit shorter. The real difference is in winter; then it gets cold, and I mean cold. There can also be mountains of snow; if you're going in winter, especially January and February, you can't take enough sweaters. Life does go on; the locals don't hibernate. If you're prepared, this time of the year has its benefits.

History

One of the continent's earliest settlements, the site of Quebec City was an Iroquois Indian village called 'Stadacone' when the French explorer Jacques Cartier landed here in 1534. The name 'Quebec' is derived from an Algonkian Indian word meaning 'the river narrows here.' Explorer Samuel de Champlain founded the city for the French in 1608 and built a fort in 1620. The English successfully attacked in 1629, but Quebec was returned to the French by a treaty and became the centre of New France. Repeated English attacks followed. In 1759, General Wolfe led the English to victory over Montcalm on the Plains of Abraham. This is one of North America's most famous historical battles and virtually ended the conflict. In 1763 the Treaty of Paris gave Canada to Britain. Despite this, in 1775, the

Samuel de Champlain

Americans had a go at capturing Quebec. They were handily turned back.

In 1791, the divisions of Upper Canada (Ontario) and Lower Canada (Quebec and the Maritime provinces) were created, with Quebec City as capital. In the 1800s Lower Canada became known as Quebec and Quebec City was chosen as provincial capital.

Orientation

Because part of the city sits atop the cliffs on Cap Diamant (Cape Diamond), it is divided into Upper Town and Lower Town. The Citadel, a famous landmark, stands on the highest point of Cap Diamant overlooking the city. Upper Town lies north of the Citadel on top of the plain. Lower Town lies mainly between the rivers and Cap Diamant by the Quebec Harbour.

The best and maybe only way to orient yourself in Quebec is to walk around. The city is surprisingly small, with nearly all things of interest to a visitor packed into one area. The city is 93 square km, but the Old City is just 10 square km, and it's here you'll want to be. If you're using the Tourist Office map, you'll soon see how large the scale is after you easily reach or pass by what you're looking for.

Lower Town is mainly the business and industrial area, lying mostly to the north-east of Upper Town. There is a small part of Lower Town in the Old City, between the river, harbour and the cliffs of Cap Diamant. There are some very old streets here such as Rue Sous Le Cap and Rue Champlain, which are only 2½ metres across. The focal point of this small area, at the south-eastern edge of Old Quebec, is Place Royale. It's in this area that most things of interest in Lower Town are found. From here, you can walk (it's not hard, nor far) or take the funicular railway (elevator) for 65c one-way to the top of the cliff or Upper Town. The funicular in Place Royale is on Petit Champlain. The ferry across the river to Levis docks here in Lower Town.

The south-western end of the upper city is still surrounded by a wall. This area, called the Old City, is where just about everything to do and see is located. Outside the wall are some things of note, including the Parliament Buildings and some restaurants. The two main streets heading west are Boulevard St Cyrille and, to the south, Grand Allee, which further west becomes Chemin St Louis and eventually Boulevard Wilfrid Laurier.

To the extreme west of the city you'll see signs for either Pont (bridge) de Quebec or Pont Pierre Laporte. These both lead to the south shore.

North of Boulevard St Cyrille is mainly residential. Then you'll encounter the cliff again; this time its northern edge. Beneath it, the section of Lower Town is of little interest and is residential or industrial. This is also true of the eastern parts of Lower Town.

Much further north in the Lower Town are the highways leading east and west. It is in this section that some of the motels are found.

Back in the old, walled section of Upper Town, the streets are pretty haphazard. Rue St Jean is a main street with many

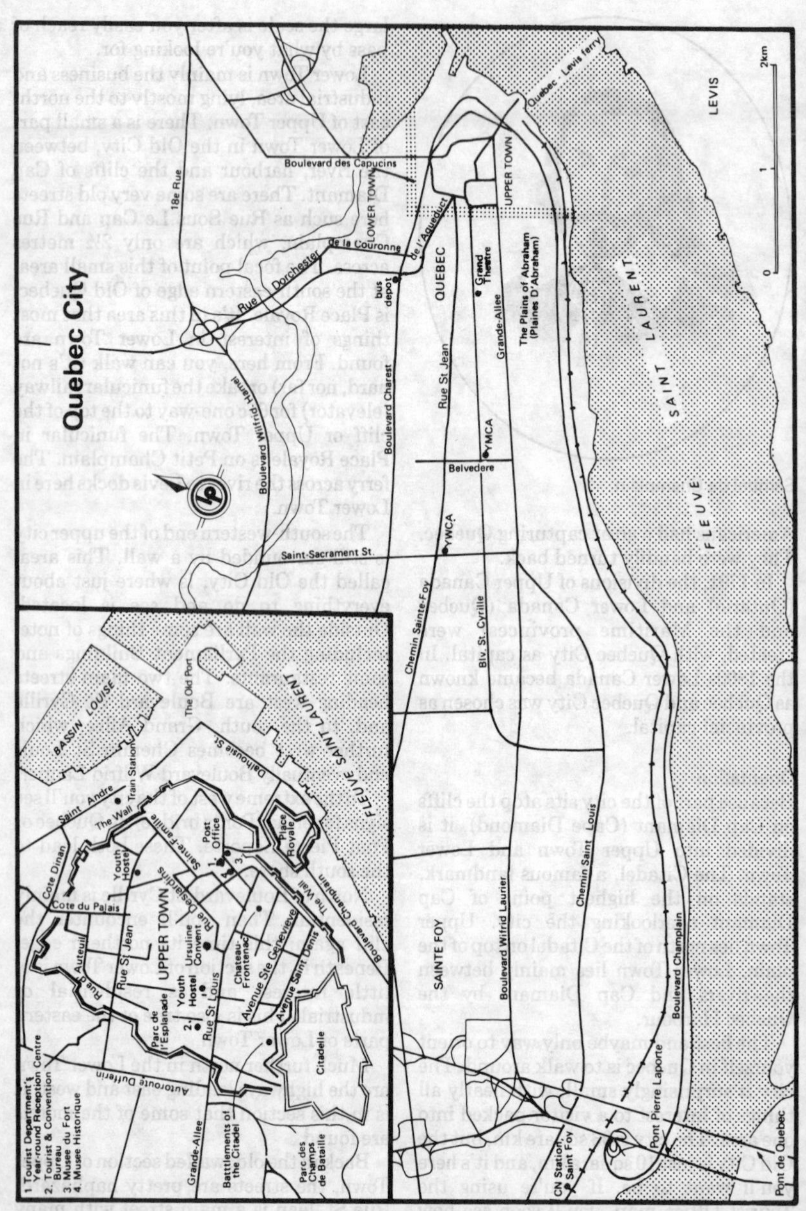
Quebec City
1 Tourist Department's Year-round Reception Centre
2. Tourist & Convention Bureau du Fort
3 Musee du Fort
4 Musee Historique
UPPER TOWN
Youth Hostel
Ursuline Convent
Chateau Frontenac
Citadelle
Parc de l'Esplanade
Post Office
Place Royale
Train Station
The Wall
BASSIN LOUISE
The Old Port
FLEUVE SAINT LAURENT
Rue St Jean
Rue St Louis
Rue d'Auteuil
Cote du Palais
Cote Dinan
Saint Andre
Sainte-Famille
Rue des Jardins
Avenue Ste Genevieve
Avenue Saint Denis
Boulevard Champlain
Dalhousie St
Autoroute Dufferin
Grande-Allee
Battlements of the Citadel
Parc des Champs de Bataille
Saint-Sacrament St.
Boulevard Wilfrid Hamel
Boulevard Charest
Rue Dorchester
de la Couronne
de l'Aqueduct
18e Rue
Boulevard des Capucins
LOWER TOWN
bus depot
QUEBEC
Grand Theatre
Rue St Jean
Chemin Sainte-Foy
YMCA
YWCA
Belvedere
Blv St. Cyrille
Grande-Allee
The Plains of Abraham (Plaines D'Abraham)
UPPER TOWN
Quebec - Levis ferry
Boulevard Wilfrid Laurier
Chemin Saint Louis
Boulevard Champlain
SAINTE FOY
CN Station Saint Foy
Pont Pierre Laporte
Pont de Quebec
FLEUVE SAINT LAURENT
LEVIS
0 1 2km

bars and restaurants. Running south from it, Cote de la Fabrique is another main street. Further south, running into Fabrique, is Rue Buade, another of the central streets. At the bottom of Buade and a little to the east is the post office, in a huge old stone building. Across from it, toward the water, is a nice little park with good views: Parc Montmorency.

A well-known landmark in Old Quebec is the copper-topped, castle-like Chateau Frontenac Hotel from 1892, which lends an old-world air. Behind the Chateau, a large boardwalk edges along the cliff with good views over the river. The boardwalk leads to the Promenade des Gouverneurs, a path which runs between the cliff's edge and the Citadel. Beyond the Citadel, outside the walls, is the huge park called Parc des Champs de Bataille. This is where the battles over Quebec took place. The park has several historical monuments and some sites within its boundaries.

Views The views are good from the boardwalk behind the Chateau Frontenac, called the Terrace Dufferin. There are always people strolling and often musicians and other street entertainers doing their numbers. At one end is the wooden slide used during the winter carnival.

For a look from higher up, go to the government building called Edifice 'G' at 675 St Cyrille Est. The observation deck on the 31st floor is open 9 am to 4 pm Monday to Friday, from March to October. Alternatives are the top floor of the Hilton where the disco is, or the restaurant at the top of Loews Le Concorde Hotel, 1225 Place Montcalm off Chemin St Louis, outside the wall.

Information

There are several Tourist Offices where the staff are bilingual and well supplied with maps and other information. Usually they will help out with off-beat questions and will even make telephone calls for you. Most of the workers are friendly, considering the crowds they get at peak times.

One office is at 60 Rue d'Auteuil, just north of Grand Allee. It's in the Parc de l'Esplanade, near the Porte St Louis.

A second one is on Place d'Armes, to the east side of the Chateau Frontenac Hotel. This one (tel 643-2280) deals with destinations anywhere in the province.

Another Tourist Office is on Place Royale, beneath the funicular in Lower Town. It's off Royal Square itself, which has a statue of Champlain in the centre.

There is a post office in the walled section of Upper Town, at the bottom of Buade, opposite Montgomery Park; another one is in St Paul near the corner of des Bains.

Things to See

Nearly every second building in Old Quebec is of some interest; to list all the sites in this area would fill a book. For a more complete guide, ask at the Tourist Office for the walking tour booklet. Following are some of the most significant sites in the old section as well as some outside the walls.

Watch for a symbol in the shape of a key on buildings and businesses around town. It indicates something of historical note is on display. The Tourist Office has a guide to the 'key' locations as well.

The Citadel

The French started to build here in 1750, when bastions were constructed for storing gunpowder. The fort itself was built by the British as the eastern flank of the city's defence system. It was begun in 1820 and not completed for 30 years. The irregularly-sided structure sits on the plain over 100 metres up from the river with an appropriate vantage point.

Today the Citadel is the home base of Canada's Royal 22s, a French regiment that developed quite a reputation through both world wars and the Korean War. There is a museum outlining their history and a more general Military Museum containing documents, uniforms and models situated in a few different buildings including the old prison at the south-east end.

The entrance fee of $2.75 includes admission to these museums and a guided tour, as well as the Changing of the Guard ceremony which takes place at 10 am daily in summer, and the Beating of the Retreat at 7 pm, Tuesday, Thursday, Saturday and Sunday during July and August. There are also cannon firings at noon and 9.30 pm from the Prince of Wales Bastion.

Parc des Champs de Bataille

This is the huge green park running west from the Citadel. Its hills, gardens, monuments and trees make it very pleasant now; however, the park was once a bloody battleground, the site of a conflict that may have determined the course of history in Canada. The portion closest to the cliff is known as the Plains of Abraham and it was here that the English finally defeated the French in 1759 with both generals dying in the process. In the park is a Martello Tower and a fountain with a lookout.

Quebec Museum Towards the south-western end of the park is this museum, with changing exhibits mainly on Quebec art – modern and more traditional, with ceramics and decorations as well. It's small and not memorable, but free. Open daily until 5 pm, on Wednesdays to 11 pm. Nearby is the old prison, now boarded up.

Old Wall (Fortifications de Quebec)

Now a National Park, the largely restored old wall fortifications can be visited for free. In fact, you can walk a complete circuit on top of the walls 4.6 km (nearly three miles) all around the old town. In the old Powder Building beside St Louis Gate, an interpretation centre has been set up, which provides a little information on the wall's history. Along the circuit are two other information booths, one on Dufferin Terrace and one on the Governors Promenade.

Artillery Park

Beside the wall at St Jean Gate, Artillery Park (Parc de l'Artillerie) has been used militarily for centuries. A munitions factory built cartridges for the Canadian Forces here until 1964. It's now an interpretation centre with a scale model of Quebec the way it was in the early 1800s. In the Dauphine Redoubt, there are costumes and displays on the soldiers for whom it was built during the French regime, and in the Officers Quarters is a history lesson for children.

Musee du Fort

This is a small museum at 10 Rue Ste Anne near Place d'Armes, dealing with more provincial military history. With the aid of a large model of 18th-century Quebec, six sieges and battles are retold using light and sound. The half-hour show isn't bad and costs $3.

Musee Historique

Also facing Place d'Armes, this is actually a wax museum with scenes depicting historical events like Columbus landing in America. Admission is $3, $2 for students.

Around Old Upper Town

In the 1700s Upper Town began to grow after Lower Town was destroyed once too often in battle.

Place d'Armes is the small square to the north of the Chateau Frontenac. It was once a military parade ground and is now a handy city orientation point.

Rue du Tresor is up, away from the water, off Place d'Armes. This very narrow street, linking Rue Ste Anne with Buade, is jammed with painters and their wares – mostly kitschy stuff done for the tourists but some pretty good work, too. At the end of Buade is the City Hall dating from 1833. Next to City Hall, the park is used for shows and performances throughout the summer, especially during festival time.

At the corner of Buade and Ste Famille is the Basilica of Notre Dame, dating from 1647. The interior is very ornate and contains paintings and treasures from the early French regime.

Ursuline Convent & Museum

This convent is on Rue des Jardins; it's the oldest girls' school on the continent. There are several buildings on the estate property, many undergoing restoration. The Ursuline Museum, which you enter at 12 Rue Donnacona, deals with the Ursulines and their lives in the 1600s and 1700s, and also displays paintings, crafts, furniture and other belongings of the early French settlers. Admission is $1.25, students 75c. The convent, chapel and museum are open daily from 9.30 am to noon and 1.30 to 5 pm. Closed Sunday mornings.

Nearby, on the same street, is the Anglican Cathedral of the Holy Trinity, built in 1804. Open noon to 5 pm.

Latin Quarter

This refers to a section of Old Upper Town surrounding the large Quebec Seminary complex. The Seminary was originally Laval University but it outgrew the space here and was moved in the 1960s to Ste Foy, west of here. Many students still live along the old, narrow streets which look particularly Parisian. To enter the Seminary grounds, go to 7 University St. In the grounds are many stone and wooden buildings, a toy museum, the University Museum and several grassy, quiet quadrangles.

Parc de l'Esplanade

Just inside the old city by Porte (gate) St Cours and Rue St Louis is this city park where many of the Quebec Winter Carnival events are held. Caleches – the horse-drawn carts for sightseeing – line up for business.

Old Lower Town

The oldest section of Quebec City, like the upper city, is well worth exploring. Get down to it by walking down Cote de la Montagne by the post office. About halfway down on the right there is a shortcut – the breakneck steps – that leads down to Rue Petit Champlain. Alternately, you can take the funicular down; it also goes to Petit Champlain, to Luis Joliet House. The house dates from 1683 and Joliet lived in it when he wasn't off exploring the northern Mississippi. Rue Petit Champlain, a very busy, attractive street, is said to be the narrowest in North America and is also one of the oldest.

Place Royale

This is the central and principal square of the area. The name is now often used to refer to the district in general. When Champlain founded Quebec, it was this bit of shoreline which was first settled. For the past few years the entire area has been under renovation and restoration, and the well-done work is now nearly complete. There are many houses and small museums to visit, some with period furniture and implements. The streets are full of visitors, people going to restaurants and cafés, and school children from around the province getting history lessons. There are small museums and houses to visit, some with period furniture and implements. Others are now galleries, craft shops and the like.

Also on the square are many buildings from the 1600s and 1700s, tourist shops (don't buy film here, it's too expensive!) and a Tourist Office at 29 Notre Dame, which offers free guided walking tours.

Church of Notre Dame des Victoires

This church on the square is the oldest stone church in the province, dating from 1688. It's built on the spot where 80 years earlier Champlain set up his 'Habitation,' a small stockade. Hanging from the ceiling is a replica of a wooden ship, thought to be a charm for good luck during the crossing and early battles with the Iroquois.

Royal Battery
This is at the foot of Rue Sous-le-Fort, where a dozen cannons were set up in 1691 to protect the growing town.

The Canadian government gives free tours of the Coast Guard base near the ferry terminal, Monday to Friday, 9 am to 4 pm. Here you'll find equipment, information and boats.

Old Port
Built around the old harbour in Lower Town east of Place Royale, Old Port is a recently redeveloped multi-use waterfront area. It's a large, spacious assortment of government buildings, shops, condominiums and recreational facilities with no real focal point but a few things of interest to the visitor.

Near Place Royale at the river's edge you'll see the *MV Louis-Jolliet*, offering cruises down-river to the Montmorency Falls and Ile d'Orleans. You'll get good views of the city, but you can also get them from the cheap ferry plying the river between town and Levis. Near the wharf is the new Man & Civilisation Museum.

Strolling along the waterfront leads to The Agora, a large outdoor concert bowl and site of many summer shows and presentations. A little further along is a warehouse-like building housing numerous boutiques.

Port of Quebec in the 19th Century
South toward the city a short distance is this National Historic Park, housed in a building on Rue St Andre. It's a large, new four-storey museum detailing shipbuilding and the timber industry, with good exhibits and often live demonstrations as well. Free admission.

Antique Shop District
The district is on Rue St Paul, around the corner from Place Royal in Lower Town very near the 'Port of Quebec in the 19th Century' museum. From Place Royale, take St Pierre toward the harbour and then turn left at St Paul. About a dozen shops here sell antiques, curiosities and old Quebec relics. There are also some good little cafés along this relatively quiet street. Right against the cliff on Cote de la Canoterie, you can walk up to Upper Town. Further along is the Farmers' Market on the right hand side, and a little further, the train station.

Outside the Walls

National Assembly The home of the provincial legislature is just off Grand Allee, not far from Parc de l'Esplanade, in this castle-like structure from 1886.

There are free tours of the sumptuous interior all day, in English and in French. The Assembly sits in the Blue Room. The Red Room, equally impressive, is no longer used as the Upper House has been discontinued.

Grand Theatre At the corner of Boulevard St Cyrille and Claire Fontaine is this grand, three-storey home to the performing arts. It's visited also for the building's design and for the gigantic epic mural by Spaniard Jordi Bonet. Free one-hour tours are given of the painting (!) which is in three parts: Death, Space and Liberty.

Le Bois de Coulonge Park Not far west of the Plains of Abraham is this large area dedicated to the plant world. Long the private property of a succession of Quebec's religious and political elite, the area of woods and extensive horticultural displays is open to the public. It's wedged between Boulevard Champlain and Chemin St Louis.

Aquarium This is in Ste Foy at 1675 Parc. They have about 300 species of fresh and saltwater fish. There's a cafeteria and out on the grounds, picnic tables. It's open daily and costs $3 for adults, children $1.50.

Events

Summer Festival (Festival d'Ete), at the beginning of July, consists basically of free shows and concerts throughout the town, including drama and dance. Ask about it at the Tourist Office; they should have a list of things going on indicating what, where and when. Most squares and parks in the Old Town are the sites of some activity daily, especially the park beside City Hall at noon and in the evening.

Winter Carnival This is the big, famous annual event in Quebec City. While the Carnival sambas in Rio and the Mardi Gras takes place in New Orleans, Quebec indulges itself in its own unique way. The festival lasts about 10 days, always including two weekends, around the end of February. If you want to go, organise the trip early as the city gets packed out (and bring lots of warm clothes). Featured are parades, ice sculptures, a snow slide, boat races, dances, music and lots of drinking. The town goes berserk. If you take the train into Quebec during Carnival, be prepared for a trip like no other.

Many activities take place in Parc de l'Esplanade. The slide is on the Terrasse Dufferin behind the Chateau. Other events take place above the Gare Saint Roche, between Pont Dorchester and the bridge of the Autoroute Dufferin.

Quebec City Provincial Exhibition This summer event is held around the end of August each year and features individual and commercial displays, handicrafts, a Black Jack parlour, horse racing and a large carnival midway with 65 rides. The fee is $7 to get in, which includes everything, even rides. Nearly three-quarters of a million people visit each year. Exhibition Park is north of the downtown centre, off the 175 autoroute Laurentide.

Places to Stay

There are many, many places to stay in Quebec and generally the competition keeps the prices down to a reasonable level. There are relatively few standard type hotels – by far the bulk of the accommodation is in small guest houses and family-run, European-like hotels. As you'd expect in such a popular centre, the best cheap places are very often full. Mid-summer and Carnival time are the heaviest periods. If you can't find a place in the Old Town, consider one of the motels slightly away from the centre or be prepared to stretch your budget.

Outside the peak periods, prices do drop. For accommodation assistance call 643-2306 or better still, go to the Tourist Office on Rue d'Auteil where they have lists of places and a phone you can use. Do not take their occupancy information as gospel, however. They may have a place down as 'full' when in fact a call will turn up a room, after everybody else has ignored it. The tourist accommodation guide also doesn't list all the places – a wander around will turn up others. Lastly, remember that morning is the best time to find a place and Fridays are often the worst.

Hostels There are at least two youth hostels here, possibly three. The best one is called *La Paix (Peace) Hotel* (tel 694-0735) at 31 Rue Couillard. It's open all year and has 40 beds. The hostel is marked with a peace sign on the white, European-looking building. Cost is $9.50 with breakfast, and $1.50 extra if you need a sleep sheet and blanket. The doors close at 2 am. The location is perfect; there is a grocery store, a drugstore, bar and restaurant all within minutes.

The other hostel, *Auberge International* (tel 694-0755), is also well located at 19 Rue St Ursule. It's usually full in summer; arrive at 10 am to get a bed. Cost is $10 with breakfast.

A third hostel did exist outside the wall

but this appears to have shut down. Ask about it.

There are no rooms at the YMCA but the *YWCA* (tel 683-2155) at 855 Holland takes couples and single women. Singles are $22 and they have a cafeteria and pool. The Y is often full, so reservations may be useful. Holland runs off Chemin Ste Foy, which becomes St John in the old section. Bus No 7 along Chemin Ste Foy goes past Holland. Walk south on Holland – it's not far.

The *University of Laval* (tel 656-2921) rents rooms in the summer from May to 21 August. Rates are $21 for singles and a few dollars less in a twin room. Students price is $12.50 or again, less if sharing a room. It's between Chemin Ste Foy and Boulevard Wilfrid Laurier to the east of Du Vallon. Bus No 8 from the Old Town will get you there; it's about halfway between the bridges and the walled area.

Tourist Homes Other than the hostels, the cheapest and best places to stay are these small, sometimes family-run hotels, often created out of old houses. There are literally dozens of them within the walls, which lets you stay in the centre of things and experience their individual characters.

Most of the cheaper ones are located in one specific area, which makes looking easy. This area is roughly bounded by Rue d'Auteuil on the west, Ste Anne to the north, the Chateau Frontenac to the east and Avenue St Denis to the south. The two most fruitful streets are Rue Ste Ursule and St Louis. Ste Anne and Laporte are also good. Again, many are nearly always full in summer. Prices at these places can be flexible, depending on time of year and other factors. On one visit, we got a single bed and a foam mattress on the floor for the price of a single, but generally the approach is more formal. Consider bargaining if you're staying for more than a couple of days.

Auberge St Louis (tel 647-9350) at 48 St Louis is one of the cheapest places in town. It has 12 rooms that start at $15 for singles, $20 doubles, and go to twice this. Parking is available but costs extra.

Next door at No 50 is *Le Gite St Louis* (tel 692-2233). They don't have extras like TV or air conditioning, but the rooms go for $15 to $25 for singles, $20 to $35 for doubles.

Further down at No 72 St Louis is *Maison du General* (tel 694-1905). There are 11 rooms ranging from $19 for singles or $24 doubles, without bath. As in many of these places, it's cheaper without TV, showers, the view or the biggest room. The cheaper places are sometimes noisier as they're often on the street.

Also on St Louis at 71 is *Hotel Le Clos St Louis* (tel 647-9305), with 15 rooms at $25 to $42 for singles, $30 to $57 doubles. You may notice signs in some store windows along here offering rooms: it's worth going in and asking. On one visit for me this turned up a small but fine low-priced room, yet on another visit, not even a 'maybe' – I think it just depends on the whim of the proprietor and whether he or she likes your face.

Running off St Louis is Ste Ursule, a pleasant, much quieter street. There are several places worth checking here. *Le Manoir La Salle* (tel 647-9361) is at 18 Ste Ursule. They have nine rooms at $21 to $35 for singles, $32 to $47 for doubles; free parking.

Le Maison Ste Ursule (tel 694-9797) at No 40, looks more expensive and is, at $32 to $40 for singles, $36 to $55 doubles, but they have a kitchenette. They also have some rooms on the adjacent side street.

Across the street at No 43 is *Maison Acadienne* (tel 694-0280). If it's sunny, the robust-looking landlady will be out on the steps sunning. Rooms are $22 to $45 depending on the number of people, size and facilities. I've stayed here – it's good, and if you're lucky you may get one of the parking spots around the back.

Le Maison Demers (tel 692-2487) at No 68, charges about the same rates for its eight rooms although the better doubles are higher and include a TV.

Further north-west off Ste Ursule is Ste Anne. *Maison Doyon* at No 9 has 20 plain, simple but clean rooms for $25 to $42 singles, $32 to $52 doubles. Take a washbasin rather than a shower and you'll save $5 to $10.

There are numerous places on and just off the Jardin des Gouverneurs to the south of the Chateau Frontenac. *Manoir Sur-le-Cap* (tel 694-1987) at 9 Avenue Ste Genevieve, has 14 rooms carved out of the old house, some with views of the park. Singles and doubles for $25 to $50.

The *Manoir de la Terrace* (tel 694-1592) is at No 4 Rue Laporte. Single rooms are $25 to $38, doubles $29 to $42.

At the corner of St Louis and Rue d'Auteuil is *Manoir de L'Espanade* (tel 694-0834), an old place recently renovated with 37 rooms ranging from singles $29 to $40, doubles $35 to $50. Corner rooms can be noisy.

Lastly, down in the Lower Town, a few blocks north of the out-of-town destination bus station, is *Maison Eldorado* (tel 524-2566) at 14 Est St Joseph. This is not a very pleasant area and it's some distance from things you'll be interested in, but if your bus arrives late it could be handy. The basic rooms are just $7 singles, $10 doubles.

Bed & Breakfasts While certainly not a tradition in Quebec, a few places providing the morning meal are now showing up. An agency to try is *Bonjour Quebec* (tel 527-1465) at 3765 Boulevard Monaco. The nine hosts they list are all quite central and priced at $35 singles, $50 doubles, give or take a few dollars.

Another place to try is *Francois Bacon's* (tel 525-9826) right in the heart of things at 300 Rue Champlain in Old Lower Town. He rents rooms at a range of prices on the third floor of his old house.

Motels I don't think I've ever seen a city with more motels than Quebec City. Whether you have a car or not, they may be the answer if you find everything booked up downtown.

There are three major areas to look in for motels, each a good distance from the Old Town, but not really far and not difficult to reach.

One area is Beauport, a section of Quebec City to the north of the downtown area. You pass by on the way to Ste Anne de Beaupre or a trip along the northern coast. The easiest way to reach it if driving from downtown is to head north up Dorchester to Boulevard Hamel. Turn right (east); Hamel turns into Rue 18 and then further east into Boulevard Ste Anne. This is Beauport. Look when the numbers are in the 1000s. Most of these motels are off the road with the river running behind them.

At No 1062 Boulevard Ste Anne is *Motel Chevalier* (tel 661-3876). Rooms are $35 to $55 for singles/doubles.

Motel de la Capitale (tel 663-0587) is at 1082 Ste Anne. The rate is $45 for singles or doubles.

Nearby, *Motel Olympic* (tel 667-8716) at 1078 Ste Anne, ranges from $38 to $60. They have just 16 rooms here.

Motel du Cosmos (tel 661-2463) at 1154 Boulevard St Anne is the cheapest of the lot with singles/doubles from as low as $28.

North-west of the centre at the intersection of Boulevard Henri IV and Highway 138 up toward the airport is *Journey's End Motel* (tel 872-5900), good value at singles/doubles $38/45. This Canada-wide budget chain is always reliable.

The second major area for motels is along Boulevard Wilfrid Laurier, west of the city. The motel section runs just east of Boulevard Henri IV, which runs into the bridges from the south shore. Check around the 3000 numbers. Prices are generally quite a bit higher here, but it is closer to town.

The *Motel Fleur de Lys* (tel 653-9321) at No 3145, has good prices with doubles from $29 all the way up to $70.

Further east after Wilfrid Laurier turns into Grand Allee, there are a few smallish, reasonably priced places in the 600 addresses. The ones closer to town are generally more deluxe and more expensive.

The third area for motels is on Boulevard Wilfrid Hamel, marked only as 'Hamel' on street signs. To get to this area, head north up Boulevard Henri IV from the river or south from Highway 40. It's about seven km from town. Start looking around the 5000 block, although the road is lined with motels.

Motel Delisle (tel 872-7476) at 5957 Boulevard Hamel, has just seven rooms but they're only $16 to $24 without extras. Open only from 15 June to 15 September.

Motel Plaza (tel 877-1552) at 5155 Boulevard Hamel, has singles from $34, doubles from $40.

Motel Rourke (tel 688-5667), 2177 Boulevard Hamel, offers singles from $22, doubles from $28.

Camping There are two provincial campgrounds fairly close to town. One is north of Quebec. To get there, take Highway 40 toward Montmorency and turn north on 369; the park is not too far, on the left. It costs $7.50.

The other provincial campground is on the south shore, east of Levis near the small town of Beaumont. It offers views out to Ile d'Orleans.

There are many private campgrounds on this south shore road. There is also a *Kampground of America* (tel 831-1813), about 10 minutes west of the city, five km west of the Pierre Laporte Bridge on the south shore. They offer tours into Quebec.

Places to Eat

There are dozens of restaurants here and the food is quite good, but recently prices have become fairly standardised at rather a high rate. Still, there are some reasonably priced exceptions, and the costlier restaurants do generally provide good service in an attractive setting. Most restaurants post their menus outside at the door, which is helpful in shopping around. If you're here for any length of time you'll likely find your own favourite.

At dinner the set menus include soup, roll, dessert and coffee. Many of these same dining rooms offer midday specials which aren't bad value, but more modest places have the usual cheap lunches of pizza, sandwiches and the like. The ethnic restaurants provide an alternative.

Upper Old Town How about breakfast? For the basic bacon & eggs there is really only one place to go – the *Au Relais de la Place d'Armes* on the Place d'Armes Square near the Chateau Frontenac. It's good, busy, friendly and doesn't cost an arm and a leg. They have good specials at all meals and a few tables outside on the square. *Wasn't that you I saw here last night having a cheap dinner?*

For a more French-style breakfast there is *Le Petit Coin Latin* at 81/2 Ursule near St Jean. Open every day, this small café has croissants, muffins, eggs, *café au lait*, etc, with low-priced lunch specials which include a glass of wine. At 25 Couillard, one east of Rue Baude, *Chez Temporal* is a little café which serves coffee, croissants, salads, etc. It's perfect for snacks, breakfasts and light meals. The café feels very French – a good place to sit in the morning and plan the day.

For lunch, *Café Buade* is right in the middle of everything on Rue Baude beside Holt Renfrew, just south of Rue des Jardins. The table d'hôte is $6 to $7. Sandwiches are all under $2.50 and soup is just $1.25.

There are a few places worth checking on Rue Garneau opposite City Hall. At No 36, *La Siesta* is a pleasant little place with a vast selection of moderately priced crepes. At No 48, *Croissant Plus* is busy day and night with snacks and light meals. Next door, the *Fleur du Lotus* offers complete dinner specials at $16 from its Thai, Cambodian and Vietnamese menu.

Top & Bottom: High and low tides near Fundy National Park, New Brunswick (RE)

Top: Quebecois Cowboy (RE)
Left: Quebec City's historic Lower Town, towered over by the famous Chateau Frontenac (ML)
Right: Modern Montreal architecture (JL)

Through Rue du Tresor from Baude you'll find the Place d'Armes. In the *Hotel du Tresor* is a dining room – very pleasant, done in wood with ceiling fans and white tablecloths. The evening meal will set you back around $20, which is about the norm.

One of the main streets for restaurants is St Jean. There are many scattered along here, both inside the wall and further out, as well as night spots. Some places act as both. At *1136 St Jean*, near Cote du Palais, is a small restaurant specialising in crepes of many kinds, starting as low as $1.40. I like it because it hasn't been dressed up for the tourists at all. You sit right up at the counter. The restaurant looks as though it's been there for a good, long while.

At No 1124 is *Le Grillon*, serving very good food. Fixed-price French food dinners are about $10 to $14 excluding drinks.

La Terrasse du Roy, at the corner of Ste Ursule, is completely modern in concept and design. The small tables, some just off the pavement, are pleasant. It looks more like a café, and true enough the menu is small, but it's a cheap and popular place with good salads.

For excellent South-East Asian fare, try *Apsara* at 71 Rue d'Auteil. Dishes are about $6.50 or a complete dinner for two is about $30. A few doors down at No 23, there's a cheap Lebanese spot.

Not far from St Jean at 48A Ste Ursule is *Le Sainte Amour*, with a $20 table d'hôte and a very good reputation. The menu offers about six meat and six fish dishes daily. For a splurge you're probably better off in a place like this, on one of the quieter streets.

There are plenty of other places for a night out, many specialising in seafood. A modest one to try is *Le Biarritz* at 136 Rue Ste Anne, which has fish dishes for $9, beef $10 to $14. It's been recommended by local people.

Cafe de la Paix at 44 Rue Desjardins is very French in decor and atmosphere and offers a varied menu of seafood, fowl and meats. It's very well-established and recommended and while not cheap, is not exorbitant either. *Restaurant au Parmesan* nearby on St Louis, is always busy. They have a large menu with most dishes $13 to $16. They also have a huge collection of about 2000 bottles.

Place Royale (Old Lower Town) At the bottom of the funicular is Rue Petit Champlain. If you're coming from Levis, walk north off the dock and veer to the left. A few doors along on Petit Champlain you'll see *Le Couchon Dingue* (with a pig for a symbol). They serve meals but it's a good place for breakfast, with *café au lait* in a bowl (as it's served in parts of France) and croissants.

The *Boulangerie Cul de Sac* on the street of the same name, at Notre Dame, sells all kinds of bread and rolls. Next door, *Le Pape-Georges* wine bar sells juice by the glass.

Le Vendome at 36 Cote de la Montagne is an expensive French restaurant which has been serving for close to 40 years.

Along St Paul, an old quiet street, there are several places. *La Bouille Cafe* at No 71 is good for light meals or a coffee. And at No 95 there is a small simple place for sandwiches, hamburgers and the like at non-tourist prices. They even have a few tables out on the pavement.

Outside the Wall Outside the city centre, things are a little quieter and not so densely packed. Rue St Jean, west beyond the gate, has numerous bars, cafés, taverns and restaurants. For eating there is Vietnamese, Lebanese and Mexican food. Keep walking and looking.

Along Boulevard St Cyrille Est is Avenue Cartier. There are a few Chinese restaurants here if you feel like a change. There are also a few standard French ones. At the corner on St Cyrille is *Restaurant La Reserve*, below which is a small delicatessen. I'm told they have the best croissants anywhere outside France.

At 821 Rue Scott south of St Jean, *La Pailotte* is a small, casual Vietnamese place.

Along Grand Allee, past the Quebec National Assembly and other government buildings, and just past d'Artigny, are about 10 alfresco restaurants. They make a good spot for a beer or lunch if you're out near the Plains. All have complete lunch specials for $6 to $8, soup to coffee, and at most places, dinners are in the $10 to $20 range. *Restaurant Patrimoine* is one of the cheapest. At No 625, *La Veille Maison du Spaghetti* offers a range of pasta dishes at below average cost.

Market The Farmers' Market is on Rue St Andre in Old Lower Town near the Louise Basin, not too far from Old Port. It's a covered open-air building where you'll find fresh bread, cheeses, fruit and vegetables. The best time to visit is busy Saturday morning.

Nightlife

Though Quebec is quite a small city, there are plenty of nightspots. Many of the cafés and restaurants – some mentioned under the eating section – have live music at night. Others are clubs open only at night. Most of the nightlife is in the Old City or just outside the walls. Brasseries – taverns for men and women – close at midnight. Bars stay open to about 3 or 4 am.

Rue St Jean is alive at night – this is where people strut. There are good places for just sitting and watching, and places with music.

Nostradamus at No 33 is a *boîte à chanson* – basically a folk club – with a casual, relaxed atmosphere.

Bar 1123 at that number, Rue St Jean, has live jazz, blues and rock. It's free; the first set starts at 10 pm. *Casablanca*, at 1169 St Jean, is a reggae club.

The upper portion of Rue St Jean near the gate is blocked off to traffic in summer and becomes a mall for people. I've always felt cities with such promenades are a little more civilised than those without.

At *Café-Terrasse*, Croque Mitaine, they often have blues music. The address is 33 Rue d'Auteuil.

Lastly, there are a couple of spots on Rue St Pierre in Place Royale. There are also lots of dancing places around town but they change quickly, so ask.

Just Sitting The restaurant with a bar at the top of the Lowes Hotel on Grand Allee at the corner of Bethelot, is good for views. Away from the clubs, if you just want to sit, Dufferin Terrace behind the Chateau is perfect. It's cool, with views over the river.

Cinema *La Boîte à Films* (tel 524-3144) at 1044 3rd Avenue, is a repertory theatre showing both English and French films, some with subtitles. There are two films nightly.

One other cinema in town shows English movies. It's near Place Quebec, the convention centre at Avenue Dufferin.

Getting There & Away

Transportation can be a bit of a hang-up here. Driving in the old section (and worse, trying to park) is a headache. The airport is a fair distance out and the bus station is none too convenient either. But the situation is better than it used to be: the new train station is central and there is an airport bus, which only recently began services again.

Air The airport is west of town, off Highway 40, near where 73 intersects it on its way northward.

The number for Quebecair information is 872-3736, reservations 692-1031. For Nordair information, ring 681-7381. Air Canada information is 925-2311.

The Air Canada fares to Montreal are $98, student $55. To Ottawa, it's $120, student $66.

Bus Voyageur Lines serve Quebec City.

The station (or *gare*) is Gare Centrale d'Autobus (tel 524-4692) at 225 Boulevard Charest Est. This is quite a way west of the downtown area. Buses to Montreal run nearly every hour; the fare is $24. They also make regular trips to Riviere-du-Loup and to Edmundston, New Brunswick. The fare to Edmundston is $30. This town is the connecting point with SMT Bus lines for Atlantic Canada destinations.

In summer, Autobus Fortin Poulin and Greyhound link up for a Boston-Quebec City trip, which takes 11 hours. If you're going to or from New York, change in Boston.

To get to town from the Voyageur station, take a No 3 or a No 8 city bus. Going to the station from downtown, take the bus to the corner of Avenue de la Canonne and Boulevard Charets. From there walk two blocks west on Charest to the station.

Train Until recently there were only two train stations, neither in downtown Quebec. One is in Ste Foy (tel 692-3940), south-west of town by the bridges over to the south shore. And there's one on the south shore in Levis, right opposite Quebec City (tel 833-8056), closer to downtown Quebec.

But there is now also the newly-renovated old station on Rue St Paul in Lower Town. Same telephone as Ste Foy above.

Trains to and from the east (Maritimes and the Gaspe Peninsula) use the Levis station, and some Montreal trains do still go to Levis. But in general, trains west, to and from Montreal and beyond, now use the new station and Ste Foy. Train schedules include:

Montreal: four daily – $27; $43 return excursion

Toronto: three daily – $79 (reservations needed)

Saint John, New Brunswick: 10.30 am daily – $68; $110 return; $92 excursion.

Car Sharing Allo Stop (tel 522-0056) at 467 Rue St Jean, is an agency that gets drivers and passengers together. Membership for passengers is $2, then you pay a portion to the agency three hours before the trip, and the rest goes to the driver. They offer good deals, such as these fares: Montreal $11, Ottawa $19, Toronto $32, New York $38, Gaspe $25.

Ferry The ferry between Quebec City and Levis runs constantly all day and most of the night. Fares are $1.25, $2.45 extra per car. You'll get good views of the river, cliffs, Quebec skyline and Chateau Frontenac. The terminal in Quebec is in Place Royale, Lower Town. In Levis, the ferry terminal is right beside the VIA Rail station.

Getting Around

Airport Transport For years there was no bus service to the airport, firstly because of a strike, and then because the strike lasted so long the company died. A new service operated by Old Quebec Tours Ltd (tel 687-9226) has arisen to save you from the $25 taxi fare. This bus makes four trips a day during the week with a reduced service on weekends. It leaves from major hotels, but will make pick-ups around town if you call at least one hour before flight time.

Bus There is a good city bus system which costs $1.25 with transfer privileges. The buses even go out as far as Ste Anne de Beaupre on the north shore. The terminal, Gare Centrale d'Autobus (tel 524-4692), is at 225 Boulevard Charest Est in Lower Town, and will supply you with route maps and information. City bus No 15 goes from downtown to the train station in Ste Foy and back regularly, all day to about midnight. You can get it on Avenue Dufferin or in Place d'Youville near the National Assembly.

To Beauport motels, take the No 53 from Dorchester.

The No 8 goes from downtown to Laval University.

Car Rentals Budget (tel 692-3660) is at 29 Cote du Palais. For sub-compacts the rate is $43 a day with 100 free km.

Driving In Quebec City, driving isn't worth the trouble. You can walk just about everywhere; the streets are narrow and crowded, and parking is an exercise in frustration. Don't bother.

Bicycle Rentals Velo Didacte (tel 648-6022) is at 249 Rue St Jean. Also central and within the old city is Location Mobylettes & Velos (tel 692-4178), at 92 Rue Petit Champlain in Lower Town, which rents scooters and bikes. You may see bikes for rent along Rue St Louis near the Chateau, too. Ten-speed and mountain bikes are available.

Caleches The horse-drawn carriages go for $30 an hour.

Tours Some companies use minibuses for rather private tours, others offer a driver and you use your own car. Several companies offer bus tours of the city.

Gray Line (tel 622-7420), runs numerous tours from Place d'Armes. Two hours around town is $12, and a 4½-hour trip to Beaufort and Montmorency Falls with a short visit to Ile d'Orleans, goes for $17. Several other companies offer similar tours but offer longer tours of Ile d'Orleans or some other variation. Gray Line seems to have the lowest prices. The Tourist Office has promotional pamphlets on the various tours available; there is also a ticket booth on Terrasse Dufferin representing many of the tour companies.

Maple Leaf (tel 687-9226) at 575 Arago West, has five different tours in and around Quebec City, at prices ranging from $15 to $46. Free pick-up from your hotel is available.

A worthwhile alternative is 'Quebec by Foot' (tel 658-4799), which provides a two to 2½-hour walking tour guided by history or architecture students. It's educational but not dry. Reservations may be made at the Musee du Fort on Place d'Armes. There are three walks a day, at a cost of $10.

Boat tours are given on the *Louis Joliet*, which has an 800-passenger capacity. Tickets (tel 629-1159) may be purchased in the Kiosque, on the boardwalk behind the Chateau or at the booth along the waterfront near Place Royale. The basic one-hour trip is $12, but there is a longer one further down-river, and two-hour evening cruises with dancing are $15.50 early in the week and $2 more at the end of the week.

Sonores (tel 692-1223), rents spoken tape cassettes which you can use for your own walking or driving tours. Rental is $6.95. The cassettes are available at tourist booths.

A new service which may last is a shuttle bus called Carrousel Touristique, which tools around old Quebec. For one fare of $3 you can hop on and off at will for the day. Pick up a copy of their stops and schedule.

A good train trip to take for the day is a tour along the St Lawrence River east as far as Pointe-au-Pic. See the Pointe-au-Pic section in this chapter for more information.

There are also excursions to Tadoussac, even further east along the St Lawrence, which are run by VIA Rail, and include accommodation, a six-hour river cruise along the Saguenay River and whale-watching trips.

Excursions Plein Air Quebec (tel 843-3750) organises canoe, bicycle and other trips around the area.

Around Quebec City

NORTH SHORE

Montmorency Falls

Just out of Quebec, these waterfalls are

higher than those at Niagara. They're set in a park with picnic grounds.

Ile d'Orleans

This 30-km-long, very green island gives a picture of traditional rural Quebec life. It offers great scenery and views, and you'll see old wooden or stone houses and cottages, some in Normandy style. Some of the villages are over 300 years old. Then, as now, the prime activity is farming for the Quebec City market. Recently, city folks have been building homes here, at least at the western end. There's lots of fruit, especially apples and strawberries. A view tower stands at the eastern tip. There's a campsite in the middle of the south side at St Jean.

Ste Anne de Beaupre

This gaudy little tourist town is justly renowned for its immaculate, mammoth church. From the mid-1600s this has been the site of Quebecois pilgrimages. The beautiful basilica now standing replaced earlier chapels and was begun in the late 1920s. Note the many crutches inside the door. There's good tile-work on the floor, and stained glass and ceiling mosaics.

Check the hotel across the street, designed like a chapel, stained glass included – yuk!

Also in town are a museum, a monastery with a seminary and a few other churches. There's a 360° painting of Jerusalem on the day Jesus died. Admission to see it is $3.

An annual gypsy pilgrimage takes place here in late July, attracting thousands. The grounds become a huge camp.

About three km north of town toward Mont Ste Anne is *La Camarine*, a fine place for a splurge on a good French meal. It's run by a woman in an old Quebec-style house and offers complete dinners from $21 and up. Not cheap but very nice.

Six km east of town, in a deep chasm, are the Ste Anne Falls, 74 metres high. You can walk across them on a suspension bridge; about $3.

Mont Ste Anne Park

This is best known as a ski area – it's the best nearby and one of the best in Quebec, and has about a dozen lifts. You can also camp here in summer. There's a gondola to the mountain's peak. Buses depart from downtown Quebec.

Cap Tourmente

This is a bird sanctuary and wildlife preserve. Flocks of snow-geese may be seen here in spring and autumn. There are walking paths through the swampy land. Open every day, 9 am to 5 pm.

The Laurentians

As in Montreal, the Laurentians north of town are a summer/winter playground. Lac Beauport is one of the most accessible resort lakes.

Laurentides Provincial Park

Considerably further north is this huge wilderness park with its wooded hills and mountains, and lots of lakes and streams. You can hike and fish here and there are campgrounds along the road through the park.

Jacques Cartier Park, in the southern portion, has camping, hiking trails and canoeing along the Jacques Cartier River. For information, call 848-3169.

SOUTH SHORE

Levis

There's not much here for the visitor. It's a cross between a smallish town and a suburb of Quebec. The ferry ride over makes a mini-cruise and the views of Quebec are good. Near the terminal is a train station (tel 833-8056) for trips east and to Montreal. For more information about trains, see the Getting There & Away section of Quebec City.

The *Hotel St Louis* opposite the train station, is run by a friendly French woman and has small, clean rooms from $28 single or $32 double. The dining room is inexpensive and neat.

Part way up the hill into town are the

remains of a fort, where there are excellent views.

Between 1865 and 1872 the British built three forts on the south shore cliffs to protect Quebec. One, known as Pointe-Levis Fort No 1 has been restored and operates as a National Historic Park, which has free guided tours. It's on the east side of Levis in Lauzon.

Eastward Leaving Quebec, the landscape is pretty flat but looking across the river you can see the mountains and hills; the large one with the ski runs is Mont Ste Anne. Going along Highway 132 through the little towns, Ile d'Orleans lies just offshore. About 100 km east of Levis is the first main point of interest.

St Jean-Port Joli

This small town, with the big two-spired church right in the middle, is a centre for the Quebec art of woodcarving. Good examples can be seen in the **Musee des Anciens**, $2. More recent carvings in the same style can be seen in the many workshops and stores, and courses can be taken in carving. Other crafts produced and sold here are ceramics and textiles.

The church was built in 1890 and the priest's house next door, even earlier in 1872.

In town you'll find a restaurant or two, including the *Dorian Casse Croute* for top-notch fries and burgers. There are a couple of motels, a campground, a youth hostel and a Tourist Office.

East along the St Lawrence

East along the river from Quebec City are some of the most scenic landscapes in the province, as the shoreline becomes more typical of that found in Eastern Canada. With neat small farms and little villages dominated by the church – usually topped by a silver spire – this is rural Quebec. With few changes, life has been pretty much the same here for well over a century. You won't hear English in this part of the province, but you won't find any hostility either.

From Quebec City you can take either the north or south shore up toward the Gaspe. Just don't take the super Highway 20, from which you'll see nothing. The north shore is hillier and more dramatic as the northern mountains come down close to the river. It also has the more physical points of interest.

There are ferries across the river at various points. The further east you go, the wider the river becomes and the more costly the ferry.

NORTH SHORE

Baie St Paul

First stop is Baie St Paul, with its old streets and big church. There are good views from the tourist chalet and a picnic area on the west side of town. A *Youth Hostel* (tel 435-5587) overlooks the bay and town, one km uphill from the highway at the eastern edge of town. Rates are $6 to $7. The bad news is it may have closed. There is good camping on Ile aux Coudres down toward St Louis. *Sylvie Chalets* has cabins for rent at low prices.

The Highway 381 north from Baie St Paul runs along the edge of Laurentide Park and offers good scenery and steep hills. In the villages along the coast here, such as St Joseph and Pointe-au-Pic, there are several small hotels with good food. In Cap-a-l'Aigle, the *Auberge des Peupliers*, with lunches at $10 and dinners $22, has been recommended.

Saint Simeon

The ferry to Riviere-du-Loup on the south shore departs from Saint Simeon.

Pointe-au-Pic

In this small town is the *Manoir Richelieu* dating from 1928 – a huge, elegant, romantic hotel worth a look.

Getting There & Away One way to see this scenic coastal district, known as Charlevoix, is by train tour from Quebec City. It travels along the river as far east as Pointe-au-Pic. The train leaves at 8 am daily, returning at 8 pm. The fare is $32 return, $24 one-way. Ring 648-1566 in Quebec. There are stops along the way and opportunities for side trips, swimming and sightseeing.

Baie Ste Catherine

Back on the road the scenery is superb around Les Eboulements, with farms running from the town's edge to the river. You may have to stop while a farmer leads his cattle across the highway. Note the piles of wood used for the long winters and the many carving outlets. At Baie Ste Catherine, you can stay at *Maison Aux Berges du Saguenay* and eat across the street. The first week in August is the Cod Festival here.

Tadoussac & the Saguenay River

The Saguenay is the largest of Eastern Canada's few fiords – a spectacular saltwater inlet, edged in part by steep cliffs and running to a depth of 500 metres along a crack in the earth's crust. Ocean-going ships can ply the deep black waters as far as Chicoutimi.

From 15 June to 15 September, a ferry runs across the river every 20 minutes from 8 am to 8 pm, then every 40 minutes. The 10-minute trip is free.

In Tadoussac, the seemingly out-of-place huge old resort *Tadoussac Hotel* used to run river excursions. (These were stopped but may recommence.) Trips upstream past the cliffs are interesting, as you lose your ability to judge size and distance against the rock walls.

The river can become very stormy very quickly. Where it meets the St Lawrence, shrimp and capelin abound, attracting beluga, finback, humpback and even blue whales. Some boat trips head out to whale-watching territory.

For a splurge, dinner prices are quite reasonable at the hotel.

Also in town is the red-and-white *Auberge du Lac* with very reasonable rates. The youth hostel is closed so for now the cheapest spot is *Manoir Audet* at 16 Rue Principale, which is about $20 for singles or doubles. There's camping two km from the ferry on Highway 138.

VIA Rail runs excursions from Quebec City to Tadoussac, which include accommodation, a six-hour river cruise and whale-watching trips.

Pointe Noire Coastal Station This is a whale study post (tel 237-4383) at the Saguenay River. There is an exhibit, a slide show and films, and an observation tower with a telescope for views over the mouth of the river. Once numbering 6000, only 500 beluga whales still remain and the area has become their refuge. Other types frequent the area; in fact, I saw a minke very close to shore. Entrance to the centre is $2.50 and recommended. Three-hour

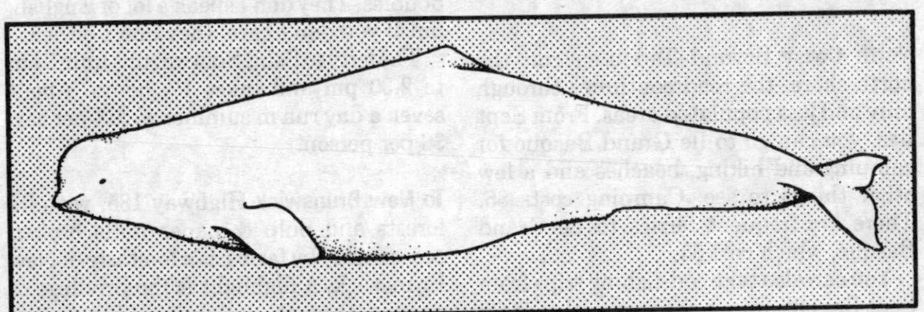

Beluga whale

boat cruises run through the summer season for $30 and go where whales are most likely to be. It is not uncommon to see a few from the ferry across the river. The station also has bed & breakfast available at $16 per person.

Societe Ecologique des Baleines This is an organisation which also runs three-hour whale-watching trips out of Grand Bergerons, further east along the coast.

Chicoutimi The roads along the Saguenay up to Chicoutimi offer good views of the river. Chicoutimi, one of the province's largest northern towns, lies not far from Lac St Jean from where the Saguenay originates. There are a couple of wilderness parks in the vicinity and boat trips south down the river and fiord from town. In Chicoutimi, see the House of Arthur Villeneuve at 669 Rue Tache Ouest. In the late 1950s when Mr Villeneuve was retiring as a local barber, he began painting. His depictions of the town and landscape along the river attracted a lot of attention and are now sold and collected around the world. The house, he and his wife's former home, is now a museum known not so much for the paintings it contains but for the painting it is. The entire house has been painted inside and out like a series of canvases in Villeneuve's bright naive folk style. It's open weekdays from mid-May to mid-October for a couple of bucks. You may well meet the artist or his wife.

North Coast Beyond Tadoussac on the north shore, the road continues through hilly and less populated areas. From Sept Iles, you can go to Ile Grand Basque for camping and hiking, beaches and a few other things to see. Camping costs $6. There are frequent ferries to Ile Grand Basque, which cost $5.

You can also take cod-fishing trips from Sept Iles out among the many islands for $15.

SOUTH SHORE

Riviere-du-Loup

As you approach you'll see the downtown area with the church along the hillside on the right. Although there is little to see, this is a pleasant town. The Tourist Office is on the east side of town, not far from the sign for the ferry. It's in the Museum of the Lower St Lawrence on Rue Hotel de Ville, which runs through town. The museum deals with local history and is all in French, but there's also a small art gallery.

The main street, Rue Lafontaine, leads up the hill from Highway 132 or Hotel de Ville. On it are a couple of places to eat and a good view of the river. East off Frontenac St, not far from Lafontaine are some waterfalls and a picnic table or two. Just west of town the river holds a smattering of islands; going eastward, it really begins to widen.

Along Highway 132 are numerous restaurants and motels as well as the Loup River. There is a *Youth Hostel* (tel 862-7566) at 46 Rue Hotel de Ville. Eastern Quebec has several other youth hostels.

Chalets Bienvenue on Route du Quai and *Motel Choo Choo* on the highway are in the $20 to $30 range. There are quite a few motels near town and prices aren't bad at all.

There is a farm bed & breakfast about 48 km south-east of town, inland at St Clement. Yvette and Georges Veilleux run the *Fermes des Peupliers* (tel 963-6120) and charge $15/18 for singles/doubles. They don't speak a lot of English, but if you don't care, they don't either.

The ferry to Saint Simeon runs from 9 am to 2.30 pm and takes 1¼ hours. About seven a day run in summer at $14 per car, $6 per person.

To New Brunswick Highway 185, with its forests and pulp & paper mills broken occasionally by farms, is a foretaste of New Brunswick. A highlight is the privilege of passing through and being able to say you've been to St Louis Ha! Ha! Also good is the beautiful green rolling landscape around Lac Temiscouta. There is some camping and a couple of motels but it remains a largely undeveloped area. In summer a ferry runs across the lake.

ALONG THE ST LAWRENCE

Trois Pistoles

The coast becomes more hilly and less populated as you head for the Gaspe Peninsula – it looks somewhat like the Scottish Highlands. People in the area cut and sell peat for garden fertiliser. The town of Trois Pistoles is dominated by a massive church. There's a ferry here (tel 851-3099), going to Les Escoumins. The trip takes 1¼ hours and costs $13.50 per car, $6 per person. It runs from May to November, with three a day in July and August.

Bic

Bic is a very picturesque little village in a beautiful setting a few km from Rimouski. The coastal views from here are excellent. The village has a good picnic spot and a large campground.

Rimouski

This is a fairly large, growing industrial and oil-distributing town. There is a good Tourist Office by the highway near the museum, and a cathedral in the centre of town. There are plenty of motels and restaurants in all price ranges. *Le Riverain*, 38 St Germain Est, has inexpensive Italian dishes and pizza as well as fish and sandwiches. *Restaurant Marie Antoinette* on the highway is also reasonable. There is a *Youth Hostel* (tel 724-9595) at 186 Rouleau St. It's open summers only, $6 to $7.

After Rimouski the land becomes noticeably more wooded as you enter the Gaspe region. At Mont Joli, Highway 132 goes south to New Brunswick for those wishing to avoid the Gaspe Peninsula.

Jardins de Metis

On the west side of Grand Metis, this oddity is worth a look. It's an immaculately tended, Japanese-like garden with streams, flowers, bushes and trees – all labelled. There's a fantastic view over the coast by the old wooden mansion. The garden was started by one Mrs Reford, who inherited the land from her uncle, the first president of Canadian Pacific Railway. Begun in 1910, it is now looked after by the government. Admission is $3.50 per car. In the house at the centre of the park is a restaurant with lunches for $6 to $9.

At Pedore, inland about seven km from Grand Metis, is a farm bed & breakfast (tel 775-5467) run by the Hartons, who speak only French. Singles/doubles here cost $20/24. It's a working farm and very quiet.

The Gaspe Peninsula

This is the rounded chunk of land that juts out above New Brunswick into the Gulf of the St Lawrence. To the people of Quebec it's 'the Gaspesie'. The peninsula really begins at Matane. In this area the trees and woods have become forests, the towns smaller and farther apart, the weather windier and cooler. The landscape is very hilly and rocky with excellent views along the rough coastline.

With fewer attractions, less development or organised tourism, the area is much less crowded than Cape Breton Island in Nova Scotia. It's probably harder to get around, but to me it's scenically more impressive.

The Gaspe is popular with cyclists, despite the hard climbs, and there are plenty of hostels, campgrounds and unoccupied woods to sleep in. The little trucks and chip wagons throughout the area make superb French fries and real meat hamburgers.

You may see some of these French signs so here's a quick run-down:

pain de menage – home-made bread
a vendre – for sale

vers – not a tasty snack, but worms
biere froid – cold beer (available at most stores)
cretons – a local pork pâté

Except for gasoline, prices in the region are quite low and a trip around this part of the country is highly recommended.

MATANE

A small, typical French town, Matane makes a good stopover point. There's an information office by the lighthouse off the highway, open daily. Rue St Jerome and St Pierre are the main streets in town.

Matane is a fishing town with salmon and shrimp among the catch. In mid-June is the shrimp (*crevette*) festival when you can feast on them.

Salmon run up the river here, beginning in June. The government has set up a monitoring system where you can see the fish heading upstream and listen to taped explanatory information. It's in the little building by the dam, adjacent to the park.

You can buy salmon and other fish at the packing plant on Rue St Pierre, at the corner of Avenue Fraser.

Behind the City Hall is a large park with an open-air theatre for summer shows.

Matane Wildlife Preserve

The preserve can be reached south of Matane off the 195. It's a huge area with camping, canoeing, hiking, fishing and boat rentals. For information call 562-3700. You'll see lots of moose here.

The road continues on to New Brunswick but don't take it. Go around the rest of the Gaspe Peninsula.

Places to Stay

The best places to stay are the motels strung out along the highway. Some are expensive; *Les Mouettes* at 298 McKinnon is one of the cheapest at $30 to $36. Similarly at the *Motel Le Beach*. In town is the world's easiest-to-find youth hostel. As you come east along Highway 132, cross the bridge and you can't help but see the big red letters (though they are now fading) – *Auberge de Jeunesse* (tel 562-2836) – on top of the hill on the right. It is not bad and has a kitchen. The rates are $6 to $7. The address is 354 Rue d'Amours. As alternatives there are the *Hotel de Roy* at 74 Rue St Pierre, or *Hotel L'Ancre* at No 292. They both offer basic accommodation for $15.

Places to Eat

For the stomach, the fairly new *Café des Iles* at 50 d'Amours is recommended. They offer three complete dinner choices from between $6 and $7.50. Prices are lower at lunch.

The *Café aux Delices* on St Jean near St Jerome St is a standard, bit-of-everything restaurant. A block away, at Bon Pasteur and St Jerome near the river is a health-food store with a few snacks and sandwiches.

Getting There & Away

Ferry The ferry to Baie Comeau on the north shore is the run furthest east. There are two a day and the trip takes two hours and 20 minutes. Cost is $16 per car, $2.50 per bicycle, $7 per person. For information call 562-6344.

Bus The terminus (tel 562-1177) is at 701 Avenue du Phare Ouest. There are two buses a day for Gaspe, four a day for Quebec City.

CAP CHAT

The locals of this small town will take you out cod fishing for $5 to $7 an hour. It's best to spend about three hours early in the morning – the waters tend to be calmer then. Try Olivier Boucher at 786-5802, Jean Lepage at 786-2143, or Raymond Amiot at 786-2229.

Lac Joffre, Lac Simoneau or Lac Paul are good for trout-fishing and there's salmon-fishing in the Cap Chat River.

Rocher Cap Chat (the rock) is a well-known landmark. It sits by the shore on the west side of town.

A good place to spend the night is the *Cabines Goemons Sur Mer*, right on the beach. The cabins have kitchens and go for $28 and up. Further east, the smaller, simpler *Cabines Skyline* are only $15/17 for singles/doubles and perfectly fine, though the location is not as good.

Le Cabillaud Restaurant on the east side of town is surrounded by flowers and is a good eating spot. However, it's not really cheap, at $6 to $20. They specialise in seafoods.

STE ANNE DES MONTS

Ste Anne is another fishing town, with smoked fish for sale down by the dock opposite the church. For a cheap, decent meal go to *Le Patriote* in Les Galeries Gaspesiennes near the junction of Highways 132 and 299. It's good for breakfast or lunch. From 25 June to 3 August, tours are given by local people (tel 763-3366), offering insights into the past and present. There's one to Cap Chat for $6 and one to Gaspesie Park for $8. They leave from the Motel la Brunante.

GASPESIE PARK

From Ste Anne des Monts, Highway 299 runs south to this excellent park. It is a huge, rugged, undeveloped area of lakes, woods and mountains. There's lots of wildlife like deer and moose. The fishing is good; hiring a boat for three people costs $25.

At Gite du Mont Albert there is camping and a lodge with a highly-praised restaurant. Rooms can be reasonable; the range is great but they start at $22 single or double.

The roads leading through the park are very rough and will take you to various hiking trails – some overnighters – and lookouts over the lumpy Chic Choc mountains.

For park info, call 763-3039. You can enter the park at Ste Anne des Monts and return to the coast highway at Mont St Pierre.

Mont Jacques Cartier – at 1270 metres – is the highest mountain in this part of the country. It rises above the tree line and epitomises the conditions of the Gaspe: cold, windy and often wet at the peak, too. Hiking up it takes about 3¾ hours for the return trip, but it's well worthwhile – the alpine scenery and views are fantastic and it is fairly common to see some of the herd of woodland caribou near the top. These are the last of the caribou found this far south; they seem to find the barrens quite fine and happily munch on lichens all day. You can also climb Mont Albert – a longer but easier hike.

MONT ST PIERRE

Not far from Ste Anne des Monts on Highway 132 is this little white village nestled in a short bay. The setting is spectacular and this small community, far from any big city, is famous for hang-gliding. The spot is considered one of the best in North America. Each year around the end of June is the two-week Hang-Gliding Festival (La Fete du Vol Libre).

There is a youth hostel, a campsite and several motel-hotels. Tours from the hostel to local sites cost $4 to $7.

The cliffs east of town are etched with interesting rock patterns. They continue like this for some km out of town. You'll see lots of signs here for *pain frais* or *pain chaud* – fresh or hot bread.

From here east, there are lots of good picnic areas with coastal views, also plenty of motels or cabins with cuisinettes (kitchenettes) and campgrounds. Good sunsets.

Other Attractions

At Anse Pleureuse, turn off to Murdochville for mine tours. Madeline Centre, a particularly beautiful village, has lots of baked goods for sale. At Pointe a la Fregate, the *Auberge*, in the old white house, has good food for $25 to $30.

FORILLON NATIONAL PARK

The park lies at the extreme north-eastern tip of the peninsula and is well worth a stop. The northern coast consists of steep limestone cliffs – some as high as 200 metres – and long pebble beaches. See Cap Bon Ami for the best of this topography. There is a telescope for whale-watching – good from May to October – and sometimes you can hear them surface.

There are good trails through the park, some with overnight camping. Two trails are 16 km – about six hours – but there are others that take 30 minutes to three hours to travel. The park service naturalists offer interpretive programmes and free guided tours. You can also use the information chalet. Boat trips to bird sanctuaries and seal colonies are possible. In the woods there are moose, deer and an increasing population of black bears.

The south coast has more beaches – some sandy – and small coves. Penouille Beach is said to have the warmest waters. Petit Gaspe is the most popular organised campground as it is protected from sea breezes.

The hike along the southern shore to Cap Gaspe is easy and very nice, with scenery that's good though not spectacular. The headlands, with a lighthouse, have viewing stations.

CAP DES ROSIERS

This is a small, old and interesting little village on the north shore. The graveyard, right on the cliff, tells the town's history – how the English came from Guernsey and Jersey, and the Irish settlers were Kavanaghs, O'Conners, etc; and how both groups mingled with the French. Generations later, the same names are still here in town.

There are a couple of places to stay. The *Chalets Cap Cabins*, about $22, are pleasantly rustic with views over the bay. There's also a restaurant in town. Saltwater sport-fishing trips depart from the wharf on the *Anna-Lucie* for $14.

At Cap Aux Os on the south shore there is a *Youth Hostel* beside the motel on Highway 132, overlooking the bay.

GASPE

After all the good scenery and attractive little villages, the town after which the entire peninsula was named seems pretty ordinary. It does have all the amenities and services, petrol stations and grocery stores, etc; also a fair bit of English is spoken.

The Jacques Cartier Monument at the north side of town is worth a look. It's different and well done. It was here in 1534 that the explorer landed, met the Iroquois and claimed the area for the king of France. He took two sons of Chief Donnacona back to see France and later returned them. Beside the sculpture is a museum showing maritime exhibits, some crafts and a bit on traditional foods. Admission is $2. Closed Saturdays and Sunday mornings.

There's camping by the Fort Ramsay Motel on the water.

PERCE

Named after the large offshore rock formation with the hole pierced through it (one of Canada's best-known landmarks), this town is the main tourist attraction of the Gaspe Peninsula. Despite this, it's a pleasant, pretty place and the Perce Rock is truly an impressive sight. Perce is the only place on the peninsula that gets busy, and because of this June or September make good visiting times. The weather is usually good then, too. The Tourist Office is in the centre of town beside the dock for boats to Bonaventure Island.

Just north of town is the Pic de l'Aurore (Peak of Dawn), which dominates the north end of town. From the next hill you'll see Perce Rock below and, further out, Ile Bonaventure, an island bird sanctuary. Other good views of Perce Rock are from the road, south of town.

You can also walk out to it anytime and even around much of it at low tide.

For $7, a boat will take you to the green Ile Bonaventure beyond Perce Rock. There are Wildlife Service-sponsored walks on the island and a gannet colony of 50,000. They also run a Wildlife Interpretation Centre south of town on the Route d'Irlande road, which is open from 10 am to 5.30 pm. There's a walking trail, film, slide-show and naturalists on hand to answer questions on the geology, fauna and flora of the area.

In town there are lots of souvenir shops selling glasswork, pottery and some good quilts. At the south end is a well-laid-out museum.

Behind the town are some interesting walks, which you can use a Tourist Office map for. Hike up to Mont Ste Anne for a great view and to see the deep crevice between two sections of mountain and the Grotto near Mont Blanc.

At nearby beaches, rock hounds can look for agate, which is abundant. There is also some diving in the area and an underwater park; check the dive shop by the Tourist Office.

At night there is often folk music or jazz at *Les Fous de Basson Café*.

Places to Stay

During the mid-summer months, a *Youth Hostel* (tel 782-2829) is open with beds for $6.50. It's up the hill in the southern portion of town beyond St Paul's Anglican Church. Turn right off Highway 132 just south of Perce Wharf.

There are a number of good-value guest houses around. *Maison Avenue House* (tel 782-2954) is on Rue d'Eglise, which runs off the main street in the middle of town. Before the church, you'll see this fine house with five rooms of varnished wood at just $10 for singles, $14 to $16 doubles. There are sinks in the very clean rooms. The guest house is in an excellent location and both English and French are spoken. The place next door also rents rooms.

A little more expensive is *Maison The Haven* (tel 782-2374) on the main street, with rooms at $15 to $25.

South of town are a few bargains. The *Etoile Chalets*, little cabins with good views, are just $12 single, $15 double. Further along on the other side of the road is *Hillside Farm Guest House*. And a few doors further is *Mahan's Guest House* (tel 782-2294), a deal at $12 single, $14 double, $16 triple. It's an 85-year-old wooden house set back from the road, six km from town. The rooms are comfortable, with some antique furniture. The woman who runs it is English and has lived in Perce all her life.

In town, *Horseshoe Cabins (Cabines Fer a Cheval)* are central, on the sea side. There are 10 units, each with a balcony and a great view of the rock and island. A small boardwalk runs along the shoreline by an indoor/outdoor restaurant attached to one of the cabins. Singles are $20, doubles $25 and up. Recommended.

Across the street, the green-and-white *Fleur de Lys* charges $25 to $45. The *Sea Gull* is $22 or $26 with TV.

There are many other places to stay, the lower-priced ones out of town a bit. There are also campgrounds with views on both sides of town.

Places to Eat

Les Fous de Basson is the café in the centre of town, beside the art gallery. They serve breakfasts of yoghurt, granola, croissants and other foods. Lunches $3 to $4. Dinners $6 to $14; seafood is on the menu too.

Biard's is on the highway in town, just slightly north of the centre. It's a standard sort of place with OK prices for such a town and cheap breakfasts. The daily special is $6; lobster is $12.

There is a brasserie (a tavern admitting women) on Rue d'Eglise. It's always good for a cheap feed and a couple of cold ones.

The *Pantagruel*, five km east out of town, has complete dinners for $7.95. They have fresh cod. Back in town, *La*

Table a Roland and *Au Pigalle* are cheap, the latter with Chinese food.

For a good splurge, the *Auberge Le Coin du Banc* is recommended. They have an extensive menu with table d'hôtes in three price ranges – \$9.95, \$14.95 and \$19.95. Good seafood, and you help yourself to six home-made desserts. The dining room is comfortably casual with a hodge-podge of antiques, odds and ends and farm tools. No credit cards accepted. It's about seven km west of Perce; you won't miss it – the yard is scattered with junk.

There's a bakery north of town, on the left-hand side.

Getting There & Away

Voyageur Buses link Perce to Matane, Rimouski, Quebec and Montreal. They also go to Edmundston and Campbellton, New Brunswick.

VIA Rail serves Perce, Gaspe and points along the south shore. The one-way fare to Levis is \$90 (\$68 for one-week return), \$132 to Montreal. The rail line goes along the north shore of the Peninsula as far as Matane.

SOUTH SHORE

The south shore of the Gaspe Peninsula is different from the north coast. The land is flatter and less rocky, the weather warmer, so farming and small industries are more important. There are quite a few English towns on this southern shore.

In Paspebiac live descendants of Normans, Bretons and Basques. New Carlisle was founded by Loyalists and has some grand colonial homes. One of these homes, on the north side of the road at the east end of town, is open for tours.

Bonaventure, a small, pleasant town by the water, has an Acadian Museum.

From Carleton there are boat excursions (tel 364-3926) for fishing or sightseeing. Daily bus tours also leave from Motel Baie Bleue. Good food is available at *Café l'Independant*, specialising in fish.

At Miguasha, a park has been set up around a fossil site. A few km west of the bridge from Pointe a la Croix, a new national park is being created to mark the battle of Restigouche. An interpretation centre explains its significance.

The ferry to Dalhousie, New Brunswick, from Miguasha is a short cut across the Baie de Chaleurs.

Islands

ILES DE LA MADELEINE (Magdalen Islands)

Out in the Gulf of St Lawrence, closer to the Maritime provinces than Quebec, lies this 100-km-long string of islands. There are about a dozen islands, 120 km north-east of Prince Edward Island, and most of them are linked by long sand spits. In fact, the islands are little more than spits themselves, so excellent sand beaches line the shores. Because of their remoteness, the quiet life, the seashore scenery of carved red and grey cliffs and the great beaches, the islands appeal to outsiders and are slowly becoming more popular with visitors.

The local people make their living mainly from fishing, as they have always done. Sealing was important until recently, but the commercial hunt is disappearing under international pressure from those opposed to it. Some former hunters are now taking tourists out on the ice to see and photograph the baby seals.

Over 90% of the population speak various French dialects, but Scottish and Irish descendants live in some number on the islands of Entry and Grosse-Isle.

The main islands are Ile du Havre aux Maisons, which has an airport, and Ile du Cap aux Meules. At the town of Cap aux Meules, the ferry from Souris, Prince Edward Island ties in, and there is an information office, (tel 986-2245).

Most of the islands' activities and sights revolve around the sea. The waters aren't tropical but are warmed by the Gulf Stream. With nearly constant breezes, windsurfing is very good and several places offer boards and lessons. Beach-strolling, and exploring lagoons, tidal pools and the cliff formations can take up days. More work can be found searching out the best vistas and poking around the fishing villages. There are also some historic points of interest: the old churches and unusual traditional buildings such as the now-disappearing hay barns. In the evenings during the summer, you may find a concert or play or an exhibition of some sort.

At Grand Entree, a lobster festival is held the first week in July. Fishing expeditions can be arranged and diving on the reefs is possible.

Places to Stay

A good portion of the Magdalen's accommodation is in people's homes or in cottages and trailers they rent out. These represent by far the best bargain and average $30 for two people. There are motels as well, at nearly double the price. Lastly there is a *Youth Hostel* (tel 969-4286) on Havre aux Maisons, and at least three campgrounds on the islands.

Getting There & Away

The cheapest and most common way to get to the Magdalen Islands is by ferry from Souris on Prince Edward Island. The boat leaves once daily except Tuesdays but if things get busy, an extra crossing may be added until things slow down again. You should make a reservation for the return trip a week in advance. The cost is about $25 per person for the five-hour, 223-km trip.

Passenger boats cruise to the islands down the St Lawrence from Montreal, but are expensive. There is also a passenger and cargo ship once a week from Montreal, which is less costly. Canadian Airlines flies in daily from Halifax, and Quebecair has two flights a day from Montreal, Quebec, Sept Isles, the Gaspe and other points.

Getting Around

Five of the main islands are linked by road but distances are small and bicycles are recommended for getting around. There are lots of rental places. As you peddle, look for the old fish-smoking houses – they're becoming scarce as the islands develop.

A ferry connects Ile d'Entree to the two principal islands.

ANTICOSTI ISLAND

A large island at the mouth of the St Lawrence, halfway between the Gaspe and the north shore, Anticosti was privately owned by different companies and individuals from 1680 to 1974. One was Henri Menier, a French chocolate whiz. The island is now a natural wildlife reserve. There are about 300 residents, mainly around Port Menier on the western tip, from where the island's lone road ventures to the interior.

There is a campground not far from town toward West Point at the end of the island. There is still no ferry from the mainland though there are flights from Sept Iles. I guess it doesn't get too crowded.

Ontario

Entered Confederation: 1 July 1867
Area: 1,068,587 square km
Population: 8,625,107

The name 'Ontario' is derived from an Iroquois Indian word meaning 'rocks standing high near the water', probably referring to Niagara Falls.

Ontario, situated smack in the middle of the country, is the centre of Canadian politics and economics, and much of the arts as well. It is by far the richest, most populous province, with about a third of all Canadians. Over 80% of Ontarians are urban dwellers, most living between Kingston and Windsor along the great waterways that make up the southern boundary. The country's largest city, Toronto, is here, as are the Niagara Falls and Ottawa, Canada's capital city. These features help make this region the most heavily visited in the country.

The area around the western shore of Lake Ontario is booming – there is as much manufacturing in Ontario as in all the other provinces combined. Hamilton is the country's iron and steel centre; nearby cities make Ontario the national leader in car production.

Further north are tremendous resources. Sudbury produces a quarter of the world's nickel; Elliot Lake sits on the largest uranium deposits known. And, of course, there are the forests.

Odd as it may seem, Ontario is also tops in farm income, although the area of excellent farmland (around the Great Lakes) shrinks each year as fields are lost to asphalt. Fruit is a major market crop and to an ever-decreasing extent, tobacco.

Despite all this, there remains much uncluttered wooded lakeland and large areas of quiet country towns surrounded by small produce farms. And, within the northern regions, vast areas of wilderness still exist.

I guess you can see why Ontario is called one of the 'have' provinces. It is also very conservative – politically and socially.

Within Ontario is the country's most southerly region, an important climatic factor. Around Niagara the summers are long, the winters mild. Lake Ontario keeps the bulk of the population from being too cold in winter. Summers can be hot and muggy. Temperatures drop progressively (and considerably) the further north you go.

Ontario has many excellent government parks for outdoor activities.

Ottawa

Ottawa is known to all Canadians with the mixed emotions worthy of a nation's capital.

It sits attractively on the south bank of the Ottawa River at its confluence with the Rideau. The gently rolling Gatineau Hills of Quebec are within sight to the north.

The government is the largest employer, and the stately gothic Parliament Buildings act as landmarks. The city attracts four million tourists a year, many to see just what the heck kind of a city the capital is. The abundance of museums and cultural activities are another enticement. And then, of course, there are the Canadian Mounties who are to be seen in numbers, but only in summer.

A surprise may be the amount of French

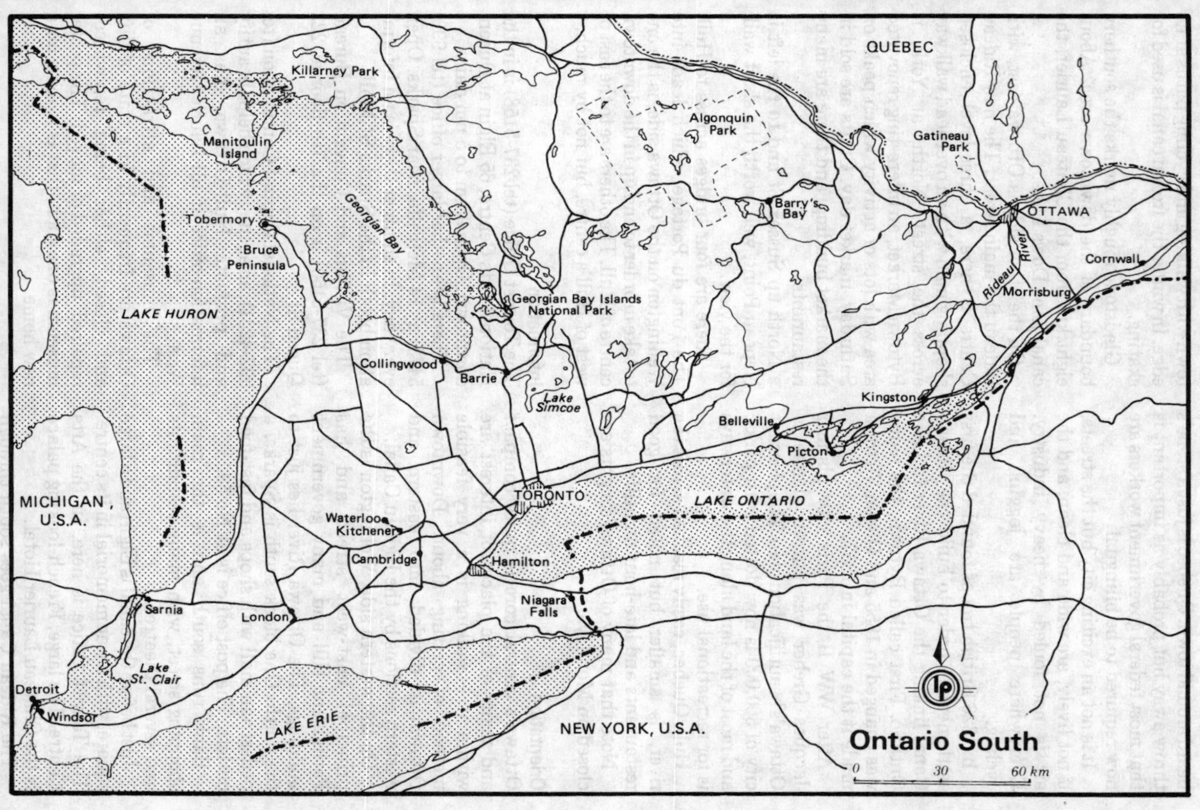
QUEBEC
Killarney Park
Algonquin Park
Gatineau Park
Manitoulin Island
Georgian Bay
Barry's Bay
OTTAWA
Tobermory
Bruce Peninsula
Rideau River
Cornwall
Morrisburg
Georgian Bay Islands National Park
LAKE HURON
Collingwood
Barrie
Lake Simcoe
Kingston
Belleville
Picton
MICHIGAN, U.S.A.
TORONTO
LAKE ONTARIO
Waterloo
Kitchener
Cambridge
Hamilton
Niagara Falls
Sarnia
London
Lake St. Clair
Detroit
Windsor
LAKE ERIE
NEW YORK, U.S.A.
Ontario South
0
30
60 km

heard around town. Quebec is just a stone's throw away but probably as important is that most federal government workers are now required to be bilingual.

It is not an exciting city but the streets, if not lively, are wide and clean, and the air is not fouled by heavy industry. Everywhere people are jogging and cycling.

In 1826 British troops founded the first settlement in order to build the Rideau Canal linking the Ottawa River to Lake Ontario. First called Bytown, the name was changed in 1855 and Queen Victoria made it the capital in 1857.

After WW II the Paris city planner Jacques Greber was put in charge of Ottawa's beautification plan. The pleasant city of 300,000 is now dotted with parks, and most of the land along the waterways is for recreational use.

Hull, Quebec, easily reached across the river, is smaller but noted for good restaurants and late-hour nightlife.

Note that many of Ottawa's sights are closed on Mondays.

Orientation

Ottawa's central core is quite compact and many of the places of interest are within it – walking is a very feasible method of getting about. Downtown Ottawa is divided into eastern and western sections by the Rideau Canal.

On the western side, Wellington is the principal east-west street and has Parliament Hill and many government buildings. The Ottawa River lies just to the north. One block south is Sparks, a pedestrian mall with shops and fast-food outlets. The post office is at No 59.

Bank runs south and is the main shopping street, with many restaurants and several theatres.

Just before the canal is Elgin and a large square, with a war memorial in its centre. The Tourist Office is here, in the Arts Centre. The large, French-looking palace is the Chateau Laurier Hotel.

The Rideau Canal goes south through town with walking and cycling paths at its edge. In winter the frozen canal is used for skating.

Gladstone roughly marks the southern boundary of the downtown area. About eight km from the Chateau Laurier, the canal joins Dows Lake.

On the other side is Ottawa east, with Rideau the main street. The new Rideau Centre is here, a three-level enclosed shopping mall with an overhead walkway across the street. North, at York, is Bytown Market, an interesting renovated area with lots of activity which peaks on Saturday, market day. Crafts are sold in the market building, and there are many restaurants.

North up Sussex St and to the left is Nepean Point, well worth the short walk for the view.

There are four bridges across to Hull. The Pont du Portage, which leads into Wellington on the Ottawa side, is the one to take in order to end up in the downtown centre of Hull. The others are to the east or west of Hull's centre, but not by much.

Information

The Tourist Office (tel 237-5158) is in the National Arts Centre, 65 Elgin at Queen, downtown. Open 9 am to 5 pm daily.

There is another larger office (tel 992-5473) at 14 Metcalfe, near Sparks. Open every day. In summer there is an information booth in the Sparks St Mall.

The Visitors and Convention Bureau (tel 237-5150) is on the 7th floor at 222 Queen St.

The National Capital Commission (tel 992-4231), an agency which helps beautify and promote Hull-Ottawa, has an information office at 161 Laurier Avenue West.

The museums and attractions of Ottawa are frequently in a state of flux and closed, either being renovated, repaired, upgraded or moved. The postal museum is one such, that is looking for a new home.

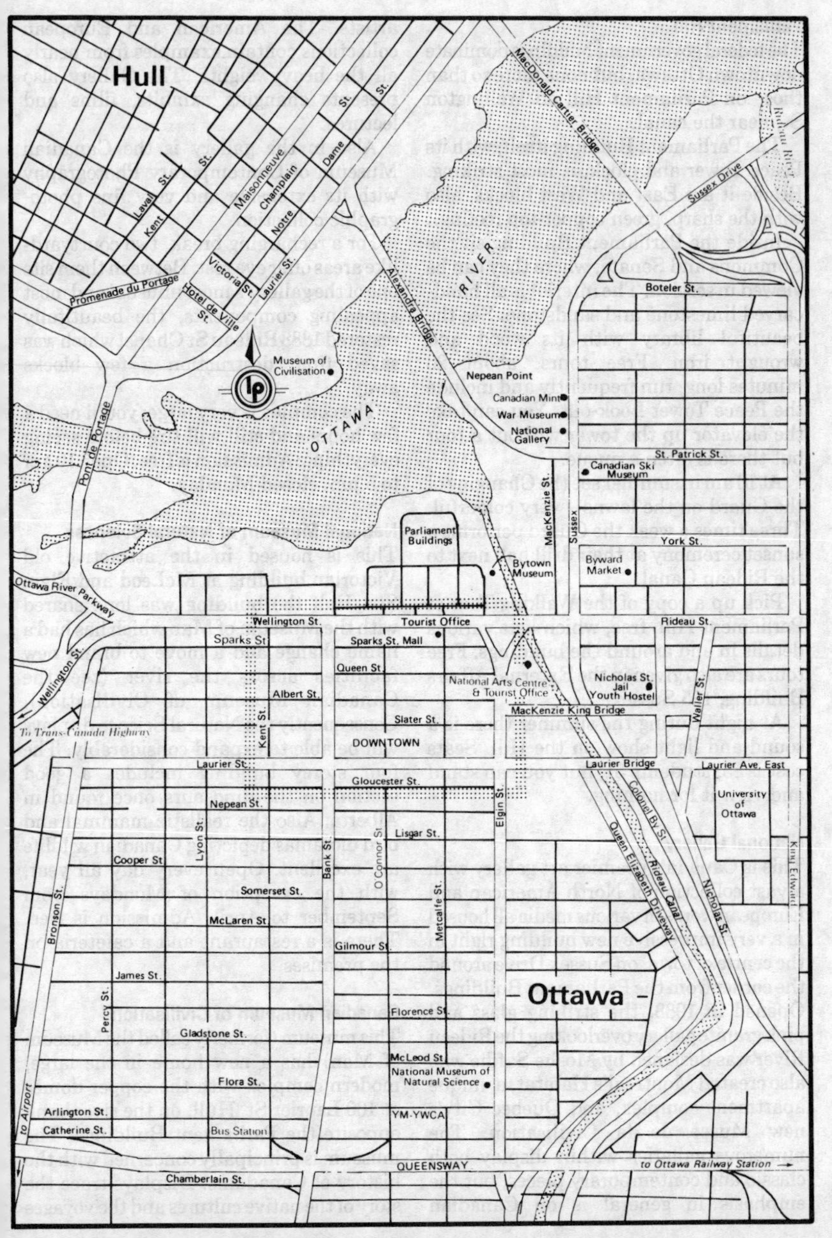

Hull
Laval St.
Kent St.
Maisonneuve
Champlain
Notre Dame St.
Victoria St.
Laurier St.
Hotel de Ville St.
Promenade du Portage
Pont de Portage
Alexandra Bridge
MacDonald Cartier Bridge
Sussex Drive
Rideau River
RIVER
OTTAWA
Museum of Civilisation
Nepean Point
Canadian Mint
War Museum
National Gallery
Boteler St.
St. Patrick St.
Canadian Ski Museum
MacKenzie St.
Sussex
Parliament Buildings
York St.
Bytown Museum
Byward Market
Ottawa River Parkway
Wellington St.
Tourist Office
Rideau St.
Sparks St
Sparks St. Mall
Queen St.
National Arts Centre & Tourist Office
Nicholas St. Jail Youth Hostel
Waller St.
Albert St.
MacKenzie King Bridge
Slater St.
Wellington St.
To Trans-Canada Highway
Kent St.
DOWNTOWN
Laurier St.
Gloucester St.
Laurier Bridge
Laurier Ave. East
Colonel By St.
Nepean St.
Elgin St.
University of Ottawa
Lisgar St.
Lyon St.
Bank St.
O'Connor St.
Queen Elizabeth Driveway
Rideau Canal
Nicholas St.
King Edward
Cooper St.
Somerset St.
Metcalfe St.
Bronson St.
McLaren St.
Gilmour St.
James St.
Ottawa
Percy St.
Florence St.
Gladstone St.
McLeod St.
Flora St.
National Museum of Natural Science
to Airport
Arlington St.
YM-YWCA
Catherine St.
Bus Station
QUEENSWAY
to Ottawa Railway Station
Chamberlain St.

Parliament Hill

The federal government buildings dominate downtown Ottawa, but none more so than those on Parliament Hill off Wellington St, near the canal.

The Parliament Building itself, with its Peace Tower and clock, is most striking. Beside it are East and West blocks, also with the sharp, green copper-top roofing.

Inside the Parliament Building sit the Commons and Senate, where they can be viewed in session. The interior is all hand-carved limestone and sandstone. See the beautiful library with its wood and wrought iron. Free tours, about 20 minutes long, run frequently and include the Peace Tower Look-out. You can take the elevator up the tower without a tour but there is often a queue.

At 10 am in summer see the Changing of the Guard on the lawns – very colourful. Three times a week the Guard performs a sunset ceremony at their drill hall next to the Rideau Canal.

Pick up a copy of the Walking Tour of Parliament Hill, free, which lists various details in and around the buildings. Free tours are also given in the External Affairs Building, 125 Sussex.

At night during the summer there is a sound and light show on the Hill. Seats cost is $3, students $1, but you can stand and view it for nothing.

National Gallery

This is Canada's premier art gallery with a vast collection of North American and European works in various media all housed in a very impressive new building right in the centre of town, on Sussex Drive around the corner from the Parliament Buildings. Opened in 1988, the striking glass and pink granite gallery overlooking the Rideau River was designed by Moshe Safdie who also created Montreal's Habitat, a unique apartment complex, and Quebec City's new Musee de la Civilisation. The numerous galleries within display both classic and contemporary pieces, but the emphasis in general is on Canadian artists. The American and European collections contain examples from nearly all the heavyweights. The Gallery also presents changing exhibits, films and lectures.

Also in the gallery is the Canadian Museum of Contemporary Photography with its extensive and very fine photographic collection.

For a recharging break, two courtyard-like areas offer eye rest. Between them sits one of the gallery's most unusual and most appealing components, the beautifully restored 1888 Rideau St Chapel which was saved from destruction a few blocks away.

The complex is very large; you'll need a few hours and still will tire before seeing everything. Admission is free. Open 10 am to 5 pm, closed Monday.

National Museum of Natural Sciences

This is housed in the attractive old Victorian building at McLeod and Elgin Sts. Half the building was long shared with the Museum of Man which has had a name change and a move to brand new facilities across the river (see the Canadian Museum of Civilisation). Consequently the Natural Science displays will be able to expand considerably. The four storey building includes a good section on the dinosaurs once found in Alberta. Also the realistic mammal and bird dioramas depicting Canadian wildlife are excellent. Open every day all year, with the exception of Mondays from September to April. Admission is free. There is a restaurant and a cafeteria on the premises.

Canadian Museum of Civilisation

This museum (formerly called the Museum of Man) has a new home in the large, modern complex with the copper domes at 100 Laurier St, Hull, on the river bank opposite the Parliament Buildings. The museum is principally concerned with the history of Canadians. Displays trace the story of the native cultures and the voyages of the country's European explorers. If you're not going west don't miss the chance to see the art of the BC Indians, especially the Haida. The Native Gallery offers various shows by Canadian artists – painting, dance, crafts and more. There are also displays on the Inuit and the development of Canada's national identity. In the Children's Museum section, exhibits permit hands-on interaction. The museum also has an IMAX and OMNIMAX theatre for realistic, large-format film presentations. Closed Mondays.

Supreme Court of Canada
This rather intimidating structure is open to non-litigants. Construction of the home for the highest court of the land was begun in 1939 but not completed until 1946. The grand entrance hall, 12 metres high, is certainly impressive. During the summer a visit will include a free tour given by a law student. It's at the corner of Wellington and Kent.

Bytown Museum
This is in the oldest stone building in the city. It's to the east of Parliament Hill beside the canal – go down the stairs from Wellington and back at the river. Used during construction of the canal, it now contains artefacts and documents pertaining to local history. Open mid-May to mid-October, 10 am to 4 pm, Sunday 2 to 5 pm. A small admission fee is charged.

War Museum
At 330 Sussex Drive, this museum contains all manner of things military and traces Canadian military history. There's a life-sized replica of a WW I trench that's good. You'll also see large displays with sound, showing the American invasion of 1775 and the Normandy D-Day landing. The museum also contains the country's largest collection of war art. Open 10 am to 6 pm in summer, in winter from noon to 5 pm. Sundays, noon to 5 pm. Closed Monday.

Royal Canadian Mint
Next door to the War Museum is the Mint. Here they produce both domestic and foreign coins and bullion. Founded in 1908 and renovated in the mid-1980s, this imposing stone building has always been Canada's major refiner of gold. Tours given every half hour show the process from sheets of metal to bags of coins. Hours are from 8.30 to 11 am and 12.30 to 3 pm Monday to Friday.

Currency Museum
For those who like to look without possessing, you can see more money at the Currency Museum in the Bank of Canada, 245 Sparks St. Open daily in summer, closed Monday in winter. Various displays tell the story of money through the ages, from whales' teeth to collectors' bank notes. The emphasis is on Canadian monies.

National Aviation Museum
This collection of over 100 aircraft is housed in a huge new triangular building (about the size of four football fields) at the Rockcliffe Airport, not too far from the centre of town. See planes ranging from the Silver Dart of 1909 to the first turbine-powered Viscount passenger carrier, to more recent jets. Peace and wartime planes are equally represented; included is the renowned Spitfire. The Cessna Crane is the very one my father trained in for the RCAF. Free, open 9 am to 9 pm. Closed Monday. The airport is off St Laurent St north-east of downtown near the river and the Canadian Forces Base. Call 998-4566 to check on opening hours as they vary according to attendance and time of year.

National Museum of Science & Technology
At 1867 St Laurent Boulevard at Russell Rd (tel 998-4566), this museum has all kinds of participatory scientific learning exhibits. Try things out, test yourself, watch physical laws in action, see optical illusions. It's great for kids; avoid

weekends for this reason. Also on display are farm machinery, trains, model ships and stagecoaches. The bicycle and motorcycle collections and the computers are good, and don't miss the incubator where you can see live chicks in various stages of hatching.

National Postal Museum

In Ottawa you'll find many museums and attractions are either being renovated, repaired, upgraded or moved. The postal museum is one such at the moment. While a new permanent location is sought, some of the displays can be seen at 365 Laurier St at the corner of Kent (tel 995-8088). Open Tuesday to Saturday 9 am to 5 pm. Also here is the philatelic library and a sales counter for various collectables.

Canadian Ski Museum

This small museum at 475 Promenade Sussex Drive, has a collection of equipment and memorabilia. It is open noon to 4 pm Tuesday to Saturday.

Bytown Fire Brigade Museum

Nearby, at 179 Clarence, this small museum has some restored antique fire trucks and some other related memorabilia.

Cathedral Basilica of Notre Dame

Built in 1839, this is one of the city's most impressive houses of worship. A pamphlet available at the door outlines the many features including carvings, windows, the organ and Gothic style ceiling.

Central Experimental Farm

At the Driveway and Carling Avenue (tel 995-5222) are about 500 hectares of flowers, trees, shrubs and gardens. The site is still used for research on all aspects of farming and horticulture. A big flower show is held here in November, and both Canadian and foreign species are shown. Tours are given, or take your own walking tour. You'll also see livestock and show-case cattle herds, an observatory and the arboretum which is good for walking through. The farm is linked to the rest of Ottawa's cycling routes. Admission is free.

Laurier House

This Victorian home at 335 Laurier Avenue was built in 1878, and was the residence of two prime ministers – Laurier and the eccentric Mackenzie King. It's beautifully furnished throughout – don't miss the study on the top floor. Free. Closed Monday.

Prime Minister's House

You can view the outside of the present prime minister's house at 24 Sussex Drive as well as Rideau Hall, the Governor-General's pad, around the corner up from the river. At the latter, built in the early 1900s, the grounds are open to the public and tours are given with stories told of some of the goings-on through the years. At the main gate there's a changing of the guard ceremony every hour on the hour from the end of June to the end of August. Both houses are north-east of the market area.

Rockcliffe Village

East along Sussex Drive, this is one of the poshest, most prestigious areas in the country. Behind the mansion doors are some very prominent Canadian citizens and many foreign diplomats.

Prince of Wales Falls

Where the Rideau River meets the canal south of town (at the junction of Colonel By St and Hog's Back) there are falls, walking and cycling paths and some historical plaques.

Log Farm

This re-creation of a 19th-century farm, complete with costumed workers, is 20 km west of Parliament Hill. Both here and at Jacques Cartier Park there are historical exhibits and activities, some of which are participatory.

Activities

In summer you can rent a boat for trips along the canal. Canoe and rowboat rentals are at Dows Lake or at the marina on Hog's Back Rd (tel 733-5065). The rates are by the hour or week at the marina.

There are several outfits in town which run white-water rafting trips – one or two days. No experience is needed, and locations are less than two hours from town. Two to call are Equinox Adventures (tel 648-2241) in Quebec, and OWL Rafting (tel 646-2263). The Ottawa and the Magnetawan are two rivers that are used.

In winter there's skiing as close as 20 km from town in the Gatineau Hills. Two resorts with variously graded hills are Camp Fortune and Mont Cascades. Tow passes are more expensive on weekends. In warmer weather it's good for walking and picnicking.

Again in winter, the Rideau Canal is famous for the skating along five km of maintained ice. Rest spots along the way serve great doughnuts to go with the hot chocolate. Ask at the Tourist Office about skate rentals.

The city has an excellent parks system with a lot of green space and several conservation areas. There are also many walking, jogging and cycling trails as well as picnic areas. You'll even find some fishing. The Tourist Office has a sheet, with map, of all the parks and a description of each. Bicycle paths wind all over town; get a map of them. For rentals see the Getting Around section.

Events

The big annual event is the Festival of Spring in May. During this time the city is decorated with 200 types of tulips, mainly from Holland. Festivities include parades, regattas, car rallies, dances, concerts and fireworks.

In July and August the outdoor stage in Major's Hill Park, known as Astrolabe, is used for concerts, dance, mime and other performances. It's open nightly and is free.

Central Canada Exhibition is an annual event held toward the end of August. There are 10 days of displays, carnival and entertainment. The exhibition is held at Lansdowne Park.

The Canada Canoe Festival celebrates native peoples and the first pioneers, fur-traders and *voyageurs*.

In late January and early February is the good and popular Winterlude, a week of festivities mainly on or around frozen Dows Lake and the canal. The ice sculptures are really worth seeing.

Places to Stay

Hostels The *YHA Hostel* (tel 235-2595), 75 Nicholas St, is in the old Ottawa Jail – see the gallows at the back. It has a good location near the Parliament Buildings. Nicholas is just east of the Rideau Canal off Rideau St. Largely restored, the hostel has 160 beds, some of them in old cells. It's bit pricey at $10 for members and $14 for non-members, but they have a sauna and cheap breakfasts are available. There is an information board, too. Open all year.

The *YMCA* and *YWCA* (tel 237-1320) are in the same building at 180 Argyle, in the southern downtown area under the Queensway. They're at the corner of O'Connor. Singles for either sex are $25 to $30, doubles $33. There's a cafeteria and a pool.

The *University of Ottawa* (tel 231-7055) downtown has some of the cheapest dormitory space in Canada. The rates for students are $11/25 for singles/doubles and for non-students $25/34 for singles/doubles. They have laundry facilities, parking and a cafeteria with cheap meals. Reception is at 100 Hastey St. The university is an easy walk south-east of the Parliament Buildings. They also offer accommodation at Little White Fish Camp in Gracefield, Quebec, where there are extensive sports facilities. It's open May through August.

Carleton University (tel 231-5510), also pretty central, has rooms for $20 singles or $32 doubles, which includes an all-you-can-eat breakfast. Athletic facilities and full meal service available. Check at the Tour & Conference Centre in the Commons Building at the university. Families are welcome.

Hotels - bottom end There are few older or budget hotels in Ottawa. Most moderate accommodation is in motels away from the town centre or in tourist homes.

The cheapest hotel is the *Albion* (tel 232-4819), 1 Daly St near the Youth Hostel, off Nicholas near Rideau. Singles $21, doubles $32. There's a cheap restaurant and bar downstairs. The place is decent and pretty well kept for an old inner-city hotel. Another no-star spot is the *Somerset House Hotel* (tel 233-7762) at 352 Somerset West, with 35 rooms starting at $21 singles, $28 doubles and rising quite a bit with more amenities.

The next two choices cost much more but have little character. The *Townhouse Motor Hotel* (tel 236-0151), 319 Rideau, charges $42/46 for singles/doubles. The *Parkway Motor Hotel* (tel 232-3781), 475 Rideau, is also close to town. Singles are $42, doubles $48. Cheap breakfasts are served in the coffee shop.

The *Butler Motor Hotel* (tel 746-4641) is comparable but a little cheaper at singles $40, doubles $45. The 95 rooms are large and it's a five-minute drive to downtown. The hotel is at 112 Montreal Rd.

Hotels - middle & top end Centrally located and good value is *Doral House* (tel 230-8055) at 486 Albert St, with 22 rooms at $44 to $49. Some with housekeeping although there is a coffee shop as well. There's a swimming pool, too. The *Beacon Arms Hotel* (tel 235-1413) at 88 Albert is much larger and has kitchen facilities, but rooms cost only slightly more at $51/56 for singles/doubles.

Hotel Roxborough (tel 237-5171), 123 Metcalfe, is more expensive, with rooms from $72 to $110, but they have some good weekend specials. *Chateau Laurier* is the one that looks like a castle at 1 Rideau, and is the city's best known hustler. Rates are from $100 to $150.

During the summer when Parliament is in recess and business traffic is light, many of the good downtown hotels offer very good daily and weekend specials. For example, the *Aristocrat Hotel* at 131 Cooper St rents its rooms for $59 for up to four people. The old stately *Lord Elgin* at 100 Elgin (with free parking) has summer prices starting at $60. Even the *Chateau Laurier* gets in on it and they have a large indoor swimming pool to take advantage of.

Tourist Homes Generally, this is the way to beat hotel prices in Ottawa. There are quite a few of these places, and most include breakfast. The Tourist Office has a list of some tourist homes, and Ottawa Bed & Breakfast (tel 563-0161) is an organisation listing such places. There are city, suburban and country members. Another such service is Capital Bed & Breakfast Reservation Service, again with a variety of places and locations. Prices start at $25/30 for singles/doubles. Some offer fireplaces or swimming pools and all have free parking.

In town, try these examples. *Daly Heritage Guest House* (tel 236-4314) is central, near the canal and market at 121 Daly Avenue. It's open in summer only, with singles $20 to $25, doubles $30 to $35. Also on Daly, at 185 is *McGee's Inn* (tel 237-6089) which has expanded to 14 rooms in a restored Victorian mansion and has prices going from $32 to $58, depending on facilities. Some rooms here have private bathrooms, which is not the norm in tourist homes, and a full breakfast is included.

At 352 Stewart is *Stewart Manor* (tel 741-1807) at $25 for singles and $30 for doubles. It has just three rooms and prices include continental breakfast. On last visit there were a couple more on Stewart so a stroll up the street may turn up others. There are some fine Edwardian houses in the neighbourhood.

Also on Stewart is the *Stewart Guest House* (tel 236-8951) at 354. Singles/doubles cost $25/35, with full breakfast; they have five rooms.

Another good street to check is Marlborough, south-east of Daly and Stewart, south from Laurier, west of the Rideau River. Its location is still quite central. *Australis Guest House* (tel 235-8461) is at 58 Marlborough and has just three rooms. Singles/doubles are $27/35, including breakfast, and there are lower weekly rates. Next door is the *Sandy Hill B & B* (tel 232-9198), which has rooms for $20 to $30. Not far away at No 80 is *Copland's Guest House* (tel 235-8458) with roughly the same prices and weekly rates. As on Stewart, others come and go along Marlborough.

Closer to downtown, *Beatrice Lyon* (tel 236-3904) has a guest home at 479 Slater, and charges $27/32 for singles/doubles. Slater runs east-west from Bank St. There is also *Albert House*, at 478 Albert, but this is more expensive: up to $45.

Lastly, one to try situated in the Bytown Market area and very central is *L'Auberge du Marche* (tel 235-7697) at 87 Guigues Avenue. It's a recently renovated older house with three rooms at $34/44 for singles/doubles.

Motels There are two main motel strips, one on each side of downtown. On the east side look along Montreal Rd, an extension of Rideau, which leads east out of town. The motels are about six km from downtown.

The *Miss Ottawa* (tel 745-1531), 2098 Montreal Rd, charges $38/46 for singles/doubles, and has a pool.

Le Normandie (tel 824-1350) is at 6825 Highway 17, and charges $30/38 for singles/doubles. They too have a pool.

Closest to town is the *Eastview* (tel 746-8115), 200 Montreal Rd charges $30/35 for singles/doubles.

On the west side of town check along Carling where there are numerous to choose from. These are about 10 km from downtown. The *Stardust* (tel 828-2748) at 2965 Carling charges $32/44 for singles/doubles for its 25 rooms. The *Bayshore* (tel 829-9411) at 2980 Carling charges $45/56 for singles/doubles.

Camping There is an excellent camping site practically right in the centre of town for $4 a night, with a stay limited to five nights. You'll find room for 200 tents at the corner of Fleet St and Booth. The site is called *Camp Le Breton*, west along Wellington past the government buildings. The camp is designed for cyclists and hikers. Open mid-May to Labour Day, early in September.

Camp Hither Hills is 10 km south of city limits on Highway 31 and charges $8. There are places both east and west of town on Highway 17. You'll also find some in Gatineau Park.

The Tourist Office has lists of others in the Ottawa area and there is camping in Gatineau Park across the river in Quebec.

Places to Eat

Hull has the very best restaurants but Ottawa has a pretty good range of places. I've grouped them by area.

Market We'll start with the market – it's central, just about everybody goes there, and there is a good selection. During the warm months many of the area eateries have outdoor tables.

The *Café Bohemian* at 89 Clarence is good for any meal. It's a busy European-type place with meals like quiche, fish and the latest trendy foods for $5 to $8. Sunday brunch is good value, with desserts and coffee. *Café au lait* is good here, especially the large size served in a bowl.

Across the street, *Bagel Bagel* has all sorts of bagel toppings and sandwiches as well as salads and other light meals and deli items. It's inexpensive and open daily. Good for breakfast.

Daphne & Victor's at 47 William St is pleasant; one side for eating, one for drinking. The place is good for snacks or a meal, $3 to $8. Try the carrot cake. There is another café, the *Fiesta*, across the street in the market building itself.

A bit less casual are two crepe places. *The Creperie*, corner of York and Byword, has salads and crepes at $4.25 to $6.95. Afternoon tea is served Monday to Friday. *La Crepe du France*, 76 Murray, has a patio bar and glassed-in terrace.

The *Khyber Pass* is a recommended slight splurge for its Afghani food – kebabs, pilau, rice and meat dishes that are less hot than Indian. Lunches are cheap; at dinnertime prices double but portions are larger, too. Nearby at 283 Dalhousie, *La Medina* has Lebanese food. Lunch $5, dinner $5 to $8.

The always reliable and economical *Spaghetti Factory* has a branch here at 126 York St, around the back. Full meals range from $6 to $10. Good value. There is a food fair in the Rideau Centre.

Downtown Along Bank St and its side streets are numerous restaurants.

Liv-eaticus at 131 Bank is an inexpensive, cafeteria-style natural-food restaurant. Pile up your plate and then pay by the weight. It's closed on weekends. At 202 Bank the *Silver Ball Cafe* is also vegetarian.

The *Brown Bag Cookery* at 113 Bank is an office-worker sandwich spot. It's a good choice for tasty, cheap food like fresh muffins and salads. Further south at 294 is the *Bank Café* in an old bank beautifully decorated in '30s style. There's also an outdoor section. Fixed-price dinners cost $15 and include a ticket to the movie at a theatre up the street. For lighter fare, the hamburgers sound good but aren't.

Suisha Gardens, on Slater St near the corner of Bank, is a highly recommended Japanese place. The food is excellent though somewhat westernised, the environment is authentic, and the service perfect. The best room is downstairs and to the left. Very inexpensive at lunch; prices are higher after 6 pm.

There are several British-style pubs around; try the *Royal Oak* at 360 Bank for British beer and food. They're friendly and you can play darts. The *Duke of Somerset* at 352 Somerset West is similar.

Flippers, upstairs at Bank and 4th, is a good fish restaurant with entrees at about $10 to $13.

Kamal at 789 Bank has good Lebanese food, $3 to $9, and is licensed. *The Avenue*, a standard Canadian greasy spoon, has the cheapest meals in town and bargain breakfasts.

Further south, the *Glebe Café* at 840 Bank is good. They offer a few Middle Eastern dishes, some vegetarian food, and burgers. Prices average from $3 to $8. It's a casual place where there are newspapers to read, local information and an entertainment notice board.

Ottawa also has a small Chinatown within walking distance of the centre. It's based around the corner of Bronson and Somerset. There are quite a few restaurants; for Cantonese food the *Yeng Shang* right at the corner is cheap and not bad.

Happy Four at Bank and Riverdale offers Sichuan as well as Cantonese food. There are also a few Chinese places on Rideau.

The Barking Fish at 1 Beechwood Avenue serves Cajun and Creole specialties.

For a splurge, *Chez Jean Pierre* is said to be good for French food.

Rideau St Across the canal from Wellington, this area has a number of eateries. The *Sitar*, not far east from the canal, is not cheap but has been recommended. Prices range from $22 to $34 for two. *Nate's*, at 316, is somewhat of a local institution. This Jewish delicatessen is known far and wide for its low prices on good food. The very popular breakfast special is the cheapest in the country – $1.25 for the works. The service is incredibly fast. They also serve blintzes, cream cheese bagels and the like. Open Sunday.

Elgin St This is another popular restaurant area with several night spots as well. *Sorrenti's* is good for pizza and the *Ritz* for other Italian food. You'll also find a couple of Middle Eastern places here.

Nightlife

Check Friday's *Ottawa Citizen* for complete club and entertainment listings.

Hooper's, 321 Bank St, has young new wave or rock bands. There's usually a small entrance fee, but admission is sometimes free. The *Penguin Café* at 292 Elgin is a fun spot on Friday and Saturday nights, with live big band music. The decor is sort of '40s style. Go for drinks or coffee and dessert. No cover charge. *Patty's Place* is a cosy Irish pub with music from Thursday to Saturday and an outdoor patio in summer. It's at Bank and Euclid.

Yuk Yuk's in the Beacon Arms Hotel, 88 Albert, has comedy from Thursday to Saturday. There's an admission charge.

There's a folk hootenanny every Sunday from 8 pm at the *Jack Purcell Community Centre*, 320 Elgin St. Admission $2. There's an open stage and nine players nightly at this local institution.

The *National Arts Centre*, known as the NAC, has theatres for drama and opera and is home to the symphony orchestra. It also presents a range of concerts and films. It's on the banks of the canal at Confederation Square.

The *Hotel Lafayette* in Bytown Market on York is good for its cheap draught beer day or night. It's your basic dive, but its character and characters attract a wide cross-section of people.

For jazz, *Friends and Company*, 221 Rideau St, has a live band Saturday afternoons and Tuesday nights. Folk music is played upstairs at night.

Hull Local jazz groups play at the *St Jacques*, Rue St Jacques, every Friday and Saturday night in Hull.

After 1 am, when the bars close, the partygoers head across the river to Hull where things are open to 3 am and later. Promenade du Portage in the middle of the downtown section has numerous nightspots, some with live music, some dressy, some quiet and dark – a good range. *Chez Henri* is an up-market disco; the deluxe *Viva* (tel 770-2216), 259 Boulevard St Joseph, is similar. *Le Bistro* attracts a more casual and younger crowd for loud dance music. It's on Aubry St at the top of the hill on the brick pedestrian mall off the Promenade. There are plenty of others in the area.

Cinema There are several repertory theatres around town, showing two films a night for $4 (non-members). They are the *Towne* (tel 745-3456), 5 Beechwood; the *Mayfair* (tel 234-3403), 1074 Bank St; and the *Phoenix* (tel 232-0456), 413 Bank St.

The Phoenix has a deal with the Bank Café down the street at 294: a three-course dinner and a movie for $15.

For what's happening in the National Arts Centre, check the box office or newspaper.

Getting There & Away

Air The airport is 20 minutes south of the city. It's surprisingly small. The main airlines serving the city are Canadian Airlines (tel 237-1380), and Air Canada (237-5000). Canadian Airlines destinations include Toronto ($129), Halifax ($202), Montreal ($103), Winnipeg ($298). All fares plus 8% tax. Excursion fares (return) are much cheaper: about half price. Air Canada fares, promotional sales aside, are pretty much the same.

Bus The bus station is at 265 Catherine near Bank St, south of downtown about a dozen blocks. The main bus line is Voyageur Colonial (tel 238-5900). One-way fares include:

Toronto – $33
Kingston – $17
Montreal – $17.50
Sudbury – $42.

Students can get a third off with a book of tickets; ask about it. Return tickets on a seven-day excursion, for example to Montreal, are considerably cheaper.

There are about 10 buses daily to Montreal and Toronto; some are express. There are frequent departures for Kingston, Belleville, Sudbury and other towns.

Train The train station (tel 238-8289) has been moved from town to a big, new centre a long way south-east of the city. It's on St Laurent Boulevard near Alta Vista Rd.

There are three trains a day for Toronto, six for Montreal, one to Vancouver. Trains for Sudbury depart Monday, Wednesday and Friday. One-way fares:

Toronto – $37
Kingston – $20
Montreal – $19
Sudbury – $45.

Ride Sharing A service called Tele-lift gets drivers and passengers together. Call 234-9927 or drop into the office at 402 Bank St to see what's available and when. Examples of costs for passengers are: Toronto $18, Montreal $8 and New York City $34. Other destinations are covered, too.

Hitching This is easy between Montreal and Ottawa, but convoluted for Toronto. Going to Montreal take the eastbound Montreal-Ogilvy bus on Rideau St which leads to Highway 17 East where you can begin. For Toronto take Highway 31 south to Highway 401 near the town of Morrisburg. The busy 401 (probably the most-travelled route in Canada) connects Toronto to Montreal and hitching is fairly common along the way.

For a more rural trip take Highway 7 to Tweed and Highway 37 to Belleville, then Highway 401 from there.

Getting Around

Airport Transport The cheapest way to get to the airport is by city bus. Take the No 5 on Elgin going south (away from the river) to Billings Bridge. Transfer to No 83 to airport.

There is also an airport bus leaving every 20 to 30 minutes from the Chateau Laurier Hotel. It costs $5.50 and takes about 25 minutes. The bus is not as frequent on weekends.

Bus Both Ottawa and Hull operate bus systems; with a transfer you can switch from one to the other, $1.05. For Ottawa information phone 741-4390 – they're very helpful. All Ottawa buses quit by 1.30 am, most earlier. Drop in to the office of OC Transpo which runs the city buses and get a Tourpass good for unlimited use for one day. The office is centrally located at 294 Albert St. You can take buses from downtown to:

Bus Station – No 4 south on Bank St
Train – No 89 or 95 east on Slater
Museum of Man – No 5 or 6 on Elgin
Aeronautical Museum – No 4 on Bank to Hemlock and St Laurent, then No 185 to airport base
Hull – No 89 west on Albert.

Bicycle Ottawa is the best city in Canada for cyclists. There is an extensive system of paths in and around town and through the parks. Get a bicycle route map from a Tourist Office.

For rentals try Cycle Tour Rent-A-Bike (233-0628) at the Chateau Laurier. They're open May to September and rent three, five and 10-speeds. ID is required. Open every day. They run tours, with discounts for hostel members, and a repair shop as well. R A Rentals (tel 237-4333) is at the Dows Lake Pavilion, 1001 Queen Elizabeth Driveway. Or try T'n'T Tandem rental at the Conference Centre, Confederation Square.

Car Rentals Tilden (tel 232-3536) is at 199 Slater and also at the airport. Their rate is

$38 per day with 250 free km, and 12c per km after that; $205 a week, 1750 free km.

Rent-A-Wreck (tel 238-5595) is at 449 Gladstone at Kent. Their rate is $9.95 to $15.95 per day with 40 free km, then 10c per km. They have mostly gas-guzzling cars.

Visitors to the city can park free at many locations; get the details at any information office.

Tours The government offers several free tours. From 9 June to 31 August there are three downtown Ottawa walking tours of 1½ hours. They depart every 15 minutes from the Visitor Centre, 14 Metcalfe.

Capitour is a system where you pay $2.25 once for the bus, and can get off and on at any of 10 places in Ottawa and Hull – all of which are near major attractions. The ticket is good all day.

A tour of Hull leaves from Place Aubrey at 11 am and 1.30 pm Monday to Saturday. There's a free minibus from the Visitor Centre to Place Aubrey. For information phone 996-4908.

A free mini-bus tour of Hull, lasting two hours, is given in summer. The tour begins at the Centre.

Gray Line (tel 741-6440) offers a 50-km, two-hour tour of the city, leaving from the north side of Confederation Square. They also do longer tours of the region.

A double-decker bus makes a similar trip, though shorter. It operates only during summer and is run by Piccadilly Tours.

Paul's Boat Lines (tel 235-8409), runs cruises on the Ottawa River and the Rideau Canal. Each takes about 1½ hours and costs $7, less for kids. There is a dock behind the Conference Centre for tickets and information. The Ottawa Riverboat Company (tel 232-4888) 173 Dalhousie St does much the same thing. Some trips include dinner and/or dancing.

Valley Cycle Tours (tel 234-5273), 110 O'Connor St, run extended bicycle tours, up to six days long.

Voyageur Bus Lines runs several day trips to attractions in Eastern Ontario, for example the Thousand Islands, Upper Canada Village and Kingston. Phone 238-5900 or ask at the bus terminal.

HULL

Across the river in Quebec, Hull is as much the other half of Ottawa as a separate city. And because it represents that in more ways than just geography, it warrants a visit. Hull now has its share of government offices and workers cross the river in both directions each day but this side remains home to most of the area's French population. On the street you'll feel the difference. The architecture is different (at least the older stuff), the top restaurants are here and the nightlife is livelier and later.

Promenade du Portage, easily found from either Portage Bridge or Alexander Bridge, is the main downtown street. Between the two bridges are numerous and varied eating spots, bars and discos as well as a few places where people have to work.

For a bite, head for *Café Le Coquetier* at 147 Promenade du Portage, an unpretentious, casual bistro with very good yet cheap food. *Le Bistro* on Aubrey just off Promenade du Portage is a bar/café serving light lunches for under $6. There's an outdoor patio in summer. A similar place is found at 44 Laval, on the corner.

Hull has long been known for its nightlife and bars that close at 3 or 4 am rather than at 1 am, as is the law in Ontario. Aside from the central area where most of the activity is, St Joseph Boulevard has several popular, dressy discos and the *Brasserie Bon Vivant* (tel (819) 771-8990), 462 Boulevard St Joseph, which brings in Quebec folk singers. It's cheap.

Gatineau Park

This 360 square km area of woods and lakes in the Gatineau Hills lies across the river, north-west of downtown Hull. It's only a 20-minute drive from the Parliament Buildings. On weekends some roads may be closed to cars.

There is plenty of wildlife in the park, including about 100 species of birds. Around the park are 150 km of hiking trails. Meach Lake, Lac Phillipe and Lac Lapeche have beaches for swimming and so are most popular. Many of the camping facilities are around Lac Phillipe. You can fish in the lakes and streams. The hiking trails are good for cross-country skiing in winter. Pink Lake is recommended for swimming; on one side are some cliffs from which you can jump or dive in. It is a short walk through the woods. The lake is best during the week when there are fewer people around. There is a nude beach at Meech Lake but don't say I told you.

Also in the park is Kingsmere, the summer estate of William Lyon Mackenzie King, prime minister in the 1920s, late 1930s and early 1940s. Here he indulged his hobby of collecting ruins, both genuine and fake. In 1941 King had bits of London's House of Commons brought over after the German blitz. His home, Moorside, is now a museum. An astute politician, King was much interested in the occult and apparently talked to both his dog and his deceased mother. There's a tearoom at Moorside.

Fall Rhapsody Occuring in September or October, the event celebrates the brief but colourful leaf-changing season; a time when the maples and birches of the Gatineau Hills are having their last fling before winter. An arts festival is part of the affair, as hot air ballooning and various concerts and competitions. Events are held in the park with a few around town as well. During Fall Rhapsody, there are cheap buses from town.

Place to eat *L'Agaric*, near Old Chelsea off Highway 5, is a good restaurant.

Rideau Trail
This hiking route takes you to Kingston; see the section on that city.

Eastern Ontario

West from Ottawa there are two main routes through Ontario. The northern one goes toward Pembroke, then either north or south past Algonquin Park on to North Bay and Sudbury. This is the route the Trans-Canada follows so it is the quickest way to western Canada.

The southern route goes to the more populated southern region of Ontario, the St Lawrence River, the Great Lakes and Toronto.

EGANVILLE

North-west of Ottawa, this small town is worth a stop for the nearby Bonnechere Caves, eight km south-east. The caves and passages were the bottom of a tropical sea about 500 million years ago and contain fossils of animals from long before the dinosaur age. You'll see some stalactites. Tours are offered through the summer months.

MORRISBURG

This small town lies just west of Cornwall on the St Lawrence River. Upper Canada Village is here, a detailed historic site fashioned to re-create a country town of 100 years ago. About 40 buildings and costumed workers bring the period to life. There's a blacksmith's shop, inn and sawmill. The setting is a nice one on the river. Several hours minimum is needed to fully explore the site, which is open from 15 May through to 15 October. Admission is $5, less for kids. Nearby Crysler Battlefield Park is a memorial to those who died fighting the Americans in 1812.

Just east of town is Auto Wonderland, a car museum with 50 vehicles, from an

1898 steam car to autos on through the years. Admission is a few dollars.

Highway 2 along the river is slower but more scenic than the 401. There are numerous provincial parks along the way, especially just west on the Long Sault Parkway.

In Cornwall there's a bridge to the USA. Tours of the power facilities at the dam are available and there are a few small museums.

BROCKVILLE

A small town along the river, Brockville is mentioned here because I find it a particularly attractive town, with its many old stone buildings and the classic-looking main street. The courthouse and jail in the centre of town date from 1842.

KINGSTON

Kingston, with a population of 60,000, is a handsome town that retains much of its past through preservation of many historical buildings and defence structures. Built strategically where Lake Ontario flows into the St Lawrence River, it is a convenient stop-off point as it lies almost exactly halfway between Montreal and Toronto.

Once a fur-trading depot, Kingston later became the principal British military post west of Quebec and was for a while the national capital. The many 19th-century buildings of local grey limestone and streets of Victorian brick houses give the downtown area a certain distinctive charm. The attractive waterfront doesn't hurt either.

There is a major university here, Queen's, and the city is also known across the country for its several prisons – both sexes are represented.

On Tuesdays, Thursdays and Saturdays, a small open-air market takes place right downtown behind City Hall on King St. It's not difficult to spend an interesting

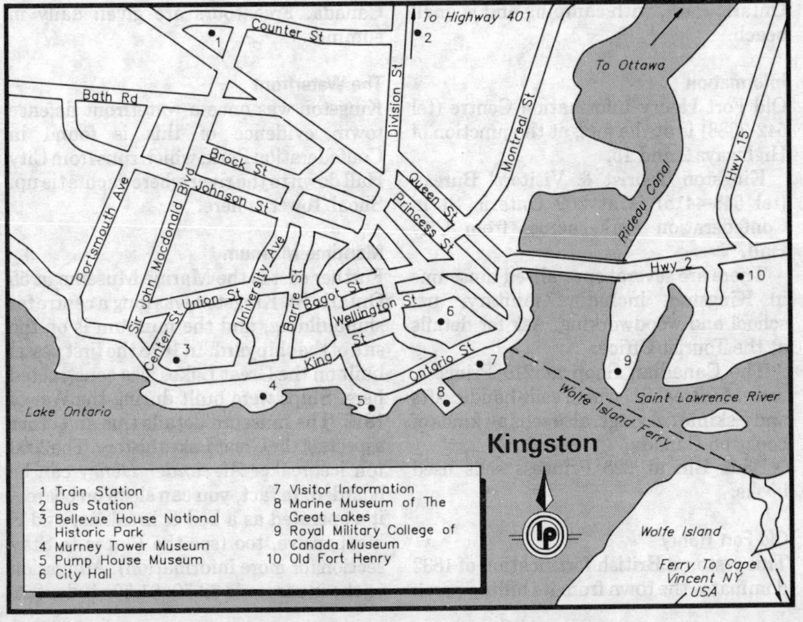

and enjoyable day or three in and around town.

Orientation
The town lies a few km south of the 401. Princess, the main street, runs right down to the river. It has many fine old buildings at its side, some limestone, others red brick. The whole city is low; few buildings are higher than two or three storeys and there aren't many modern ones either.

At the bottom of Princess, Ontario St runs along the harbour by the start of the Rideau Canal to Ottawa. This is the old, much-restored area with the Tourist Office, old military battery and Martello Tower. There are views across the mouth of the canal to the military college. The market is at Brock and King St East.

King St leads out along the lake's shore toward the university. Here you'll see many nice 19th-century houses and parkland. The impressive limestone County Court House is near the campus facing a small park. Further out is Lake Ontario Park, with camping and a small beach.

Information
Old Fort Henry Information Centre (tel 542-7388) is at the fort, at the junction of Highways 2 and 15.

Kingston Tourist & Visitors' Bureau (tel 548-4415) is at 209 Ontario St in Confederation Park, across from City Hall.

There are several specialised museums in Kingston, including military, art, school and woodworking. Ask for details at the Tourist Office.

The Canadian Shop at 219 Princess, near Montreal St, which sells handicrafts and Eskimo carvings, also sells all kinds of books on Canada.

Book Bin at 225 Princess sells used books.

Old Fort Henry
This restored British fortification of 1832 dominates the town from its hilltop perch and is the city's prime attraction. It's a bit of a disappointment though, as there is more space inside than anything else. But the beautiful structure is brought to life by colourfully-uniformed guards trained in military drills, artillery exercises, and fife & drum music of the 1860s. Entrance is $4, less for kids, and includes a 20-minute film and guided tour. If you just want to walk around on your own, it's free. The soldiers put on their displays periodically throughout the day. They're best at 7.30 pm on Mondays, Wednesdays and Saturdays when there is a rifle-firing, cannon-blasting ceremonial military retreat, mid-season only. Inside the fort's rooms are artefacts, uniforms, weapons and more. Good views. Open daily. Closed 15 October to 15 May.

City Hall
The grand City Hall is one of the country's finest classical buildings. Built of limestone, it dates from 1843, when Kingston was capital of the then United Provinces of Canada. Free tours are given daily in summer.

The Waterfront
Kingston was once a waterfront defence town; evidence of this is found in Confederation Park, which runs from City Hall down to the river where yachts tie up. Shoal Tower is here.

Maritime Museum
Further east is the Marine Museum at 55 Ontario St. Kingston was long a centre for shipbuilding, and the museum is on the site of the shipyard. In 1678 the first vessel built on the Great Lakes was constructed here. Ships were built during the War of 1812. The museum details this and other aspects of the Great Lakes history. The 3000 ton icebreaker *Alexander Henry* can be boarded. In fact, you can sleep on board – it's operated as a bed & breakfast and is inexpensive, too (see the Places to Stay section for more information). Admission to the museum is $2.50, $1.50 students.

Top: Rainbow over Niagara Falls (JL)
Bottom: Niagara Falls from the top (RE)

Top: Downtown Toronto from the observation level, CN Tower (RB)
Bottom: Roadside novelty, Highway 132, Quebec (ML)

Macdonald Park

At the corner of Barrie St and King East is Macdonald Park, right along the river. Just offshore in 1812, the British ship *Royal George* battled with America's *USS Oneida*. At the western end of the park is the Murney Martello Tower, dating from 1846. This round defence structure was part of the early riverside fortifications and is now a museum housing historical tidbits from the area. There's a small admission fee. Open daily in July and August, weekends in spring and fall. There are walking and bicycle paths along here and further west by the water's edge.

At the corner of King East and West Sts is a big city park with a statue of Sir John A Macdonald.

Bellevue House

This national historic site (tel 542-3858) is an immaculately maintained Tuscan-style mansion, which apparently means a very odd-shaped, balconied, brightly painted architect's field day. It works, though, and in the garden setting this is an impressive and interesting house. It was once the home of Canada's first prime minister, Sir John A Macdonald. The mansion houses many good antiques. Open daily all year, 9 am to 5 pm. Free. The address is 35 Centre St.

Brock St

Brock St was the middle of town in the 1800s, and many of the original shops still stand by its side. It's worth a walk around. Take a look in *Cooke's Fine Foods* at 61 Brock St. It's a gourmet shop with old wooden counters and a 100-year-old pressed-tin ceiling. There are great smells and a curious assortment of goods and shoppers, including local professors drinking the fresh coffee at the back of the store.

Pump House Steam Museum

This is a one-of-a-kind, completely restored, steam-run pump station. First used in 1849, it now contains several engines and some scale models, all run on steam. The address is 23 Ontario St. Open mid-June to Labour Day but closed Fridays.

Fort Frederick Museum

This museum is in the grounds of the Royal Military College Museum, in a Martello Tower. You have to wonder how or why, but here lies the small arms collection of General Porfirio Diaz, the President of Mexico from 1886-1912. Also outlined is the college history. The museum is just east of town, off No 2. Open daily in summer.

Hockey Hall of Fame & Museum

At the corner of Alfred and York Sts, this collection honours the history and stars of Canada's most loved sport. Lots of photos and mementoes. Open from mid-June to mid-September daily and the rest of the year weekend afternoons only. A small admission fee is charged.

The Thousand Islands

This is a very scenic area just east of Kingston, consisting of quite a few more than 1000 islands which dot the river between the two national mainlands. In spring the islands are an undulating white with the blooming trillium, the provincial flower.

Boat tours from Kingston trip around some of the islands. A couple of companies run daily trips in summer. The Miss Kingston boat line is at 549-1123. Cost is $10.50. The *Island Queen* Showboat provides live entertainment and has a three-hour evening cruise. Others leave from Rockport and Gananoque ('gan-an-ok-way'), two small towns east down the river a bit. Most tours are about 3½ hours, cost $9.50 and include glimpses of some of the island curiosities like Boldt Castle.

Wolfe Island

It is possible to have a mini cruise for free by taking the car ferry from Kingston to

Wolfe Island. The 20-minute trip affords views of the city, the fort and a few of the Thousand Islands. Wolfe Island, the largest in the chain, lies halfway to the US and is basically flat farmland, although many of its inhabitants now work in town. There is not a lot to see on the island, but there is the *General Wolfe Hotel*, a short walk from the dock, with its three busy and highly regarded dining rooms. Moderate to slightly expensive.

From Wolfe Island another ferry links Cape Vincent, New York, but on this segment a toll is charged, at least if you have a car.

St Lawrence Islands National Park
Within the gentle, green archipelago, the park covers 17 islands scattered along 80 km of the river. There are primitive campsites on 13 of them, accessible only by boat. You can take a water-taxi from Mallorytown Landing on the mainland. Located here are the park headquarters and a 60-site campground.

Rideau Canal
This canal/river/lake system is 200 km long and 150 years old; it connects Kingston with Ottawa. The historical route is good for boating or canoeing trips, with many places to stop along the way. Boats moor at the 47 old lock systems. There are parks, small towns and lakes along the route. The old defence buildings along the way have been restored.

Roads parallel much of the canal, so walking or cycling the route is also possible. Ask about the boat that will take passengers through the system. Several places along the canal rent houseboats so you can meander about at your own speed. The Tourist Office has information on history, times, lock fees (minimal) and boat rentals.

Rideau Trail
This is a hiking trail system 400-km-long which links Kingston to Ottawa. It passes through Westport, Smith Falls and many conservation areas on the way. Forests, fields and marshes as well as some stretches of road are used. There are some historic sites on the route and you'll see the Rideau Canal. There are also 64 km of side loops. Most people use the route only for day trips but longer trips and overnighting are possible. The main trail is marked by orange triangles; side trails by blue triangles. The Rideau Trail Association prints a map kit for the entire route. They have an office in Kingston.

Camping Between Kingston and Smith Falls are numerous camping spots. The rest of the way camping is less available but there is commercial accommodation. Camping on private land is possible but permission should be asked of the owner.

Activities
Bicycle rentals are available at Alford's Sports Shop, Princess St, or at Rent a Bike, 35 Johnson (near City Hall), by the hour, day or week.

Windsurfing Kingston has a shop at 93 Princess. A windsurfing school with an office at the foot of West St at the waterfront rents sailboards, sailboats, paddleboats, canoes and bikes.

Crafts
The Canadian Shop, 219 Princess, near Montreal St sells handicrafts, including Cowichan sweaters from Vancouver Island for about the same price they are there. The shop also sells Eskimo carvings and all kinds of books on Canada.

Places to Stay
Hostels The *Youth Hostel* (tel 546-7203) is at 323 William, which is within easy walking distance of most places, and has 23 beds. Members $7.50, non-members $10.50. Continental breakfasts are available. Open early May to early September only. During the rest of the year there is a programme of home hostels; call the same

number for details or ask at the Tourist Office.

Rooms are available in residences at *Queens University* (tel 547-2775) from mid-May to mid-August. Rooms are $20.50, $13 for students. Meals are available. The campus is at the corner of the University and Union.

Waldron Tower (tel 544-6100) is a residential complex of the Kingston General Hospital. It's great if you can get in, but it's usually full so call ahead. The rate is $19 a day with a good weekly rate. Single rooms only. They have a cafeteria, kitchens, all manner of facilities and a view over the river to boot. The tower is on 17 King St West near Macdonald Park.

The *YM-YWCA* (tel 546-2647) is at 100 Wright Crescent. It has beds for women only. There are kitchen facilities and a pool.

There's a *Salvation Army* (tel 548-4411) here for men who are broke or close to it.

Bed & Breakfasts Mrs Ruth MacLachlan (tel 542-0214) runs a bed & breakfast agency in Kingston, at 10 Westview Rd. There are about 25 participating homes in and around town. Tell her where you want to be and what your interests are, and you'll be matched up suitably. Rates are $27 for singles and $38 for doubles, full breakfast included; and $5 to $10 for children. Cheaper rates are available for extended stays.

A unique bed & breakfast is on a moored, retired icebreaker which is part of the Marine Museum situated right downtown. Beds are in the former crew's quarters and a continental breakfast is served from the cook's galley. You can wander all over the ship. Singles cost $25 and doubles $35 – more in the captain's cabin. Rooms are available during summer only.

Hotels Kingston has very few hotels, and nearly all the accommodation is in motels.

The *Plaza Hotel*, 46 Montreal St at Queen, is mainly used for the bar downstairs but it's not badly kept. Not a family place but cheap at $22/28 for singles/doubles, with own bathroom.

Better is the *Queens Hotel* at 125 Brock, a few blocks from City Hall, which is another older, small hotel with rooms at $30/40 for singles/doubles.

Offering more services are the *Princess* and the *Shamrock*, 720 and 671 Princess respectively. They charge $42/55 for singles/doubles; less after September.

The *Prince George Hotel* dates from 1809 and is now restored with National Heritage recognition. It has comfortable rooms with balconies overlooking the lake at splurge prices ranging from $40 to $80.

Motels There are plenty of these. In town at 1454 Princess St is *Journey's End* (tel 549-5550), a two-storey place. Rooms are cheaper upstairs and range between $41 to $45 for singles or doubles.

A little cheaper is the *Hilltop* (tel 542-3846) at 2287 Princess, at $28/34 for singles/doubles. There are many other motels on Princess and some along Highway 2 on each side of town.

Camping There are quite a few places to camp in the area. *Hi-Lo Hickory* on Wolfe Island is reached by ferry from Kingston. There's a beach. A bridge on the other side connects the island with New York State. The campground is east of the Kingston ferry about 12 km. *KOA* (Kampgrounds of America, seen all over the continent) has a location 1.6 km north of the 401 off Highway 38. They're usually very plastic with as little to do with camping as possible. They're also expensive, but big and generally pretty busy. Mainly trailers but there are some tent sites here.

Places to Eat

Kingston is a pretty good eating town, especially for its size.

The *Sunflower Restaurant*, serving

good vegetarian food, is a bright spot with sturdy wooden tables and batiks on the walls. Meals run from $5 and there are lots of desserts and snacks. It's at 20 Montreal St and is open until 9 pm daily except Sunday.

Hanley's at the corner of Ontario and Johnson is good for lunch downstairs. Burgers, salads, finger foods cost $3 to $6. The dining room upstairs for dinner is more expensive, with steaks and fish. Nearby on Clarence, the *Brew Pub* has meals washed down with beer made on the premises.

Cultures at 335 King is recommended for its sandwiches and excellent yoghurt smoothies. Try the chicken salad thing – it's a meal.

Kresge's Store at the back of 124 Princess has probably the cheapest food counter in town. You can get a meal for under $4. Also very cheap is the small *Madras Café* at 177 Division St, with vegetarian and non-veg Indian meals. Another Indian place is the *Curry Village* at 169A Princess. Quite inexpensive, and for the evening meal a tandoori oven is fired up.

For a better-heeled place try the *Canoe Club* in the Prince George Hotel near the waterfront. It's across from Confederation Park and is a nice place, but moderate in price. Seafood is the specialty.

E P Murphey & Sons & Daughters at 70 Brock has been around for ages and though the restaurant upstairs is closed, fish & chips are still offered in the store front. At 76 Brock, there are good burgers to be had at *Simon's*.

For a splurge there's *Chez Piggy*, probably the city's best-known restaurant, in a renovated early 19th-century building at 68 Princess. At lunch, 11.30 am to 2 pm, soup and entree is $5. Dinners from 6 pm range from $6.50 to $12.50. The selection includes lamb, steaks and omelettes. They have interesting appetisers.

For coffee and sweets check out the *Tea Cozy Tea Room* on Johnson, halfway between King and Ontario. It's open in the afternoon only and offers fresh pastries in a real English setting.

Lino's, corner of Division and Ontario, is open 24 hours.

Nightlife

The *Cocama* is a huge dance bar down near the water styled after the Limelight in New York City. *Dollar Bills* in the Prince George is one of several student drinking spots with videos and dancing.

The *Manor*, 28 Yonge St, never has a cover charge for rock, new wave bands or contests. The *Dockyard Tavern*, 76 Princess near King, is a pub-like place with bluegrass music nightly, and movies upstairs.

The *Duke of Kingston Pub* serves English beers amidst an English-style decor. It's on King St East at Brock, near City Hall.

Cinema The *National Film Theatre* (tel 547-3059) is in the Ellis Hall Auditorium on University Avenue. Admission is $3.50 for US or foreign films, and shows start at 8 pm.

Getting There & Away

Bus The Voyageur station (tel 548-7738) is at 959 Division St, a couple of km south of the 401. There are special excursion return fares to these cities and also smaller towns like Pembroke, Cornwall. Ordinary services include:

Montreal: at least eight buses daily, all hours, some express – $23

Ottawa: at least eight daily, all hours – $15

Toronto: about eight daily – $22.

Train The station (tel 544-5600) is very inconvenient, a long way from downtown. It's on Counter St near the corner of Princess, north-west of town. There are no city buses; you can try hitching or take a taxi. The train services include:

Montreal: six to eight daily, morning, noon and night – $28

Ottawa: 11.52 am, 7.37 pm – $19

Toronto: 10 daily – $28.

Getting Around

For information on Kingston Transit call 544-5289. The city bus office is at Barrack and King.

There is a city bus stop across the street from the bus station to get into town. It departs quarter to and quarter after the hour.

For car rentals there's a Rent-A-Wreck at the corner of Chatham and Princess. They charge from $10 a day for the small cars.

Tours

The Tourist Office has a pamphlet which outlines a detailed self-guided walking tour, or you can rent a cassette which leads you through the historic section of town.

Three and five-day cruises along the St Lawrence River are offered by Rideau St Lawrence Cruise Ships on their replica steamship sailing out of Kingston.

AROUND KINGSTON

East East of Kingston between Ganonoque and Mallorytown Landing, a small road – the Thousand Islands Parkway – dips south of the 401 and runs along the river. This route is recommended and offers good views and picnic areas. Boat cruises around the islands depart from Rockport and Gananoque. Sixteen km east of town in Grass Creek Park is the MacLachlan Woodworking Museum.

West West of Kingston in Amherstville is Fairfield Historical Park along the shoreline, which includes Fairfield House, one of the province's oldest. It was built by Loyalists from New England in 1793. North about 10 km in Odessa is the historic Babcock Mill, a working water-powered mill which once again produces the baskets originally made here in the mid-1800s.

North North of Kingston is the Rideau Lakes region, an area of cottages, lodges, marinas and fishing and camping.

New Frontenac Provincial Park straddles both the lowlands of southern Ontario and the more northern Canadian Shield so the flora, fauna and geology of the park are an admixture. There is one campground, at the main gate, but the park is really designed for overnight hikers and canoeists. Trails have been mapped out and campsites are located through the park. Though the park is large, there aren't many designated camping sites; but this has not yet been a problem as the park remains relatively unknown. The entrance and information centre are at Otter Lake, off the 5A north of Sydenham. The swimming is excellent and I drink the water straight from the lakes. There are no bears to worry about and pretty good bass fishing.

North-west from Kingston, up the 41, is Bon Echo Provincial Park, also pretty good for canoeing. Some of the lakes are quite shallow and get very warm. There is walk-in hiking or roadside campgrounds with facilities. At Mazinaw Lake there are Indian rock paintings on granite cliffs. This is one of the largest parks in eastern Ontario and generally speaking, the larger the park the better, because you can lose your fellow humans for a spell.

Belleville & Area

There's not much for the visitor in this town of 35,000 – it's more a departure point for Quinte's Isle to the south. It does have the Waterfront & Folklorama Festival, which is held in July and consists of three days of events, music and shows.

North of Belleville up the 37, roughly 10 km north of the 401, is Mapledale Cheese, worth a visit to buy some of the excellent cheddar.

The 37 continues north through old Tweed to the 7 which is the main route to

Toronto from Ottawa. It's a bit slow with only two lanes, but the scenery is good and there are a couple of parks along the way and several places to eat.

QUINTE'S ISLE

Irregularly shaped Quinte's Isle is a quiet, rural, scenic, historic retreat from the bustle of much of southern Ontario. The rolling farmland is reminiscent of Prince Edward Island and, in fact, Quinte's Isle is also known as Prince Edward County. Many of the little towns were settled in the 18th and 19th centuries, the cemeteries adjacent to the village churches revealing clues to these earlier times.

It's only been in the past several years that the island has been somewhat discovered and developed for visitors to any degree but it still hasn't changed very much.

Things to See

Traffic is light on most of the island's roads which lead past large old farmhouses and cultivated fields. The St Lawrence is never far away and many routes offer good views. Fishing is quite good in the Bay of Quinte and the locals use the waters for sailing. The island is popular with cyclists; it's generally flat and some of the smaller roads are well shaded.

The excellent strawberry-picking in late June draws many outsiders.

There are three fine provincial parks: North Beach, The Outlet and Sandbanks. Sandbanks, the only one offering camping, is one of the most popular in the province. Book ahead, as reservations are definitely required for weekends when a fair bit of partying goes on. The park is divided into two sections, the Outlet with an excellent strip of sandy beach and Sandbanks, itself, containing most of the area's sand-dunes, some over three storeys high. There's a large undeveloped section at the end of the beach, good for walking and exploring the dunes and backwaters.

Picton

This small town is the only town of any size on the island and has one of the six district museums. There is a Tourist Office here with detailed maps of the island. Pick up the walking tour guide of Picton, which leads you past some of the fine historical buildings in town. Another guide lists various island attractions. One of them is Bird House City which has dozens of birdhouses painted to resemble the buildings of a human city, including a fire station and a courthouse.

Lake on the Mountain Park

On the other side of the island, this is really nothing more than a picnic site but is worth a visit to see the unusual lake. It sits on one side of the road at a level actually higher than that of the road, while just across the street is a terrific view over Lake Ontario and some islands hundreds of feet below. Geologists are still speculating as to the lake's origins. The local Mohawk Indians have their own legends to the lake, which apparently has no source they know of.

Tyendinaga Indian Reserve

This is just off Quinte's Isle and is also mainly farmland. In mid-May the original coming of the Mohawks is re-enacted in full tribal dress.

Places to Stay

There are several commercial campgrounds nearby which aren't quite as busy if you can't get in to Sandbanks. There's a large one opposite the Outlet, geared mainly for trailers and quite a nice one good for tenting as well, out at the tip of Salmon Arm. Minimal facilities but great sunsets. There are also numerous resorts, cottages, motels and bed & breakfasts in a range of prices.

TRENTON

This small town is known as the starting point of the Trent Canal, which goes 386 km through 44 locks to Georgian Bay in Lake Huron. Yachties and sailors follow this old Indian route.

There is now a cruise ship which plies the route, taking seven days. Shorter, four-day trips are also available. These are not cheap. Inquire in Peterborough.

Presqu'ile Provincial Park is west of town and has a long, sandy beach. There's camping and bird-watching in spring and fall. At Beach 3, you can rent boats of various types, sailboarding equipment and bicycles.

KAWARTHA LAKES

Peterborough

This is a mid-size Ontario town, more or less at the centre of the Kawartha Lakes vacation region. The older downtown area has some fine buildings and it's all very green. Trent University is here.

The Trent-Severn Waterway (a canal), passes through the large hydraulic-lift lock, a major landmark in town. Cruises through the locks and along part of the system are available.

In late July or early August is the Summer Festival, with various events and shows.

Century Village South-east of Peterborough is Century Village, a pioneer village with costumed workers, demonstrations and 20 buildings from 1820-1899.

Lakefield A few km north is Lakefield, a very small town with a boys' school that our Queen saw fit to send Prince Andrew to.

Canoeing There are several possibilities for canoeing. From Peterborough you can get to Serpents Provincial Park. Possibilities are easy trips on the canal or tougher white-water trips in spring on rivers in the area. Ask at the Tourist Office in town. The Ministry of Natural Resources publishes a map called 'North Kawartha Canoe Routes', which shows some possible trips and their portage distances.

Other Many of the pretty towns in the region have a good restaurant or two and, usually, a couple of antique dealers. Bobcaygeon and Fenelon Falls are two examples and are worth dropping into if you're up this way. (The former also hosts a big fiddle contest annually in July).

Nearby, Balsam Lake is popular for swimming and fishing. In Lindsay, a more generic small town, don't miss the *Dutch Treat* on Kent St for excellent, very cheap food: good home-made muffins and various treats. This town has a summer theatre programme.

At Burleigh Falls who could resist a place called the *Lovesick Cafe*? It's a typical country shop with food, souvenirs, fishing tackle, etc. The date squares are recommended.

Parks The district has some interesting parks as well. Petroglyphs Provincial Park has probably the best collection of prehistoric rock carvings in the country. There are, they say, 900 figures carved into limestone ridges, only discovered in 1954. The easily-seen collection is much smaller than that figure suggests and, though interesting, is not an overwhelming sight by any means. Recently the rocks have had to be covered with glass or plastic to protect them from acid rain, a serious problem over much of the province. The people in positions to do something about the situation continue to sit on their butts. The area and small lake within the park remain important spiritual sites for the local Indians.

Serpent Mounds Park is the site of an ancient Indian burial ground. The Warsaw Caves Conservation Area contains tunnels eroded into limestone; there are walking trails here.

NORTH OF THE KAWARTHA LAKES

Continuing north you come to a less busy, less populated hilly region known as the Haliburton Highlands. Highway 507, leading up from Bobcaygeon through Catchacoma and Gooderham (which has a small waterfall), is the narrowest, oldest-looking highway I've driven anywhere in the province, often looking more like a country lane.

Bancroft

This is the district centre, well known for its minerals and the big gem festival held each August. Examples of 80% of the minerals found in Canada can be dug up in the Bancroft area.

Combermere

Combermere Catholic Commune (tel 756-5031) is a religious, co-operative farm, run by J Scanlon. Primarily run as a learning experience and as a place to practice the group's ideas (originally of Russian origin), the farm will take in travellers for a few days in exchange for work around the farm. Interesting. Also in Combermere is the Madonna House Pioneer Museum.

Barry's Bay

This old lumber town is now supply centre for the cottagers in the area on and around Lake Kaminiskeg. It's also pretty close to Algonquin Park and is on the main highway to Ottawa. Odd as it may seem, this is the centre for a sizeable Polish population attracted to the hilly, green topography which is much like that along the Baltic in northern Poland. Nearby Wilno was the first Polish settlement in Ontario. The entire region has cottages for rent and lakeside resorts, but advance reservations are a very good idea. Pembroke, east at the Quebec border, is the nearest town of any size.

Toronto

Toronto is the country's major urban centre. Already the largest Canadian city, it is one of the fastest growing municipalities on the continent. With the booming economy of the past few years it is well entrenched as the nation's financial and business capital as well as being the main focus for English culture.

Among the first things you'll notice in Toronto is the vibrancy and cleanliness of the downtown area. These two factors alone separate it from the bulk of large North American cities, but another great thing is that Toronto is safe. The streets are busy at night, with all the restaurant and entertainment doors open, and the parks and subway are generally used without hesitation. Of course this isn't the English countryside either and women alone should always take precautions after dark.

There is a lot of central housing in the city and this plan has kept the city well-rounded and liveable. Despite high costs, there are no areas of concentrated poverty. Throughout the city, various ethnic and immigrant groups have collected in fairly tight communities to form bustling, prosperous districts. These various neighbourhoods are one of the best and most distinctive aspects of the city and have helped to warm up what has been the rather stand-offish character of Toronto.

Toronto celebrated its 150th birthday in 1984 but has only recently attained its prominent stature and international attention. It was about 20 years ago that the city scored points in its traditional rivalry with Montreal by surpassing it in size. Since this largely symbolic achievement, Toronto has grown in every way. It is the busiest Canadian port on the Great Lakes and is a major centre for banking, manufacturing and publishing. The Toronto Stock Exchange is one of North America's most important and the city is the provincial capital.

As you will notice, Toronto is new and shiny. Much of the downtown area has been rebuilt in the past 15 years. I swear every time I turn around there's a new building up. This rapid modernisation and embracing of progress and change was not always so, however.

The Seneca Indians first lived here in

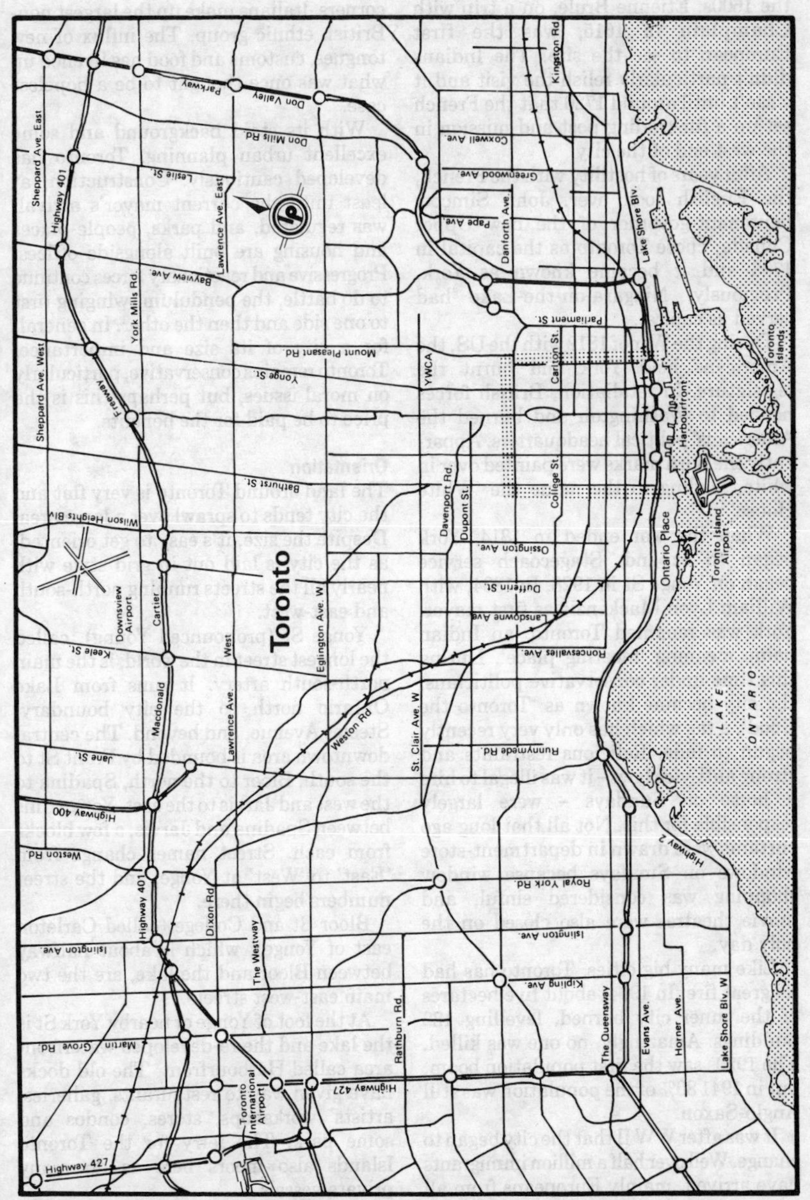

Toronto
Highway 401
Highway 400
Highway 427
Highway 2
Sheppard Ave. East
Sheppard Ave. West
Don Valley Parkway
Don Mills Rd.
Leslie St.
Lawrence Ave. East
Lawrence Ave. West
Bayview Ave.
York Mills Rd.
Mount Pleasant Rd.
Yonge St.
Freeway
Bathurst St.
Wilson Heights Blv.
Downsview Airport
Cartier
Macdonald
Keele St.
Jane St.
Weston Rd.
Eglinton Ave. W
West
Islington Ave.
Dixon Rd.
The Westway
Martin Grove Rd.
Rathburn Rd.
Toronto International Airport
Kingston Rd.
Coxwell Ave.
Greenwood Ave.
Pape Ave.
Danforth Ave.
Lake Shore Blv.
Parliament St.
Carlton St.
YWCA
College St.
Davenport Rd.
Dupont St.
Ossington Ave.
Dufferin St.
Lansdowne Ave.
Roncesvalles Ave.
St. Clair Ave. W
Runnymede Rd.
Royal York Rd.
Kipling Ave.
The Queensway
Evans Ave.
Horner Ave.
Lake Shore Blv. W
Harbourfront
Toronto Islands
Toronto Island Airport
Ontario Place
LAKE
ONTARIO

the 1600s. Etienne Brule, on a trip with Champlain in 1615, was the first European to see the site. The Indians didn't particularly relish the visit and it wasn't until around 1720 that the French set up a fur-trading post and mission in the west end of the city.

After years of hostility with the French, the English took over. John Simcoe, lieutenant-governor of the new Upper Canada, chose Toronto as the capital in 1793 and it became known as York. Previously, Niagara-on-the-Lake had served as capital.

During the War of 1812 with the US, the Americans held York and burnt the legislature. In retaliation, British forces headed to Washington and burned the Americans' political headquarters. Apparently the burn marks were painted over in white, leading to the name the 'White House'.

When the war ended in 1814, York began to expand. Stagecoach service began on Yonge St in 1928. In 1834, with William Lyon Mackenzie as first mayor, York was renamed Toronto, an Indian name meaning 'meeting place'. During this time under conservative politicians, the city became known as 'Toronto the Good', a tag which has only very recently begun to fade. Religious restraints and strong anti-vice laws – it was illegal to hire a horse on Sundays – were largely responsible for this. Not all that long ago curtains were drawn in department-store windows on Sundays because window shopping was considered sinful, and movie theatres were also closed on the holy day.

Like many big cities, Toronto has had its great fire. In 1904, about five hectares of the inner city burned, levelling 122 buildings. Amazingly, no one was killed. The 1920s saw the first population boom, but in 1941 80% of the population was still Anglo-Saxon.

It was after WW II that the city began to change. Well over half a million immigrants have arrived, mainly Europeans from all corners. Italians make up the largest non-British ethnic group. The influx of new tongues, customs and food has livened up what was once thought to be a hopeless case.

With its staid background and some excellent urban planning, Toronto has developed cautiously. Construction, at least until the current mayor's arrival, was regulated, and parks, people-places and housing are built alongside offices. Progressive and reactionary forces continue to do battle, the pendulum swinging first to one side and then the other. In general, for a city of its size and importance, Toronto remains conservative, particularly on moral issues, but perhaps this is the price to be paid for the benefits.

Orientation

The land around Toronto is very flat and the city tends to sprawl over a large area. Despite the size, it's easy to get oriented, as the city is laid out in grid style with nearly all the streets running north-south and east-west.

Yonge St (pronounced Young), called the longest street in the world, is the main north-south artery. It runs from Lake Ontario north to the city boundary, Steeles Avenue, and beyond. The central downtown area is bounded by Front St to the south, Bloor to the north, Spadina to the west and Jarvis to the east. Yonge runs between Spadina and Jarvis, a few blocks from each. Street names change from 'East' to 'West' at Yonge, and the street numbers begin there.

Bloor St and College (called Carleton east of Yonge), which is about halfway between Bloor and the lake, are the two main east-west streets.

At the foot of Yonge or nearby York St is the lake and the re-developed waterfront area called Harbourfront. The old docks have given way to restaurants, galleries, artists' workshops, stores, condos and some park. The ferry for the Toronto Islands also moors here as do many private vessels.

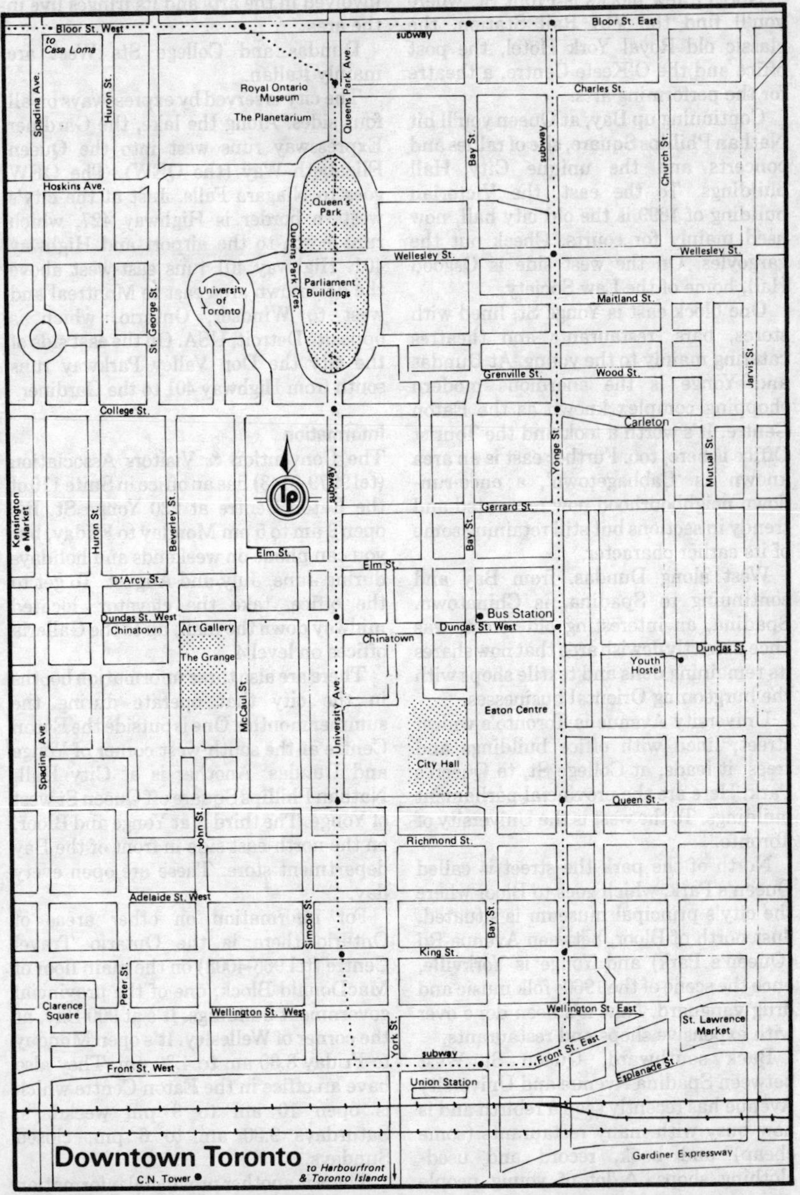
Bloor St. West
to Casa Loma
subway
Bloor St. East
Spadina Ave.
Huron St.
Royal Ontario Museum
The Planetarium
Queens Park Ave.
Charles St.
Bay St.
subway
Church St.
Hoskins Ave.
Queen's Park
Queens Park Cres.
Wellesley St.
Wellesley St.
University of Toronto
St. George St.
Parliament Buildings
Maitland St.
Grenville St.
Wood St.
Jarvis St.
College St.
Carleton
Yonge St.
Mutual St.
Kensington Market
Huron St.
Beverley St.
subway
Gerrard St.
Bay St.
Elm St.
Elm St.
D'Arcy St.
Dundas St. West
Chinatown
Art Gallery
The Grange
Bus Station
Dundas St. West
Chinatown
Dundas St.
Youth Hostel
McCaul St.
University Ave.
Eaton Centre
Spadina Ave.
City Hall
John St.
Queen St.
Richmond St.
Adelaide St. West
Simcoe St.
King St.
Peter St.
Clarence Square
Wellington St. West
York St.
Wellington St. East
St. Lawrence Market
subway
Front St. East
Front St. West
Esplanade St.
Union Station
Gardiner Expressway
Downtown Toronto
to Harbourfront & Toronto Islands
C.N. Tower

North a few blocks is Front St, where you'll find the VIA Rail Station, the classic old Royal York Hotel, the post office and the O'Keefe Centre, a theatre for the performing arts.

Continuing up Bay, at Queen you'll hit Nathan Phillips Square, site of rallies and concerts and the unique City Hall buildings. To the east, the Victorian building of 1899 is the old city hall, now used mainly for courts. Check out the gargoyles. On the west side is Osgood Hall, home of the Law Society.

One block east is Yonge St, lined with stores, bars, restaurants and theatres catering mainly to the young. At Dundas and Yonge is the enormous modern shopping complex known as the Eaton Centre. It's worth a look and the Tourist Office is here, too. Further east is an area known as 'Cabbagetown', a once-run-down neighbourhood now renovated and trendy in sections but still retaining some of its earlier character.

West along Dundas, from Bay and continuing to Spadina, is Chinatown. Spadina, an interesting old street, was once a strictly Jewish area that now shares its remaining delis and textile shops with the burgeoning Oriental businesses.

University Avenue is Toronto's widest street; lined with office buildings and trees, it leads, at College St, to Queen's Park. Here are the provincial parliament buildings. To the west is the University of Toronto.

North of the park the street is called Queen's Park, which goes to Bloor where the city's principal museum is situated. Just north of Bloor, between Avenue Rd (Queen's Park) and Yonge is Yorkville, once the scene of the 1960s folk music and drug vanguard. Now it's been done over with expensive shops and restaurants.

Back southward, Queen St West between Spadina Avenue and University Avenue has recently seen a rebirth and is now busy with many restaurants (some cheap) and book, record and used-clothing shops. A lot of young people involved in the arts and its fringes live in the area.

Dundas and College Sts West are mainly Italian.

The city is served by expressways on all four sides. Along the lake, the Gardiner Expressway runs west into the Queen Elizabeth Way (the QEW). The QEW goes to Niagara Falls. Just at the city's western border is Highway 427, which runs north to the airport and Highway 401. Highway 401 runs east-west above the downtown area east to Montreal and west to Windsor, Ontario, which is opposite Detroit, USA. On the east side of the city the Don Valley Parkway runs south from Highway 401 to the Gardiner.

Information

The Convention & Visitors Association (tel 9979-3143) has an office in Suite 110 of the Eaton Centre at 220 Yonge St. It's open 9 am to 5 pm Monday to Friday, but you can phone on weekends and holidays during June, July and August. To get to the office, take the elevator, located midway down the mall, up to the Galleria offices on level 4.

There are also three information booths in the city that operate during the summer months. One is outside the Eaton Centre at the south-west corner of Yonge and Dundas. Another is at City Hall, Nathan Phillips Square off Queen St west of Yonge. The third is at Yonge and Bloor, on the north-east side in front of the Bay department store. These are open every day.

For information on other areas of Ontario there is the Ontario Travel Centre (tel 965-4008) on the main floor of MacDonald Block, one of the provincial government buildings. It's at 900 Bay, at the corner of Wellesley. It's open Monday to Friday 8.30 am to 4.30 pm. They also have an office in the Eaton Centre which is open 10 am to 9 pm weekdays, Saturdays 9.30 am to 6 pm, closed Sundays.

There is another provincial information

office (tel 965-4008), more conveniently located on the lower level of the Eaton Centre which is at 220 Yonge St at the corner of Dundas. It's open until 9 pm during the week, 6 pm on Saturdays and is closed on Sundays.

The main post office with general delivery is on Front St between Yonge and Bay.

The Youth Hostel head office is just a few doors from the hostel itself at 217 Church St.

CN Tower

The highest free-standing structure in the world, the CN Tower has become a symbol and landmark of Toronto. The top antenna was put in place in 1975 by helicopter, making the tower 533 metres high. Its primary function is communications – radio and television signals – but up at the top there is a restaurant, disco and two observation decks. The one outside is windy. On a good clear day you can see about 160 km, which easily includes American cities across the lake.

The glass elevator travels up the outside of the tower. The tower is in the south end of the city near the lake, south of Front St West at Walkway. Phone 360-8500 for information. Cost is $7.50 for the elevator plus $1 for the observation tower, reduced if you're eating or drinking up top. Open every day and night. The time and weather display at ground level is worth a look.

At the base of the tower is the Tour of the Universe. This simulated futuristic space trip to Jupiter is by all accounts very well done and good fun. Admission of $11 is separate from visiting the top of the tower.

Views

For a very pleasant and free view of the city, head to the rooftop bar of the Park Plaza Hotel. It's at the corner of Bloor St West and University. You can sit under the sun at white wrought-iron tables and chairs and sip a cool one above the masses.

The Harbour Castle Hotel at the foot of Yonge St at the lake's edge has a quiet bar way up high with windows on all sides. The Aquarius Lounge atop the Manulife Centre at the corner of Bay and Bloor is similar. Drinks aren't cheap at either but there is no admission charge.

Royal Ontario Museum (ROM)

The museum, at the corner of Queen's Park Avenue and Bloor St West, is Canada's largest and has exhibits covering the natural sciences, the animal world and the history of humans. For several years the museum has been undergoing extensive renovation and modernisation, a process which will not be complete until 1992. Even though several galleries are not yet open, the museum covers five floors and is large.

The collection of Chinese crafts,

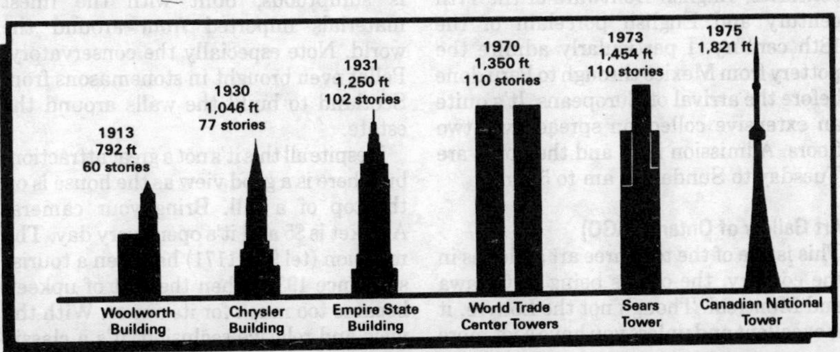

textiles and assorted arts is considered one of the best anywhere. The Egyptian, Greek, Roman and Etruscan civilisations are also represented. The newly designed dinosaur and mammalogy rooms are very good with the latter containing a replica of part of an immense bat cave found in Jamaica. Another section outlines the history of trade between the east and west from the ancient caravan routes through to more modern times. In-depth touring exhibits are often on view – these are generally excellent but a surcharge is added to the admission fee.

The museum is open daily 10 am to 6 pm and until 8 pm Tuesday and Thursday. Admission is $5, less for seniors and students; seniors get in for free on Tuesday evenings. If you go to the planetarium the same day, a discount can be had.

An annexe to the museum is the Canadian Decorative Arts Department, down the street in the Sigmund Samuel Building at 14 Queen's Park Crescent West. The focus is on Canada's early artists and craftsmen. It's free and open daily from 10 am to 5 pm and Sundays from 1 pm to 5 pm.

George R Gardiner Museum of Ceramic Art
At 111 Queen's Park, this museum is also part of the ROM which lies just across the street. The collection is divided into four periods of ceramic history: pre-Columbian, Italian maiolica from the 15th and 16th centuries, English Delftware of the 17th century and English porcelain of the 18th century. I particularly admire the pottery from Mexico through to Peru done before the arrival of Europeans. It's quite an extensive collection spread over two floors. Admission is $2 and the hours are Tuesday to Sunday 10 am to 5 pm.

Art Gallery of Ontario (AGO)
This is one of the top three art galleries in the country, the others being in Ottawa and Montreal. Though not the Louvre, it is excellent and unless you have a lot more stamina than I do, you'll need more than one trip to see it all. It houses works – mainly paintings – from the 14th century to the present. There is also a Canadian section and rooms for changing exhibitions, which can sometimes be the highlight of a visit. The gallery is best known for its vast Henry Moore sculpture collection. One room holds about 20 of his major human form sculptures.

The gallery is on Dundas St West, two blocks west of University Avenue. There is a cafeteria if you need a break, and a good gift/book store. At the door, pick up a schedule of the films and lectures that go on in the gallery. Hours are Tuesday to Sunday 11 am to 5.30 pm, Wednesday 11 am to 9 pm, closed Mondays. Admission is $3.50, students $1.50, free on Wednesday evenings. The Ontario Art College is next door.

The Grange The Grange is a restored Georgian house adjoining the AGO. The door is down in the basement beside the cafeteria. Admission is included with the gallery ticket. Authentic 19th-century furniture and workers in period dress represent life in a 'gentleman's residence' of the time. Also closed Monday.

Casa Loma
This is a 98-room medieval-style castle-cum-mansion built between 1911 and 1914 by Sir Henry Pellat, a very wealthy and evidently eccentric man. The interior is sumptuous, built with the finest materials imported from around the world. Note especially the conservatory. Pellat even brought in stonemasons from Scotland to build the walls around the estate.

Despite all this it's not a great attraction, but there is a good view as the house is on the top of a hill. Bring your camera. A ticket is $5 and it's open every day. The mansion (tel 923-1171) has been a tourist site since 1937, when the cost of upkeep became too much for its owner. With the view and relative seclusion, it's a classic spot for couples to go 'parking' at night. The address is 1 Austin Terrace off Spadina. From the corner of Dupont St and Bathurst, it can clearly be seen, perched impressively above the surroundings.

Provincial Parliament Buildings
The attractive pinkish sandstone legislature sits in Queen's Park just north of College on University Avenue. The stately building was completed in 1892 and is kept in superb condition. Free tours are given frequently throughout the day. For a flashback to your First Grade class, head for the visitors' gallery when Parliament is in session, roughly October to December and February to June.

City Hall
Located in Nathan Phillips Square at Queen and Bay, this distinctive new building represented the beginning of Toronto's emergence as an important and modern city. It was completed in 1965 to Finnish architect Viljo Revell's award-winning design. The twin clamshell towers, with a flying saucer-like structure between them at the bottom, are unmistakable. Free tours are given throughout the day. The square out front is a meeting place and location for concerts, demonstrations and office-worker lunches.

Ontario Science Centre
This centre (tel 429-4423) has an interesting assortment of scientific and technological exhibits and demonstrations, most of which you can take part in. It's a museum where you can touch, pull and squeeze everything. You might even learn something, although it's best for children and on weekends there are hundreds of them. The fitness-testing machines are worth challenging. You'll find good changing exhibits here, too. The design of the centre and its location in a small ravine are assets. It's at the corner of Eglinton Avenue East and Don Mills Rd. To get there, take the subway to Eglinton, transfer to the Eglinton East bus, and get off at Don Mills. Open 10 am to 6 pm daily, admission is $4 and parking $1.50. On Friday nights it remains open to 9 pm and is free from 6 pm to closing, parking included.

Fort York
Fort York (tel 366-6127) was established in 1793 by the British to protect the town, then called York. It was largely destroyed at the end of the War of 1812 against the Americans, but was quickly rebuilt. Now restored, it has eight original log, stone and brick buildings. In summer, men decked out in 19th-century British military uniforms carry out marches and drills, and fire musket volleys. Open every day, all year, 9.30 am to 5 pm, admission $3.50. It's on Garrison Rd which runs off Fleet St which in turn is near Bathurst Avenue near the corner with Front. Take the streetcar south on Bathurst.

Planetarium
McLaughlin Planetarium (tel 586-5750), next door to the ROM, 100 Queen's Park, has entertaining and informative shows about the solar system and universe. The realistic and interesting programmes last 45 minutes. On the second floor, the Astrocentre includes hands-on exhibits, slide shows, astronomy equipment and a solar telescope enabling viewers to watch sun flares as they actually occur. Admission is $3, students $2 and this fee entitles you to $1 off the admission to the museum on the same day. Laserium or laser rock shows are given a few nights a week at $5. Arrive early – once the programme begins you cannot get in. Phone for programme details and times. By subway get off at the Museum stop.

City Neighbourhoods
Toronto has a very wide variety of ethnic groups, some in large, concentrated numbers. Throughout the city, these neighbourhoods maintain the homeland cultures, and offer outsiders glimpses of

foreign countries. These areas are good for restaurants and several are mentioned in the 'Places to Eat' section. All these neighbourhoods have changed considerably through the years and continue to do so as other groups such as West Indians and Latin Americans arrive in Canada. Here are a few of the most prominent districts.

Chinatown Toronto has a huge (and growing) Chinatown right in the centre of town. The original old area runs along Dundas from Bay St, by the bus station west to University. There are many restaurants here, but this area has become rather touristy and isn't really where the local Chinese shop. The newer, bigger and more interesting segment of Chinatown is further west. Also on Dundas, it runs from Beverly, near the Art Gallery, to Spadina Avenue and includes some of Spadina, north and south. Again there are lots of restaurants but also variety and grocery stores, jobbers, herbalists and places selling many things known only to the customers. The area gets packed on weekends and restaurants do good business. There are also a few Japanese and more and more Vietnamese places in the area.

Elm Avenue One of the city's wealthiest areas is just north-east of the corner of Yonge and Bloor. Driving or walking up Park Rd north of Bloor leads to Elm Avenue where nearly every house on the north side is listed by the Historical Board as being architecturally or historically of note. All the streets branching from Elm contain some impressive domains, however. East along Elm, Craigleigh Gardens is a fine, old park.

Cabbagetown Cabbagetown, east of Yonge St, is both a residential district, which ranges from the poor to the very comfortable, and a commercial district. Aside from the differences between its denizens, the area is distinguished primarily by its 19th-century Victorian row houses. It's bounded roughly by Gerrard St East to the south, Wellesley St to the north, Parliament St to the west (which is the main business centre) and Sumach to the east. The last 20 years have seen considerable gentrification of the once very run-down area and there are some very attractive and interesting-looking houses, no doubt about it. The new money has meant a certain uniformity to the neighbourhood but the remaining unrenovated places add a little conflict. The Necropolis off Sumach St at Winchester St is one of the city's oldest and most interesting cemeteries.

Danforth Avenue In the east end of town along Danforth, roughly between Pape and Woodbine, is a large Greek community. There are many restaurants, smoky men's cafés, and also a few big, busy, colourful fruit & vegetable and flower stores which stay open into the night.

Little India Also out this way is Little India, where you'll see numerous specialty stores and women in saris. It's along Gerrard St East, one block west of Coxwell.

St Clair Avenue West Italians, in number, are found in many parts of the city but if there is one centre of the community it's probably on St Clair Avenue West, east and west of Dufferin. Here you'll find Italian movies, clothing stores, espresso cafés and pool halls for the young men. The area went nuts when Italy won the World Cup Soccer Championship a few years ago. I've heard that the crowd that gathered was the largest ever recorded in Toronto. Another significant Italian area is on College between Manning and Ossington.

Nearby is a Portuguese neighbourhood based along Dundas St West between Ossington and Dufferin.

Yorkville

Once Toronto's small version of Greenwich

Village or Haight-Ashbury, this old counter-culture bastion has become the city's trendy boutique area. Along the narrow, busy streets are many art galleries (including one for Inuit work), cafés, restaurants and expensive shops. The whole area has been renovated and in summer can be pleasant with the outdoor cafés and people-watching. It's worth a stroll but the pretension gets a bit nauseating. I mean, a boutique that sells only men's underwear? Watch where you're going, too, or you'll get hit by a Corvette. The district is very central, just above Bloor between Yonge and Avenue Rd. It's centred around Cumberland Avenue, Yorkville Avenue and Hazelton.

Markham Village

As you approach the corner of Bloor and Markham (one block west of Bathurst) you'll see Toronto's most colourful, gaudy store, the zany *Honest Ed's*. Giant signs say things like 'Don't just stand there, buy something'. Hardly subtle but you won't believe the queues outside the door before opening time. Most patrons are from the nearby Italian and Portuguese neighbourhoods. There are some good buys – cheap running shoes, T-shirts and various household necessities. With the money Eddie has made, he has established quite a reputation and become a major patron of the arts. Markham St, south from Bloor with its galleries, boutiques and bookshops, is mostly his doing.

There are some interesting little specialised import shops to browse in. The *Mirvish* bookshop has good sales on Sundays. Bloor St around this area is fun to stroll and has numerous restaurants and bars, patronised for the most part by a mix of students and immigrants.

Harbourfront

Harbourfront is a strip of lakefront land running from the foot of Bay St westward to roughly Bathurst Avenue. Until the past couple of years, redevelopment had usurped old warehouses and factories and converted them to a good, park-like place with community-oriented exhibitions, displays, artists' workshops, craft shows and concerts. Since then, it's now generally acknowledged that construction has been let to run amok and too much of the waterfront is blighted by ugly condos. My blood boils to think of what might have been.

For visitors the centre of activity remains the attractive York Quay, 235 Queen's Quay, where there is an information office. Something goes on nearly every night; it might be a dance or a concert or who knows what. There are a couple of nearby restaurants and a place or two for a drink. Some presentations are free. They may be held outdoors or inside in the various theatres and galleries.

Just to the east is the impressive looking Queen's Quay Terminal with the green glass top, a refurbished 1927 warehouse now containing some interesting specialty and gift shops, restaurants and, up above, offices and apartments.

Contemporary art is displayed in the Power Plant, an old power station, near Queen's Quay. Free.

On weekends the area is popular for a walk along the pier or a browse in the antique and junk market. Try the French fries from one of the many chipwagons. The Canoe School rents canoes which can be used for an enjoyable paddle out to the harbour or along the shore either east or west. Various boats offer trips out on the water.

To get to Harbourfront, first get to Union Station, the train station on Front St, a few blocks north of the lake. The subway will take you this far south. From here either walk south on Yonge St or take the free shuttle bus which runs to Queen's Quay Terminal every 15 minutes from 9.30 am to 9.30 pm daily. Look for the bus with the large key sticking out of the roof. Parking in the area can be a headache and/or costly.

The Islands

From the foot of Bay St near the Harbour Castle Hotel, you can take a 10-minute ferry ride out to the three Toronto Islands – Ward, Centre and Hanlan's Point. Once mainly residential, the islands are largely park now, and very pleasant. Centre Island has the most facilities, many summer events and the most people. Boats can be rented, there is a small animal farm and an amusement area for kids. Beaches line the southern and western shores.

Hanlan's, to the west, is the best beach. You may see some nude sun-bathing at Hanlan's southern end – it's popular with homosexuals – but it is illegal, even though the law is only sporadically enforced. Inland from the beach are picnic tables and some barbecue pits. Toward the city on Hanlan's Point is a small private-craft airport.

Ward Island, the one on the east side, still has quite a few houses that are lived in all year. There is a small restaurant here for snacks and light lunches out on the lawn.

Ferries run frequently, especially in summer, and cost just $2 return. A ferry ride is as good as a harbour tour, with views of the city. You can walk around the islands in under two hours. The cool breezes are great on a hot, sticky day, and it's pretty quiet during the week. Bring a bottle of wine. Riding along the islands' boardwalk on the southern shores is nice. You can take bicycles on some of the ferries or rent them on Centre Island.

Ontario Place

This is a 40-hectare recreation complex built on three man-made islands offshore from the CNE grounds, 955 Lakeshore Boulevard West (tel 965-7711). The futuristic buildings and parkland contain about a dozen restaurants, beer gardens, an outdoor concert stage called the Forum and a Cinesphere for 70 mm films with a six-storey-high curved screen. Check what film is showing; the effects can be amazing. There is also a large, well-stocked, supervised playground with wading pool and slide for kids where you can just let them go nuts.

In summer there are concerts every night, with everything from ballet to rock and they are free with admission to the grounds. Even on a hot day bring a sweater; it gets cold at night down by the water. At the western end is another stage with a waterfall as a curtain where amateurs or lesser names perform concerts, shows, etc. Also here is the new 0.7-km-long flume water-slide with simulated rapids and tunnels. This is an additional $2.50. A new attraction is the Baseball Hall of Fame & Museum.

The park is open from mid-May to October, 10 am to 1 am, admission $5. After 9.30 pm admission is just $1.25. If there is a concert you really want to see or if the act is a big name, arrive early, or even better, very early, with a picnic dinner. If you are driving, parking is another $4.50. Take a subway or streetcar to Bathurst and then the streetcar south down Bathurst to the CNE exhibition grounds. There may also be a new shuttle bus running from downtown to the site, but you'll have to inquire.

Moored off one of the islands is the *Haida*, a destroyer, open to visitors.

High Park

The city's biggest park is another people-place used for picnics, walking and jogging. There is a small children's zoo and a lake with boat rentals. Some parts of the park are well-maintained garden; others are left as natural woods. No cars are allowed on summer weekends. Also in the park is Colbourne Lodge, built by one of Toronto's first architects. The ghost of the architect's wife, who died in the bedroom here, is said to still inhabit the place. Open daily. The park is off Bloor St West at Parkside and runs south down to Lakeshore Boulevard, west of the CNE.

Leslie St Spit

Also known as Tommy Thompson Park, this man-made landfill site extends out into the lake and has become an unexpected, phenomenal wildlife success. It was designed to improve and develop shipping facilities but within a few years became the second largest ring-tail seagull nesting place in the world. Terns and other bird species nest here too. The spit is now a sanctuary for ducks, geese, swans and sandpipers as well as plantlife. Nearly 300 kinds of plants, some found nowhere else in Toronto, have also taken root. Even mammals such as foxes, rabbits and mink are arriving – from where?

The area is open to the public on weekends and holidays only. It's still under construction and arguments over development continue. At the least, some marinas are likely to be built. It's south of the corner of Queen St East and Leslie.

In summer, there may be a bus that runs the length of the spit. And maybe a bus from the corner of Leslie and Queen down to the beginning of the spit.

The Beaches & the Bluffs

The Beaches is a rather wealthy, mainly professional neighbourhood along Queen St East at Woodbine down by the lakeshore. For non-area residents, the Beaches means the beach itself and the parkland along the lake – very popular in summer even if the water has been condemned and is off limits. The sandy beaches are good for sun-tanning and picnicking and a long boardwalk edges along the sand. Sailboards are for rent, with or without lessons. Beach Park is the centre of things, although there are other adjacent parks. At the west end, in Woodbine Park, there is a swimming pool for public use.

About five km further east are the Scarborough Bluffs, 90-metre-high limestone cliffs set in parkland. Erosion has created some odd shapes and revealed layers of sediment indicating five different glacial periods. There are paths here with views. Below, in the lake itself, landfill has been used to form parkland and boat-mooring space. Access to the bluffs is from several points but one main one is from Brimley Rd, which runs south from Kingston Rd. Look for Cathedral Bluffs Park.

Not far (by vehicle) east of the park is the Guild Inn with its large lakefront grounds. From behind the Inn there are good views along the shoreline to bluffs. In the garden is a collection of statues and sculptures as well as many columns and gargoyles that were taken from old buildings being demolished. There is one nearly complete facade that looks like something from the Parthenon. Tea is served on the patio in the afternoon. The Inn (which does rent rooms) is on Guildwood Parkway, south from Kingston Rd at Livingstone Rd.

Other Parks

Allan Gardens is an often-mentioned, much-publicised park that's pretty overrated. The highlight is the large old greenhouse open daily from 10 am to 5 pm. Plants include tropical specimens. The rest of the park is unsavoury enough that visits aren't recommended after dark. The park is a few blocks east of Yonge at Carleton and Jarvis Sts.

The city does have some very fine, largely natural parks located in numerous ravines formed by rivers and streams running down to the lake. Start in Edwards Gardens, corner of Lawrence Avenue West and Leslie. It's a big, cultivated park with flower gardens, a pond and picnic sites. You can take a ravine walk from the gardens via Wilket Creek Park. The Science Centre backs onto the park here. Along Wilket Creek you can walk for hours all the way down to Victoria Park Avenue, just north of Danforth. Much of the way is through woodland.

From the corner of Yonge and St Clair, walk east to the bridge and the sign for the

Nature Trail. This leads down into the Don River Valley, another good walk.

Markets
Kensington Market is the city's prime one; it's a colourful and lively multi-ethnic old-style market squeezed along Baldwin and Augusta off Spadina Avenue, just south of College and east of Bathurst. It's open every day but is wild on Saturday morning. The cheese shops are good, and there's all manner of fresh fruit & vegetables. You can bargain over prices. This was the heart of the city's Jewish area, but as you'll see, people from many countries have changed that. There are a few small restaurants in the area, too. On Saturdays don't even think of driving down here.

The St Lawrence Market is on Front St at Jarvis in what was Toronto's first city hall in 1844. Here nearly everyone is English and the atmosphere is closer to sedate – there are even classical musicians playing – but it is also very lively on Saturdays. On Sundays there is an antique and flea market here. Just north of this building is St Lawrence Hall, topped with its clock tower. It is one of the city's finest old buildings; used as a public meeting hall in the last century, it is now – among other things – used by the National Ballet for rehearsal.

The Market Gallery on the 2nd floor of the market building is the city's exhibition hall and displays good, rotating shows (paintings, photographs, documents, artefacts) on Toronto's history. Free. Closed Mondays, Tuesdays and holidays.

Historical Sites
There isn't a lot for history buffs as the city is so new, but the few small sites are well done. The Tourist Office has a guide to the historic homes and sites. Many of these remaining old buildings stand where the old town of York was situated – in the southern portion of the city. Here are some of the best sites.

Mackenzie House was owned by William Lyon Mackenzie, the city's first mayor. The mid-Victorian home is furnished with antiques from the 1800s. In the basement is an old print-shop, where it's said the machines can be heard mysteriously working some nights. The house is at 82 Bond St, a couple of blocks east of Yonge. Afternoon tea is served.

Churches At the corner of King and Church, the town's first church was built in 1807. St James Cathedral now stands here and is the city's tallest church. Nearby at Queen and Parliament, the first Catholic church was constructed in 1822. On this site a second St Paul's Anglican Church now stands, one of Toronto's most impressive Renaissance-style buildings.

Spadina House was the gracious mansion of local businessman James Austin. Built in 1866, the impressive interior contains fine furnishings and art collected over three generations. About 10 of its 35 rooms are open to the public. The family gave the house to the historical board in 1982. The address is 285 Spadina Rd, just east of Casa Loma, and it's open daily, admission $3.

Campbell House is downtown at the corner of Queen and University. Once the residence of the chief justice of Upper Canada, it is a colonial-style brick mansion furnished in early 1800s style. The house is open daily in summer, weekdays in winter; there is a small admission.

Colbourne Lodge This house in High Park, built in 1836, is a Regency-style cottage and contains many original furnishings, including possibly the first indoor flush toilet in the province! Informative tours are offered by the costumed staff and may include baking or craft demonstrations. Admission is inexpensive and the site is quite popular.

Montgomery's Inn was built in 1832 by an Irish military captain of the same name, is a fine example of Loyalist architecture. It has been restored to the period 1830-1855. Costumed staff answer questions, bake bread and demonstrate crafts. Open daily, it's at 4709 Dundas St West at Islington Avenue, in the city's far west end.

Enoch Turner Schoolhouse dates from 1848. It's a restored, simple, one-room schoolhouse where, during the week, classes are held to show kids what the good old days were like. It's open to the public at weekends. The address is 106 Trinity St and it's near the corner of King and Parliament.

Post Office Toronto's first post office, from the 1830s, is at 260 Adelaide St East. Letters can still be sealed with wax and sent from here.

The northern part of the city also has a few historical attractions. Gibson House at 5172 Yonge St shows the 1850 farmhouse of a prosperous surveyor and politician.

Todmorden Mills Historic Site near the location of an important 1794 sawmill and gristmill on the Don River preserves two houses, complete with period furnishings and a brewery from about 1825. Also on the site is an old train station moved from nearby and a former paper mill now used as a playhouse. The park is at 67 Pottery Rd and is open from May to December. A small admission is charged.

The large, red-brick houses found all over downtown Toronto were built around the 1920s.

Black Creek Pioneer Village

A replica of an Ontario village of 100 years ago, this is the city's top historic attraction (tel 661-6610). It's about 30 minutes' driving from downtown, at the corner of Steeles Avenue and Jane St in the north-west section of town and is accessible by public transportation. Restored buildings and workers in authentic dress give a feeling of rural life in the 19th century. Crafts and skills of the times using the old tools and methods are demonstrated. One reader raved about the herb garden. You can buy the results of the cooking and baking. In one of the barns is a large toy museum and woodcarving collection. Open daily, late May to late September. Admission $5. Special events are offered regularly through the season.

Toronto Zoo

Opened in 1974, this huge zoo has quickly gained an excellent reputation and, although still expanding, is one of the country's best. There are over 4000 animals on the 283 hectares, some in natural-setting pens the size of football fields. Of course, with enclosures that large, it takes a lot of walking. In fact, there's a small train that goes around the site, but walking is best. A full day is needed to see it all.

The animals are divided into five areas, each covering a major world geographical area. Each area has outdoor and climate-simulated indoor pavilions. A good idea is the black-light area that enables you to observe nocturnal animals. Through the use of lights, the animals' days have been turned upside down so we can see them at their active time. There's also a pets area for children.

The zoo is good for cross-country skiing in winter; equipment is available. You may want to take your lunch as *McDonald's* has an exclusive food contract for the grounds. The zoo is on Meadowvale Rd, north of Highway 401, at the eastern edge of the city. To get there, take the subway to Warden or the No 86a bus to the zoo. Admission is $6, less for kids. Summer hours are 9.30 am to 7 pm daily.

Wonderland

Away from the centre of town, Wonderland (tel 832-2205) is Toronto's – I guess Canada's – newest large-scale attraction:

a Canadian Disneyland opened in May 1981. The $120-million theme park has exhibits, games, animals, shows and, of course, rides, including some killer roller coasters, one going 80 km/h. There is a huge man-made mountain with a waterfall and areas made to look like scenes from fairy tales.

Covering 150 hectares, the park can't be seen all in one day. Get a guidebook at the entrance and decide what you want to see the most. Prices vary but are not low. A one-day pass good for all attractions and rides is $20. A ticket which includes some rides and attractions is $17 and straight admission to the grounds is $13. Kids' passes are less. Parking is another $3. Top-name entertainers are presented through the summer at the Kingswood Theatre but tickets for these shows are extra. Wonderland is open from approximately the beginning of June to the beginning of September, and weekends a month before and after these dates. Hours are 10 am to 10 pm in peak season, 10 am to 8 pm the extra weekends.

Wonderland is on Highway 400, 10 minutes north of the 401. Exit at Rutherford Rd if you're travelling north, Major Mackenzie Drive if you're going south. There are buses from Yorkdale and York Mills subway stations.

Sunshine Beach Water Park

Open daily from June to September, this huge water park offers about half a dozen twisting water-slides and a couple of steep, high, straight speed slides, along with a wave pool and huge whirlpools. Picnic grounds are provided and there are food concessions. An all-day ticket is $13, less for kids. The park is 1.6 km west of Highway 427 on Finch Avenue north-west of the centre of Toronto.

Marine Museum of Upper Canada

Located in the officers' quarters of an 1841 army barracks at Exhibition Place, this museum shows the history of the city as a port. On exhibit are models, old ship relics and, moored outside, a restored steam tugboat. Admission is $2. Open Mondays to Saturdays 9.30 am to 5 pm, Sundays from noon.

Police Museum

This museum has a small collection of equipment and details of some cases. It's in the lobby of the headquarters at 311 Jarvis and admission is free. Open 6 to 9 pm Thursday and Friday and from 1 to 5 pm on weekends.

Museum of the History of Medicine

Another specialty museum, this one outlines healing practices and health care from before recorded history. It's central at 288 Bloor St West and is free.

Toronto Dominion Gallery of Inuit Art

Housed on the ground floor of the IBM Tower of the Toronto Dominion Centre, corner of King and Bay, this gallery displays a good collection of far northern art mainly from WW II to the present. It consists primarily of sculpture in stone and bone which is the foremost form of Inuit art. The gallery is free and open daily.

Toronto Stock Exchange

The new exchange is Canada's largest and one of the most modern anywhere. Stock worth $100 million is bought and sold each day so it's a fairly hectic place. There is a visitors' centre and tours are given Monday through Friday. The exchange is in the Exchange Tower, Canadian Place, at the corners of King or Front and Bay St, right in the centre of the city's financial district.

Ecology House

Ecology House (tel 967-0577) offers a free tour on Sunday at 2 pm. Otherwise, wander around by yourself reading the explanations that show how houses can be made more energy and conservation-efficient. You can pick up some good ideas, especially if you want to buy or build a house. It's at 12

Madison Avenue at Bloor St West and is open Wednesday to Sunday, noon to 5 pm. Admission is free.

Events

The Canadian National Exhibition (CNE) CNE claims to be the oldest (nearly 100 years), and the largest annual exhibition in the world. It includes agricultural and technical exhibits, concerts, displays, crafts, parades, a good air show, horse show, midway and fireworks. The exhibition is held during the last two weeks of August at Exhibitions Place, which is by the CNE football stadium on Lakeshore Boulevard West, at the lake. Admission to the grounds includes a free entrance to Ontario Place.

Mariposa Now over 25 years old, Mariposa is a festival of mainly folk but also bluegrass and American Indian music. Having grown from just a three-day event, the festival now schedules concerts throughout the year at various venues around town. The main annual event is often held in Molson Park just out of Barrie, north of Toronto. The three-day affair is usually held in July. Workshops, jam sessions and ethnic folk dancing are featured as well. For information on all the events call 363-4009.

Carabana An ever-growing annual West Indian Festival, Carabana will celebrate its 25th year in 1991. It takes place around the beginning of August and is a weekend of reggae, steel drum and calypso music & dance held on Centre Island.

The main attraction, however, is the very lengthy and colourful parade down University St to the ferry, featuring fantastic and outrageous costumes à la carnival in Rio. This parade can have perhaps 6000 people in it and can take five hours or longer to pass by!

Caravan This is a nine-day event of cultural exchange where ethnic groups offer music, dance and food native to their homelands. There are about 50 different ethnic pavilions set up around the city. A passport entitles you to entry into all the pavilions. The event takes place during the last days of June. A passport is about $10 and buses travel between the pavilions. Ask the Tourist Office for a complete list of events and things to see and do. The Japanese pavilion is rated highly and has taken top prize in recent years.

International Picnic At the beginning of June each year, the huge International Picnic is held on Centre Island. Admission is free and there's music, dancing, contests and lots of food. The picnic's purpose is the welcoming of summer.

Queen's Plate The year's major horse race and one of North America's oldest (since 1859), the Queen's Plate is held at the Woodbine Track on the last Saturday in June. Get lucky and your trip will be paid for.

Toronto Star Great Salmon Hunt This annual fishing derby attracts anglers to Lake Ontario from far and wide, hoping to catch some of the hundreds of thousands of dollars in prizes for landing the big one.

Film Festival The annual film Festival of Festivals is now a prestigious and major international cinematic event. It lasts about a week and a half and features films of all lengths and styles, gala events and well-known stars. The festival is usually held in September; you can get more information from the Tourist Office. All the papers have special guides and reviews as well. You can obtain tickets for individual screenings or buy expensive, all-inclusive packages.

Jazz Festival The annual Molson Jazz Festival is held at Harbourfront in July or August. It features three days and evenings of generally traditional, swing and Dixieland jazz with both local and American players. Free.

Activities

Cycling For cyclists, the Martin Goodman Trail is a bicycle route along the waterfront which stretches from the Beaches in the east end, past Harbourfront and the downtown centre, to the Humber River in the west end. From here, it connects with paths in parkland running along the Humber northward. This section is a really fine ride and you can go as far as Eglinton, at least. That's quite a few km. Visit the Tourist Office for a free pamphlet detailing sights along the path.

The Toronto Bicycling Network runs short, medium and long weekend trips (some overnight) throughout the summer. Give them a call for the upcoming schedule and more information.

Other At two of the better camping stores, Trail Head at 40 Wellington St East and Mountain Equipment Co-op nearby at 35 Front St East, you can get information on adventure trips such as white-water canoeing and wilderness hiking.

You can go windsurfing at the Beaches in east-end Toronto; rentals are available.

Free public pools can be found in High Park, the Sunnyside Natatorium south of the park at the lake, and Woodbine Park at the Beaches in east-end Toronto.

There are two places to go ballooning near Toronto but it's big bucks at about $125 an hour. The choices are the Balloonery in Acton, or the Millcroft Inn, just outside of Acton near Caledonia on summer weekends.

Places to Stay

Hostels Toronto finally has a permanent *Youth Hostel* (tel 368-0207) after years of frequent change. The three-storey renovated brick building opened in 1982. Its location, three blocks east of the Eaton Centre on Yonge St, is excellent and central. The address is 223 Church St, just south of Dundas St East; the subway stop is Dundas. The hostel is open all year and there are about 90 beds. While there's no kitchen, there is a fridge and a kettle. It's closed from 10 am to 5 pm and there's a midnight curfew. The hostel is a little expensive at $9 for members and $13 for non-members. If you don't have a sleep sheet it's 75c. The *Ontario Hostelling Association* (tel 368-1848) has an office a few doors down.

The *YWCA* (tel 923-8454), for women only, is also central at 80 Woodlawn Avenue at Yonge St. There's a cheap cafeteria and pool. The price ranges from $31 to $36 for one and there is also a dormitory where a bed goes for $14, but either way a continental breakfast is included. The YMCA in town no longer has rooms for rent.

The *University of Toronto* (tel 978-8735) rents rooms in various college residences. The campus is by the corner of University and College. Rooms are available mid-May to late August. Singles are $27 and doubles $34, and there are very good weekly rates. Rooms are also available at another campus which is smaller and more suburban, and there are still more beds in other downtown residences such as Trinity College.

York University (tel 667-3098) has a similar deal. They rent rooms from May to the end of August. They have good recreational facilities, but the trouble with accommodation here is that it's a long way from downtown, at the northern boundary of the city. The address is 4700 Keele at Steeles Avenue. Reservations are required; singles are $25 and doubles are $37, with breakfast included.

Neil Wycik College Hotel (tel 977-2320), an apartment-like residence, is at 96 Gerrard St East, right downtown by Ryerson Polytechnical Institute. It's good value and in an excellent location. They rent their very small rooms from 14 May to 5 September. Singles are $24 and doubles $31, but there is a student standby rate after 8 pm which is quite a bit cheaper.

Weekly rates are 10% less. There are shared kitchens and a student-run cafeteria for breakfasts. Larger family rooms are available.

Tartu College (tel 925-4747) at 310 Bloor St West, not far from Yonge, rents rooms in the summer. A single is $125 (per week) and must be rented by the week or longer.

Tourist Homes There aren't a lot of commercial guest houses in town but the ones that do exist are generally very centrally located, pretty well established and fairly priced. *Karabanow Guest House* (tel 923-4004) is recommended by the Hostel Association. It has a good location at 9 Spadina, just above Bloor St West. The tariff includes parking, daily cleaning and cable TV. Singles are $30 and up, and doubles range from $45 to $55 – less with a Youth Hostel card. The weekly rate saves the cost of a night or two.

Very conveniently situated just north of College St at 322 Palmerston Boulevard, a quiet tree-lined avenue, is the *Burkin Guest House* (tel 920-7842). It's a well-kept large older house with eight guest rooms and a pleasant second-storey balcony. Prices are a little higher than the others at $40 to $50 for singles and $50 to $55 for doubles.

On King St West at 1233 is the simpler *Candy Haven Tourist Home* (tel 532-0651). It's right on the King streetcar line; look for the bright paint job and sign. It's central and there are sinks in the rooms. Doubles go for $30 to $35.

Further west on King St is the *King-Jameson Tourist Home* at 1409 King St West (tel 432-4822). Kitchen facilities and free parking are available. There are just four rooms here, ranging from $25 to $35 for singles and $35 to $50 for doubles.

Still further west at 1546 King St, near Roncesvalles Avenue, is the *Grayona Tourist Home* (tel 535-5443). It's a recently renovated old house run by Marie Taylor, a friendly, enthusiastic Australian. Singles range from $30 to $45 and doubles are $40 to $55. More expensive rooms have cooking facilities. A few doors down there is another guest house.

Bed & Breakfasts There are now three bed & breakfast associations in town which check, list and book rooms in the participating homes. Indicate where you'd like to be and any other preferences, and attempts will be made to find a particularly agreeable host. Prices start at $30 for singles and $40 for doubles and go up quite a bit.

Toronto Bed & Breakfast (tel 233-3887, 233-4041), Box 74 Station M, M6S 4T2, seems to have the best rates. They have about 30 members.

Metropolitan B&B Registry (tel 964-2566, 928-2833) is the largest outfit with members in and out of town. The office is at 72 Lowther Avenue. Foreign languages are spoken at some and, as is the norm generally, smokers will be told to butt out. One example of their listings is the *Ringeval's* house (tel 363-7449) near King St West and Strachan, close to the CNE and streetcars. They charge $32 for singles and $39 for doubles. The man is French, the woman from New Zealand.

Thirdly, there is the *Downtown Toronto Group of B&B Guest Houses* (tel 977-6841) at PO Box 190, Station B, Toronto, M5T 2W1. Their rooms are all downtown in renovated Victorian houses and cost $40 for singles and $50 to $65 for doubles. The association's founder, Susan Oppenheim, rents rooms in her own house and serves breakfast in a kitchen that you won't forget.

Hotels – bottom end & middle Toronto has an abundance of large, new, modern hotels and more are being added continually. There are many downtown, plenty around the edges and a good number out around the airport. Of course, they tend to be rather pricey and sterile to boot. The city, unfortunately, lacks smaller, older hotels which offer character. There are a few exceptions, but most of these fall into the middle price ranges rather than low-budget. Many hotels offer weekend packages at lower than usual rates.

The *Strathcona* (tel 363-3321) is an older place that has been overhauled and upgraded and has all the usual amenities and yet is, for downtown, moderately priced at $50 for singles and $70 for doubles. It is excellently located at 60 York St, very near the train station. There's a dining room, coffee shop and a bar.

The similar but much smaller *Whitehouse Hotel* at 76 Church St is a narrow, unobtrusive place that takes up nine floors with its 35 rooms. It's good value, with singles for $50 to $60 and doubles for $55 to $65. Nearly everything downtown is within walking distance.

The *Quality Inn* (tel 362-6061), part of a chain, is always dependable, and is central at 300 Jarvis St. Singles/doubles are $65/75. The *Bond Place* (tel 362-6061) is busy with vacationers – there are often tour buses out front. It has a great location near the Eaton Centre at 65 Dundas St East. Prices vary but average $74/82 for singles/doubles.

One of the best of the small, old downtown hotels is the *Victoria* at 56 Yonge St, near its southern end. The hotel has recently changed ownership and has been completely refurbished. Some of the features remain (eg the fine lobby), and the place has a lot of history, but it's no longer the real bargain it was. Prices are now in the $80 to $100 category.

More like a motel but perfectly good and far cheaper is the *Executive Motor Hotel* (tel 595-1975) at 621 King St West. The 75 rooms are priced from $40/45 and up for singles/doubles. The streetcar goes right by.

The inner city still does have some older, cheaper hotels and a good portion of these are found in the Jarvis and Sherbourne Sts area east of Yonge. Sections of this part of town can be a little on the rough side and some hotels' rooms are used for more than sleeping. Single women may not like walking in the area alone at night and may well be asked their price.

The *St Leonard* (tel 924-4902) at 418 Sherbourne is worn but clean and friendly. They have 22 simple rooms, some with private bath and TV. Prices start at $38 for singles and rise to $46 for doubles.

The *Selby* (tel 921-3142) at 592 Sherbourne, near the Isabella Hotel, is in Gaytown and is known basically for its bars and patio used by men of that persuasion, but the place has an old, interesting history. Ernest Hemingway once lived here when he worked for the *Toronto Star* in his younger days, before heading to Paris. Rooms cost from $35 and up.

For connoisseurs of classic dives, there's the *Gladstone* at 1214 Queen St West. It's a beautiful old building long past its day with plenty of 'rubbies' throwing 'em back in the bar downstairs. Rates are cheap: $18 for singles, $24 for doubles.

Hotels – top end The costliest rooms in town are found at the *Four Seasons* in Yorkville at 21 Avenue Rd where prices are around $200 a night and up. Also very well appointed with a good reputation is the *Westin*, right in the centre at 145 Richmond St West. Singles/doubles cost from $135/155. The *Toronto Hilton Harbour Castle* has a fine location right at the edge of the lake opposite the Toronto Islands. The address is 1 Harbour Square; it's very near the bottom of Yonge St. They offer a revolving restaurant & bar which provide good views over the city and lake. Prices start at about $20 less than the Westin.

Lastly, the venerable *Royal York* at 100 Front St opposite the train station deserves mention. Among the top class hotels it's the oldest and has served rock stars to royalty. You can grab a single here from just over $100.

Apartment Hotels Fully furnished rooms

with kitchen facilities have sprung up in some number in recent years and can provide quite good value. One of the longest running is the *Avenue Park Hotel* (tel 961-2444) at 138 Pears Avenue, where all rooms come with small kitchens. Singles/doubles cost about $60/70, with weekly and monthly rates available. There's a bar and restaurant downstairs. Pears runs west off Avenue Rd, north of Davenport. The hotel is near the corner of Bloor and University.

Executive Travel Suites (tel 273-9641) have four such properties in the downtown area with prices starting at $75 a day with a three-day minimum. Each unit has a separate bedroom and living room and each building offers one or more extras, such as a pool, balconies, roof deck or restaurant. The Tourist Office will know of other apartments for rent on a short term basis.

Motels For such a large city, Toronto is rather short on motels and consequently, in summer they are often full. There are two main districts for motels in the city and others scattered throughout and around the perimeter.

On the west side of town, a strip of motels (now threatened with redevelopment) can be found along the lake on Lakeshore Boulevard West, formerly Highway 2. Many are between the Humber River and Park Lawn Avenue, just west of High Park. The further out you go (motels dot the road all the way to Hamilton), the cheaper the motel and the greater your chances of finding a vacancy. The area by the lake is nice, with several parks nearby on the waterfront. There are cool breezes in summer and good views of the city and islands. You'll find about 10 motels beside each other, which are busy in summer.

This district isn't too far from downtown and is still on the streetcar line from Yonge St. To get there, take the Queen or King St streetcar from downtown to Roncesvalles, and continue on the Queen car to the Humber River. Switch (no charge) to the Humber car, which goes along the lakeshore.

The *Sunshine Motel* (tel 255-1121) is a green place at 2171 Lakeshore Boulevard West. It's small and one of the older ones but OK. The rates are $32 to $45.

The *Palace* (tel 259-7671) at 2083 Lakeshore is small, very plain and white with red doors, and charges $30 to $40.

The *Rainbow* (tel 259-7671) is close to Sunshine Motel at 2165; it's the blue & white place. Rooms cost from $40.

Another one to check is the *North American*. It's bigger and more modern, a greenish two-storey place at 2147 Lakeshore Boulevard West. Prices range from $35 to $55 for singles and $36 to $60 for doubles.

Back closer to town, the *Inn on the Lake* at 1926 Lakeshore Boulevard West is very popular with American visitors; the parking lot reveals cars from all over the States. The *Lakeshore Inn* next door is also busy. Both are in the $50 to $70 range.

Not too far away but west on The Queensway, try the *Queensway Motel* (tel 252-5281), at 638 The Queensway. It's sort of away from the traffic, and may have rooms when others have booked up. Its prices are lower.

More motels although not in great numbers, can be found along Dundas St West, west of Highway 427 which is in the suburb of Mississauga rather than Toronto proper.

The other main motel district is on the east side of town, on Kingston Rd, which is an extension of Queen St East and later turns into the old Highway 2 to Montreal. Motels start just east of where Danforth begins branching off from Kingston Rd.

The *Royal Motel* (tel 264-4381) is at 2746 Kingston Rd just past Bluffers Park, and has rooms for $38 to $55. Next door is the *Avon* (tel 267-0339), which costs $30 to $50 and has TV, radio and a heated pool.

Several other motels are nearby. Try the *East Side Motel* (tel 265-3500) at 3300

Kingston, with rooms at $30 to $40. Further east at 3370 Kingston Rd is the *White Swan* (tel 261-7168), a brick place with blue & white sign. The rates are $28 to $44. They have weekly rates, too.

The *Roycroft* (tel 267-9941) is a neat, clean, white & brown place at Highway 3137. There's a small pool and colour TV and they charge $35 to $55. Further out at 4275 is the *Montoro* with blue & white awnings, corner of Galloway. The rate is $35 to $60.

Camping There are several camping/trailer grounds within 40 km of the city. The Tourist Office has a complete list.

Two of the closest are: *Clairville Conservation Area* (tel 678-1233), north up Indian Line Rd in Downsview, beside the airport. It's near Steeles Rd. Follow Highway 427 past the airport. This is probably the best one for tenters. The second is *Glen Rouge Park* (tel 947-8092), on Kingston Rd (Highway 2) at Altona Rd, near Sheppard Avenue East. It's at the border of Scarborough – part of Toronto – and the town of Pickering at the eastern edge of the city and is on the lakefront. There are about 120 sites.

Moodies (tel 683-1995) is at 248 Kingston Rd, west of Pickering. It's east of town. There are 40 sites from $8.

KOA is on RR1 Bradford at Highway 400 and Highway 88. It costs a little more than others at $13 to $15.

Places to Eat

Toronto has a good selection of restaurants in all price categories and a very wide variety to choose from, thanks to the many nationalities represented in the city. For the most part, the following are centrally located and accessible by public transport.

Yonge St in the downtown centre has, in general, become swamped with fast-food franchises and cheap take-out counters. But there are exceptions on and near the city's main street although they are geared more to lunch than dinner. At the hole in the wall *Papaya Hut* at 515 Yonge, the home-made vegetable soup, a sandwich such as avocado and tomato, and a papaya drink or smoothie provide an alternative to the nearby junk food. Another bargain can be had at *Aida's* which at 597 Yonge is even smaller but cranks out quite decent and cheap felafels, tabouli and a very limited number of other Lebanese basics. At 362 Yonge St, *Swiss Chalet* is an outlet of the very popular Canadian Roast Chicken chain. The meals are tasty and good value.

A world apart is *Taiko Sushi* downstairs at 607A Yonge. It's a small, low-key Japanese sushi bar where an inexpensive snack or an expensive meal can be put together while you sit and watch at the counter. Green tea is on the house and the box lunches to go are reasonably priced.

British-style pub grub can be had with a brew at one of the city's four *Nag's Head Taverns*. The Eaton Centre has the slickest and most expensive one; the corner of King and Yonge holds the working class version. More Englishy and offering a variety of beers and an outdoor patio is the *Artful Dodger* on Isabella, east a few doors from Yonge St.

The large, crowded, noisy cafeteria at Ryerson Polytechnical Institute serves up reasonable student-price meals. Food is served at meal times only in the cafeteria in Jorgenson Hall, which is at Gerrard St East and Victoria St.

The *Vegetarian Restaurant* at 4 Dundonald St, just a few doors from Yonge St, is one of the few of its kind in the city and is recommended. The tasty and inexpensive fare includes daily specials, soups, salads and create-your-own-sandwiches, all offered cafeteria-style. They have good desserts. It's a very quiet, low-key place open every day, but on Sundays it's closed until late in the afternoon.

There are several places with outdoor patios nearby, especially on St Joseph St. The *Fair Exchange* at 4 Irwin is good for lunch or dinner and is licensed and moderately priced. Further north, the *Apple Cafe*, at 15 Haydn east off Yonge, is good for a tea or coffee and a sweet.

All along Yonge St, usually on corners, are *Mr Submarine* outlets where they make good sub sandwiches for $3.50 and up. A simple cheese sub, microwaved, is good.

Over at 131 Jarvis, *The Groaning Board* is a casual, semi-self-serve place with some vegetarian dishes but meats as well. The soup is good, as are the sandwiches and there is a large salad bar, but the hamburgers are not recommended. Folk music is presented on weekends. The rest of the week they show a two-hour reel of the year's best commercials chosen at Cannes.

For a splurge on a good steak, try *Harry's* at 518 Church, an established place in an area of many new restaurants. The restaurant offers soft lights and attentive service. On Mondays and Tuesdays there is a complete fixed-price dinner at $16.

Bloor St offers all sorts of eating along its considerable length. Around Yonge, an area of expensive shops and fashion boutiques, there is a very good never-advertised spot: the *Fresh Market* on the third floor of Holt Renfrew, a department store at 50 Bloor West. It used to be a real bargain but at last visit the increases were a bit of a surprise. However, the afternoon tea with scones and Devon cream is still a little pleasure. Open 10 am to 5 pm on retail sales days.

A very cheap place worth going if you're in the area is the *Masters' Restaurant*, 310 Bloor St West in the University Faculty of Education Building, just east of Spadina. Mostly for students, it's open 7 am to 7 pm Monday to Friday. Cafeteria-style meals like lamb, sole and shepherd's pie are served for under $5. Complete breakfasts are available at rock bottom prices.

Bloor St West around Bathurst is a lively student area with many good and generally cheap restaurants, a few cafés, the *Brunswick Tavern* and the popular Bloor Cinema.

The Continental, a Hungarian place at 521 Bloor West, is a cosy place with the usual red & white checkered table-cloths. About five meal choices are offered each day, including rice dishes and schnitzels. Meals average $7.

By The Way Café, with the former 'Lickin' Chicken' sign still in place, is a popular sitting and meeting place which also serves pretty decent food – Middle Eastern or vegetarian. The desserts are excellent. There are some outdoor tables. The café is on the north-western corner of Bloor and Brunswick.

Queen St West between Spadina and University has been the site of a mini-boom in restaurants in the midst of a general area revival. First claimed by the arts community and their followers, numerous shops and eateries sprang up, many to be replaced as the money moved in. Some of the places cater more to trend than quality but it's a very interesting and varied area with some good and reasonably priced restaurants.

One of the better and more stable of the eateries is the comfortable *Queen Mother* at 208 Queen West. They offer a good, varied menu for meals and serve coffee and snacks all day.

Barney's at 385 Queen West is definitely not a newcomer. In 35 years, this has become one of the small elite of classic local institutions that North American inner cities seem to produce. The few mini-tables and 13 stools are usually full at lunch and you'll be reminded that dawdling is *verboten*. The chilli, corned beef and breakfasts are highlights.

Many of the area's younger residents and more impecunious artists have now moved further west to between Spadina and Bathurst and along here are various new, small restaurants and specialty stores including quite a few bookshops.

Much further west but still on Queen in a bit-of-everything area known as Parkdale, *Thumpers* has the best hamburgers in town and good salads, shakes and home-made pies to accompany them. It's at No 1336.

Down at King St and Simcoe St is Ed Mirvish's one-man development complex. Centred around the Royal Alexander Theatre are his famous restaurants, which are famous for the garish exteriors, the sumptuous interiors and the straight, simple food served at low prices. The meats are good, the instant potato and frozen vegetables just filler.

Old Ed's is a fairly casual place with dinners from $8 to $11 and lunches for a dollar or two less. Selections include lasagne, chicken, fish, ribs and veal. As in all Ed's restaurants, which run in a line linked by the white signs and lightbulbs, the entree comes with potato, salad and rolls. *Ed's Warehouse* (tel 593-6676) is a bit more up-market. No jeans are allowed and jackets are required. At the door they usually have some jackets and ties to hand out to those without. Call ahead to make sure, if you don't have one. Here prices are $12 to $15 at dinner, and a few dollars less at lunch. The menu offers a couple of selections of roast beef and steak only.

The main attraction to both these places is the decor – a wild, sense-stunning compilation of antiques and oddities lit by dozens of Tiffany lamps. Wedged in and around these two are now others specialising in either Italian, seafood or Chinese foods. I'm telling you, this guy leaves no stone unturned. The restaurants are one block north of the CN Tower.

Around the corner on John St and up two blocks is the *Amsterdam Cafe*, which is Toronto's first brew pub and a good place for a quaff after a show or trip up the tower.

Toronto, like nearly all Canadian cities of any size, has its *Spaghetti Factory*. This one is at 54 The Esplanade behind (south of) the O'Keefe Theatre on Front St near the corner of Yonge. This is an area very popular with visitors as well as residents. The restaurant offers good value with meals from salad through dessert starting at $7, and served in an interesting, eclectic, colourful atmosphere. Lunch can be had for around $5. It's a popular family and teenager spot. They make numerous spaghettis and other Italian dishes like lasagne and chicken cacciatore.

Nearby are numerous other places to eat, many with large outdoor sections. At 6 Market St across from the market building, the *Old Fish Market* with lots of nautical adornments offers a variety of food from the sea at $10 to $15 at dinner, or standard English fare like shepherd's pie for $5 at lunch.

Toronto has a huge Chinatown downtown, based around the corner of Spadina and Dundas St West and it is home to scores of restaurants. As the area developed, so did the tastes of restaurant patrons. As well as the standard Cantonese fare, the city now has Sichuan, Hunan and Mandarin places. Browse around reading menus. For tasty, spicy Sichuan food, try the *Great Wall* at 444 Spadina. The hot spiced chicken with peanuts is a great dish, as is the Hunan hot beef. Under $40 for four at dinner. *Lee Garden* at 358 Spadina offers a consistently good and unusually varied Cantonese menu and is also not expensive at all.

Until recently, it was the Jewish community which dominated Spadina. Despite the Chinese influx, a few restaurants, textile shops and jobbers remain. *Switzers* at 322 seems to have been there forever. It's a popular deli with dishes such as smoked meat and pickles with prices from $5 or $6. *Moishes* at 440 Spadina is another perennial spot. Once tattered-looking with 'autographed' celebrity photos, it has recently cleaned up and looks a little plastic but the service and food haven't changed. Meals average $5. It's popular with U of T students.

Formerly just around the corner but now a little further, the *Kensington Kitchen* at 124 Harbord St is a very fine and comfortable Middle Eastern café. They serve generous portions; try the soup with a felafel or grilled cheese. Afterwards I'll bet you'll have a favourite little lunch spot in Toronto. Also the appetisers are definitely worth sampling. About $6 at lunch, $10 at dinner.

Little India, based on Gerrard St East just west of Coxwell, has numerous inexpensive restaurants. The *Moti Mahal* at 1442 is very plain but the food is good and ridiculously cheap. The *Bar-Be-Que Hut* (peculiarly named) at 1457 is plusher than most; again the food is good but the portions are pretty small. The *Madras Durbar*, a tiny, exclusively vegetarian place serves South Indian dishes. The *thali* plate is good and makes a complete meal for only $4.50. The address is 1435 Gerrard St East. After dinner, take a walk around the area and pop into one of the shops to ask for a *paan* made to order. With or without tobacco, this is a cheap, exotic taste experience.

My personal Indian favourite is nowhere near this part of town. It's the *Indian Rice Factory* at 414 Dupont St in the west end. Quite unlike Gerrard St's choices, this is a sedate, tastefully decorated dining room. The food is top rate and offers a little more subtlety than the norm, yet prices are certainly reasonable. The only drawback is the interminably slow service. Open every day.

The Greek community along the Danforth is also a good place to get a meal. Some are in the old style where you can check out the kitchen and tell the chef what you'd like. The *Byzantium* at 401 Danforth offers this approach for its presentation of most of the Greek standards. Kebab houses have become popular in the past few years and there are now quite a few in the neighbourhood. One that's good and cheap – just look for the queue – is *Omonia* at 426 Danforth. The outside tables are a little quieter.

Also out this way is a good seafood restaurant, *The Round Window* (tel 465-3892) at 729 Danforth. Phone for reservations – it gets full. A meal with a glass or two of wine runs $30 to $40 for two. The food is always fresh and simply cooked without much in the way of sauces or spicing. Good value.

The Peasant's Larder on Carleton at Parliament is a small, friendly place for Mexican food that runs from mild to very spicy. The garlic chicken is said to be good. Meals average $10 to $12.

An excellent and very cheap meal of Thai food can be had at *The Thai Shan Inn*, 2039 Eglinton Avenue West. Open every day. The trip to this part of town is well worth it. Meals average $20 for two. Don't miss the *kang ped*, a hot, spicy beef dish with lemon grass.

Another good Asian place is the *Ole Malacca*, a Malaysian restaurant at 886 St Clair Avenue West. Satay (kebabs), that you cook at your table over a small barbecue grill, are good to start with. About $25 to $30 for two.

If you're down at Harbourfront, the *Water's Edge Café* in York Quay isn't bad. When the weather is fine and the windows are all open, lunch with a beer can be pretty nice. There are several restaurants nearby in the Queen's Quay Terminal, too.

For the best ice cream, try *West D Kones* on Edward St, just off Yonge in the Atrium complex.

Nightlife

Toronto is busy after dark with countless nightspots, concerts, films, lectures and the country's largest theatre scene.

Bar hours are from 11 am to 1 am, as they are all over Ontario. Numerous clubs stay open after-hours to 3 or 4 am without serving any more alcohol; but who knows how many unofficial boozecans there are where pricey drinks can be had at all hours.

Beer can be bought retail at Brewers Retail Stores and liquor and wine at Liquor Control Board of Ontario (LCBO) outlets. Some of the latter are self serve, in others you have to read the boards, write down the desired number and give it to the cashier. Addresses for both outlets can be found in the yellow pages of the phone book. There are plenty of shops around town but hours vary and they are all closed Sundays and holidays. The drinking age in the province is 19 and drunk driving is a very serious offence.

Drinking During good weather, Ontario Place or Yorkville are good spots to sit outside for a drink. Ontario Place usually has nightly concerts, included in the admission price to the grounds. There are several bars here and it's cool and festive on a summer night. Yorkville is one area where there is some concentration of outdoor cafés and restaurants, which, until very recently, the city has sorely lacked. It's a place to be seen and a bit pricey but still OK if you're in the right mood.

Live Music The small, crowded *El Mocambo* on Spadina, just south of College, is one of the local institutions and the city's best-known bar. It has a long, celebrated history, and the Rolling Stones once played here. Shows feature live rock and blues. Admission varies with the band and can be a bit high, but downstairs entrance is free and there's cheaper drinking to a local band.

Just down the street at 379 Spadina is *Grossman's*, which is bright and grubby but one of the cheapest in town. They sometimes have very good bands and there's usually an interesting, mixed crowd. Admission is free.

Further down Spadina at King is the *Cabana Room* in the Spadina Hotel (tel 368-2864). Entertainment includes live rock, art school bands and new wavish groups. Entrance is about $4 and the drinks are fairly cheap.

The *Bamboo* at 334 Queen is very popular with excellent music in the ska, reggae, African and similar genres. Great dancing music and it's always busy. In summer they have a rooftop patio to catch a breath and in addition the kitchen serves tasty, spicy meals. Admission is in the $3 to $6 range.

The Blue Note attracts a 30-ish crowd with its live rhythm & blues and dancing. The address is 138 Pears Avenue.

Hotel Isabella, 'the Izzy' (tel 921-4167) at 566 Sherbourne, has more than one drinking room and there's always live music in at least one of them. Blues is the specialty and the cover charge, if there is one, is low. Again, the place is busy most nights.

Yonge St has numerous places. *The Gasworks* is a long-time and popular heavy metal and hard rock bar.

The *Brunswick*, 481 Bloor St West, is a funky place, a bit like a pub and a bit like a frat house and often a lot of fun. It has good, well-known jazz or blues players upstairs and downstairs, where there is never a cover and all kinds of entertainment from contests to bizarre amateur nights. Cheap.

There's live folk music at the *Free Times Cafe* at 320 College St.

For jazz, there's *East 85th* at Front St East, with new bands each week. For more experimental music, the *Music Gallery* is at 1087 Queen St West. *Meyer's Deli* at 69 Yorkville has more conventional jazz.

Club 22 at 22 St Thomas, just south of Bloor near Bay, is a small, seemingly very straight piano bar that often has an odd and enjoyable little quirk to the atmosphere.

Disco For dancing to recorded music try *Nuts & Bolts* at 77 Victoria near Yonge. Open till 4 am Friday and Saturday nights. They play mainly new wave music and offer good drink prices. *The Copa* at Yorkville and Yonge is a huge, sort of New York-style disco-dancing bar with videos. Garb ranges from jeans to dressy. It's a few bucks to get in. Open after hours. Free and fun is the video bar right by the lake in York Quay, Harbourfront. It's open Friday and Saturday nights and the drinks are not costly.

Cinema There are several repertory film houses around town. The *Revue* (tel 531-9959) is at 400 Roncesvalles, in the west end. They feature different films nearly every night. Each screening is $3.50. The *Roxy* (tel 461-2401) in the east end at 1215 Danforth Avenue, shows mainly pop, cult and rock movies, mostly for young people. Loud, smoky parties accompany the movie. Midnight shows are sometimes offered.

The *Bloor Cinema* (tel 532-6677) at 506 Bloor St West is popular with the many students of the area. A double feature is shown nightly at $3 per movie without a membership card. A wide variety of films are shown – American, European, old and new.

Theatre There is more theatre in Toronto than any other Canadian city. Also big is dinner theatre. Check newspapers or the guides to Toronto available at hotels. The cost is about $20 to $30 per person for a meal and show.

The Dream in High Park is a great summer theatre presentation in which one play is put on each night through July and August, free. The Toronto Free Theatre's production and acting is top rate. For details, call their downtown theatre. Shows begin at 8 pm, but go very early with a blanket and picnic or binoculars will be required.

Five Star Tickets (tel 596-8211) sells theatre and dance tickets at half-price for shows the same day with leftover seats. They have a booth at the Eaton Centre, corner of Dundas and Yonge. You can't place telephone orders. Open noon to 7.30 pm daily, Sunday 11 am to 3 pm.

For complete listings of theatre, events and concerts, see *Now* magazine, available free in many bars, record stores and cafés or from newsstands. Or check Thursday's entertainment guide in the *Globe & Mail* newspaper or Friday's *Toronto Star*.

Sports The Toronto Blue Jays play major league baseball at the CNE Stadium and will move to the Skydome when construction is complete. Sipping a beer and watching the game on a warm night is pleasant and the cheap seats are very low priced. Take a jacket – things cool off down here near the water. For horse racing, Greenwood track is quite central at the corner of Queen St and Woodbine Avenue on the streetcar line. Last time I went I could do no wrong and won $144. It's just $2 to get in and a bet need only cost another deuce.

Other Toronto has a place for comics called *Yuk Yuks* (tel 967-6425) at 1280 Bay St. Presentations are sometimes funny, sometimes gross, sometimes a joke. Admission is $5 on weekdays, $8 on weekends, and includes several comics. On weekends there is a dinner package, too.

The Toronto Symphony plays at the new *Roy Thompson Hall*, 60 Simcoe, not far from the CN Tower. The Canadian Opera Company performs at the *O'Keefe Centre* in early fall. The National Ballet of Canada is based in town and also performs at the O'Keefe.

Getting There & Away

Air The airport, Pearson International, is about 24 km north-west of the city in Malton. All major Canadian airlines fly in and out of Toronto, as do many of the international companies.

Some one-way fares on Air Canada (tel 925-2311) are:

Montreal – $150, youth standby (under 22) $75

Halifax – $247, youth standby $124
Calgary – $424, youth standby $212.

Canadian Airlines (tel 675-2211) has virtually the same prices, which vary only during special promotions.

Wardair runs charters out of Toronto to numerous Canadian destinations, a few American points (mainly Florida and California) and to western Europe at good rates.

A small and relatively new airline, City Express (tel 979-0000), connects Toronto to other nearby centres quite economically. Flights arrive and depart from the Islands airport at the lake at the foot of Bathurst St. The short take-off and landing aircraft get you to where you're going a lot quicker than the major carriers because you don't have to drag yourself all the way out to the airport. A shuttle bus runs to the airport from the Royal York Hotel in Toronto; major hotels are also used as depots in the other cities served. To Montreal the fares start at $59, to Ottawa $49. American cities are soon to be added to the list.

Also from this airport, General Aerospace offers flights over to Buffalo for just $19. How's that for an international flight? The trip takes half an hour and there are quite a few daily.

It is not uncommon for Canadians (and visitors) to skip over to Buffalo to take advantage of the generally much cheaper American airfares. For example, a flight from Buffalo to Seattle could be hundreds of dollars less than say, Toronto to Vancouver. At either end, a short bus ride links the Canadian city. The real heyday for gutbucket American fares seems to have ended with the demise of People Express. When it was in full swing, a shuttle bus ran from downtown Toronto to the Buffalo airport from where $19 would fly you into New York City. For longer trips it's still worth calling some US carriers such as Continental or American.

Bus The bus station for out of town destinations (tel 979-3511) is centrally located on Bay St at Dundas in Chinatown, a few blocks west of Yonge. Destinations and one-way fares include:

Ottawa: 8 am, 9.30 am, 11.30 am and frequent through afternoon and evening – $33

Thunder Bay: 8 am, 12.45 pm, 5.30 pm, 1 am – $88 (about 20 hours)

Montreal: buses run regularly all day – $36

Niagara: 8.15 am, 10 am and every hour to 7 pm – $14.25 (about two hours).

Return tickets used within 10 days provide substantial savings.

Train Union Station (tel 366-8411) is also conveniently situated. It's on Front St (which runs east-west) at the extreme south end of the city at the bottom of University, York and Bay Sts. The subway goes right into the station; the stop is called Union.

Ottawa (direct): 9 am, 1 pm, 5 pm – $45 (about six hours); others go to Kingston with bus connections for Ottawa

Sudbury: 11.59 pm – $39 (seven and a half hours)

Montreal: six daily – $51.

Reservations are needed for all trains. Return trips, providing a Friday isn't a travel day, are better value.

Road For drive-away cars, check the business personal columns in either the *Toronto Sun* or the *Star*. Also check the yellow pages in the phone book. One company is Toronto Drive-away Service (tel 225-7754), with cars for Canadian and US destinations.

Highway 2, the old east-west highway, is still there, going along the lakeshore. It's slower by far, but more interesting.

Getting Around

Airport Transport There are several ways to get to the airport. The cheapest is to take the subway to Kipling on the east-west line. From there, take the Kipling or Martingrove bus (Nos 45 or 46) north up to Dixon Rd. Transfer to the Malton Nos 58A or 58C, which go west to the airport.

Keep your transfer from the subway, but the second bus will cost $1.10 extra. Take the same route to get from the airport to downtown.

From the Islington subway stop (one before Kipling), at the far western end of the Bloor Line, there is a direct bus to the airport. It leaves every 30-40 minutes, takes 25 minutes and costs $4.25. For details call 979-3511. The bus also leaves from the Yorkdale and York Mills subway stations.

There are also buses to and from major hotels such as the Royal York, Sheraton and the Holiday Inn, which is very near the bus terminal. The fare one-way is $7.50 and the trip takes about 40 minutes.

Of course, there are taxis and, for a couple more bucks, limousines.

TTC The city has a good subway-bus-streetcar system, called the TTC (tel 484-4544). Fares are $1.05 cash or eight tickets for $7. Tickets are available in the subway or at some convenience and corner variety stores. Once one fare is paid, you can transfer to any other bus, subway or streetcar within one hour. One ticket can get you anywhere the system goes. Get a transfer from the driver, or in the subway from the machine inside the turnstiles where you pay the fare.

The subway system is clean, safe and fast. There is one east-west line which goes along Bloor and Danforth and two north-south lines, one up Yonge St. The Spadina line is the newest; the stops are decorated with the work of Canadian artists. The subway runs until about 1.30 am. Bus hours vary; some run late but are infrequent.

Streetcar You may want to try the streetcars. Toronto is one of the few North American cities still using them and in fact has added some new models to the old yellow & red fleet. Find them on College, Dundas, Queen, King and St Clair Sts. The King car runs from one end of the city to the other, 24 hours a day.

For transit and route information call 484-4544, daily from 7 am to 11.30 pm.

GO Train The GO train system leaving from Union Station, 7 am to 11.30 pm daily, services the suburbs east and west of Toronto. Deposit half the ticket as you enter and save the other half for when you get off. Service is fast and frequent.

Driving All over Ontario you can turn right on a red light, after stopping. Parking is expensive, usually about $1.25 to $1.50 for the first half hour, then slightly less. Rush hours are impossible so avoid them. Pedestrians use the painted crosswalks across the street and traffic will stop. If you're driving watch out for these – you must stop. Hitting someone on a cross-walk in Toronto is a big no-no.

Car Rentals If you're renting a car, be aware that many places require that you be 21 years old or more, some 23. If you're under 25, many will ask for a credit card. If you don't have one, be prepared for a hefty ($200 to $300) deposit requirement.

Downtown Car Rental (tel 947-0212) rents used cars. The office is very central at 123 Dundas St East. I haven't had much luck with these from other companies; maybe theirs are more reliable. Prices are from $10 a day during slow periods and more like $26 in summer with the usual mileage charges.

Tilden (tel 364-4191) is in Union Station. Their rate is $35 per day, 200 free km, 11c per km over. They offer weekend specials; book early.

Avis (tel 964-2051) is in the Bay Department Store at the corner of Yonge and Bloor. Their rate is $34 a day, 200 km free, 11c per km over. On weekdays it's $20 a day, minimum three days, maximum four, 800 or 1000 free km respectively. Reservations are required. Both rates quoted are for the smallest cars available.

Another major company is Budget and all of them have many more offices around town and one at the airport.

Bicycle Rentals Brown's Sports & Cycle (tel 763-4176) is at 2447 Bloor St West, near Jane and on the subway route. They rent 10-speeds for $11 a day with a good weekly rate.

There are also rentals on Centre Island. Try Toronto Island Bicycle Rental (tel 365-7901) on the south shore.

You Pedal It (tel 862-7684) is another. It's found at 180 Queen's Quay West in the harbourfront area. Lastly, High Park Cycle (tel 532-7300) at 1168 Bloor St West will rent you wheels.

When bicycling, be careful on the streetcar rails – cross at right angles or you'll land on your ear.

Pedicab A recent appearance on Toronto streets are pedicabs – deluxe bicycle rickshaws peddled by sweating students. You see them along Yonge St and in Yorkville. Prices are about $6 for 15 minutes.

Hitching Thumbing is illegal on the expressways in the city. On city streets there's no problem. You can hitch on Highway 401 out of town or on the lead-in ramps in town. If you're heading east for Montreal, best bet is the city transit to roughly the corner of Port Union Rd and the 401 in Scarborough, near the Metro Zoo.

To get there from downtown is a bit complicated and the fastest way takes about 1½ hours. Take the subway east to Kennedy stop. From there catch the 86A Scarborough bus to the corner of Sheppard Avenue and Meadowvale Rd. Transfer (free) to the Rouge Hill bus down to Highway 401.

If you're going west, take the subway to Kipling. Transfer to the West Mall bus, Nos 112 or 112B, and go to the corner of Carlingview Drive and Highway 401. This is just at the city limits so you are OK on the highway, but it could be very busy and difficult for cars to stop at rush hour. The bus takes about one hour from downtown.

If you're northbound back up to the Trans-Canada at Sudbury, it's a bit tricky. I think the best bet is to take the bus to Barrie and then hitch the rest of the way on Highway 400.

Tours The reliable Gray Line (tel 979-3511) runs two-hour inner-city tours for $12. Various other tours from 1½ hours and up are offered, with stops at sites included. Two others are 'Toronto by Night' and to Niagara Falls. They pick up passengers at hotels and the office is at the Elizabeth St bus terminal, right across from the main bus station at 610 Bay St.

Gray Coach offers numerous one-day trips around Toronto ranging from $25 to $40. Examples are Elora and Georgian Bay. They are also in the bus station.

At the Tourist Office pick up a copy of *A Walking Tour of Old Toronto*, free, for a self-guided tour starting at Union station. It covers about four blocks and 25 buildings of the city's early downtown.

A similar map/information sheet is available for the Canadian National Exhibition Grounds in west Toronto. Twenty historical buildings and monuments are highlighted.

The University of Toronto (tel 978-5000) runs free guided tours of the campus through the summer, three times daily. This is the country's largest university and the campus has some fine buildings.

A unique tour takes visitors around the inner city on a restored 1920s trolley car. The very popular 90-minute tour departs four times daily from the west side of the Sheraton Centre on York St south of Queen. St. The trip costs $14, less for kids, and tickets should be obtained in advance. They can be purchased at Ontario Travel Desks (tel 869-1372), which are found in the larger downtown hotels, including the Sheraton. Unfortunately, there has recently been talk of discontinuing the tours due to the costs of maintaining the old clangers.

Several companies run boat tours in and around the harbour and the islands. Most depart from Harbourfront around Queens Quay, York Quay or John Quay. The Island Queen has a one-hour cruise for $7. Toronto Tours (tel 869-1372) also run harbour tours around the islands. Their hour-long trip with narration on history and other facts is the same price. Hourly departures take place May to October from 145 Queens Quay West, at the foot of York St.

Boat Tour International (tel 364-2412) at 5 Queens Quay West offer a similar tour of about the same duration and price but to 10 pm, when the skyline is lit up.

Some privately owned sailing ships and schooners offer trips of varying lengths as far as Niagara-on-the-Lake. Some boats are geared for fishing. Snoop around the dock area; you'll see signs.

Remember that the island ferry has good views of the city and is only $2. If you're visiting the islands, remember to check the time of the last return trip. In summer they run about every half an hour but not very late at night.

AROUND TORONTO

Within approximately 1½ hour's drive or less from the city are a large number of small, old towns that were until fairly recently centres for the local farming communities. Some of the country's best land is here but working farms are giving way to urban sprawl and many of the old downtowns are now surrounded by modern housing developments. Day trips around the district especially on a Sunday are popular. There is still some nice rolling landscape and a few conservation areas which are basically parks incorporating a river or other geographical feature for walking or picnicking. Quite a few of the towns attract antique hunters and craft and gift shops are plentiful.

Caledon is one of the larger and closer examples and is set in the Caledon Hills. Not far south-west in Terra Cotta is an inn which makes a good place to stop later in the day for afternoon tea served with scones, cream and jam. Terra Cotta is also one of the closest points to Toronto for access to an afternoon's walk along the Bruce Trail which runs for 700 km north-south.

The Hockley Valley area near Orangeville is more of the same. The Credit River has trout fishing and in winter the area is not bad for cross-country skiing but the hills aren't high enough for downhill.

Kleinburg

The McMichael Collection is a small but excellent art gallery, just north of the city in the village of Kleinburg. The gallery of hand-made wooden buildings in a pleasant rural setting displays a large Canadian painting collection. Very well represented are Canada's best-known painters, known collectively as 'The Group of Seven'. If you're going to see northern Ontario, where much of the group's work was done, it makes a visit all the more worthwhile. The work of other Canadian painters is also on view. A new second floor exhibits Inuit and West Coast Indian Art which includes sculpture, prints and paintings. Admission $2.50, students $1. School kids often visit weekday mornings. Open daily in summer, from November to April closed on Mondays.

Kleinburg is 18 km north of the corner of Islington Avenue and Highway 401 in Toronto. To get there by car go north up Highway 427 to Highway 27 and continue north. Turn right at Nashville Rd. By bus first take the Toronto subway and then bus to Islington and Steeles Avenue. From there the Vaughan bus will drop you at the gallery gate. For times of buses call 832-2281. Another method is GO Transit. For their information call 630-2295.

Dunlap Observatory

Just north of the city limits, the observatory (tel 884-2112) has what was once the world's second largest telescope and which remains the biggest in Canada. Except in winter, it is open to the public Saturday evenings. A brief introductory talk is given to accompany a slide show and a look through the scope. It's free. Call ahead weekdays for reservations. To reach the observatory drive up Highway 11 (Yonge St's continuation) toward Richmond Hill and you'll see the white dome on the right.

African Lion Safari

Here you'll see about 1000 animals and birds in one vast park, where there are no cages. You drive through, sometimes getting very close to lions, tigers and other animals. Monkeys climb all over the car. Or you can take the park tour bus. Open from April to October and the longest hours are in July and August but it still closes then at 5.30 pm. The park is between Hamilton and Cambridge on Highway 8.

Ontario Agricultural Museum

With 30 buildings on 32 hectares of land, the museum brings to life the farming history of the area through demonstrations, displays, and costumed workers in historical settings. It's near Milton, 52 km west of Toronto, about a 45-minute drive. It's on Townline (also called Tremaine Rd). Open daily from the middle of May to October.

Kortright Waterfowl Park

This is a wildlife area and waterfowl research centre with 3000 birds and 75 species. There is an observation tower, nature trails and an interpretive centre. Open daily, all year. Admission $2.50. The park is near the city of Guelph on Kortright Rd, west of Highway 6 on the Speed River.

Pickering Nuclear Plant

About 40 km east of Toronto on the Lake Ontario shoreline is this nuclear power station with portions open to the public. Whether pro or con nuclear plants, you could find out something you didn't know. Free films, displays and a drive around the site explain the operation. Open 9 am to 4 pm daily. Look for the signs on Highway 401 – the plant is at the foot of Liverpool Rd. If your kids are born glowing in the dark, don't blame me.

Local Conservation Areas

South-western Ontario is an urban area. To offset this somewhat, the government has designated many conservation areas here – small nature parks for walking, picnicking and sometimes fishing, swimming and cross-country skiing. These are not wild areas by any means and some are not even pretty but they are close and do offer some concrete relief. The Tourist Office has a list of these around Toronto and within 160 km of town.

One which makes a good quick escape on a nice summer day is the large Albion Hills Conservation Area. This one also allows for decent cross-country skiing. On the west side of town take Indian Line (by the airport) north. It becomes Highway 50 which leads to the park. In this basic region is also the Kortright Centre for Conservation located near Kleinburg. There are trails here, too, but it's more of a museum with displays and demonstrations on resources, wildlife, ecology, etc. It's open daily to 4 pm.

On the east side of town one not too far away is Milne Lake. To get to this conservation area, go north on Markham Rd, which later becomes Highway 48.

Cullen Gardens

I haven't been to the gardens so am not recommending it, but here is a brief description. In a garden setting is a miniature village representing historic buildings from around southern Ontario. Flower shows are put on here. I wouldn't go out of my way.

Canadian Automotive Museum

Further east near Oshawa, a centre for car

assembly, is this museum with a collection of over 50 cars. Included are a 1890 Redpath Runabout from 1890, a Model T of course, and various automotive memorabilia. It's at 99 Simcoe St. Open daily.

Parkwood

Also in Oshawa, at 270 Simcoe St North, Parkwood is the estate of R S McLaughlin who once ran the Canadian division of General Motors. The property consists of a 55-room mansion with antique furnishings set amidst large gardens. Admission is $3 and it's closed Mondays. Afternoon tea is served during summer.

Cathedral of the Tranfiguration

It seems nobody builds churches anymore, especially on the grand scale of the old world. But north of Toronto straight up Highway 404 in Markham is one heck of an exception. Opened in 1987, this Byzantine Catholic cathedral is one of the country's largest and stands 62.7 metres high at the tip of the copper-topped spire. Based on a smaller version found in Czechoslovakia, this is a 1000-seater. One of the impressive features is the French-made main bell ringing in at 16,650 kg, second only in size to the one in Paris' Sacre Coeur. Also it is the first cathedral in the western hemisphere to be blessed by a pope – John Paul II did the honours in 1984.

North of Toronto

BARRIE

A little over an hour north of the big city is the town of Barrie, which is more or less the unofficial gateway to Toronto's cottage country. Around Lake Simcoe, north through the Muskoka's region (named after one of the larger area lakes) and along the vast Georgian Bay shoreline the largely wooded hills, scores of lakes and rivers and numerous parks make for fine summertime R&R. Fishing, swimming, camping, lazing – just what the doctor ordered. In winter the area is busy with winter recreation: skiing, snow-mobiling and lots of ice fishing. In September and October the region is toured for nature's annual brilliantly-coloured tree show.

Travel Information Centres can be found in Barrie, in the County Administration Building; in Collingwood, 101 Hurontario St; and in Orilla on Sundial Drive. Many other towns have small information booths where you can pick up the local information on sights, events, festivals and places of historical interest. Despite the emphasis on outdoor activities this is a pretty busy and developed area. For more space or wilderness head north or to the larger government parks.

From Toronto, Barrie is straight up Highway 400. From here buses go in all directions. For a snack on the way stop at *Webber's*, a hamburger joint so popular a pedestrian bridge had to be put in. It's on the 11, south of the Severn River. On Friday afternoons and Sunday nights expect a lot of traffic.

WASAGA BEACH

Wasaga is the beach resort closest to Toronto. Around Wasaga Beach and the strip of beaches (about 14 km) running up along the bay are hundreds of cottages, a provincial park and several private campgrounds. Centre of activity is the excellent beach with fine swimming at Wasaga Beach Provincial Park. A very popular weekend spot, Wasaga is nearly empty during the week. Some areas of the beach are more for families, others (like those around the snack bars) are more for the younger crowd although drinkers are now often fined on the spot. Water-slides are one of Canada's fastest-growing diversions and Wasaga Beach now has one right at the shore. It's over 100 metres long.

For accommodation assistance in the area call 445-0748. There are several motels along Main St or Mosley and they range from $25 single to $50 double, cheaper by the week. Also check Rural

Route 1. Others are right on the beach. Lots of cottages with housekeeping facilities as well.

COLLINGWOOD

In the centre of the Blue Mountain ski area and right on the water, this little resort town has a reputation for being pretty but it isn't. The surroundings are scenic enough with the highest sections of the Niagara Escarpment nearby. The escarpment runs south all the way to Niagara Falls. The caves along it near town are heavily and misleadingly promoted as they are not what you and I expect of that term but are really more like overhangs and caverns. There is some good walking, however, and the hour-long trail by the caves loops over interesting terrain and the views are excellent. A chairlift runs to the top of Blue Mountain where there is a choice of it or a water-slide down in summer.

The area is known for its 'blue' pottery which is very nice but not cheap. A bluegrass music festival is held here in summer.

Places to Stay

Collingwood has an excellent youth hostel. *Blue Mountain Hostel* (tel 445-1497) is open all year but is often booked out. There are about 60 beds and a kitchen in a chalet-like building. The hostel also has a sauna. You'll find it on Rural Route 3, near the ski hills north of Craigleith – two hours from Toronto. Members are charged $8.50 in summer, $12 in winter; the rate is quite a bit more for non-members.

There are plenty of motels here, too. The *Fireside* (tel 445-1917) on Rural Route No 2 is small and a good deal at $20 to $24. Also offering budget accommodation is the *Glen Lake Motel* (tel 445-4280) on the same street and the *Village Store* (tel 445-1617) on Rural Route No 3, close to the Blue Mountain Slides. Of course, there are more expensive places in the area.

MIDLAND

This small commercial centre in the area known as Huronia has a number of sites relating to the early native population and the arrival of the white man. Huron Indian Village is a replica of what the native settlements were like until the early 1600s. Things changed not long after this date when in 1639 some French Jesuits arrived on a soul-saving drive. 'Sainte-Marie Among the Hurons' is an historical site which reconstructs the 17th-century Jesuit mission and tells the story of a pretty dramatic chapter in the book of Indian/European clashes. Graphic depictions of missionaries' deaths by torture are forever etched in the brains of countless Canadians by elementary school history texts. Six of the eight martyred missionaries in North America were based at the Sainte-Marie mission. Martyr's Shrine here is a monument to them and the site of pilgrimages each year. Even the Pope showed up in 1984.

Also in town is a small museum but there are other attractions in the area unrelated to human history. The Wye Marsh Wildlife Centre provides boardwalks, trails and an observation deck over the marsh which houses abundant birdlife. Displays offer information on the flora and fauna found in the area. Canoe trips through the marsh are also possible.

From the town dock, four-hour boat cruises depart for Georgian Bay.

PENETANGUISHENE ('pen e tang wish een')

Slightly north of Midland, this smaller town has reconstructed its naval base. It was built by the British after the War of 1812 against the Americans, but never used. The site contains 15 buildings and a ship replica.

Between Penetanguishene and Parry Sound the waters of Georgian Bay are speckled with 30,000 islands – the highest concentration in the world. Three-hour tours depart from both towns and are popular not only in summer but fall as well when the leaves are all reds and yellows. At this end try the *Georgian Queen*, a three-decker.

For somewhere to eat try the place down at the docks. You can't miss it.

CHRISTIAN ISLAND

Off the north-west edge of the peninsula and connected by toll ferry, this island, part of an Ojibway reservation, is the site of an archaeological dig which will form the basis of a tourist draw for the Indian Band. Two thousand years of Indian settlement will be surveyed and excavated and work is focusing on a very well preserved 650-year-old fort. It was built by the Hurons in an attempt to protect themselves and some French soldiers and priests from the Iroquois. The Iroquois decided to starve them out. Inside the Jesuits controlled the very limited rations and exchanged food for the Hurons' attendance at Mass. Within a year 4000 Indians had starved to death, spelling the end of that band as a significant people in the area.

AWENDA PROVINCIAL PARK

Awenda, right at the end of the peninsula jutting into Georgian Bay, is one of the newest provincial government parks. Though relatively small and busy with both day visitors and overnighters, it's pretty good. The campsites are large, treed and private. There are four good beaches, all connected by walking paths. The first one can be reached by car and the second and third are the sandiest. There are also a couple of longer trails through the park, one supplying a good view of the bay. Awenda is north of Penetanguishene, where food and other supplies should be bought. Basic staples can be bought not too far from the park entrance.

The campsites cost $8.50 and reservations are advised for weekends, or arrive early. There are no electrical hookups so many people are tenters. Cooking grills are available free for use over fires. The park office has a list of commercial campgrounds in the district.

SIX MILE PARK

Another provincial park in the region, Six Mile Lake (tel (705) 728-2900), is on Highway 69 north of Port Severn. There are 192 basic sites; no showers or electricity. Boat rentals are nearby and the park has access to a canoe route. There's swimming too.

GEORGIAN BAY ISLANDS NATIONAL PARK

This park, consisting of some 50 islands in Georgian Bay, has three completely separate sections. One of these segments is not far from Six Mile Lake – take Highway 400 from Toronto then the 69 to Honey Harbour. Once there, water taxis can be taken to the islands.

Beausoleil is the largest island and is the park centre, with campgrounds and an interpretive centre. Several of the other islands have primitive camping at just $4 a site. The islands are home to the now quite rare Eastern Massasauga rattlesnake. You may like to know that it is rather small and timid – usually.

Recreation includes swimming, diving, snorkelling and fishing: the bay is great for bass and pike. Boating is very big in the area, what with all the islands and the Trent-Severn Canal system. Many boaters (and they range from those putting along in aluminium 14-footers to would-be kings in their floating palaces), tie up for a day or night at the park islands so they are fairly busy.

For park information, there is an office (tel 765-2415) in Honey Harbour near the grocery store. In summer a shuttle service runs over to Beausoleil quite cheaply. In contrast, the plentiful water taxis offer flexibility as to destinations and pick-up times but are rather costly.

Section two of the park, consisting of a number of smaller islands, is further north up the bay, about halfway to Parry Sound.

The third section of the park is off Tobermory on the point south of Manitoulin Island. See the section on Tobermory for more information.

ORILLIA, GRAVENHURST, BRACEBRIDGE & HUNTSVILLE

These four towns from south to north are the principal centres of the Muskokas. They supply cottage country. None of them is especially attractive as a destination but there are a few things of interest. Orillia was the home of Canada's best-known humourist, Stephen Leacock. He wrote here and built a house in 1919 which can now be visited.

In Gravenhurst is the Bethune Memorial House in honour of China's favourite Canadian, Dr Norman Bethune, who travelled throughout China in the 1930s as a surgeon and educator, and died there in a small village. The house details this and other aspects of his career and life.

All of these towns have numerous places to eat and nearby motels and resorts.

ALGONQUIN PROVINCIAL PARK

This is Ontario's largest park and one of Canada's best known. Just 200-odd km north of Toronto, it offers hundreds of lakes in nearly 7800 square km of near wilderness. There are 1600 km of charted canoe routes to explore, many of them interconnected by portage paths. There is one road, Highway 60, which runs through the southern edge of the park. Off it are lodges and nine campgrounds as well as wilderness outfitters who rent canoes and just about everything else. Maps are available at the park. If you want some peace and quiet, I highly recommend this park.

There is a lot of wildlife in the park and not bad fishing either. And you can drink the water right out of the lakes. The canoe route maps available for $2 have a lot of good information on the reverse side about the park and camping advice.

At two access points off Highway 60 – Canoe Lake and Opeongo Lake – there are outfitters for renting canoes. This is where most people begin an interior canoe trip. Canoes are about $15 a day. At all other access points you must bring your canoe. Because summer weekends are busy, a system of admitting only a certain number of people at each point has been established. Arrive early or book, at Algonquin Interiors (tel (705) 633-5538 or 633-5725), PO Box 219, Whitney, Ontario, K0J 2M0. The further in you get by portaging, the more solitude you'll find. I've had a whole lake to myself. A good trip takes three to four days. I find the western access points – Nos 3, 4 and 5 on the Algonquin map – good, with fewer people, smaller lakes and plenty of moose.

Rick Ward's (tel (705) 636-5956) in Kearney, north of Huntsville, rents canoes for just $12 a day, including paddles and life jackets. Interior camping is $3 per person per night. At the campgrounds a site is $8 or more, but here there are showers and real toilets.

The park runs its own wilderness canoe trips which include all equipment – canoe, food, supplies, and even sleeping bags – for $32.50 per day or less for longer trips. Phone 633-5622 or visit the outfitting stores mentioned. Commercial outfitters can be found outside the park at either end.

PARRY SOUND

Boat cruises of the 30,000 islands on the *Island Queen* push off from Government Wharf in this small commercial centre about midway up Georgian Bay. The trips are about three hours long. There is a lookout tower in town with views over the bay.

The *Sound House* (tel 746-8806) is a bed & breakfast place at 67 Church St, and charges $45 for doubles. There are literally dozens of motels and cottages for rent in the area, some quite reasonably priced.

KILLBEAR PROVINCIAL PARK

Georgian Bay of Lake Huron is huge enough and grand enough to dwarf most of the world's waters. It's cool, deep, windy and majestic. The deeply-indented, irregular shoreline along the eastern side with its myriad islands is trimmed by slabs of pink granite barely supporting wind-bent pine trees. This unique setting represents for many central Canadians, in words taken from the national anthem, . . . *our home and native land* . . . . The country's best known painters, The Group of Seven, have in their work linked this landscape to the Canadian experience.

Killbear Park is one of the best places to see what it's all about. There is shoreline to explore, three short but good walking trails, numerous little hidden sandy beaches and camping. Of course it's popular; in July and August call ahead to determine camping vacancies. I was there in September, however, and it was less than half full. Many of the visitors spent the day painting and photographing. May and June would also be less busy. Highly recommended even if an afternoon is all you have.

From Parry Sound east to Burk's Falls is more lake and timber-land with numerous cottages, both private and commercial. Out of the summer season things are pretty quiet up here.

SHELBURNE

A rather nondescript small southern Ontario country town between Toronto and Owen Sound, Shelburne comes alive once a year for the old-time fiddler's contest. It's held for two days in August and has been running for the last 35 years. There's a parade and free music shows, and the contest finals are only $3. Saturday night grand finals are $7 and those tickets must be reserved.

Many people make rooms in their homes available for the weekend; phone (519) 925-5535. For camping, contact the Kinsmen Camp, Box 891, Shelburne.

Durham

Slightly to the north and west of Shelburne, this little town is the location of the annual North American banjo contest.

Bruce Peninsula & Manitoulin Island

OWEN SOUND

Owen Sound, with a population of 20,000, is the largest centre in the region and if you're going up the Bruce Peninsula or north to Manitoulin Island you'll pass by. It sits at the end of a deep bay surrounded on three sides by the steepness of the Niagara Escarpment.

Although still a working port it is not the shipping centre it was from the 1880s to the first years of this century. In those early days before the railway, the town rocked with brothels and bars battled by the believers. One intersection had a bar on each corner and was known as Damnation Corner, another had four churches and was called Salvation Corner. I guess the latter won out because the churches are still there. In fact for 66 long years from 1906 to 1972 you couldn't get a drink: the town was dry! There aren't too many seaman on the waterfront now but sections of it have been restored and it's an attractive setting for the marinas and restaurants.

The Sydenham River drifts through town dividing it between east and west and the main street is Second Avenue. Quite a few of the original brick buildings remain and there are some pretty old stores still open for business. Check out McKay Brothers with its old floors, cabinets and a cash register system that takes your money in a little box along a pulley line to the rear of the store, where your change is made and then sent back the same way. Apparently there are only three such systems left in the country. And don't miss the mannequin heads either, with their real hair and teeth. There are others, too, from the turn of the century. A folder for a two-hour, self-guided historical walking tour of the city is available at city hall.

Saturday is market day. It's held beside City Hall.

Harrison Park
This is the large, green park right in town and along the Sydenham River. It has picnic areas, trails, fishing and even camping.

Tom Thomson Memorial Art Gallery
Thomson was a contemporary of Canada's 'Group of Seven' and is one of the country's best-known painters. He grew up here and many of his works were done in this part of the country. The gallery displays the work of some other Canadian painters as well. It's at 840 1st Avenue West. Open daily in July and August; closed Sundays and Mondays other months.

County of Grey & Owen Sound Museum
Here you can see exhibits on the area's geology and human history. There's a half-size replica of an Ojibway Indian Village as well as an eight-metre birch bark canoe on display. The address is 975 6th St East.

Mill Dam & Fish Ladder
In spring and fall it's interesting to see the struggle trout must go through to reach their preferred spawning areas – this dam and ladder was set up to help them.

Billy Bishop Heritage Museum
Home-town boy Billy Bishop, who became the flying ace of WW I, is honoured here. The museum is in the Bishop home. He is buried in town at the Greenwood Cemetery.

Kelso Beach
North of downtown on Georgian Bay is Kelso Beach. Free concerts are held regularly here in summer.

Inglis Falls
Six km south of town, off Highway 6, the Sydenham River falls over the Niagara Escarpment. The falls of 24 metres are set in a conservation area which is linked to the Bruce Trail. The trail runs from Tobermory south to the Niagara River. See under Tobermory for details. The segment by Owen Sound offers good views and springs, as well as the Inglis, Jones and Indian Falls. It makes a nice half-day walk.

Events
The three-day Summerfolk music festival held annually around the second or third weekend of August is a major North American festival of its kind. The event is held in Kelso Park right along the water and attracts crowds of up to 10,000. Musicians come from around the continent. Tickets are about $14 a day – and each day is a full one. There's camping nearby.

Places to Stay
Hotels The old downtown hotels such as the Seldon on the corner at 1005 2nd Avenue East which was built in 1887 are being converted to other uses but new, more expensive places are springing up around town and along the waterfront. An example is The *Inn on the Bay* with 60 rooms at 1800 2nd Avenue East.

Motels Most accommodation here is motels. Ninth St has several. The *Key Motel*, 11 km south of town on Highways 6 and 10, is one of the more moderately priced with rooms for $34 to $38.

Camping Very conveniently, there are campgrounds right in town. One is across the road from Kelso Beach, ideal for the music festival. Another is in Harrison Park (tel 376-5151), which charges $8 per site without electricity, and you can use the heated pool (Georgian Bay is known for its cold water).

Places to Eat
The *Erie Belle* is quite Englishy with pub grub and British brews. *Norma Jean's* with a Marilyn Monroe theme serves burgers,

salads and other casual, inexpensive fare. There are a few places along the waterfront and most offer seafood. One, the *Jolly Rodger* is on a boat moored off the harbour.

PORT ELGIN

This is a little town on Lake Huron west of Owen Sound. MacGregor Provincial Park is located here. There are sandy beaches, the warm waters of Lake Huron and camping. Further south is the Bruce Nuclear Plant, which is controversial of course, as are all nuclear plants in Canada. They offer free tours and a film on nuclear power.

SAUBLE BEACH

Sauble Beach is a summer resort town due to the excellent, sandy, 11-km beach. There are plenty of hotels, motels and cottages for rent as well as entertainment diversions. Cottages tend to be somewhat cheaper than motels. *Chilwell's Cottages* (tel 422-1692) at 31 3rd Avenue North has six small cottages and is one of the cheapest at $25 to $30 for doubles. Prices generally range from $35 to $65.

There are also many campgrounds in the area, all busy on summer weekends. Best is the *Sauble Falls Provincial Campground*. Reservations are a good idea. Further north along the road are several commercial grounds – for example, *White Sands* (tel 534-2781) in Oliphant. Four of us in two tents paid $18 for one night here. The sites at the back are treed and quiet.

Brown House (tel 422-2504) at 24 Graham Crescent is a guest house about two km south of the town's main intersection. Singles/doubles cost $25/35.

The coast all along here is known for good sunsets.

DYER'S BAY

If you have a car, a good scenic drive can be made by Dyer's Bay about 20 km south of Tobermory. From the No 6 take Dyer's site road into the village and then the road north-east along the coast. It's not long, but with Georgian Bay on one side and the limestone cliffs of the escarpment on the other, it is impressive. The road ends at the Cabot Head Lighthouse. Before arriving there, you'll pass by the ruins of an old log flume where logs were sent over the escarpment.

The road south of Dyer's Bay is also good, leading down to another flowerpot formation, this one known as the Devil's Monument. This secondary road goes to Lion's Head, where you can connect back with the main highway.

DORCAS BAY

On Lake Huron about 11 km south of Tobermory there is a preserve owned by the Federation of Ontario Naturalists. It's not developed at all but attracts plenty of walkers and photographers mainly for the abundance and variety of wildflowers. Up to 50 species of orchids can be spotted. To reach the site turn west from Highway 11 toward Lake Huron. You're there when you reach the parking lot with a few picnic tables and a toilet.

TOBERMORY

This small town sits at the northern tip of the Bruce Peninsula, which juts into Lake Huron. On one side of the peninsula are the cold, clear waters of Georgian Bay, and on the other is the much warmer main body of Lake Huron. There is not much to see in town itself but it is a busy spot in summer for a couple of reasons. First, the ferry to Manitoulin Island departs and arrives here. Many people driving across Ontario take this route as it saves time driving around Georgian Bay. Manitoulin has its own charms as well.

Tobermory is the centre for several government parks and marks the end of the Bruce Trail. The town is also a diving centre; the waters offshore contain 50 known sunken ships.

There are many places to stay in and around town but prices are a little high.

The *Grandview* right by the harbour has a fine view and the meals are quite good. Nearby motels are less costly.

Bruce Trail

Tobermory marks the north end of this 700-km footpath, which runs from Queenston on the Niagara River to this point on the tip if the Bruce Peninsula on Georgian Bay, over private and public lands. You can hike for an hour, a day or a week. The scenery is good as the trail edges along the Niagara Escarpment, much of it inaccessible from the road.

The most northerly bit from Dyer Bay to Tobermory is the most rugged and most spectacular.

The Bruce Trail Association (tel 529-6821) puts out a detailed map of the entire route for about $10. The head office is at Raspberry House, PO Box 857 Hamilton, L8N 3N9. There is also an office in Toronto. The Grey-Bruce Tourist Association has a map of the top portion of the trail for $1.50. Other Tourist Offices can tell you where there are access points. Some parts of the trail are heavily used on summer weekends. Near Hamilton at the south end is a popular day walking area at Rattlesnake Point Conservation Area. Another southern one is at Terra Cotta not far from Toronto. Yet another is at the forks of the Credit River.

There are designated areas for camping along the path, although in the gentler, busy southern sections some huts are provided where even a shower can be taken.

In another section there is accommodation in bed & breakfasts or old inns. Country Host is a network of bed & breakfasts which caters to hikers with homes along the trail. Prices are about $35 to $45 for doubles. Contact Grace Conin (tel (519) 941-7633), Rural Route 1, Palgrave, L0N 1P0.

Don't drink the water along the trail and bring good boots: much of the trail is wet and muddy. And don't forget the insect repellent.

Activities

Diving The waters here are excellent for scuba diving, with the many wrecks, geological formations and very clear water. The water is also very cold, however. Boats and programmes are available for beginners to advanced divers. Equipment is available in town. Snorkelling is possible in some areas, too. The Ontario government has a pamphlet listing dive sites with descriptions, depths and recommendations. It's available free at the Tourist Office.

Parks & Canoeing Between Tobermory and Wasaga Beach are three provincial parks and several river canoe routes. Local Tourist Offices have information on them. The Saugeen River has been divided up into sections ranging from 20 km (four hours) to 40 km (5½ hours). There's camping along the way. A shorter trip is along the Rankin River.

Just south of Tobermory is Cypress Lake Park, with camping for $8. One section is for vans, another is for tenters only. Swimming in Georgian Bay in August can be good and warm; otherwise, the shallow lake in the park can be used. Part of the Bruce Trail – right along the bay – goes through the park, and a good day's hike is possible. You may even see one of the rare Ontario rattlesnakes.

GEORGIAN BAY ISLANDS NATIONAL PARK

One of the three parts (the other two are listed under 'North of Toronto', and are near the town of Bracebridge) of this park lies five km offshore from Tobermory.

Flowerpot Island, with its unusual, precarious-looking rock columns formed through years of erosion, can be visited by boat from town. There are various trails on the island, taking from a little over an hour for the shortest one to 2¼ hours for the more difficult. The island has cliffs, caves, picnic spots and just a few camping sites. Reservations are needed and you should take all supplies.

Various companies offer boat trips to

the island, where you can hop off if you wish and catch a later boat back. The cost is $8. The *True North* boat doesn't charge any extra to drop you at Flowerpot. The price also includes a cruise past some of the shipwrecks visible in the very clear waters. The offices for boat trips are all around the harbour in Tobermory.

FATHOM FIVE PROVINCIAL PARK

Ontario's first underwater park, Fathom Five was developed to protect and make more accessible this interesting area. Nineteen wrecks lie in the park's waters, scattered between the many little islands. There is a Visitor's Centre on Little Tub Harbour in Tobermory. They have displays and can offer information and advice.

A new National Park to be known as the Bruce Peninsula National Park is now being set up and will include Cypress Lake, Fathom Five, Flowerpot Island and some of the Georgian Bay coastline and Niagara Escarpment.

MANITOULIN ISLAND

The world's largest freshwater island, Manitoulin is basically a rural region of small farms. About a third of the population is native Indian. Recently tourism has become the island's main money maker and many southerners own summer cottages.

The island has a scenic coastline, some sandy beaches, 100 lakes, lots of small towns and villages and has remained pretty undeveloped. The two principal attractions for visitors are the fishing and boating. There are several fishing camps around the island. For cruising, the 225-km North Channel is superb. The scenery is great: one fiord, Baie Finn, is 15 km long with pure white quartzite cliffs. And the water is clean enough to drink from the side of the boat.

The island also makes a good short cut if you're heading to northern Ontario. Take the ferry from Tobermory, cross the island and then cross the bridges to the north shore of Georgian Bay. The route can save you a few hours of driving around the bay and is pleasant. The ferry is called the *Chi-Cheemaun* and gets very busy even though it can hold 600 passengers and about 140 cars. In midsummer there are four crossings daily. From Tobermory times are 7 am, 11.20 am, 3.40 pm and 8 pm. Tickets are $8 per person and $17 for a car, slightly cheaper in spring and fall. There's a small charge for bicycles. The ferry season is from early May to mid-October and out of the peak period just three runs are made daily. The trip of 50 km takes about 1¾ hours and there is a cafeteria on board. For reservations call 1-800-265-3163 toll free.

From the ferry landing on the island, 3½-hour bus sight-seeing tours are operated during July and August. Tel 282-2848 on the island.

South-western Ontario

This geographic designation covers everything west of Toronto to Lake Huron, which borders Michigan in the US. For the most part the area is flat farmland – the only area in Ontario with little forest – and population density is high. With the warm climate and long growing season, this southern tip of Canada was settled early.

Arching around Lake Ontario is a continuous strip of urbanisation. This 'Golden Horseshoe' helps make the region one of the most industrialised and one of the wealthiest in the country.

Hamilton, the largest city in the area, is a major steel town. Niagara, with its famous falls, is an important fruit-growing district.

Further west, the soil becomes sandier and the main crop is tobacco although this is changing as the cigarette market shrinks. Around Kitchener and London the small towns are the centres for mixed farming of the region. Lake Erie and Lake

Huron both have sandy beaches. In some of the older country towns crafts and antiques are available.

Windsor – like its counterpart across the river, Detroit, Michigan – is an auto-manufacturing centre.

Because the area is heavily populated and America is close by, attractions and parks do get busy in summer. This is an area for people-related activities and pastimes, not for nature or rugged landscapes.

HAMILTON

Hamilton, sometimes referred to as Steeltown, is a heavily industrialised city of about 450,000, situated halfway between Toronto and Niagara Falls. This is the centre of Canada's iron and steel industry and unfortunately it's notorious for its pollution problems. While Hamilton is obviously not a tourist town, there are nonetheless a few good things to see in and around town.

Orientation

King St (one-way going west) and Main St (parallel and one south of King, one way going east) are the two main streets. King has most of the downtown shops and restaurants. King and John is the core of the downtown area. The Convention Centre with the art gallery is at King and Macnab. Just south across Main is City Hall. The bus terminal is on Rebecca, off John, about three blocks from the centre of town.

Information

The Tourist Office (tel 526-4222) is in the Hamilton Place Convention Centre complex in the centre of town, between King and Main Sts at Macnab. It's only open from Monday to Friday but the reception desk has maps and a few pamphlets.

Art Gallery

The art gallery, the province's third largest, is new, very spacious and has a good selection of Canadian and international painting. They also run an interesting film series with screenings at lunchtime and some evenings. Tours of the gallery are given every Thursday at 1.30 pm and on Sundays. Open Tuesday to Saturday 10 am to 5 pm, Sunday 1 to 5 pm, closed Mondays and holidays. Admission $2, students $1.

Hamilton Place In the same complex as the art gallery is this theatre-auditorium for the performing arts. Shows of various types are featured almost nightly. The local symphony plays here regularly. Tours are available.

Botanical Gardens

The Royal Botanical Gardens – 2000 acres of flowers, natural park and wildlife sanctuary – is probably the big attraction in the area and is one of the largest of its kind in the country. It is a little out of town on Plains Rd at Highway Nos 2 and 6. The grounds are split into sections with trails connecting some areas. In July and August, best are Trial Garden – the rock and herb gardens – and Hendrie Park. It's free, but donations are invited.

Hess Village

Two blocks west of the Convention Centre on Hess St is this renovated area of old houses now containing boutiques, restaurants and cafés. It is well promoted but small and not particularly interesting.

Dundurn Castle

This is actually a 36-room mansion once belonging to Sir Allan Napier McNab, the prime minister from 1854 to 1856. Concerts are held on the grounds. The mansion is on York Boulevard just out of town.

Warplane Museum

The museum has 35 planes, all in flying condition. Together with newer planes, they are part of an excellent two-day air show in June.

Stelco & Defasco Companies

These two steel giants offer free guided tours of their steel mills, including the furnaces. The tours are quite good.

Wentworth Heritage Village

A re-created town from the 1850s, this complex has about 30 buildings, costumed staff, displays and exhibits.

Museum of Steam & Technology

The old pumphouse from 1860 was built to supply clean water when cholera and typhus menaced the city. Now restored, these steam engines are among the largest in North America. Trimmed with mahogany and brass, they are quite attractive objects. Also featured are photographs and engine exhibits. Admission costs $1.75; closed Saturdays. The address is 900 Woodward Avenue.

Confederation Park

Not far north of town on Centennial Parkway, this park has a water-slide, a swimming pool with waves and a beach along Lake Ontario.

Events

The Festival of Friends happens each August in Gage Park and features music, crafts and foods from many countries.

Places to Stay

There are few hotels in the downtown area and those there are not inexpensive. On the outskirts, motels abound. In town I'd try the *Cobblestone Lodge* (tel 545-9735), a huge old place now a tourist home at 684 Main St East, at the corner of Holton Avenue. It is often busy and the owner, Aileen Harvey, prefers to see you rather than speak over the phone, but it's worth a try. Rooms run from $25 per couple to $45 depending on facilities.

The *Town Manor Motor Hotel* is central on Main St at Caroline, near Hess Village. They charge $38 for a double bed.

The *Manhattan Motor Hotel* (tel 528-7521) at 737 King St East is cheaper. Further out, close to McMaster University at 1870 Main St West, the *Mountain View Motel* is $36 to $46 for two people.

Places to Eat

King St downtown has numerous restaurants, including various ethnic places like Chinese, Greek and Italian. At Ferguson, the *Black Forest Inn* is pleasant and reasonable with soups, sandwiches and a variety of schnitzels. Across the street at 234 King is *Ganges Exotic Curry House*, and just below King of John is the *Old Spaghetti Factory*, always good value for money. In Hess Village the *Gown & Gavel* serves sandwiches and beer under the umbrellas. There are other more costly places here for dinners.

NIAGARA-ON-THE-LAKE

This small, pretty village is about 20 km downstream from the falls. It's considered one of the best-preserved 19th-century towns in North America and in the 1790s was made the first capital of Ontario. The main street has many shops from the 1800s, well restored. With the lakeside location, tree-lined streets and old houses, it makes a nice place to see before or after the falls. The village gets very busy on good summer days, though generally only on the main street. Stroll down the side streets and you'll get a quiet taste of former times in a prosperous small Ontario town.

Main Street

The town's main street is the prime attraction. In restored and well-maintained wooden buildings and shops are antiques, bakeries, various specialties and restaurants. Note particularly the apothecary from 1866 fitted with old cabinets, remedies and jars. I recommend a jam sample from the Greaves store, fourth-generation jam-makers. There are a couple of fudge shops too.

Museums

Also in town is the Fire Museum with fire-fighting equipment that dates from 1816 to 1976.

The Historical Museum at 43 Castlereagh is the oldest local museum in the province. It opened in 1907 and has a collection of early 1900 items. Open daily. The Court House on Main St is now undergoing renovations.

Events

The Shaw Festival is an internationally respected theatre festival held here annually (May-September). It features the plays of G B Shaw and his contemporaries, played by top actors and actresses. There are three different theatres, and location has a bearing on ticket prices. Cheapest are the week day matinees. Tickets range from $8 up to $34 for the best seats in the house Saturday night. Rush seats available the day of performance are $10 and go on sale at 10 am. There are brief lunchtime plays and dance performances for $7.50 and Sunday music concerts at St Mary's Church for $8, students $5. The box office (tel 468-2172) is open from 10 am to 9 pm every day from June to the middle of October.

In Simcoe Park, right in town, there are often free classical music concerts on summer Saturdays.

Tour

C Peter Neufeld (tel 468-7347) runs Gardenland Tours every day but Sunday around town, including visits to 19th-century houses and a farm market. The tour costs $6.

Places to Stay

There are some very fine inns in town and several hotels. For budget accommodation, several tourist homes have rooms. The one at 139 Victoria St (tel 468-4033) charges $35 per couple, which includes breakfast. Non-smokers only.

Another is at 69 Platoff St (tel 468-3573), just off Main. It offers use of the pool and breakfast.

Lastly, *Mrs Lynda Kay Knapp* (tel 468-3935) offers rooms for $30 singles, $35 doubles with breakfast. Her house is close to the centre of town at 390 Simcoe.

The Chamber of Commerce (tel 468-2326) can give you a list of about 35 other tourist homes.

Places to Eat

There are a number of good places to eat in town. In fact, for the money, you're better off eating here than at the falls, especially at lunch.

The *Angel*, just off Queen on Regent, dating from 1823, is a good spot for lunch. it is an English pub-type place with fish & chips, sandwiches and various beers. Prices range from $3 to $6.

The *English Tea Room*, 65 Main, is the perfect place for a tea and scone or piece of freshly baked pie.

Julio's Pizza & Spaghetti House is housed in a fine old building on Main St. Good value. The *Old Time Ice Cream Shoppe & Restaurant* has inexpensive breakfasts and sandwiches. The *Prince of Wales Hotel* has a good dining room for finer eating.

Getting There & Away

There are buses between here and Toronto on Tuesdays, Thursdays and Saturdays but only during the summer. The fare is $12.05 one-way.

A local bus, the Blue Bird, runs between here and Niagara Falls, leaving from the Prince of Wales Hotel and going to the Canada Coach Terminal in Niagara Falls. The express bus is $7, the milk run $4.50 or $4.25 for students. It leaves Niagara-on-the-Lake at 10 am and 6 pm.

NIAGARA FALLS

The roaring falls make this town one of Canada's top tourist destinations. It's a very busy spot and you'll hear and see people from all over the world.

The falls themselves, spanning the

Niagara River between Ontario and upper New York State, are impressive, particularly the Canadian Horseshoe Falls. They look good by day or by night, when spotlights flicker across the misty foam. Even in winter, when the flow is partially hidden and the edges are frozen solid – like a stopped film – it's quite a sight. Some people prefer the iced version.

It is said that Napoleon's brother rode from New Orleans in a stagecoach with his new bride to view the falls and that it has been an attraction ever since. In fact, the town is sometimes humourously but disparagingly called a spot for newly-weds and nearly-deads.

The city now has an incredible array of man-made attractions which together with the hotels, restaurants and flashing lights produce an environment as close as Canada comes to the gloss and garishness of Las Vegas. It's a sight in itself.

Orientation

The town of Niagara Falls is split into two main sections. Around the train station, on Bridge St, is the town where the locals go about their business. There's little to see or do. About three km south along the river are the falls and all the trappings of the tourist trade – restaurants, motels, shops and attractions.

The Youth Hostel is in the upper section of town, not far from the train station. The bus station, on the other hand, is near the falls. Many of the area's tourist homes are between the two sections. Along the river is scenic parkland which runs from the falls upstream about 40 km to Niagara-on-the-Lake.

Niagara is approximately two hours from Toronto by the Queen Elizabeth Way (QEW), past Hamilton and St Catherine's.

Information

There are several Tourist Offices in the area. One of the major year-round offices (tel 358-3221) is at 5629 Falls Avenue by the falls. There's also a new, large Ontario Travel Information Centre (tel 358-3221) at 5355 Stanley Avenue, Ontario L2E 7C2. Open 8 am to 8 pm. They have information on places all over the province but also have detailed knowledge of Niagara Falls. There is another office downtown by the Skylon Hotel, and one further south of town at Marineland.

For information on rooms and help finding one you can call 356-6061.

The Falls

The 56-metre falls are the great sight – close up, just where the water begins to plunge down, is the best spot. Also good is the observation deck of the souvenir shop by the falls, which you can use at no charge. After checking out all the angles at all times of day, you can try several services offering still more approaches. For overall views you can try the Skylon Tower at 5200 Robinson St, with its outside glass elevators. There is also an observation deck in Maple Leaf Village, a boutique-style shopping mall at 5705 Falls Avenue by Rainbow Bridge. The *Maid of the Mist* boat takes passengers up to the falls for a view from the bottom – loud and wet. The ride costs $5.60. From Queen Victoria Park at the falls you can pay $3.75, don a raincoat and walk down through rock-cut tunnels for a close-up (wet) look, from behind the falls and halfway down the cliff. If I was going to bother with any of these extras, this is the one worth paying for. It's a good way to cool off on a hot day.

Further north along the river is the Great Gorge Trip, an elevator to some rapids and whirlpools. Don't bother. They also have a collection of barrels and vessels that many of the wackos attempting to shoot the falls have used. Surprisingly, a good proportion of those who have gone over live to tell about it. But only one who took the trip accidently has lived to tell about it. He was a seven-year-old boy from a tipped boat upstream who did it without even breaking a bone. Mind you, I don't think he wants to do it again.

Niagara Falls Museum
Here is another 'daredevil collection' of the objects in which people have gone over the falls. Also on display are curios and artefacts from around the world, including Egyptian mummies. The address is 5651 River Rd. Open all year.

Conservatory
There is a a year-round floral display here, just south of Horseshoe Falls, and it's free.

Marineland & Game Farm
Of the dozens of commercial attractions, this is probably one of the best. It's an aquarium with special family shows by dolphins, sea lions and killer whales. Admission includes the game farm which has buffalo, bears, lions, deer and others in an outdoor park setting. There is also a large roller coaster. It's open from 9 am to 6 pm (tel 356-8250). Admission is about $6. It's about two km from the falls, south on Portage Rd.

Clifton Hill
This is the name given to the part of the downtown area near the falls. Here is every type of commercial attraction in Disney-like concentration. You name it – museums, galleries, displays like Ripley's Believe It or Not, Madame Tussaud's, Houdini's Museum – they're all here. Looking is fun but in most cases paying the entrance fee will leave you feeling like a sucker. I know – I've done it. They don't live up to their own hype. Also in this bright, busy section are dozens of souvenir shops and restaurants.

Wine Tours
Niagara is in the prime fruit and grape-growing district of Eastern Canada. Several of Canada's wineries are here, including Bright's (tel 357-2400), the oldest. Free one-hour tours with wine sampling are given at 10.30 am, 2 pm and 3.30 pm every day except Sundays and holidays. Bright's is at 4887 Dorchester Rd, Niagara, north off Highway 420.

There are others but they are out of Niagara. In St Catherine's around the shoreline toward Hamilton is Jordan and St Michelle at 120 Ridley Rd. Tours are held Monday to Friday, 10 am, 1 pm and 3 pm.

Also there is Barnes (tel 682-6631), open Monday to Saturday, offering free tours with a taste at the same times as the above. It is off Martindale Rd near the QEW Highway. Or you could try Andre's free tours and samples. It's in Winona, close to Hamilton on the lake (between Hamilton and Grimsby). Lastly, try Chateau des Charmes (tel 262-4219) in St David's, between the falls and Niagara-on-the-Lake. It's on Line 7 off Four Mile Creek Rd, not far from the highway, and is open all day, Monday to Saturday.

Events
The Blossom Festival is held in early or mid-May, when spring flowers bloom in the many parks. Featured are parades and ethnic dances.

The annual Niagara Grape & Wine Festival is held in late September. There are many events, including parades and tours of five major wineries. In addition, activities are planned throughout the region.

Places to Stay
Hostels Best bet in town is the *Brock Hall Youth Hostel* (tel 357-0770), 4699 Zimmerman Avenue, off River Rd near Queen St in the old town. It's near the train station. The hostel is in a nice, Tudor-style house near the Niagara River, and has good facilities. Members are charged $8, and non-members $12. There is only room for 25 males and 20 females. Open all year. They offer bicycle rentals and discounts for some of the museums and *Maid of the Mist* boat.

The *YWCA* (tel 357-4555) is at 6135 Culp St, not far from the bus station. They have rooms for women only, costing $18. The YMCA has no residence.

Tourist Homes Other than the hostels, these are the best bargains here. They are cheaper than either motels or hotels and are usually more pleasant. Many are centrally located. The season is from May to October, when they're all open. The cheapest ones are on River Rd or Lundy's Lane. The Tourist Office has a complete list. Prices range from about $20 to $40 with the average $25 for singles and $30 for doubles. Good value. A couple to try are *Mrs W Beacham* (tel 354-4979), 6964 Lundy's Lane; or at 6986, *Mrs Wilma Slack*.

River Rd links the falls area with Old Niagara Town, three km upriver. There are quite a few tourist homes along here, with good views of the river and a convenient location. Two of the less expensive ones are *Noel Downer* (tel 356-4607) at 5077 River Rd, and *Sylvia Gran* (tel 358-7283) at 5239.

There are also three guest houses on Robert St. *Mrs H Hamilton's* (tel 358-8376) at 4998, has rooms starting from only $20. Another street to check is Victoria. Many of these guesthouses have a sign out front.

Bed & Breakfasts A bed & breakfast programme also operates in town; phone 358-8988 or go around to 2631 Dorchester Rd, where the service is run. Prices are generally $35/45 for singles/doubles, including full breakfast.

Hotels There are few hotels in town; most accommodation is in motels, and the hotels tend to be new and expensive. A budget alternative is the *King Edward* at the south end of Queen St, in the older part of town not far from the train station. Rock music is played downstairs in the bar. The basic rooms are $24/28 for singles/doubles.

The *Royal Inn Hotel* is at 4152 Bridge St, near the train station (turn left on exit). It's kind of a sleazy place with mostly permanent residents, but they might have a vacant room. About $15.

Motels There's millions of 'em. The cheapest ones seem to be along Lundy's Lane which leads west out from the falls and later becomes Highway 20. The wide price ranges are partially because many have honeymoon rooms with double bathtubs, waterbeds and other price-bumping features. Rates vary dramatically by season but are most costly in July and August. Later it's a buyer's market.

The *Thunderbird Motel* (tel 356-0541) at 6019, has rooms for $29 all the way to $65. Also small, with 20 rooms, is the *Bonanza* (tel 356-5135) at 6267. Prices here are $28 to $55.

The *Caravan Motel* (tel 354-6038), 8511 Lundy's Lane, charges $23 to $48. *A-1 Motel* (tel 354-6038) at 7895 charges $44 to $75 and has 20 rooms and a pool. At 7742 Lundy's is the *Alpine Motel* (tel 356-7016). Their rate is $36 to $48, and they also have a pool. The *Melody Motel* (tel 227-1023) at 13065, charges $35 to $60 and has a pool. The street has literally dozens of other motels.

On Main St the *USA Motel* (tel 295-4481) at 6541 and Georges Parkway is modestly priced. Ditto for the *Lennox Motel*, 3769 Macklem, which is only $25.

Leeland Cabins (tel 295-3898) is six km south on Niagara River Parkway. Individual cabins are $28 to $34; not a bad deal.

Camping There are campgrounds all around town. Three are on Lundy's Lane, leading out of Niagara, and two are on Montrose Avenue south-west of downtown. They are decidedly not primitive.

At the government-run *Miller's Creek Park* (tel 871-6557), each large site has some privacy and a fireplace. It's open from mid-June to early September. Sites are $8.50 with no electricity.

Places to Eat

Down by the falls around Clifton Hill there are scores of restaurants. Some offer breakfast and/or lunch specials. Just look around. Taking a leaflet from one of the hustlers on the street can lead to a good bargain. The *Rascal House*, 5575 Victoria Avenue, not far off Clifton Hill Rd, has an all-you-can-eat spaghetti deal.

In the northern, older section of town there's *The Café* on Erie Avenue just up from the train station. It's cheap and pleasant. On Queen St is *Woolworth's*, which has a cafeteria serving breakfasts and full lunches and dinners under $5.

Getting There & Away

Bus The station is south-west of downtown, near the falls and the Panasonic Tower. It's at the corner of Dunn and Oakes Drive. Between Niagara Falls and Toronto, service is very frequent – there is one bus per hour. The trip takes about two hours and the fare is $14.25. Tickets are on sale from 6 am to 9 pm. For buses to Niagara-on-the-Lake, see under that section.

Train The station is in the older part of town on Bridge St, close to this area's downtown section. Tickets are on sale from 6 am to 9 pm.

Departure times for VIA Rail trains to Toronto are 9.40 am, 1.30 and 5.40 pm. The trip takes about two hours and costs $14. There is a special if you go and return between Toronto and Niagara on the same day and it's $22 return within five days provided you don't use a Friday. There is one train daily west to London at 1 pm, for which the fare is $16.

Getting Around

Walking is best; most things to see are in a small area. The Niagara River Sightseeing Package Tour takes in most of the area's sights and includes admission to a number of attractions and *Maid of the Mist* boat trip. The tour takes about six hours, costs $26.50 and includes a meal. Tickets and information are available at Table Rock House (by the falls) or in the Victoria Park Restaurant.

English double-decker bus tours run along the river during a 50-km trip for $7.50. Gray Line offers seven different bus tours. Their depot is opposite the Panasonic Tower.

Bicycles can be rented at Cupulos, on Ferry at the corner of Stanley, open 9 am to 9 pm.

AROUND NIAGARA

A slow 20-km trip along the Niagara Parkway to Niagara-on-the-Lake is most enjoyable. Riding a bike for the excursion would be well worthwhile. Along the way are parks, picnic areas, good views over the river and a couple of campgrounds. Fort George, dating from 1797, is one of several historic places. It's open daily but there's not really much to see. Maybe best of all are the fresh fruit stands with cold cherry ciders and juices.

At Queenston is the southern end of the Bruce Trail, a hiking path which extends 700 km to Tobermory on Georgian Bay. There are numerous access points in the Niagara and Hamilton area. For more details on the trail see under Tobermory.

South from Niagara Falls, along the parkway, is a reconstruction of Fort Erie which the Americans seized in 1814 before retreating home. There are a museum, military drills and uniformed soldiers. Admission is $2.

The town of Fort Erie across from Buffalo is connected to the US by the Peace Bridge. This is a major border-crossing point and buses from Toronto connecting to many eastern American cities use it. On summer weekends expect queues. Many air travellers now find it worthwhile to bus to Buffalo from Toronto and vicinity to take advantage of cheaper US airfares. For example, a flight from Buffalo to Seattle is much less than from Toronto to Vancouver and means only short bus trips at each end. There are buses from Toronto direct to the Buffalo airport, some connecting with specific flights, such as the ones to New York City which have very low fares.

Back in Ontario slightly further south is Crystal Beach, a beach-cottage resort with Canada's largest amusement park. Open 10 am to 10 pm daily.

BRANTFORD

West of Hamilton and surrounded for the most part by farmland, Brantford is known for several things. It has long been associated with Indians as Chief Joseph Brant led the Six Nation Indians in an area stretching from here to parts of Upper New York State. The Brant County Museum has information and artefacts on Brant and his people. Her Majesty's Chapel of the Mohawks is the oldest Protestant church in Ontario and the world's only Royal Indian Chapel. The Woodland Indian Museum has displays on the various original peoples of Eastern Canada.

Brantford was the home of Alexander Graham Bell, the telephone's inventor. The Bell Homestead displays some of his other inventions and is furnished the way it was when he lived in it.

The town is also known for native son Wayne Gretzky, the greatest hockey player the world has yet produced.

There are some additional attractions such as Myrtleville House, dating from 1837, and the interesting eight-sided (what else?) Octagon House.

KITCHENER-WATERLOO

These twin cities – amalgamated to form one – are about an hour west of Toronto in the heart of rural southern Ontario. About 60% of the 190,000 inhabitants are of German origin. The city also acts as a centre for the Amish and Mennonite religious farming communities. It is these two factors that attract visitors and make the town stand out from its neighbours. There is not a lot to see, and at a glance things here are much the same as in any other large town. However, it's worth a short visit, particularly if your timing is right and you arrive for Oktoberfest. The towns share two universities and therefore have a fair number of young people.

Orientation

Kitchener is the southern portion of the city and is nearly three times the size of Waterloo, but you can't really tell where one ends and the other begins. The downtown area refers to central Kitchener. King St is the main street and runs roughly north-south. The farmers' market at the corner of King and Frederick Sts marks the centre of downtown. This area of town has the train and bus stations, hotels and restaurants. King St runs south to Highway 8, which continues to Highway 401 for Windsor west and Toronto east.

Highway 8 west at the junction of King St heads to Stratford. King St runs north right through the city to the two universities and beyond.

Information

Maps and information are available at the Kitchener Chamber of Commerce (tel 576-5000), 67 King St East on the second floor of the Canada Permanent Trust Building. Open 9 am to 5 pm weekdays.

Farmers' Markets

One market is in a new building right downtown at the corner of King St East and Frederick. The market began in 1839 and features the products of the Amish and the Mennonites – breads, jams, many cheeses and sausages as well as handicrafts such as quilts, rugs, clothes and hand-made toys. Whether they like it or not, it is the farmers themselves who are often the main attraction. Some of these religious people, originally from Germany via Pennsylvania, live much the way they did in the 19th century. They use horse-drawn buggies for transportation, and don't drink, vote or use the courts. Some do not use any modern machinery. The strict Old Order members are easily recognisable, with the bearded men in black suits and hats, and the women in bonnets and ankle-length skirts. The market takes place Saturday mornings 5 am to 2 pm and in summer on Wednesdays too, from 6 am.

Across the street, at the corner of King and Benton, is a 23-bell glockenspiel that rings at noon and at 5 pm.

The Waterloo Market is another, more authentic version with horse and buggy sheds still in place. It's near St Jacobs, a small town a few km north of the city. It's open the same days as the other market, but doesn't begin as early in the morning.

On Sundays you may see the wagons rolling down the country roads and lining up outside the old wooden churches of the district.

Woodside National Historic Park

This park contains the 100-year-old mansion where former Prime Minister William Lyon Mackenzie King (Canada's 10th Prime Minister) once lived. It has been restored and refinished in upper-class 1890s style. The basement houses displays on the life of Mackenzie King. On weekends see demonstrations of period crafts, music and cooking by guides in costume. The park is at 528 Wellington St North in Kitchener, is open daily and admission is free.

Universities of Waterloo & Wilfrid Laurier

In Waterloo, west off King St, these two universities are right beside each other and have attractive, green campuses. Waterloo has an art gallery and the Museum of Games which depicts the history of games around the world. Open Monday to Friday.

Doon Heritage Crossroads

This is a re-creation of a pioneer settlement located just south of Kitchener. The 27 buildings include a general store, workshops and sawmill. There is also a model of an original Mennonite village in Russia and a replica of an 1856 railway. The site is down King St, right on Fairway, left at Manitou and left again at Homer Watson Boulevard. Open spring to fall. Admission is $3.50; less for students. Special events are often held on weekends.

Joseph Schneider Haus

At 466 Queen St South, not far from the market, is this Heritage Canada site, the restored house of a prosperous German Mennonite. It's a museum depicting life in the mid-1850s, with demonstrations of day-to-day chores and skills.

Seagram Museum

Set in part of the original Seagram distillery in Waterloo, this is a museum (tel 885-1857) showing the history and technology of booze production. On display are 2000 artefacts from around the world and many different time periods. You'll see some beautiful tools and equipment. Explanatory films are shown. The address is 57 Erb St. Open Tuesday to Saturday noon to 8 pm, Sunday noon to 5 pm.

The Centre in the Square

At the corner of Queen and Ellen Sts is this new arts complex with the art gallery and theatre.

Entertainment Parks

Sportsworld is a new entertainment park containing, among other diversions, a waterslide, wave pool, go-kart track and snack bars, and can be found at 4370 King St East, close to the 401. Bingeman Park at 1380 Victoria St. North on the Grand River offers much the same thing but is older and not as big.

Events

Oktoberfest is the event of the year and is the biggest of its kind in North America, attracting 350,000 people annually. The nine-day festival starts in early to mid-October and includes 20 beer halls, German music and foods, and dancing. A huge parade wraps up the festivities on the last day. For more information, ring Oktoberfest Inc on 576-0571.

The Mennonite Relief Sale is a large sale of home-made foods and crafts and also includes a quilt auction. It's held the last Saturday in May in New Hamburg, 19 km west of Kitchener-Waterloo.

Places to Stay

Hostels There is no Youth Hostel here. The Y's are a reasonable alternative. The *YMCA* (tel 743-5201) is at Queen and Water, across from the courthouse. The rate is $16 to $19 per day; it's cheap by the week. The *YWCA* (tel 744-6501) is at Frederick and Weber, also in Kitchener. Both are central. The YW charges $23 per night and offers weekly rates. They take women only.

The *University of Waterloo* (tel 885-1211) has rooms. Singles/doubles are $25/40, including breakfast. Other meals are available.

At *Wilfrid Laurier University* (tel 884-1970) contact the housing officer, 75 University Avenue West. Singles/doubles are $20/33. Rooms are available from 1 May to 15 August. The dining room is open.

Hotels For the dollar conscious, the *Mayfair*, right downtown at the corner of King and Young Sts, close to the bus station, is basic but gets the job done. Singles/doubles cost $20/28 with toilet and shower. There's a bar downstairs.

For shoestringers, the *Station Hotel* right beside the train station is a bit of a dump and often full but costs only $15/18 for singles/doubles.

In a different league altogether is the *Walper Terrace Hotel* (tel 745-4321) also central at 1 King St. It's an old place that has been restored and has won a heritage award. They have over 100 rooms ranging in price from $65 to $85.

During Oktoberfest many people rent out rooms. For information call Oktoberfest Inc, 576-0571.

Motels Motels are numerous, good and clean. Most of them are on Victoria St, which runs east-west off King St just north of downtown Kitchener. Two of the cheapest are *El Rancho* (tel 743-4167), at 1191 Victoria, which costs $31/40 for singles/doubles, and the *Shamrock* (tel 743-4361), at 1235, with singles/doubles at $28/34.

Places to Eat

There are many restaurants on King St. At Water on King is *A la Cape Breton*, serving crepes and breakfast specials. It has a salad bar as well. At Cedar and King is *Checkerboard*, a small, quick lunch spot serving home-made soup, chilli, pies and real hamburgers. At 258 King St is *Angelo's Pizza & Spaghetti House* with all manner of Italian food between $4 to $8. *Harvey's*, further down, is the best of Canada's hamburger chains.

The Rathskeller, at 151 Frederick, offers German food.

Getting There & Away

Bus The station is on Gaukel St, west off King and two blocks down, in central Kitchener.

Train The station is at the corner of Victoria and Weber Sts, an easy walk north of the Kitchener downtown.

AROUND KITCHENER-WATERLOO

St Jacob's

Just north of town is St Jacob's, a small historic village with the Meeting Place, a little museum on the Mennonites and their history, and numerous arts & crafts shops housed in original buildings from the 1800s. There is an inn and a guest house in town as well as a couple of restaurants if you want to stay. Either way, drop into the bakery.

An Area Drive

Take the 401 past Kitchener (going west) to the Doon exit and go to New Dundee. From there, travel north-west to Petersburg, where you'll find the Blue Moon Pub.

Then on to St Agatha with the church steeple, followed by St Clements and Lindwood – both Mennonite towns with some interesting stores. Drive back east to Hawkersville, with its blacksmith shop, and take a gravel road with fine scenery to St Jacobs. Continue north up to Elmira and over to West Montrose, where there is a covered bridge – one of the few left in Ontario.

ELORA

Not far from Kitchener-Waterloo, north up Highway 6 from Guelph, is this small, heavily-touristed little town. Named after Ellora in India, with its famous cave temples, this was once a mill town using the falls in the Grand River which runs through town. These, the old mill, the pleasant setting and nearby gorge and park make the town a popular one-day trip for visitors and Ontarians.

Not far from town, at the Elora Gorge Conservation Area, the river flows through a deep limestone canyon. Much of the area is park and trails lead to cliff views and caves at the water's edge. Riding the water in a rubber inner tube is a fun way to spend a warm afternoon. There are also picnic areas in the park. The nearby quarry is worth a look.

The Grand River is good for canoeing and overnight trips are possible. The river can actually be paddled all the way to Lake Erie. More information is available at the park.

Elora Tours (tel 846-5567) offers minibus trips around town, with historical commentary. The tour takes only an hour and includes the gorge and park, and costs is $4.50, $4 students. Their address is 201 Smith St.

For shoppers there are plenty of small stores in Elora offering crafts, jewellery, paintings and pottery, etc, much of it produced by the numerous local artisans.

Places to Stay

The *Desert Inn* also operates a very pleasant bed & breakfast just down the street from the café with rooms for $60 per couple. Other residents offer lodging; for information call Mrs Groves (tel 846-0640) at 36 David St. Average price is $35 for two including breakfast. The *Elora Mill Inn* is the place to stay in town offering views of the river and fireplaces but you may have to look in both pockets. There is a large campground at the Elora Gorge Conservation Area which, though usually full on holiday weekends, has a number of sites that can be reserved one week in advance.

Places to Eat

The town has several good eating spots near the mill. I've eaten several times in the *Desert Rose*, a sort of health-food, home-made-foods specialty place with a Mexican slant, and always found the food good. They serve soups, salads and sandwiches. Nearby, across the street, is the *Elora Gourmet Café & Delicatessen*, open 10 am to 3 pm only. They serve simple but tasty lunches at reasonable cost. Others along the street and the dining room of the *Mill Inn* offer more expensive menus.

FERGUS

Fergus is Elora's neighbour and a quiet, farm-area town. As the name suggests, the heritage here is Scottish and this is best appreciated at the annual Highland Games held the second week of August. Included are Scottish dancing, pipe bands, foods and sport events such as the caber toss. It is one of the largest Scottish festivals and Highland Games held in North America.

Many of the town's buildings are of limestone, again suggesting the old country. Another event is the Old Time Fiddle & Step Dance Contest, held every year on the second weekend in July.

Canoes can be rented in town at Templin Gardens for a paddle down the gorge to Elora. An oddity in town is the painted fire hydrants.

As in Elora, lodging is in short supply and rather costly. The *Newson family* run a bed & breakfast at their farm 3.2 km east of town on Orangevill Rd. It's a large stone house – look for the blue mail box. Singles/doubles cost $18/22, and $2 for breakfast. Another is called *Washa Farms* (tel 846-9788) seven km north of town, which is $30 for two with breakfast. It's on an 88-hectare working farm.

For food try the *Honeycomb Cafe* at 135 St David North, which has homemade soups, breads and desserts.

Between Fergus and Elora is the Wellington County Museum with artefacts relating to the history of the county.

ELMIRA

Not far north of Kitchener-Waterloo and slightly west is this, another Mennonite centre. In spring there is a Maple Syrup Festival with street activities and pancake breakfasts. The Sap Bucket is a store specialising in local crafts, including the fine quilts, but these are not given away. Brox's Old Towne Village is a shopping centre designed to look like an earlier era. Brubacher's Country Store in the complex is a 19th-century general store. You'll find antiques and restaurants in the centre.

There are quite a few bed & breakfasts in the area, many on farms and with owners who speak Pennsylvania Dutch or German.

STRATFORD

With a population of 25,000, this commercial centre surrounded by farmland is a fairly typical slow-paced Ontario town, though rather prettier than most. What makes it different and special is the now world-famous Stratford Shakespearean Festival. Stratford's Avon River and its swans, the green lawns and theatres, give the town a deliberate, successful resemblance to Stratford-Upon-Avon in England. The town is about 60 km east of London, two hours or so from Toronto. Ontario St is the main street and everything is close to it.

The Festival

Begun humbly in a tent in 1953, the theatre now attracts worldwide attention. I've never studied nor been overly interested in Shakespeare, but I find these plays excellent. The productions are first rate, as are the costumes, and respected actors are featured. The season runs from June to October each year. Tickets range from $7.50 to $30 and go on sale the first week of March. By showtime, nearly every performance is sold out. Tickets are available by mail at the Festival Theatre Box Office, PO Box 520, Stratford, Ontario, N5A 6V2, by telephone (519) 273-1600, or at the box office.

There are three theatres – all in town – that feature contemporary drama and music, operas, and works by the Bard.

The Gallery

This is a good art gallery in a fine old building near Confederation Park on 54 Romeo St North. Featured are changing international shows of modern painting, with emphasis on Canadian works. Three shows are presented at any given time. Closed Monday.

Queen's Park

Down by the river, near Festival Theatre, this park is good for a picnic or walk. Footpaths from the theatre follow the river past Orr Dam and a 90-year-old stone bridge to the formal English Flower Garden.

Shakespeareland

This is a miniature model of Stratford in England, in a park setting on Romeo St North. It's open daily from June to September, and admission is $4. There's a good reduction for students.

Places to Stay

There is often a *Youth Hostel* here but it changes location and comes and goes. Check in Toronto or at the local Tourist Office.

The *Queen's Inn* at 161 Ontario St at

Waterloo, is 130 years old, the oldest hotel in town. Refurbished and re-opened in 1988 it's a fine place to stay, with a double going for $55 in summer, less the rest of the year.

There are also nearly 10 bed & breakfasts in town charging about $25 for singles, $35 for doubles. They're open in summer only. The *Four Swans* (tel 271-5385) is at 266 Ontario St. They have a kitchenette and are central. A little more expensive is *Crackers* (tel 273-1201), a house dating from 1888, at 433 Erie St, which is one km from downtown. Happy hour is 5.30 pm, with complimentary wine and cheese. They have four rooms.

Close to the theatre on Ontario St are three guest homes open during the summer. They charge about $20 for a bed, one or two people. *Heinbuck Tourist Haven* is at 411, *Tourist Riviera* at 417 and *Duck Inn* at 456.

Motels are expensive. Try the *Noretta* (tel 271-6110) on Highway 7 toward Kitchener. Rooms cost from $45 for a double. The *Majers* (tel 271-2010), a little further out, is slightly more expensive.

Places to Eat

Most places are expensive and cater to the theatre crowd. The *Jesters Arms* on Ontario in the centre of town is like an English pub with lunches from $5. There are a few fast-food joints further up the street heading out of town.

Getting There & Away

There is no train service. The bus stops on Ontario St, at the opposite end from the theatre. There's no real terminal, so ask.

TILLSONBURG & DELHI

These two small towns are in the centre of the sandy tobacco-growing region. Look here around the second week of August for casual work picking tobacco. Try Canada Manpower. Jobs last roughly a month. It's hard work but room and board are often thrown in with the wage, and it can be a good time. Watch your valuables in the bunkhouse.

LAKE ERIE SHORELINE

The shallowest of the five Great Lakes, Erie suffered not long ago from extreme pollution. While not to be confused with a mountain stream, improvement in the past few years has meant it's coming back from the nearly doomed. All along its northern Canadian shoreline, from Windsor to Buffalo, there are government parks, some with camping, some day-use only. Aside from these, the area is mainly farmland, small towns and summer cottages. The parks are good for camping and fishing (Turkey Point and even more so, Long Point are good and popular), although Huron and its parks are much better for swimming. Most are busy on summer weekends.

Further west, Point Pelee is a national park on the southernmost point of mainland Canada and is primarily known for the thousands of birds that show up in spring and autumn on their migrations. Up to 342 species have been seen here – about 60% of all the species known in Canada. The region also contains some plants found nowhere else in the country, for example, the prickly pear cactus. There is a 1.5-km boardwalk through the marsh and sandy beaches. Camping is not allowed but there are private places nearby.

Hillman Marsh, north of Point Pelee on the shoreline, offers good bird-watching as well; there's an observation tower and a boardwalk. Nearby in the town of Wheatley, *Burton House* (tel 825-4956) is a moderately-priced bed & breakfast.

Quite close to Windsor are the lakeside towns of Leamington and Kingsville from where ferries run to the largest island in the lake, Pelee Island, which lies halfway across to Ohio. Some good beaches.

LONDON

This is the most important town in the Lake Erie area, with a lot of industry and a large university. Despite the activity, London preserves a quiet, conservative atmosphere highlighted by the tree-lined streets and old houses. The city harks back to London, England; the Thames River flows through town, in the centre is Hyde Park and there are many street names paralleling names in England's London, like Oxford. Not much to do here, but it may be a convenient stopping point if you're coming from Detroit. The town is about halfway between the USA-Canada border at Detroit-Windsor and Toronto.

The main east-west street is Dundas. Richmond is the main one north-south.

Information

For information the Tourist Office is in City Hall on Dufferin at the corner of Wellington.

Things to See

In town, the beautiful university campus is nice to stroll around. At 481 Rideout is Eldon House, the city's oldest house dating from 1834 and now a historical museum. East of the city is a Pioneer Village with demonstrations of skills and crafts. Sixteen km west of the city is Ska-Nah-Doht Indian village, a re-creation of a small community using longhouses.

The first week in June there is an international air show and in mid-September is the Western Fair, a 10-day agricultural and amusement-park event.

Places to Stay

Hostels There is no hostel, but the *YM-YWCA* (tel 432-3706) which burned down a few years ago is operating again. The address is 433 Wellington, which is central. They have mostly singles but also a few rooms for couples as well as a cafeteria and pool.

The *University of Western Ontario* has rooms in Saugeen-Maitland Hall (tel 679-2980); see the manager there. Singles are $17.50 and doubles $25. The student rate is $13. Breakfast is included. Accommodation here is mostly for people with business at the university.

Hotels Most of the small downtown hotels are alcoholic city. If you don't mind too much, they're cheap enough and there are several on Dundas St. Otherwise, read on.

On King St at 186 the *Park Lane* is the best alternative with prices in the $60 range.

Tourist Homes There is a *Tourist Home* (tel 434-2474) at 256 Wharncliffe Rd South. A single is about $20 and there is a community kitchen.

Bed & Breakfasts The local bed & breakfast association (tel 471-6228) at 720 Headley Drive has a list of places to stay, with prices around $20/35 for singles/doubles.

Betty & Doug Rose (tel 433-9978) offer two rooms in their 110-year-old house. It's central at 526 Dufferin Avenue. The rate is $20/25 for singles/doubles with breakfast. *John & Terry Herbert* (tel 673-4598) at 87 Askin, off Wharncliffe, are also fairly central, with two rooms as well. Their rate is $23 for singles, $28 for doubles. The house was built in 1871.

Motels Most commercial accommodation is in motels. On Wellington coming in from Highway 401 is the *White Oaks*, with singles for $38, doubles for $52. At 767 Wharncliffe is the *New London Motel* (tel 681-2302), which has singles/doubles for $34/38. The *Rossholme* across the street is cheap and rents beds, not morals. And at 1739 Dundas St East, the *White Village Motel* (tel 451-5840), has better but pricier rooms at $50/55 for singles/doubles.

Places to Eat

For eating there's the unchanging *London Café* downstairs on Dundas, just east of Richmond. They serve plain, simple lunch specials from $4.50.

Covent Garden, beside the market, is pretty similar. The market is behind Simpson's, at the corner of Richmond and

Dundas. It's a good place to buy food, including cheeses and fruit. Check out old Mac the Macaw in the pet shop – he's been there for years. Sometimes he talks, sometimes he bites, sometimes he just sits.

Pickles Restaurant, on Richmond just south of Oxford, is recommended. They serve various excellent hamburgers – try the caps burger, $6. The wedge fries are very good at $2. Pickles Restaurant is also known for its desserts.

Mother's Pizza, on Richmond just south of Mill St on the way to the university, is very good.

At night there's the pleasant *Change of Pace Coffee House* at 355A Talbot St. Good music is featured from Thursday to Saturday – mostly folk. The coffee house serves alcohol.

The *Ceeps* in the CPR Hotel at Richmond and Mills Sts is the spot for drinking university students. And I mean drinking.

Getting There & Around

Both the bus and train stations are at the foot of Richmond, on York St. They offer frequent services to Toronto.

For inner-city buses (LTC) there's an information office with ticket sales on Richmond at the corner of Dundas.

LAKE HURON SHORELINE & AREA

North of Windsor on the southern tip of Lake Huron is Sarnia, an industrial and oil refining centre. Across the St Clair River is Port Huron in Michigan.

Along Lake Huron as far up as Tobermory on the Bruce Peninsula are numerous and popular parks, good sandy beaches and small summer resort towns and cottages. The water is warm, the beaches broad and sandy.

About 40 km north-east of Sarnia at Kettle Point is a 350-million-year-old attraction. Along the shoreline are a series of spherical rocks called kettles or to geologists, concretions. Some of these calcite formations which sit on beds of softer shale are nearly one metre in diameter. Though rare, they are found in other countries but are often underground and this collection is considered top rate.

A little further up the coast, both Ipperwash and the Pinery Provincial Parks south of Grand Bend have camping. The Pinery, a large park with 1000 sites, long had a reputation as a party spot but has quietened down in the past couple of years. The beach is 10 km long and trails wind through the woods. Further north is Point Farms Park, about the size of Ipperwash.

Grand Bend is one of the Lake Huron resort towns, similar to Sauble Beach. It's a lively spot in summer with a few places for a drink along the shoreline.

Goderich is a small, rather attractive town with a circular main street that acts as a regional centre. There's a good, small *Youth Hostel* (tel 524-2442) on Black Point Rd. At dusk in town, a spot to view the 'world's best' sunsets is by the museum in the Historic Huron Jail. It's set on a cliff over the water.

For more information on the northern section of the lake, see the North of Toronto section.

WINDSOR

Windsor, with a population near 200,000, sits at the south-western tip of the province across the river from Detroit, Michigan. It is not in any way a tourist city but, like its counterpart across the border, is a heavily industrialised car-making centre. With easy access across the Detroit River, this is a major point at which to cross the American border. From here it's about two hours to London, 4½ hours to Toronto. From Detroit there are routes down to Chicago.

The International Freedom Festival combines Canada's 1 July national holiday with America's 4 July Independence Day celebrations for an event of parades, concerts, dances and one of the continent's largest fireworks displays to end the affair.

If you arrive at night, most accommodation is in motels and the place to look for modestly priced ones is Division Rd. The *Casa Don Motel* (tel 969-0630) at 2130, charges $32 to $38. The slightly lower priced *Lorna Doone* (tel 969-1060) is at 1425. Another street with even more motels is Huron Church Rd.

For eating, the *Himalaya* on Quellette is said to be good for curry.

Northern Ontario

Northern Ontario is a vast, underpopulated region of lakes and forest. How large an area it is will quickly become evident if you're going over Lake Superior to or from Manitoba.

Commercial activity up here is almost all involved with natural resources – forestry and mining and their spin-offs. The big cities on the Great Lakes are major ports and shipping centres. Outside the widely-spaced towns, much of the land is wild; the waters are clean and wildlife abounds. This would have to be one of the best regions for your traditional Canadian outdoor activities. But make the most of your time in summer; it's fairly short.

NORTH BAY

North Bay with a population of a little over 50,000 sits at the eastern end of big Lake Nipissing and at about 350 km north of Toronto is the southernmost of the north's major towns.

The Trans-Canada Highway which connects Sudbury to the west with Ottawa to the east passes through town. North Bay is also an access point to the many mining towns above it which straddle the Quebec-Ontario border. There is also some fine wilderness in the region which attracts outdoor enthusiasts, fishermen etc.

Orientation

Main St is the main street; south of town it becomes Lakeshore Drive. The centre of town is found between Cassells and Fisher. Ferguson is the principal cross-street and runs from the waterfront east to the North Bay by-pass which connects Highways 11 and 17. Lakeshore Drive going south turns into Highway 11 for Toronto. Algonquin leading north becomes the 11 for Timmons and also links to the 17 east and west.

The bus station is at the corner of 2nd and Cassells and the train station (VIA Rail and Ontario Northland) is at 2nd and Fraser.

Information

The Tourist Office is on Highway 11 near the junction of the 17 to Ottawa.

Things to See

Boat cruises on Lake Nipissing follow the old voyageur paddle strokes to the Upper French River. The six-hour trip includes a film.

All along the shore in town is sandy beach with scattered parks and picnic tables. Sunset Park is good at the end of the day.

At Canadore College, north-west of downtown, one of the several walking paths leads to Duchesnay Falls and good views.

Beside the Tourist Office, the Quints Museum contains articles relating to the Dionne quintuplets born in 1934 and the most famous Canadian multiple-birth story. The museum is actually the family log farmhouse, moved and restored.

Places to Stay

The bulk of the city's accommodation is in motels. Many can be found along Lakeshore Drive in the south end of town. The *Star Motel* at 405 Lakeshore Drive costs $32 to $39 for doubles and, like all of them, is cheaper in the off season. Across the street the *Holiday* is a few dollars more but the rooms are a little newer. Both are

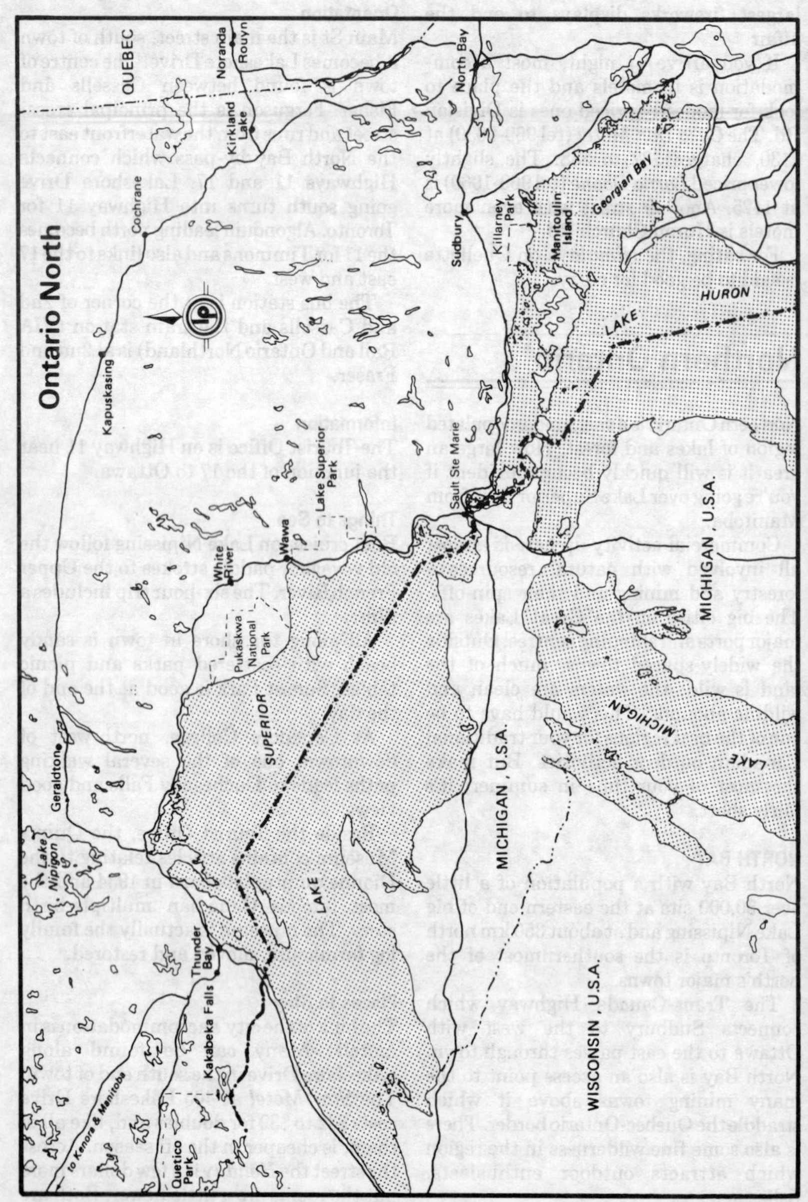
Ontario North
QUEBEC
Noranda
Rouyn
Kirkland Lake
North Bay
Cochrane
Sudbury
Killarney Park
Manitoulin Island
Georgian Bay
LAKE
HURON
Kapuskasing
Sault Ste Marie
Lake Superior Park
Wawa
White River
MICHIGAN, U.S.A.
Pukaskwa National Park
LAKE
SUPERIOR
LAKE
MICHIGAN
Geraldtone
Lake Nipigon
Thunder Bay
Kakabeka Falls
Quetico Park
to Kenora & Manitoba
MICHIGAN, U.S.A.
WISCONSIN, U.S.A.

friendly. Others can be found further afield on Highway 11 both north and south of town.

Places to Eat

I'd try *Maltilda's* at 725 Main St East at Maingate. It's a small, plain place that serves up very good, inexpensive homemade Italian dishes. There are a few tables right at the front and a dining room at the back. And don't forget the fresh baked butter tarts, excellent. Closed Sundays.

The *Windmill Cafe* downtown at 168 Main St East is the best of the central basics, and serves low-priced BBQ chicken or fish dinners. For breakfast come back here or head to *Smitty's* out on Lakeshore Drive for pancakes.

Mike's Seafood with two locations, one on Main St and one on Lakeshore, is good and the prices are reasonable. The fish & chips are quite decent. *Casey's* is a popular something-for-everyone place as well as a drinking hole for local youth.

At 174 Worthington, the *Lion's Heart Pub* is very Englishy, even serving old country brew. It has cheap meals and some evenings live entertainment, too.

Getting There & Away

Ontario Northland runs both a rail and a bus service north of North Bay. Their rail lines link North Bay, Timmons, Kirkland Lake, Cochrane and Moosonee as well as numerous small destinations in between. Connecting buses go further afield, to Sudbury and Sault Ste Marie for example.

TEMAGAMI

Temagami is a small town north of North Bay on Lake Temagami. More importantly, the name also refers to the fabulous wilderness of the area renowned internationally for its 300-year-old red and white pine forest, an excellent interconnected canoe route system, numerous archaeological sites and Indian pictographs, and scenery which includes waterfalls and some of the province's highest terrain. There are few roads (one of the major assets) and the area can be accessed by a visit to Lady Evelyn Smoothwater Provincial Park. The area is under some threat by logging interests which are being opposed by local conservation groups as well as the respected International Union for Conservation, based in Switzerland.

Just two km from the town of Temagami is Finlayson Provincial Park with a commemorative plaque for English author Grey Owl, who lived with the local Ojibway for several years and then convinced the world through his writing on nature and its preservation that he was an Indian himself.

SUDBURY

For 100 years, Sudbury, sitting on the rocky Precambian Shield, has been supplying the world with nickel. Inco Ltd, the world's largest nickel producer, is the town's biggest employer and until recently, its lifeblood. While still vitally important, Inco and its rival, Falconbridge, have seen their fortunes decline with the drop in international demand and price. But Sudbury, for the first time in its history, is trying to get away from the precarious 'one-industry town' syndrome and is slowly diversifying.

The city is not pretty; it's been a rugged mining town a long time and is best known for its treeless, moon-like landscape. In fact parts of the surroundings are so like what the US space team expected to find on the moon that astronauts trained here before the real lunar launch.

The bleakest area is seen from the train, though if you're driving you'll pass by the dull, brown-grey hills west of town. The complete lack of vegetation is mainly due to discharges from the mining and smelting operations but the naturally very thin soil covering doesn't help matters.

Inco recently built a giant smokestack, which allowed some plants and grasses to take hold in previously barren, dead areas. As for the districts where the wind now blows the effluvium . . . try and avoid them.

Despite all this, much of the town and vicinity is not strikingly dessert-like and, ironically, Sudbury is surrounded by a vast area of forests, hills and lakes, making it a centre for outdoor and sporting activities. Even on the east side of town, away from the mineral operations, the land is green and wild-looking. There are over a dozen lakes just outside of town, including the large Ramsey Lake at the south-east edge of the city. And Sudbury gets more hours of sunshine than any other industrial city in Ontario.

Sudbury isn't the place to make an effort to get to, but if you're heading cross country you'll probably pass through, and there are a few interesting things to see and do, mostly related to mining. You may also be surprised to find a very large French population here.

Orientation

The main streets downtown are Elm running east-west and Durham going north-south. The core runs along Elm from Notre Dame to Lorne St.

On Elm is the new shopping centre complex, City Centre, and the Holiday Inn. The post office is across the street. Nearby is where the local bus routes start.

Elgin St running south off Elm divides Elm East from West and at its southern end has the VIA Rail station. As you head east on Elm at Notre Dame you'll encounter the green-bulbed Ukrainian Church. Further east the street changes names several times. It goes by a commercial strip of gas stations, fast-food spots, motels and the bus station, and eventually becomes Highway 17 to Ottawa.

South from town, Drinkwater turns into Highway 69 for Toronto. It also passes through a long, commercial district.

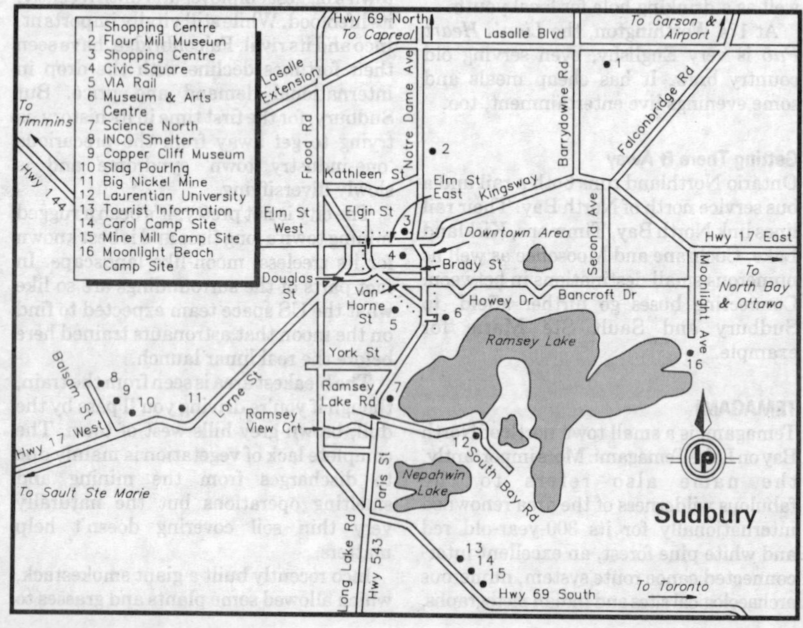

Going west, Lorne St leads to Highway 17, Trans Canada. There are motels along the way, the Big Nickel coin park, Inco, smelters and Copper Cliff.

Laurentian University lies on a hill on the far side of Ramsey lake south-east from downtown. Good views.

Information

The Tourist Office (tel 675-4346) is central at 199 Larch St. They are helpful and are open all year, Monday to Friday.

There is a large, new tourist centre on Highway 69, eight km south of town. There is also a booth, open in summer only, a long way from town on Highway 17 west toward Sault Ste Marie and another on Highway 144 north from town. The Chamber of Commerce (tel 673-7133) at 40 Elm West has information as well.

Science North

Opened in the mid-80s, this large participatory science centre (tel 522-3700) at the south-west end of Lake Ramsey has quickly become a major regional attraction. The museum complex is conspicuously housed in two snowflake-shaped buildings built into a rocky outcrop at the lake's edge.

Inside, after you enter by tunnel through the 2½-billion-year-old Canadian Shield, is a collection of exhibits and displays on subjects ranging from the universe to insects, communications to fitness, animal life to rocks. Visitors are welcome to get involved with the displays through the many computers, the hi-tech equipment and the helpful, knowledgeable staff many of whom are from the university.

Some personal highlights were the white quartz crystal displayed under spotlight appearing like a lingam in an Eastern temple, the excellent insect section (how about patting a tarantula?) and lying on a bed of nails. The fitness test is fun but can be humbling as well. They told me if I was an athlete I'd be a golfer. And lastly, the 3-D film presented in the pitch black cave is quite remarkable. Just reach out and grab that fish.

Also in the complex is a cafeteria and a science and book shop. At the swap shop you can trade anything natural for anything else from nature's wonders.

From the dock at the centre boats depart for one-hour cruises of Lake Ramsey.

A ticket is $5 or $8 for this and the Big Nickel which costs $4. Another ticket also includes a bus tour around town. Hours are 9 am to 7 pm daily in summer, till 5 pm in spring and fall and from October to May 11 am to 5 pm, closed Mondays. Buses run from the centre of town to Science North every day. Catch the No 18.

Big Nickel Numismatic Park

Just west of town on Highway 17 West, up on the hill, is the Big Nickel, the symbol of Sudbury. The huge nickel, however, is actually made of stainless steel. At the site there are four other large mounted coins including a penny and a Kennedy memorial. Also in the park is the Big Nickel Mine. You can go down a 20-metre mine shaft, view equipment and see an exhibit of mining science and technology and history. The mine is open every day from mid-May to mid-October and keeps the same hours as Science North. Entrance to the park is $4, and city bus No 940 will get you there. From up at the nickel there's a good view of the surrounding area.

Path of Discovery

From the Big Nickel this 2½-hour bus tour takes visitors on a geological tour around the city on the rim of the Sudbury basin, a 56 km-long, 27 km-wide depression or crater formed two billion years ago. The principal theories for the origin of the basin are volcanic activity or a crashing meteorite. The trip includes a look at the deepest open pit mine in the country. A ticket costs $7 and may be combined with the above two attractions at a small saving.

Inco Metals Tour

Inco (tel 682-2001) runs a free tour of their giant surface operations just west of town, including a look at the mill, smelter and refinery. The tours operate every day in summer from 9 am to 2.30 pm; each is about 1½ hours long.

Falconbridge Nickel Mines

This company (tel 693-2761) also offers free tours which include surface or underground trips at either Strathcona or Falconbridge mine. The mine is more genuine than Big Nickel mine. Phone for information on times and exact location. Tours are held every day from 9.30 am to 1.30 pm. Falconbridge is about 18 km east of town, near the Sudbury airport.

Copper Cliff Museum

On Balsam St in Copper Cliff, where Inco has its operation, this pioneering log cabin with period furnishings and tools is open June to August. Times are 10 am to 5 pm during the week, early afternoons on weekends.

Flour Mill Heritage Museum

This is a similar place – a pioneer house (tel 675-7621) with period implements, artefacts and furnishings from the late 1800s. The museum is at 514 Notre Dame and is named after the three flour silos on this street. Open Monday to Friday 1 to 5 pm.

Slag Pouring

When wind conditions are right, there are good views at night from Highway 144. Tonnes of slag – like molten lava – are poured, lighting up the sky. Another viewing spot is from Highway 17 just west of the Big Nickel.

Event

Voyageur Days is a 10-day summer festival starting about 15 July each year.

Places to Stay

Hostels There's a new *Hostel* (tel 674-0104) in town at 307 Struthers St, not far from downtown or Lake Ramsey. They have 20 beds, open May to September. *G Carpenter* (tel 673-8863) used to run a type of hostel in a private house which had been partially converted into a rooming house; call to see if he is still renting rooms. The location is good, at 278 Lloyd, which is an extension of Elm and leads out of town to Highway 17 for Ottawa. It's past Notre Dame, up the hill a few blocks and on the left. Prices are comparable to hostels and there are kitchen facilities.

Laurentian University (tel 675-1151, ext 300) on Ramsey Lake Rd rents rooms from mid-May to mid-August. There is a cafeteria (closed on weekends), vending machines and use of physical education facilities. The only problem is that the university is away from the downtown, south-east around the other side of Ramsey Lake. The views are good and the area is nice, though. They charge $20/27 for singles/doubles.

The *YWCA* (tel 674-2210) is at 111 Larch St, downtown. They have a few rooms for women only, but they are used mainly as a crisis accommodation. If there are rooms left over they will rent you one for $15. They have a cafeteria. You can't stay at the *YMCA* (tel 674-8315), as it burned down a few years ago and has been rebuilt at 185 Elm St East without accommodation facilities.

There's a *Salvation Army* for men in trouble, on Elm St a few blocks from the corner of Notre Dame.

Bed & Breakfasts There is a bed & breakfast at 212 Elm St (tel 674-2528); the location is very central. It operates during summer only. Single/doubles cost $25/35, with breakfast. There are just two rooms.

Another is the *Red Geranium Guest House* (tel 675-8000), on the corner of Paris and Van Horne. Singles/doubles cost $29/36.

Hotels For budgeters the *Elgin* is a small, almost Asian-looking Chinese place at 196 Elgin, on a strip belonging to the street people. Lots of gritty urban life, grubby hotels and busy lunch counters. But the Elgin is not bad, with singles/doubles for $14/17. The hotel closes at 3 am nightly, 1 am on Sundays.

The *Ledo* (tel 673-7123) is also on Elgin, right opposite the train station. The place is reasonably clean and there are 25 rooms at $18/24 for singles/doubles, although they are more for semi-privates. Ask in the bar about the rooms.

The *Hotel Coulson* (tel 675-6436), downtown at Durham and Larch, is a friendly and better place still in the low budget category. Their rate is $28/32 for singles/doubles. There are two bars downstairs – one with strippers, one with live rock or country music. Both are very popular.

A good central hotel is the *New President* at 99 Elm St W. with rooms ranging from the low $40s to the mid-$60s. Similar but not as good is the *Senator* at 390 Elgin St.

Motels The bulk of Sudbury's accommodation is in motels found around the edges of town.

Highway 17 West is called Lorne near town. A few km from the centre there is a collection of motels. At 965 is the *Canadiana* (tel 674-7585) with the new glassed porch and the black & white sign. Single and double rooms cost $40. The *Imperial* (tel 674-6459) at 1111 Lorne, is a colourfully painted place where breakfast is served. Singles/doubles cost $32/38.

The better motels are found south of town on Highway 69. The *Cedar Motel* (tel 522-3757) is here 16 km south of town. They have singles/doubles for $32/39. The *Brockton Motor Hotel* is five km south on Highway 69. Rooms cost $30 to $32.

There are other motels along the 69 or on Kingsway leading to the 17 East. Along the latter both the *Sorrento* and the *Ambassador* are overpriced but the small and simple *Medallion* is fine at $30 per double.

Camping Sudbury is surrounded by rugged, wooded, lake-filled land. There are quite a few government parks within about 50 km of town. One is *Halfway Lake* on Highway 144 north-west of town. *Windy Lake Park* is on the way. Closer to town, there is a campground on Ramsey Lake at Moonlight Beach.

Places to Eat

As with the accommodation and bars, many of the eating spots are out of the centre. Downtown *Grandma Lee's* on Elm near the corner of Elgin is good for a soup and sandwich and has the distinct advantage of being open on Sundays.

The *Friendly* on Elgin is a typical Canadian working-class spoon. Friendly (like the sign says), cheap, long hours and good for breakfast. *Frank's* is a deli on Durham near Larch. A newer place is *Delights* at 115 Larch with salads, quiches and other light fare. Cheap beer, too.

There is a good cafeteria, the *Richmond Room*, in Kresge's on Elm at Durham. Good-value breakfasts are served from 8 to 11 am, with five choices from $2. There are eight daily specials, for example, roast beef dinner is $4.25. Closed Sunday. At 302 Notre Dame a few blocks from Elm is the *Continental Cafe* with German and European fare, most notably the wiener schnitzel. Open every day. Low dinner prices before 7 pm.

Regent St South (Highway 69 to Toronto) is a commercial strip which has a few restaurants. Among the many offerings are *McDonald's* and *Marconi's*, specialising in Italian and steaks with an extensive salad bar, and *Smitty's Pancakes* where the pancake breakfast is good value. Best is the *Ponderosa Steak House* with lunches from $4 and up and dinner from $6 to $9. Dinner includes a small steak and an all-you-can-eat salad bar. This restaurant chain often has promotional specials. The full meals are good, filling and a bargain.

On Lasalle Boulevard at 1893 is *Teklenburg's*, a good seafood house. Watch for the lighthouse.

Casey's at 1086 Kingsway is a loud, popular restaurant with a very varied menu. Nothing great but there's something to satisfy most people.

The Friday or Saturday newspaper lists the weekend restaurant specials and Sunday brunches.

Nightlife

Pat & Marios, away from the centre at the corner of Lasalle Boulevard and Barry Downe Rd near two big shopping malls is a popular drinking and carousing spot. Fairly dressy.

Downtown, the low-brow *Coulson Hotel* at Durham and Larch draws a mixed crowd for live rock or country music. There is no admission charge, and drink prices are good.

My Place (tel 675-3210) in the Northbury Hotel, 50 Brady St, has commercial rock music nightly. Admission is a few dollars. Women are admitted free on Wednesdays.

Joe's Rock Palace (tel 522-5270) brings in good bands. It's on 69 South.

Getting There & Away

Air Companies flying here are Air Canada and Norontair.

Bus The Greyhound Bus Station (tel 560-1444) is west of town at 200 Falconbridge Highway, about five km from downtown at the corner of Kingsway (which is Highway 17 East).

Eastbound: five a day for North Bay/Ottawa/Montreal

Westbound: five a day for Sault Ste Marie/Winnipeg/Vancouver

Northbound: to Timmins, 6.15 am

Southbound: 10 a day for Toronto, some express.

Fares one-way: Ottawa $39, Sault Ste Marie $24.75, Toronto $34.

Train The VIA Rail station (tel 1-800-268-9520, 673-4771) is at the corner of Minto and Elgin, about a 10-minute walk from the centre of town. It's in the low grey building that is mostly black roof.

North Bay to Ottawa to Montreal: 11.30 pm daily

Thunder Bay to Winnipeg to Vancouver: 8 am daily

Cartier to White River to Chapleau: 9.40 am Tuesday, Thursday and Saturday.

Fares one-way: North Bay – $11, Ottawa – $44, Thunder Bay – $61.

Hitching Highway 17 or Kingsway in town goes east to Ottawa. Drinkwater St runs south from town into Highway 69 south to Toronto. If westbound, head out along Lorne St, which eventually becomes Highway 17 West.

Getting Around

For transit information call 560-1111. The city buses collect on Lisgar beside the post office between Elm and Cedar, right downtown near Eaton's. The No 940 goes to the Big Nickel site, quarter to and quarter after each hour. The No 40 goes to Copper Cliff Mine Smelter site.

Car Rentals Hertz (tel 566-8110) is at 1090 Kingsway Boulevard. Their rate is $130 per week.

Tours are given, free, of the Civic Square – Sudbury's new government building – Monday to Friday. The tours depart from the information desk. There are also tours of Laurentian University.

AROUND SUDBURY

The area around and north of Sudbury is both one of the richest mining districts in the world and a destination for those seeking outdoor adventure and recreation. The fishing, camping and other activities attract visitors from the populated southern regions and the US.

Many of the mines and smelters are

open to the public; the Tourist Office has a 'Mine Guide' of the area. For sportspeople there are endless lodges, camps and guide services – usually fairly costly, especially the fly-in trips.

French River

South of Sudbury, the French River is famous for its fishing. There is also white-water canoeing. One group which organises such trips here and elsewhere is the Voyageur School of Canoeing (tel (705) 932-2131) in Millbrook, Ontario. There is also white-water rafting on the Spanish River.

Killarney Provincial Park

A large forested area about 80 km south-west of Sudbury on the shores of Georgian Bay, this is one of Ontario's three wilderness parks and has few conveniences. It's generally considered to be one of the best for isolated beauty. Access around the park is by canoeing, hiking or skiing. There is excellent scenery of birch and pine forest edged by the La Cloche mountains. There is a campground at the village of Killarney and at Lake George but to really see the park, venture to the interior via 75 km of portages. There's tenting along the way and outfitting at Killarney village. You'll encounter lots of wildlife – and bugs.

Halfway Lake Provincial Park

This is one of the many small, relatively developed parks with camping that surround Sudbury. Within this park are various hiking trails of four, 10 and 34 km. There are several scenic look-outs. The park is about 80 km north-west of town on Highway 144.

Gogama

Continuing north, about half way to Timmons up the 144 at Gogama is the Arctic watershed from which point all rivers flow north to the Arctic Ocean. Did you notice it was getting a bit cool?

TIMMONS

Way up here in northern Ontario is Timmons, the largest city in Canada. In area that is. This notwithstanding it's a small (about 50,000 people) and particularly neat northern town. Originally the centre of the most productive gold mining area in the western hemisphere, the city still acts in the same capacity but the local mines are now silver and zinc. The world's largest zinc mine is here as is Canada's second largest silver mine. One mine is the country's deepest, going down nearly 2.5 km! Together with the rest it makes up well over 2000 km of underground workings in the area. Forestry products are also important in this rough, rugged cold region of primary industry. And, oddly, there are 45 registered trap lines within city limits. Not a bad idea for New York City.

Orientation

Highway 101 passes through the centre of town, where it is known as Algonquin St, on its way west to Lake Superior and east to Quebec. In town the main streets are Third, which runs parallel to the highway, Pine and Cedar. The central core is marked by the brick streets and old-style lampposts.

The rail and bus stations are in the same building on Spruce not far from Algonquin. The Ontario Northern Railway connects from here to Cochrane for the Polar Bear Express.

As in much of north-east Ontario there is a large French population in and around town and native Indians are a significant ethnic group.

Information

The Chamber of Commerce east of town on the the main road has information on industrial tours in the Porcupine-Timmons area and sells the tickets for them.

Gold Mine Tour

The still-worked Pamour Schumacher mine can be visited and includes demonstrations of some of the procedures to get at the gold stuff. Take a sweater; other equipment is supplied. The tour is good and with an introductory video lasts 2½ hours. It's not cheap, though. Get tickets at the Chamber of Commerce. Tours are offered from the end of June to September except Saturdays.

Mill Tour

Tours are offered at The Pulp & Paper Path Mill in Iroquois Falls three times daily, Monday to Friday. The mill is a major newsprint producer.

Ukrainian Museum

This museum at 98 Mountjoy has articles and information on this group in general and on their life in Canada. First arriving in Canada in 1891, many Ukrainians settled across northern Ontario. Admission is free.

Timmons Museum

In South Porcupine at 220 Algonquin East, this museum is good and doubles as an art galley presenting changing exhibits ranging from paintings to masks to performances and more. In the museum section see the prospector's cabin which gives an idea of the life they lead. The history of the area is outlined. Open every day but afternoons only on weekends. Admission is free.

Other

As a resident told me there is really very little to do so people drink. And she wasn't lying. Sports are also popular, but winter sports as there isn't really much of a summer. These two characteristics are common to all northern towns.

Places to Stay

Accommodation is limited and includes a couple of motels on each side of town. The *Matagami Motor Hotel* on the west side gets the job done at $35 for doubles, and there's a restaurant. In town there are a couple of basic hotels and the good *Venture Inn*.

Places to Eat

Pedro's has Mexican and finger foods and is open late on weekends and on Sundays. *Casey's* east of town is a popular general restaurant and place to have a beer.

COCHRANE & MOOSONEE

The Polar Bear Express is the best known line of the small, Ontario Northland rail service. It runs north out of Cochrane, a town of 5000, roughly 100 km north of Timmins. The Polar heads 'down' through northern wilderness to Moosonee on the edge of James Bay, part of vast Hudson's Bay. There is a one-day return trip or a slower, cheaper two-day trip. The express is run primarily for tourists or those in a hurry and leaves early in the morning and returns later the same day, taking 4½ hours each way, allowing for a look around Moosonee and Moose Factory. The slower local train is an odd mix of tourists, Indians, trappers and geologists. Both are run by Ontario Northland and the fare is the same ($32 return) with reservations worth looking into. Trips are run from 21 June to 1 September. Three, four and five-day trips can be booked out of and depart from Toronto.

Moosonee is as far north as most people get in Eastern Canada. There are no roads and it sits near the tundra line. Once there, see the historic sites and the two museums. Boat trips take people around the bay and freighter canoes go to Fossil Island for $12. Fossils over 300 million years old can be found. Sometimes the northern lights are visible.

If you're staying overnight in Moosonee, which is very likely if you take the overnight train, there are a couple of places to stay although they are not cheap. Rooms at the *Polar Bear Lodge* (tel (705) 336-2351) and *Moosonee Lodge* (tel (705) 336-2345) are $52 for singles or doubles. The *Lilly*

Pad (tel 336-2353), is slightly cheaper at $42/50 for singles/doubles, with breakfast. Reservations are a good idea. You may be able to camp; ask about it in Cochrane.

From Cochrane, Ontario Northland also connects south to Timmons, North Bay and other regional towns. In addition there are buses between these points.

Northern Route

West from Cochrane, Highway 11 runs west eventually connecting to Thunder Bay. It's the province's most northerly major road and cuts across rough forest through several mining towns. There are campgrounds along the way.

THE BUDD CAR

This is the local nickname for a one-car train that three times a week makes the trip through northern bush past Chapleau to White River above Lake Superior. It's an interesting eight-hour trip through sparsely populated forest and lakeland. For many villages and settlements – some nothing more than a few buildings and the odd tourist lodge – this is the only access in and out. The train stops and starts as people along the way flag it down, often wilderness seekers with their canoes and gear. A moose or bear on the track also means an unscheduled stop. There's lots of birdlife, too, including hill cranes and Great Blue herons. Sometimes there is even time for a bit of fishing or berry picking if you're stuck waiting for a freight train to pass. The train doesn't make money and once again there is talk of cancelling it.

ESPANOLA

This is the largest centre between Sudbury and Sault Ste Marie and how it got its name is an interesting tale. In about 1750 the Ojibway Indians of the district went on a raid down south in what is now the US but at the time, was under Spanish control. They brought back a captive woman who later taught her children Spanish. When the French explorers arrived on the scene I guess they were a little surprised to hear familiar Spanish being spoken. They called the settlement Espanole which was subsequently anglicised to its present form.

It's a pulp & paper town (EB Eddy, one of Canada's biggies, has a mill here) and also acts as a gateway for the Manitoulin Island ferry. The island can be reached by road on this side but connects to southern Ontario by ferry. (See Tobermory).

There are a couple of standard motels and a few places to grab a bite. White-water rafting is offered on the Spanish River.

SAULT STE MARIE

The Soo, as the city is called, sits strategically where Lake Huron and Lake Superior meet. Once a fur-trading outpost, the city is now an industrial town important as a shipping centre. For here, on St Mary's River, are a series of locks which enable ships to navigate the sea-way system further west into vast Lake Superior. Aside from the busy canal, the steel, pulp & paper and lumber mills are major employers.

The International Bridge connects the city to its twin in Michigan, USA. Going west to Winnipeg it's slightly shorter via Michigan and Duluth than going over the lake, but not as impressive.

With the bridge and the Trans-Canada, the Soo is a convenient stop-over place and acts as a tourist supply centre. I find it the most appealing of the northern cities and there are some fine outdoor possibilities within range to complement it. With a population just shy of 85,000 it's the last big town until Thunder Bay to the west. Sudbury is a few hours east.

Orientation

The approach to the city from the east or west is a long row of eateries, gas stations and motels. Highway 17 North becomes the Great Northern Rd and then Pim St in town. Highway 17 West becomes Wellington, which is the northern edge of the downtown core. If you're passing through, you can use the by-pass to avoid traffic hassles.

The city itself is quite small with pretty much everything on the long, recently upgraded Queen St. South below Queen St is the waterfront area, which also has undergone a fair bit of renovation in the past few years. Several of the sites, the bus station and the Tourist Office are down in this section.

A couple of interesting buildings in town are the imposing Court House in the middle of Queen St and the Precious Blood Cathedral constructed of local red-grey limestone in 1875, and originally a Jesuit missionary.

Queenstown refers to the renovated downtown core.

Information

There is a huge, modern tourist information centre (tel 253-1103) in town on Huron at Queen St West, just north of the International Bridge leading to the USA. Here you can get maps, guides, advice and change money. Open daily in summer. There are also booths on the highway on each side of town.

The Chamber of Commerce, 360 Great

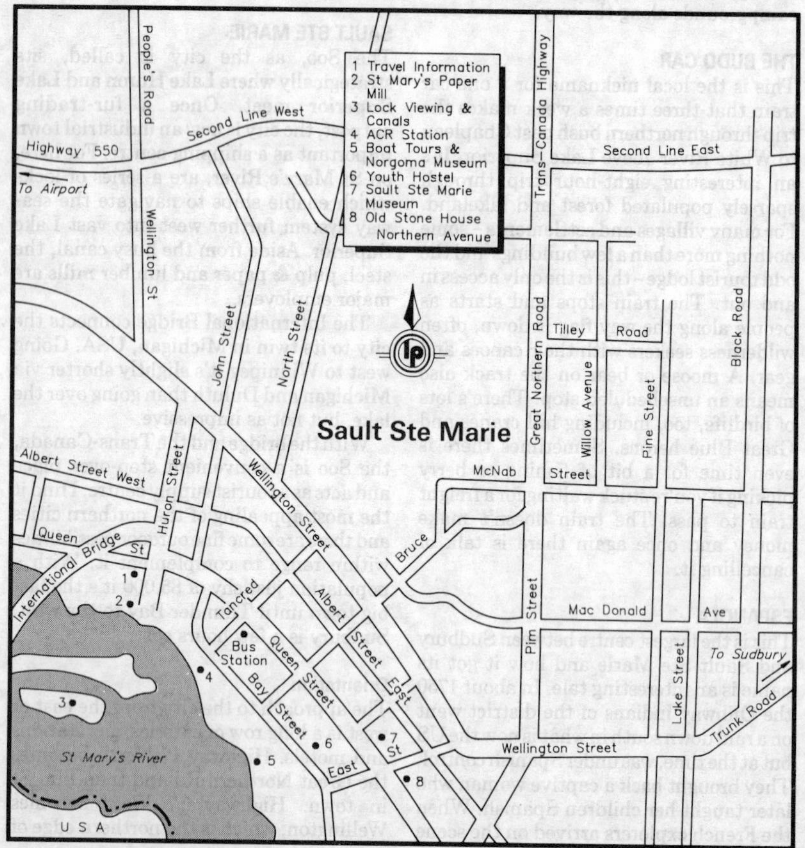

Northern Rd (Highway 17 North, near the large white mushroom-like water tower), also has an information desk. It, however, is closed on weekends.

Locks & Canals

At the south-west corner of downtown, at the bottom of Huron St (by the bridge), are the locks linking Lake Superior to Lake Huron. Joining the two great lakes is the small St Mary's River with its rapids. It is here that the locks were built in 1895, enabling lake freighters to make the journey hundreds of extra km inland.

Lake Superior is about seven metres higher than Huron. The often continuous lake traffic can be watched from a viewing stand or anywhere along the locks, no charge. There are four American and one Canadian (the oldest) lock.

Walking trails from the locks lead to the islands and canals in the river under the International Bridge. The paths, winding through the woods, make a nice retreat and there are views of the shorelines and ships. The oldest canal, built in 1895, is here on the Canadian side and is now used by small pleasure craft. There's a boardwalk, the rapids and picnicking over on Whitefish Island which has been designated a National Historic site. For 2000 years the Ojibway Indians fished the plentiful waters here.

Boat tours (tel 253-9850) of the locks depart from the dock by the Holiday Inn at the foot of Elgin St. Two boats operate several times daily from June through October. The two-hour cruise which includes passing through the Canadian lock costs $7.50 to $8.50 and for my money doesn't offer anything you can't see from shore.

MS *Norgoma*

Moored near the foot of Elgin St in the main waterfront area, this ship, now a museum, was the last one built for passenger use on the Great Lakes. Open daily.

Steel Tours

On my last visit Algoma Corporation had stopped the tours of their plant, Algoma Steel, one of the largest mills in Canada. The tour showed the entire process from raw material to steel and was worth seeing. Ask the Tourist Office if it's been reinstated. The mill is on Queen St West.

St Mary's Paper Mill

This mill, on Huron St on the south-east edge of downtown offers walking tours on Tuesday and Thursday afternoons.

Sault Ste Marie Museum

Housed in an Ontario Heritage building at the corner of Queen and East Sts is a small but well-put-together museum. Various displays depict the exploration, fur trading, lumbering, native people, geology and other aspects of the area. Another section, on the Inuit is very good. In the turn of the century exhibits, the cigarettes for asthma relief are a lark. Open 10 am to 5 pm Monday to Saturday, afternoons only on Sundays. Admission by donation.

Historical Museum

This museum (tel 256-2566) has a small collection of artefacts and curios from the city's past. It's on the second floor of the Pine St Armoury at McDonald and Pine. Admission is free and it's closed Sunday, Monday and holidays.

Bellvue Park

On the water two km east of town along Queen St by the university, this is the city's largest park. There is a small zoo, picnic areas, sports fields and marina.

The Old Stone House

Also known as Ermatinger House (tel 949-1488), this was built in 1814 by an English fur trader and his Ojibway wife. It's the oldest stone house west of Toronto and was where many explorers put up for the night, including the likes of Simon Fraser and Mackenzie. Inside, the house has been restored and contains furnishings from the 1800s. Someone there will answer questions. It's open every day in summer, Monday to Friday other seasons, and admission is free. The museum is on Queen St near the corner of Pine.

Forest Research Centre
The centre (tel 949-9641) at 129 Queen St East runs free tours Monday to Friday at 10 am and 2 pm. The work here, and therefore the tour, is mostly about bugs.

Forest Ecology Trail Also operated by the government forestry service is this self-guided nature trail at the Research Centre. There is an attendant to answer questions.

Mini Aquarium
Down near the locks is a sea lamprey control and research centre. You can see lampreys and some fish. Open Monday to Friday. At night you can still see into the lighted building. Summers only and very mini.

Kinsmen-Crystal Creek Conservation Area
Known locally as Hiawatha Park, this is about a 10-minute drive from Great Northern Rd, north-west of downtown. Stop at the big Hiawatha Lodge from which there are lots of walking trails ranging in length from two to 10 km, a swimming pond and waterfalls in Crystal Creek. Admission is free.

Gros Cap
Twenty-odd km west on Highway 550 is this ridge about 150 metres above Lake Superior and Blue Water Park. Hike up the cliffs for excellent views of Lake Superior where there's usually a ship or two cruising by. Or take Voyageur Trail marked by white slashes which winds up along the ridge edge. Views of St Mary's River and the lake.

Beside the park and parking lot is the *Blue Water Inn*, a great place to eat, and is popular on weekends when the Yugoslavian owner puts on big barbecues. Open in summer only.

Agawa Canyon
This is a wilderness area accessible only by the Algoma Central Railway (ACR) train. The 200-km route due north from town to Hearst goes through a scenic area of mountains, waterfalls, valleys and forests. The one-day return trip gives you a two-hour stopover for a quick walk, fishing or lunch. There are also trips that allow you to stay over in Hearst for as long as you wish. The one-day return is $29. There is a dining car on board. The train departs daily at 8 am from June to October, arriving 3½ hours later in Hearst. The trip is spectacular in the fall when the leaves have changed colour and the forests are brilliant reds and yellows. Normally the colours are at their peak in the last two weeks of September and early October. During winter a snow and ice run is added on weekends only.

The ACR station (tel 254-4331) is at the corner of Bay and Tancred. A second train, primarily for local people rather than visitors short on time, follows the same line, making stops at many tiny communities along the way. It's a much slower trip which might appeal if you wish to meet some of the area's inhabitants.

Places to Stay
Hostels There is a *Youth Hostel* (tel 256-7233) at 452 Bay St near the corner of Elgin. It's in an old house and has room for 20 as well as kitchen facilities. The hostel is close to the bus and train stations. It's open all year, and the charge for members is $8.50.

Hotels There are few hotels and they tend to be either bottom basement or very expensive. The *Beaver Hotel* (tel 256-8411) at 569 St West, west of the International Bridge, falls into the first category and is primarily a bar but the rooms are cheap enough.

At 2 Queen St East is the refurbished

Royal Hotel (tel 254-4321) with an interesting-looking entrance. The location is good and what with the improvements room are now up to $40 to $50 for a double. The bus station is across the street.

Better still is the *Empire Inn* at 320 Bay St, opposite the Algoma Central Railway (ACR) train station, right downtown. All mod cons at $50 to $85 for two.

Motels Sault Ste Marie's location means a lot of people pass through. Consequently, it's one of those places with scores of motels. Most are on Highway 17 either east or west of town, some downtown. Prices vary but average $30 for singles and $35 to $45 for doubles – a little higher than other places, perhaps because the visitor season is short. Generally, the closer to town, the more costly.

The *Shady Pines Motel* (tel 949-4980) out a ways east at 1587 Highway 17 is a good bargain. It's one of the cheapest around and though ugly at the front is very good. Big, modern rooms open out on a treed back yard with picnic tables and barbeques. Singles/doubles cost $25/30.

The *Evergreen Motel* (tel 253-4241) at 1447 Highway 17 East has singles/doubles for $28/32.

The *Travellers Motel* is the white one at 859 Trunk Rd, which is part of Highway 17 East. It has colour TV, and kitchenettes are available. Doubles cost $34 to $50.

The *Holiday* (tel 253-4381) is at 435 Trunk Rd. Singles or doubles are $32.

Lastly, *Journey's End* is good value at $35 a double. Very new, neat and busy. It's part of a Canadian chain. Save a few bucks by taking the second floor rooms. It's on Great Northern Rd north of Northern Avenue, north of downtown.

Camping There are several campgrounds, and they are close to town, if not very rustic. *Rock Shop Campground* is 12 km from town on Highway 17 North (called the Great Northern Rd in town).

KOA (tel 256-2806) tent & trailer park is eight km north of town on Highway 17. Turn west at the flashing amber light, 5th Line. The park is on a river and is equipped with laundry, store and pool.

A little further is *Pointe des Chenes* on St Mary's River, 12 km west on Highway 550 to Highway 565, then 10 km south past the airport to the community park. There are 82 sites.

All these campgrounds cost about $8 to $12 for two people tenting. There are others close to those listed here.

Places to Eat

Most of the restaurants, many of which are the ubiquitous franchises, line the highway but I've listed mainly local establishments found in the city centre. Queen St has a real assortment of good, atmospheric old lunch-counter type beaneries.

The *Coral Coffee Shop*, 470 Queen near Spring is a basic classic. They offer good prices for home-made soups, muffins, chili and the like, and have cheap breakfasts and various specials. It's the only place I've ever seen braille menus.

Recommended is *Country Life* at 326 Queen, a health-food store and vegetarian restaurant. Excellent, inexpensive food without meat or dairy products. Try the avocado/tomato sandwich. They only open between 9 am and 5 pm and are closed on Saturdays.

Tiny *Mike's* with just half a dozen stools at 518 Queen has been serving its very regular customers since 1932. Meals for under $5 at this friendly time warp.

At Queen St East near the corner of East St is the old-fashioned *Mary's Lunch*, which serves a lot of home-made stuff, including bread. Mary is quite a character, too.

Two town specialties are lake trout and whitefish and both turn up on menus all over town. *Vavalas* on the corner of Queen and Dennis at the western end of town offers them as well as various specials like a complete meal with cabbage rolls for $4. Can't beat that, and it's open Sundays.

Moving up the scale, *Aurora's* is a

fancier seafood place where the lobster is said to be good. Italian food is very popular in town and *Soriano's* is well patronised.

Barsanti Small Frye, 23 Trunk Rd (Highway 17 East), is recommended for its basic good food, low prices, friendly waitresses and style. They've been in the business for 60 years and have it right. Open daily, 6 am to midnight.

The *Movieola Cafe* on Great Northern is open late on weekends with finger foods, burgers, Mexican and dancing to pop music.

On Wednesday and Saturday mornings a farmer's market is held in the parking lot at Memorial Gardens Arena downtown.

Getting There & Away

Air There are regular Air Canada and Nordair flights.

Bus The bus station (tel 949-4711), with Greyhound buses, is right downtown at Queen St East and Tancred.

Ottawa: 7.15 am, 5.50 pm – $59
Toronto: four or five a day – $55
Winnipeg: four or five a day – $92
Detroit: 11.55 am
Chicago: 6.30 pm.

Train There is no VIA Rail service in or out of Sault Ste Marie.

Hitching This is a major drop-off point for those thumbing east and west. In summer there are plenty of backpackers hanging around town. If you're going west, remember that from here to Winnipeg is a long way with little to see in between. Nights are cold and rides can be scarce. Try to get a through ride to Thunder Bay (715 km) and then go on to Winnipeg from there.

Getting Around

The city bus terminal is at the corner of Queen and Dennis. The Riverside bus goes from downtown east to Algoma University near Belvedere Park.

The airport is 13 km west on Highway 550, then seven km south on Highway 565. There are airport buses between the airport and the major hotels like the Holiday Inn and the Empire Hotel.

Tours Hiawathaland Sightseeing Tours (tel 253-3235) has a ticket booth next to the Algoma Central Railway depot and runs six different bus tours in and around the city. The double-decker bus city tour is a two-hour trip costing $6. Out-of-town trips stop at various beauty spots and sites. There is a night tour and now also a trip out of town through some of the area's forest land.

AROUND SAULT STE MARIE

Batchawana Bay

North of town along the lake's edge, Batchawana Bay offers beach, swimming (the water is cool) and numerous motels, resorts and cottages for rent. Chippewa Falls here is called the centre-point of Canada and it probably is pretty close. The area has a couple of waterfalls, two provincial parks and what with the shoreline, an enjoyable afternoon can be spent poking around. And you can visit the garbage dump at Camp River in the evening to watch bears waddle in for a snack. It's not a bad idea to stay in your car.

St Joseph Island

St Joseph lies in the channel between Michigan and Ontario, 50 km east of Sault Ste Marie. It's a rural island visited for swimming and fishing and for Fort St Joseph National Park. The fort ruins date from the turn of the 18th century and the new museum displays Indian, military and fur-trade artefacts. A bird sanctuary surrounds the fort. It's reached by a toll-free bridge off Highway 17.

NORTH AROUND LAKE SUPERIOR

From Sault Ste Marie to Thunder Bay the Trans-Canada is one of the few roads cutting through the thinly populated northern Ontario wilds. This huge area is rough, lake-filled timberland. So far, development has been slow to penetrate and the abundant minerals and wildlife remain undisturbed. There are areas where logging operates but these are rarely seen. You may see areas that have suffered a forest fire; these are common each year.

This is a quiet, beautiful part of the country presided over by awesome Lake Superior – once known as Gitche Gumee (Big Sea Water) to the Ojibway Indians. The largest of the five Great Lakes (and one of the world's largest), it's sometimes pretty, sometimes brutal, but always worthy of respect and admiration: a symbol of nature itself. Even today there are disastrous shipwrecks here when the lake gets angry, and according to a Canadian folk song, Superior 'never gives up her dead'.

Several of the Canadian Group of Seven painters were inspired to work here, as was the poet Longfellow. Along the highway are many provincial parks, which make good places to stay to get a feel for the lake and surrounding forest.

LAKE SUPERIOR PROVINCIAL PARK

Highway 17 runs for 80 km through this large natural park north of Sault Ste Marie, so luckily you can't miss it. It's a beautiful park with a few things to see even if you don't stay. The rugged scenery is good, with rivers in the wooded interior and a shoreline with rocky headlands or sandy beach. Several Group of Seven painters worked in the park.

There are three campgrounds, short and long hiking trails usually accessible from the highway, fishing, and seven canoe routes. Naturalists give talks and guided walks. A variety of mammals live in the park, including the odd bear.

At Agawa Bay, see the Indian pictographs on the shoreline rocks which are believed to commemorate a crossing of the lake. There is no charge. Note the crevices in the rocks along the path. Further along, stop at Sand River and walk down to the beach. Though the water is cold, the beautiful sandy beach, long and empty, looks like it's been lifted from a Caribbean island.

Those who want access to the eastern side of the park can catch a train at Frater at the southern end of the park or at Hawk Junction east of Wawa and north of the park.

Distance hikers and canoeists should cross their fingers for good weather – this is one of the wettest areas in Ontario. Trails are often enveloped in mist or fog, which lends a primeval, spooky air to the woods. As always, interior camping is a few dollars less than the campgrounds with their facilities.

WAWA

This small mining centre has a big, bad reputation for hitch-hiking. The story is told of one man who got stuck here waiting so long for a lift that he finally had to get a job. He ended up meeting a woman, getting married – and still lives here. As traffic has picked up over the years and the locals have mellowed, things aren't like they were but it's still better to get a ride right through. There is nothing down at the highway here and it can be a cold place at night, even in midsummer. A lot of cars have passengers by the time they get here.

Thousands of geese stop off here during migration; see the huge steel statue of a goose at the edge of town.

CHAPLEAU

Chapleau is a small logging and outdoors centre inland from Wawa. There are numerous provincial parks in the area, three within 80 km. Missinaibi Lake Park is in the middle of Chapleau Game Reserve, the largest in the western hemisphere. You can go wilderness camping or fishing here. The Tourist Offices around the area have a listing of canoe routes. There are 12 trips ranging from one to 14 days with five to 47 portages. The longest one is a river & lake circle route going through part of the reserve; it's good for viewing moose.

WHITE RIVER

Back on the Trans-Canada, this is called the coldest place in Canada, with temperatures recorded as low as -50°C. Get your picture taken near the thermometer.

PUKASKWA NATIONAL PARK

Find out how tough you are. There is no road into this park, (pronounced 'puk-a-saw') and access is by hiking or boat. From Heron Bay off the highway near Marathon is a small road which goes to the edge of the park. The park officially opened in 1983 and now has a small, simple campground. There is also the old 68-km coastal hiking trail with primitive camping spots along the way. The terrain is rough but beautiful, and the weather is very changeable, switching from sun to storm quickly. The interior offers some challenging canoe runs.

QUIMET CANYON

Not far west of Thunder Bay, north of the highway on gravel roads, is this small park with a great canyon 150 metres both wide and deep. The walls on either side of the chasm are virtually perpendicular. Recently, fences and viewing stations have been built, preventing you from getting so close to the edge that you hear your heart pounding, but the views are better now. The canyon is definitely worth a quick stop. Officially, there's no camping.

THUNDER BAY

Known as 'The Lakehead,' Thunder Bay on the northern shores of Lake Superior is an amalgam of the two towns of Fort William and Port Arthur. Despite being so far inland, Thunder Bay is a major port and is as far as ships using the St Lawrence Seaway get westward. The main cargo switching hands here is prairie wheat going to market. The docks make the city the world's largest grain handler.

The city, halfway between Sault Ste Marie and Winnipeg – 720 km to either one – is a good stopoff point. The town itself may not hold you long, but the setting is scenic and it makes a handy centre for experiencing some of the things to see and do in northern Ontario's rugged timberland.

The first Europeans here were a couple of Frenchmen who reached the area is 1662. For hundreds of years this was a fur-trading settlement. In 1869 the Dawson was begun, the pioneer's road westward. In 1882, the CP railway arrived, and soon after the prairie's first shipment of wheat was heading east.

Coming into town from the east on the Trans-Canada, you'll pass mountains and see the city at the edge of the bay. Along the shoreline are pulp mills and grain elevators. Out in the harbour, ships are moored, and beyond is a long rock formation and an island or two. The unusually shaped mass of rock offshore is important to Indian legend and is said to be the Great Spirit, Nana-bijou, who turned to stone after a promise to him was broken. Today the formation is known as the Sleeping Giant.

Orientation

The city still has two distinct downtown areas which are connected principally by Fort William Rd and Memorial Avenue. The area between the two is pretty much a no-man's-land of fast food outlets, the large Inter City Shopping Mall and little else. Port Arthur (Thunder Bay North), closer to the lakeshore, appears more prosperous, is more modern and generally more attractive. The main streets are Red River Rd and Cumberland St. Port Arthur Landing, not far from the Pagoda tourist booth off Water St, is redeveloped waterfront and includes parkland, the marina, fishing charters, a small art gallery and restaurant, and the old rail station. This half of Thunder Bay has a sizeable Finnish population with several restaurants on Bay St.

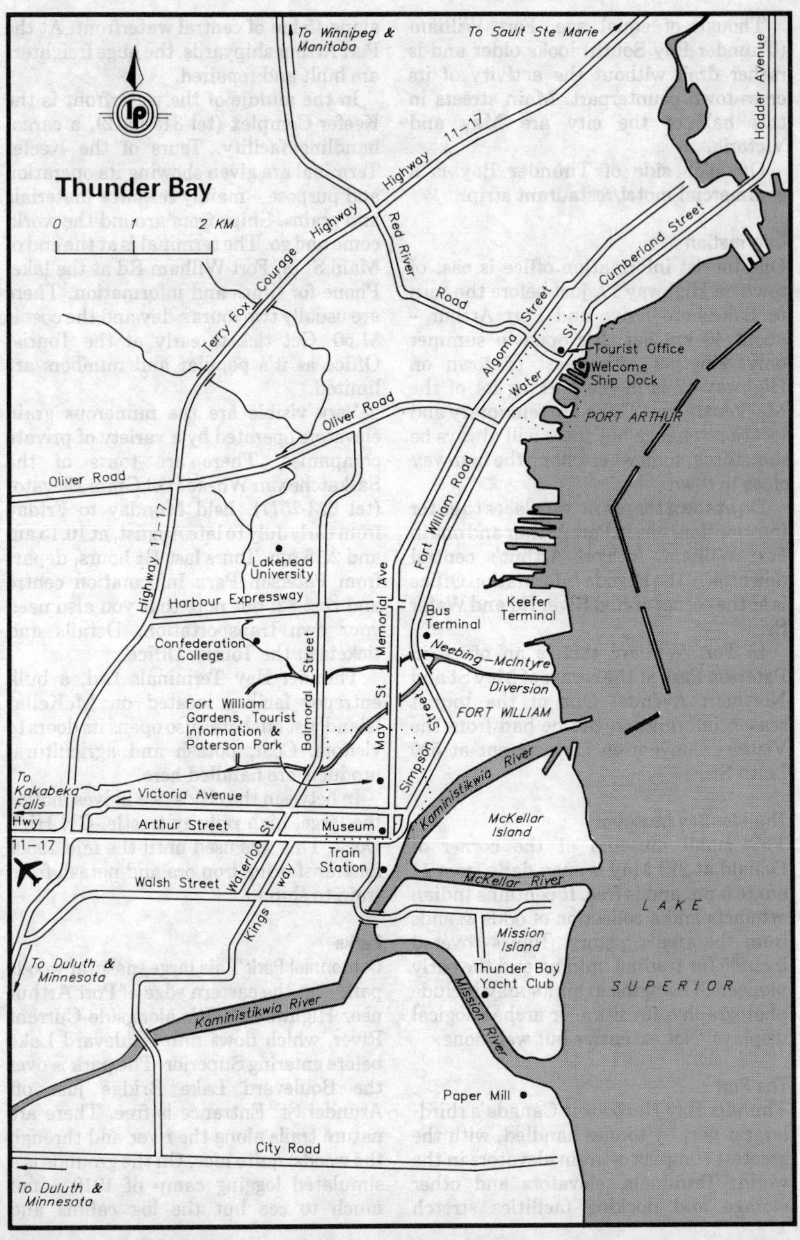
Thunder Bay
0 1 2 KM
To Winnipeg & Manitoba
To Sault Ste Marie
Highway 11-17
Terry Fox Courage Highway
Red River Road
Hodder Avenue
Cumberland Street
Algoma Street
Water St
Tourist Office
Welcome Ship Dock
PORT ARTHUR
Oliver Road
Oliver Road
Fort William Road
Highway 11-17
Lakehead University
Harbour Expressway
Memorial Ave
Bus Terminal
Keefer Terminal
Confederation College
Balmoral Street
Neebing-McIntyre Diversion
Fort William Gardens, Tourist Information & Paterson Park
May St
Simpson Street
FORT WILLIAM
Kaministikwia River
To Kakabeka Falls
Victoria Avenue
Hwy 11-17
Arthur Street
Waterloo St
Museum
Train Station
McKellar Island
Walsh Street
Kings way
McKellar River
LAKE
Mission Island
To Duluth & Minnesota
Thunder Bay Yacht Club
SUPERIOR
Kaministikwia River
Mission River
Paper Mill
City Road
To Duluth & Minnesota

Though of equal age, Fort William (Thunder Bay South) looks older and is rather drab without the activity of its cross-town counterpart. Main streets in this half of the city are May and Victoria.

On each side of Thunder Bay is a commercial motel/restaurant strip.

Information

One tourist information office is east of town on Highway 17, just before the turn to Lakeshore Drive and Port Arthur – about 40 km out. It's open in summer only. Another office east of town on Highway 17 is in the parking lot of the Mackenzie Inn. These are temporary and locations change but there will always be something, somewhere along the highway close to town.

Downtown there are two places to go for information: one in Port Arthur and one in Fort William. In Port Arthur's central downtown, the Pagoda Information Office is at the corner of Red River Rd and Water St.

In Fort William there's an office in Paterson Park at the corner of May St and Northern Avenue. Out of the tourist season information can be had from the Visitors Convention Department at 520 Leith St.

Thunder Bay Museum

This small museum at the corner of Donald at 219 May is open daily from 11 am to 5 pm and is free. It contains Indian artefacts and a collection of odds & ends from the area's history. Topics covered include fur trading, mining and the early pioneers. Changing exhibits may include photography, furniture or archaeological displays. Not extensive but well done.

The Port

Thunder Bay Harbour is Canada's third-largest port by tonnes handled, with the greatest complex of grain elevators in the world. Terminals, elevators and other storage and docking facilities stretch along 45 km of central waterfront. At the Port Arthur shipyards, the huge freighters are built and repaired.

In the middle of the waterfront is the Keefer Complex (tel 345-6812), a cargo-handling facility. Tours of the Keefer Terminal are given showing its operation and purpose – mainly resource materials and grains. Ships from around the world come and go. The terminal is at the end of Main St off Fort William Rd at the lake. Phone for times and information. There are usually two tours a day and the cost is $1.50. Get tickets early at the Tourist Office as it's popular and numbers are limited.

Very visible are the numerous grain elevators operated by a variety of private companies. There are tours of the Saskatchewan Wheat Pool Grain Elevator (tel 623-7577), held Monday to Friday from early July to late August, at 10.15 am and 2.15 pm. Tours last 1½ hours, depart from Paterson Park Information centre and cost $2, but note that you also need your own transportation. Details and tickets at the Tourist Office.

Thunder Bay Terminals Ltd, a bulk entrepot facility located on McKellar Island just offshore, also opens its doors to visitors. Coal, potash and agricultural products are handled here.

In between the city's two halves, notice the large, high railway trestle, CN High Dock. This was used until the mid 1980s for transferring iron ore and potash from train to ship.

Parks

Centennial Park This large, natural woods park is at the eastern edge of Port Arthur near Highway 17. It's alongside Current River, which flows into Boulevard Lake before entering Superior. The park is over the Boulevard Lake Bridge just off Arundel St. Entrance is free. There are nature trails along the river and through the woods: quite nice. On the grounds is a simulated logging camp of 1910 – not much to see but the log cabins and buildings themselves are good. A small museum has a cross-cut section of a 250-year-old white pine tree on display. Various dates in history are marked at the corresponding growth rings. It's amazing to think what has gone on while this tree quietly kept growing. You'll find canoes and boats for rent here as well. Up the road from the park is the Bluffs Scenic Lookout for a view of the lake and shore.

International Friendship Gardens This good-sized city park is off Victoria Avenue near Waterloo. Various local ethnic groups such as the Finns and Hungarians have erected monuments and statues. There is a pond and some flowers but no extensive gardens. The park is west of downtown Fort William on Victoria Avenue.

Waverly Park Another city park, free summer concerts are held here on Wednesday evenings and Sunday afternoons in summer at the Rotary Thundershell.

Thunder Bay Art Gallery
This gallery at Confederation College campus collects, preserves and displays contemporary art by Canadian Indians. Works include paintings, prints, masks, sculptures and more. There are displays from the permanent collection as well as travelling exhibits which are usually by non-native artists. Norval Morrisseau, perhaps Canada's best-known Indian painter, was born in Thunder Bay and some of his work is on view. Admission is free, and the gallery is open Tuesday to Thursday noon to 8 pm, Friday to Sunday noon to 5 pm. The city bus to the campus will take you there.

Biloski Site
This Indian archaeological site was discovered in 1984 when the Cherry Ridge subdivision was being developed for new houses. The site is just west of Highway 11/17 by the shoreline. Many of the tools and weapons found are on display, along with explanations in the Thunder Bay Museum.

Boat Cruises
The *Welcome* ship trips around the harbour for two hours for $9. I would say, though, you'd do better to pay a dollar extra and cruise up the Kaministikwia River to Fort William. From there the bus trip back is included in the cruise price, although entrance to the park is not. The half & half method can be done in either direction. Neither gives you a long time at the fort but you can always catch the city bus back when you're ready. Food and drinks are available on board. The ship departs the Port Arthur Marina at the foot of Red River Rd. For details phone 344-2512.

Old Fort William
Some of the city's best-known attractions are some distance from downtown, as is this, the old fort settlement (tel 577-8461). The historic site is west of town, not far past the airport off Broadway Avenue. City buses go to the fort from the terminal in either William or Arthur every hour; the last bus from the fort leaves at 5.45 pm. Or see 'Boat Cruises' above for a different way to get to the fort.

This is not one of the best Canadian historic sites or re-created forts but there are some good displays and woodwork, and it seems each year there are expansions and good new ideas. Fort William from 1803 to 1821 was the headquarters of the North West Furtrading Company. In 1821, with much haggling and hassling, the company was absorbed into its chief rival, the Hudson's Bay Company. The fort re-creates some aspects of these early fur-trading days through buildings, tools, artefacts and documents. Workers will answer questions. Good home-made and cheap food is available in the fort's canteen. Entrance is $4.25, $2 for students, but throughout the summer are free special-event days. Open mid-May to early October from 10 am.

Kakabeka Falls

The waterfall is about 40 metres high, and is set in a provincial park 25 km west of Thunder Bay off Highway 17. It's most impressive in spring when the water in the river is at its highest. Sometimes the water flow is very small, as it's dammed off for power. Most people go to take pictures at the falls but the park itself isn't bad. There's camping, swimming at small beaches, and picnicking.

Mount Mackay

Mount Mackay is the tallest mountain in the area's north-western chain, rising to 350-odd metres. It offers excellent views of Thunder Bay and environs. However, the lookout is on an Ojibway reservation and, in keeping with the Indians' new-found assertiveness, they charge $4 per car. It's not really worth it. The lookout is south-west of Fort William. Take Edward St to the City Rd on the west side of Kaministikwia River and follow signs.

Amethyst-Searching

Amethyst, a variety of quartz, is a purple semi-precious stone found in many areas around Thunder Bay. It is mined from veins which run on or near the earth's surface, so looking for the stone and digging it out are relatively easy. Within about 50 km of the city are six sites where you can go looking for your own. Each site has some pre-found samples for sale if you should strike out. Shops in town sell jewellery and finished souvenir items made of the purple quartz. There are many superstitions surrounding amethyst, including the early Greek one that it prevents drunkenness. The Greeks often fashioned wine cups from the stone.

Two of the mines are off East Loon Lake Rd east of Thunder Bay off Highway 17. East Loon is east of the 587 south. Thunder Bay Amethyst Mines is a huge property where entry is $1. Nearby is N Dzuba's, which is free. It's run by a friendly and unpredictable old man and his wife. Check out the huge chunk in the parking area. You pay by the quality of what you find and want to keep. The road to the sites from the Trans-Canada is long, rough and steep in places. In town, a shop at 122 May St sells some stuff produced with the finished stone – mostly pretty tacky. The stone generally looks better raw. The Tourist Office will be able to direct you to other area mines.

Terry Fox Courage Highway

A segment of the Trans-Canada Highway east of town has been named after the young Canadian who in the early 1980s, while dying of cancer, attempted to run across Canada to raise money for cancer research. After having one leg amputated, he made it from Newfoundland to Thunder Bay, raising millions and becoming a national hero before finally succumbing. A monument sits at a lookout just east of town.

Chippewa Park

At the edge of Lake Superior, just beyond the southern end of Fort Willam at the foot of City Rd, Chippewa Park has a beach, picnic and camping sites, a small amusement park and some wildlife.

Sibley Provincial Park

This is a larger, more natural and scenic park further out and on the east side of the city. The scenery is good – woods, hills, shoreline. There are some good walks, one out along the top of the Sleeping Giant rock formation, where there are views. You can get details on this Indian legend at the park. Activities include swimming, fishing and camping. The park makes a good stop if you don't want to go into town to sleep. Note that it is further in off the Trans-Canada than it looks on the map. Last trip in just after dark we saw three foxes at the road's edge, and there are moose in the park.

Tours

Forty-five minute historical walking tours

are available daily (not Sunday) from the Pagoda tourist booth.

In the booth pick up a folder on a self-guided architectural walking tour of Port Arthur. The firehall, some churches, various houses of note and other buildings are pointed out and described.

Bayway (tel 345-3673) offers city and area bus tours which may include the falls or a visit to an amethyst mine. All buses depart from the Pagoda. One tour goes to Quimet Canyon which otherwise is difficult to reach without a car. Phone for information and prices.

Great Lake Forest Products (tel 475-2641), one of the city's largest employers, shows visitors the paper-making process in their mill. Tours are free and start at at 9 am and 1 pm in June, July and August – times may vary according to demand. Follow Highway 61 to Broadway Avenue; turn left and then right at the mill.

Summer tours are also offered of the Thunder Bay Thermal Generating Station. Ontario Hydro operates this coal fired electricity-generating station on Mission Island over Jackknife Bridge. The 1½-hour tours run through July and August on Tuesdays and Fridays and must be booked in advance on 623-2701. They won't take you if you're wearing sandals or high heels. The station is on 108th Avenue.

See the Port section for details of tours there.

Activities & Events

Canoeing Wildwaters Outfitters at 119 North Cumberland St offer various canoe expeditions of varying lengths and costs. They include wildlife, photography, fishing and a special trip for women only. With everything included, the cost is about $50 a day. Some white-water trips are offered as well.

From Thunder Bay to Kenora there are almost limitless fishing camps and lodges. Many people fly in to remote lakes. Tourist Offices will have more information. I'm sure they're nice, but ask me if I can afford them. There are also places for canoe rentals.

Jamboree This is an annual sailing event in the harbour with festivities centred around the Marina at Prince Arthurs Landing, at the waterfront in Prince Arthur.

Sauna You can get a sauna at Kanga's (tel 344-6761), 379 Oliver Rd. Finnish saunas are popular in the region. At Kanga's there are also some Finnish eats and good desserts.

Places to Stay

Hostels There is a good youth hostel here called *Longhouse Village Hostel* (tel 983-2042), which is a member of the Canadian Association. It's a fair way from town – 22 km east – but worth it. Most beds are in a big log house, co-ed. Other rooms for women only are in the main house. The couple who run it, Lloyd & Willa Jones, spent six years as missionaries and Baptist teachers in Borneo. You'll see mementoes all over the place. The Jones are knowledgeable about things to do around Thunder Bay and there is swimming and walking nearby. Basic food is available and you can use the kitchen. Beds cost $8 for members, $10 for non-members. Camping on the lawn is $4. The hostel is on Lakeshore Drive. From the highway head down Mackenzie Station Rd, and it's near the corner – the only hostel I've seen with an electric sign. Note that there are no buses into town, but see the Getting Around section. Open all year.

YM-YWCA has no beds for rent.

There are places available in the *Lakehead University Residence* (tel 345-2121) from 1 May to 20 August. Singles/doubles cost $18/28, and $16/26 for students. The university is at 855 Oliver Rd between the two downtown areas and slightly west. The cross-town city bus goes past the campus in both directions.

There's a *Salvation Army* on Cumberland around the 500 numbers. It's free to men for a night or two if you're hard up.

Bed & Breakfasts Also cheap are the bed & breakfast places run from people's homes. They generally cost around $25 to $33 for doubles, with breakfast. Unfortunately, most are out of the downtown areas, and some are on farms. These tend to change quickly, and the Tourist Office should have a fairly accurate picture.

Near downtown Fort William, below May on Dease at Highway 213, *Holly Rigby* (tel 622-2470) has two rooms for rent. *Mrs Paul's* (tel 623-1807) at 723 Catherine St is not far from the fort and airport. Again, there are two rooms and the breakfast is substantial. Singles cost $30.

North-east of downtown Port Arthur, near the Expressway, is *Zena Whitlums* (tel 344-1358) at 120 David St. They have two doubles and one single.

Between the two downtown areas is the *Galbraiths'* (tel 344-6887) at 215 Winnipeg Avenue. It's just above Memorial Avenue, off Beverly. Accommodation is three double rooms.

The *Prince Arthur*, 17 North Cumberland, is a renovated older place with views over the lake. Rooms are large and the dining room very good. The place is a definite splurge – it's expensive.

Hotels For a reasonable price in Port Arthur there is the *Shoreline Motor Hotel* on Cumberland at the corner of Camelot. It's good, very central and good value at $32/36 for singles/doubles.

I guess the best place in town is the nearby *Ramada Inn* on Cumberland at Red River, right by the Tourist Office. It's large with several places to eat or drink.

Over in Fort William, which is more convenient for the airport, train and bus stations, a decent cheap place is the *Intowner* (tel 623-1565) at Arthur East and Brodie South. There is an adjoining restaurant and you can use the pool in the health club. Singles cost $31.50.

Best of the skid-row specials is the *Hotel Empire*, with singles/doubles $15/22 plus $2 for the key. A snack bar and a drinking bar are downstairs.

Motels Most of the moderate-priced accommodation is in the newer motel strips. There are two areas of heavy motel concentration, one on each side of the city, and there are a few pretty good places in between the two downtowns along Memorial Drive. The *Circle Inn* and the *Sleeping Giant Motor Hotel* are here with 50 rooms each and prices from $34 to $40. The *Venture Inn* is close by and a little more upmarket.

The motel area in Port Arthur is on and around Cumberland. It heads out to Hodder Avenue, which then leads to the Expressway or Highway 17 east. The motels are mainly found near the grain elevators along the lakefront. Cumberland leads right into the downtown area of Port Arthur.

The *Strathcona* (tel 683-8351) at 546 Hodder is a very small, well-kept blue & white place. Singles or doubles range from $24 to $28.

The *Hodder Avenue Motel* (tel 683-8414) at 321 Hodder is a nice place. Singles/doubles are $22/26.

The *Lakeview* is the pale yellow place at 391 Cumberland on the left-hand side approaching town. Singles and doubles are $30; there's cable TV.

The other motel district is along Arthur St heading out of town from downtown past the airport. There are a few motels side-by-side on Kingsway Avenue, off Arthur, but these are priced higher than they're worth.

The *Ritz Motel* (tel 622-4112) is at 2600 Arthur St East. Rooms cost from $38 to $47 in this red brick building close to town.

Camping There are a couple of places close to town, east of Port Arthur, just off Highway 17. Between Hodder Avenue and the Youth Hostel on Lakeshore Drive is *Wild Goose Park*, about 20 km from the city. Camping at this pleasant, quiet spot costs just $3.50.

Nearby, off Highway 17 at the junction of Highway 800, coming from the east on the Trans-Canada, is a *KOA* campground. It's about $8 for a site. Look for the road to the Mount Baldy ski area: it's nearby on the opposite side of the road. Continuing west on Highway 17 past Hodder Avenue on the right is the *Towbridge Falls* camping site.

There is also camping at Chippewa Park on the lake not far north of downtown Fort William at the end of City Rd.

Places to Eat

Port Arthur The *Appolon Restaurant* on Red River Rd not far from Cumberland has good-value daily specials. Complete standard meals run about $5 and they serve cheap breakfasts too.

On Red River is *Grandma Lee's*, a pretty fair soup & sandwich shop. Also in this area is the *Prospector*, a steak and roast beef house serving meat from a local cattle ranch. Steaks are $14 to $16. It's on Cumberland at the corner of Park Avenue.

The *Hoito*, 314 Bay St, is a Finnish place set up about 60 years ago. It is known for its home-made food served in plain surroundings. They give large portions and offer a smorgasbord. There are a couple of similar places in this Finnish neighbourhood.

The shopping malls are also a source of restaurants. *Doodles* in the Keskus Mall, Red River Rd, serves mainly crepes and salads – not bad. Also here, the *Office* is a pub with inexpensive meals and live music at night. Inter-city Mall has a cheap food fair.

On the corner of Red River and Court St, *Kresge's*, a Woolworth's-type variety store, has a lunch counter offering simple, very cheap meals.

Fort William The *Pastry Pedlar* at the corner of May St and George has croissants, pastries, muffins and sandwiches. Good and inexpensive. Closed Sundays. The *Columbia Grill & Tavern* at 123 May St is a good basic place, fine for a cheap breakfast and you can get a beer here, too.

Trifons Pizza & Spaghetti House on May and Mills sells pizza half-price on Wednesdays.

Bombay Bistro Club is a small place at 219 Brodie offering various Indian-like dishes. It's a trendy sort of place and therefore a little pricey. The *Polish Legion* at 730 Simpson St has a small coffee shop where they serve up large portions at low prices. This kind of food will hold you a while.

Victoria Mall or the Victoria Centre right in the centre of town has a food fair. *Cardigan's Bar & Grill* is new at the corner of Donald and Syndicate. There's pizza next door at *Button's*.

There are numerous spots offering hamburgers and similar fare on Memorial Avenue, which links the two parts of the city. Best is *Ponderosa Steak House* where full meals are about $8 with an all-you-can-eat salad bar. They serve fish as well.

Entertainment

Expressway in the Landmark Inn, corner of the Expressway and Red River Rd, brings in rock groups from around the province. They also have DJ dancing. Admission varies.

The *Innplace* is another motor hotel bar. It's located in the Inntowner, Arthur St at Brodie. Entertainment is live commercial pop-rock; shows change frequently, as does the cover.

The *Elephant & Castle* in the Intercity mall is a pub sort of place. *Kelsey's* at the top of Red River Rd near the highway is a popular, dressier place.

There is a summer theatre programme in Chippewa Park, called Moonlight Melodrama.

Getting There & Away

Air Lakehead Airport is west of town, about 15 minutes' driving, at the junction of Highway 17 (Trans-Canada) and Neebing Avenue.

Air Canada (tel 623-3313) and Nordair (tel 577-6461) offer flights to:

Winnipeg – $170, youth standby $76

Toronto – $210, youth standby $94.

Norontair (tel 623-3313) services the region and other northern portions of the province.

Bus The Greyhound Bus Terminal (tel 345-2194) is in Fort William at 815 Fort William Rd. It's not far east of the downtown area, toward the lake.

Winnipeg and Calgary: 12.30 am, 4.40 am, 8.40 am, 9.40 am, 2.45 and 10.30 pm

Sault Ste Marie and Toronto: 3.25 am, 6.20 am, 10.50 am, 7.35 and 10.35 pm

Sudbury: 6.45 pm.

Fares one-way: Winnipeg $46, Sault Ste Marie $63, Toronto $91 and Sudbury $86.

Train The VIA terminal is in the CPR Passenger Station in Fort William. It's on Syndicate just south of Arthur St near City Hall. For information call 623-4742. There is one trip daily to Winnipeg ($60), Toronto ($93) and Ottawa ($98).

Road From Thunder Bay, it's 720 km to Sault Ste Marie, 731 km to Winnipeg and 315 km to Duluth, Minnesota, USA.

A circular tour of northern Ontario can be made by car from Thunder Bay by backtracking to Lake Nipigon and following Highway 11, the most northerly provincial route, through Geraldton, Kapiskasing and returning south via Timmins, Sudbury or North Bay. Provincial parks are found at regular intervals along Highway 11. Towns are small.

Hitching Westbound head out to Arthur St; the airport bus will take you to a good spot. If you're eastbound, anywhere on the Highway 17 is OK. For $2.50 the eastbound Greyhound bus will take you to the edge of town.

Getting Around

Airport Transport An airport bus departs from the local city bus terminal, beside the Paterson Park Tourist Office (in Fort William at the corner of May St and Miles). One leaves every 20 minutes until 6 pm, then every 40 minutes. The ride takes about 15 minutes.

A city bus, the Arthur Route, also goes from town to the airport. It's much slower but costs less. Catch it anywhere on Arthur St.

Bus There is a good city transit (bus) system which covers all areas of the city and costs 80c. For information call 344-9666, extension 189.

In Fort William the terminal for the local buses is across the street from the Tourist Office at the corner of May St on Miles. To get to the Port Arthur end of town take the Memorial bus on May St, or the Mainline bus along Fort William. Same thing going the opposite way.

In Port Arthur the terminal is at Water St and Camelot, just below Cumberland by the waterfront. The Pagoda Tourist Office is next door.

The Cross-town bus from either end goes to the university. The Neebing bus goes to Old Fort William from the Fort William terminal.

For the Youth Hostel there are no city buses, so take the eastbound Greyhound bus from the terminal. For $2.50 they'll take you to Lakeshore Drive – or better, to Mackenzie Station Rd, which leads off the highway. From there it's a good walk straight to the hostel.

City buses go to and from the motel and fast-food strips on both sides of town.

Car Rentals Avis (tel 577-5766) is at 1475 Walsh St West. They charge $25.95 a day with 200 free km. Additional km are 15c each.

Budget Rent-a-Car (tel 577-7571) is at

1220 Commerce St. Rent-a-Wreck is at 522 Memorial Drive.

There are several agencies with desks at the airport.

WEST OF THUNDER BAY

Quetico Provincial Park

A huge wilderness park joined to Superior Park in Michigan, Quetico is very undeveloped for the most part but has one major organised campground. It offers excellent canoeing, primarily for those wanting peace and quiet. The park is a maze of lakes and rivers, with lots of wildlife and some Indian pictographs. It can be accessed from several points. There are outfitters and maps available in and around the park.

Atikoken This is the supply town for the park and it has two small museums.

There's lots of camping in the district but you really need topographic maps.

Between here and Ignace lies White Otter Lake, site of White Otter Castle, a well known local oddity, built in 1904 by a Scottish immigrant, Jimmy McOuat. He did it all by himself and nobody knows why, since he was a bachelor and it's a huge timber place with a four-storey tower.

Fort Francis

Situated on Rainy Lake opposite International Falls, Minnesota, this is a busy American border-crossing point. Both sides are popular outdoor destinations with countless lakes, cottages, fishing, camping, etc. In town a paper mill can be visited. A causeway across Rainy Lake toward Atikokan offers great views of the lake and area. North Highway 71 connects to Kenora and Winnipeg.

Kenora

Kenora is the closest town of any size to the Manitoba border. It is a pulp & paper town and centre for much of the tourist activity in the area, which is mainly fishing and hunting. The setting is a nice one on the Lake of the Woods.

Cruises of the lake are available and last two hours. There's an international sailing regatta in late July, in and around the 14,000 islands in the lake. Provincial parks are nearby. A folk festival is held each year in early July.

Many Indians still live in the area; they hand pick the Canadian wild rice which grows locally, which is $10 a pound and delicious.

Manitoba

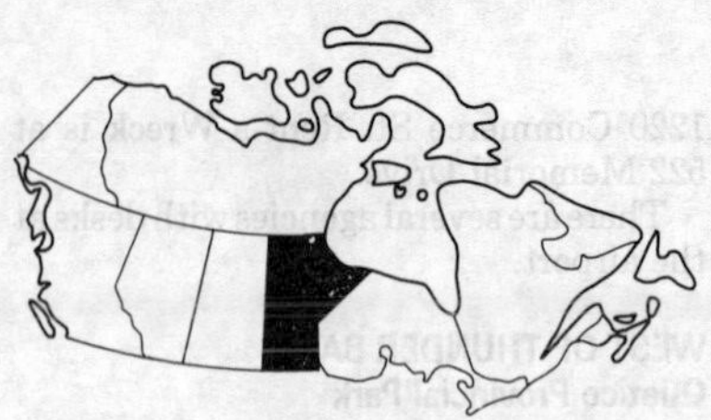

Entered Confederation: 15 July, 1870, the fifth province
Area: 650,090 square km
Population: 1,026,000

The name Manitoba probably comes from the Algonkian Indians. 'Manito' means 'great spirit'; and in Lake Manitoba there is a strait where the water hits the limestone edges, making an odd echoing sound; the Indians associated this sound with the 'great spirit' and named the spot 'Manito Waba', which means Manito Strait. Manito Waba became Manitoba.

The province is the first of the three prairie provinces as you head westward. The southern half is low and flat, the western edge best for farming. Much of the land is forested and dotted with lakes and rivers. The Canadian Shield, which covers about half the country, cuts across northern Manitoba, making it rocky, hilly forest.

The winters are long and cold but the summers can be hot. Generally there is a decrease in temperature from south-west to north-east. There's about 130 cm of snow a year.

Manufacturing is the main source of income; food processing and clothing factories are also important.

Wheat is the most important farm product, with various other grains and cattle following closely. In the northern Shield area there are good deposits of gold, copper, nickel and zinc.

Fishing and hunting attract many visitors to this province, especially Americans. A map indicating all the campgrounds in Manitoba is available from the Tourist Office, as well as an excellent guide detailing canoe routes around the province (including some wilderness trips). In addition there is a farm vacation programme.

A little novelty you'll notice if you enter the province by road is the 'put your garbage in orbit' signs, referring to the spherical containers at the highway's edge.

Winnipeg

Winnipeg sits in the geographical centre of the country but it feels very much like a western town. Although Toronto has the reputation, I'd say Winnipeg seems like the most American city in Canada. Actually, it is often compared to Chicago – its mid-western, grain handling, transportation counterpart. Winnipeg also feels much bigger than it is, although it is the fourth largest Canadian city at 650,000. About half of Manitoba's population lives here.

The Cree Indians called the area 'Winnipee' or 'Muddy Water'. They shared the land Winnipeg now occupies with the Assiniboines, before La Verendrye, the first white trader, arrived in 1738. In the early 1800s the area was the centre of rivalry between the Hudson's Bay Company and the North-West Company. In 1812 Lord Selkirk led Scottish and Irish immigrants to the first permanent settlement. Later Fort Garry was built. The railway arrived in 1881, bringing people and industry.

The 1970s saw urban redevelopment upgrade the city. The main street, Portage, has recently undergone a massive change with the building of a mega-mall complex, taking over several blocks. Today the wide downtown streets,

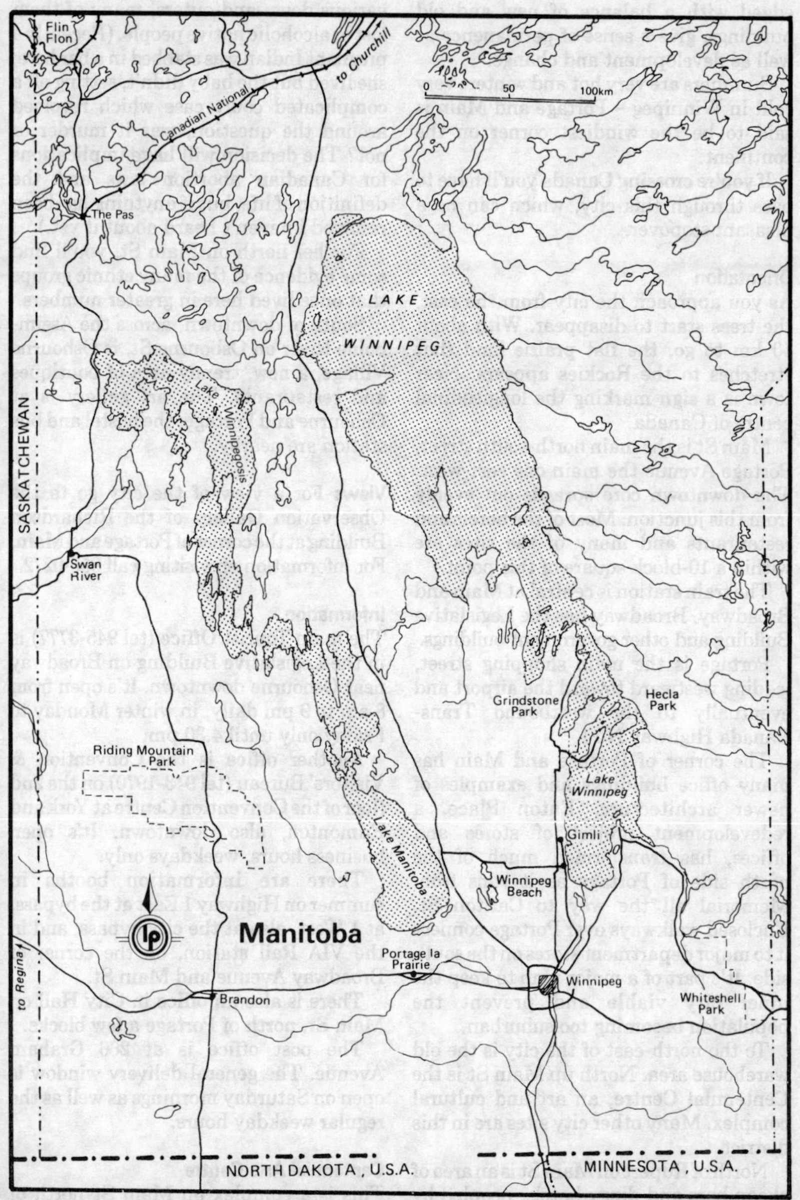
Flin Flon
to Churchill
Canadian National
0 50 100km
The Pas
LAKE
WINNIPEG
Lake Winnipegosis
SASKATCHEWAN
Swan River
Grindstone Park
Hecla Park
Riding Mountain Park
Lake Winnipeg
Lake Manitoba
Gimli
Winnipeg Beach
lp
Manitoba
to Regina
Portage la Prairie
Winnipeg
Brandon
Whiteshell Park
NORTH DAKOTA, U.S.A.
MINNESOTA, U.S.A.

edged with a balance of new and old buildings, give a sense of permanence as well as development and change.

Summers are very hot and winters very cold in Winnipeg – Portage and Main is said to be the windiest corner on the continent.

If you're crossing Canada you'll have to pass through this city, which can be a pleasant stopover.

Orientation

As you approach the city from the east, the trees start to disappear. With about 50 km to go, the flat prairie land that stretches to the Rockies appears. Near town is a sign marking the longitudinal centre of Canada.

Main St is the main north-south street, Portage Avenue the main one east-west. The downtown core spreads out evenly from this junction. Most of the hotels and restaurants and many of the sites are within a 10-block square of this point.

The train station is central at Main and Broadway. Broadway has the Legislative Building and other government buildings.

Portage is the main shopping street, leading westward toward the airport and eventually to the westbound Trans-Canada Highway No 1.

The corner of Portage and Main has many office buildings and examples of newer architecture. Eaton Place, a redevelopment project of stores and offices, has transformed much of the north side of Portage as it runs from Memorial all the way to Carlton St. Enclosed walkways over Portage connect it to major department stores on the south side. It's part of a major plan to keep the inner city viable and prevent the population becoming too suburban.

To the north-east of the city is the old warehouse area. North up Main St is the Centennial Centre, an art and cultural complex. Many other city sites are in this district.

North of Rupert on Main St is an area of cheap bars and dingy hotels, peopled by various down-and-outers, many of them lost or alcoholic native people. (Recently a pregnant Indian was stabbed in a bar here; she lived but the baby didn't, setting off a complicated court case which revolved around the question, was it murder or not? The decision will have implications for Canadian abortion laws and the definition of life, but if anything has been resolved I haven't heard about it yet.)

Further north on Main St, you'll find some evidence of the many ethnic groups that once lived here in greater numbers.

South of downtown, across the Assiniboine River on Osbourne St, is Osbourne Village, a new, trendy area of boutiques and restaurants. The art gallery is at Osbourne and Portage; the hostel and bus station are nearby.

Views For a view of the city go to the Observation Gallery of the Richardson Building at the corner of Portage and Main. For information on visiting call 956-0272.

Information

The main Tourist Office (tel 945-3777) is in the Legislative Building on Broadway near Osbourne downtown. It's open from 8 am to 9 pm daily, in winter Monday to Friday only until 4.30 pm.

Another office is the Convention & Visitors' Bureau (tel 943-1970) on the 2nd floor of the Convention Centre at York and Edmonton, also downtown. It's open business hours, weekdays only.

There are information booths in summer on Highway 1 East at the bypass, at 1 West, also at the city bypass, and in the VIA Rail station, on the corner of Broadway Avenue and Main St.

There is also an office in City Hall on Main St, north of Portage a few blocks.

The post office is at 266 Graham Avenue. The general delivery window is open on Saturday mornings as well as the regular weekday hours.

Centennial Arts Centre

This is a complex on Main St north of

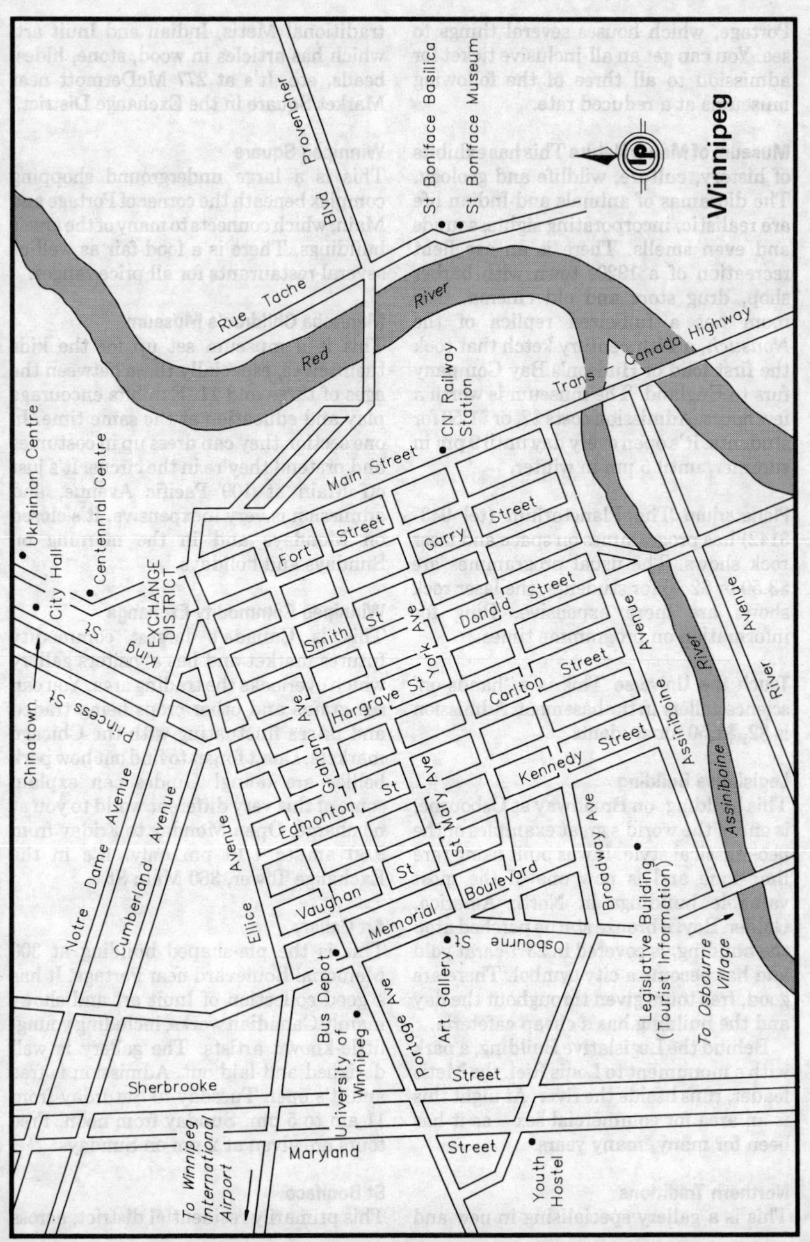
Winnipeg
St Boniface Basilica
St Boniface Museum
Provencher Blvd
Rue Tache
Red River
Trans Canada Highway
CN Railway Station
Main Street
Ukrainian Centre
Centennial Centre
City Hall
Chinatown
Princess St
King St
EXCHANGE DISTRICT
Fort Street
Garry Street
Smith St
Donald Street
York Ave
Hargrave St
Carlton Street
Graham Ave
Edmonton St
St Mary Ave
Kennedy Street
Notre Dame Avenue
Cumberland Avenue
Ellice Avenue
Vaughan St
Memorial Boulevard
Broadway Ave
Osborne St
Assiniboine Avenue
Assiniboine River
River Avenue
Legislative Building
(Tourist Information)
To Osbourne Village
Bus Depot
University of Winnipeg
Portage Ave
Art Gallery
Sherbrooke Street
Maryland Street
Youth Hostel
To Winnipeg International Airport

Portage, which houses several things to see. You can get an all-inclusive ticket for admission to all three of the following museums at a reduced rate.

Museum of Man & Nature This has exhibits of history, culture, wildlife and geology. The dioramas of animals and Indian life are realistic, incorporating sights, sounds and even smells. There is an excellent recreation of a 1920s town with barber shop, drug store and old cinema. One room has a full-sized replica of the *Nonsuch*, a 17th-century ketch that took the first load of Hudson's Bay Company furs to England. The museum is worth a few hours. Admission costs $2, or $1.50 for students. It's open every day until 9 pm in summer, until 5 pm in winter.

Planetarium The Planetarium (tel 943-3142) has programmes on space and laser rock shows. The usual programmes are $3.50 or $2.50 for students; the laser rock shows are more expensive. Ring for information on programme times.

Touch the Universe This is a 'hands-on' science gallery in the basement. Admission is $2, $1.50 for students.

Legislative Building

This building, on Broadway at Osbourne, is one of the world's great examples of the neo-classical style. It was built using rare limestone and is now one of the most valuable buildings in North America. Golden Boy, a bronze statue perched atop the building, is covered in 23½-carat gold and has become a city symbol. There are good, free tours given throughout the day and the building has a cheap cafeteria.

Behind the Legislative Building, a park with a monument to Louis Riel, the Metis leader, runs beside the river. At night this is an area for commercial sex – as it has been for many, many years.

Northern Traditions

This is a gallery specialising in new and traditional Metis, Indian and Inuit art, which has articles in wood, stone, hides, beads, etc. It's at 277 McDermott near Market Square in the Exchange District.

Winnipeg Square

This is a large underground shopping complex beneath the corner of Portage and Main, which connects to many of the area's buildings. There is a food fair as well as several restaurants for all price ranges.

Manitoba Children's Museum

This is a museum set up for the kids themselves, especially those between the ages of three and 11. Exhibits encourage play and education at the same time. In one section they can dress up in costumes and pretend they're in the circus. It's just off Main at 109 Pacific Avenue, and admission is very inexpensive. It's closed on Mondays and in the morning on Sundays and holidays.

Winnipeg Commodity Exchange

This is Canada's largest commodity futures market and has a visitors gallery which overlooks the trading area. You can see grains and other crops being traded and prices fluctuating with the Chicago markets. Don't forget to find out how pork bellies are doing! Guides can explain some of this very different world to you at no charge. Open Monday to Friday from 9.30 am to 1.15 pm only. It's in the Exchange Tower, 360 Main St.

Art Gallery

This is the pie-shaped building at 300 Memorial Boulevard near Portage. It has a good collection of Inuit art and shows mainly Canadian works, including young, little-known artists. The gallery is well designed and laid out. Admission is free and it's open Tuesday to Saturday from 11 am to 5 pm, Sunday from noon. Free tours are given at 2 pm on Sundays.

St Boniface

This primarily residential district, across

the Red River on Boulevard Provencher, is one of the oldest French communities in Canada. There's not much to see, but the facade of the St Boniface Basilica of 1818 is worth a look. The rest of the church was destroyed by fire. In front, facing the river, is a cemetery for the local French from the 1800s to the present. Louis Riel, the Metis leader, is buried here. The Metis people are of mixed North American Indian and French Canadian ancestry, who founded a culturally and politically distinctive society in the late nineteenth century. In 1885 Riel led an unsuccessful rebellion against the British government of the east, and was later executed.

Next door at 494 Rue Tache is a museum in what was the nunnery around 1850. It contains artefacts and relics of Riel and other French, Metis and Indian settlers. Admission is by donation. In summer, it's open from 10 am to 9 pm Monday to Friday, noon to 5 pm Saturday and 1 to 9 pm Sunday; in winter it closes at 5 pm. At 330 River Rd is Riel House which details his life here in the 1880s. Open every day, 9.30 am to 6 pm, free. The St Boniface Historical Society offers walking tours of older parts of the area discussing history and culture.

Royal Canadian Mint

This is south-east of town at the corner of Lagimodiere Boulevard and the Trans-Canada Highway. The ultra-modern glass pyramid building contains some of the most modern minting machinery in the world. There are free tours every half hour, which show the procedures used in cranking out two billion coins a year. The Mint produces coins for many other, especially Asian, countries. It's open Monday to Friday, 9 am to 3 pm. (No free samples!)

Ukrainian Centre

This centre, on 184 Alexander near the museum, contains a gallery and museum. Set up to preserve and present the culture of the Ukraine, the museum has costumes, textiles, ceramics and *pysankys*, painted Easter eggs. The gallery displays both old and contemporary works. A specialised library holds 40,000 volumes relating to these people. Free, open Tuesday to Saturday from 10 am to 4 pm, Sunday from 2 to 5 pm.

Assiniboine Park

This, the largest city park, is open from 10 am until dark and is free. The grounds hold an English garden and a 40-hectare zoo with animals from around the world. There are also playing fields. It's south of the Assiniboine River and just off south Portage Avenue, about seven km west of the downtown area.

Assiniboine Forest

South of the Assiniboine Park between Shaftsbury and Chalfont Avenue is this largely undeveloped forest area which is even larger than the park itself. In the middle there's a pond with an observation area for bird-watching, and you can see deer along the winding trails. Free.

Exchange District

To my mind this is one of the city's most interesting and unique features. It's a 20-block area of fine, turn-of-the-century commercial buildings and warehouses now being restored for housing, restaurants and a variety of businesses. There's some very substantial architecture here, as well as distinctive old advertising signs, painted directly on to the brick walls of numerous buildings. Though rarely seen in most of Canada today, this form of billboard seems to be undergoing a mini-revival in this part of Winnipeg.

The various Edwardian and Victorian buildings here arose at the junction of the Red and Assiniboine Rivers to fill the needs of the many stock and commodity exchanges which boomed in the city from 1880 to the 1920s. Market Square, at the corner of King St and Bannantyne Avenue, is a focal point of the area and there's often something going on here: on weekends either a flea market or some live music, for example. The Tourist Office has maps to follow for an informative walk in the district, or free walking tours are offered daily in the summer, beginning in the foyer of the Museum of Man & Nature. The area also contains many of the city's theatres and some clubs, so it doesn't close up after dark.

Macdonald House

Near the Legislature at 61 Carlton St is this beautiful Victorian house, also called Dalnavert (tel 943-2835). It was built in 1895 for the son of John A Macdonald, Canada's first prime minister. The house is decorated with period pieces. It's closed on Monday and Friday, and admission is $2.50.

Seven Oaks House

This is the oldest habitable house in the province, a big house built (without nails) in 1851. It's about four km north of Portage and Main on Ruperts Land Avenue. Open daily from July to Labour Day and weekends in spring.

Grant's Old Mill

This is a reconstruction of an 1829 water mill thought to be the first use of hydro-power in the province. There's not really very much to see, although grist is ground every day and offered for sale. Open from 10 am to 8 pm from Monday to Saturday, from 2 pm Sundays. It's at the corner of Booth Drive and Portage West near Sturgeon Creek.

Upper Fort Garry Gate

In the small park on Main St, near Broadway and across from the train station is the old stone gate and some remaining wall (restored in 1982) of Fort Garry. Since 1738, four different forts have stood on this spot, or nearby. The gate dates from 1835 and was part of the Hudson's Bay fort system. There are also some photographs and written descriptions.

The Prairie Dog Central

This is a 1900s-style steam train which takes passengers on a two-hour, 50-km trip north to Grosse Isle and back. The train makes two trips a week on Sundays at 11.30 am and 3 pm, from June to September, costing $8. The station (tel 284-2690), a bit hard to find, is on Portage Avenue West near Kehaston Boulevard, just behind Manitoba Hydro across from the Viscount Gort Motor Hotel.

North Point Douglas

This section of the city is the only area west of Montreal to be classified an historic area. Many of the houses are over 100 years old. Plaques and monuments commemorate various historical events.

St James-Assiniboine Historical Museum

This small museum has a collection of pioneer and Indian artefacts. It's at 3180 Portage Avenue and is open from 10 am to 6 pm from Monday to Saturday, from noon onwards on Sunday. Admission is $1. Next door is a 100-year-old log house with authentic furnishings.

Western Canadian Aviation Museum

This museum (tel 786-5503) is for plane buffs only. They have a few historical aircraft, including Canada's first helicopter, and other exhibits. It's at the International Airport in Hangar T-2.

Events

The annual Winnipeg Folk Festival (tel 453-2983) is probably the country's biggest and best known. It takes place for three days in summer with about 100 performers, shows and workshops. The festival is held at Bird's Hill Park.

Folklorama is the city's ethnic festival of nations. The Tourist Office will have up-to-date details.

Black-O-Rama is an annual summer festival of music, dance and poetry of West Indian origin.

Top: Windswept shore of Ontario's Georgian Bay (ML)
Bottom: Brilliant fall display, Ontario (ML)

Top: Tundra buggies, Churchill, Manitoba (RB)
Bottom: Dog sleds, Churchill, Manitoba (RB)

Activities

Swimming A couple of swimming pools in the city are open to the public. There's Central Outdoor Pool, administered by the City of Winnipeg Parks & Recreation Department, and the Pan-Am Pool (tel 284-4031), which is one of the country's largest. Admission here costs $1.50 and the pool is at 25 Poseidon Bay.

Canoeing Manitoba is a lake-filled province and there are many canoe routes around it. A lengthy list of these routes is available from the Tourist Office.

Parks There are numerous parks in and around the city, some quite large. One is Little Mountain Park, which has hiking trails and examples of local forest and prairie vegetation. It's two km east of Sturgeon Rd off Oak Point Highway.

Places to Stay

Hostels The *Youth Hostel* (tel 772-3022) is good and central. It's in an old yellow-and-brown renovated house at 210 Maryland, near the corner of Broadway and Sherbrooke by the bus station. The hostel has kitchen facilities. In summer it's often full so arrive early. The rates are $7 for members, $11 for non-members.

The *YMCA* (tel 942-8157), for men only, is at 301 Vaughan, quarter of a block from Portage near the Bay Department Store. A single room is $19 plus $3 key deposit. It has a cheap cafeteria open from 7 am to 4.30 pm, closed Sunday, and a pool, gym and sauna. Unfortunately, at my last visit it was about to close for a major renovation, so future plans were uncertain.

The *YWCA* (tel 943-0381) is nearby at 447 Webb, one block from Portage. Rates are $19 for a dorm bed, $24 each to share a double room, $26 for a single. They also have a cafeteria and pool. You must check in before 11 pm.

The University of Manitoba rents rooms from mid-May to mid-August. They're not cheap at $25 for a single room, $36 for a double, and they're only available with a reservation and one night's deposit. For information, contact the Conference Co-ordinator (tel 474-9942) at 26 MacLean Crescent, Pembina Hall.

Bed & Breakfasts The province has a bed & breakfast programme with many places in town. The Tourist Office has a complete list. Prices range from $20 for singles and $45 for doubles and breakfast is included, although some offer continental breakfasts and others a complete meal. Two in the central area are *Marie & Peter Kowal* (tel 772-5681), 1140 Ellice Avenue; and *Daisy Paully* (tel 772-8828) at 141 Furby St.

Hotels – bottom end Winnipeg has lots of small, older hotels in the downtown area. Most of these are pretty basic and cater to locals on the skids, but are cheap. Others are much better but still moderately priced.

For cheapies, the *Windsor* (tel 942-7528) at 187 Garry St south of Portage is not bad, and clean and central. Singles cost $17, doubles $22. The *Garrick* at No 287 is pretty bad.

The *Oxford Hotel* (tel 942-6712) is old but OK, in a good location in the warehouse district. Rooms start at $13 for singles, $15 for doubles; rooms with a bath cost more. There's a bar and restaurant. The hotel is on the corner of Notre Dame and Albert Sts.

There are other, similar hotels in this area; all these types of hotels have very low weekly rates.

A few blocks up Main from the train station is the *Winnipeg Hotel* (tel 942-7762), which is clean and friendly. Singles cost $11, doubles $13.

One of the best of the cheapies is the white stucco *Aberdeen Hotel* at 230 Carlton, downtown, which has a pub downstairs. Singles are $23 to $30, doubles $26 to $34.

The *Gordon Downtowner Motor Hotel* (tel 943-5581) is central at 330 Kennedy St, a few blocks from Portage. It has a restaurant and a couple of bars. Singles/doubles are $36/38.

Down in Osbourne Village is *Osbourne Village Motor Inn* (tel 942-6712). The 32 rooms are reasonably priced at singles $32, doubles $34.

Hotels - middle The *Balmoral* on the street of the same name is at the corner of Notre Dame and has singles and doubles for $44.

The *St Regis* (tel 942-0171) is a good, very central hotel with all the mod cons. It's at 285 Smith St just south of Portage, and charges $42 for singles, $47 for doubles.

Two other good value places are the *Brittany Inn* (tel 943-1375) at 367 Ellice Avenue, downtown, which has singles or doubles for $50 to $55, and *The Charterhouse*, which is a mid-size, mid-price, very central place at the corner of York and Hargrave. Each room here has a balcony and the rates are $48/55 for singles/doubles.

Hotels - top end The *Delta Winnipeg* (tel 956-1410) at 288 Portage Avenue has singles/doubles for $85/95. The *Westin* (tel 228-3000) at 2 Lombard Place, has singles for $99, doubles for $120 and up.

Motels The *Assiniboine Garden Inn* at 1975 Portage Avenue on the park, has singles or doubles for $46 and a dining room offering good prices. *Down's Motor Inn* at 3740 Portage charges $36 for singles and $40 for doubles.

Kelly's Inn at 745 Pembina has singles for $30 to $38, doubles for $36 to $40. *Journeys End Motel* (tel 269-7370) at 3109 Pembina, is immaculate with rates at $40 singles, $45 doubles.

There are many other motels that are newer, better and more expensive. Generally the larger ones cost more.

Camping There are a few places to camp around town but most are way out, off the main highways.

Whitehorse Plains Campground (tel 864-2366), is 14 km west on Highway 1. Unserviced sites are $8. *KOA* (tel 253-8168) has a site on the Trans-Canada East at Murdock Rd, with rates of $11 to $12. Both campgrounds are open from May to mid-October.

J & J's Camping is west of Portage, and at just $6 for a tent, is good value. It's grassy and quiet, with lots of trees.

Places to Eat

The cheapest place to eat in town is the *Cafeteria* in the Administration Building, in the cluster of government offices between Main and King at William. Different lunches are served each day. The cafeteria is on the 2nd floor and opens from 8.30 am to 4.30 pm Monday to Friday. I don't know if you have to be an employee to eat here, but you shouldn't have any problems getting in unless you look like you've slept in the woods for a week.

The *Cafeteria* in the Legislative Building is similar and is definitely open to the public.

Downtown on a Sunday you'll find most things closed, but there are several *Salisbury House* restaurants around town which tend to be open early and late every day. There's one at 212 Notre Dame, serving the usual simple, inexpensive stuff.

The *Old Chocolate Shop Restaurant* at 269 Portage is a likeable place whether you go for lunch, dinner, coffee and sweets or for the popular tea cup and tarot card readings. Moderately priced.

Mr Greenjeans in Eaton Place at the corner of Hargrave and St Marys offers finger foods, chicken and ribs, all served with rock music. Not too far away at 349 York is the *Garden Creperie*, a trendy-looking sort of place serving lunch crepes for about $6 and various dinners at a little less than twice that. Closed Sundays.

The *Old Swiss Inn* at 207 Edmonton St offers steaks, veal and seafood. Good, priced at $15 to $22.

Grapes at 180 Main St near the train station is a big bar-restaurant with lots of wood and plants. The menu offers a bit of everything. The food's not great but OK with a few beers.

Down in the Heritage District are numerous eating spots. Around Market Square on Albert St is *Chopin's Cafe*, a small comfortable place with straightforward food at cheap prices. There are also chip wagons which park all around the park.

Nearby, the *Stage Door Cafe* at 120 King St is a very good Jewish deli open until 4 am on weekends. They have Reuben sandwiches (hot grilled sandwiches with cheese, meat and sauerkraut), blintzes, cheesecake, etc, done well.

Winnipeg has an *Old Spaghetti Factory*, always reliable and good value if not stupendous. It's at 219 Bannantyne and offers very reasonable complete Italian meals at lunch or dinner in a well-designed space. More expensive Italian food is available at *Cibo's*, a few doors down by the park. Also more costly is *Fingers* for ribs, on Rorie at Bannantyne.

At 180 King St is the new Chinese Dynasty Building with the Heritage Gardens out front and the adjacent Chinese gate over the street. Slightly beyond is the city's small Chinatown on Rupert, Pacific and Alexander Sts. The restaurants are mainly on King. *Marigold* is the biggest and poshest restaurant. The *VIP* on Alexander is cheaper and also has some Vietnamese dishes.

There are several places worth getting to in the Sherbrooke-Broadway area. At 106 Sherbrooke is the busy *Impressions Cafe*, licensed and open every day to midnight. It has a nice European atmosphere with paintings and photographs on display, and sells sandwiches, bagels and omelettes; everything is priced under $5. The freshly baked cinnamon buns at breakfast with a tea or coffee make life worth living.

Bistro Dansk at 63 Sherbrooke is a perennial favourite with well prepared food and good lunches at $6. Also dinner specials. It's open from 11 am to 9.30 pm daily, closed on Sunday.

Down near the corner of Broadway at 218 Sherbrooke is the *Fondue Bistro*, a congenial, moderately-priced spot for a dinner out. Try the bouillon fondue; there are non-fondue items on the menu as well.

Nearly next door, across from the gas station, *Champions* serves pretty decent basic Chinese and Vietnamese food.

Over on Broadway at No 595 is the *Indian Curry House*, offering vegetarian and meat dishes. Main courses are priced at $6 to $7. This place is said to be very good. It's open every day.

An off-beat place to try in this neighbourhood is *Mrs Liptons* at 962 Westminster at Lipton St. It's a vegetarian/natural foods place in a funky old storefront corner building. Open only to 8 pm and closed Mondays.

Main St North has a number of good, cheap places. At No 1100 is *Kelekis*, a locally famous Jewish restaurant with traditional photographs of stars and pseudo-stars on the walls. It has modern decorations now, but has actually operated since 1931, and still packs 'em in with its sandwiches, burgers and meals for under $5.

Further north at No 1134 is *Betsy's Place* run by Betsy de Boer who makes cheap and good Indonesian food. Satay, *udang goreng* (a shrimp dish) and other rice plates are priced at $3 to $8.

Up the street at 1322 Main St North is *Simon's*, an old-style, unrenovated delicatessen full of members of the Jewish community. Pastrami and corned beef sandwiches are $2.75. Also on the menu are blintzes, soups and *kreplach*, meat dumplings usually served in soup. Everything is under $6 and you can buy smoked meat by the pound.

Sabrina's, a Jamaican place, has been recommended.

At 911 Main the *Blue Bay Cafe* has Ukrainian food.

In Osbourne Village there are many

restaurants, mostly pretty good. *Basil's Café* at 117 Osbourne has various specialty items and European snacks and sweets as well as sandwiches and salads. They have a selection of teas and 12 different coffees.

Simply Delicious at 100 Osbourne is very cheap, with all deli items $2.50. Daily soup and sandwich costs $3.25. The place is comfortable and casual. It's open to 2 am on weekends.

Carlos & Murphy's at 133 Osbourne is a Mexican place with an outdoor patio, a big menu and moderate prices. *Baked Expectations* is primarily for sweets, open late and not too pricey. *Pasquale's* has cheap pizza and spaghetti and other more expensive Italian dishes, and opens until 2 am.

There are many others restaurants here, some a fair bit pricier those just mentioned. The *Tea Cozy* is a posher place with highly rated food.

The downtown shopping centres have basement food fairs and the Convention Centre has a cheap cafeteria. Also, many of the better downtown hotels have Sunday brunches at noon, which are good value.

Out of the downtown area, St Boniface has several French restaurants and Pembina Highway has numerous restaurants.

Nightlife

To find out what's going on in the city, the *Winnipeg Free Press* has complete bar and entertainment listings on Fridays.

Music On weeknights in summer, you can listen for free to music played in the park off Preston Avenue near the youth hostel, from 6.30 to 11 pm.

Wellington's (tel 942-2079) at 22 Albert St has live rock'n'roll and new wave music. The cover charge varies. The *Black Knight* at 1738 Ellice, has rock and heavy metal music. The *Norlander Rock Room* in the Motel Hotel at 1792 Pembina Way also has rock music. Admission prices vary. The *Rory St Marble Club* is a dressy, trendy dance spot.

The *Blue Note* at 220 Main has live blues and jazz until very late. *Yuk Yuk's* in Osbourne Village presents stand-up comics. There are several nightspots on McDermott near Rorie, such as *Act II*, for late night reggae and jam sessions.

The boat *River Rouge* has night cruises with pop bands on Wednesdays to Saturdays, and jazz music on Sunday and Monday nights.

Theatre The *Royal Winnipeg Ballet* has an excellent international reputation. Their new home is downtown at the corner of Graham and Edmonton Sts, and they offer student rates on tickets.

The *Winnipeg Symphony Orchestra* is also good; their seasons usually run from November to May.

Various plays and concerts are performed at the *Centennial Arts Centre*, 555 Main St.

Cinema The *Festival Cinema* (tel 772-7786), at 801 Sargent Avenue, shows two films a night, at 7.30 and 9.30 pm. Another repertory cinema is the *Cinema 3* on Ellice and Sherbrooke. Finally, the *Art Gallery* has films on weekends.

Getting There & Away

Air The International Airport is about 20 minutes north-west of the city centre. Several airlines serve Winnipeg, both for local trips and destinations in the USA.

Nordair (tel 786-4435) flies to Sault Ste Marie twice daily. The phone number for Air Canada is 943-9361.

Canadian Airlines flies to Churchill four times a week but it ain't cheap. If you want to go, book at least two weeks in advance for the best deal. For more information about Churchill, see the separate section at the end of this chapter.

Bus The station for both Greyhound and Grey Goose Lines is the Mall Centre Bus

Depot at 487 Portage. Its location is central and the station is open from 6.30 am to midnight.

Greyhound (tel 775-8301) covers all Ontario points and many western cities. They run five buses daily, both am and pm schedules, to Thunder Bay ($46), Toronto ($96) and Saskatoon ($53).

The Greyhound desk also handles the small Beaver Bus line which serves Fort Garry and other points north of town. There's at least one an hour.

Grey Goose Lines (tel 786-8891) serves Regina, Thunder Bay and many of the small towns in the area.

There are also buses here for Selkirk (Fort Garry).

Train The VIA Rail station is centrally located where Broadway meets Main St. In summer there's a tourist information booth in the station.

Regina, Calgary, Banff, Kamloops, Vancouver: daily at 8.55 pm

Saskatoon, Edmonton, Jasper, Vancouver: daily at 9.35 pm

Thunder Bay, Sudbury, Ottawa, Montreal: daily at 10.35 am.

One-way fares: Calgary – $105, Vancouver – $153, Thunder Bay – $60.

There is also a train to Churchill; see the separate section in this chapter for more information.

Getting Around

Airport Transport A city bus departs for the airport every 20 minutes from Vaughan at the corner of Portage. It's called the Sargent bus and costs 95c exact change.

The airport limo runs from 9 am to nearly 1 am from the better hotels and costs about $5. If there are three of you a taxi works out the same.

Bus All city buses cost 95c exact change. For transit info, you can call 284-7190, 24 hours a day. Routes are extensive but you need a transfer if you're changing buses.

From 11 am to 3 pm the city operates Dash, a free bus service around the downtown core. Broadway, Main and the Exchange area are covered.

Car Rentals Hertz is in The Bay department store on Portage.

Budget (tel 786-5866) is at the corner of Sherbrooke and Ellice. Their rates are $29 with 100 free km, 12c per km over. Weekly rental is $132 with 1500 free km. They'll pick you up at no charge.

Dominion (tel 943-4477) is at 405 Ellice and offers three-day specials.

Hitching For hitching west out of town, take the Express St Charles bus along Portage. After 6 pm take the Portage St Charles bus.

For hitching east on Highway 1, catch the Osbourne Highway 1 bus or the Southdale bus on Osbourne St South at the corner of Broadway.

Bicycle There are bicycle routes through town and some out of town. Ask at the Tourist Office about them.

The youth hostel (tel 772-3022) rents bicycles; there's a repair shop at 185 Sherbrooke St.

Tours Free 'Historic Winnipeg' walking tours begin at the museum information booth. They take place on Mondays to Saturdays at 11 am and 1.30 pm, Sundays 1 and 3 pm, Wednesday and Thursday evenings at 7 pm. The tour lasts one hour.

Gray Line has nine boat and bus tours ranging in price from $10. The downtown bus tour is $6, lasting three hours. An evening dinner-dance cruise is $27.

MS *Lord Selkirk* has dinner cruises, dance cruises and Sunday afternoon cruises. The boat docks beside Redwood Bridge north up Main from Portage.

Rouge Line (tel 663-4083) offers double-decker bus tours and river boat trips. Some trips include a bit of each.

Destination Adventure (tel 256-9192) have a wider selection of more detailed, personal and further afield minibus tours, many highlighting interesting geographical or cultural places; some are overnighters.

VIA Rail runs excursions to Churchill by train, bus and plane, including sightseeing and accommodation. Enquire at the station.

AROUND WINNIPEG

Dugald Costume Museum

Dugald, not far from Winnipeg, is the home of a collection of 5000 items of dress and accessories, dating from 1765. The costume museum is open daily from 10 am to 5 pm during summer. Admission is $2.50.

Museum of Childhood

About 25 km east of town on the Trans-Canada Highway, this museum has a collection of furniture, toys, clothing and other articles which may remind visitors of their youth. Admission is also $2.50.

Oak Hammock Marsh

Southern Manitoba has several very important, very large marshes. These critical wetlands are home to thousands of waterfowl and other birds and act as way stations along major migration routes for thousands more.

Oak Hammock Marsh is a swamp area just north of the city, about halfway to Lake Winnipeg and eight km east of Stonewall. It's noted as one of the best bird sanctuaries on the continent; over 260 species can be seen. You can amble about on viewing boardwalks and there is an information centre. You can also go canoeing.

Lower Fort Garry

Fort Garry, 30 km north of Winnipeg on the banks of the Red River, is a restored Hudson's Bay Company fort from 1830. It's the only stone fort from the fur-trading days still intact.

Although the fort was a failure as a fur trading post, it remained in use as a police-training centre, a penitentiary, lunatic asylum, Hudson's Bay residence and later a country club.

The buildings are furnished and the grounds are busy with costumed workers who'll answer questions. Go early in the day to avoid the crowds, and see the film at the entrance for the historical background. You should allow one or two hours for a visit. Admission to the fort costs $2.75.

To get there, take the Beaver Bus Line from the main depot and tell the driver you're going to the fort – the fare is about $5 return.

Around Manitoba

LAKE WINNIPEG

This huge lake, Canada's fifth largest, lies about 50 km north of the city. The eastern shoreline is lined with beaches, including Grand Beach, which has light coloured sand and dunes as high as eight metres. It's very popular and a good place to relax.

The other side of the lake is less accessible as much of it is privately owned, many people having cottages in the area. However, there are some good, popular public beaches, such as Winnipeg Beach – very good for windsurfing.

There are motels and restaurants along the strip at Winnipeg Beach.

Gimli

Ninety km north of Winnipeg, on the western shores of Lake Winnipeg, this is the centre of a large Icelandic fishing and farming community. There's a museum showing the history and some artefacts of the local settlement. Every summer around the beginning of August the Icelandic Festival is held, which comprises three days of games, contests, parades and folk music.

Hecla Provincial Park

This new provincial park is on a peninsula and islands in Lake Winnipeg. There are lots of birds as well as other wildlife; it's good for hiking, camping and fishing.

SNAKE PITS

Snake lovers: you're in luck. Here in Manitoba is the world's largest population of garter snakes, concentrated in wiggling mega-dens for up to 10,000 of the little funsters. Researchers, pet dealers and those with a taste for the macabre come from distant continents to view the snake pits about six km north of Narcisse, off Highway 17. In fact, the attention on them has resulted in a drastic decline in the numbers of snake dens, and harvesting regulation is likely. The mating ritual, when tens of thousands emerge from their limestone sinkhole lairs to form masses of entwined tangles, takes place the last week in April and the first two weeks in May.

Bring the camera and the kids. You can really make a day of it by visiting nearby Komarno where there's a statue of the world's largest mosquito.

WHITESHELL PROVINCIAL PARK

This 259-square-km park lies along the Ontario border due east of Winnipeg. Though some parts are heavily commercialised (particularly around Falcon Lake), other areas, especially northward, are less developed. The park contains 200 lakes and all kinds of outdoor activities are available, summer and winter. There are some good hiking trails – short or up to 60 km long.

The park has 17 campgrounds and there are moderately-priced lodges which are rented by the day or week.

BANNOCK POINT

Here, not far from Betula Lake, are centuries-old Indian petroforms, which are rocks carved in the shapes of fish, snakes and birds.

ATIKAKI PROVINCIAL PARK

Heading north, the province quickly becomes pretty wild. This wilderness park is best visited by canoe. In it, along the Bloodvein River, there are remnants of Indian cliff paintings thought to date back 6000 years.

BRANDON

The second largest city in the province, Brandon has little to recommend it. It's a purely functional centre. The town's main street is Rossen Avenue.

There are plenty of motels and hotels to stay at if you don't want to haul into Winnipeg. The *YWCA*, at 148 11th St, charges $16. The Brandon *Youth Hostel* is conveniently located, 150 metres from the Trans-Canada Highway on the hospital grounds. Beds here cost $7 to $9.

RIDING MOUNTAIN NATIONAL PARK

This park is 300 km north-west of Winnipeg in a highland area, on a forested escarpment. Clear Lake is the developed area but most of the park is wilderness. Canoe rentals are available; you could use the list of canoe routes in the province, available from the Tourist Office in Winnipeg. There are over 300 km of hiking trails and a small herd of bison in the park. Camping is not expensive.

NORTHERN WOODS & WATER ROUTE

This is a series of roads – now linked as one – which connects Winnipeg across northern portions of Saskatchewan and Alberta, to British Columbia. Most of the roads are surfaced though there are stretches of gravel. There are no cities but many small communities, nine provincial parks and numerous campgrounds along the way. You'll see lots of lakes and woods up here as well as fishing areas and wildlife. Nights are cool.

From Winnipeg the route leads to The Pas in the north-west of the province, continues on to Prince Albert in Saskatchewan (near the Prince Albert National Park), on into Alberta, ending up at Dawson Creek, British Columbia. The road is marked by signs with 'NWWR'.

CHURCHILL
This is one of Canada's few northern outposts that is relatively accessible, with a train line running right up to it. Despite its forbidding location and extremes of weather – July and August are the only months without snow – it has always been of importance. Explorers, traders and the military have all been here and it has been one of the largest grain-handling ports in the world. Now, due to the decline in grain handling, it is relying on its natural resources to draw business.

Tourism has become very important and the town bills itself as the Polar Bear Capital of the World. It sits right in the middle of a polar bear migration route, which means the great white bears are often seen in and around town. Visitors are also taken out on the frozen tundra in large motorised buggies to see the huge and very dangerous bears.

Things to See
Churchill is a great spot for viewing the phenomenon known as the 'aurora borealis' or northern lights, and is excellent for observing wildlife, including beluga whales, seals, caribou and birds. Listed here are the best times to visit for certain attractions:

Northern lights: September-April
Polar bears: September-October
Whales: July-August and early September
Birds: May-June and early July
Fishing and flowers: all summer.

Visitors' Centre
This is in town; it shows films on the area, its history and the polar bears. There's also a display of furs from the Hudson's Bay Company, which opened up the area with a post about 250 years ago.

Eskimo Museum
This museum has a good collection of Inuit artefacts and carvings, including kayaks from 1700 BC. You can also visit the remains of Fort Prince of Wales built by the Hudson's Bay Company (HBC). Various stores sell contemporary Inuit arts and crafts.

Fort Prince of Wales
Water taxis run (tides and weather permitting) across the Churchill River from town to Fort Prince of Wales (not Whales!), now a national historic park. This partially restored stone fort was originally built to protect the fur-trading business of the Hudson Bay Company from possible rivals. The French, however, took it over later in the century. From 1 July to 1 September, guides working for the Environment Canada ministry are on hand to tell the fort's story. A second battery is by the mouth of the river.

Sloop's Cove
Private operators also run boat trips to Sloop's Cove, three km upriver from the fort. The cove was used by European boats out on whaling excursions and on trading trips with the local Inuit. Names of some of the early HBC men, including that of Samuel Hears, the local 18th century governor, can be seen scratched into the seaside rocks.

Cape Merry Centennial Parkway
Tours are also given by Environment Canada three km from town at the end of the Cape Merry Centennial Parkway. Here a plaque honours Sir Thomas Button, believed to be the first European to have sailed into the mouth of the Churchill River. Guides are on duty from 15 June to 15 September.

Bird Cove
Bird Cove, about 15 km east of town and accessible by vehicle (tours are available) is known for its abundant bird life. There is the wreck of a freighter which went down in a storm in 1961 at the western edge of the cove.

York Factory
Further afield and accessible only by air or

a vigorous canoe trip, is York Factory, a fur-trading post that operated for 250 years. Run by the HBC (who else?) it, too, is now a national historic site.

Places to Stay

Churchill is not a cheap place to visit. However, there are about half a dozen places to stay and a few more to eat at. Accommodation costs about $40 to $55 for singles and $45 to $70 for doubles. Meals run to about $5 to $12. The *Churchill Motel* reportedly has doubles, each with TV, fridge and bathroom, for $30.

Getting There & Away

There is no road to Churchill; you must either fly in (Canadian Airlines has four flights a week) or catch a train. There are three trains a week, at 9.55 pm on Sunday, Tuesday and Thursday; the fare from Winnipeg is $115 one-way for the 1600-km trip. VIA Rail also runs very popular excursions to Churchill which include accommodation and sightseeing. Enquire at VIA in Winnipeg for more details.

Saskatchewan

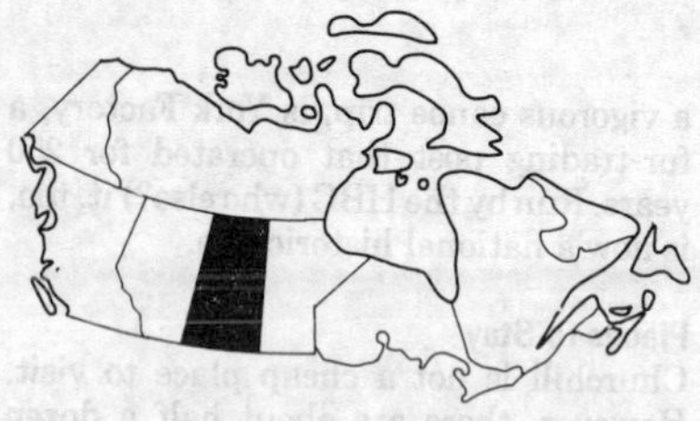

Entered Confederation: 1 September 1905
Area: 651,903 square km
Population: 968,313

Saskatchewan is a Cree Indian word which refers to the Saskatchewan River and means 'river that turns around when it runs'.

Saskatchewan and wheat are pretty much synonymous. The province is the greatest grower of wheat in North America and, with over a third of Canada's farmland, produces two-thirds of Canada's crop. Besides wheat, other grains such as barley and rye are important, as are sunflowers and beef cattle.

Many find the scenery boring and monotonous; the south of the province is mercilessly flat, often without a tree in sight. But such wide open space is a scene much of the world cannot even imagine. And the sight of golden, ripening wheat rippling in all directions to the horizon can be beautiful. The sky becomes a major part of the landscape – the sunsets, sunrises, cloud formations and night skies are all fantastic.

The far north of the state – part of the Canadian Shield – is rocky timberland and a wilderness of lakes and forests with few people. Of those who do live here, many are Metis – people of both Indian and white blood.

Between this area and the bald, open prairie of the south is a transition zone stretching across the province covering the lower middle section of Saskatchewan in rolling hills and cultivated farmland. This range is called the parklands and contains some large government parks and both the North and South Saskatchewan Rivers.

The weather in Saskatchewan is very changeable and extreme. Generally winters are long and cold, with temperatures getting down to –50°C. Summers are warm and short, but temperatures can get to 40°C as well. I've always found August and September warm and dry months, but even then, the nights are cool. It's common to see weather fronts moving across the sky, so you usually know what's coming.

In the past few years, oil has become increasingly important; you'll see the slowly cranking rigs in the fields. The province also has the richest potash deposits in the world. Along the Trans-Canada Highway, some of the soil is jet black – this is natural because the area was once totally submerged under water. Occasionally you'll see large patches of white stuff which looks like snow. This is sodium sulphate and occurs only in certain climatic conditions. It's used in various industries, like detergent preparation.

In the north of the province, 55 canoe routes have been mapped out, and there are canoe outfitters in Flin Flon, just over the Manitoba border, and Lac La Ronge.

With so much farmland in the province, it's possible to stay on a farm, which can be a reasonably-priced arrangement; the Tourist Offices have more information.

Regina

Regina is Saskatchewan's capital. It is the largest city and acts as the commercial, financial and industrial centre of the

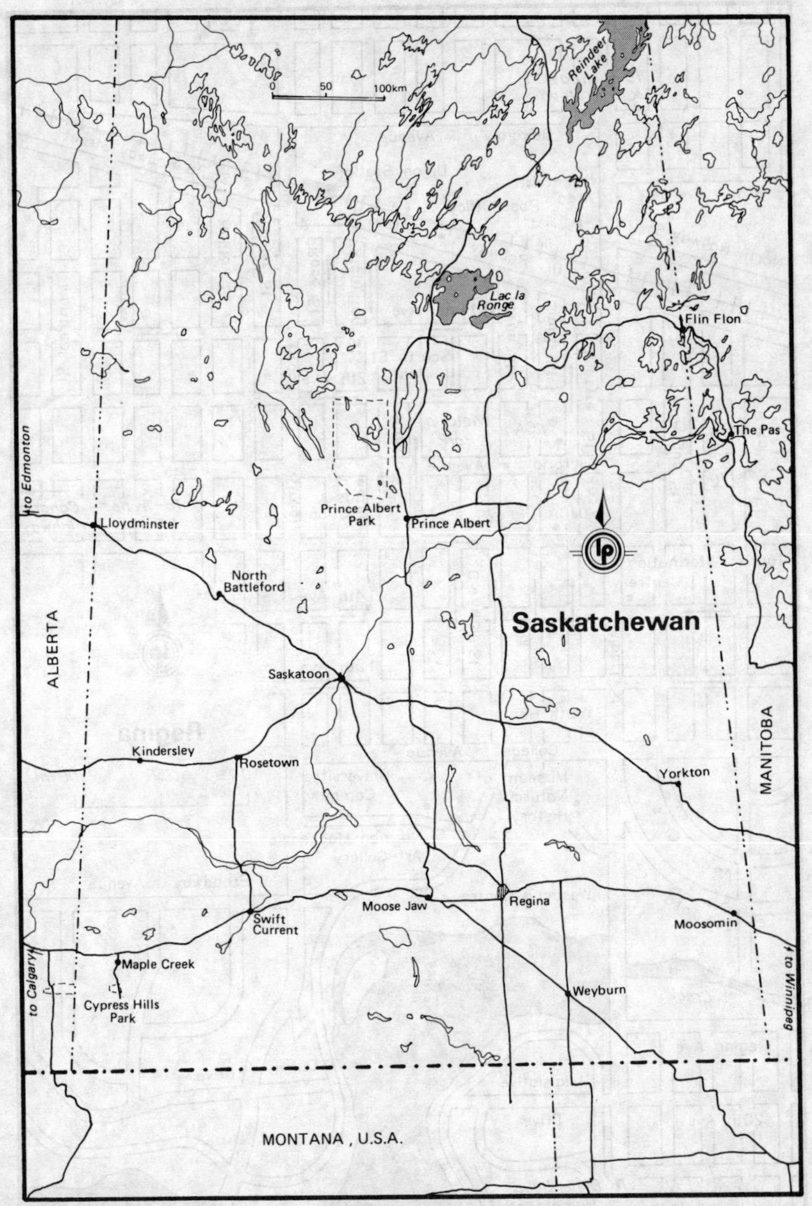

0
50
100km
Reindeer Lake
Lac la Ronge
Flin Flon
The Pas
to Edmonton
Lloydminster
Prince Albert Park
Prince Albert
North Battleford
Saskatchewan
ALBERTA
Saskatoon
MANITOBA
Kindersley
Rosetown
Yorkton
Swift Current
Moose Jaw
Regina
Moosomin
Maple Creek
to Calgary
Cypress Hills Park
Weyburn
to Winnipeg
MONTANA , U.S.A.

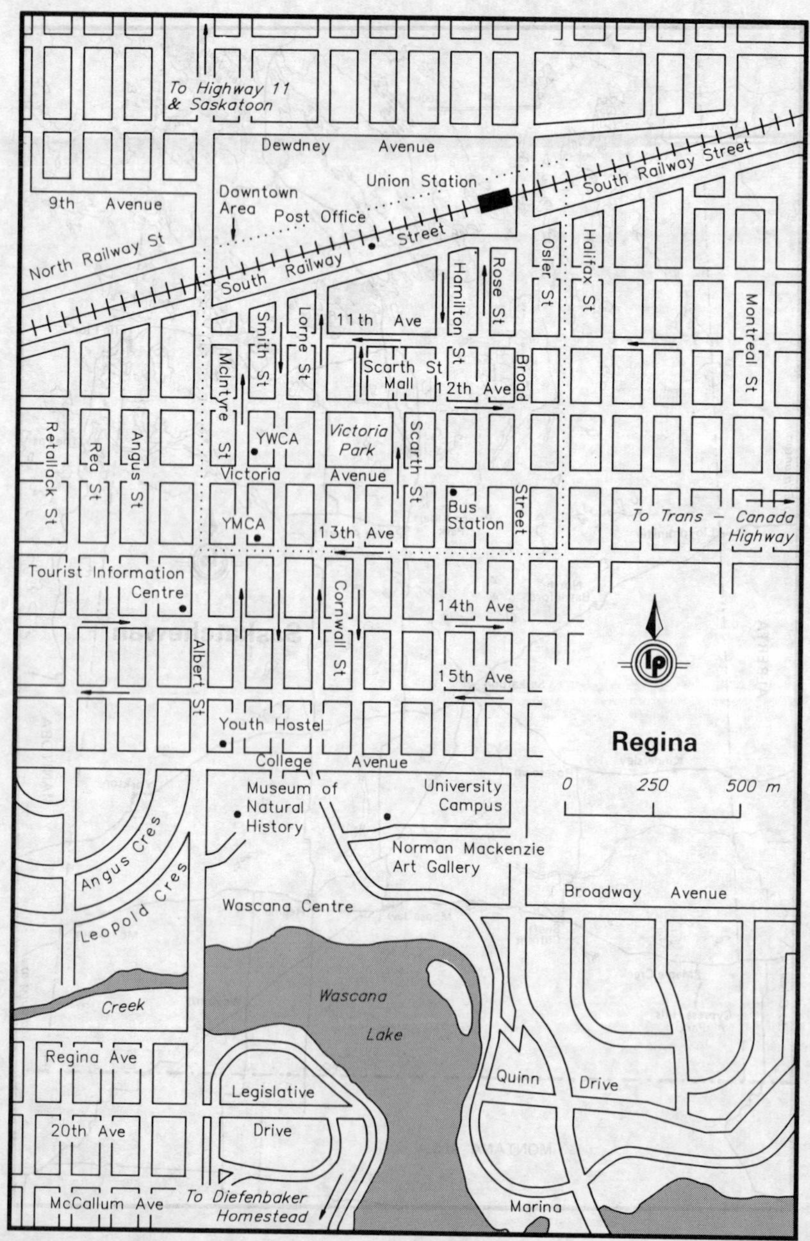

To Highway 11
& Saskatoon
Dewdney
Avenue
Union Station
9th
Avenue
Downtown
Area
Post Office
North Railway St
South Railway
Street
South Railway Street
Hamilton St
Rose St
Osler St
Halifax St
Montreal St
11th
Ave
Smith St
Lorne St
McIntyre St
Scarth St
Mall
12th
Ave
Broad
Street
Retallack St
Rea St
Angus St
YWCA
Victoria
Park
Victoria
Avenue
Scarth St
Bus
Station
YMCA
13th
Ave
To Trans – Canada
Highway
Tourist Information
Centre
Cornwall St
14th
Ave
Albert St
15th
Ave
Youth Hostel
College
Avenue
Museum of
Natural
History
University
Campus
Norman Mackenzie
Art Gallery
Regina
0
250
500 m
Angus Cres
Leopold Cres
Wascana Centre
Broadway
Avenue
Creek
Wascana
Lake
Regina Ave
Quinn
Drive
Legislative
Drive
20th Ave
McCallum Ave
To Diefenbaker
Homestead
Marina

province, but it's still a small, quiet town that pretty much closes down after dark.

The Cree Indians lived in this area, butchering buffalo and leaving the remains along the creek, which prompted the first European settlers to dub the settlement 'Pile o' Bones'. In 1882 the city was made capital of the Northwest Territories and its name was changed to Regina in honour of Queen Victoria. The Northwest Mounted Police used the city as a base from the 1880s, and in 1905 it became the capital of the newly-formed Saskatchewan.

In 1933, the Co-operative Commonwealth Confederation (CCF), a socialist party, held its first national meeting in Regina and called for the end of capitalism. In 1944 they became the first socialist party to form a Canadian provincial government. The CCF merged with the New Democratic Party (NDP) in 1961, to form Canada's present left-wing party.

The population of Regina is approximately 170,000.

Wascana Creek and its parkland run through town, providing a change from the dry, golden wheat fields stretching in all directions.

Two interesting little city tidbits: it's the sunniest capital city in Canada and, oddly, every single tree you see anywhere was planted by hand.

Orientation

The city's two main streets are Victoria Avenue, running east-west and Albert St, going north-south. Both streets are lined with fast-food places and petrol stations.

Victoria Avenue going east becomes the Trans-Canada Highway No 1 to Winnipeg. Highway 1 West continues off Albert St in the far south of town. Albert St North leads into Highway 11 for Saskatoon.

Wascana Centre, a 1000-hectare park, dominates the city. It lies four blocks south of the corner of Victoria and Albert.

The downtown core is bounded by Albert St to the west, 13th Avenue to the south, Osler St to the east and the railway tracks to the north.

Victoria Park sits in the middle of the downtown area. Scarth St and 12th Avenue, which edge the park, are important shopping streets. Scarth, between 11th and 12th Avenues, has been converted into a mall which, though small, is pleasant with bunches of trees. On the corner is the old city hall housing a theatre, shops and a museum. The new Continental Bank Building on the south corner is unusual and interesting with its pyramidal shapes.

The area on and around Osler gets pretty tacky at night even though the new police station is here. Be careful downtown after dark; the streets get very quiet and wandering around is not advisable.

The airport south-west of downtown is about a 15-minute drive.

Views

SGI Building This building, at 2260 11th Avenue, offers a good view of the city. The cafeteria on the 18th floor is open from 8 am to 5 pm.

Gallery on the Roof This art gallery for provincial artists (tel 566-3174) has an observation deck offering great views of the city. It's on the 13th floor of the Power Building, 2025 Victoria Avenue; free.

Information

The handiest information office is in the old streetcar (tel 789-5099) on the Scarth St mall. It's open from Monday to Saturday, 9.30 am to 6 pm.

There is a Travel Information Centre in the Bank of Montreal Building, 2103 11th Avenue, open year-round.

The Chamber of Commerce (tel 527-4658) at 2145 Albert St, also provides local information; open Monday to Friday only.

In summer there are two or three temporary booths set up around town but locations change.

For Saskatchewan information, there's an office at 2103 11th Avenue, downtown.

The train station is at the corner of South Railway St and Rose St. The post office is also on South Railway, a few blocks west of the station. The bus station is on Hamilton St just south of Victoria.

Wascana Centre
Regina is blessed with many parks, nearly all of them adjoining Wascana Creek which meanders diagonally through the southern portion of the city. Wascana Centre Park is the largest of these, at about eight times the size of the city centre. The park begins five blocks south of 12th Avenue – take Scarth or Rose St south and it extends south-east from there. In July and August, cheap 50-minute guided tours of the park on London double-decker buses leave from the Legislature flower garden daily in the afternoon.

Within the park are the man-made Wascana Lake and a waterfowl park with 60 species of birds. A boardwalk leads into the marsh; naturalists work weekdays. Besides picnic areas and sports fields, this green area contains many of the city's sights. Free Sunday afternoon concerts are given at the Bandshell.

The Marina at the eastern edge of the park rents bicycles, roller skates and boats.

Wascana Centre, north of the marina, is the park headquarters. There's not really much of interest but a view can be had from the fourth level of the building. The bus tours can also be boarded here.

Provincial Legislature This building is just off Albert St on the park's west side. It's a beautiful building, done in loose English Renaissance style in 1919 at a cost of $3,000,000. Inside, 34 kinds of marble were used. The building is open all day and there are tours given on the hour except at lunch.

Museum of Natural History This museum is inside the park, south of College Avenue at Albert St. Upstairs there are very realistic displays of North American wildlife, particularly animals native to Saskatchewan, with good explanations accompanying the exhibits. Downstairs the displays outline the biology of insects, birds, fish and animals and attempt to explain their behaviour. Space is given to palaeontology (fossils) and archaeology; another room gives the Indian history of Saskatchewan.

There are often films on a variety of topics; a visit will take about one hour. Admission is free.

Norman Mackenzie Art Gallery Next door is this gallery which specialises in Canadian painting, much of it by local artists. Exhibits change and may be historical or contemporary. Free; open daily in the afternoons.

Diefenbaker Homestead This is also in the park. It's the boyhood home of this former prime minister, and is furnished with pioneer articles, some from the politician's family. Open daily.

University Campus This is on the east side of the park.

Plains Historical Museum
This museum is on the 4th floor of the old city hall at the corner of Scarth and 11th Avenue. There are several women working in the place who will guide you around, lovingly telling stories about the various items from Saskatchewan's past. It's open Monday to Friday from 11.30 am to 5 pm, weekends from 1 pm. Admission is $1, or 50c for students and seniors.

The Trial of Louis Riel
This is a theatrical dramatisation of the 1885 court battle fought over this leader of the Metis (Canadian half-breeds of French and Indian stock). One of Canada's most famous historical figures, Riel led two uprisings against the

government. The re-creation of the trial brings out issues that are still important as well as the animosity between the country's French and English. It's presented in authentic costumes in Government House, near the corner of Dewdney Avenue and Pasque St. There are shows three nights a week in summer. Tickets – which are inexpensive – are available at the Chamber of Commerce, 2145 Albert St, or at the door.

Government House, the restored home of the Lieutenant Governor of the Northwest Territories and Saskatchewan from 1891-1945, contains period furnishings and is free to visit. Open afternoons but closed Mondays.

RCMP Barracks & Museum

This museum (tel 780-5838) details the history of the Royal Canadian Mounted Police, or Mounties, from 1874 when they first headed west to keep the peace. It was in this part of the country that their slogan 'we always get our man' became legend. On display are uniforms, articles, replicas and stories of some of the famous or notorious exploits of the force. You can tour the training facilities and see the daily drill at 1 pm on weekdays. Open every day, the museum is at Dewdney Avenue West.

Also at the depot is the very popular RCMP Sunset Ceremony, a formal drill spectacle of drumming and marching surrounding the flag-lowering. It's a bit slow – call it a long hour – but the uniforms are colourfully impressive, and hey, the Mounties are one of Canada's native symbols! The ceremony is free but held only once a week in July and August at 6.45 pm. Ask the Tourist Office for details.

Science Centre

The new science centre (tel 352-2797) with hands-on types of exhibits is in the old SPC Power House building in Wascana Centre at 2026 Broad St.

Sports Hall of Fame

This small provincial museum at 2205 Victoria Avenue honours local athletes and teams. Open daily, free.

Firefighters Museum

You can see displays of old firefighting equipment here, at 1205 Ross Avenue. Open weekdays only; also free.

Wild Slides

This is a water-slide park with picnic area. It's 1.6 km east of town on Highway 1. Open from June to September.

Events

The big annual event is Buffalo Days – a 12-day celebration held toward the end of July. Stores put up special decor and some workers wear pioneer garb. A talent stage is set up offering free entertainment and the days are filled with competitions, pancake breakfasts, a beard-growing contest, parades and a big barbecue in Wascana Park. The Exhibition features midway rides, music shows, a casino and various displays and exhibits. A fireworks display wraps up the festival.

Through the summer there are free Sunday performances in the Bandshell in Wascana Center.

Mosaic is a three-day multicultural event with ethnic foods, music and entertainment. It's held in early June.

The three-day Folk Festival at the university is also usually held in early June.

Activities

You can visit the Regina Court Club with $2.50 and a youth hostel card. Use the racquetball, badminton or squash courts for an hour, then hop into the whirlpool, sauna or shower. Racquet rentals are 50c.

For $4 you can get a pass at the YMCA to use their courts, gym or pool. Men can use the facilities during the day, women after 6 pm.

Youth Hostel members have free use of the university's physical education facilities, including pool, courts and gym. The fee is $1 for a locker.

Hostellers can also go to the top floor of the public library to listen to music, view 8 mm films or read. It's a good place for a rainy day. You must get a day card; ask at the hostel.

The Tourist Office can tell you about swimming at public pools. There's a pool in Wascana Centre.

There's roller skating at 'Great Skate'. Call for times and skate rental prices.

The Devonian Pathway is 11 km of paved bike routes through four city parks. Bicycle rentals are available in Wascana Park.

The Regina Astronomical Society has a telescope set up on Broad St opposite the CBC building by Wascana Park and is open on Wednesday nights in summer for public viewing.

Places to Stay

Hostels The youth hostel, called *Turgeon Hostel* (tel 522-4200) at 2310 McIntyre St, is not right downtown but is close and quite central. The rates are $8 for members, $11 for non-members. They have 50 beds and cooking facilities, a laundromat and canoe rentals.

The *YMCA* (tel 527-6661) at 2400 13th Avenue rents only to men at $18. There is a cheap cafeteria and pool you can use (see the Activities section for details).

The *YWCA* (tel 525-2141) at 1940 McIntyre St, is a little more at $26.50 plus a $2 key deposit. They have a cafeteria, pool and kitchen.

For men in need there's the *Salvation Army* on Osler between 11th and 12th. As in many cities, they'll offer a free bed and breakfast. The place is not especially pleasant.

Bed & Breakfasts There are quite a few of these around the province – most in small towns – and they are not expensive. In Regina there is *B & J's* at 2066 Ottawa St, only about three blocks from downtown, just south of Victoria St. In this two-storey house on a residential street there are four rooms at $15 for singles, $25 for doubles with breakfast.

Hotels The best of the low-budget places is the *Georgia Hotel* (tel 352-4696) at 1927 Hamilton St, about a block north of the bus station. It is good and clean, and the bar and restaurant have recently been renovated. They offer full meals at budget prices. Single rooms are $20 without bath, $24 with; doubles are $23 without, $27 with. There are 65 rooms.

The *Lasalle Hotel* (tel 522-7655) at 1840 Hamilton, has some renovated rooms. Prices vary quite a bit depending on the room and facilities, with rates at $17 to $30. This place is central but basic.

Cheaper and still more basic is the *Empire*, 1718 McIntyre, corner of South Railway. It is north-west of central downtown but an easy walk. They have clean, simple rooms without toilet or bath but with a sink. Singles are $15, doubles about $20. There are many other cheap hotels around town but most are pretty grim.

Moving up the scale is the large and good *Relax Inn*, 1110 Victoria Avenue East, with nearly 200 modern rooms. Rates are $33 to $44 for singles or doubles.

Other hotels in the downtown area are costlier, though the *Plains Motor Hotel* is an exception, with rooms from $28 to $40. *Sheraton Centre* (tel 569-1666) at 1818 Victoria Avenue is $67 and way up. *Regina Inn* (tel 525-6767) at 1975 Broad St has rooms for $70 to $87. *Hotel Saskatchewan* (tel 522-7691) on the corner of Scarth and Victoria is $69 to $150.

Motels Most of the motels are on Highway 1 east of town. Cheapest is the *Siesta* at the corner of Park and Victoria by the Pump Bar with singles at $24 to $36.

The *North Star* (tel 352-0723), a few km from town, is the last motel on the north side of the highway. It's pale blue and set back from the road. Rooms are $23 to $50 for singles or doubles with air-conditioning.

The *Coachman Inn Motel* (tel 522-8525) is closer to town. It's the orange place at 835 Victoria. Rooms vary in price from $29 to $34.

The *Sunrise* (tel 527-5447) is near the overpass on Highway 1 East just out of town. Rooms with TV and air-conditioning are $32 to $60.

The *Intowner*, 1015 Albert St, has rooms at $34 to $50.

Camping As you approach Regina from the east on Highway 1 there are a few crappy campsites, mainly for trailers. One might prove useful for a short stay.

Places to Eat

Many restaurants in Regina are closed on Sundays, but the Saturday newspaper is full of ads for Sunday brunch buffets offered around town.

A clean, friendly place for simple meals is the *Pantry Restaurant* on Rose, north of 11th. For a snack they serve cinnamon buns and muffins. *Grandma Lee's* at the corner of Albert St and 7th Avenue is a chain specialising in soups and sandwiches on their own breads. It's in the midtown Plaza.

Mr Mike's at 302 Albert St has small steak dinners with a potato, bread and all-you-can-eat salad bar. Good value.

The Elephant & Castle, a British-style pub is found in the Cornwall Centre, which you enter at the corner of 11th and Scarth. Part of the restaurant facade is from the bank building built on the site in 1911. Also in the mall on the 2nd level is a cheap food fair.

The 1928 Warehouse Village Shopping Mall, a restored building at the corner of 11th and Lorne has the *Post & Beam*, an inexpensive spot. There's also a coffee shop downstairs.

Perky's, at the corner of 12th and Broad, is a chain similar to Smitty's or Sambo's: a bit plastic, with no pretensions. Meals are $4 to $6, coffees are refilled. It's a good place for breakfast as it opens at 6 am.

For Chinese food there's *Pagoda Gardens*, 1745 Broad St. It opens at 4.30 pm and closes late. The decor includes red-and-white tablecloths with vinyl chairs (what else?) But the food is cheap and not bad. A Vietnamese place, the *Vien Dong*, at 1841 is better.

On Scarth opposite the park the *Taker Outer* makes fresh sandwiches to go and the nearby *Copper Kettle* is open all day seven days a week and offers pizzas, Italian and Greek dishes and cheap breakfasts.

The restaurant at the Wascana Marina in the park near Broad St is recommended. It's a small place with some pleasant outdoor tables run as a teaching restaurant by a youth organisation; good value. They're open every day but don't do dinners on Sunday. Try a bison burger.

For a splurge, *Roxy's Bistro* is within walking distance from the town centre at 1844 14th Avenue. They have a fairly extensive and well balanced menu with an emphasis on French influences. The breads and desserts are made on the premises. Closed Sunday and Monday.

Nightlife

Barthelby's on the corner of Broad and 12th is a nicely decorated restaurant-bar where the food is slightly more than 'budget', though it's a good place for a beer and chat. No music. Young locals frequent the place.

The *Copper Kettle* is a restaurant, though it's popular with students as a place for beer. No music either.

In the 1928 Warehouse Mall on the corner of 11th and Lorne, the *Speak Easy* is a small, quiet bar with a real 'speakeasy' in the front door to talk through.

The better hotels have lounges: some quiet, some with live music.

The Saskatchewan Centre of the Arts has performances of opera, musicals and the symphony orchestra.

Other than the places mentioned, there's lots of bingo played in Regina.

Getting There & Away

Air The airport is a 15-minute drive west of downtown.

Air Canada (tel 525-4711), with an office at 2015 12th Avenue, has flights east and west, with the following standard one-way fares: Vancouver $239, Thunder Bay $216 and Montreal $362 – all plus a little over 10% tax.

Norcanair (tel 525-8711) serves smaller points around the province.

Bus The station is near downtown on Hamilton St, just south of Victoria. There are lockers for 50c and a quick-lunch counter. Three bus companies operate out of the station: the Saskatchewan Transportation Company covers the small towns in the province; Moose Mountain Lines does more or less the same. Greyhound (tel 565-3340), is the most important one, with five trips daily to Calgary and Vancouver, and four daily to Winnipeg and Toronto. One-way fares: Winnipeg $38, Calgary $50 and Montreal $90.

Train Union Station is at the corner of South Railway St and Rose, one block west of Brock. It's in the northern downtown area, an easy walk from anywhere in town. There are lockers in the station which cost 50c for 24 hours.

Calgary and Vancouver: one train daily, in the evening

Toronto and Montreal: one train daily, in the morning

Saskatoon and Prince Albert: 5.30 pm.

One-way fares: Calgary – $68, Thunder Bay – $100 (about 24 hours).

Getting Around

Airport Transport The airport is about a 15-minute drive. There's an airport bus which connects major hotels with each flight arrival or departure. You can get it at the Hotel Saskatchewan at Scarth and Victoria. It operates on weekdays only, leaves one hour before flights and costs $4. It doesn't run on weekends.

A 'limo', a taxi at half the price, can be had by asking at the better hotels.

Bus Regina Transit (tel 569-7810) operates several bus routes around the city.

Car Rentals Holiday Rentals (tel 525-1377) is at 1975 Broad St. Other companies are Hertz and Avis.

Bicycle Western Cycle at 1745 Hamilton St is a good cycle shop. Rentals are available in Wascana Park, and there is a system of 11 km of paved bike routes through four city parks, called the Devonian Pathway.

Hitching For hitching east take the No 4 from downtown. At Lindsay on Victoria is *Robin's Donuts*, open 24 hours. It's a handy place to go if you're cold, tired, or just need a break from the road.

Tours There are 20-minute boat tours on Wascana Lake available. They leave from the landing north of the Legislature.

The Saskatchewan Wheat Pool (tel 569-4411), offers assistance in planning a visit for those interested in seeing a grain elevator or a livestock-selling yard.

Lastly, Prairie City Tour Guides (tel 949-5727), 918 Garry St North, offer various city and area tours.

MOOSE JAW

Moose Jaw is a small, typical farm-supply town. It has a wild animal park with mainly local animals including bison, and a museum which displays the development of transportation in the west and has old carts, cars and trains. Admission costs $2. The museum is one of four Western Development Museums around the province, each specialising in an area of provincial history. The town also hosts an international band festival annually. It's a bad place to get stuck hitching.

LOUIS "Scoop" Lewry, the mayor of Moose Jaw, Sask., was trying yesterday to get in touch with impressionist Rich Little, who made several jokes about the city on TV Wednesday.

The Canadian comedian was host of a show called Rich Little and Friends which aired on the CBC in Saskatchewan at 9 p.m. In one of the segments, Little said Moose Jaw is so small they had to close the zoo when the chicken died.

He joked that Moose Jaw's fire department is a 4-year-old who wets his bed. He also said Moose Jaw has no weather and the hooker is a virgin.

Is Lewry upset? Is he stompin' angry, fit to be tied and ready to shoot Little on sight?

"No . . . no," Lewry replied yesterday. "I've always said, 'I don't care what you say about me as long as you spell my name right.' "

Lewry, who used to be the local radio station's news director, was trying to get Little's address so he could send him some brochures about the city of 35,000 which is on the Trans-Canada Highway 70 kilometres west of Regina.

By the way, the fire department has a staff of 40 and six vehicles. The Moose Jaw Wild Animal Park has more than 200 animals and is still open.

Southern Saskatchewan

BIG MUDDY BADLANDS

South of Regina and Moose Jaw down near the US border are these badlands: a vast, hot area of sandstone formations, hills and valleys once used by stagecoach robbers, cattle rustlers and all the other bad-guy types you see in western movies. In fact, the outlaw Butch Cassidy used to ride here.

CYPRESS HILLS

This is a small region in south Saskatchewan and Alberta offering geographical respite from the prairies. It's a pretty area of small lakes, streams and green hills up to 1400 metres high. Much of the land is park which stretches across the provincial border. There's organised camping on the Alberta side around the lakes where tenting costs $7, but it gets very crowded in summer.

A dirt road links this area to Fort Walsh, where there's a national historic park. The fort is a remnant of the district's rich but sad history.

The hills, always a sanctuary for animals, were at one time a sanctuary for Plains Indians. Information at the old Northwest Mounted Police fort tells the story of the time when 'a man's life was worth a horse and a horse was worth a pint of whisky'.

GRASSLANDS NATIONAL PARK

Not yet developed, this new park near Val Marie, south of Swift Current, will preserve shortgrass prairie land, a prairie dog town, badlands, some historic Indian sites and other geographical features. Ask for latest details.

GREAT SAND HILLS

Just west of Swift Current (or north of Maple Creek and Sand Hills) is a semi-desert with dunes and near-arid vegetation.

Saskatoon

Saskatoon, a small, quiet city, sits smack in the middle of the Canadian prairies. The clean, wide streets, low skyline and flat surroundings give the city a western flavour and with the South Saskatchewan River drifting through, makes for a peaceful, easy-paced community. The largest employer in town is the university.

However, Saskatoon, as the second city of the province, is a farm trading centre. It also acts as a transportation, communication and commercial centre. Six bridges link the city across the river.

In 1883, 35 members of the Temperance Colonisation Colony founded a settlement on these Cree lands. The town stayed but the ban on alcohol didn't. In 1890 the railway hit town and growth began. The city has had its ups and downs but is now patiently waiting for the potash boom to begin and for the uranium mines in the vicinity to be developed. Some of the world's largest potash deposits are nearby.

There isn't a lot here for the visitor and with a short look-see you'll have a feel for the place. Accommodation is reasonable and you can get a fair meal.

Just off the main thoroughfares, residential streets are lined with small, neat square houses – some old, some new.

Orientation

The South Saskatchewan River cuts through the city diagonally north-east to south-west. The main downtown area, which is small, lies on the west bank; the university is on the opposite side.

Idylwyld Drive divides the city into east and west. Out of town in each direction Idylwyld becomes Highway 16, Yellowhead Highway. Twenty-second St splits the city into north-south sections.

The downtown core is bounded by the river to the south, 1st Avenue on the west, 25th St to the north and Spadina Crescent and the river again (which has shifted direction) to the east.

Streets run east-west, avenues north-south. The main street is 2nd Avenue. Another important street, with lots of stores, is 21st St East. The Bessborough Hotel, the large chateau-like place, sits at the bottom of 21st St, by the river.

Behind the Bessborough is one of the city's large parks, Kiwanis Memorial. The park runs beside the river. At each end of the park, Spadina Crescent carries on along the river.

Just west of Idylwyld on 20th St West is an interesting old area with many restaurants. Most are Chinese but there are also a few cafés with Ukrainian food. In between are a couple of cheap hotels, pawnshops, a second-hand bookshop and a Kentucky Fried Chicken.

Information

The Saskatoon Visitor's Bureau (tel 242-1206) is at 304 Spadina Crescent, near the river not far from the town centre. It's closed on Sundays and in the evenings. There might also be one in Market Mall, corner of Preston Avenue and Louise St.

In summer there are small booths in and around town, including a couple on the main roads leading in to town; open daily.

The lobby of the town's oldest and largest hotel, the Bessborough, has a desk for tour information and has maps and pamphlets on attractions.

For provincial information, Tourism Saskatchewan is in the Bank of Montreal Building, 2103 11th Avenue.

Western Development Museum

You open the door of this museum and *voila!* you're looking down Main Street, circa 1910. It looks like a movie set and contains stores, workshops, a hotel, a printing shop and other establishments. The general store is good. Don't miss the model of men playing chess. There are all manner of goods, tins, relics and supplies

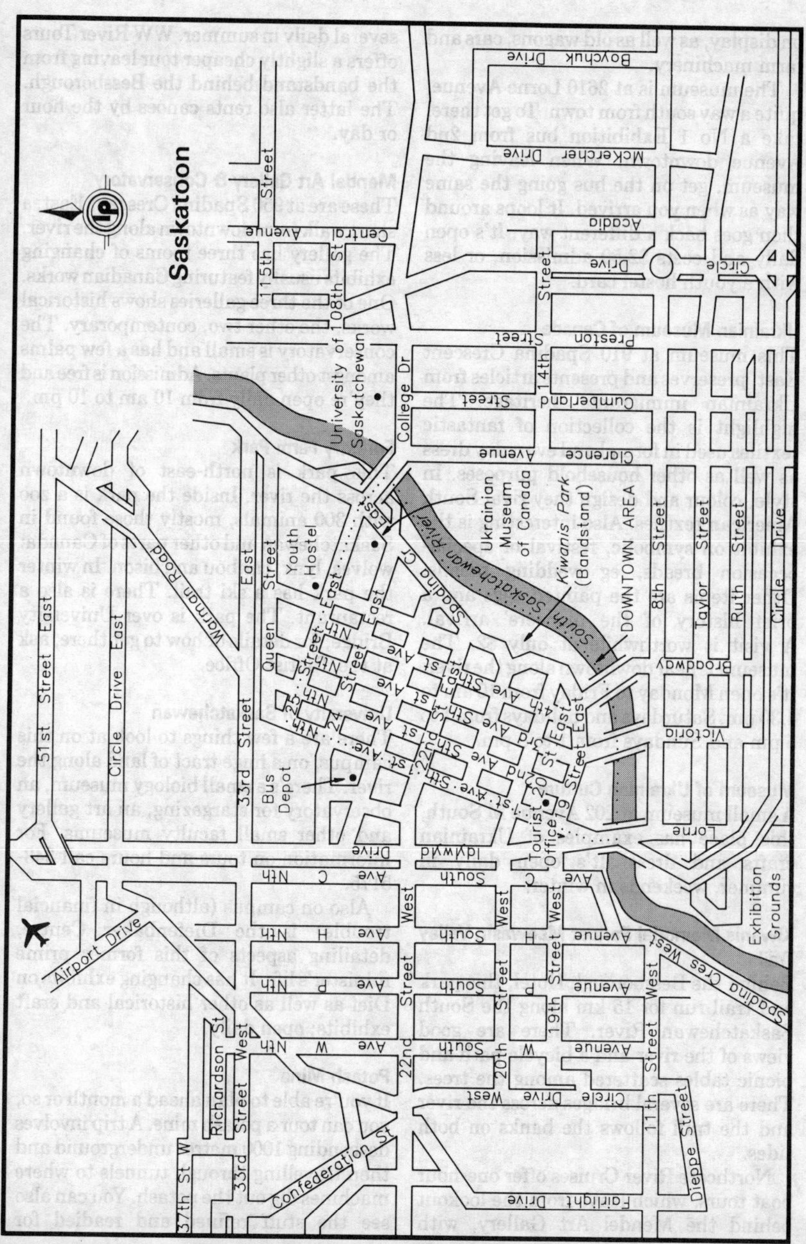
Saskatoon
Boychuk Drive
McKercher Drive
Acadia Drive
Circle
Preston
14th Street
Cumberland Avenue
Clarence Avenue
College Dr
University of Saskatchewan
108th St
Central Avenue
115th Street
Ukrainian Museum of Canada
Kiwanis Park (Bandstand)
South Saskatchewan River
DOWNTOWN AREA
8th Street
Taylor Street
Ruth Street
Circle Drive
Broadway
Victoria
Lorne
Exhibition Grounds
Spadina Cres West
Spadina Cr East
Youth Hostel
Queen Street
25th St East
24th St East
23rd St East
22nd St
21st St
20th St East
19th Street East
1st Ave
2nd Ave
3rd Ave
4th Ave
5th Ave
Bus Depot
Tourist Office
Idylwyld Drive
Ave C North
Ave C South
Ave H North
Ave H South
Ave P North
Ave P South
Ave W North
Ave W South
33rd Street West
22nd Street West
20th Street West
19th Street West
11th Street West
Circle Drive West
Dieppe Street
Fairlight Drive
Warman Road
Circle Drive East
51st Street East
Airport Drive
Richardson St
33rd Street West
37th St W
Confederation St

on display, as well as old wagons, cars and farm machinery.

The museum is at 2610 Lorne Avenue, quite a way south from town. To get there, take a No 1 Exhibition bus from 2nd Avenue downtown. When leaving the museum, get on the bus going the same way as when you arrived. It loops around then goes back a different way. It's open daily and costs $2.50 admission, or less with a youth hostel card.

Ukrainian Museum of Canada

This museum at 910 Spadina Crescent East, preserves and presents articles from Ukrainian immigrants' heritage. The highlight is the collection of fantastic textiles used in formal and everyday dress as well as other household purposes. In style, colour and design they rival South American textiles. Also interesting is the exhibit on symbolic, festival or special-occasion breads, eg wedding breads. Other items are the painted eggs and a brief history of the pioneers' arrival. A visit is worthwhile at only $2. The museum is near downtown along the river. It's open Monday to Friday from 10 am to 4.30 pm, Saturdays and holidays from 1 to 5 pm and Sundays from 1 to 8 pm.

Museum of Ukrainian Culture

A small museum at 202 Avenue M South, this place has examples of Ukrainian crafts and dress. It's open daily in summer, weekends in winter.

Kiwanis Memorial Park at Meewasin Valley Trail

Behind the Bessborough Hotel, this park and trail run for 15 km along the South Saskatchewan River. There are good views of the river and a bicycle path and picnic tables scattered among the trees. There are several bridges across the river and the trail follows the banks on both sides.

Northcote River Cruises offer one-hour boat tours, which leave from the lookout behind the Mendel Art Gallery, with several daily in summer. WW River Tours offers a slightly cheaper tour leaving from the bandstand behind the Bessborough. The latter also rents canoes by the hour or day.

Mendel Art Gallery & Conservatory

These are at 950 Spadina Crescent East, a short walk from downtown along the river. The gallery has three rooms of changing exhibits usually featuring Canadian works. One of the three galleries shows historical works, the other two, contemporary. The conservatory is small and has a few palms amongst other plants. Admission is free and they're open daily from 10 am to 10 pm.

Forestry Farm Park

This park is north-east of downtown across the river. Inside the park is a zoo with 300 animals, mostly those found in Saskatchewan and other parts of Canada: wolves, lynx, caribou and bison. In winter the park has a ski trail. There is also a restaurant. The park is over University Bridge; for details of how to get there, ask at the Tourist Office.

University of Saskatchewan

There are a few things to look at on this campus, on a huge tract of land along the river. There's a small biology museum, an observatory for stargazing, an art gallery and other small faculty museums. For information on tours and hours call 343-5175.

Also on campus (although in financial trouble) is the Diefenbaker Centre, detailing aspects of this former prime minister's life. It has changing exhibits on Dief as well as other historical and craft exhibits; open daily.

Potash Mine

If you're able to plan ahead a month or so, you can tour a potash mine. A trip involves descending 1000 metres underground and then travelling through tunnels to where machines dig out the potash. You can also see the stuff refined and readied for shipping. For details call 664-5543 or write to 'Tours', Public Affairs Department, Potash Corporation of Saskatchewan, 500-122 1st Avenue South, Saskatechewan.

Events
Folkfest is a festival that takes place in late summer and early September. The fee of $7 gets you into 20 multicultural pavilions set up around the city, presenting food, crafts, music and dances.

The Exhibition is a five-day event in mid-July with concerts, rides, parades and exhibits.

Rocktoberfest is a big beer bash with rock and Bavarian music held in October.

Places to Stay
Hostels The *Youth Hostel* (tel 244-0944) is set up in the YWCA, 220 24th St East, but is open only in summer, usually from June to the first week in September. The rate for a bed is $5.75.

The *YWCA* at 5th Avenue North on 25th St East rents rooms all year round to women for $20 for singles. Look for the blue sign near 3rd Avenue. They have a pool and a small kitchen.

Males, if they're in need, can stay at the institutional *Salvation Army* (tel 244-6260), at the corner of 19th St and Avenue C in south Saskatoon. If you arrive after 10.30 pm you'll need a slip from the police station before they'll let you in. A bed in a dorm and meals are free but you can only stay a few days.

Bed & Breakfasts If you don't mind going out of town a bit, *Northbound Acres* (tel 239-4710) is a bed & breakfast on a working farm. Singles are $15, doubles $20, plus $3 per breakfast. It's 32 km north-east of Saskatoon, 6.4 km north-east of Osler.

Hotels The *Patricia Hotel*, 345 2nd Avenue North at 25th St East, is the best and cleanest of the low-budget places. It's good value at $19 for singles, $22 to $32 for doubles depending on facilities.

The *Senator*, right in the centre of town at the corner of 3rd Avenue South and 21st St East, is old but was recently renovated. The rooms are good and $32 for singles includes breakfast.

There are a couple of cheapies on 2nd Avenue at 20th St, across from the visitor centre.

Moving up the scale, there are several moderately priced places. The *Westgate Inn* (tel 382-3722) is at 2501 22nd St West with rooms from $30 to $38.

At the corner of 2nd Avenue and 20th St is the *Capri Motor Hotel* (tel 244-6104). They have 64 rooms with rates varying a lot, from $28.

The *King George* (tel 244-6133) at 157 2nd Avenue North, is large and central, and slightly more expensive.

Motels The *Travelodge Motel* (tel 242-8881), near the airport, is like the others in the chain. It's pale yellow with an orange name sign. The motel section has rooms for $49 to $95. You'll find it at 106 Circle Drive West, at the corner of Idylwyld.

The following motels are all quite close to town.

The *Colonial Motel* is at 1301 8th St East, near the university. Rooms are $24 to $32.

Journeys End (tel 934-1122) at 2155 Northridge Drive near the airport offers good value with rooms for $36 to $43.

The *Relax Inn Motel*, 102 Cardinal Crescent, has singles/doubles at $34/39 and is very good and clean.

Top End There are quite a few expensive hotels out around the airport as well as these two:

Holiday Inn (tel 244-2311) at 90 22nd St East, has rooms from $45 to $90.

Hotel Bessborough (tel 244-5521) at 601 Spadina Crescent East, costs $56 to $92.

Camping There's a site called *Tourist*

Campsite, south of downtown off Spadina Crescent West, by the river.

Places to Eat

The *Adonis* on 3rd Avenue on the corner of 22nd St is recommended for lunch. It serves soups, salads, sandwiches, vegetarian offerings and some Middle-Eastern items, all fresh and inexpensive. There are outside tables, too. Very busy.

The *Commodore Restaurant*, at the corner of 2nd Avenue North and 22nd St East, is a basic restaurant with a varied menu. They offer good value breakfasts. The dinner special from Monday to Wednesday from 5 pm consists of a large sirloin steak, potato, dessert, salad and coffee, all for $6.95. A lasagne costs $4.95. Open daily until late, Sundays from noon.

Next door is a quick deli with tasty vegetarian sandwiches.

Maxim's on 2nd Avenue right downtown, offers good value buffets, dinner specials and cheap steaks.

Johnny's Inn at the corner of 22nd St East and 3rd Avenue is a small cafeteria popular with workers, which has good hamburgers. They also serve home-made chillies and large sandwiches.

On 21st St East between 2nd and 3rd Avenues are the very unassuming cafeterias of *Kresges* and *Woolworth's* (five-and-dime stores). Both offer a full meal for $3.29, a lighter lunch of soup and sandwich for $2.89, and just about everything is under $3.50. The food is decent and quick, if plain.

The *Artful Dodger* at 119 4th Avenue South, is an English sort of pub with typically British meals.

Even Saskatoon has a modern Canadian-style trendy spot. It's called *St Tropez Café*, 243 3rd Avenue South, and serves the standard quiche or crepes for about $6. Open-face sandwiches with salad are $4.25. Continental breakfast is $2.25 for a croissant, bun, cheese and fruit. Dinners are more expensive but the fondue for two is a nice deal. The surroundings are pleasant and the food is well prepared. The café is open from 9 am to 11 pm.

Lucci's on 3rd Avenue offers good but pricey Italian food.

There are a number of restaurants along 20th St West. The *Trio Café* at No 509 is ordinary but serves three or four Ukrainian dishes, cabbage rolls and *varenyky* (stuffed savoury pastry).

The *Dragon House* a Chinese place, has cheap lunch specials. There's a large, cheap, Chinese buffet offered in the *Capri Motor Hotel* downtown, lunch or dinner. The *Haiping* at 617 20th St West is good for Cantonese and Mandarin food. They have a Sunday smorgasbord and dim sum daily.

Eightieth St East and 22nd St West, offer abundant choices for those with wheels.

Out of town, *Taunte Maria's Mennonite Kitchen* (tel 212-2750) on the corner of Faithful Avenue (coincidence?) and 51st St offers basic, healthy farm food.

Shopping

A store that might be worth checking out is the large old Army & Navy at the corner of 21st St East and 3rd Avenue South. They have really cheap clothes and some camping supplies.

Nightlife

The *North 40 Inn*, on the corner of 20th Avenue West and 6th St, has live country music. Admission is a few dollars.

Capper's Place brings in Canadian rock bands. It's at 215 2nd Avenue South.

At the *Capri* in Club Soda there's rock and blues music. It's at the corner of 2nd Avenue South and 20th St East.

The *London Bridge Inn* at 3120 Laurier is an English-style pub with British beer on tap and (sometimes) entertainment.

Getting There & Away

Bus The big new bus station (tel 933-5700) for destinations all over Saskatchewan, is at 23rd St East and Pacific Avenue; there's a cafeteria here.

Regina: daily at 8 am – $15

Winnipeg, Edmonton, Calgary: two a day to each; one during the day, one at night.

Fares: Jasper $60, Winnipeg $53, Edmonton $36.

Train You won't be too happy with this station's location – it's way out, a long way west from downtown on Chappell Drive. A taxi fare gets close to $10 and the bus service to major downtown hotels is $4, but a city bus runs from the curling rink across from the station to town at a quarter to and quarter after each hour. For train information ring 1-800-665-8630.

Edmonton-Jasper-Vancouver: late in the evening – $68 to Jasper

Winnipeg-Toronto: early in the morning – $62 to Winnipeg

Regina: daily at 8 am – $22.

Getting Around

Bus For city bus information call 664-9100. Most things are within walking distance.

Bicycle Recycles (tel 652-7877) at 221 20th St West, rents bicycles and does repairs.

Car Rentals Rent-A-Wreck (tel 933-4353) at 518 Circle Drive East charges about $10 a day plus mileage.

There are other local and well-known companies around town and at the airport.

Tours Heritage Tours (tel 382-1911) run a 2½-hour trip around town, taking in some old homes, the university and city parks. They run another one focussing more on history. Also offered are more extensive tours out of town, one an overnighter all the way to Prince Albert National Park.

Around Saskatchewan

Prince Albert National Park

A large wilderness area, the park is 200 km north of Saskatoon on Highways 2 and 263. The park is typical wooded lakeland of the prairie north. Hiking and good canoeing in summer provide access. The system of inter-connected rivers and lakes is a good one. There's fishing, camping for $6 and cross-country ski trails in winter. The park's service centre is Wakesiu on the lake of the same name, where you'll find swimming, lodgings, groceries and petrol.

South of the park is the town of Prince Albert, also called PA. The area north of town is known as the lake district. It's a relatively undeveloped area of woods, bush, lakes and cottages. Aside from those of the National Park, other mega-lakes are Candle Lake and Montreal Lake.

North of the National Park is pretty much untouched wilderness.

Lac La Ronge Provincial Park

Some of the 55 provincial canoe routes are here; you can hire canoes and other gear.

Flin Flon

Just over the border in Manitoba, Flin Flon has several canoe outfitters for canoeing the northern lakes.

Yorkton

Yorkton, a major town in east central Saskatchewan, reflects the area's Ukrainian heritage with its onion-domed churches. There's a branch of the provincial museum system here, which depicts the various immigrant groups.

Nearby are two provincial parks, Good Spirit, which has good swimming and the larger Duck Mountain Provincial Park, on Manitoba's border.

Place to Stay The *Corona Motor Inn* at 345 West Broadway has been recommended. It cost $42 for doubles and has very good service, quiet rooms, a restaurant and bar.

Veregrin

Veregrin has a small Doukhobour Heritage

Village and a statue of author Leo Tolstoy, who helped this religious group emigrate from Russia in 1898-99. The town is 265 km north-east of Regina.

Fort Battleford National Historic Park
This park is about 140 km north-west of Saskatoon off the Yellowhead Highway. The Northwest Mounted Police built the fort in 1876 to help settle the area and police the Indians, traders and white settlers. Inside the walls are five buildings you can visit which contain police and Indian artefacts, tools and memorabilia. Open daily, free. There's also a museum in North Battleford dealing with agricultural history.

Meadow Lake Provincial Park
Similar to Prince Albert National Park, this one runs along a chain of lakes by the Alberta border. There are nature trails and a series of longer hiking trails which allow for wildlife viewing. There is a lot of wildlife in the park, and good beaches on many of the lakes. Aside from campsites, visitors can stay in simple, privately-operated rental cabins.

The park is north of Meadow Lake off Highway 55, and is part of the Northern Woods & Water Route, a road system that begins in Manitoba and ends in British Columbia.

Alberta

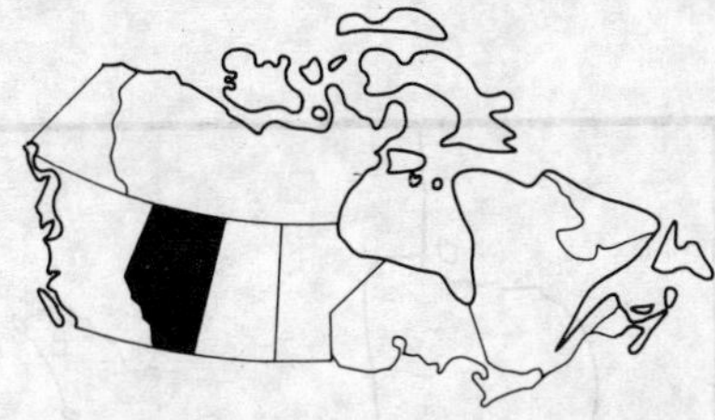

Entered Confederation: 1 September 1905
Area: 661,188 square km
Population: 2,238,000, fourth largest

Not long ago Alberta was just a vast tract of land with a few scattered trading posts. Then came the farms and huge ranches that the west is known for.

But in the early '70s this began to change. Oil was discovered, lots of it. And then natural gas, lots as well. For over a decade, people and money poured in from all parts of the country. Edmonton and Calgary became booming, modern cities, the fifth and sixth largest in the country.

Recently things have taken a new turn. With the fall in the price of oil and grains, the economy base, the boom has ended and hard times have quickly come to many. Some native Albertans have left the province but most of the departing are going back to the homes they left in the middle of the Alberta rush. Still, there is a lot of wealth and potential and the province now has more political clout than it had in the past. Development continues, although at a much reduced rate and, of course, things can change quickly depending on the world oil markets. Alberta has a strongly independent, individualistic rancher mentality and this remains intact.

Aside from gas and oil, Alberta makes money through coal and other minerals, and through a good agricultural base of wheat, barley, rye and beef.

Visitors can take advantage of the lowest petrol prices in Canada and the lack of any sales tax.

The western edge of the province rises from foothills into the Rocky Mountains; the east is a continuation of the prairies. The northern area is rugged, lake-filled forest, while the south is very dry and flat with badlands in some areas.

As for its climate, Alberta has more sunshine per year than any other province. August and September are particularly good for travelling: in my trips west I've almost never seen rain in late summer. In the mountains summers are short and it's always cool at night.

The Tourist Office has produced a provincial canoe map and has an adventure guide describing various outdoor activities, trips and tours.

Edmonton

Edmonton, like Calgary and the west in general, is in a period of reassessment after a series of fluctuating fortunes. Once known as 'The Gateway to the North', its title changed to 'Oil Capital of Canada' in the 1970s when the entire province boomed. Calgary had the head offices and oil management but Edmonton had the technicians, the scientists and the wells – some 7000 of them within a 160 km radius.

They were heady days. Edmonton, Alberta's largest city, experienced explosive growth; the downtown area was totally transformed and modernised. The last few years have seen a dramatic downturn in the oil business and consequently the two main cities have eased up on development and are now forging identities in a less hectic atmosphere.

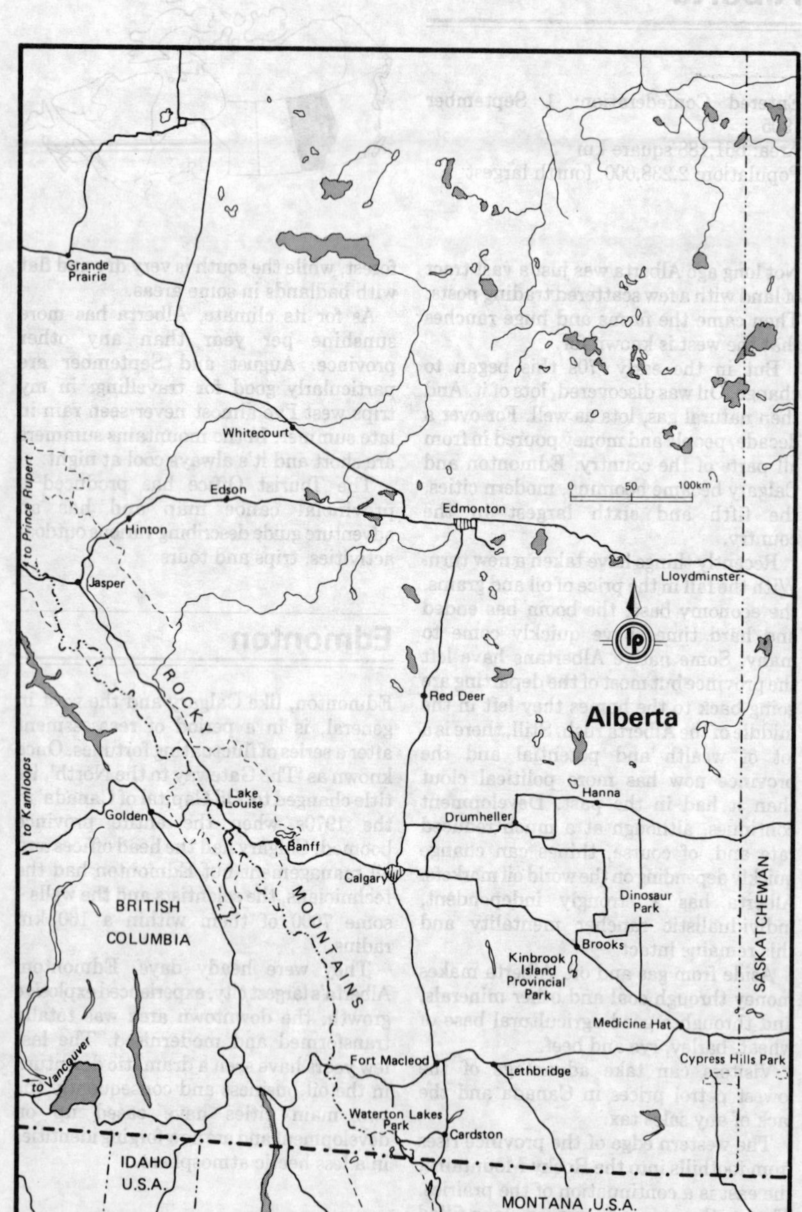
Alberta
Grande Prairie
Whitecourt
Edson
Edmonton
Hinton
Jasper
to Prince Rupert
to Kamloops
to Vancouver
Lloydminster
0 50 100km
Red Deer
ROCKY MOUNTAINS
Lake Louise
Golden
Banff
Calgary
Hanna
Drumheller
BRITISH COLUMBIA
Dinosaur Park
Brooks
Kinbrook Island Provincial Park
SASKATCHEWAN
Medicine Hat
Cypress Hills Park
Fort Macleod
Lethbridge
Waterton Lakes Park
Cardston
IDAHO U.S.A.
MONTANA ,U.S.A.

History

Before the Hudson's Bay Company built a fort in 1795, the area was populated by Cree and Blackfoot Indians. The small settlement grew as a fur-trading centre until about 1870, when the Canadian government opened up the area for pioneers. By 1891 the railway had arrived from Calgary and in 1892 the town of Edmonton was officially incorporated. In 1905, with the creation of Alberta, Edmonton – now with 8000 people – became the capital. WW I brought a large influx of people, mainly to work on the Alaskan Highway. In 1938, North America's first mosque was built here by 34 Muslims.

It was in the 1960s and '70s that real development in Edmonton began, when wells started hitting oil with great regularity.

The rapid changes to the city have caused some continuing problems. Many of the city's 25,000 Indians have little education or job training and the changes have made life harder for them in particular. Despite the lack of much physical evidence around town, the city does have a fairly long history and the native people played a major part in it.

Although the population has decreased somewhat, many of the newcomers now consider themselves Edmontonians. The steep prices of a few years ago have levelled off and the cultural life a city needs has grown noticeably. The downtown area is shiny, high-rise new with a complementary subway system.

The city averages over six hours of sun per day, although temperatures are cool. Summers are short but generally dry.

Orientation

Edmonton sits right in the middle of Alberta. The Rockies are about 300 km to the west, the rough lake country and Alaska Highway to the north. The North Saskatchewan River, which starts in the Columbian ice fields, drifts through the centre of town.

The main street, Jasper Avenue, is very long and runs east-west. All avenues go east-west; streets run north-south.

Though the city is spread out, the downtown core with the bus and train stations, restaurants and hotels is quite small. The central downtown area is bounded by 104th Avenue to the north and 100th Avenue to the south. The western edge is marked by 109th St, the eastern side by 95th St. The area is easily walkable.

The main intersection is Jasper Avenue and 101st St. At 100th St, two blocks north of Jasper, is the new Civic Centre with several municipal buildings. Here is the City Hall with lots of flags on top and a small green area in front with flowers and benches. To the east are the art gallery and law courts.

Another block north to 104th Avenue will bring you to the train station and main post office.

This entire area is very new and clean with many mirrored, 1970s-design, high-rise buildings. The bottom of 100th St is the office section. Many of Canada's banks have new buildings in the area. This is also the theatre and shopping district, with Eaton's and the large Edmonton Centre housing all types of stores in its mall.

A few blocks east of downtown there are a couple of sleazy streets, especially 96th St. The bars and hotels here aren't recommended. Along 97th St are many pawnshops, cash-for-goods stores and an Army & Navy Surplus which might be useful. A few blocks further will take you to the hostel.

West a few blocks from City Hall are a number of hotels in all price ranges, and the bus station. Jasper Avenue has mainly stores and restaurants.

Beneath the downtown area are underground walkways called 'pedways' which connect shopping malls with City Hall and the VIA Rail train station.

There is a good view of the south side of Edmonton from behind the Hotel

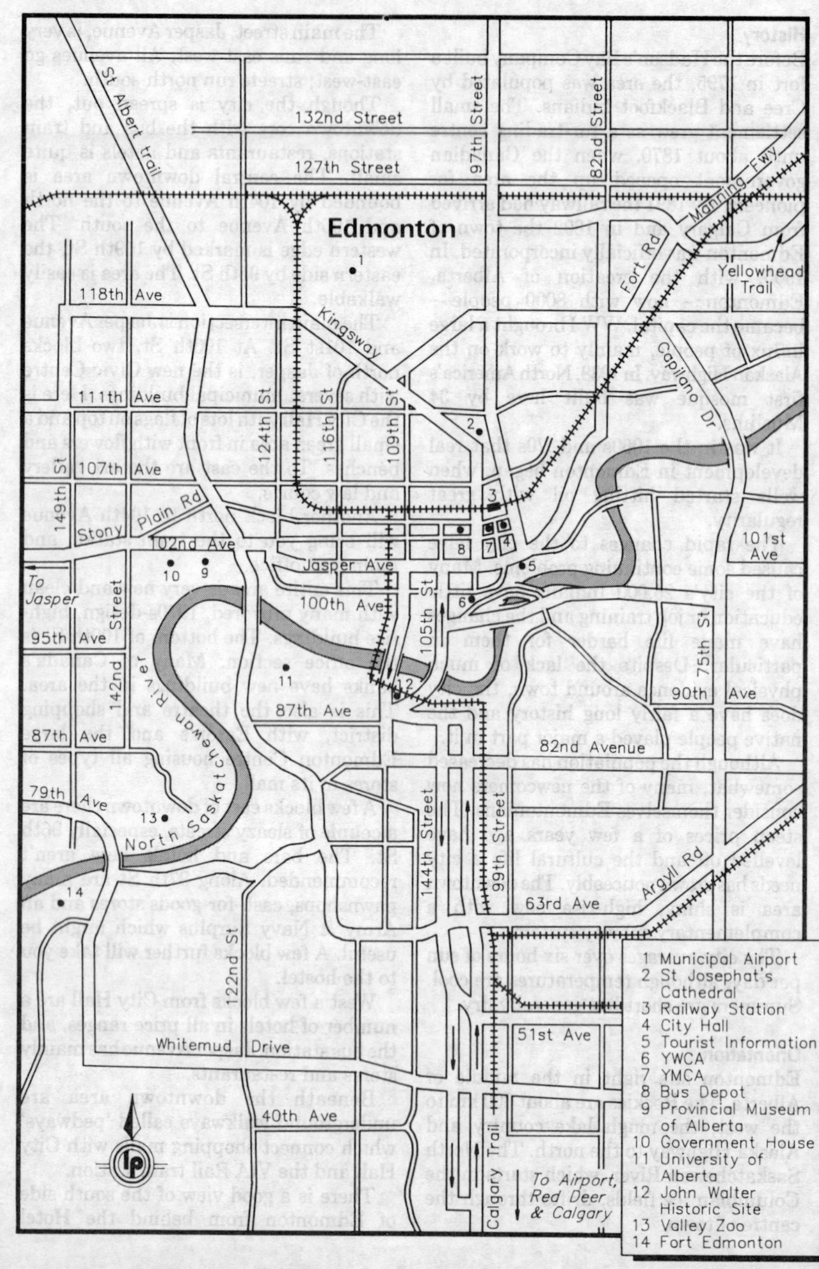
Edmonton
St Albert Trail
132nd Street
127th Street
97th Street
82nd Street
Manning Fwy
Fort Rd
Yellowhead Trail
118th Ave
Kingsway
Capilano Dr
111th Ave
124th St
116th St
109th St
107th Ave
149th St
Stony Plain Rd
102nd Ave
Jasper Ave
101st Ave
To Jasper
100th Ave
142nd Street
105th St
75th St
95th Ave
North Saskatchewan River
90th Ave
87th Ave
87th Ave
82nd Avenue
79th Ave
144th Street
99th Street
Argyll Rd
63rd Ave
122nd St
51st Ave
Whitemud Drive
40th Ave
Calgary Trail
To Airport, Red Deer & Calgary
1 Municipal Airport
2 St Josephat's Cathedral
3 Railway Station
4 City Hall
5 Tourist Information
6 YWCA
7 YMCA
8 Bus Depot
9 Provincial Museum of Alberta
10 Government House
11 University of Alberta
12 John Walter Historic Site
13 Valley Zoo
14 Fort Edmonton

Macdonald at 100th St and McDougal Hill.

West of the downtown centre, 124th St between 109th and 102nd Avenues is an expensive shopping district, with fashion boutiques, art galleries and a few bistros and restaurants.

South across the river, 82nd Avenue, also called Whyte, is a main street. On 82nd Avenue around 104th St there's a mini-downtown area with many stores and restaurants, including numerous Chinese ones.

To the east is Old Strathcona, a district with many old buildings that date from when this area was distinct from Edmonton itself. The area has undergone some low-key redevelopment and is a very agreeable part of town with a good selection of restaurants.

At the west end of 82nd Avenue is the university, and following the river south-west, Fort Edmonton, where the town began. Most of the south side is residential.

Calgary Trail leads south to the airport, Red Deer and Calgary.

Back on the north side of the river, both Jasper and 102nd Avenue go west from town through a middle-class residential area. They then lead into Stony Plains Rd, a commercial strip which becomes Highway 16 to Jasper. The strip includes motels and lots of fast-food restaurants, including Ponderosa and McDonald's.

Up 97th St north from town is the municipal airport. By the airport, 118th Avenue and one block north, the Yellowhead Trail, Highway 16, goes east to Saskatoon and west to Jasper.

Information

The Central Tourist Information Office is at 9797 Jasper.

South of town, just off Highway 2 to Calgary, by the big oil derrick (the city's symbol), is another office (tel 434-5322). They're open daily from 9.30 am to 4.30 pm and on weekends too, year-round. The address is 5068 103rd St.

For information on other parts of Alberta, go to Travel Alberta in the Imperial Oil Building at the corner of Jasper Avenue and 100th St.

Out of the centre there are also offices open in summer only, one on Highway 16 east and one on Highway 16 west.

Note that on Sunday, many places are closed in Edmonton.

Jobs For temporary work, try Northern Alberta Personnel Services at 11109 95th St; go in person at 6 am. Also check out the Chamber of Mines; it's in the phone book.

Parks

On each side of the North Saskatchewan River, which runs basically west-east through the city, is parkland. This appears to be one long park, though it's actually a series of small parks joined together. You can walk, jog or cycle all day along the system using the many trails and bridges. In Laurier Park, near the Valley Zoo, are nature paths which become cross-country ski trails in winter. Whitemud Park has a hang-gliding area. Throughout the parkland are dozens of picnic spots. Many of the city's other sites are in this green belt area.

Provincial Museum

This is another excellent western museum, well laid out with exhibits artistically displayed. The museum is divided into four parts: Habitat, Anthropology, Natural History and History. The Habitat section displays animals and birds of Alberta in incredibly realistic nature settings.

The Anthropology section covers the Indians of Alberta, with drawings, photos and examples of various plants and how the Indians used them. Some were used for medicine, some for spice and tea while others were smoked; at Blackfoot feasts, Saskatoon berries were mixed in a soup of buffalo fat and blood and used for dessert. A large display tells the story of one of the most important Blackfoot festivals, a social

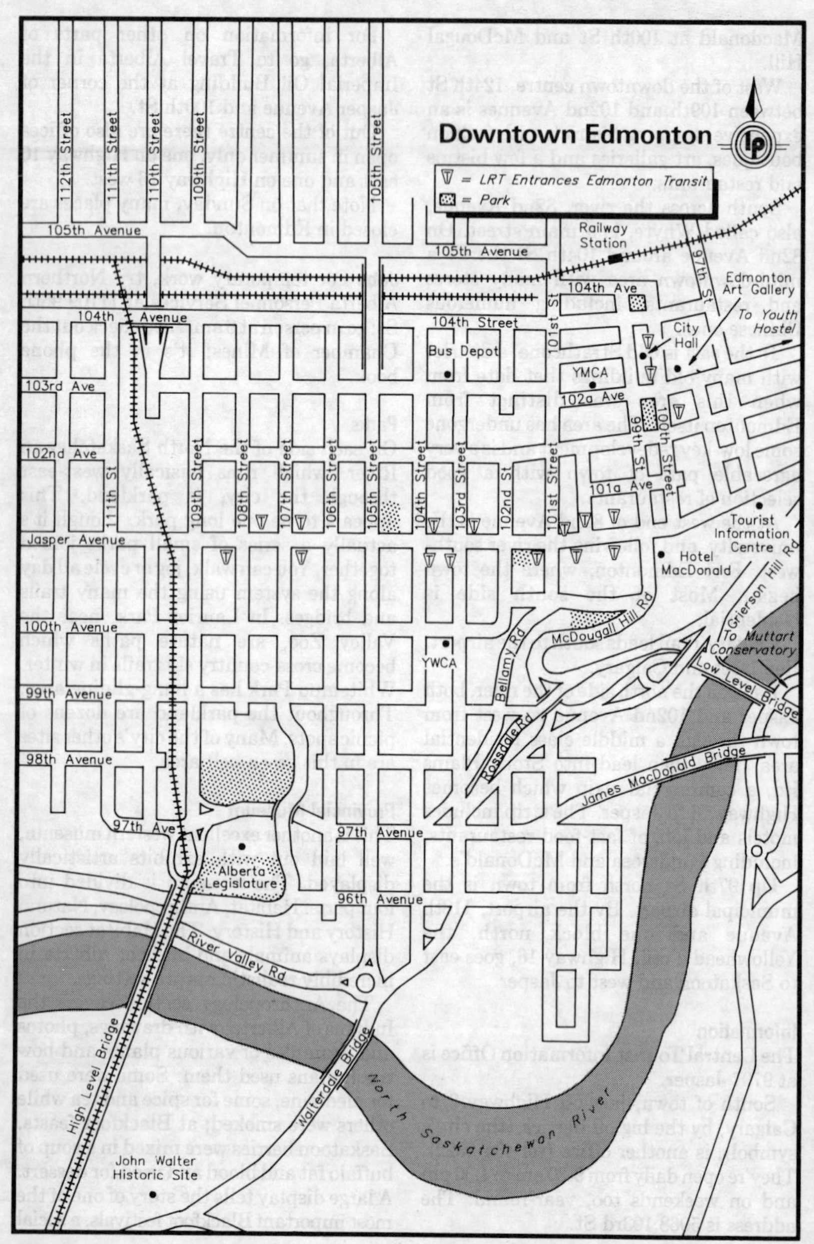

Downtown Edmonton
= LRT Entrances Edmonton Transit
= Park
112th Street
111th Street
110th Street
109th Street
105th Street
105th Avenue
105th Avenue
Railway Station
97th St
Edmonton Art Gallery
To Youth Hostel
104th Ave
104th Avenue
104th Street
101st St
City Hall
Bus Depot
YMCA
103rd Ave
102a Ave
99th St
100th Street
102nd Ave
111th St
109th Street
108th Street
107th Street
106th Street
105th Street
104th Street
103rd Street
102nd St
101st Street
101a Ave
Jasper Avenue
Tourist Information Centre
Hotel MacDonald
Grierson Hill Rd
100th Avenue
McDougall Hill Rd
Bellamy Rd
YWCA
To Muttart Conservatory
Low Level Bridge
99th Avenue
Rossdale Rd
98th Avenue
James MacDonald Bridge
97th Ave
97th Avenue
Alberta Legislature
96th Avenue
River Valley Rd
High Level Bridge
Walterdale Bridge
North Saskatchewan River
John Walter Historic Site

Top: Beware the bears on the beach, Hudson Bay, Churchill, Manitoba (RB)
Bottom: Bear-proof shack, Churchill, Manitoba (RB)

Top: Ice-bridge, Athabasca Glacier, Jasper National Park, Alberta (RB)
Left: The town of Banff in the Rockies, Alberta (RB)
Right: Calgary cowboy tests his strength (JL)

and religious event called the Sun Dance Ritual. There are amulets incorporating the wearer's umbilical cord and many artefacts and crafts, too.

The Natural History section has a large display of stones and minerals. The History area covers the pioneer days and settlement of Alberta.

The museum also has frequent cultural shows, eg Mexican dancing, and free film programmes. It's at 12845 102nd Avenue. To get there, take a No 1 bus from Jasper Avenue. Opening hours are 10 am to 9 pm daily and admission is free.

Government House
This is the large and impressive structure beside the museum, used for government conferences. It can be visited on Sundays. For information call 427-7362.

Alberta Legislature
This is built on the site of the original Fort Edmonton. A beautiful Edwardian building of 1912, it is surrounded by manicured lawns overlooking the river. Its dome has remained one of the permanent landmarks of Edmonton. Free tours are given daily, offering interesting details about the building and the government. The tours start from a very Italian-looking lobby and last about half an hour. They begin at noon on weekends, 9 am weekdays. The Legislature is at 97th Avenue and 109th St.

Fort Edmonton
On the south side of the river over the Quesnel Bridge, this is a reconstruction of the old Mounted Police fort and the surrounding town, circa 1885. The fort contains the entire post of 1846 which was built to promote the fur trade (not as a military fort), and was presided over by Chief Factor John Rowland, head of Saskatchewan District from 1828 to 1854. Being new, it lacks some authentic feel, but the carpentry, meant to re-create the times through furniture, tools and constructions, is excellent.

Outside the fort is a street re-creating downtown Edmonton between 1871 and 1891, when the railway arrived. It's quite interesting, with good explanations of the buildings, though hard to visualise as Jasper Avenue. Along the wooden sidewalks are examples of the various merchants and their goods, such as a newspaper office and a schoolhouse. Check all the cabinets, bottles and vials in the chemist's. Rides on the train and horse-trailer are included in tickets, which cost $4, less for kids.

Fort Edmonton is open from 10 am to 6 pm daily in summer, from 1 to 5 pm on weekends only in September and is closed in winter.

On the grounds beside the fort is the Nature Centre. There are a few examples of both living and dead local animals, insects and reptiles. You'll see educational exhibits in simulated natural environments; best is the live bee display. It's open on weekdays from 9 am to 4 pm, weekends 1 to 7 pm. If they start charging an admission, forget it.

Vista 33
This is the name of the observation deck on the 33rd floor of the AGT Tower at 10020 100th St, which is the head office of Alberta Telephones. On clear days you can peer out over 6475 square km of the flat land surrounding Edmonton. Nearly one-third of the population of Alberta lives in the area viewed. It's open until 10 pm for night viewing and is only 50c. Included in the price, and on the same floor, is a small but interesting museum of telecommunication equipment, including old telephones and switchboards. Some of the exhibits are meant to be played, in an attempt to expose the magic of the hardware.

St Josephat's Ukrainian Catholic Cathedral
This church on 97th St at 108th Avenue is worth a visit: you don't see too many of these in North America. With its rounded domes outside, it'll remind you of Turkey,

whether you've been there or not. Inside the Byzantine structure, pastel paintings cover the walls. Check the figure on the ceiling in front of the altar. There's a lot of gilt-work here, including the large screen fronting the altar.

Muttart Conservatory

Off James Macdonald Bridge at 98th Avenue and 9th St, this comprises four spacey-looking pyramids you can see from the north side of the river. There are some interesting photos to be taken of the place. It also offers good views of the city.

Each of the four pyramids contains a different climate and the plants that go with it. One is desert, one Canadian, one jungle and the last experimental. If you walk up the hills you can look without going in, but you miss the best part – the feel and smell.

The conservatory is open from 11 am to 9 pm daily and costs $2. It's on transit routes 44 and 51.

Police Museum

This small museum is on the 3rd floor of the Police Headquarters building at 9620 103A St, downtown. Using artefacts, historical notes, uniforms and photographs, it tells something of the history of the Royal Canadian Mounted Police (RCMP) which formed in 1873, as well as that of the local city police department. Included in the displays are firearms, handcuffs, an old jail cell and even a preserved rat which became an early RCMP mascot. Admission is free; opening hours are Tuesday to Saturday from 10 am to 3 pm and Thursday and Friday evenings.

Aviation Hall of Fame

This is a an extensive collection of models, photos, displays, films and biographies of important figures in Canadian aviation. On display is the country's first commercial flight simulator, an exact duplicate of a Douglas DC-6B cockpit. It's in the Convention Centre Mall at 9797 Jasper Avenue, downtown. Admission is free and it's open daily.

Space Sciences Centre

Out of town a bit at 11211 142nd St is a complex of several attractions in Coronation Park. The city planetarium (tel 452-9100) presents multi-media programmes on the solar system and universe. The shows are entertaining, educational and life-like. Imax (large-format cinema) has a film theatre here as well, with changing films. Rock music laser shows are offered frequently in the Star Theatre.

The planetarium also has galleries using photographs, video, film and hands-on exhibits to explain or show various aspects of the planets, the history of astronomy and star-gazing equipment. Don't miss seeing the Bruderheim meteorite which fell near Edmonton in 1960. It's 4.6 billion years old – older than any rock on earth; as old as the solar system itself.

There's a small science shop with some fun little items and a restaurant.

Outside, telescopes and an observatory permit sun and star observation, free. There are also picnic tables in the grounds.

The galleries are free but there are admission charges for the rest; a combination ticket saves a bit over buying singles. The city bus gets you to within a block or so.

Next door the Coronation Swimming Pool, indoors, is open to the public in the afternoon.

Edmonton Art Gallery

This is part of the Civic Centre and sits opposite City Hall. The gallery has changing exhibits which are well spaced and lit. Mainly modern Canadian painting is shown, with some American. One room shows a few samples of Canadian work from the late 1800s to the present. I've seen several photography shows here.

It's open Mondays to Saturdays from

10 am to 5 pm, Thursdays and Fridays until 10 pm and Sundays and holidays from 1.15 to 5 pm. Admission is $2 or $1 for students; free on Wednesdays between 5 and 9 pm.

John Walter Historic Site

This site (tel 433-7853) comprises four historic buildings, including the first home south of the river. This glimpse of early Edmonton includes its first telegraph station. It's at 10627 93rd Avenue; open daily in summer from 10 am to 6 pm; free.

Rutherford House

This house (tel 427-3993) was built by Alexander Rutherford, the first premier of Alberta. Completed in 1911, the mansion is said to symbolise the end of the pioneer architectural style. The building has been restored and contains many antiques. Admission is free and it's open in summer from 10 am to 8 pm daily, in winter on weekend afternoons only. The address is 11153 Saskatchewan Drive; it's beside the University of Alberta. A bus services the campus.

Valley Zoo

This zoo in Laurier Park at the south end of Buena Vista Rd has about 500 animals and birds, but it's mainly a children's zoo with models of storybook characters. Open daily in summer. Admission is $3, kids $1.50. The zoo is on local bus transit routes 50 and 123.

Ukrainian Museum

This museum has a small collection of costumes, Easter eggs, dolls and very fine tapestries. It's at 10611 110th Avenue, on tourist routes 41, 42. It's open in July and August on Sunday afternoons; free.

West Edmonton Mall

I thought perhaps I'd seen everything. I thought a shopping centre had no place in this guide. Wrong. This place is really something else. More than just the world's largest shopping mall and largest indoor water-park, it's a self-contained city complete with roof. You could live inside for years or until brain-dead, whichever came first. There are over 800 stores, a hotel, an amusement park, a water-park with beach, an ice rink, a mini-golf course, cinemas, submarines in simulated oceans, restaurants galore and lots more, plus thousands of people. A few highlights are the Drop of Doom, a ride in Fantasyland guaranteed to put your stomach in your mouth (and that's just watching!), the pool complex with slides and waves, the ice rink with skate rentals and the ersatz New Orleans Bourbon Street, complete with statues of prostitutes.

If you get too tired to make it around everything they'll rent you a little powered scooter. I'd have to say it's so overwhelming it's worth a visit, but don't let it become a habit.

The Mall is at 2872 170th St on the west side of town. City buses, including an express run, do the trip from downtown in about 25 minutes.

Wild Waters Aquatic Park

At 21512 103rd Avenue (Highway 16 West) is this water-slide complex. In the past few years these have been springing up all over Canada. Open every day in summer.

Farmers' Market

The city market is in downtown Edmonton at the corner of 102nd Avenue and 97th St. It's best on Saturdays.

Strathcona

The area south of the river, by 82nd Avenue and 106th St, was once the town of Strathcona. It amalgamated with Edmonton in 1912. Though now absorbed into the city, this area is rich in historical buildings dating from 1891. There are about 75 houses built prior to 1926 in the residential district and about 40 buildings of note in what was the commercial core.

You can pick up a walking tour map of

the district at the Tourist Office or the Old Strathcona Foundation Office (tel 433-5866) at 8520 104th St. The tour will take you past the old train station, a hotel, movie theatre, church and many other gems. Along 82nd Avenue from 103rd St to 105th St has been spruced up with brick sidewalks, old-style lampposts, etc. It's a pleasant area with numerous cafés, restaurants and bookshops.

Activities

For information on park and recreation facilities like swimming pools, skating and skiing areas or bicycle paths, ring 428-3559.

The Kinsmen Sports Centre (tel 428-4182) at 9100 Walterdale Hill, has public swimming and other programmes.

Milkwood's Recreation Centre (tel 463-8550), 7207 28th Avenue, has saunas, ball courts and other facilities.

You can go hot-air ballooning to 1000 feet – every day if the weather is fine – with Windship Aviation (tel 436-6418). Their address is 5965 103A St.

Events

Klondike Days This is Edmonton's biggest festival, held at the end of July. Street festivities last five days; the Northlands Park Exhibition goes on for another five. The event honours the gold rush days of 1898, when the Klondike Trail to Dawson City, Yukon, put Edmonton on the map. During the festival, locals dress up the streets, the stores and themselves in period style; stages dot the road and are alive with singers and dancers; parades run through the streets; the Coliseum presents nightly entertainment of rock, pop or western music; a Klondike village, with old-time stores and a gambling saloon, is set up in Northlands Park; Citadel Theatre puts on 'heroes and villains' melodramas, and City Hall serves up open-air breakfasts. Check out the show in the Macdonald Hotel at Jasper Avenue and 98th St.

Other In August the city holds a folk music festival and a jazz festival. Ask at the Tourist Office.

'Gone with the Fringe' is a nine-day event of alternative theatre. It's a fairly new programme that brings live theatre to the public through free noon and evening performances and low-cost shows at numerous venues. Again, ask at the Tourist Office for details.

Places to Stay

Hostels The CYHA *Youth Hostel* (tel 429-0140) is good and within walking distance of downtown and the bus or train station. It has a view across the river to the south side of Edmonton, a kitchen, and sells a few basic staples. But it's a bit more expensive than usual at $7.50 for members, $11 for non-members. The high price keeps it from becoming a flop-house, which could easily happen in a boom town like Edmonton. It closes at midnight and operates from May to 15 September. To get there from downtown, walk east on Jasper or 103rd Avenue – which soon turns into Jasper Avenue anyway – down to 91st St. The hostel is down a few doors on the left on 91st. Between downtown and the hostel are a couple of run-down blocks which are not great at night, especially for women alone.

The *YMCA* (tel 421-9622) at 10030 102A Avenue beside the Edmonton Centre, takes in men only. The single rooms are $16.50 with a $5 key deposit. It's in a good location close to the train and bus stations. There's a TV room and pool you can use and a very cheap cafeteria, which has breakfasts for $1.99 and dinners for $2.75. It closes at 6.30 pm and on weekends and holidays.

The *YWCA* (tel 424-8047) at 10305 100th Avenue, at the corner of 103rd St, is also central. They take women only and charge from $6 on the floor to $28 in a private room. Sheets are supplied in all the rooms. There's a good, cheap cafeteria that anyone can use.

The *University of Alberta* rents out

rooms in the summer in the Lister Hall Complex. The campus is in South Edmonton next to the Jubilee Auditorium. It has good facilities and cheap cafeterias. Rates are $25 for singles, $28 for doubles. Contact the Conference Coordinator (tel 432-4281), 44 Lister Hall, 87th Avenue and 116th St.

The *Single Men's Hostel* (tel 427-2735) is at 10014 105A Avenue. They take in men and give them bed and breakfast for nothing. It's not meant for travellers and few stay here, but you may find it useful for a day or two. At last visit it was about to move so check the address.

Bed & Breakfasts The Alberta Bed & Breakfast Association (tel 462-8885) is at 4327 86th St. They keep a changing list of participants. Doubles fall in the $40 range.

Hotels Edmonton is not blessed with a great selection of cheap central hotels. There are a few basic, torn around the edges places which may fill your bill.

The *Grand Hotel* (tel 429-7521) at 103rd St and 103rd Avenue is very central, right beside the bus station. Their cheapest rooms are $16/19 for singles/doubles, and up to $20/23 with extras. All have colour TV. The hotel – including the shared bathrooms – is very clean. There's a bar downstairs with snacks and TV. The rooms are mainly used permanently rather than for overnighters.

Hotel Cecil (tel 428-7001) at 10406 Jasper is a little rougher, especially in the bar. It's old and worn but clean, and the rooms are fine. Some have a bath; all have sinks and are comfortable. The basic rate is $17/20 for singles/doubles; new rooms with shower cost $21/24. Downstairs there's a friendly, cheap restaurant.

West of town there's the *Klondiker Hotel* (tel 489-1906) at 153rd St and Stony Plain Rd. The lobby has a gold rush feel and a mural symbolising that period. The rooms – at $30 to $35 – are alright. There are three bars downstairs so you won't go thirsty. The hotel is pretty popular and features live music at night.

Better is *Hotel Vega* (tel 423-1650) at 10815 Jasper Avenue. A double room with shower is $29, with a bath, $35. An extra person is $5. This hotel is good value and central. The *Downtown Motel* at 102nd Avenue near 96th St is similar, with an inexpensive restaurant. It's central near Chinatown. Better still is the *Best Western Ambassador Motor Inn* (tel 423-1925) at 10041 106th St. Singles or doubles cost between $40 and $50; they offer cable TV in all rooms.

About the same price and standard is *Adventure Inn* (tel 428-9710) at 9710 105th St, but a small breakfast is thrown in.

In South Edmonton a cheapie to try is the *Commercial* at 10329 Whyte Avenue (also called 82nd Avenue), which has live music in the bar downstairs and costs around $20 for a single or double room. A pretty good deal nearby is the *Park Hotel* (tel 433-6441) at 8004 104th St, just below 82nd Avenue. It's got a good location and rates, with singles at $30, doubles at $36. Clean.

Lastly, the *Alberta Place* (tel 423-1565) is an apartment hotel with complete cooking facilities which is expensive by the day but weekly and monthly rates are available. It's central at 10049 103rd St on the north side of the river.

Motels The bulk of the city's mid-price range accommodation is in motels. Most motels have plug-ins (electric sockets for engine heaters) for your car – a good thing for Edmonton winter mornings. There are two areas near town where most are located. One area is along the Calgary Trail, and Highway 2 South on the south side of the river. The other is on Stony Plain Rd, north of the downtown area. To get to this area you head out along Jasper Avenue. This turns into Stony Plain Rd, where most of the motels are. Further west, Stony Plain Rd is called Highway 16 West or the Yellowhead Trail.

Royal Scot Motel (tel 447-3088) is on

Highway 16, about 1.5 km from Edmonton. It has singles/doubles for $26/34 or $2 extra for a kitchen.

The *Parkland Motel* (tel 470-4455) is 3.2 km from town on Highway 16. There are 40 units with colour TV, priced at $25 to $32.

The *West Edmonton Motor Inn* (tel 484-1136), closer to town at 18245 Stony Plain Rd, has singles or doubles for $36. Weekly rates are available, as is a laundromat.

One main street south of the Yellowhead Highway is 118th Avenue; further east it leads into the Yellowhead.

The *Beverly Motel* (tel 479-3923) is at 4403 118th Avenue. It's small with just 12 rooms, with singles/doubles at $28/30, triples at $32. The rates include use of the kitchen.

South of town try the *Derrick Motel* (tel 434-1402) at 3925 Calgary Trail. There's quite a few motels along this strip, most pretty fairly priced. This one's $28 for singles, $32 for doubles with kitchenette available.

There are many other motels, mostly more deluxe.

Top End *Westin Hotel* (tel 426-3636) at 10135 100th St, costs $90 and up.

Chateau Lacombe (tel 428-6611) at 101st St at Bellamy Hill, is also $90 and up.

Camping There are several camping areas close to town. Some of them, run by the Alberta government, are free.

Androssan Campground, 18 km east of Edmonton on Highway 16, has 24 free campsites. There are firepits but nothing else, and no water.

Bretona Campground, 18 km southeast of Edmonton, is on Highway 14. Here again there are no facilities other than picnic tables and fireplaces. Free.

The privately owned *Half Moon Lake Resort* charges but has every convenience and then some. It's 29 km east of Edmonton, four km north and four km east off Highway 14. The resort is very large and there is swimming on the lake.

Places to Eat

The Silk Hat, 10251 Jasper Avenue, was one of Edmonton's first restaurants. It still has the old, small wall jukeboxes at the booths and good prices. They have breakfast and lunch specials. This is the hang-out for a lot of local characters.

The *Cafeteria* in the Alberta Legislature serves plain, decent food at the best prices in town. Open 9 am to 4 pm, with lunches from 11.30 am to 1.30 pm Monday to Friday. Have something on the taxpayers of Alberta.

The *YWCA Cafeteria*, centrally located, is open to both men and women, resident or not. It's open daily at meal times only, and closes at 7 pm. There's not a lot of choice but prices are good.

Tivoli Gardens, 10432 Jasper Avenue, does simple food well. A cafeteria-style office-worker lunch spot, it specialises in soup and sandwich-type lunches for $3. Open Monday to Friday 7.30 am to 6 pm, Saturday 8.30 am to 4 pm.

Ye Olde English Restaurant is the pub-like building at the corner of 103rd Avenue and 102nd St. It specialises in fish & chips but has other things too.

Albert's Deli & Bar has outdoor tables and umbrellas, and is busy at lunch serving sandwiches and burgers. It's at the corner of 111st and Jasper.

The *Russian Tea Room* is ideal for a late afternoon pick-me-up, especially for teas, coffees, cakes, pastries, etc.

Around the corner of 101A Avenue and 100A St right in the centre of downtown, a small restaurant district and people-place sanctuary has sprouted amidst all the office towers. Trees have been planted and there are benches for lingering. Most of the restaurants have outdoor sections.

Right at the corner, the *Mongolian Food Experience* is pretty good. A sizeable black bean beef special with a beer was tasty and set me back $8.50.

Down a couple of doors is the *Bistro*

Praha, a European-style spot good for coffees, cakes and pastries. They also serve wine by the glass. Meals are about $10, salads between $3 and $4. During non-meal hours it's pleasant for a coffee and a flip through a newspaper.

Nearby on 101A Avenue by 100th St is the *Sherlock Holmes*, a British-model pub for both food and brew.

Another grouping of meal spots can be found in the Boardwalk Market on the corner of 103rd St and 102nd Avenue, a renovated old building also containing offices and stores. *The Old Spaghetti Factory* is always reliable with decent food at low prices in an interesting environment – lots of plants and Tiffany lamps. It's open Monday to Thursday from 11 am to 11 pm, Friday and Saturday 11.30 am to midnight and Sunday 3 to 10 pm.

Next door is *Bones* for ribs and chicken and a few doors down, *La Creperie* offers a range of crepes. There are other places here both more and less expensive. Walk through the building and have a look-see.

For moderately-priced dinners, *Mother Tucker's* at 10184 104th St is open daily. Dishes like baked chicken, fish or steak include vegetables, bread and a trip to the huge salad bar. Similarly priced ($12 to $15) is the *Schnitzel House* on 103rd St south of Jasper, with a dozen types of schnitzel offered.

The small Chinatown bounded by 97th Avenue, 102nd St, 96th Avenue and 102A St a few blocks east of the downtown core doesn't have a whole heck of a lot to recommend it. Best of a poor lot is the *Dragon Garden* on 96th Avenue with a daily dim sum lunch special. Open daily.

Across the river on the south side of town in the Old Strathcona area is an altogether different story. There are a good number of decent eateries here which for the most part fall into the same casual, comfortable and cheap category.

At the corner of 104th St and 82nd Avenue is *Uncle Albert's Pancake House*. I've heard it's good, although I couldn't get in on a Saturday morning, the line was so long. They have meal specials. It must be cheap, judging by the young crowd. Players from the city's sports teams often stop in here.

There are several places on 82nd Avenue. The *New York Bagel Café* is recommended. This is a small, very comfortable little spot serving espresso and light foods. The address is 8209 104th St and it's just north of 82nd Avenue.

Back a street at the corner of 103rd St and 81st Avenue, the *Bella Festa* is a dressier, more expensive Italian spot.

In Strathcona Market Square along 82nd Avenue at 105th St, the basement is a food mart with a bakery and various other food shops, with restaurants and boutiques upstairs.

One of the best eating buys in Edmonton is at one of the places with a lunch buffet or Sunday brunch, a relatively new Canadian phenomenon. Check the Saturday newspaper for places and times.

The *Holiday Inn*, 10001 107th St, has a lunch buffet every weekday. This is a recommended buy; a good feed here can last you till the next day's breakfast. For $6.95 you can eat until you're sick. The buffet includes hot and cold meats, potatoes, salads, vegetables and desserts; the roast beef alone is worth the money. The atmosphere is nice and the service good. Buffet hours are 11.30 am to 1.30 pm.

Nightlife

The *Bullet* is a local entertainment paper. It's free around town.

Music & Theatre *Andante* at 8230 103rd St brings in rhythm & blues and funk bands. There's a cover charge. The *Commercial* at 10329 Whyte Avenue (82nd Avenue) in the Commercial hotel features live blues music. The *Southside Pub* at 4404 Calgary Trail is a hard rock bar.

The *Yardbird Suite*, 10203 86th Avenue, is the jazz bar in town. Admission is $3 to $8, less for students.

The *Coliseum, Jubilee Auditorium* and *Sub-Theatre* all bring in name acts on a regular basis. Tickets cost $4 to $16 for performances that range from rock music to ballet.

For straight drama, try the *Citadel* at 101A Avenue and 98th St in the new brick and glass building. This is the city's foremost playhouse and first-class plays are presented in the two theatres. The larger theatre has tickets from $9 to $13. In the smaller *Rice Theatre*, they range from $5.50 to $9.

Laser shows are held at the *Space Sciences Centre* (tel 452-9100) for $6.

Cinema The *Princess Repertory Theatre* (tel 433-5785) is Edmonton's main outlet for good, varying films at below-normal cost. They show two different films per night and charge non-members $4.50 for each one. The movie house itself is a historic site – it was the first marble-fronted building west of Winnipeg and at one time showed first-runs of Mary Pickford films. It's on 82nd Avenue near 104th St.

Getting There & Away

Air The International Airport is 16 km south of the city on Highway 2, down Calgary Trail, about a 45-minute drive from downtown. This airport handles most flights.

There's another airport, the Municipal, closer to town, north of the downtown area off 97th St near 118th Avenue. City buses run between here and town but it's generally used only for smaller planes, therefore shorter flights. This airport is used for many flights in Alberta, including the Calgary Express. I landed here coming in from Saskatoon on one trip.

Time Air (tel 552-8007) is Alberta's commuter airline. They have daily services between Grand Prairie, Calgary, Edmonton, Lethbridge, Medicine Hat and Red Deer.

Canadian Airlines (tel 421-1808) flies to the Yukon, Vancouver and major cities in eastern Canada. They also the commuter service to Calgary with flights all day long for the 40-minute trip. If you're not on business you'll probably find it a bit pricey at $70.

Bus The bus terminal is at the corner of 103rd St and 103rd Avenue, very close to the train station and centrally located. It's new, large and modern and serves both Greyhound and Coachways, which has the northern routes.

Bus fares are usually cheaper than taking the train.

Greyhound (tel 421-4211) goes east to Winnipeg several times a day. The one-way fare is $75. Greyhound also goes west to Vancouver ($65) and Jasper ($24), and south to Calgary.

Another bus line serving Calgary is Red Arrow Express. They have four buses a day which leave from the CN office tower by the train station and cost $21. You travel on deluxe buses with kitchenette. The Red Arrow Express office is also in the CN Tower.

Coachways has two buses daily to Whitehorse, Yukon. From there it goes to Beaver Creek on the Alaska border, where you can get a connection on the Alaskan bus line to Fairbanks, Alaska. From Edmonton to Whitehorse the fare is $151.

Train The VIA Rail station is at 10004 104th Avenue at the corner of 100th St, near the bus terminal, beneath the white CN Office Tower. The station has a coffee shop and newsstand. For fares and reservations call 1-800-665-8630 toll-free.

Saskatoon, Winnipeg, Toronto, Ottawa, Montreal: daily at 4.15 pm

Jasper, Kamloops, Vancouver: daily at 2.30 pm.

There is now no train to Calgary.

Fares, one-way: Jasper – $32, seven-day return – $51; Saskatoon – $44; Toronto – $199.

Getting Around

Airport Transport The international airport is about 16 km south of town. City buses don't go this far. You can catch the Grey Goose Airporter Bus (tel 463-7520), which leaves from the Macdonald Hotel every half hour from 5.15 am to 12.15 am, for a fare of $6.50. It also departs from other top hotels. But if there are several of you a taxi works out about the same.

City buses run to and from the Municipal Airport.

Bus & LRT Edmonton Transit operates city buses and Canada's newest and smallest subway system. The subway, called Light Rail Transit (LRT) is sometimes above and sometimes below the surface. It runs east-west along Jasper Avenue and then north all the way to 139th Avenue. There are eight stops and more planned. Between 9 am and 3 pm Monday to Friday and 9 am to 6 pm on Saturdays, the four downtown stations are in a free zone.

Using either the LRT or the bus get a transfer – you can switch from one to the other and it's also your proof of payment. For route information call 421-4636 or visit the information office at Jasper and 100A St. Visitors can also buy unlimited-use tickets for $2.50 from the Tourist Office at the Churchill LRT station (corner of Churchill and 102 Aenue). Weekly passes for visitors are also available.

Buses cover all parts of the city but may be a little slack on Sundays. Bus Nos 46 and 64 go from downtown to the university and back. Bus No 50 goes from downtown south-west to the Valley Zoo in Laurier Park.

Bicycle River Valley Cycle & Sports (tel 421-9125) is at 9701 100A St. They have guided history tours by bike.

Car Rentals Budget (tel 428-6155) at 10016 106th St charges $24.95 a day with 200 free km, then 10c per km.

Rent-A-Wreck (tel 423-1755) at 10140 109th St charges $8.95 to $17, plus 7c per km.

Tours The Edmonton Youth Hostel (tel 429-0140) runs a couple of tours. There is a three-day Rockies trip and five-day Alberta tour. The hostel also arranges trips to various fairs and festivals throughout the summer.

For bus tours around Edmonton enquire at the bus terminal. Gray Line offers several day tours lasting about three hours and costing around $11.

Edmonton Transit operates the Discovery Run on Sunday and holiday afternoons for a basic fare. This route, No 123, takes a circular tour of the city, passing by many of the sites, including the museum, Fort Edmonton and the university.

Royal Tours (tel 424-8687) offer three tours of town, each taking 3½ hours. The cost is $17.

Wood Buffalo Tours (tel 489-8730) at 8804 160th St, runs three and four-day tours of Wood Buffalo National Park, in the far north of Alberta. Contact Lila Ward.

AROUND EDMONTON

Strathcona Archaeological Centre

This centre (tel 427-9487) offers visitors a glimpse of an archaeological dig, with explanations at the Interpretive Centre. The site is a stone-age industrial plant where people living around 3000 BC worked making tools and weapons. It's a project of the Alberta Museum and makes an interesting and cheap (free) look at historical discovery. The site is open daily in summer and is close to town, near Highway 16 and 17th St.

Alberta Pioneer Railway Museum

This museum has a collection of steam and diesel locomotives and rolling stock depicting the railways from 1877 to 1950. There is also an artefact exhibit. Admission is free although the non-profit organisation that runs the museum asks for a donation.

To get there, drive three km north-east on Highway 15 to Oliver Rd; turn left one block to the right for eight km. The museum opens at noon.

Alberta Wildlife Park
This park (tel 921-3918) is 22 km north of Edmonton on Highway 28, then 13 km north on Lily Lake Rd. It's open daily year-round from 10 am to dark. Admission is $3. The 400-hectare park holds 100 species of wild animals from around the world. How do they stand the winters?

Polar Park
Polar Park (tel 922-3401), 22 km south-east of town on Highway 14 East, is run by the same man who started the Alberta Wildlife Park. This park specialises in animals of the north. Snow leopards, polar bears and caribou are some of the 100 species. There are good walking and cross-country ski trails. It's open all year and admission is $3.

Elk Island National Park
Thirty-five km east of Edmonton on Highway 16 is this 19,500-hectare reserve of original forest that is actually a wildlife sanctuary. There are free-roaming herds of elk and plains buffalo and a small herd of endangered wood bison. About 35 other mammals inhabit the park. It's a popular weekend spot with camping, hiking and swimming in summer and cross-country skiing in winter.

Ukrainian Cathedral Heritage Village
Forty-eight km east of Edmonton on Highway 16, the village pays homage to Russian immigrants. There is a replica pioneer home and other exhibitions of the first settlers in the area. It's open daily from 10 am to 6 pm from mid-May to the end of August. Free.

Lac Ste Anne
For about 100 years, since prayers at the lake by the Roman Catholic Mission to end a drought were answered, it has been believed these waters have God-given curative powers. Here, 50 km west of Edmonton, an annual pilgrimage takes place in July drawing about 10,000 native people from around the province and across North America. It's a five-day event.

Vegreville
The Ukrainian community in this town (120 km east of Edmonton) has constructed the world's biggest *pysanka* or painted Easter egg. It sits, 9.1 metres tall, just off the highway on the east side of town. The Ukrainian Festival takes place in early July.

Red Deer
Halfway to Calgary, this large town is in the centre of grain and cattle country. An international folk festival is held here every July.

Northern Alberta

ST PAUL
The land north of Edmonton is a vast area of farms, wilderness, lakes and oilfields. Two hundred km north-east of Edmonton is St Paul, a trading centre and gateway to the lake district. In the town is a flying-saucer landing pad waiting for its first customer.

WOOD BUFFALO NATIONAL PARK
Wood Buffalo is one of the world's largest parks. Bigger than Switzerland, it lies two-thirds in Alberta and one-third in the Northwest Territories.

This wilderness park has the world's largest free-roaming bison herd – about 6000 – and is the only nesting ground of the diminishing, rare whooping crane. Moose, caribou, bears and wolves abound as well as many smaller animals, and over a million ducks, geese and swans pass by in autumn and spring on their migratory routes.

Vegetation in the park ranges from forest to plains to bogs and marshes.

Most of the scenic areas in the park are not visible from the roads; the roads themselves are not always open. Check with the park offices.

If you want to get a glimpse of what the early fur traders accomplished, this is a good place to look.

Fort Chipewyan

This is the oldest settlement in Alberta. Wood Buffalo Tours runs three and four-day trips in the park leaving from here. For information, contact Lila Ward (tel 489-8730) at 8804 160th St in Edmonton.

Activities

You can explore the deltas of the Peace and Athabasca Rivers by canoe or hike on the marked trails. The park staff run field trips and overnight camping trips or buffalo-observing hikes. In winter there are cross-country ski trails.

Places to Stay

There are few comforts in Wood Buffalo National Park. There is one small campground in the park but in addition there are a couple just outside the park's border. Within the park there are also numerous designated basic campsites for individual campers. They offer some primitive facilities such as an outhouse and perhaps a fire-pit. The more adventurous may set off on their own and camp anywhere they find agreeable.

Getting There & Away

Wood Buffalo National Park is not easily accessible by road. To get there, you go up the Mackenzie Highway north-west of Edmonton to Great Slave Lake in the Northwest Territories and then around to the eastern side of the park. The other way to get there is to fly into Fort Chipewyan.

Calgary

The name Calgary, meaning 'clear, running water' in Gaelic, comes from Calgary Bay on the Isle of Mull in Scotland.

The area was initially home to the Blackfoot Indians. In the 1800s the Indians were at war and there was trouble with white trappers and traders, so the Northwest Mounted Police were sent to cool things down. They established a fort in 1875. The Canadian Pacific Railway was built this far in 1883. Settlers were offered free land and the population jumped to 4000 by 1891. Soon, cattle herders from the US were pushing north looking for better grazing. Calgary became a major meat-packing centre and cowboy metropolis. It's now a major transportation-distribution point and is still the leading cattle centre.

In recent years the city has had to deal with some dramatic ups and downs, having exploded from a fair-sized cow town to a brand new city of steel and glass in under 20 years. It was labelled everything from a rootless boom town to a major new urban centre to a depressed area. But through it all, the city has continued to develop and remains quite a phenomenon. Calgary's fortunes and reputation got a big boost when it hosted the Winter Olympics in 1988.

The reason for Calgary's changeable fortunes is simple: oil. In the late 1960s, the black gold was found in vast quantities across the province. The energy crisis in the 1970s bumped prices up sharply. With this, the city took off, becoming one of the fastest growing cities in the country. It became the headquarters of 450 oil companies and home to more Americans than any place outside the USA.

The population mushroomed to 640,000 and the city centre was transformed. For years it looked like a construction site as buildings seemed to rise with the morning sun.

After a brief breath-catching period, the cultural side of the city began to develop as well. However, the last few years have been tough. With the bottom falling out of the oil market and 70% of the workforce relying on it, things turned sour quickly. Just when the city was struggling, attempting to maintain what it had become, it was granted the Olympics. Calgary is now maturing and will continue to grow in size and importance.

The city is dry and very sunny. It gets hot in summer but remains amazingly cool in the shade. In winter the warm 'chinook' wind blows off the mountains, raising temperatures – at least temporarily.

One of Alberta's greatest assets, Banff National Park, is just 120 km to the west.

Orientation

Calgary, like the plains around it, lies on flat ground. It began at the confluence of the Bow and Elbow Rivers and has spread equally in all directions, but the downtown area is still bounded by the Bow to the north. The Elbow cuts across the southern portions of the city.

I'm sure the person who originated the street-numbering system thought it great, but it's a jumbled mess. One travel writer has said only Central London matches it for sheer muddle. It'll take you a good few days to get a grip on this.

The city is divided into four geographical segments: north-west (NW), north-east (NE), south-west (SW) and south-east (SE). These abbreviations are important as they're marked on street signs.

All city streets run north and south, all avenues run east and west. The downtown streets are all one-way except for 7th Avenue. Here all cars go west to east but there's one bus and taxi lane which goes the opposite way.

Around the downtown centre the 'Plus 15 Walking System' refers to pedestrian bridges and over-the-street walkways (enclosed sidewalks) which are at least 15 feet (five metres) above the ground. Various buildings and shops are connected in this way.

The north-south sectors of the city are divided by the Bow River and Memorial Drive, approximately. The east-west sectors are divided by Centre St downtown and Macleod Trail to the south.

The Calgary Tower, right downtown on 9th Avenue at Centre St, is a good orientation point. If you look across the street up Centre St, you're looking north toward the downtown area.

Ninth Avenue is lined with brand-new buildings – offices, expensive hotels, banks and parking lots as well as the Convention Centre and the Glenbow Museum and Art Gallery complex.

Continuing north up Centre St will take you through town. Eighth Avenue between 3rd St SW and 1st St SE is a very long pedestrian mall. It's lined with shops, including the large department stores. The mall has trees, benches, stores, restaurants and fast-food places. There are also a lot of vendors selling crafts, odds & ends and souvenirs.

On and just off Centre St, before it heads north over the river, is the small Chinatown

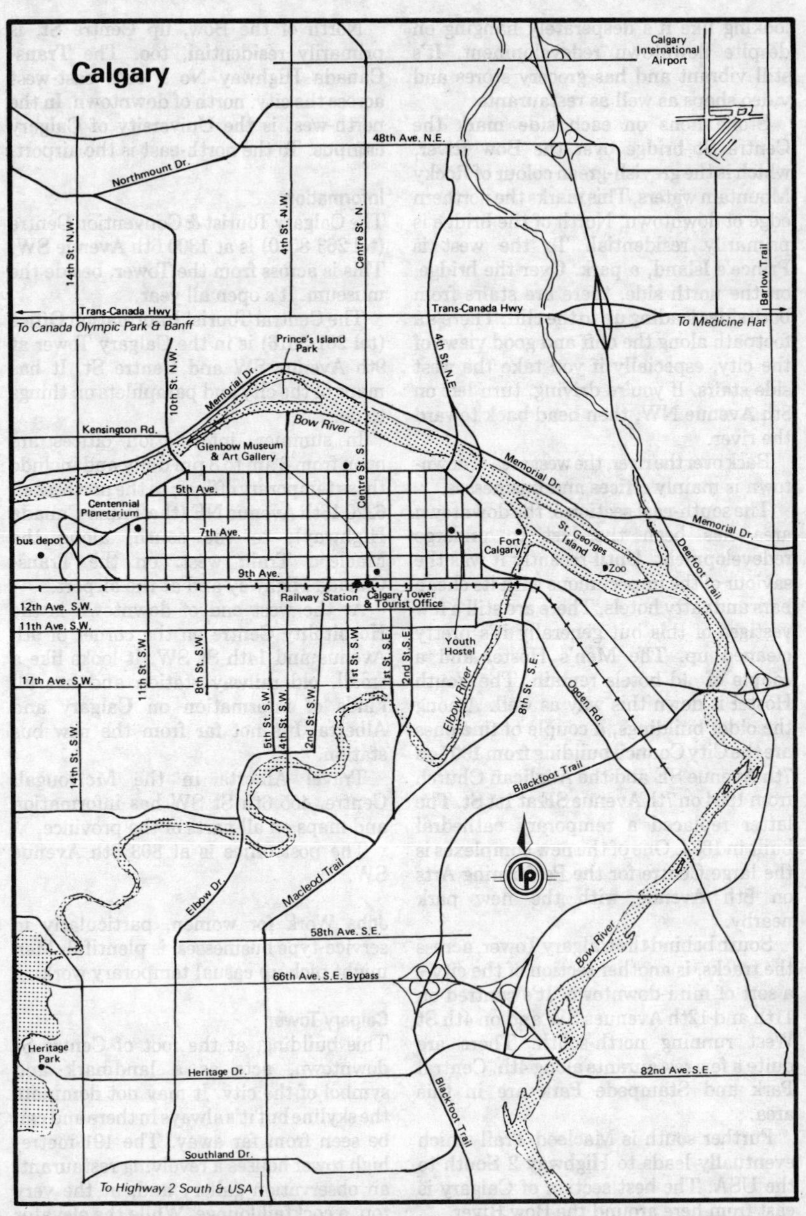
Calgary
Calgary International Airport
48th Ave. N.E.
Northmount Dr.
14th St. N.W.
4th St. N.W.
Centre St. N.
Trans-Canada Hwy
To Canada Olympic Park & Banff
Trans-Canada Hwy
Barlow Trail
To Medicine Hat
4th St. N.E.
Prince's Island Park
10th St. N.W.
Memorial Dr.
Bow River
Kensington Rd.
Glenbow Museum & Art Gallery
5th Ave.
Centennial Planetarium
7th Ave.
bus depot
9th Ave.
Railway Station
Calgary Tower & Tourist Office
Centre St. S.
Memorial Dr.
Memorial Dr.
Fort Calgary
St. Georges Island
Zoo
Deerfoot Trail
12th Ave. S.W.
11th Ave. S.W.
17th Ave. S.W.
14th St. S.W.
11th St. S.W.
8th St. S.W.
5th St. S.W.
4th St. S.W.
2nd St. S.W.
1st St. S.W.
1st St. S.E.
2nd St. S.E.
Youth Hostel
Elbow River
8th St. S.E.
Ogden Rd.
Blackfoot Trail
Elbow Dr.
Macleod Trail
lp
Bow River
58th Ave. S.E.
66th Ave. S.E. Bypass
Heritage Park
Heritage Dr.
82nd Ave. S.E.
Blackfoot Trail
Southland Dr.
To Highway 2 South & USA

looking like it's desperately hanging on despite downtown redevelopment. It's still vibrant and has grocery stores and video shops as well as restaurants.

Stone lions on each side mark the Centre St bridge over the Bow River, which is the greyish-green colour of Rocky Mountain waters. This marks the northern edge of downtown. North of the bridge is primarily residential. To the west is Prince's Island, a park. Over the bridge, on the north side, there are stairs from both sides leading up to the cliff. There's a footpath along the cliff and good views of the city, especially if you take the west side stairs. If you're driving, turn left on 8th Avenue NW, then head back toward the river.

Back over the river, the west area of downtown is mainly offices and businesses.

The south-east section of the downtown area has been the last to undergo redevelopment. Until recently it was the saviour of the impecunious with its cheap bars and tatty hotels. There are still a few vestiges of this but generally it's pretty cleaned up. The Men's Hostel and a couple of old hotels remain. The Youth Hostel is down this way as well. Among the older buildings, a couple of fine ones are the City Council building from 1907 on 7th Avenue SE and the Anglican Church from 1904 on 7th Avenue SE at 1st St. The latter replaced a temporary cathedral built in 1884. One of the new complexes is the large Centre for the Performing Arts on 8th Avenue with the new park nearby.

South behind the Calgary Tower, across the tracks, is another section of the city – a sort of mini-downtown. It's centred on 11th and 12th Avenues SW and on 4th St West running north-south. There are quite a few restaurants along 4th. Central Park and Stampede Park are in this area.

Further south is Macleod Trail which eventually leads to Highway 2 South to the USA. The best section of Calgary is east from here around the Bow River.

North of the Bow, up Centre St, is primarily residential, too. The Trans-Canada Highway No 1 cuts east-west across the city, north of downtown. In the north-west is the University of Calgary campus. To the north-east is the airport.

Information

The Calgary Tourist & Convention Centre (tel 263-8510) is at 1300 6th Avenue SW. This is across from the Tower, beside the museum. It's open all year.

The Central Tourist Information Office (tel 261-8616) is in the Calgary Tower at 9th Avenue SW and Centre St. It has maps of the city and pamphlets on things to do.

In summer, information offices are open from 8 am to 8 pm daily and include these temporary offices: to the north-east, 6220 16th Avenue NE (the Trans-Canada Highway); to the south, along the Macleod Trail; west, on the Trans-Canada Highway and at the airport.

At the west end of downtown is the Hospitality Centre on the corner of 9th Avenue and 14th St SW. It looks like a small, old railway station and has all kinds of information on Calgary and Alberta. It's not far from the new bus station.

Travel Alberta in the McDougall Centre, 455 6th St SW has information and maps on all parts of the province.

The post office is at 803 8th Avenue SW.

Jobs Work for women, particularly in service-type businesses, is plentiful. Men might pick up casual temporary work.

Calgary Tower

This building, at the foot of Centre St downtown, acts as a landmark and symbol of the city. It may not dominate the skyline but it's always in there and can be seen from far away. The 191-metre-high tower houses a revolving restaurant, an observation gallery and, at the very top, a cocktail lounge. While the elevator takes just 63 seconds, walking the 762 emergency steps might take a bit longer.

The Observation Terrace is open from 8 am to midnight daily except Sunday, when it closes at 11 pm. A ticket costs $2.75.

Glenbow Museum & Art Gallery

This is excellent and well worth a visit. The collections are varied and interesting, the displays effectively laid out. Opened in 1966, the complex shows part of human history through artefacts and art.

The 2nd floor contains frequently changing exhibitions of international, national and local art. I saw British photographs, Bolivian textiles, Amish quilts, American painting and some Group of Seven (Canada's best-known painters) works all in one visit. There is always some Inuit (Eskimo) art and a painter's work on show.

The 3rd floor has historical displays, mainly to do with the Canadian West. There is a superb collection of Indian dress and jewellery. Woodcarving from coast to coast is also represented. There's a section with Eskimo tools and a kayak, the traditional one-person boat.

There is also a huge collection on pioneer days that includes old wagons, tractors, CPR relics, saddles and cowboy tools and implements. Another area presents an interesting collection of stuff from the 1920s and '30s. Articles include old washing machines, a car, slot machines, bathing suits and a 1930 brassiere.

On the 4th floor is the military and arms collection. There are figures dressed in Japanese samurai armour and armoured knights of Britain's Middle Ages. The WW I and WW II posters are interesting; newspaper headlines make it all come alive.

The museum is open Tuesday to Sunday from 10 am to 6 pm and costs just $2, students $1. It is across from the Calgary Tower at 130 9th Avenue SE.

Heritage Park

This is an area of 24 hectares portraying life in a town of the Canadian West prior to 1914. The park sits on a peninsula jutting into the Glenmore Reservoir formed out of the Elbow River. It's south-west of downtown and offers views of the Rockies on a good day. The reconstructed frontier village includes a Hudson's Bay Company fort, a working grain mill, an 1896 church and many stores full of artefacts and antiques.

The well-laid-out grounds have a ranch house, a teepee, a trapper's cabin and other housing. The old schoolhouse with its desks and slates is interesting. There is an excellent collection of horse-drawn buggies in Section E, which includes stagecoaches, traps and surreys, and the chemist's and general store are particularly good. Also be sure to see the two-storey outhouse.

The park actually covers more than just pioneer days, encompassing development into the early 1920s. There are old cars, a railway exhibit of old coaches and a working steam engine.

Around the site are several eating places and you can buy fresh bread from the bakery. The park is open daily until 6 pm and admission is $4. To get there, take the No 53 bus south from downtown.

Devonian Gardens

This place makes a pleasant sanctuary from the concrete of downtown Calgary. Built entirely indoors, it's a one-hectare park with more than 20,000 plants and the smell and freshness of a greenhouse. There's over a km of pathways skirting fountains, pools, benches and a sculpture court. There's a small stage for regular entertainment, often during weekday lunch hours, and a special display area for art exhibitions. The gardens are 15 metres above street level on the 4th floor of Toronto Dominion Square, which is a complex on the 8th Avenue Mall, between 2nd and 3rd Sts SW. They're open daily from 9 am to 9 pm; free. Outside regular business hours, elevators must be used to reach the gardens.

Fort Calgary

This is not really a fort but a 16-hectare park where Calgary's original settlement began. In the park is an interpretive centre, the remains of the fort and two of Calgary's earliest houses.

At this point, where the Bow River meets the Elbow River, the first detachment of the Northwest Mounted Police arrived in 1875. They built a fort and called the developing settlement 'The Elbow'. Later it became Fort Calgary and remained a police post until 1914, when it was sold to the Grand Trunk Railway. Of the fort itself all that remains are a few foundations. Plaques give some of the history.

The fort site is pleasant with views and you can follow paths down to the river, walk across the footbridge to St Patrick's Island and on to Calgary Zoo.

To the east, across the Elbow River, is Hunt House, probably the oldest building in the Calgary area. It was believed to be built by the Hudson's Bay Company for one of their employees. Next door is the larger Dean House, built in 1906 for the commanding officer and partially renovated.

The Interpretive Centre (tel 232-1875) tells the story of Calgary's development. There are displays and a slide show on the Northwest Mounted Police every 30 minutes in the theatre. The park is open every day and is free. It's east of town at 750 9th Avenue SE.

Energeum

This outlines the development and uses of Alberta's energy resources. Models and charts depict the formation, discovery and exploitation of coal and oil, and include a good explanation of the province's valuable yet problematic oil sands. Some interactive computers supply further details, as does a film. I liked the gorgeous 1958 Buick the best. The display is free and open from 10.30 am to 4.30 pm Monday to Friday and Sundays during the summer. It's on the main floor of the Energy Resources Building at 640 5th Avenue SW.

Telecommunications Hall of Fame

This is a small telephone museum with exhibits on Alexander Graham Bell and other inventors. Also on view are various phones and systems and a couple of audio-visual displays. It's on the 2nd floor of the AGT Tower, 411 1st St SE.

Natural Gas, Light, Heat & Power Museum

That's quite a mouthful (and it's not even the complete title); it's a lot of name for a pretty superficial display in the Natural Gas Company's lobby at the corner of 11th Avenue SW and 8th St SW. The gas stove/oven from 1912 is quite a sight but beyond that, the few home appliances and old photographs don't amount to much. Admission is free.

Prince's Island Park

This is a pretty park on an island in the Bow River north of the downtown area, connected to both sides of the river by pedestrian bridges. It's a cool, quiet spot with lots of trees and flowers, picnic tables and jogging paths. On a hot summer day in Calgary this is a good antidote. As the signs say, the water is dangerous for swimming; not only does it move fast, bear in mind that the Bow River is melted snow from the Rockies. The bridge to the Island from downtown is at the top (north end) of 3rd St SW. Free.

Lunchbox Theatre

This is a professional performing arts stage (tel 265-4292) catering to downtown shoppers, workers and passers-by at lunch hours during the week. Shows vary from comedy to drama to musicals and change regularly. They start around noon, usually with an additional afternoon programme each week. Admission is $3.25. The theatre is in the Bow Valley Square at the corner of 6th Avenue and 1st St SW.

Planetarium

This is an entertaining and educational complex. The main attraction is the ever-changing one-hour show about a specific phenomenon of our universe. There are shows every day and night. Weekend nights are given over to laser rock music shows. The planetarium is at 7th Avenue SW and 11th St SW. Admission is $4.

Also on the premises is a small observatory with telescopes focused on the moon, the planets and star clusters. This is open every night if the weather is good. In the display area, exhibits vary from scientific presentations to models of parts of our galaxy. Admission is about $3.

Calgary Zoo

This zoo (tel 262-8144), one of Canada's largest and best, is near Fort Calgary on St George's Island in the Bow River. The zoo brings together 300 species of mammals, birds and reptiles, many in enclosures simulating the animals' natural habitats. Underwater viewing areas allow you to see polar bears, seals and other creatures as they behave beneath the water. Special blacked-out rooms enable you to see nocturnal animals. There is a section on Australian animals and pens for large, exotic mammals like tigers, giraffes and Himalayan cats. Hundreds of tropical birds are kept in greenhouses full of plants and flowers of warmer climes.

The zoo is open year-round and charges $4, less for kids. In summer the hours are 10 am to 7 pm, in winter 10 am to 5 pm. Picnic areas dot the zoo and island and there is a restaurant at the site.

Prehistoric Dinosaur Park

This is an extension of the zoo on St George's Island. This three-hectare park contains fossil displays and life-size replicas of dinosaurs in natural settings. Like the zoo, the park is about a 10-minute bus ride from downtown and is open every day. Take the Forest Lawn bus from downtown.

Inglewood Bird Sanctuary

This reserve (tel 269-6688) is at 9th Avenue and 20A St SE, south-east of downtown on a forested section of the Bow River flats. The area is home to many birds and a resting spot for those on the migratory trail. Trails lead through the sanctuary.

Calgary Stockyards

The stockyards, at 21st Avenue St SE, are one of the centres for western livestock dealing. If you want to see the goings-on, there are cattle auctions on weekdays.

Military Museums

On the Canadian Forces Base (tel 240-7322) on Crowchild Trail between 33rd and 50th Avenue NW are two military museums. Each pays homage to one of Calgary's two home regiments – Lord Strathcona's Horse and Princess Patricia's Light Infantry. There are collections of uniforms, weapons, badges, toys and memorabilia from both the 19th and 20th centuries. Both museums are open only on weekdays; the Lord Strathcona closes at 3 pm, the Princess Patricia at 4.30 pm. As they are on the base, you may be asked for identification; calling ahead is a good idea.

Fish Creek Park

On the southern edge of Calgary, quite a way from downtown, is this huge 800-hectare tract of land running along Fish Creek, which flows into the Bow River. It acts as a shelter for many animals and birds as well as people on weekends. Park interpreters present slide shows and walking tours to explain some of the local ecology. For details drop into the administration office or call 278-5640. To get there from downtown take the Macleod Trail south.

Calaway Park

This is a large amusement park about five km west of town on the Trans-Canada Highway. It features over 50 rides, a 180°

cinema, restaurants and entertainment events. It costs $7 to get in and see the shows, or $11 which includes rides.

Winter Olympics Site

Calgary hosted the 15th Winter Olympics in 1988, a first for Canada. Some of the locations and facilities were already in place, others were specially built for the Olympics, but they all remain in use. Canada Olympic Park, a 15-minute drive west of town on the Trans-Canada Highway, is interesting to visit. Here you can see the 70 and 90-metre ski jumps – from the top you realise how crazy those guys were – and the bobsled and luge runs built of concrete. There's an Olympic Hall of Fame and a Visitor's Centre, as well as the facilities now used as the Olympic Training Centre. The adjacent downhill ski area is open to the public in winter. But the real alpine skiing took place 55 km west of town at Nakiska on Mt Allan, where the slopes were newly constructed for the Games, and where skiers can now challenge themselves.

Bow River

The Bow River begins as clean, clear, barely melted ice in Bow Lake in the Rockies not far from Banff, and flows swiftly through Calgary about 140 km away. From Calgary it slows and warms and eventually reaches Medicine Hat near the provincial border. Here it melds with other meandering rivers, changes name and eventually slips into Hudson Bay.

The Bow in its middle section – the 60 km from Calgary east to Carseland – is considered one of the best trout-fishing rivers in North America and the best dry fly fishing river in the world. The fish, mainly brown and rainbow trout, are numerous and big, too. And the river will just float you along with no effort required. Sounds good even for those who don't fish. Swimming is out, though – the water here is still far too cool.

A good access point is just at the south edge of Calgary's city limits under the Highway 22X bridge. There are numerous fishing guide services in town as well as sporting goods stores for fishing tackle and information. One place to try that combines the two is Country Pleasures.

Activities

Calgary has 180 km of bicycle and hiking trails, many in the parks and nature areas. There are maps available from the City Parks Department.

There are two leisure centres in town run by the City Parks Department (tel 278-7542), which include giant wave pools, year-round skating, racquet courts and hot tubs.

Calgary Stampede

The Calgary Stampede is a wild 10-day festival that includes everything you can think of. The festival, which began in 1912, commences in the second week of July each year. The town and nearby countryside is packed for the duration. Most organised events take place in Stampede Park but many of the streets are full of activity too. Stampede Park comes alive with concerts, shows, exhibitions, dancing and eating. There is also an amusement area with rides, a gambling hall and lots of contests. It's all kicked off with a huge parade.

Highlights are the chuck wagon race and the rodeo, which is said to be the biggest and roughest in North America. Events include rides on bucking broncos and bulls, and calf-roping and branding. At night the Stampede Stage Show takes over, with singers, bands, clowns and dancing girls.

Tickets for the main events go early and range in price from about $7 to $25. Prices all over town go up, so beware, and arrive early to find a place to stay.

For more information or tickets write to Calgary Exhibition & Stampede, Box 2890, Calgary, Alberta.

Places to Stay

Hostels The CHA *Youth Hostel* (tel 269-

8239) is at 520 7th Avenue SE. The hostel opens at 5 pm and closes at 11.30 pm. In the morning you have to be gone by 10 am. It is a new, large hostel with complete facilities. There's washing equipment in the basement and a small park next door. It can get very crowded in summer; take care with valuables. Rates are $7 for members, $9 for non-members.

A few doors up from the youth hostel on the opposite side of the street is the government-run hostel for the needy, the *Single Men's Hostel* (tel 261-6269) at 631 7th Avenue SE. You can stay here and get a breakfast, too, for nothing, but the atmosphere can be pretty grim.

The *Salvation Army* (tel 262-2756) nearby at 515 1st St SE is much the same thing. It's opposite the Calgary Board of Education with its Family of Man sculpture on the lawn.

The *YMCA* (tel 269-6701) is at 332 6th Avenue SW. This is the old, very central, inexpensive YMCA which was unfortunately slated for demolition on my last visit. There are plans to open a new one, not far away, probably at the corner of 3rd St SW and 1st Avenue SW, but it may not offer rooms. In the meantime, this one has a cafeteria, pool and gym.

The *YWCA* (tel 263-1550), for women only, is also central at 320 5th Avenue SE. The single rooms are $22 without bath, $29 with, plus a $3 key deposit, but there are doubles, triple and bunk rooms for less. A simple, hostel-like room is about $7. They also have a cafeteria but it's closed on weekends. Rooms are clean and you can use the pool.

The University of Calgary rents rooms in the dormitories from mid-May to mid-August. For details and information call the Special Functions office (tel 284-7243) at Room 03 in the dining centre. The normal rate is $27 for singles and $38 for a twin room, but much less for students. All prices include breakfast. There are good facilities on campus, including a gym and a cheap cafeteria.

Bed & Breakfasts An association which checks and lists houses offering bed & breakfasts is Welcome West Vacation (tel 258-3373). They have places in and around town with prices from $15 to $25 for singles, $25 to $45 for doubles.

Hotels Central Calgary doesn't have an abundance of lodgings in any price range and many of the hotels are around the edges of town. In the city the south-west section, once a pretty rough and tumble area, was the centre for cheap hotels but as the area has been cleaned up the small, older places disappeared. There are still a couple hanging on and we'll start with them.

The *Cecil* (tel 266-2982) is my top choice amongst the low-budget spots. It's at the corner of 4th Avenue SE and 3rd St SE. It has a new yellow-and-brown paint job and is better maintained than most. Rooms are $18 for singles or doubles with no TV, no phone and no bath, but a sink in each room. There's a bar downstairs where you can get basic food. They require a key deposit but offer free parking.

The *St Louis* (tel 262-6341) at 430 8th Avenue SE is pretty basic, but shoestringers will find it cheap at $14 or a couple of dollars more for a room with bath and TV. There's a busy blues bar and simple restaurant downstairs.

Much better is the very central *York Hotel* (tel 262-5581) at the corner of Centre St and 7th Avenue SW. The place is good, clean, modern and safe. Rooms are $38/42 for singles/doubles with all comforts.

Also good but a bit costlier is the *Lord Nelson Inn* (tel 269-8262) at 1020 8th Avenue SW. Singles and doubles go for between $40 and $50. It's got full facilities, including a fridge in each room.

In the expensive range there's the *Calgary Centre Inn* (tel 262-7091) over at 202 4th Avenue. It's a large place with bar, restaurants and floors for non-smokers. Rates are in the $60 to $70 range. The *Sandman* (tel 237-8626) at nearly twice the size is about the same price and standard and also central at 888 7th Avenue SE.

Motels Much of the cheap and moderate accommodation is found outside the central core. Calgary has dozens of motels in all parts of the city, but there are some areas of very heavy concentration, making it easy to shop around. One of these is along Macleod Trail which heads south from the city, eventually leading to Highway 2 South to the USA. Macleod Trail is a commercial strip with petrol stations, fast-food restaurants, furniture shops and motels.

The *Flamingo Motor Hotel* is marked by – you guessed it – a large pink flamingo. It's at 7505 Macleod, near the corner of 75th Avenue SW. Rooms are $50/55 for singles/doubles with a TV in each room, a pool and a sauna. The treed grounds are pleasant. There are restaurants nearby and a laundromat on the property.

Relax Inn, 9206 Macleod near 90th Avenue SE, is the brown-and-white two-storey building which contains a pool and whirlpool. Singles cost $35, doubles $43, with TV. You can get a room cheaper if it's used only between 8.30 am and 5 pm. Good value.

The *Travelodge* (tel 253-1111) is also good value at about the same price, and has a pool. It's at 7012 Macleod Trail South.

Another motel area is in the north-west section of the city on and just off Highway 16, which is also Highway 1 – the Trans-Canada Highway.

Near the University of Calgary, Highway 16 meets Crowchild Trail. Linking the two on a diagonal, making a triangle, is Banff Trail. Banff Trail is also called Highway 1A. Because of the many motels in and around this triangle, the area is called 'Motel Village'. It's a fair way from town, close to where the Bow River crosses the Trans-Canada Highway.

The *Panama Motor Inn* (tel 289-2561), in Motel Village at 2440 16th Avenue NW, is fairly priced in the mid-$30s; some rooms have kitchenettes.

The *Budget Motor Inn* (tel 288-7115) is along 16th Avenue at No 4420. It's simple but fine and has free coffee.

Cheapest of the lot is *Circle Inn Motel* (tel 289-0295) at 2373 Banff Avenue. They have a pub and kitchenette for a few extra dollars.

Camping There are several campgrounds near the city for both trailers and tents. They all have good facilities and are cheaper than other accommodation but are very developed and organised.

Closest to town is the *Max Bell Park* (tel 248-4707), three km east of the zoo in the triangle between Deerfoot Trail, Mermaid Drive and Barlow Trail. The entrance is on Barlow. Tenting is $9 for two people and there are 60 sites; showers are available; the city bus is nearby. The park is open from 19 June to 31 August.

Bow Bend Trailer Park (tel 288-2161) is up near Motel Village in north-west Calgary. It's beside Shouldice Park and the Bow River at 5227 13th Avenue NW. Two tenting are charged $10 and there are showers and a laundromat. The park is open all year. To get there, turn off Highway 1 at Home Rd, then west on 13th Avenue. If it's full there are two others further out along Highway 1.

Whispering Spruce Campground (tel 274-4211) is about 15 minutes north of the city limits along Highway 2. They have complete facilities, including a small grocery shop. Open 15 May to 31 October.

Places to Eat

The Café 1886 is an interesting little place in the old Calgary Water Power Company building, established in 1886. It's open for breakfast and lunch and serves only omelettes, but they have every kind and they're big. With toast, they cost about $5. All the Colombian coffee you can drink is $1.25. The place is open from 9.30 am to 2 pm on weekdays, and 10 am to 3 pm on weekends. It's in a worn white wooden building by the river right beside the walking bridge for Prince's Island, corner of 3rd St SW and 1st Avenue SW. It's sort of hidden away as there are no other restaurants or stores nearby. Watch for the beautiful old yellow car out front – I think it belongs to the restaurant's owner.

Henry's is a much more plastic place at 509 8th Avenue SW, but is open every day for standard breakfasts and meals for $3 to $7. The place has weird counter chairs which look like pilot seats.

For lunch or dinner, check out the second floor of the Lancaster Building at 304 8th Avenue SW. There are 17 food kiosks serving cheap Chinese, Mexican, deli and other foods. You get street views, too.

Three other reliable, cheap places are *Woolworth's* in the mall, *Mr Submarine* at the corner of 6th Avenue SW and Centre St and the restaurants in The Bay department store, on the corner of 1st St SW and 8th SW.

There's good pizza at the *Baby Blues Cafe Bar*, 937 7th Avenue SW. Try the one with the spinach. They have live music at night.

More agreeable is the *Unicorn Pub*, a busy, friendly pub which serves inexpensive food like quiche, fish & chips, and steak & kidney pie. It's downstairs at 8th Avenue SW on the corner of 2nd St SW.

The 8th Avenue Mall has numerous other places, most of the quick variety. The *Sahara Club* at No 120 offers the usual sandwiches but also quite a few Middle Eastern dishes at fair prices, and all-you-can-eat buffets. Other places set up tables in the mall in fair weather.

For dinners downtown, *The Three Greenhorns* at the corner of 4th Avenue SW and 4th St offers pretty decent value steaks and seafood. The *Thames & Ganges* is at 915 6th Avenue SW. As the name suggests, this place blends English and Indian fare, doing it inexpensively and well. It's closed on Sundays.

For other ethnic fare there's *Sara's Pyrohy Hut* at 1216 Centre St, a Ukrainian place with all the usual specialties and good, solid food at moderate prices. *Chalet Heidi's* is a more expensive Swiss place at 122 16th Avenue NE. They serve mainly veal dishes but offer reindeer, too and have lots of soups on the menu.

At the *Keg'n'Cleaver* with three outlets around town, you can try fresh Alberta steaks.

There is a small Chinatown on 2nd and 3rd Avenues at Centre St. *First Delight* and *A A Seafood* both offer dim sum lunches. *Ho Won* has been recommended. The *Chinatown Mall* on the corner of 3rd Avenue SE and 1st St SE is fun on a Sunday around noon when the whole area is packed. Lots of fresh pastries are offered. The *Diamond Bakery* at 111A 3rd Avenue SE is a tiny place offering tasty Chinese treats and sweets. There are also a couple of Vietnamese places in this district.

For desserts, try the casual *European Cascade Grill* at 817 1st St SW. Meals and wines are also offered, with music on Monday nights.

South across the train tracks below 9th Avenue there are also a couple of good areas for food searching. The misnamed *Cedars Deli* on the right side, just after the underpass on 1st Avenue SW, is worth the short walk for good, cheap Lebanese food in the green-and-white setting.

Along 10th Avenue you'll find two good places to eat. The *Pearl of the Orient*, a Vietnamese restaurant at No 351, is inexpensive and their spring rolls have been described as 'beyond delicious'. Next door, *Mother Tucker's* is a popular, moderately-priced steak and chicken place with a huge salad bar.

Further south, 17th Avenue SW is lined with a wide range of restaurants as well as a variety of other businesses including many antique shops. Fourth St SW, south of 17th has boutiques, a few galleries and yet more eating places and night spots. Along 17th Avenue, the *Soup Kitchen*, near 7th St SW, is a small, pleasant café with good sandwiches. *Bagels & Buns* across the street is also good for casual breakfasts and lunches. There's a variety of places around the corner of 17th Avenue and 4th St – Indian, Greek, French, delis, etc.

Outside the downtown area, the commercial strips mentioned in the motel section are lined with eating places. Both Macleod Trail to the south and Highway 1 east-west across the northern section have many familiar chains.

The Saturday *Herald* has lots of ads for Sunday brunch bargains.

Nightlife

For complete entertainment guides pick up a copy of *Key to Calgary* in one of the good hotels and read the local newspapers, especially on Friday or Saturday.

Music Downtown, *The Old Scotch* at 820 10th St SW, on the corner of 9th Avenue SW, brings in good country, folk and jazz bands. There are jam sessions on Sunday nights. For rock, there's the *Cecil Hotel* on the corner of 4th Avenue SE and 3rd Avenue SE, and *Frankie & Johnny's* in the North Centre Inn, corner of Centre St and 16th Avenue.

The *Tiki Tiki* in the downtown Holiday Inn is a quiet spot with the usual Polynesian motifs.

Marty's Cafe is an excellent funky little spot for blues, jazz and a varied asortment of music on 17th Avenue SW near 4th St SW. There are other places along the street, some with dancing.

Kensington, a district based on Kensington Rd and 10th St NW, is an old city neighbourhood with plenty of restaurants and nightspots; *Kensington's Delicafe*, at 1414 Kensington Rd, is both. There's cheap food, a relaxed atmosphere, live music and an outdoor patio. Open every day and good.

South of town way out at Lake Bonavista the *Inn* there, with views of the lake and mountains, is a spiffy place for a drink.

Theatre The *New Calgary Centre for the Performing Arts*, known as The Centre, is on the 8th Avenue Mall at 1st St SW. It has lots of theatre, the symphony and more. The city has several other live theatre venues as well as a couple offering dinner and the show. Sun-Ergos often presents dance performances.

Cinema The *National Film Board Theatre*, 222 1st St SE, shows free movies on Tuesdays from 11.45 am to 1.15 pm.

The *Plaza Theatre* (tel 283-3636) at 1113 Kensington Rd NW, has two different shows a night plus midnight performances on Fridays and Saturdays. They present off-beat American and foreign films.

The University of Calgary often has films in either 148 Science Theatre or the Boris Roubakine Recital Hall. The films are mainly foreign.

Getting There & Away

Air The Calgary International Airport is about 15 km north-east of the centre of town – a 25-minute drive.

Air Canada (tel 265-9555), flies to many Canadian cities. Its commuter runs to Edmonton are very frequent, especially from Monday to Friday. The best fare for any destination is standby, but it's only available for those aged 22 or under. Full fares, one-way include:

Vancouver – $170
Thunder Bay – $310
Montreal – $450 (standby $166).

Train The VIA Rail station is very conveniently located in the shopping mall beneath (and slightly to the west of) the Calgary Tower. Ring 1-800-665-8630, toll-free. For lost and found ring 262-6308.

The westbound train for Banff and Vancouver leaves daily at 2.05 pm. The eastbound Toronto/Montreal train leaves daily at 3.15 pm. There are no trains to Edmonton.

Fares, one-way: Banff $13, Vancouver $71, Winnipeg $105.

Bus There's a big new bus station (tel 265-9111) in Calgary, a bit away from the centre. It's walkable but most people opt for the city bus which goes to the door. The station is at Bow Trail at 9th Avenue SW.

The Greyhound station (tel 265-9111) is a very busy, crowded depot with buses going in all directions. It's at 125 4th Avenue SW. The fares in the following information are all one-way:

Edmonton: about 15 buses daily – $19

Vancouver, through Rodgers Pass and Fraser Canyon: 7.30 am, 2.30 pm, 4.30 pm, 6.30 pm, 10.30 pm, 1.15 am

Vancouver, through the Okanagan: 7 am, 12.30 pm, 10.30 pm

Vancouver, through Crownest Pass: 8.15 am, 10.20 pm

Banff: six or seven a day – $9.15

Drumheller: 8 am, 6 and 10.45 pm – $10.45

Fort Macleod and Lethbridge: six a day

Winnipeg, Toronto, Montreal, New York: 8 am, 11.45 am, 2 pm, 9 pm – $75 (to Winnipeg).

Red Arrow Express runs four buses daily to Edmonton ($21) from the Calgary depot at Westward Inn, 119 12th Avenue SW.

Getting Around

Airport Transport The best way to and from the airport is the Airporter Bus, which runs from 5.30 am to 11.30 pm between all major downtown hotels and the airport and costs $6. One departs every 20 minutes from the Westin Hotel on 4th Avenue SW.

A taxi to the airport costs about $15.

Bus & LRT Calgary Transit operates the bus, streetcar and Light Rapid Transit (LRT) train system. The downtown office (tel 276-7801) is at 216 7th Avenue SW, opposite the Bay Store. They have route maps, information and tickets. One fare entitles you to transfer to other buses or the LRT train. This train, called the C train, is free in the downtown area along 7th Avenue. If you're going further or need a transfer, buy your ticket from a machine on the C train platform.

Bus Nos 3 and 53 go north-south up Centre St to the northern areas of the city. Bus No 51 runs east-west along 16th Avenue-Highway 1 (Trans-Canada Highway). Westbound, it goes to the university.

Note that most places in the downtown area are within walking distance of each other.

Car Rentals Rent-A-Wreck (tel 237-7093) requires reservations for small cars.

Mini-Drive (tel 262-4400) at 117 5th Avenue SE, has Hondas and Chevettes for $23 a day, $139 a week, 200 free km included. They're open every day.

Cheap Mobile (tel 276-7389) is another car rental business.

Hitching Thumbing within the Calgary city limits is illegal and subject to very heavy fines. The law's enforced, so forget hitching here. Take the No 51 bus east or west and ask the driver if there's a connecting bus going further. If not, walk to the city boundary before attempting to hitch.

Tours Call the Alberta Historical Resources Foundation, 102 8th Avenue SE, to see if they still run their free guided walking tours.

The cheapest bus tour of town is to take the No 10 bus from the CN Tower. For $1.25 this city bus goes on its two-hour, 45-minute circular route past old and new areas, the highest point of the city with views to the foothills, the university and some wealthy districts.

Brewster Gray Line runs tours of Calgary and various Rocky Mountain locations from Calgary. The tour of Calgary takes four hours, covers about 50 km and costs $20 ($9.50 in the off-season). It includes Fort Calgary, Heritage Park and the downtown area, with admissions included in the ticket. A history of the city is given.

There are daily trips leaving from the Greyhound Bus Station.

Canwest (tel 938-5111) gives helicopter rides over the city which cost $20 each for two passengers or $30 for a single. Rides depart from the downtown heliport at Bow River and 7th St SW, on Saturday and Sunday from 10 am.

Other tours offered by Brewster and Greyhound go to the Columbia Icefield, Banff or some of the mountain lakes. The Brewster Mountain Lakes tour, taking about 10 hours, includes Banff, Lake Louise, Moraine Lake and some of the Bow River Valley. It runs in summer only and costs $32. For more information visit their office in the Palliser Hotel, downtown at 9th Avenue and 1st St SW, or call 276-0766.

Pacific Western Transportation (tel 243-4990) also run bus tours.

Southern Alberta

LETHBRIDGE

Southern Alberta is ranching country, although wheat is very important, too. This is the largest town in southern Alberta and a centre for the local agricultural communities.

Things to See

Nikka Yuko Japanese Gardens is an authentic Japanese-style park. The garden consists of ponds, rocks and shrubs but no flowers. The buildings and bridges were built in Japan and reassembled here. Admission is $1.25, students 50c.

On the west side of the city is Indian Battle Park and Fort Whoopup, a replica of a notorious whisky trading post. The site is open in summer only.

There is another small museum displaying artefacts from Lethbridge history.

FORT MACLEOD

West of Lethbridge, two hours south of Calgary, is this reconstruction of a Northwest Mounted Police fort of 1874. The fort (tel 553-4703) is still patrolled by Mounties in their traditional red uniforms, but only from Wednesdays to Sundays in July and August. Inside there is a small local history collection.

HEAD-SMASHED-IN BUFFALO JUMP

This recently accredited UN World Heritage Site is the oldest, biggest and best preserved bison jump site in North America. For thousands of years Indians used it to run buffalo, their 'living department stores', over the edge of the cliff. They then used the meat, hide, bone, horns and nearly everything else for their supplies and materials. Opened in 1987 by the Duke and Duchess of York, the Interpretation Centre provides explanations of the site and how the Indians' work was achieved. Heritage Hikes, a private business run by an archaeologist, offers a series of day-long hikes beyond the actual jump site into the surrounding valley, with a maximum of 15 per group. Ancient petroglyphs (prehistoric carvings or drawings on rock) can be seen.

The site is 20 km west of Fort Macleod.

WATERTON LAKES NATIONAL PARK

In far south-west Alberta is this national park, opened in 1895. It is now joined with the Glacier National Park of Montana to form an international park. The land here rises from the prairie into rugged, beautiful alpine scenery with many lakes, waterfalls and valleys. The whole park is much less visited than its two more northerly sisters, Banff and Jasper. Partly because of this, spotting wildlife here is more common.

The park has over 160 km of trails – good for hiking or riding – and boat tours on Waterton Lake run daily from mid-May to late September. This cruise, which costs $8, crosses the border and stops in Goat Haunt, Montana. The town of Waterton is smaller and much more low-key than Banff.

Accommodation in the park consists of campgrounds and a couple of hotels.

DINOSAUR PROVINCIAL PARK

This 70-million-year-old graveyard is a must if you're going by. It's 78 km north of Brooks, halfway between Calgary and Medicine Hat, and it's free.

The 'badlands' of the park are a dry, convoluted lunar landscape. But they weren't always like this: at one time the Gulf of Mexico reached this far; the area was a jungle-like swamp and dinosaurs loved it. Their remains and fossils lie buried all over the valley. There are four display areas where nearly complete skeletons have been uncovered, dusted off and encased in glass, just the way they were found. Close to 120 skeletons have been found, many sent to museums around the world.

There are guided walks through the strange, eroded landscape. Ask about them at the office. Good photographs are easy here; look for the hoodoos, a mushroom-like geological oddity. Take plenty of water along in summer; walking in the valley can be as hot as hell.

Place to Stay

There is a pretty good campground in the park by a river, making a small, green oasis in this stark place.

KINBROOK ISLAND PROVINCIAL PARK

This is a good camping spot on the way to or from Calgary. It's 19 km south-west of Brooks, by a man-made lake. You can swim and fish, or simply escape the very flat, totally treeless stretch of highway between here and Medicine Hat.

MEDICINE HAT

This city was formed in 1883 when the Canadian Pacific Railway, drilling for water, hit natural gas. They subsequently found enough of it to prompt Rudyard Kipling to label it 'the city with all hell for a basement'. Today Medicine Hat still has very cheap heat, light and hot water.

Things to See

If you miss Calgary's Stampede, there's one here at the end of August.

Free tours are given at the Altaglass Factory where glass is still blown in the traditional manner.

CYPRESS HILLS PROVINCIAL PARK

This park straddling the Saskatchewan border is described in the Saskatchewan section.

DRUMHELLER

A small city in a strange setting, Drumheller is about 150 km north-east of Calgary. It sits 122 metres below prairie level in a valley carved out by glaciers. As you come into town you'll see heavy farm machinery lined up for sale, looking like the work of a mad sculptor. Thousands of years of wind and water erosion have generated the surrounding badlands which reveal millions of years of earth's animal and geological history. The area is renowned for its fossils of dinosaurs, petrified wood and weird land formations.

There are privately-owned campgrounds in the area.

Things to See

The Dinosaur Museum, open from 9 am to 8 pm, gives a good introduction to the badlands and has remains and fossils on display. Tickets cost $1.50. One display is a pieced-together edmontosaurus, a four to five-tonne, nine-metre-long beast found in 1923.

Forget the Homestead Antique Museum for $2 and Prehistoric Park, a hokey collection of dinosaur models.

Drumheller is at the beginning of Dinosaur Trail, a 48-km loop around the area taking in all the attractions, for which you need a car. The scenery along the trail is really good, as is the view from

Horsethief Canyon Point. There are trails here leading down into the valley where you can poke around in the petrified oyster beds. The Hoodoos, 14 km south-east of Drumheller on Highway 10, are the best example of this weird, time-telling formation.

Along North Dinosaur Trail (Highway 838) north-west of town is the new Tyrell Museum of Palaeontology. This modern museum uses displays, videos, films, computers, etc, to outline the study of early life on earth. Fossils trace evolution and best of all is the extensive display of dinosaurs. It's open daily from 9 am to 9 pm in summer and is free. The rest of the year it's closed on Mondays.

In Midlands Provincial Park (no camping) there are tours of old mines at 10 am and 3 pm daily, except Wednesday and Thursday.

The Rockies

Much of the mountain area of Alberta, running along the British Columbia border, is contained and protected in two huge, adjacent national parks – Banff to the south and Jasper to the north. The Icefields Parkway links the two, though there is no real boundary.

The entire area is one of spectacular beauty with some of the best scenery, hiking and skiing to be found anywhere. With the Canadian Rockies there are 644 peaks over 6000 feet (1829 metres) and 144 over 10,000 feet (3048 metres).

The two principal parks offer jagged, snow-capped mountains, peaceful valleys, rushing rivers, natural hot springs and alpine forests. The colour of many Rocky Mountain lakes will have you doubting your eyes.

Both parks also have modern conveniences or back-country trails to choose from. Wildlife abounds, particularly in Jasper.

Banff was Canada's first national park and is now the best-known and most popular, attracting three million visitors annually. The skiing and climbing are world famous. The larger Jasper park is wilder and less-explored but, like Banff, offers excellent hiking trails.

The small towns of Banff and Jasper act as focal points for orientation, supplies and information.

There is a $3 fee to drive into either park and this permit is good for four days. A $12 ticket is good in any national park for a year.

BANFF

Banff is Canada's No 1 resort town in both winter and summer, and as such is really the centre of the Rockies. Despite that, it's very small, consisting of one main street, and so can get crowded. The heaviest months are July and August. Although this can cause problems, the many vacationers generally create a relaxed and festive atmosphere. Many of the workers in and around town are newcomers, 'gorbies' (tourists) or long-term visitors themselves.

The town is clean and pleasant, the surroundings unbeatable. It makes a good R&R spot after travelling awhile, or hiking.

There are stores selling and renting skiing, hiking and camping equipment and supplies. Many good day trips and hikes can be done from Banff.

Orientation

Banff Avenue, the main street, runs north-south through the whole length of town. It heads off north to the Trans-Canada Highway. The street is lined with stores, restaurants and souvenir shops which sell over-priced junk. Lately they've been catering to the heavy Japanese trade. Over the bridge at Banff Avenue's south end is the Administration Building. This is a good place for a view and a photo of the town. Behind the building are flower gardens with a stream, ponds and a few benches.

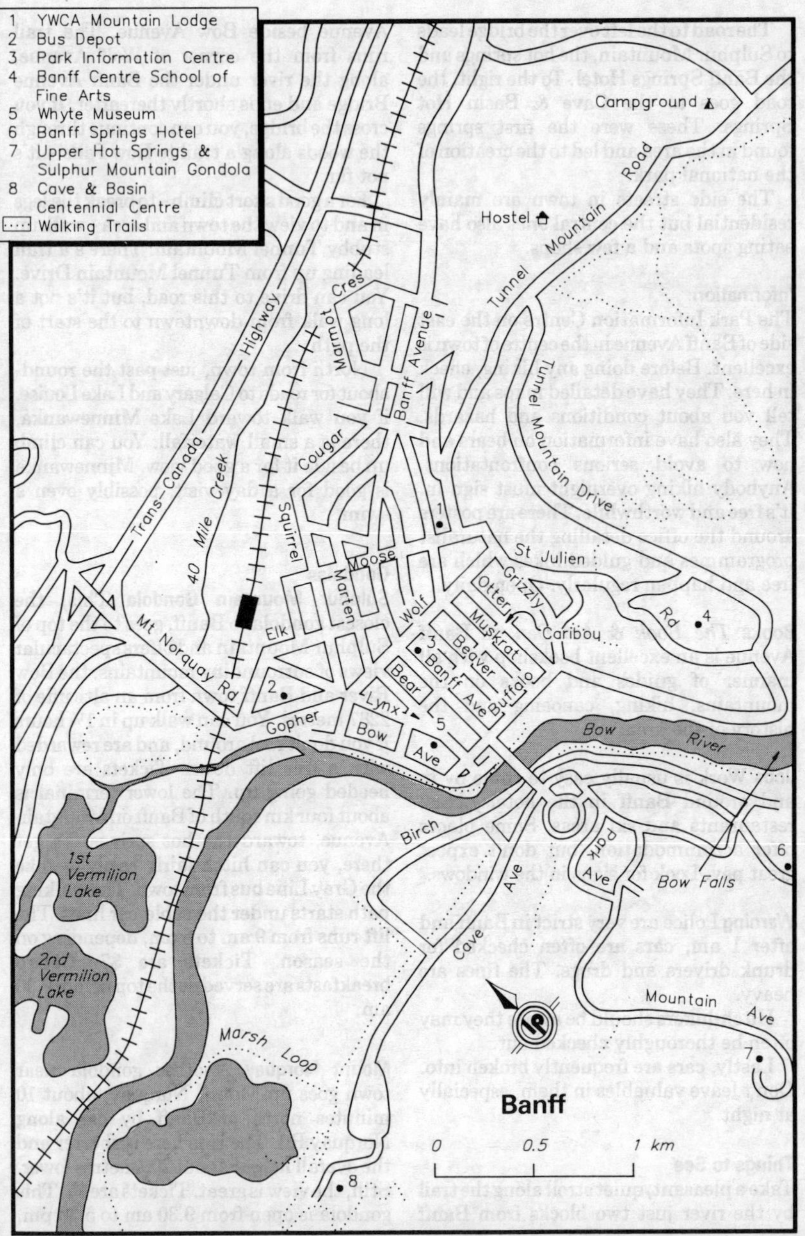
1 YWCA Mountain Lodge
2 Bus Depot
3 Park Information Centre
4 Banff Centre School of Fine Arts
5 Whyte Museum
6 Banff Springs Hotel
7 Upper Hot Springs & Sulphur Mountain Gondola
8 Cave & Basin Centennial Centre
Walking Trails
Campground
Hostel
Tunnel Mountain Road
Tunnel Mountain Drive
Trans-Canada Highway
40 Mile Creek
Marmot Cres
Banff Avenue
Cougar
Squirrel
Moose
Marten
Wolf
Elk
St Julien
Grizzly
Otter
Caribou
Rd
Muskrat
Beaver
Buffalo
Banff Ave
Bear
Lynx
Bow Ave
Gopher
Mt Norquay Rd
Bow River
Birch
Park Ave
Bow Falls
Cave Ave
1st Vermilion Lake
2nd Vermilion Lake
Marsh Loop
Mountain Ave
Banff
0 0.5 1 km

The road to the left over the bridge leads to Sulphur Mountain, the hot springs and the Banff Springs Hotel. To the right, the road goes to the Cave & Basin Hot Springs. These were the first springs found in the area and led to the creation of the national park.

The side streets in town are mainly residential but the central ones also have eating spots and a few shops.

Information

The Park Information Centre on the east side of Banff Avenue in the centre of town is excellent. Before doing any hiking, check in here. They have detailed maps and will tell you about conditions and hazards. They also have information on bears and how to avoid serious confrontations. Anybody hiking overnight must sign in. It's free and worthwhile. There are posters around the office detailing the naturalist programmes and guided hikes which are free and happen regularly. Open daily.

Books *The Book & Art Den* on Banff Avenue is an excellent bookshop with all manner of guides and books on the mountains, hiking, canoeing and the history of the area.

Jobs Work is usually easy to come by in and around Banff in the hotels, bars, restaurants and ski areas. Some places offer accommodation, but don't expect great pay. Look for signs in the windows.

Warning Police are very strict in Banff and after 1 am, cars are often checked for drunk drivers and drugs. The fines are heavy.

Hitch-hikers should be aware they may often be thoroughly checked out.

Lastly, cars are frequently broken into. Don't leave valuables in them, especially at night.

Things to See

Take a pleasant, quiet stroll along the trail by the river just two blocks from Banff Avenue beside Bow Avenue. The trail runs from the corner of Wolf Avenue, along the river under the Banff Avenue Bridge and ends shortly thereafter. If you cross the bridge, you can continue through the woods along a trail to Bow Falls – it's not far.

For a good short climb – to break the legs in and to view the town and area – walk up stubby Tunnel Mountain. There's a trail leading up from Tunnel Mountain Drive. You can drive to this road, but it's not a long walk from downtown to the start of the path.

North from town, just past the roundabout for roads to Calgary and Lake Louise, if you walk toward Lake Minnewanka, there is a small waterfall. You can climb up beside it for a good view. Minnewanka is good for a day visit, possibly even a swim.

Gondolas

Sulphur Mountain Gondola This, the closest gondola to Banff, goes to the top of Sulphur Mountain and offers spectacular views of surrounding mountains, the Bow River and Banff town from an altitude of 2287 metres. You can walk up in 1¼ hours if you don't fool around, and are rewarded with a free lift down. Tickets are only needed going up. The lower terminal is about four km south of Banff on Mountain Avenue, toward the hot springs. To get there, you can hitch fairly easily or take the Gray Line bus from town. The walking path starts under the cable-car lines. The lift runs from 9 am to 8 pm, depending on the season. Tickets are $7. Cheap breakfasts are served at the top before 9.30 am.

Mount Norquay Another gondola near town goes up Mount Norquay, about 10 minutes north of Banff by car along Norquay Rd. The ride here is shorter and the overall height about 200 metres lower. Still, the view is great. Tickets are $5. This gondola is open from 9.30 am to 5.30 pm,

1 April to 13 September. There is a restaurant at the top.

Sunshine Village A third gondola ride is found at Sunshine Village. It's the longest at five km. There is a hotel at the top which isn't too badly priced and a restaurant. This is a major ski centre in winter. The round trip is $7, one-way $5. The village, a 15-minute drive west of Banff, has long and short trails and a restaurant. On one of the trails, you can walk interstate into British Columbia.

Hot Springs

There is a soothing hot pool and steam room at the Upper Hot Springs spa, which is out of town toward Sulphur Mountain. Bathing suits and towels can be cheaply rented. Admission is $2 for the pool. This is quite a walk from town. To get there, take Mountain Rd at the fork for the Banff Springs Hotel. The hot springs are open from 9 am to 9 pm in summer. Ahhhhhh.

South-west of town is the Cave & Basin Centennial Centre with swimming pool and complex rebuilt to the original style of 1914. The mineral water here is not as hot as that of the Upper Hot Springs but it's still comfortably warm, with swimming from May to September. The rented bathing suits are fun – they're also 1914-style. There's a couple of nice short walks here as well as the cave and a coffee shop.

Banff Museum

This museum has a collection of mammals, birds, plants and animals found in Banff National Park. Included are two small stuffed grizzlies and a black bear so you can study the difference. There's also an 1841 tree graffiti carving. The old wooden building which houses the museum dates from 1903. Open 10 am to 6 pm daily, free. It's before the bridge at the south end of town.

Natural History Museum

This museum has displays on early life forms, including Canadian dinosaurs. It

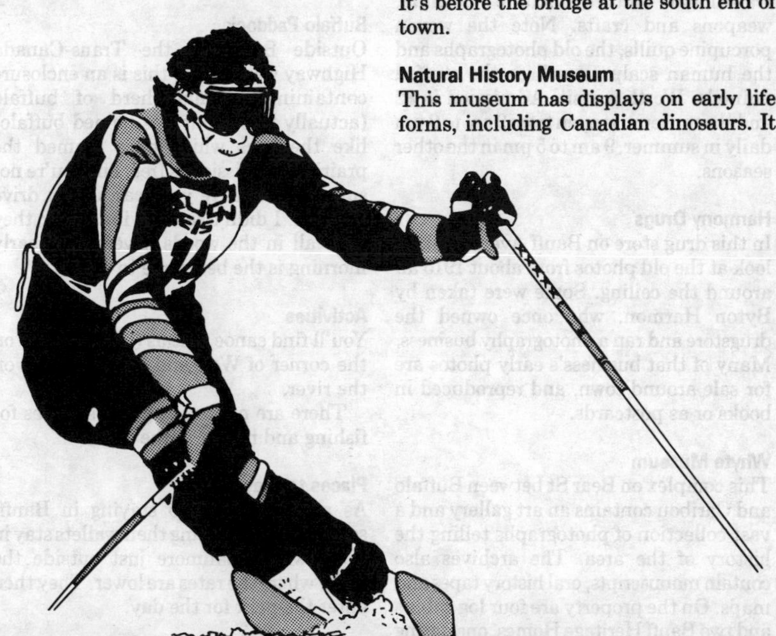

has film and slide presentations and features a model of the notorious Sasquatch, the abominable snowman of the Rockies. The Loch Ness of Western Canada, he's said to be eight to 10 feet tall and spotted 500 times. You can also read descriptions of Castleguard Cave, one of Canada's biggest at 12 km long, which is in northern Banff Park. The museum is open daily until 10 pm and admission is $1.50. It's on the second floor in the Clock Tower Mall, 112 Banff Avenue.

Luxton Museum

Usually called the Indian Museum, the Luxton is in the fort-like wooden building beside the river, to the right of the bridge over the Bow River (behind the Indian 'craft' shop). It deals mainly with the Plains Indians but also covers tribes from all over Alberta. Displays, models and re-creations depicting aspects of their traditional culture include clothing, weapons and crafts. Note the woven porcupine quills, the old photographs and the human scalp as well as the stuffed animals. Worth a visit. Admission is $2 and the museum is open from 9 am to 9 pm daily in summer, 9 am to 5 pm in the other seasons.

Harmony Drugs

In this drug store on Banff Avenue take a look at the old photos from about 1915 all around the ceiling. Some were taken by Byron Harmon, who once owned the drugstore and ran a photography business. Many of that business's early photos are for sale around town, and reproduced in books or as postcards.

Whyte Museum

This complex on Bear St between Buffalo and Caribou contains an art gallery and a vast collection of photographs telling the history of the area. The archives also contain manuscripts, oral history tapes and maps. On the property are four log cabins and two Banff Heritage Homes, one dating from 1907 and one from 1931. Guided tours are offered of the latter. The foundation presents films, lectures and concerts regularly. It's open daily in summer and costs $2, less for seniors and students. There are tea and cookies served on Fridays to Sundays from 2.30 to 4.30 pm.

Banff Centre School of Fine Arts

This centre contains one of Canada's best known art schools with facilities for dance, theatre, music and the visual arts. There are often exhibits, concerts and various other events taking place. Throughout the summer, in the Festival of the Arts, students, together with internationally recognised artists, present their works in workshops and performances. There is usually something each day, usually free. The Tourist Office will have a complete schedule.

The Banff Centre is not far from downtown on St Julian Rd.

Buffalo Paddock

Outside Banff on the Trans-Canada Highway westbound, this is an enclosure containing a small herd of buffalo (actually bison, but mis-named buffalo) like the ones which once roamed the prairies. Admission is free, but you're not supposed to leave your car as you drive through. I didn't see a living thing; they were all in the woods. Evening or early morning is the best time to visit.

Activities

You'll find canoe rentals (tel 762-3632) on the corner of Wolf and Bow Avenues on the river.

There are numerous guide services for fishing and hiking in the area.

Places to Stay

As an alternative to staying in Banff, some people watching their wallets stay in the town of Canmore just outside the park, where the rates are lower. They then enter the park for the day.

Hostels Banff has a large new *Hostel* (tel 762-4122) three km from the town centre. It's got 150 beds in small rooms, a cafeteria, laundry facilities and a common room with fireplace. Members pay $9, non-members $12. It's on Tunnel Mountain Rd, away from the town centre.

Spray River Hostel (tel 283-5551) is 4.8 km south of town. It is on the Spray River fire road which begins at the Banff Springs Hotel but is closed to cars. From here you must hike in but it's not far. They have room for 47 and are open all year. Rates are $4.50 for members.

The good *YM-YWCA* (tel 762-3560) at 414 Muskrat St takes men and women. Dorm beds are $8, singles are $14 and doubles $18; couples are OK. There are no cooking facilities. This nice looking lodge is near the corner of Moose St, central, and is very popular and often full.

Hotels & Tourist Homes Generally, accommodation here is pretty costly. The numerous motels are usually moderately priced, the hotels expensive. Easily the least expensive and, in many cases, the most interesting places to stay are the private guest houses. The Tourist Office will have an up-to-date list of people renting rooms in their houses or in small separate cabins.

The prices for tourist homes vary, depending on their size and facilities and your duration of stay, but are in the $20 to $45 range for a single or double. Most are about $30 to $35. There are quite a few but you should telephone around first. Some prefer at least a week's stay, some prefer not to take young people or may ask if you're married. They get busy on weekends, so calling saves legwork. A selection of tourist homes follows.

Mrs J Cowan (tel 762-3696) at 118 Otter St, rents rooms all year.

The *Holiday Inn Lodge* (tel 762-3648), run by Mrs Iva M Lindow, is one of the nicest in town. It's bright yellow, immaculately maintained and covered in flowers. You can't miss it. The owner is a warm and friendly person and rents her extra rooms for $34 for singles or doubles. Out the back is a cabin which holds four and goes for $45. The address is 311 Marten St.

Mrs W Allan (tel 762-2441) at 132 Otter St has one double room.

On my last visit I stayed at *Mrs Miller's* (tel 762-3684) at 137 Muskrat St, which is very central. The rooms are small and simple but fine; anyway I sleep with my eyes closed and was pleased with the price of $15. Others upstairs are $20 to $25 for singles/doubles. It's easy to meet people in these homes. I ended up meeting two Swiss girls here and we went to Calgary a few days later in a car they'd picked up in California.

Mr Harnack (tel 762-3619) at 338 Banff Avenue, has 10 double rooms at $25 each and some larger self-contained cabins out the back. One for four people is only $45.

Mrs McHardy (tel 762-2176) at 412 Marten St offers cabins with hot plates for $30 a double.

Mrs Wray (tel 762-3612) at 206 Otter has two singles at $20 and two double rooms which are $25.

For a good central hotel there's the *King Edward Hotel* (tel 762-2251) at 137 Banff Avenue. Popular with young people and those on a budget, it's often full. Rates are $30 for singles or doubles but cheaper in the off-season. Most of these rooms have a sink only; rooms with complete facilities are about $10 more.

In the expensive range, the *Banff Springs Hotel* has rooms for about $100.

Motels Most accommodation here is in motels and they are not cheap. These are the budget places.

Johnson's Canyon Resort (tel 762-2971) is one of the cheaper motels but it's 26 km west of town on Highway 1A. It's $36/42 for singles/doubles and opens from 15 May to 20 September. Groceries are available.

Red Carpet Inn (tel 762-4184) at 425 Banff Avenue is close to town and charges

Vermillion Lake, Banff National Park

$45/50 for singles/doubles. It's usually full in summer.

The Spruce Grove (tel 762-2112) at 545 Banff Avenue, charges $48 for singles and $55 for doubles for standard rooms with colour TV.

Irwin's on Banff Avenue is also not badly priced.

The Cascade Inn (tel 762-3311) has been recommended at $28 for singles, $30 for doubles, but you have to ask for the simplest rooms with sink only. Others have a toilet and still others are complete with full bathroom. The rooms are clean and they all have TV.

There are many places geared for skiers,

Left: Sentinel Pass, Banff National Park, Alberta (JL)
Right: Jasper National Park, Alberta (JL)
Bottom: Chuck wagon race, Calgary, Alberta (JL)

Top Left: Columbines (JL)
Top Right: Alpine Forget-me-nots (JL)
Bottom Left: Alberta Rose (JL)
Bottom Right: Alpine wildflowers (JL)

which offer kitchens and can be good value if there are four of you or more. Of course, there are also many deluxe places around too if you're looking to really splurge.

Camping There are many campgrounds in the area around Banff and Lake Louise. Tunnel Mountain is close to town and has three sites – one for trailers only and two with sections for tents only; $11 per tent. This place is not bad. At night you may hear coyotes yelping and howling.

In order to preserve the region the Canadian Parks Service controls visitor impact by designating specific park areas as campgrounds, picnic sites, fireplaces, service centres and townsites. Please stick to these areas when camping. Bears and other wildlife can be encountered anywhere in the park so exercise caution. All campgrounds are busy in July and August so you'll need to book in by noon.

Places to Eat

Like any resort town, Banff has plenty of restaurants. It's a good place to catch up on a meal or two if you've been in the back country. You have lots to select from but prices tend to be a bit high. Prices in Banff have actually risen more in the past few years than those in the rest of the country.

The *Banff Café*, in the middle of town, has been here since 1926 and is really an institution. Although now expanded and a little on the expensive side for its sandwiches, burgers and special dinner fare, it will always have a special place in my heart. Many years ago I was hitching through and got caught in the rain here. It poured all day, but the manager at the time filled my coffee cup countless times for the price of one until the rain stopped. They don't serve refills now, but the walls and decor are still plain and ordinary and there's a certain homey quality to the place. To give you an idea of prices, soups are $1.50, sandwiches $4 to $5 and a full meal is about $7.

Coriander Snack Bar is upstairs in the Sundance Mall, across the street from the Tourist Office. It's mainly a health-food shop but also has four tables for serving food. They have fresh daily soups, lots of sandwiches and salads, which cost $3.50 to $5.

Smitty's Restaurant across from the Banff Avenue Tourist Office is always reliable if not great. It's open from 6 am to 10 pm daily. The best value is the five pancakes with syrup for $3.45.

Down the street, the *Rundle Restaurant* is one of the few steady, long-term places that doesn't even try to be trendy. It's straightforward, reasonable and a good spot for breakfast.

Nearby at 321 Banff Avenue, the *Picadilly Fare* is a small sandwich bar/deli with espresso coffee. They also have burgers and cheap spaghetti on Monday nights. Next door is the bakery.

For something a bit tastier try the *Magpie & Stump* at the corner of Caribou and Bear. Built like an old-style saloon with cosy browns inside, it serves mainly Mexican food like tacos, enchiladas and burritos for about $8. Guacamole salad is $4.95. They also serve steaks. Open until 2 am.

Also up the ladder a rung is *Melissa's Missteak*, looking sort of like a wood cabin inside and sort of like an English cottage outside. It specialises in deluxe heavy-duty hamburgers that make a meal, not a snack. There are 10 varieties, each $6. The blue cheese is yummy. The rest of the menu includes pizza, and steaks for $14. It's on Lynx St, one west of Banff Avenue near Caribou.

Drifters Inn in the Sundance Mall has good-value lunches at $4 to $5. On the menu are red snapper, stew, chilli and spaghetti. Dinners of mainly fish are $12. Steak specials are available day and night.

The Balkan in the middle of Banff Avenue on the eastern side is a moderately-priced Greek restaurant with a very good reputation. They offer a couple of vegetarian dishes for those inclined that way.

For a splurge, *Grizzly House* at 207 Banff Avenue is recommended. It's basically a fondue place with prices of about $21, depending on volume and what your preference is – beef, seafood, etc, but also has escargots and steaks. Appetisers of French onion soup are $3.50. There's live jazz and recorded music nightly from 9 pm to 1 am. Open daily from 11.30 am to midnight.

There are several other places for splurges – steaks, seafood, Italian or French. The expensive *Beaujolais* is highly rated. *Bumpers* out toward the highway has good beef at fair prices, a salad bar and a casual atmosphere. The *Banff Park Lodge*, on the corner of Caribou and Lynx, has been recommended for its good-value buffet feasts on Sundays at noon.

For those of you who would rather be eating chocolate, go to *Bernard Callebaut* in the Charles Reid Mall on Banff Avenue. It's great for on the trails, and besides, you're burning calories off, right?

Nightlife
Banff is the social centre of the Rockies and a fair bit of drinking goes on. There is not an abundance of places but a few popular bars have decent prices and entertainment.

The *King Edward Hotel*, affectionately known as the King Eddie, is busy day and night. This perfectly Canadian bar at the corner of Banff Avenue and Caribou St is a casual place, popular with young and old. No backpacks or skis, though.

The *Cascade Inn* is on the east side of Banff Avenue, dead centre of town. Inside are two rooms: the piano bar which is free and can get quite rowdy, and the room opposite which has a cover charge of a dollar or two and live rock music. Both are busy with their clientele of young people and have good prices on beer and drinks. Closing hour is 1 am.

The Banff Centre School of Fine Arts often presents movies, theatre and concerts, and the Peter Whyte Gallery has free movies on Thursday nights.

Getting There & Away
Train The station (tel 762-3722) is the ochre building at the top of Elk St, close to downtown. The office is open from 10 am to 7 pm.

To Calgary, there's a train at 6.35 pm costing $13.

To Lake Louise, there is one train there and one back to Banff daily; a ticket costs $7. You can also go to Field (Yoho National Park). The train from Banff to Lake Louise goes on westward to Field (for trips to Yoho National Park) and beyond to Vancouver. Going from Lake Louise to Banff, you're actually boarding the Vancouver to Montreal train.

Bus The Greyhound station (tel 762-2286) is beside the train station.

Jasper: 8 am, 4.15 pm – $24
Calgary: seven daily – $9.15
Vancouver: 10 daily – $55
Lake Louise: $6.

All Vancouver buses stop at Lake Louise, some also stop in Kelowna or Kamloops. One bus makes the journey via Radium.

You can stop off at Lake Louise for free with a ticket on to Vancouver.

Brewster Bus Line at 130 Banff Avenue runs between Calgary, Banff and Lake Louise and charges $5 from Banff to Lake Louise.

For Calgary, note that some buses go into downtown, others straight to the airport.

Getting Around
There's a bus every hour from the bus station to the Sulphur Mountain Gondola and the Banff Springs Hotel, which costs $2.50. You can also get on this bus at the King Edward (King Eddy) Hotel on Banff Avenue.

Hitching is common in and around town.

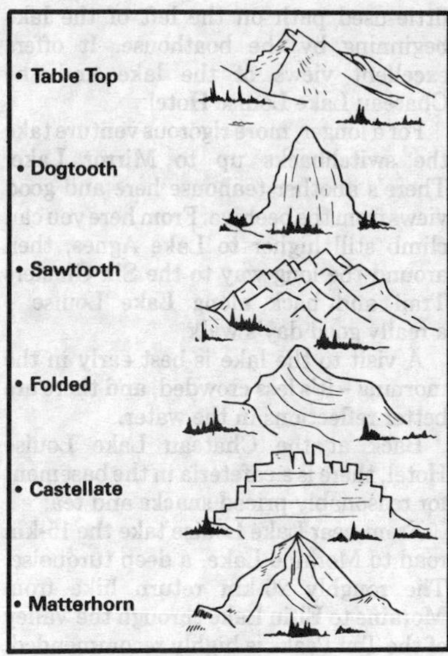

Major mountain formations

The local happy bus leaves from the King Edward Hotel and runs to various hotels, including the Banff Springs. It's cheap but may run only in the evenings.

Bicycle The Park & Pedal on Wolf St around the corner from Banff Avenue rents bicycles. They're open from 9 am to 9 pm and have a one-hour minimum. Most bikes cost $2.50 an hour or $10 a day; mountain bikes cost more.

The Spike'n'Edge, across the street, rents 10-speed bikes by the hour or day.

You can rent a moped at Mountain Mopeds in the Sundance Mall.

Car Rentals Banff Used Car Rentals (tel 762-3352) at 215 Banff Avenue in the Sundance Mall, has cars for about $20 per day. No extra charges.

Tilden (tel 762-2688), at Lynx and Caribou, charges $23 plus 13c per km for the smallest cars. By the week it's $120 plus the km charge. Other cheap car rental firms are Mobile and Avis.

Tours All sorts of trips are available, from tours where you hire an auto tape (cassette) and drive yourself around, to bus trips, to white-water rafting and even helicopter skiing. Ask at the Tourist Office and shop around on Banff Avenue. Some companies offer wilderness camping trips and in winter, various ski packages are available. Make sure you know what you're getting.

Warner & Mackenzie Outfitting, with information in the Trail Rider Store at 132 Banff Avenue, offer horseback trips from one hour to one week in length.

The reputable Brewster Bus Line (tel 762-2241) at 130 Caribou has trips to the more famous spots around the Rockies. Not bad value. The four-hour round trip to Lake Louise is $21. You can also make trips to Jasper, Yoho National Park and the Athabasca River for rafting.

Rocky Mountain Cycle Tours (tel 762-3477) run bicycle trips.

AROUND BANFF

Hikes

There are many good short hikes, day walks and drives around the Banff area; the Tourist Office has a list of them. Some good walks begin more or less right in town, like Tunnel Mountain and the Hoodoos. Others begin a little further out.

The nearby Vermillion Lakes are good for wildlife viewing.

One nice hike, not difficult, begins at Johnston Canyon. This is on the old highway, the 1A, that branches off from the Trans-Canada Highway en route to Lake Louise. It later joins back in. The 12-km trail goes by many waterfalls, including two large ones, to some underground-fed crystal-clear pools known as 'inkpots'. Here in the meadow is an ideal picnic spot.

Along the 1A highway watch for Castle Mountain, also called Eisenhower, on the left. It's a huge piece of rock that catches the late afternoon light.

One of the most popular overnight trips

is to nearby Egypt Lakes. It begins at the Sunshine Village ski area off the highway west of Banff. It's a long, steady climb with great scenery over the Healy Pass, including views to Mt Assiniboine, the highest in the park at 3618 metres. You'll see lots of butterflies and flowers in the alpine meadows. You can take hikes to the higher lakes and fish for cutthroat trout. At the lakes is a basic hut that sleeps about 10, but you should register before you go – it may be booked. There's tenting too.

For information on Yoho and Kootenay National Parks, see the separate sections at the end of the British Columbia chapter.

Places to Stay

There are a couple of campgrounds along the 1A highway route. More camping is available near Lake Louise, the cheapest sleep by far. There are also two youth hostels between Banff and Lake Louise.

Precautions

In the past few years it has been recommended that water be boiled before drinking when in the back country, due to 'Beaver Fever' (*Giardia lamblia*). This bug, an intestinal parasite, is spread by animal waste. I've never taken precautions and haven't had trouble: it's up to you.

If you're heading into wilderness regions, read the pamphlet on bears.

The trails heavily used by horse trips are a real mess; long-distance hikers will want to avoid them.

LAKE LOUISE

About 50 km west of Banff is Lake Louise, the jewel of the Rockies. Don't be put off by Lake Louise Village but carry on to the lake itself, a much-visited but gorgeous lake sitting in a small glacial valley, surrounded by green, snow-capped mountains. There are some good walks and hikes.

One walk takes you beyond the lake to the Plain of Six Glaciers. At the end of the lake and up a bit is a teahouse. There's a little-used path on the left of the lake beginning by the boathouse. It offers excellent views of the lake and the Chateau Lake Louise Hotel.

For a longer, more rigorous venture take the switchbacks up to Mirror Lake. There's another teahouse here and good views from the beehive. From here you can climb still higher to Lake Agnes, then around the long way to the Six Glaciers Trail and back along Lake Louise – a really good day's walk.

A visit to the lake is best early in the morning – it's less crowded, and there are better reflections in the water.

Back at the Chateau Lake Louise Hotel, there is a cafeteria in the basement for reasonably priced snacks and tea.

From near Lake Louise take the 15-km road to Moraine Lake, a deep turquoise. The roughly 20-km return hike from Moraine to Elfin Lake through the Valley of the Ten Peaks is highly recommended. Take a quick detour to Larch Valley where, if you don't have a canteen, there's a stream and superb scenery. Better still, hike to Moraine Lake via Paradise Creek and Sentinel Pass. This is a full day's hike with some steep parts but is an excellent route, with great scenery. You can do it the other way round but that's doing it the easy way! Once at Moraine Lake you can hitch back to your car if you left it at the other end. Getting up through Sentinel Pass is a long, scree-filled trek but well worth it. At the top, 2600 metres high, it's cool and breezy. There are other trails in the area as well.

It is common to see pikas (also called conies), plump furry animals, and the larger, more timid marmot along these trails. You often hear ice rumbling on the slopes, too.

There's a gondola up nearby Mt Whitehorn, from which there are views of Lake Louise. It costs $6 for the round trip, $4 one-way.

In the village of Lake Louise there isn't much. In the mall area you can buy basic grocery supplies. From here it's about four to five km uphill to the lake. There are buses there for about $2.50, which depart from the Post Hotel at the rate of about one per hour. I found it better to hitch. At the lake is a bicycle rental outfit. Buses connect to Banff and straight up to Jasper.

ICEFIELDS PARKWAY

This is the 230-km road linking Banff and Lake Louise with Jasper. It runs through the Eastern Main Ranges – the highest, most rugged and maybe the most scenic in all the Rockies. The highway is new and good but slow as animals such as goats, bighorn sheep and elk are often beside or on it. It follows a lake-lined valley between two chains which make up the Continental Divide. You can drive the route in a couple of hours but stopping at the many viewpoints, picnic spots, sights and hikes along the way can easily make it a full day or even longer.

On the way you'll see Peyto Lake, one of the world's most beautiful glacial lakes. Moose are plentiful around Waterfowl Lake.

About halfway to Jasper is the Athabasca Glacier, a tongue of the vast Columbia Icefield. Parts of the icefield are nearly 900 metres thick. You can take a 45-minute truck ride out on the ice for $12, but this is a waste of money. The Tourist Office across the street has a display and film on glaciers for free. They also organise free walking tours daily except Wednesday at 1.30 pm, but you must have good boots. Ask them about other walks.

Other points of interest are Sunwapta and Athabasca Falls, closer to Jasper. There are picnic and photography points along the way as well as many trails leading into the back country. Information offices will have trail details.

If you're cycling, it's much easier going from Banff to Jasper than vice versa.

Places to Stay

The route is lined with a good batch of rustic youth hostels charging only $4.50 for members, $5.50 for non-members. The Tourist Office has a map showing them all. Most are quite close to the highway in scenic locations. Most are also small and without showers but usually there's a 'refreshing' stream nearby.

Mosquito Creek Hostel is excellent, with a sauna, cooking facilities and friendly wardens.

You'll also find campgrounds along the way. The one at Mosquito Creek is inexpensive.

JASPER

Jasper is Banff's northern counterpart. Its setting is less grand, it's smaller and has fewer things to see and do, but some people prefer its quieter streets and less full-scale pandering to tourists. It's a good connecting point with highways going in all directions and the cross-country train running east and west.

The town is a good supply centre for trips around Jasper Park, which is teeming with wildlife and has excellent back-country trails of various lengths.

Orientation

The main street, Connaught Drive, has virtually everything including the bus and train stations, the banks, restaurants and souvenir shops.

Outside the toy-like train station is a 21-metre totem pole carved by a master Haida Indian from British Columbia's Queen Charlotte Islands. Nearby is an old CN steam engine.

Off the main street, the town is made up of small wooden houses, many with flowered gardens befitting this alpine setting.

Information

Right in the centre of town, with a large lawn out the front, is Canada's nicest Tourist Office (tel 852-4401), a wooden cabin covered in flowers and plants. They have information on trails in the park and will offer suggestions to your specifications. They have a good publication on day hikes

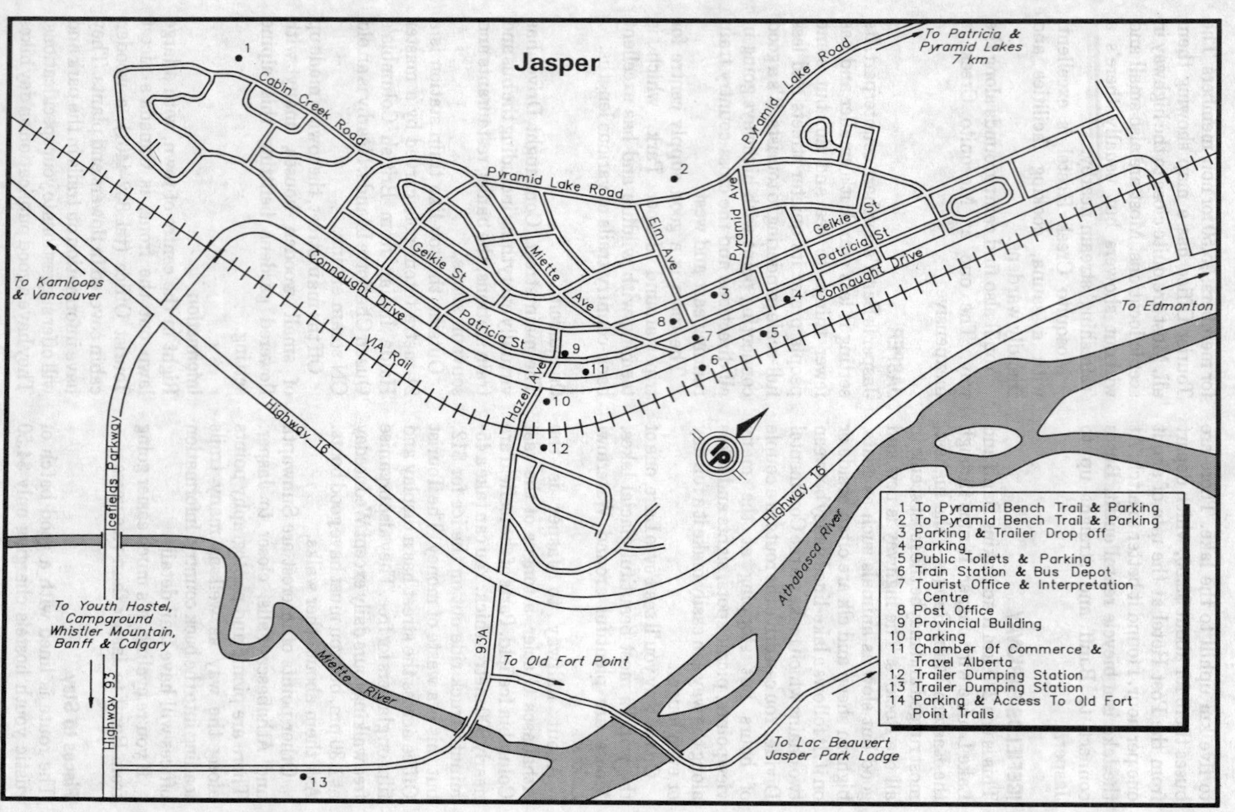
Jasper
To Patricia & Pyramid Lakes 7 km
Pyramid Lake Road
Cabin Creek Road
Pyramid Ave
Elm Ave
Miette Ave
Geikie St
Patricia St
Connaught Drive
Hazel Ave
VIA Rail
To Edmonton
To Kamloops & Vancouver
Highway 16
Icefields Parkway
Athabasca River
Miette River
93A
To Old Fort Point
To Lac Beauvert Jasper Park Lodge
To Youth Hostel, Campground Whistler Mountain, Banff & Calgary
Highway 93
1 To Pyramid Bench Trail & Parking
2 To Pyramid Bench Trail & Parking
3 Parking & Trailer Drop off
4 Parking
5 Public Toilets & Parking
6 Train Station & Bus Depot
7 Tourist Office & Interpretation Centre
8 Post Office
9 Provincial Building
10 Parking
11 Chamber Of Commerce & Travel Alberta
12 Trailer Dumping Station
13 Trailer Dumping Station
14 Parking & Access To Old Fort Point Trails

in the area and a list of tourist homes in town. The lawn is a popular meeting place and usually has people and backpacks lying all over the place.

At the south end of Connaught Drive is the Chamber of Commerce & Travel Alberta Information. Here you can get maps and information on other parts of the province.

The post office is on Patricia St near Elm.

The Chata Cinema in town shows the movie *Challenge* three times a day in summer. It chronicles kayaking, skiing, climbing and other activities in the Rockies well enough to have been shown at the Cannes film festival. It lasts one hour and costs $4, students $3.

On Patricia, one block from the Tourist Office, is a laundromat where you can wash sleeping bags and yourself as well. Showers cost $1.50 for seven minutes. It's open from 8 am to 10 pm.

Jasper Tramway

Six km south of Jasper, this 'skytram' (tel 852-3093) goes up Whistler Mountain in seven minutes and offers views south 75 km to the Columbia Icefield and west to Mt Robson. The upper terminal is at 2500 metres. There's a restaurant and you can hike up and around the top on trails. The tramway is open every day in July and August and costs $6.50. If you go between 7.30 am and 9 am, you'll get 20% off the ticket price.

Patricia & Pyramid Lakes

North-west of town about eight km are Patricia and Pyramid Lakes, which are small and relatively quiet and have picnic sites and beaches. It's not uncommon to see deer, elk, coyotes or bears in the vicinity.

At Pyramid Lake, canoes and kayaks can be rented.

Places to Stay

In general, prices here are better than those in Banff, but hotel and motel prices are still pretty steep. The tourist homes are the best bet after the hostel or campground.

Hostels There are only two places to sleep very cheaply, the youth hostel or the nearby campground. The *Whistler Hostel* is on the road toward the Jasper Tramway, south of town about five km; the last two km are uphill. The hostel is one of the few big modern ones in the Rockies and has showers and a large kitchen. It opens at 5 pm, closes at 11 pm and you're woken up at 7 am. Members pay $6, non-members $9.

Tourist Homes The Tourist Office has a list of about 30 tourist homes, all clean, most close to town and nearly all charging the same prices. In July and August, many fill up, so it's a good idea to book ahead.

The cheapest of the lot is *J Maclay's* (tel 852-4543) at 719 Patricia St. It's open all year and has a double room for $21. Use of the kitchen is $5. You need two people to make this a reasonable price.

Mrs G Beilard (tel 852-4338) along Patricia at No 114 offers three rooms at $25 for two people.

R W Bowen (tel 852-4532) at 228 Colin Crescent has a couple of rooms and charges $15 for a single, $20 for a double.

Hotels, Motels & Bungalows In town the *Athabasca Hotel* and the *Astoria Hotel* are less than $60 a night but aren't strictly tourist hotels; they're busy with the pubs and entertainment.

Motels and bungalows charge $60 and up. *Patricia Lola Bungalows* are reasonable. *Tekkara Lodge* (tel 852-3058), eight km south of Jasper on the Miette and Athabasca Rivers is comfortable with fireplaces in the cabins. Rooms are cheaper in the lodge itself. Open mid-May to mid-September.

Camping The campground is down the hill from the hostel near the corner of the Icefields Parkway. It's quite good but, though large, does get very crowded. In summer, films and talks are presented nightly.

A herd of wapiti (American elk) lives in the park amongst the tents at certain times of the year. A male looks after a large number of females, the harem, in the autumn and his bawling instructions are heard far and wide.

Places to Eat

Mountain View Café, across the street from the train station, is a good health-food café and shop. Since getting rid of the pool tables there's a lot more room for sitting and eating the soups, sandwiches and huge muffins. They've got good desserts; try the carrot cake. The shop also sells granola, nuts and other foods for hiking.

The *L & W Pizza & Spaghetti* place at the corner of Patricia and Hazel is plastic-looking but serves decent pizza, spaghetti or lasagne for about $6 and up.

The *Astoria Motor Inn* on Connaught has good lunch specials from 11.30 am to 3 pm. Dinner includes a salad bar.

Whistler's Hotel on Connaught is a basic place, ideal for breakfasts. The hotels in town also have restaurants.

There is also an *A & W*, *Kentucky Fried Chicken* and a *Smitty's*, the pancake house, in town.

At the corner of Patricia and Miette is a very good bakery.

Nightlife

The *Athabasca Hotel* has live rock music. Admission is $3.

Getting There & Away

Bus The station (tel 852-3962) is in the VIA Rail station on Connaught. It's open from 7 am to 1.30 am daily.

There are three buses to Kamloops, Vancouver and Edmonton daily. One-way fares: Edmonton $24, Vancouver $48 and Banff $24.75.

The bus to Banff will drop you off at campgrounds or youth hostels along the way. It also goes to Lake Louise. There's only one a day, in the afternoon. Book ahead a few hours if possible. It's a 4½-hour trip to Banff.

Train The station (tel 852-3168) is on Connaught Drive. From here trains go west through Kamloops to Vancouver and east through Edmonton to Saskatoon, Winnipeg and beyond.

One-way fares: Edmonton $32, Vancouver $58.

Getting Around

Car Rentals Budget Rent-A-Car (tel 852-3330) is at 638 Connaught. Rates are $33 for one day with 200 free km, 10c per km over.

Avis Rent-A-Car (tel 852-3970) is at 300 Connaught. Their rates are $30 per day, with 120 km free and 14c per km over.

Bicycle You can rent five-speed bikes in the shop beside the A & W on Connaught Drive. They're $15 for 24 hours.

Rentals are also available at Jasper Park Lodge, Mountain Air at 622 Connaught, or Freewheel Cycle at 600 Patricia.

Tours Brewster (tel 852-3332) at 314 Connaught, arranges many trips and excursions, including tours along the Icefield Parkway and to Lake Louise. The Maligne Lake tour leaves at 8 am and costs $28.

The Jasper Travel Agency at 626 Connaught co-ordinates and sells tickets for various tours, river trips, sightseeing tours and adventures.

Jasper Raft Tours (tel 852-3613) run trips along the Athabasca River. The cost includes the bus trip and two hours on the river.

AROUND JASPER

If you're planning to do any walking, pick up a copy of *Day Hikes* at the Tourist Office.

The 17-km hike around Valley of the

Five Lakes from Jasper is relatively flat and pleasant.

Further south, the scenic Maligne Lake is the largest of the glacier-fed lakes. You can hike near it for a good view or take a boat tour for $15. The 40-km trip takes two hours.

Near town, Lakes Annette and Edith, at about 1000 metres, are warm enough for a quick swim. There are trails, picnic areas and boat rentals in the wooded parks around the lakes.

There are quite a few two and three-day hikes in Jasper Park. The Skyline Trail, 45 km long, is nearly all above the tree line, with great scenery. Watch for grizzlies. If the weather has been wet. you may want to avoid the lower trails where horse trips are run for those too lazy to walk. They make the path a mud bath.

There are also a few four, seven and 10-day hikes. Wildlife is more plentiful in Jasper than in Banff and hikers are generally fewer. Topographic maps are available for all routes.

Out toward Edmonton is Miette Hot Springs, a good spot for a bath. The old spa has been renovated and has two pools, one deep and one suitable for kids. Although off the main highway, the road to the springs has been improved and is now pretty quick. On the way out of the park from Jasper it is common to see goats along the highway's edge.

Out of the park, leading north and south of Hinton, is the Adventure Highway. It goes south nearly as far as the American border, though not in a straight line. Much of it is only gravel. You'll find campgrounds but few other services or amenities, apart from the ranger stations along the way.

Places to Stay

Mt Edith Hostel is just south of Jasper but off the highway quite a distance. There's another hostel at Maligne Canyon which is small, good and cheap; there's walking in the area.

At Nordegg, a crossroads halfway to Calgary, there's a *Youth Hostel*.

British Columbia

Entered Confederation: 20 July 1871
Area: 948,600 square km
Population: 2,744,467

British Columbia, known simply as BC, is, I think, the most beautiful province in the country. The Rocky Mountains are on the east side and the northern interior is full of mountains, hills, forests and lakes. The southern interior even has a small desert – Canada's only one. The Pacific coast is ruggedly beautiful. In short, there is every type of landscape, whatever your preference.

The general atmosphere in BC, particularly on the south-west coast, is different from the rest of Canada. The culture, more permissive and life style-conscious than that found in the east, partially reflects the influence of California.

These factors combine to make tourism – in a province with many lucrative industries – the third largest money-maker.

The other major industries are fishing, mining, forestry and fruit. Casual work is often available in these industries. Recently, however, with a downturn in resource-based businesses and on-going labour troubles, the province has been weak economically. Unemployment is high in this, Canada's most unionised workforce.

As in California, much of the early settlement was due to gold fever here around the 1850s. More than half the population lives around Vancouver and Victoria so there is a lot of uncluttered space. New, inaccessible areas of the province are still being developed. The bulk of the population is of British ancestry, although Vancouver has a large Chinese community.

Temperatures on the coast are mild, with coolish summers and warm, wet winters. The interior is much drier, much hotter and much colder. In the mountains, summers are short and nights always cool.

Vancouver

Vancouver lies nestled between sea and mountains in the extreme south-western corner of British Columbia. Its physical setting and features make it easily one of the most attractive Canadian cities. The hilly terrain it's built on and the many bridges offer beautiful views of the ocean, sheltered bays and the city itself. The parks are numerous and large. One – Stanley Park – is the size of the downtown business area. Sandy beaches dot the shoreline, and like the towering mountains just out of the city, can be used for sports and recreation. Few cities can match Vancouver for its number and variety of interesting sights.

The port, the busiest on North America's west coast, operates all year round in the beautiful and practical natural harbour. It handles nearly all Canada's trade with Japan and the East.

History

The Vancouver area was first inhabited by Salish Indians. The first European to see the region was the Spanish explorer Don José María Narvaez in 1791. There wasn't a real settlement until 1865, when Hastings Timber Mill was built. In 1867 a town sprang up around 'Gassy Jack'

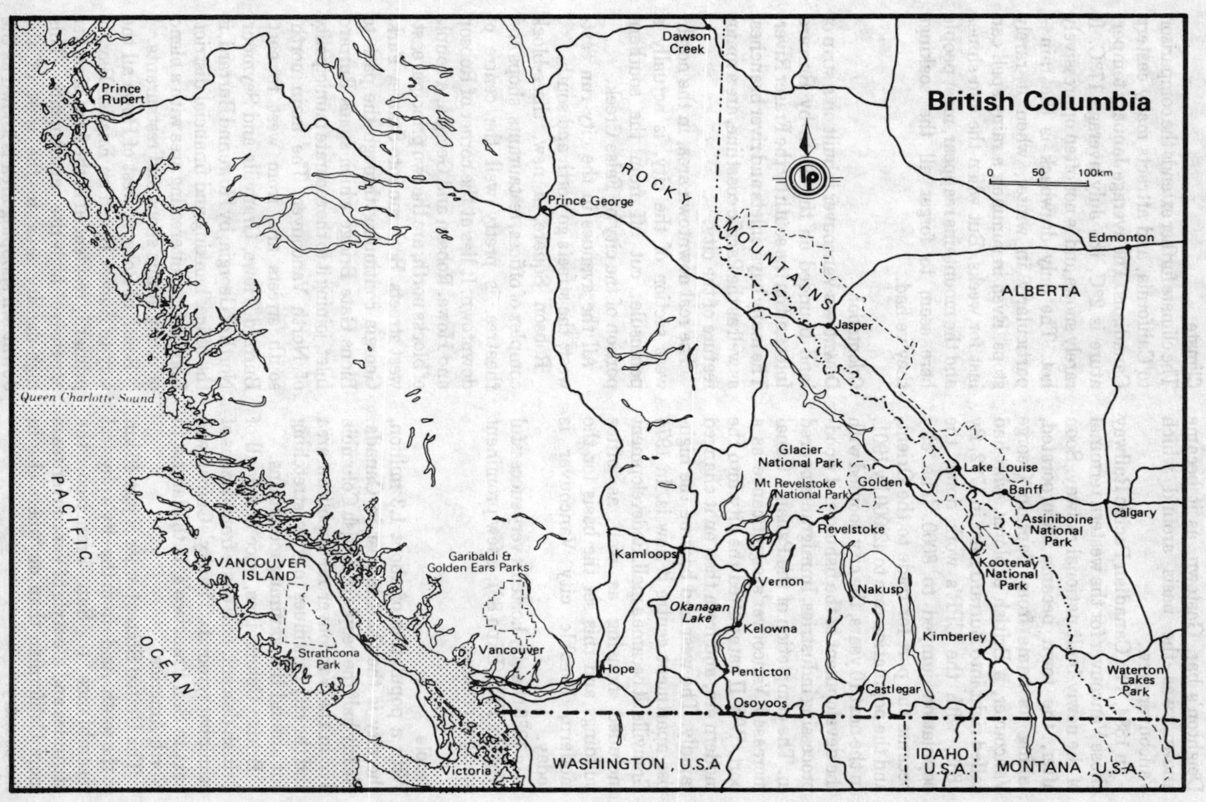

British Columbia
0 50 100km
Dawson Creek
Prince Rupert
Prince George
ROCKY MOUNTAINS
Edmonton
ALBERTA
Jasper
Queen Charlotte Sound
Glacier National Park
Mt Revelstoke National Park
Golden
Lake Louise
Banff
Calgary
Assiniboine National Park
Revelstoke
Kamloops
Kootenay National Park
Vernon
Nakusp
Okanagan Lake
Kelowna
Kimberley
PACIFIC
VANCOUVER ISLAND
Garibaldi & Golden Ears Parks
Strathcona Park
Vancouver
Hope
Penticton
Castlegar
Waterton Lakes Park
OCEAN
Osoyoos
Victoria
WASHINGTON, U.S.A
IDAHO U.S.A.
MONTANA, U.S.A.

Deighton's bar. Gastown, as it became known, was the basis around which Vancouver grew.

In 1884, The Canadian Pacific Railway chose Vancouver for the western terminal of the newly-built national railway. Soon after, the town became incorporated, taking its name from Captain George Vancouver, a British explorer, who had sailed right into Burrard Inlet in 1792. By 1889, with the CPR's work done, the population jumped to 8000. The city became the port for trade to the Orient, and the population rose to 42,000 by 1901. In the next 10 years, the city boomed with the development of the fishing and wood-processing industries. Immigrants poured in. The completion of the Panama Canal increased Vancouver's significance as a port. WW II catapulted the city into the modern era, and from then on it changed rapidly. The west end became the high-rise apartment centre it now is. In 1974 Granville St became a mall. Redevelopment included housing as well as office buildings and this set the basis for the modern, liveable city Vancouver is today.

In 1986 the city hosted a very successful World's Fair (Expo 86); a few prominent vestiges remain.

People

With a population of about 1.3 million, the city is the third largest in Canada. Nearly half the people of British Columbia live in the Vancouver metropolitan area and the city continues to grow, stretching out around the confining mountains.

British Columbians, once nearly all of British descent, now come from dozens of ethnic backgrounds. The city's Chinatown, next to San Francisco's, is the largest in North America.

The United States border is just 40 km to the south. Aside from the city's physical resemblance to San Francisco, the attitudes and life style of Vancouverites is more Californian than anywhere else in the country.

Climate

The climate further extends the comparison to California, and attracts many eastern Canadians. The average January temperature is 2°C, the July average 17°C. It rarely snows and is not often oppressively hot. The only drawback is the rain – particularly in winter, when it rarely stops. Even in summer, a rainy spell can last for weeks. But when the sun shines and the mountains reappear, most people here seem to forget all the soakings they've had.

Orientation

Downtown Vancouver is built on a strip of land bounded on the north by Burrard Inlet and on the south by the Fraser River. The many bays, inlets and river branches, as well as the Pacific coastline, are a major feature of the city.

The real downtown area, in the north-west section of the city, is actually a peninsula, cut off from the southern portion of the city by False Creek.

All the avenues in the city run east-west; the streets go north and south.

Robson Square, a new, three-block complex of offices, restaurants, shops and theatres, is pretty well the centre of downtown. It lies at the corner of Robson and Howe. Robson and Georgia, a couple of blocks north, are the two principal east-west streets. Both run into Stanley Park, Georgia continuing through the park to Lions Gate Bridge which spans Burrard Inlet, joining it to the separate municipality of North Vancouver. The main north-south streets are, from west to east: Burrard, Howe, Granville and Seymour. North of Georgia, by Howe and Burrard, is the office, banking and financial district. Robson is an interesting area with a blend of many ethnic shops and restaurants.

South of Robson, west of Howe all the way to Sunset Beach on English Bay, is primarily residential in the form of rather expensive high-rise apartments. This high-density area to the west of the downtown shopping area is known as the

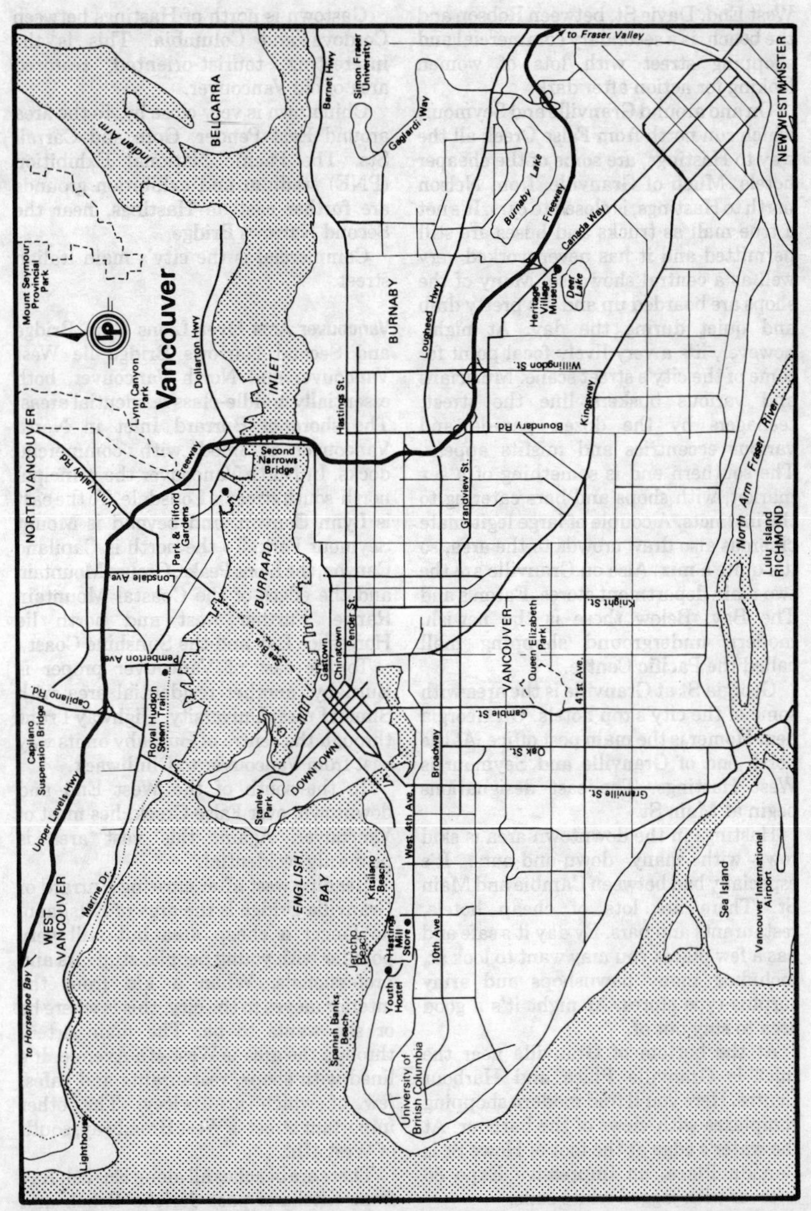
Vancouver
to Fraser Valley
NEW WESTMINSTER
Simon Fraser University
Barnet Hwy
Gaglardi Way
BELCARRA
Indian Arm
Mount Seymour Provincial Park
Burnaby Lake
Freeway
Canada Way
Deer Lake
Heritage Village Museum
Lougheed Hwy
BURNABY
Willingdon St.
Kingsway
Boundary Rd.
Hastings St.
INLET
Dollarton Hwy
Lynn Canyon Park
NORTH VANCOUVER
Lynn Valley Rd.
Freeway
Second Narrows Bridge
Park & Tilford Gardens
Lonsdale Ave
BURRARD
Sea Bus
Pemberton Ave
Capilano Rd.
Capilano Suspension Bridge
Royal Hudson Steam Train
Gastown
Chinatown
Pender St.
DOWNTOWN
Stanley Park
Upper Levels Hwy
WEST VANCOUVER
Marine Dr.
ENGLISH BAY
Kitsilano Beach
Hastings Mill Store
Jericho Beach
Youth Hostel
Spanish Banks Beach
University of British Columbia
Lighthouse
to Horseshoe Bay
West 4th Ave.
Broadway
10th Ave.
Oak St.
Cambie St.
Granville St.
Grandview St.
Queen Elizabeth Park
VANCOUVER
41st Ave.
Knight St.
North Arm Fraser River
Lulu Island
RICHMOND
Sea Island
Vancouver International Airport

West End. Davie St, between Robson and the beach, is a secondary commercial and shopping street with lots of women looking for action after dark.

On and around Granville and Seymour, which run north from False Creek all the way to Hastings, are some of the cheaper hotels. Much of Granville, from Nelson north to Hastings, is closed to cars. It's not a true mall as trucks and buses are still permitted and it has never worked very well as a central showcase. Many of the shops are boarded up and it's pretty drab and quiet during the day. At night, however, it's a very lively focal point for some of the city's street scene. Musicians and various buskers line the street, teenagers by the dozen parade and various eccentrics and misfits appear. The southern end is something of a sex market, with shops and bars catering to the instincts. A couple of large legitimate cinemas also draw crowds to the area, so it's quite a mix. Also on Granville are the two main department stores, Eaton's and The Bay. Below these is the newish, modern underground shopping mall called the Pacific Centre.

Georgia St at Granville is the area with some of the city's top hotels. On Georgia near Homer is the main post office. At the north end of Granville and Seymour is West Hastings. The east designations begin at Main St.

Hastings in the downtown area is skid row, with many down-and-outs. It's especially bad between Cambie and Main St. There are lots of cheap hotels, restaurants and bars. By day it's safe and has a few places you may want to look at, including many pawnshops and army surplus-type stores. At night it's a good area to stay out of.

At the bottom of Granville near the Inlet is Granville Place and Harbour Centre. Here you'll find modern shopping complexes with views of the harbour. At the water's edge at the foot of Howe St is Canada Place, an impressive Expo 86 leftover with jagged white sails.

Gastown is north of Hastings between Cordova and Columbia. This is the interesting, tourist-oriented, restored area of old Vancouver.

Chinatown is very close by, in the area around East Pender, Gore and Carrall Sts. The Pacific National Exhibition (PNE) stadium and exhibition grounds are further east on Hastings, near the Second Narrows Bridge.

Commercial is the city's main Italian street.

Vancouver Area Over Lions Gate Bridge and Second Narrows Bridge lie West Vancouver and North Vancouver, both essentially middle-class residential areas. The shore of Burrard Inlet in North Vancouver is lined with commercial docks. In North Vancouver the principal north-south street is Lonsdale. To the east is Lynn Canyon, and beyond is Mount Seymour Park. To the north is Capilano Canyon, the Lions Peaks, Grouse Mountain and the edges of the Coastal Mountain Range. Further west and north lie Horseshoe Bay and the Sunshine Coast.

To the east of Vancouver proper is Burnaby, another residential area with Simon Fraser University. Highway 1 runs through the centre of Burnaby on its way east from Vancouver to Chilliwack.

To the south of the West End and downtown, over False Creek, lies most of Vancouver. Again, this vast area is primarily residential.

Heading west after crossing Burrard or Granville Bridge is the area of Kitsilano, no longer a cheap area but still very popular with young people, students and professionals. When a kid from the interior moves to the city, this is where he or she wants to be. The main artery through the area is West 4th Avenue. It's lined with shops, restaurants and cafés, few of which are pricey. The other important street is West Broadway, south of West 4th.

There are beaches all along English Bay from Kitsilano past Jericho Beach and

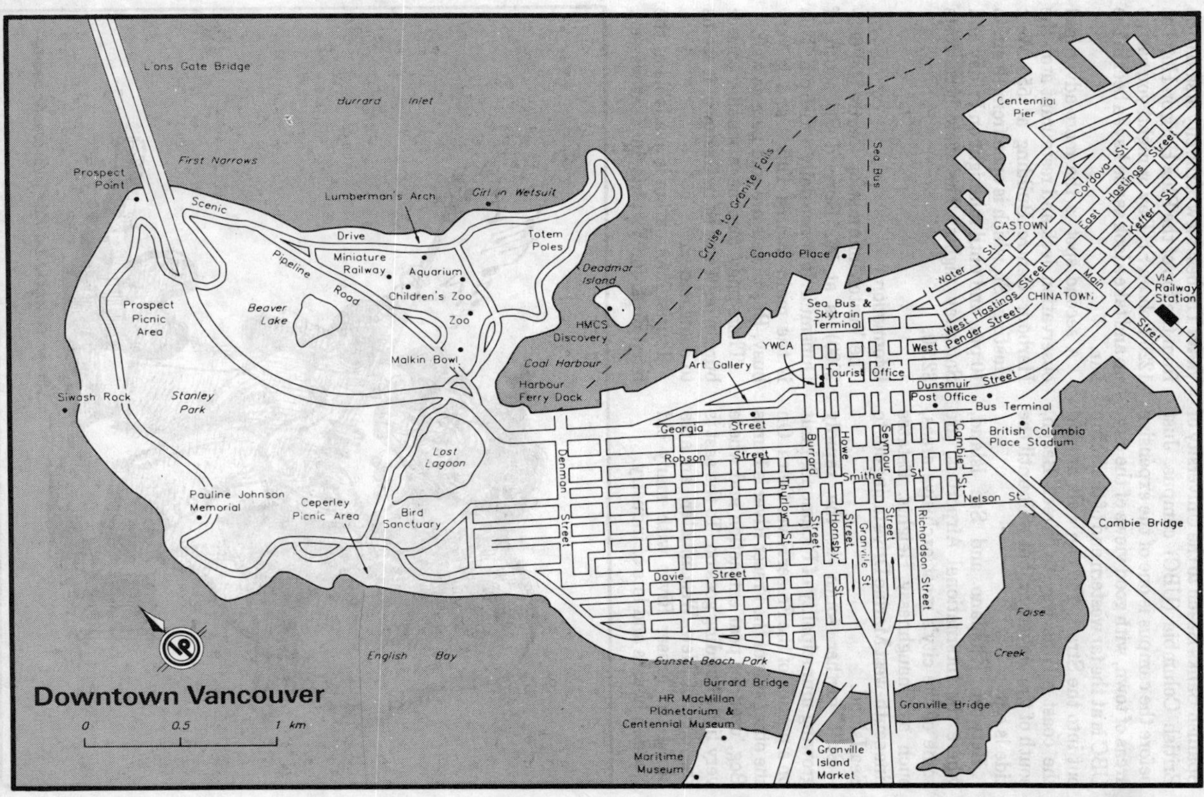
Downtown Vancouver
0
0.5
1 km
Lions Gate Bridge
Burrard Inlet
First Narrows
Prospect Point
Scenic
Drive
Lumberman's Arch
Girl in Wetsuit
Totem Poles
Deadmar Island
HMCS Discovery
Coal Harbour
Harbour Ferry Dock
Pipeline
Road
Miniature Railway
Aquarium
Children's Zoo
Zoo
Malkin Bowl
Beaver Lake
Prospect Picnic Area
Siwash Rock
Stanley Park
Lost Lagoon
Pauline Johnson Memorial
Ceperley Picnic Area
Bird Sanctuary
English Bay
Sunset Beach Park
Burrard Bridge
HR MacMillan Planetarium & Centennial Museum
Maritime Museum
Granville Island Market
Granville Bridge
False Creek
Cambie Bridge
Cruise to Granite Falls
Sea Bus
Centennial Pier
Canada Place
Sea Bus & Skytrain Terminal
YWCA
Art Gallery
Tourist Office
Post Office
Bus Terminal
British Columbia Place Stadium
GASTOWN
CHINATOWN
VIA Railway Station
Water St
Cordova St
East Hastings Street
Keefer St
Main Street
West Hastings Street
West Pender Street
Dunsmuir Street
Georgia Street
Robson Street
Davie Street
Denman Street
Thurlow St
Burrard Street
Howe Street
Hornsby St
Seymour Street
Smithe St
Granville St
Richardson Street
Cambie St
Nelson St

Spanish Banks Beach to the University of British Columbia (UBC) campus. Just before the campus is one of the expensive areas of town, with good views of the city. UBC is at the far western end of the hump out into the Strait. You can walk around the coast all the way to Wreck Beach, south of the university, but wait until the tide is out.

Between Kitsilano and Sea Island, where the International Airport is, are some of the city's most exclusive areas, such as Shaughnessy Heights. Estates line south-west Marine Drive facing out to Sea Island.

Still further south is the rapidly growing municipality of Richmond, built on a portion of the Fraser River Delta. On the other side of the Fraser River is Burns Bog, used for peat extraction and where very little building goes on. To the east is the city of New Westminster, an area along the Fraser River with many old wooden houses and lots of industry.

Views The best view of the city is said to be from the top of the Blue Horizon Hotel at 1225 Robson St. Day or night, you can go up and take a look as you have a beer in the bar.

A second spot is the more-advertised observation deck and restaurant atop the Harbour Centre Building at 555 West Hastings St, which is open from 10 am to 10 pm, and until midnight on Friday and Saturday nights. The view here costs $2.50.

Information

The Visitor Information Centre (tel 683-2000) is at 562 Burrard St, south of Dunsmuir. It's open daily until 6 pm. This is the main Tourist Office and is very busy. Bus tickets are sold here as well.

There may also be a smaller visitor bureau on Water St in Gastown; it seems to come and go.

Tourist information is available at the ferry dock for Victoria in Tsawwassen.

Senior citizen busker, Vancouver. CANADA

There are information booths at either end of the George Massey Tunnel under the Fraser River on the way to Tsawwassen. If you're coming from the east along the Trans-Canada Highway you'll see the signs as you get closer to town. There are a couple on the route.

The Youth Hostel has a notice board that lists rides, plane tickets and goods for sale, and sometimes has job offers.

Vancouver lacks expressways, and with no subway, traffic congestion is a problem. On a wet or snowy day it's worse: try to avoid rush hours. Parking in the downtown area is a hassle and/or costly.

Downtown

Gastown

This name is taken from 'Gassy' Jack Deighton, an English sailor who forsook the sea to open a bar servicing the developing timber mills. When a village sprang up around his establishment, it was called Gassy's Town. The name stuck and Vancouver was on its way. The Gastown area today is bounded by Cordova and Carrall Sts, with Water St the main thoroughfare. Burrard Inlet is just to the north. A statue of Gassy Jack has been erected in Maple Street Square, where Cordova meets Water St.

The whole Gastown area gradually became a skid row and, in the 1970s, it was restored and renovated. The old Victorian buildings now house restaurants, bars, boutiques and galleries. The brick streets have been lined with old lamps. Street vendors and buskers add to the holiday feel of the area.

At the west end of Water St is the world's first clock run by steam. You can see it work through the side glass panels and will hear it toot every 15 minutes.

There is a wax museum at 21 Water St, open daily in summer, which charges $3.50 admission, $2.50 for students. There are 150 life-size figures and, of course, a chamber of horrors.

In the mall at 131 Water St is Perry's Old Time Portraits, a photography studio that will dress you in 1890s style, or as a 1920s gangster if you prefer, and have your picture ready in five minutes. They make good quality souvenirs. Also worth looking at in Water St is the Inuit Gallery of Vancouver, one of just three galleries in Canada devoted exclusively to Inuit Art. It's open Monday to Saturday from 9.30 am to 5.30 pm. The art is free to look at, big bucks to buy.

Chinatown

This is the best kind of Chinatown – the sort you can smell before you see. More than 30,000 people of Chinese descent live in the area around West Pender St, roughly bordered by Abbott and Gore. For the most part it's genuine, serving the locals. The streets are full of people shuffling into stores of hanging ducks and chickens. There are scores of cheap hotels, restaurants and little grocery shops. Even some of the young people don't speak English. The colours, signs and occasional old Chinese-style balcony can make you believe for a second that you're in the East. Note the Chinese characters on signs for banks and Hertz Rent-a-Car.

The world's thinnest office building – according to Ripley's 'Believe It Or Not' – is somewhere near Pender and Carrall. It must be very small because I couldn't find it. There are tourist and souvenir shops interspersed with the community businesses. This is not a good area at night, particularly around Hastings. After dark it's advisable to stay out of the side streets in Chinatown.

Dr Sun Yat-Sen Classical Chinese Garden

The only full-scale classical Chinese garden found outside China is a must. Months after visiting, I still think of this place. It's a very subtle attraction but exquisite in execution and effect. Modelled after the Ming Dynasty gardens best represented in the city of Suzhou, it makes a real sanctuary in the centre of the city. The Taoist principles of yin and yang are incorporated in numerous ways throughout the garden. The guided tours are included in the admission and are well worthwhile. Also, if possible, go during the week when it won't be too busy. It's at 578 Carroll St behind the Chinese Cultural Centre in Chinatown. It opens at 10 am daily and admission is $3. The adjacent park, built by local craftsmen using Chinese materials is similar in design and free. It's well done but don't miss the real thing.

Robsonstrasse
This is the local name given to the section of Robson St between Howe and Broughton Sts. At one time mainly German, the area is now known for its many ethnic restaurants and shops. There are Italian, French, Vietnamese and Danish places among them. For detailed information on restaurants, see the Places to Eat section. On my last visit, the number and variety of places to eat had declined and it seemed as though many of the shops were giving way to cheap touristy souvenir dealers. This may be a temporary trend fuelled by Expo. The bottom of the street, down toward Stanley Park, has less souvenir shops and some of the newer, better restaurants.

Stanley Park
This 400-hectare park is one of the best in the country. With its wooded hills, parkland, trails, sports fields, swimming pools and beaches, there's something for everyone. The 10-km sea wall which encircles the park makes a good walk or bicycle ride even if you don't go all the way round. From various points there are good views of downtown Vancouver, the north shore and out to sea toward the islands.

Along the west side are several sandy beaches; Lions Gate Bridge extends from the northern tip. Just to the west of Lions Gate Bridge is Prospect Point, a popular point for views of the narrows and passing ships. There's a restaurant here as well; it's a nice spot for a coffee on the terrace. Near Brockton Point there is a good collection of totem poles. There is a small, free zoo near Brockton Oval. Off the southern side, near the yacht club, is Deadman's Island, once used, it's said, by a Northern Indian tribe as a camp for women captured in raids. Later it became a burial ground for Indians and Chinese.

Within the park is the Vancouver Aquarium (tel 685-3364), Canada's largest, with 9000 sea creatures. Most popular are the dolphins and killer whales that put on shows several times a day. There is also a special tank for Beluga whales. Other exhibits include octopuses, crocodiles, eels, piranhas and a wide variety of local sea life and freshwater fish. The aquarium is also used for research. It's open every day from 9 am to 6 pm, until 9 pm in summer. Admission is $4.50.

Vancouver Art Gallery
The city's new art gallery is right at the centre of things, at 800 West Georgia. It has a large collection of Emily Carr's work, a resident of the area and one of Canada's best-known painters. There's also a survey collection of other Canadians and some US and British paintings. The gallery is open from 10 am to 6 pm Tuesdays to Saturdays, until 9 pm on Fridays and from 1 to 6 pm on Sundays. It's closed on Mondays. Admission costs $2.50, $1 for students and unemployed or if you go on Tuesdays, it's free.

City Art
Worth a look (duck your head) is the swaying 26-metre sculptural piece called Pendulum in the Hong Kong Bank of Canada. It's on Georgia St opposite the Vancouver Art Gallery.

Expo 86
Surprisingly, there is very little left of the world's fair, as the majority of the buildings developed for it were dismantled. There are, however, some noteworthy exceptions. Foremost among these is the unmistakable Canada Place jutting into the harbour at the foot of Howe St. The

Haida indian, southward bound on the BC Ferry for Vancouver Chrismas shopping.

white sail-like roof, designed to visually link the ships of the inlet to the downtown office towers, has become a major city landmark. The complex now contains the Trade & Convention Centre. At the northern end are the promenade shops and restaurants and outside, good views. Also here is an IMAX film theatre with a five storey-high screen showing films made exclusively for these theatres.

The main pavilion area for Expo was along False Creek, off Pacific Boulevard and behind the BC Place stadium. There is precious little here now. Behind the stadium are a few remaining bars and restaurants soon slated to disappear. One structure that is to remain is the geodesic dome not too far from here. It may become a new science centre.

Arts, Sciences & Technology Centre

This is a museum (tel 687-8414) where you can get involved through touching and testing the displays. Hands-on exhibits and experiments help explain scientific and physical phenomena. It's rather a mishmash, aimed primarily at children. Most exhibits are simplistic demonstrations of various scientific and biological principles. Plans are afoot to expand and move into the geodesic dome at False Creek built for Expo. This will probably mean a considerable improvement. It's not worth the $3 admission, but students pay only $1.50. It's at 600 Granville St near Dunsmuir. Opening hours are Monday to Saturday 10 am to 5 pm, Sundays and holidays 1 to 5 pm.

Vancouver Discovery Show

This is a half-hour film telling the city's story in a rah-rah style. It's in the Harbour Centre Building, a shopping and restaurant complex at 555 West Hastings St.

Port

The commercial harbour area stretches along Burrard Inlet from Stanley Park to the Second Narrows Bridge. The plaza at Granville Square, beside the Seabus terminal, or Canada Place's observation deck, offers a view where you watch the many types of vessels moving in and out of the harbour. For a closer look visit Vanterm, the Vancouver Container Terminal. Here you can see the inner workings of a port facility – the warehouse, cranes, containers and the guys slugging freight. The port viewing area is at 1300 Stewart Avenue at the foot of Clark Drive. It's free and there is an audio-visual show included. Open Monday to Friday from 9 am to 12 midday and 1 to 3 pm.

BC Place

This name refers to both a large tract of city land being totally redeveloped and the new stadium which kicked off the entire project. The land runs along the waterfront at False Creek at the end of Robson St, near the Granville Bridge. Formerly an area of disused rail lines and warehouses, it will contain apartments, parks, a theatre, museums and a rapid transit station as part of a 25-year plan. At 1 Robson is BC Place Stadium, the world's largest dome. Opened in 1983, it has an air-supported fabric roof and seats 60,000 for sporting events, concerts and trade shows. One-hour tours are given at 11 am, 1 pm and 3 pm daily. The cost is a few bucks.

Vancouver West Area

Granville Island

On the south side of False Creek under the Granville Bridge, this formerly industrial little island has been redeveloped into a busy blend of businesses, restaurants, arts and entertainment. Major attractions include two important performing-art centres, numerous theatre companies, and, on the north-western tip, a market with fresh fruit, vegetables and fish. A few prepared food counters sell small meals and snacks. La Baguette opposite the market makes fresh French breads and rolls and sells cheeses and pastries, too.

There are several shops where local painters, jewellery makers and weavers make and display their crafts. Prices are fairly reasonable. There is also an art gallery in the Emily Carr College.

The Granville Island Brewery is worth visiting. It's a small company producing pure beer, without chemicals. They give free tours with a sample at the end.

If you've got the energy for canoeing or kayaking, Vancouver Canoe & Kayak rents equipment.

A good restaurant to try is *Isadora's* for snacks, cheap lunches or full meals. There are more up-scale places to eat, and a new hotel.

On the north-eastern edge it's interesting to have a look at the attractive, pricey floating houses.

To get to the island from either Gastown or Granville St downtown, catch the No 50 False Creek bus. There's an information office where the bus stops. Alternately, there is the False Creek mini-ferry which shuttles between the Aquatic Centre on Sunset Beach on English Bay, Granville Island and the Maritime Museum on Kitsilano Point. Other stops are at the east end of False Creek, including one by the BC Place Stadium.

Centennial Museum

This is at 100 Chestnut St just west of the Burrard Bridge in Vanier Park on English Bay. Also called the Vancouver Museum, it specialises in local history. On display are old photos of BC and sections on the archaeology of the area, concentrating on the Salish Indians and ethnology. There are a few examples of most Indian crafts. The basketry is impressive, especially the baskets made of cedar and pine roots. The part of the museum on the exploration and settlement of Vancouver is interesting. The last of the Hudson's Bay forts was here – Fort Victoria. Open 10 am to 5 pm daily, Thursday till 9 pm. Admission costs $2.50 or $3 for entrance to the Maritime Museum as well.

Maritime Museum
This is a five-minute walk from the Centennial Museum at the foot of Cypress St. It is divided into two sections. The museum itself is strictly for boat buffs – lots of wooden models and some old rowboats on display. Admission is $2 or $3 if you buy a ticket to the Centennial Museum as well. Students pay half. The other section, actually a National Historic site, is good, and free. On display is the *St Roch*, a 1928 sailing ship which was the first to navigate the legendary North-west Passage in both directions. There are interesting free guided tours on the ship every half hour or so. To get there, take Bus No 22 from Burrard downtown.

Macmillan Planetarium
This planetarium (tel 736-4431) is at 1100 Chestnut St, in Vanier Park. It has entertaining and educational shows projected on a 20-metre dome which change regularly. The shows are very popular, so make reservations early. Admission is $4 or cheaper with a youth hostel card. The planetarium is closed on Mondays. The observatory (tel 738-2855) is also open to the public.

Old Hastings Mill Store
Built in 1865, this was the first store on Burrard Inlet. It survived the Great Fire of 1886 and was moved in 1930 to where it stands today on Point Grey Rd at Alma. It's the large, off-white, barn-like building with brown trim, close to English Bay. There is a small collection of Indian artefacts and some local memorabilia. Admission is free.

University of British Columbia
This is at the most westerly point in Vancouver, on the spit jutting out into the Georgia Strait. The huge campus serving 30,000 students is spread over 400 wooded hectares; apart from these attractive grounds, there are several points of interest on it.

UBC Museum of Anthropology This museum is excellent. The exhibits include art and artefacts from cultures around the world. Asia, Africa and the Pacific are all well represented. The slight emphasis on the work of BC's Indians includes a terrific totem pole collection – both indoors and out. The collection has some fine sculptures and carvings. One thing I found unique is that all the items are stored in glass filing cabinets. Everything is numbered and catalogued, so you can look up details and cross references yourself. The museum is open from noon to 9 pm Tuesday, noon to 7 pm Wednesday to Sunday and is closed Monday. In winter it's open to 5 pm. The admission charge of $2 is waived on Tuesdays.

Nitobe Memorial Gardens These beautiful Japanese-style gardens are near the museum. Designed by a leading Japanese landscape architect, they're a perfect display of this symbolic Eastern art form. Get a guide at the gate when you buy a ticket. The gardens are open from 10 am to dusk in summer, until 3 pm in winter. Admission is 50c.

Totem Park, near the gardens, has carvings and buildings representing part of a Haida village. Free.

Wreck Beach Along Marine Drive, past the Rose Garden and Museum on the campus, are markers for trails into the woods. Follow trail Nos 3 or 4 down the steep steps to Wreck Beach, a pleasant and quiet – if notorious – nude beach. If you don't fancy that, the campus aquatic centre (tel 228-4521), with pools, saunas and exercise areas, is open to the public. The No 10 bus from Granville St downtown runs up to the university every 10 minutes.

Queen Elizabeth Park
This park, near Cambie St and 33rd

Avenue, is the city's second largest park. Up the hill to the conservatory there are great views of the city in nearly every direction. There's a well-designed sunken garden surrounded by small cliffs which has some fantastic plants, one with leaves a metre across. Next to the parking lot is an unusual, Oriental-looking garden consisting of many pools and fountains. The garden is mostly cement, but is dotted with wooden frames holding plants and flowers. There is a restaurant and a cheaper coffee shop for snacks or tea.

Bloedel Conservatory The conservatory at the park has tropical plants beneath its plastic dome, but for the admission prices of $1.50 or 60c for students, it's not really worth it with all the flowers and gardens around for free.

Vandusen Botanical Gardens

This new 55-acre park contains a small lake and a large collection of ornamental plants from around the world. It's open daily from 10 am to 8 pm in summer. Admission prices are $3.50, students $2. The gardens are at 37th Avenue and Oak St, not far from the Queen Elizabeth Park. Take Bus No 17 from downtown.

Vancouver East Area

Simon Fraser University

This university sits atop Burnaby Mountain in Burnaby, several km from town along East Hastings St. Its intriguing modern architecture and excellent vistas make it a worthwhile visit. The design, incorporating unusual use of space and perspective, was – and remains – controversial. There are huge courtyard-like quadrants and many fountains, including one on a roof. Some areas of the complex I found reminiscent of Mayan ruin sites in Mexico.

Other attractions of the university are the Ethnology Museum, which has a collection of Indian artefacts, and a very cheap cafeteria. For information on tours around the university, call 291-3111. To get there, city buses run from downtown.

Heritage Village Museum

This museum (tel 294-1231) is beside Deer Lake in Burnaby's Century Park. It's a replica of a village community which attempts to preserve both the artefacts and atmosphere of a south-west British Columbia town in the years 1890-1925. There's an old schoolhouse, printing shop, drug store and other establishments. Workers are in period dress. Recently, a large, working steam train model has been located next to the village. It's open daily from 11 am to 4.30 pm; closed Monday. Admission is $4, $3 for students.

Teleglobe Canada

This display has exhibits on satellite and undersea international communications, videos, telecommunications artefacts and related electronic equipment. Free guided tours are offered Monday to Friday from mid-June to Labour Day. It's in the Vancouver International Centre, 3033 Beta Avenue, Burnaby, off Canada Way. To get there, go south of the Trans-Canada Highway on Willingdon, 13 km from downtown.

North Vancouver

Lonsdale Quay Market

Major redevelopment has transformed the area by the Seabus terminal on the north shore. Foremost among the changes, which include a water's edge park, offices and residential complexes, is the market building. The first floor is devoted to fresh and cooked food; the second floor is mainly specialty shops but with a restaurant with views. As you depart the ferry, there's an information booth to offer guidance on the North Vancouver attractions. The local bus depot is here as well.

North Shore Museum

The small museum located at 209 West 4th St offers rather good changing exhibits on a wide range of subjects. I saw coastal Indian basketry and some local transportation history. Admission is free and it's open Wednesdays to Sundays from 1 to 4 pm.

Capilano Suspension Bridge
This bridge (tel 985-7474), at 3735 Capilano Rd on the left-hand side going north, spans the Capilano River for 140 metres at a height of 70 metres. Open daily, it's very tourist oriented, and with little else in the small park is really not worth the $4, students $3 admission. To get there, take Bus No 246, 'Highlands', going west on Georgia.

Lynn Canyon Park
Set in thick woods, this park gives a good glimpse of the rainforest vegetation so different from that found in eastern Canada. There are many hiking trails, and you can find your own picnic and swimming spots. Over Lynn Canyon is a suspension bridge; although not as big as Capilano, it's much the same and free. At Ecology House, a small museum, are displays about the biology of the area. It's open daily from 10 am to 5 pm and costs $1. To get to the park, go over Second Narrows Bridge and take Lynn Valley Rd. Go east on Peters where you'll see signs that lead you into the park.

Capilano Salmon Hatchery
This is a fish farm run by the government to help stop the depletion of valuable salmon stocks. Although you can't see the holding pools, there are exhibits with good explanations of the whole process. Salmon in various stages of growth are on display in tanks, and you can see how they are channelled from the river into the hatchery when they head upstream to spawn. Admission is free. It's in Capilano Park, off Capilano Rd not far north of the suspension bridge.

Cleveland Dam
The dam blocks Capilano Lake, which supplies much of Vancouver's drinking water. You'll get good views of the Lions – two peaks of the coastal mountains. There are picnic areas and trails. Free. The dam is slightly further north of the salmon hatchery, up Capilano Rd.

Grouse Mountain
Grouse Mountain, off Nancy Greene Way North at the end of Capilano Rd, is famous for its Swiss-built Superskyride cable car. From the top – 1250 metres – you can see all of Vancouver, the coast, part of Vancouver Island and northward over the mountains. It's an expensive ride at $8 or $6 for students. An open chair lift goes from the upper plateau to the peak but this is a further couple of bucks. There are restaurants at the top and bottom of the mountain.

If you take the Superskyride, make sure it's a clear day. If it's raining, foggy or at all hazy with low clouds, forget it: by the time you reach the top you won't see a thing. Go in late afternoon; then you can see the city by day and night.

Grouse Mountain has great skiing in winter, and is very popular for hang-gliding, with a championship held here every year. You'll probably see some hang-gliders soar by the cable car.

To get to the mountain from downtown, you can use the city bus system: the Seabus and one transfer.

Royal Hudson Steam Train
This 1930s steam engine pulls restored coaches on a 5½-hour return excursion to Squamish. The route follows the coast northward through some beautiful scenery. The cost is $16. The train leaves from the BC Railway Station at the foot of Pemberton Avenue on Burrard. For details of the rather complicated schedule call 687-9558. A variation is to take the train one way and cruise back on the MV Britannia.

Park & Tilford Gardens
This is a 1.2-hectare flower garden developed by the distillery of the same name. There are some unusual tree specimens, tropical birds and lots of flowers. Although free, they're not highly recommended; they're used mainly by wedding photographers. Open daily from

8 am to 11 pm. The gardens are at 1200 Cotton Rd, North Vancouver.

Out of Town

Mount Seymour Provincial Park

This park, 15 km north-east from downtown, is a quick, close escape from the city. There is a road up most of the way; a chair lift goes to the peak. The views of Vancouver's surroundings are beautiful. There's skiing here in winter.

There are parking lots for trailers but no real tent campground; you can pitch a tent along the many alpine trails. Some areas are very rugged, so visitors going on overnight trips should register.

Lighthouse Park

This park has a stand of original forest and contains some of the largest trees in the Vancouver area. Trails lead to the lighthouse and bluffs, with views of the Georgia Strait. The park is at Point Atkinson in West Vancouver, eight km to the left on Marine Drive after going over Lions Gate Bridge.

Sunshine Coast

This name refers to the coastal area from Horseshoe Bay to Powell River. The scenery is excellent: hills, mountains, forests, inlets, harbours and beaches. The highway along the coast is broken at two separate points, and ferries are necessary. The road ends completely at Powell River, where there is a ferry over to Comox on Vancouver Island. The Nanaimo ferry leaves from Horseshoe Bay. The ferries are all rather expensive if you take your car. For detailed information about the ferries, call BC Ferries (tel 669-1211).

In Powell River itself is the Beach Gardens Dive Resort at 7074 Westminster Avenue. They rent some equipment and run charters out to diving spots. There is good diving around Egmont by Earl's Cove, south of Powell River, and wrecks off the coast in the area.

Horseshoe Bay is a pretty spot, but commercial and expensive. Following Highway 99 north from Horseshoe Bay leads to a few interesting places.

Shannon Falls

Squamish is the main town in this resort area. South of Squamish, the Shannon Falls tumble over a cliff just off the road in a park. There's hiking and camping in summer, skiing in winter.

Garibaldi Park

This park is a 2000 square km mountain wilderness, 64 km north of Vancouver. Most of the park is undeveloped and it's a full day's hike from the parking lot to the campground. There's some good hiking and cross-country ski trails. For more information and a map of the park, stop at a tourist information booth.

Whistler Mountain

Just outside Garibaldi Park is this major new resort area geared mainly for skiing. Whistler Village offers hotels, lodges, restaurants and bars. In summer you can go hiking, take the gondola up the mountain or visit an aquatic park.

There's a good *Youth Hostel* (tel 932-5492), five km from Highway 99 on Alta Lake (West) Rd. It's open all year, with room for 30 people. Meals are offered. There's camping at the nearby provincial park. Hotels are not cheap but there are quite a few.

Maverick Coach Lines has a daily bus service from Vancouver.

George C Reifel Waterfowl Refuge

This is a 340-hectare bird sanctuary on Westham Island, 10 km west of Ladner, south of Vancouver. Each year, over 230 bird species pass through, including herons, eagles, falcons and swans. There are about three km of pathways and an observation tower for bird-watching. It's open to 6 pm in summer, 4.30 pm in winter.

Buddhist Temple

Out in Richmond, south of town at 9160

Steveston Highway is this Buddhist centre consisting of a temple, garden, small museum and library. You may also catch an art show or tea ceremony. The temple, in Chinese style, is ornate and has some fine work but compared to the temples of the far east, it may seem a little clean, modern and sterile. The centre is free and open daily. It's accessible by city bus.

Steveston

This little town, on the coast near the Buddhist temple, is heavily promoted as a quaint fishing village. That's rather a promotion man's con. There's certainly nothing overly wrong with the place and you can get some alright fish & chips, but a quaint fishing village it ain't. There's a wharf where some of the fishing fleet moors and a place to buy fresh seafood.

Whiterock

Still further south on Semiahmoo Bay is Whiterock Beach, with expanses of sand and warm waters. Every summer a major sand castle competition is held, with entrants even coming from overseas. This is definitely not just dumping a pail of sand upside down. All summer long the beach strip is quite a scene; strut your stuff if you've done your sit-ups.

Fort Langley National Historic Park

This fort (tel 534-4232), erected in 1827 and serving as a Hudson's Bay Company post until 1858, was established long before Victoria or Vancouver. It was here in 1858 that BC was proclaimed a Crown colony. Most of the buildings were restored in 1956 and you can see the old palisades, utensils and furnishings. It's 48 km east of Vancouver along the Trans-Canada Highway.

Vancouver Game Farm

This 48-hectare site (tel 856-6825) has 60 different kinds of animals in large, open pens, including tigers, lions, elephants and buffalo. It's about 12 km east of the fort in Aldergrove; open daily.

Events

Polar Bear Swim (1 January): This popular, chilly affair has been taking place on English Bay Beach annually since 1819. If you can't handle the water, watching is allowed.

Chinese New Year (mid-February): Chinatown provides the setting for one of Vancouver's most colourful events, with dancers, music, fireworks and food.

Folk Festival (1 July): This is the province's largest multi-cultural festival. Main events take place in Gastown, Robson Square and the Orpheum Theatre – all free. There is music, dance, performances and of course, traditional costumes and foods. For information call 736-1512.

Vancouver Sea Festival (mid-July): During this festival there is entertainment like concerts, parades and salmon barbecues which take place on the shores of English Bay. For details and times call 669-4091 or the Tourist Office.

Vancouver Folk Music Festival (mid-July): This is three days of music, including concerts and workshops, from some of the best North American folk musicians. Most of the action takes place at Jericho Beach near UBC. For information and tickets call Vancouver Ticket Centre, 687-4444.

Carnival (1-3 August): This event also celebrates various ethnic cultures with pavilions scattered around town offering music, dance, foods, etc.

Abbotsford International Air Show (early August): I've heard this is a fantastic spectacle – it's known as Canada's National Air Show and has been voted the world's best. The three-day event, which celebrated its 25th anniversary in 1986, has everything that flies, from fighters to the Concorde. It's held 56 km east of Vancouver near the US border in Abbotsford.

Pacific National Exhibition (late August to Labour Day): Known as the PNE, this big fair features a little bit of everything – sports, competitions, international exhibits, concerts and shows, as well as amusement park rides. It starts off each year with a two-hour parade. The exhibition lasts about two weeks. The PNE grounds are on East Hastings Avenue near the Second Narrows Bridge.

Oktoberfest (weekends, late September to early October): Held at the beginning of October, this event takes place at BC Place. There's the usual oompah and Tyrolean music, Bavarian dancers, beer and more beer. It usually lasts until 2 am.

Activities

Swimming & Water Sports You can swim at city beaches, eg Sunset Beach or Second and Third Beach in Stanley Park.

At the Aquatic Centre (tel 689-7156), 1050 Beach Avenue, there is a heated saltwater pool, gym and sauna open for visitors. There's another pool at Kitsilano Beach, outdoors.

Windsure Windsurfing School (tel 734-7245) gives lessons and rents boards. Its offices are at English Bay Beach, Kits Beach and Jericho Sailing Center.

English Bay is a popular area for salmon fishing, for which the west coast is famous. Boats and equipment are for hire and there are expensive guided charters.

At Vancouver Canoe & Kayak (tel 688-6010) they rent by the hour, day or week. The office is at 1666 Duranleau on Granville Island in False Creek.

Divers World has equipment and scuba trips. It's at 1523 West 3rd Avenue.

Other Wine tours are held at the Jordan Ste Michelle Cellars (tel 576-6741) in Surrey, 30 minutes from town and 12 km from the US border. A free tasting is included.

In summer, every Friday at noon, there are concerts at the Orpheum for $1. The program varies each day but you might hear folk, blues, jazz or classical music.

Places to Stay

Hostels The *YHA Youth Hostel* (tel 224-3208) is in the southern part of Vancouver, south over False Creek, in Kitsilano. The rates are $8 for members, $10 for non-members and the hostel has 280 beds. The other facilities include a kitchen, cafeteria, laundry room, notice board and parking. Ask about the places in town where the hostel card will get you reductions, eg Camps Bike rentals, UBC and the Planetarium. It's in Jericho Park, which has a beach on English Bay about 20 minutes from downtown by bus. From downtown take the 4th Avenue bus from Granville St to Jericho Park. Continue west on 4th Avenue to Discovery St, turn right (or north) and you'll come to it – the big white building on the left. This is one of the country's more stable hostels, so it's likely to stay in the same place.

The *YMCA* (tel 681-0221) is right downtown at 955 Burrard St. It has recently been upgraded and is good, but prices reflect the change. Singles are $25; the best value are the triples. Women and couples are allowed and quite a few travellers stay here. There are gym and pool facilities and a small inexpensive restaurant serving the best roast beef sandwich I've ever had; good value breakfasts, too.

The *YWCA* (tel 662-8188) for women only, is very central at 580 Burrard St. It's really like a hotel, with full facilities including a pool. Singles are $30 to $39, doubles $40 to $49 and rooms for four are only $55.

For students there is *Redford House Student Hotel* (tel 294-6873) out in Burnaby at 1850 Rosser Avenue. Singles cost from $16, doubles from $20. There are buses from town.

The University of British Columbia rents rooms in the Walter Gage Residence from about the first week in May to the end of August, at the rates of singles/

doubles $24/40. Contact the Conference Centre Manager (tel 228-2963) at 2071 West Mall, Vancouver. Self-contained apartments are also available. There is a cafeteria, laundromat and sports facilities and the campus is pleasant. To reach it from downtown take the UBC bus from the corner of Robson and Granville. From the university to downtown, take the No 14 Hastings. The bus trip takes about 30 minutes.

The *Salvation Army*, for men only, is on Dunsmuir between Seymour and Richards. If you're hard up you can get a bed and a meal here for nothing.

Bed & Breakfasts Bed & breakfast accommodation has really mushroomed across the country, perhaps more in BC than anywhere. The Tourist Office has information on agencies who select, inspect and book individual houses. A couple to try are Born Free B & B (tel 298-8815) at 4390 Frances St, Burnaby, and Old English Bed & Breakfast Registry (tel 986-5069) at 1226 Silverwood Crescent, North Vancouver. *Town & Country Bed & Breakfast in BC Canada* is a home accommodation guide – now in its sixth edition – which also offers a reservation service for the Vancouver area (tel 731-5942). Another is *Host International*. Prices average $30 to $45 for singles, $40 to $60 for doubles.

Other operators run independently and many have advertisements at the Tourist Office. Some are very central but nearly all have only a couple of rooms, so you may have to call several to get a room.

Hotels – bottom end Many people find the hostel or University dorms too far from the centre and prefer one of the older, cheap central hotels. Vancouver, despite its rapid growth, has a great number of them, right in the downtown core. Many are well-kept and offer good value, but Vancouver is one of Canada's biggest tourist towns so rooms in summer may be rather scarce. In winter you may get places a little cheaper, and if you'll be a week it's worth asking for a reduction any time of year. There are also numerous third-class (and below) hotels; the city has more hotels serving the downtrodden and the fringe than any other Canadian city.

There are more cheapies than you can shake a stick at in Gastown, Chinatown and Hastings Avenue; Cordoba and Abbot Sts have several too; a few of these are all right for shoestringers. Rooms are rented by the day, week or month. Nightly rates are from as low as $12; weekly rates range from $60.

Easily one of the city's best deals is the spotless *Spinning Wheel Inn* (tel 681-1627) in a great location in the centre of Gastown. Singles are $22, doubles $25. Housekeeping rooms are $35 or $165 a week. The address is 210 Carrall St. This small, newly renovated place was once the historic Kings Hotel.

The *Old Dominion Hotel*, from 1899, at 210 Abbot St is also in Gastown, at the corner of Water St. The renovated rooms go for $25 for singles and $35 for doubles, including breakfast. There are many others in the area but most are bottom-of-the-line.

The affable man who looks after the old *Metropolitan* at 320 Abbot charges $14.

The *Hazlewood* at 344 East Hastings costs $18 for a single room without bath, $28 with. Weekly rates are available. You might have to wait a while for the desk clerk to appear.

The *Patricia* (tel 255-4301) is much better. It's large, clean and well-kept, and good value at singles/doubles for $21/24 with sink only. Double rooms with bath cost $36. It's at 403 Hastings East.

A reader has recommended *Vincent's Guest House* (tel 254-7462), which offers free breakfast, free pick-up from the bus station and airport, and many other amenities. Shared rooms are $10, singles/doubles are $20/35. It's at 1741 Grant St.

The downtown area also has a good

selection of hotels, ranging from basic ones through moderate to expensive.

At 435 West Pender is *Hotel Niagara* (tel 681-5548) with a sign depicting Niagara Falls tumbling four floors. It's old but good, with rates from $25 for singles without bath to $35 for doubles with bath and TV.

Nearby, the *Piccadilly* (tel 669-1556) has 45 small, simple but modern,

comfortable rooms from $25 for singles, $30 for doubles. The location is very central at 622 West Pender St.

The *St Regis* (tel 681-1135) at the corner of Dunsmuir and Seymour, is a little more costly. All rooms come with bath and there is a bar and restaurant. Singles are $35 and up, doubles start at $45.

The *Marble Arch* at the corner of Richards and West Pender has recently been cleaned up and offers bathless singles for $25 including breakfast.

Also in the area is the *Kingston Hotel* (tel 684-9024) at 757 Richards. It was the city's first bed & breakfast hotel and still offers the morning meal. Prices depend on your room and facilities, but are around $30. The hotel is a very nice one, with a sauna and guests' laundry.

Down Robson St toward its foot are several good, moderately priced places. The *Robsonstrasse City Motor Inn* is about $40 to $60. Across the street at No 1431, the *Riviera* (tel 685-1301) is the same price and rooms come with kitchens.

There are several hotels down Granville. There is nothing special about the area and it's one the streetwalkers use, but a couple of hotels are all right.

A cheap central one is the *Gresham Hotel* at 716 Granville, which has singles for $15 and doubles for $17. The rooms are plain, a bit tattered but vacuumed, and the beds are OK. It's a place used mainly by young transients and is run by a friendly Chinese man.

The *Austin Motor Hotel* (tel 685-7235) at No 1221, is fine and big with singles from $30, doubles from $36. There's free parking and full facilities.

For budgeters, the *Cecil Hotel* at 1336 Granville near the Burrard Bridge has simple rooms which aren't bad at $24/26 for singles/doubles. There's a popular bar downstairs with exotic dancers working to loud rock music.

The nearby *Hotel California* on Granville St is cheap and central.

Montrose Hotel Pension (tel 988-5141) at 170 West Esplanade, North Vancouver has singles/doubles for $30/35; some rooms come with bath. The Montrose is close to Seabus and Lonsdale, the shopping-restaurant street of North Vancouver.

Hotels – middle The *Abbotsford* (tel 681-2331) at 921 West Pender is central and has a pub as well as a dining room. All rooms are self-contained. Singles range from $50 to $65, doubles from $55 to $75.

The *Dufferin Hotel* at 900 Seymour has recently upgraded and offers similar rooms to the Abbotsford. Rooms are $40 to $50 for singles, $50 to $65 for doubles. There's free parking and that's a plus.

There's a pretty good dining room. There's also a *Travelodge* at the bridge end of Granville.

Hotels – top end *Hotel Georgia* (tel 682-5566) at 801 West Georgia St has singles/doubles for $105/120.

Century Plaza (tel 687-0575) at 1015 Burrard St has singles/doubles for $100/115.

Hotel Vancouver (tel 684-3131) at 900 West Georgia St, has singles ranging from $110 to $180 and doubles from $130 to $200.

Apartment Hotels There are quite a few of these around town. The *English Bay Hotel* (tel 685-2231) at 1150 Denman St, charges about $34 to $37 for singles/doubles with kitchen. It's got good views. Or try *Shato Inn* at 1825 Comox off Denman. Single rooms are from $35 to $50, doubles from $45 to $60. Weekly rates are usually in the $200 range.

Motels There are three distinct areas where you'll find motels around Vancouver. They're all outside the downtown area but not a great distance away and with a car, they're very accessible. Some of the cheaper ones follow.

The closest strip to downtown is along Hastings East around Exhibition Park and east into Burnaby. This is a convenient area, close to Second Narrows Bridge over to North Vancouver.

Rainbow Auto Lodge (tel 298-1828) at 5958 Hastings East is also a trailer camp and has a laundromat. Basic single rooms are $35, the doubles are $37. Some units have a kitchen, which is well worth the $3 extra.

Martin's Motel (tel 298-5445) at 6574 Hastings East, is very close to Exhibition Park. Singles/doubles are $40 to $50; the more expensive have colour TV. The rooms with kitchen are $5 more.

The *City Centre Motel* at 2111 Main St has been highly recommended. It has singles/doubles for $30/$34, free coffee and is well situated.

The second major motel area is along the Kingsway, a major road which was the old highway running south-east out of downtown through Burnaby and New Westminster across the Fraser River. It's also called Highway 1A and is south of the Trans-Canada Highway. Most of the motels are in Burnaby, about a 20-minute drive from downtown.

Blue Haven Motel (tel 524-8501) is at 7026 Kingsway, Burnaby. This place has both sleeping and housekeeping rooms, TV and laundromat. Singles or doubles range from $35 to $80; use of the kitchen is $5 extra.

The other motel area is on the north shore, over Lions Gate Bridge. Look along Marine Drive and north up Capilano Rd. There are also a couple of spots on Esplanade which runs east-west along the north shore of Burrard Inlet, past the Seabus depot.

Avalon Motor Hotel (tel 985-4181) is at 1025 Marine Drive, North Vancouver, about five minutes east of the bridge. Singles/doubles cost $42/$47 for rooms with colour TV and phone.

Canyon Court Motel (tel 988-3181) is at 1748 Capilano Rd, North Vancouver. Singles range from $40 to $65, doubles from $50 to $75 and use of a TV or kitchen is $4 extra. All rooms are cheaper after 1 October. There's a laundromat, free coffee and a swimming pool. The motel is close to Lions Gate, Stanley Park and Grouse Mountain. It offers good value for a motel.

Camping The trailer parks right in Vancouver do not allow tenting. The closest camping areas that do are south of the city, on or near Highway 99, which runs to the US border. There are also a couple near the ferry terminal for Vancouver Island in Tsawwassen.

Timberline Campsite (tel 531-1033) for tents and trailers is at 3418 King George Highway (99a) Surrey. A site costs $10 and there's a laundromat and showers. The campsite is half an hour's driving from Vancouver, six km from the US border.

On the east side of town is the *Cedar Acres Trailer Court* (tel 464-6929) which has some places for tents. It's 25 km from the city centre, 275 metres east from the junction of Highways 7 and 7a. Highway 7 is also called the Lougheed Highway.

There are several places to camp along Beach Rd, White Rock. *Oddfellows & Rebeka Campsite* (tel 531-5600) is at 16249 Beach Rd, White Rock, 40 km from Vancouver. It has hot, coin-operated showers, and a beach. Tenting is just $7. *Parklander Motor & Trailer Court* (tel 531-3711) at 16311 8th Avenue, White Rock, has campsites for $12. Showers are available and the campground is surrounded by trees.

Places to Eat

For many years Vancouver has had a reputation as a good town for eats. This is true now more than ever, with the recent rapid increase in population and sophistication. As in many places known for good restaurants, the quality and variety filters down through all budget levels.

Downtown I guess I have to start with the *White Spot*, a BC chain begun in 1928. They're nothing fancy, but family restaurants serving not bad food at good prices, and open every day. The chocolate milkshakes are excellent. There are numerous White Spots in Vancouver. In town there's one at Georgia St near Denman and one on Seymour and W Georgia.

For lunch there's *Glen's Fabulous Sandwiches*, giving the office workers a break from brown baggin' it. It's at 420 Howe near W Hastings.

Another good place for lunch is *Papaya Gardens* at 950 Granville. It has mainly vegetarian and health-foods although chicken is also on the menu. There are very good value lunch specials which could include a piece of carrot cake.

There's a good fair in Robson Square, down a level at Robson and Howe; at 1610 Robson the Public Market has a bakery, cheese shop, fruit stalls, etc.

Pepita's at 1169 Robson offers very good Mexican meals with quite a bit of seafood on the menu.

For a good, inexpensive dinner, the *Saigon* is a very popular Vietnamese place at 1500 Robson. Meals cost around $6 to $9.

A long-time favourite of mine is the *India Gate* at 616 Robson. They have an extensive menu of Indian vegetarian and meat dishes, with prices at about $10 to $15 per meal at dinner or less for the lunch menu.

For European fare, the *Heidelberg House* at 1164 Robson has been serving various German specialties for years. The reasonably priced menu includes goulashes, schnitzels and a variety of sandwiches.

Another national cuisine is Portuguese, represented by the *Tesca*. This is a very highly rated restaurant with main courses – primarily of seafood – in the $12 to $15 bracket and lunches as low as $5. It's on Robson in the 1600 block.

A couple of pubs with great names are the *Jolly Taxpayers* at 828 W Hastings near Howe, and the *Elephant & Castle* on Dunsmuir at Granville.

The *Punjab Restaurant* at 746 Main St at Union has long opening hours: 11.30 am to 11 pm daily. Complete meals are about $12 for vegetarian food, $14 with meat. It's small, quiet, rather posh and was nearly full when I saw it. Service is excellent. An Indian resident of the city informed me that they serve the best Indian food in Vancouver.

Another minor splurge is the *Ferguson Point Tea House* in Stanley Park. With its wicker furniture, hanging plants, large windows and a view over the ocean, the atmosphere is right out of The Great Gatsby. The best prices are at lunch time, which is from 11.30 am to 2 pm Monday to

Friday. Dinner is served from 5.30 to 10 pm seven days a week. The entrees are mainly seafood; fisherman's soup at $4 is nearly a meal; the salads are good and wine is served.

Also in Stanley Park, *Prospect Point Cafe* has a varied, continental menu, worth a small splurge on the pricey hamburger or to share a pizza and some wine. If it's a little overpriced, it's also a great spot with an outdoor patio and views across the inlet.

At 363 East Hastings is the *Buddhist Vegetarian Restaurant* with lots of soups and dishes that just about fool you with simulated meats. Not expensive.

Denman Denman St has become a very lively, pleasant street to visit around evening meal time. There's a good selection of eateries, particularly toward the Georgia St end, and lots of people strolling and menu-reading. The choice includes Mexican, French and Greek food, as well as the selections which follow.

Not far from Georgia on the east side, the *Japanese Restaurant* is cosy, casual and cheap. On the other side of the street, *Cafe Slavia* is an inexpensive place for food with a Slavic slant like goulash and *pierogies* (dumplings) for $5 to $6. The *Dover Inn* on the corner of Barclay (with the English phone booth) serves mainly fish. For fish & chips go to *Budd's* at 1007 Denman; it'll be packed. *Ciao!* at No 1074 is a small espresso bar with croissants, etc.

Gastown Area *The Only Fish & Oyster Café* at 20 Hastings East is a Vancouver institution and a must – it's been going for 70 years and hasn't changed a bit. There's no toilet, no liquor licence and seating for only 25, mostly on stools. And there's always a queue: about 500 people eat here daily and over 200 litres of chowder are served every day. The people create the atmosphere; there are all types, including tourists on every kind of budget and no shortage of drunks. The fare consists of large portions of seafood fresh from the docks which is served quickly by the Chinese waitresses. A bowl of clam chowder with one piece of warm fresh French bread and two pieces of fresh brown bread is $3. A full meal of clams, oysters or various fish is between $5 and $8. They'll also boil, steam or fry whatever fish you want. The Café is open Monday to Saturday from 11.30 am to 10.30 pm; closed on Sundays.

Just down the street is *White Lunch* at 124 West Hastings. This is another place of character, attracting many European immigrants and old men, and serving cheap meals at small wooden booths.

The *Old Spaghetti Factory* at 55 Water St is good food value. This is a branch of the popular Canada-wide chain. The decor is interesting; it's lined with all types of old machinery, stained-glass Tiffany lamps and even a 1910 Vancouver streetcar. Complete meals go for $6.50 to $9. It's open daily until 10 pm, on Sundays until 9 pm.

La Brasserie de l'Horlage is at 300 Water St, right across the street from the steam clock. In English the name means 'Brasserie of the Clock'. This was once the Regina Hotel, built in 1875 and the only major building to escape the Great Fire of 1886. Inside it looks reasonably like a French bistro and serves French items like quiche and *croque monsieur*. The food's good and reasonably priced with lunches at $5 to $6 and dinners for $9 to $14. It's open Monday to Friday from 11.30 am to 3 pm, and Saturday from noon to 3 pm and 5 pm to midnight; closed Sunday.

The *Kilimanjaro* at 328 Water serves Ugandan food, based on Indian dishes. There's a restaurant upstairs and a bistro downstairs. It's a very attractive place with quality food and good prices. In the same price range, the new *Eat Your Heart Out* at 217 Carrall serves French and Italian dishes. Dinner for two with wine costs about $25.

For soup & sandwich lunches, try the *Cottage Deli* at 131 Water, which has views of the inlet; or, at the corner of Carrall where the statue of Gassy Jack stands, there are several cafés which have had rapid changes of ownership but remain good value places. *Orlando's Fresh Pasta Bar* is on Abbot near Water. They serve very cheap pastas and breakfasts and have some outdoor tables, too.

Chinatown For good value, simple Chinese food you can't beat *Yang Sheng* at 207a East Pender. They have six lunch specials every day, priced at $3.25. A big pot of tea is plonked down before you even order. An à la carte menu is available too, which is more expensive but still reasonably priced. *On On Tea Garden* at 212 Keefer is small, inconspicuous and cheap but has good Cantonese food. *Maxim's Bakery & Café* at 257 Keefer has tasty pastries and cakes.

Ming's at 147 Pender St East has excellent dim sum between 11 am and 2 pm daily. A wide variety of dishes are served from a cart whirled around by the waitress, each priced at about $1.50. Arrive early for the best selection.

Kitsilano & 4th Avenue Area This is an area of students, alternate lifestylers, cafés and second-hand stores. In recent years, it's also become very desirable, attracting more professionals. Between Burrard and Alma, 4th Avenue has a large, varying selection of eating spots with many nationalities represented. Broadway also has numerous spots for stomach satisfaction.

The *Lifestream Natural Food Store & Restaurant* is at the corner of 4th and Burrard. Good, cheap food is served cafeteria-style and there's lots of choice. You'll find a big noticeboard of local activities here too.

At 1754 4th Avenue is the *Heaven & Earth Curry House*. They serve meat or vegetarian dishes, priced at about $8 to $9. The place is established and good.

Topanga's at 2904 4th Avenue is a good Mexican place. *Dar Lebanon* is a small, pleasant and cheap Middle-Eastern café. It's at 1961 4th and opens every day.

One of the many Greek places in the area is *Simpatico* at 2226 4th. It's a very attractive, open-sided Greek tavern. Moderate dinners.

NAAM at 2724 4th Avenue is a good, inexpensive 'new age' vegetarian and health-food restaurant . It's very casual and has live folk music every night. At No 1938, *Pistachio's* is a nice little café for breakfast, snacks and light meals.

Over on West Broadway in the 3000 block, the ethnic mix includes *Da Tandoor* at No 3135 with a good, two-person Indian dinner special, a German place and a couple of Greek ones.

Little India The Vancouver area has the largest Indian community in the country and the majority are Sikhs from the Punjab. The focal point of the population is on Main St between 49th and 51st Avenues. Here you'll find Indian groceries, sari and spice shops and shops selling Indian records and tapes. *The Bombay Sweet & Restaurant* at 6556 Main St is a simple place offering very cheap lunch and dinner buffets, including half a dozen or so curries, lentil dishes and various breads. Next door and along the street are places specialising in Indian sweets.

North Vancouver The new complex at Lonsdale Quay where the Seabus ties in has a few places to munch at, including the British-style *Cheshire Cheese Inn* pub, where they sell traditional British food like ploughman's lunch and bubble & squeak.

Restaurants have been appearing along Esplanade St recently and several are concentrated at the corner of Lonsdale. *Corsi Trattoria* is an Italian place where everything is made on the premises, including the pasta and bread. Meals are in the middle price range.

At 69 Lonsdale *The Jageroff* specialises in schnitzels and also serves deer and

Top: Saw logs in Lake Kamloops, British Columbia (RB)
Left: Cascade Lakes, Yoho National Park, British Columbia (JL)
Right: Vancouver Harbour, British Columbia (ML)

Top: The *Bluenose II* (CG)
Bottom: Icebound fishing boats (CG)

reindeer meat. Prices are about $7 for lunch, $11 for the main dinner course.

Frankie's Inn at 59 Lonsdale is close to the Seabus terminal, near the corner of Esplanade St. It's basically a greasy spoon with the usual Western food, but there's a Vancouver twist: Japanese dishes like sukiyaki, tempura and teriyaki are available, served with chopsticks. Meal prices average $4. This spot is popular with workers from the nearby docks.

Up at No 1344, *Cafe Nairobi* is a rather posh Indian restaurant with an African slant. Meals are costlier but not exorbitant. Next door, the *Casbah* is a cheaper, more casual Greek-Lebanese place.

Shopping

There are several shops in Vancouver which sell Indian wares. Most have fairly poor quality stuff; one store that has only good quality is Hill's Indian Crafts at 165 Water St and also at 34 Nicol St in Nanaimo. They have a good selection of carvings, prints, masks and the excellent Cowichan sweaters for about $175. These sweaters are hand-knitted and 100% wool. Originally from the Lake Cowichan area on Vancouver Island, they are now made in many places.

Pack & Boots Shop (tel 738-3128) at 3425 West Broadway, is run by the Hostelling Association. This store has all kinds of camping equipment, boots and tents.

Nightlife

The best source of information on entertainment in Vancouver is the *Georgia Straight*, which comes out every Friday. The daily newspapers also have complete entertainment listings, including theatre, dance and the Vancouver Symphony.

For theatre tickets check the little booth on ground level in Robson Galleria, 1025 Robson. Open just noon to 1 pm and 4.30 to 6 pm from Monday to Saturday. They sell tickets for local shows at half price, usually close to showtime.

There is a fair bit of nightlife in the Gastown area. The inexpensive *Savoy*, 6 Powell, is a long-standing casual bar with live rock and reggae. The *Spinning Wheel*, 212 Carrall, is small but comfortable with mainly rhythm & blues bands. Monday to Wednesday, admission is also good for the nearby *Town Pump* with rock bands. At 231 Carrall the *Classical Joint Coffee House* is a small, informal, low-key place with jazz, folk, classical and blues. It's good for talking, not hustling. *Punchlines* is a comic club at 15 Water St. Cordove St has several pubs.

The Railway Club, corner of Seymour and Dunsmuir is a pub-like place with good quality and often original rock and jam sessions on Saturday afternoons. Nearby, Granville St is interesting after dark with lots of street activity. *Richards on Richards* is a dressy singles bar.

For live jazz there is the *Hot Jazz Society*, 2120 Main St. Admission is $3.50 to $5, less for students. The *Landmark Jazz Bar* in the Sheraton Landmark Hotel, Robson at Nicola, has shows that range from standards and bebop to New Orleans. Most bars close at 1 am, pubs earlier.

Sunset Beach at sunset is beautiful and busy. A stroll is highly recommended. There are cafés on the corner, as well.

Cinema The following repertory theatres show a mix of foreign and North American films. *Hollywood Theatre* (tel 738-3211) is at 3123 West Broadway. Two movies cost $3.50. *Ridge Theatre* (tel 738-6311) at Arbutus St corner of 16th Avenue, charges $5, $6 for two films.

Getting There & Away

Air The airport is about eight km south of the city on Sea Island – between Vancouver and the municipality of Richmond. Major Canadian airlines fly to Vancouver, as do many American and Asian airlines.

Some fares with Canadian (tel 682-1411) include:

Toronto – $481 plus tax, full fare
Edmonton – $177 plus tax
Seattle – $87 including tax.

On Air Canada (tel 688-5515), fares vary a lot depending on the flight's time of day, the day of the week and how far in advance you've bought the ticket. The more notice, the cheaper the fare. Generally, prices are the same as those of Canadian.

Air BC (tel 278-3800) is a local airline serving Vancouver Island, some points in the interior and Seattle. Twin Otter to Victoria is $72 one-way.

Pacific Western (tel 684-6161) flies to Seattle about eight times daily. The one-way fare is $69 plus tax. You may want to do this to get a flight to New York – it's likely to be cheaper from Seattle than a Canadian point.

On United Airlines, Seattle one-way is $87. Some flights carry on to San Francisco or various US connections from either point. Many people going across the continent find it cheaper to go, say, Seattle-Buffalo than Vancouver-Toronto.

Bus connections can be made between the Canadian and US airports at either end. Flights to Asia also may be cheaper from US west coast cities than Vancouver.

Northwest Airlines, Alaska Airlines and Wien fly to Alaska.

Fares can be cheaper if notice is given and may vary with the day of the week. Those given in this section are all full economy fares.

Bus The terminal for Greyhound is at 150 Dunsmuir, corner of Cambie. For information call 662-3222, 7 am to 11.30 pm. One-way fares are:

Banff: seven daily – $55
Kelowna: four daily – $30
Calgary: $55
Nanaimo (with ferry): 12 daily, 3½ hours – $13
Victoria (with ferry): 16 daily, 3½ hours – $15.25.

Maverick Tours (tel 255-1171) operate As Quick As Air, a bus from town to Seattle Airport. The one-way fare is $32.

Train Vancouver is the western terminus for VIA Rail. The station is at 1150 Station St at the corner of National Avenue. It's marked 'Canadian National' and has a big park out in front. The closest main intersection is the corner of Main and Pryor. For 24-hour information on fares and reservations, call 1-800-665-8630.

Kamloops, Banff, Calgary, Winnipeg, Sudbury, Ottawa, Montreal: 3.10 pm daily

Kamloops Junction, Jasper, Edmonton, Saskatoon, Winnipeg, Toronto: 4 pm daily

Fares one-way, coach: Banff $62, Calgary $71. Stopovers are permitted but you must re-reserve. There is now no train connection to Seattle. To join the American railways system, Amtrak, you must take a bus.

Car Sharing Car Drive-Aways (tel 985-0936) is at 211 West 1st St, North Vancouver. Check the newspapers for other drive-aways and the hostel noticeboard for ride opportunities.

Road If you're coming from the US (Washington), you'll be on Highway 5 until the border town of Blaine. At the border is the Peace Arch Provincial and State Park. The first town in British Columbia is White Rock. Highway 99 veers west, then north to Vancouver. Close to the city, it passes over two arms of the Fraser River and eventually turns into Granville St, one of the main thoroughfares of downtown Vancouver. Following Granville will take you right through the city to the north side. The only catch is that Granville is broken in the centre of town into a pedestrian mall, and ordinary traffic is forbidden.

If you're coming from the east, you'll nearly certainly be on the Trans-Canada, which takes the Port Mann Bridge over the Fraser River and snakes through the eastern end of the city, eventually meeting with Hastings St before going over the Second Narrows Bridge to North Vancouver. If you want downtown, turn left when you reach Hastings.

Getting Around

Airport Transport There are two ways to get to the airport but the quickest is to take the airport bus – known as 'The Hustle Bus' – from the Greyhound Terminal for $6. It also goes to top hotels. The bus leaves every 30 minutes starting at 6.50 am. The last bus departs the airport about 12.15 am. For the latest city bus route call Information (tel 324-3211).

For the city bus (85c), take the No 20 Granville south on Granville. Transfer at 70th Avenue to the No 100 Airport. Total travel time is one hour.

Bus, LRT & Ferry Vancouver doesn't have a subway, but does have a widespread bus system and the new light rapid train, Skytrain, and ferry links. For local transit information call 324-3211. Try to avoid buses at rush hour as the traffic jams are unbelievable.

The bus fare is $1.15, but at rush hour goes up to $1.55 and exact change is required. All-day bus/ferry/Skytrain passes are $3; buy one at the Seabus or Skytrain stations.

The No 4 bus goes from downtown to the Youth Hostel; No 17 goes the opposite way. No 11 bus from Hastings goes to Stanley Park.

For the US border take bus No 22 'Knight Rd' from 4th Avenue and MacDonald. Get off at Melville and Dunsmuir and catch a White Rock No 351, 352, or 353 bus to the border.

For Swartz Bay, take the No 601 bus, 'South Delta', to Ladner. Take the No 640 bus, 'Valley to the Sea', to the Tsawwassen Ferry Terminal. One-way costs $4.

For Grouse Mountain take the No 246 bus from Georgia and Granville. Transfer to No 232 'Queens' to Grouse Mountain Skyride. There are buses to other attractions, like the Capilano Suspension Bridge.

Driving If you're driving, you'll notice the city doesn't have any expressways; everyone must travel through the city. Congestion is a big problem, especially around the bridges and right downtown. It's also very difficult to find a parking spot in the inner city.

BC Ferries A good, if expensive, government ferry system links the mainland with Vancouver Island in several places. The Tourist Office will have the latest schedules and fares. The two main routes are from Tsawwassen to Swartz Bay and from Horseshoe Bay to Nanaimo. The fare is $4.50 per adult, $16 per car. There are about 15 ferries in each direction daily in summer. There is usually a one or two-ferry wait, particularly on weekends and holidays. There are also ferries to the Strait Islands along the Sunshine Coast north to connect with Powell River. Horseshoe Bay is the departure point for ferries northward on the mainland.

Transferring from city buses downtown or at the hostel, you can get to Tsawwassen. On the other side, a city bus goes into Victoria.

Hitching Thumbing is legal and common within the city, and seems to be pretty good.

For hitching east take the No 9 bus from Broadway and Granville. Go to the end of the line, Boundary Rd. Walk south to Grandview Highway and stick your thumb out.

Bicycle Stanley Park Rentals (tel 681-5581) is in Stanley Park opposite the Stanley Park Bus Loop. Open seven days a week, they have three, five and 10-speeds and tandems. Bayshore Bicycles (tel 689-5071) at 1876 West Georgia also rents bikes.

Car Rentals Rent-A-Wreck (tel 876-7155),

225 Kingsway, charges $8.95 a day plus mileage and insurance.

Lo-Cost (tel 689-9664) is at 1105 Granville St. Rent-a-Car (tel 734-6622), 1122 West Broadway, is cheap. Canada Camper (tel 688-0511) down near the US. border rents campers good for three to four adults. Free delivery to the airport.

Seabus These super-modern catamarans zip back and forth between downtown and North Vancouver across the Burrard Inlet. The terminal in Vancouver is at the bottom of Granville, in North Vancouver; it's the bottom of Lonsdale. They leave every 15 minutes during weekdays, every half hour at other times, and cost $1.15. A transfer is usable on connecting buses. The trip lasts only 12 minutes but gives a good cruise of the harbour and at night offers an excellent view of the city skyline. Avoid rush hours when many commuters crawl aboard. At peak times the fare for this and the city buses is $1.55.

Tours Gray Line Bus Company (tel 681-8687) offers more than 15 tours, ranging from Vancouver itself to the immediate surroundings to an eight-day tour of the Rockies. Most tours begin at the Hotel Vancouver. All major hotels sell tickets. The most complete tour of Vancouver is called the Deluxe Grand City Tour. It costs $43, lasts 6 hours and will acquaint you with many varying districts within Vancouver. The tour stops at a few attractions. A shorter introduction to the city costs $15.

There are other tours, some cheaper, some more costly, that include visits to the Botanical Gardens and the Aquarium. One company tours the sights of North Vancouver and includes a ride up Grouse Mountain. This one lasts four hours and costs $32.

Another company with local area tours is Town Tours (tel 733-4711).

Pacific Coast Lines (tel 662-3222) operate a number of one-day excursions for about the same price as a normal bus ticket. It's at 150 Dunsmuir St. Some destinations are Vancouver Island, the Sunshine Coast and Fort Langley.

These companies charge about the same prices; they all have trips to Victoria. Landsea Tours use mini-buses but their tours are a little more costly.

A different sightseeing trip is the boat and train tour run by Harbour Ferries (tel 687-9558), which is at the foot of Denman St adjoining Stanley Park. The 6½-hour trip past good scenery goes up Howe Sound to Squamish. You'll travel one way by the MV *Britannia* and return by the Royal Hudson Steam Train. The cost is $40, $35 for students. The tour is not offered on Mondays or Tuesdays. Take your own lunch. They also run shorter harbour tours, narrated, but the cheap Seabus gives you much the same thing.

For a self-guided tour you can rent a cassette player and tape for $20. Renting the cassette only costs $10. The rentals include a map for you to follow in your own car. The tour takes about two hours. You can find out more at the Gray Line tour desk in the lobby of the Sheraton-Landmark Hotel, 1400 Robson St, 8 am to 6 pm.

City Nature Sightseeing (tel 254-5015), 2091 East 6th Avenue, offers personal and detailed but leisurely tours in and around the city specialising in flora, fauna and geology. Some driving and some walking is involved.

You can rent a boat at Granville Island (tel 682-6287).

Vancouver Island

Vancouver Island, the largest off the west coast of the Americas, ranges from rugged wilderness to the grand rooms of the provincial legislature.

Though 450 km in length, there are only 500,000 people and nearly all of them are along the south-eastern coast.

The geography is scenically varied.

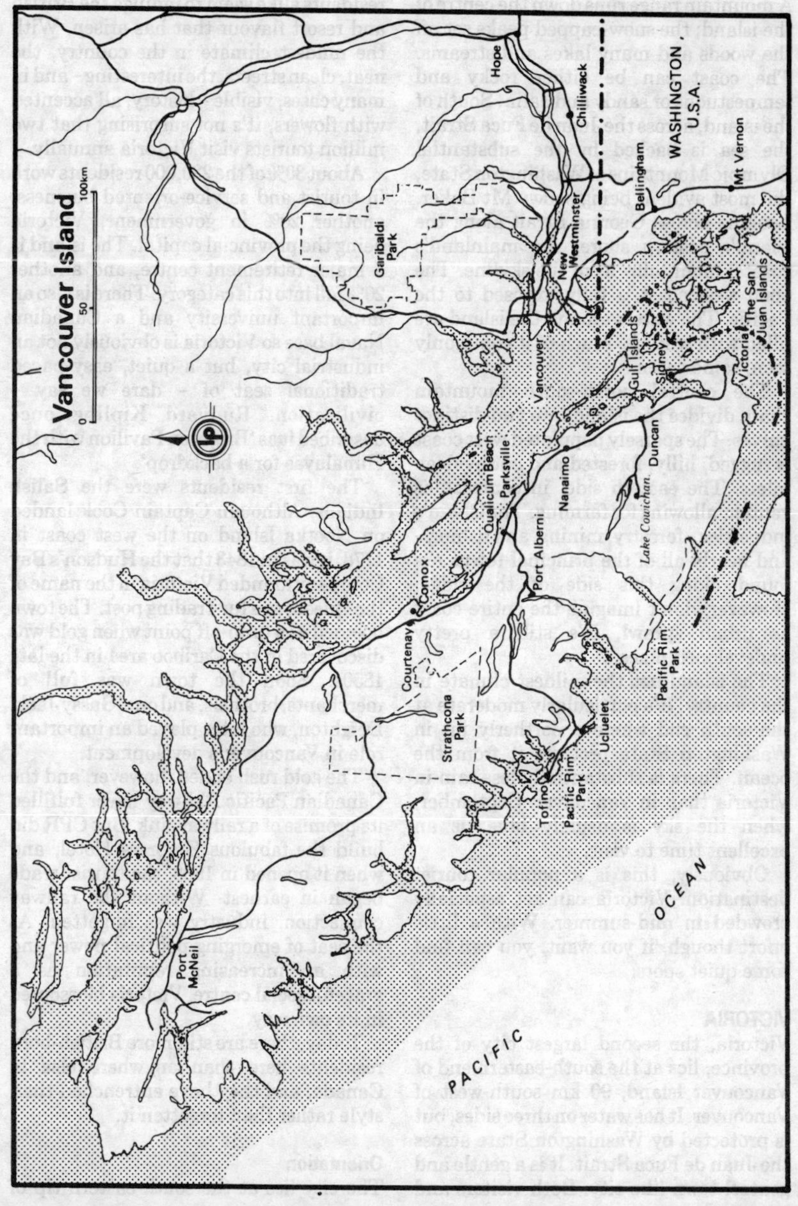
Vancouver Island
0
50
100km
Garibaldi Park
Hope
Chilliwack
WASHINGTON
U.S.A.
Bellingham
Mt Vernon
New Westminster
Vancouver
Gulf Islands
Sidney
Victoria
The San Juan Islands
Duncan
Nanaimo
Lake Cowichan
Qualicum Beach
Parksville
Port Alberni
Comox
Courtenay
Strathcona Park
Pacific Rim Park
Ucluelet
Pacific Rim Park
Tofino
Port McNeil
PACIFIC
OCEAN

A mountain range runs down the centre of the island; the snow-capped peaks set off the woods and many lakes and streams. The coast can be either rocky and tempestuous or sandy and calm. South of the island, across the Juan de Fuca Strait, the sea is backed by the substantial Olympic Mountains of Washington State, the most evident being snowy Mt Baker. Looking across Georgia Strait along the island's eastern shore, the mainland's coastal mountains form the skyline. The open west coast is fully exposed to the Pacific. The waters around the island are filled with wildlife, much of it commonly seen, some eaten.

The central north-south mountain chain divides the island into two distinct halves. The sparsely populated west coast is rugged, hilly, forested and cut by deep inlets. The eastern side, in contrast, is gentler, allowing for farming. The island's industries – forestry, mining, and fishing – and nearly all of the principal towns are found along this side of the ridge. However, don't imagine the entire coast as urban sprawl. It's still a pretty undeveloped place.

The island has the mildest climate in the country. It's particularly moderate at the south end where a northerly jut in Washington State protects it from the ocean. There is substantially less rain in Victoria than in Vancouver. September, when the sky is usually blue, is an excellent time to visit.

Obviously, this is a popular tourist destination. Victoria can get especially crowded in mid-summer. With a little effort though, if you want, you can find some quiet spots.

VICTORIA

Victoria, the second largest city of the province, lies at the south-eastern end of Vancouver Island, 90 km south-west of Vancouver. It has water on three sides, but is protected by Washington State across the Juan de Fuca Strait. It is a gentle and genteel town-like city. Both visitors and residents alike seem to indulge the British and resort flavour that has arisen. With the mildest climate in the country, the neat, clean streets, the interesting – and in many cases, visible – history, all accented with flowers, it's not surprising that two million tourists visit Victoria annually.

About 30% of the 230,000 residents work in tourist and service-oriented business, another 20% in government, Victoria being the provincial capital. The island is a major retirement centre, and another 20% fall into this category. There is also an important university and a Canadian Naval base so Victoria is obviously not an industrial city, but a quiet, easy-paced traditional seat of – dare we say – civilisation. Rudyard Kipling once described it as 'Brighton Pavilion with the Himalayas for a backdrop'.

The first residents were the Salish Indians. Although Captain Cook landed on Nootka Island on the west coast in 1778, it was in 1843 that the Hudson's Bay Company founded Victoria in the name of the Queen, as a fur-trading post. The town boomed as a drop-off point when gold was discovered in the Cariboo area in the late 1850s. Soon the town was full of merchants, brothels, and one 'Gassy Jack' Deighton, who later played an important role in Vancouver's development.

The gold rush ended, however, and the Canadian Pacific Railway never fulfilled its promise of a railway link. But CPR did build the fabulous Empress Hotel, and when it opened in 1908, the tourist trade began in earnest. Without the railway connection, industry was forgotten. As the seat of emerging political power and with an increasing reputation as a graceful social centre, Victoria blossomed in its own way.

Today, there are still more British-born residents here than anywhere else in Canada, and they have entrenched their style rather than forgotten it.

Orientation

The city lies at the south-eastern tip of

Vancouver Island, actually closer to the USA than the Canadian mainland. The downtown area is simply laid out and really not very large. Bounded on two sides by water, the central area of the city is easy and pleasant to explore on foot, so you'll have little trouble getting your bearings. The city is low, with very few high-rises, enabling you to see a long way.

The focal point is Inner Harbour, a section of Victoria Harbour which fronts several of the most important structures. Facing out to Inner Harbour across its lawns is the Empress Hotel, still very much the hub of the wheel. Across the way are the enormous Provincial Parliament Buildings. In between the two, on the corner beside the Netherlands Carillon bell tower, is the Provincial Museum. To the east of it is Thunderbird Park with its totems, and south of this is Beacon Hill Park, the city's largest. Surrounding the park, down to the ocean, are well-kept residential houses, many with attractive lawns and gardens.

North up Wharf St from the Empress Hotel is the Central Tourist Office at the corner of Inner Harbour. Following Wharf along the water will take you through Old Town, the original area of Victoria which has now been restored.

Meeting Wharf St at right angles are Fort, Yates and Johnson. Just up a few steps from Wharf is Bastion Square, the Old Town's square, lined with historic buildings.

Parallel to Wharf and a couple of blocks east is Government St, one of the major downtown streets. It holds numerous government buildings, including the large Central Post Office between Yates and Bastion Square. Opposite the post office is Trounce Alley, once the tiny by-way where miners sold their gold, now renovated with boutiques - some selling gold.

Near the harbour at Johnson and Wharf is Market Square, two storeys of shops and restaurants built around a courtyard shaded by trees. The wooden stairs and balconies make the place seem like part of a pioneer museum.

One block east is Douglas, the main commercial street of Victoria. The area around Douglas, Government and Bastion Square is the centre of the business area, with banks, offices and department stores.

City Hall is at Douglas and Cormorant. The brownish-purple building with the mansard roof, built in 1890, is worth noting. With the clock tower and flowers, it's a very accessible-looking municipal office. Most look intimidating.

Fort St from around Blanchard up a few blocks away from town has numerous antique and bric-a-brac shops. Good browsing.

On Fort St between Douglas and Quadra there are numerous antique shops.

East again is Blanchard, running near the edge of the downtown area. Going further leads you into residential areas. Marine Drive along the waterfront east of town is a wealthy district. There are parks and beaches along the Drive.

The northern boundary of downtown is Fisgard, an interesting street for its Chinese-style buildings, including one that houses the Chinese Public School. It has a pagoda-type roof.

Around Fisgard and Government is a small Chinatown, with Oriental-style street lamps, Chinese characters on the street signs, and, of course, restaurants. The area is remarkably neat and clean but very colourful due mainly to the colour schemes recently painted on the buildings. Fan Tan Alley, halfway between Government and Wharf off Fisgard, has many crafts and artisans. About 125 years ago when this, Canada's first Chinatown, was in its heyday and much bigger, the alley was lined with opium dens and gambling houses.

Both Douglas and Blanchard lead north out of the city to either Highway 1 or Highway 17 for the Swartz Bay Ferry

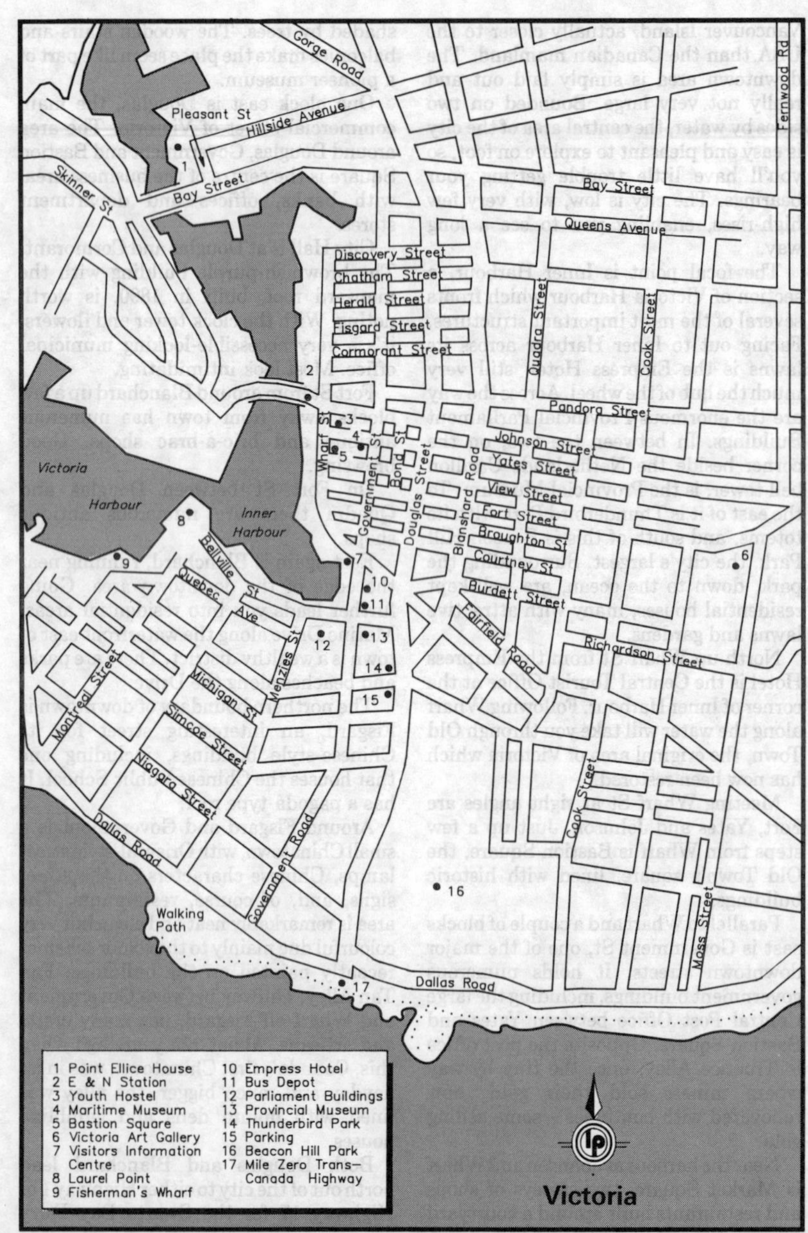
Gorge Road
Pleasant St
Hillside Avenue
Skinner St
Bay Street
Bay Street
Queens Avenue
Fernwood Rd
Discovery Street
Chatham Street
Herald Street
Fisgard Street
Cormorant Street
Quadra Street
Cook Street
Pandora Street
Johnson Street
Yates Street
View Street
Fort Street
Broughton St
Courtney St
Burdett Street
Richardson Street
Wharf St
Government St
Bond St
Douglas Street
Blanshard Road
Fairfield Road
Victoria
Harbour
Inner
Harbour
Bellville St
Quebec Ave
Menzies St
Montreal Street
Michigan St
Simcoe Street
Niagara Street
Dallas Road
Government Road
Cook Street
Moss Street
Walking Path
Dallas Road
1 Point Ellice House
2 E & N Station
3 Youth Hostel
4 Maritime Museum
5 Bastion Square
6 Victoria Art Gallery
7 Visitors Information Centre
8 Laurel Point
9 Fisherman's Wharf
10 Empress Hotel
11 Bus Depot
12 Parliament Buildings
13 Provincial Museum
14 Thunderbird Park
15 Parking
16 Beacon Hill Park
17 Mile Zero Trans-Canada Highway
lp
Victoria

Terminal. Highway 1A, which cuts across both Douglas and Blanchard, runs west along the gorge and is one area of heavy motel concentration. Highway 1A meets up with Highway 1 for Nanaimo further west.

Information

The Visitor Information Centre (tel 382-2127) is on the water at Inner Harbour, across from the Empress Hotel. The address is 812 Wharf St. There is also an office two km from the Swartz Bay ferry landing.

Things to See

Victoria has just about every kind of commercial attraction you can imagine, and more. Most charge $4 to $6 and for my money aren't worth it, although if there's something you're particularly interested in, you may find it worthwhile. The Tourist Office will have pamphlets on all these diversions. There are gardens, replicas and museums of every sort, and more than a few novelty attractions. Some are excellent, others created just for the heavy tourist trade.

Provincial Museum of Natural History & Anthropology

This excellent museum is a must, even for non-museum-goers. This is so, even though admission has recently and controversially jumped from free to $5. The wide variety of displays is artistically arranged, beautifully lit and accompanied by informative, succinct explanations. Models and display cases are incredibly realistic, making the traditionally dry manner of presentation obsolete. There are sections on geology, vegetation, wildlife and ethnology.

In the areas devoted to the BC Indians, see the detailed models of villages, the 1914 documentary film, *In the Land of the War Canoes* on the Kwakiutl Indians, and the rock on which a man fell from the sky. Also look at the Haida craftwork in argillate, a dense black carbon shale. The pipes represent some of the best aboriginal art anywhere.

There's a town made up of 19th-century and early 20th-century buildings and goods, including a Model T Ford. Chaplin movies are shown in the old movie theatre. They also have an interesting collection of artefacts from the 1920s through the 1970s.

The museum is open daily 9.30 to 7 pm in summer, until 5.30 pm in winter.

Parliament Buildings

These are dominated by the palatial Victorian building facing Inner Harbour on the corner across from the Empress Hotel. This multi-turreted structure was designed by Francis Rattenbury and finished in 1898. On top is a figure of Captain George Vancouver, the first British navigator to circle Vancouver Island. Rattenbury also designed the Empress Hotel and Parthenon-like Wax Museum which was once a CP ticket office.

There are free tours of the building from 8.30 am to 5 pm Monday to Friday. They last about 20 minutes and are worthwhile. The paintings in the lower rotunda depict scenes from Canadian history. Around the upper rotunda are paintings of four of British Columbia's main industries. The Legislative Chamber is where all the laws of British Columbia are made. You can view the debates from the public gallery when the session is in. The site should actually be called the Legislative Buildings because provincially, there is only one house; there is no Senate as in the true Parliament Buildings in Ottawa.

On the lawn is a statue of Queen Victoria and a sequoia tree from California planted in the 1860s. The building is spectacularly lit at night. In the Legislative Library is the dagger that Captain Cook was murdered with.

Old Town

The original Victoria was centred along

Wharf St and Bastion Square. This was where the first fur-trading ships moored. The street was once busy with miners, merchants and all those heading for the Klondike.

Bastion Square held the courthouse, the gaol, the gallows and the whorehouse.

At the foot of Fort Street on Wharf is where Fort Victoria once stood. Next door is the Provincial Capital Commission Planning Office. All that remains of the fort are a couple of steel moorings, marked by a plaque in a small grassy square.

Up a few steps from Wharf St is Bastion Square. The whole area has been restored and re-developed. The square is pleasant for strolling or sitting and holds the Maritime Museum. Many of the old buildings are now restaurants, boutiques and galleries. A few are offices.

The same is true of Wharf St, where some of the old buildings have been interestingly painted in two-tone pastels. Check out Peter London's of Edinburgh Antiques Shop; he's got some nifty items.

Further north up Wharf St you'll come to Market Square on the left. This is a quadrangle of buildings dating from between 1894 and 1900. Renovated in 1975, it now has 40 shops and restaurants in this compact, attractive area.

Art Gallery of Greater Victoria

The gallery (tel 384-4101) is best known for its excellent Asian art, including the Japanese and Chinese collections, but it has artworks from around the world and from widely varying periods of history – pre-Colombian Latin American objects through to contemporary Canadian painting. There are some good Inuit pieces. It's in a Victorian mansion at 1040 Moss St, 1½ km east of downtown, just off Fort St. Take the No 11 Uplands bus, or No 14 University from downtown. Open 10 am to 5 pm, Sunday from 1 pm. Closed Monday. Admission $1.50, students 75c. They have a restaurant too.

Emily Carr Gallery

At 1107 Wharf St, this gallery pays homage to one of Canada's best-known and liked painters, a native of Victoria. Many of her paintings included totem poles of the west coast Indians. The gallery shows changing exhibits and four films daily about the life and career of Carr. Admission is free. Open 10 am to 8 pm in summer, 10 am to 4 pm Tuesday to Saturday in winter. Prints from originals are sold.

Maritime Museum

This collection of artefacts, models, photographs and naval memorabilia is for nautical buffs only. They'll find it at 28 Bastion Square, near Government St at the big anchor. Open 10 am to 4 pm, admission $3, students $1.

Beacon Hill Park

Just south-east from downtown, this 62-hectare park is Victoria's largest. It's a very well cared for oasis of trees, flowers, ponds and pathways. Trees of this size you don't see anywhere but on the west coast. Also in the park is the 'world's tallest totem'. And a cricket pitch (told you it was British here). The southern edge overlooks the ocean and offers good views of the coastline. At the look-out above Dallas Rd is a direction marker pointing out various places, eg Seattle, and in the case of mountains their elevations. At the south-west corner of the park, the path along the water meets the Mile 0 marker, the Pacific terminal of the Trans-Canada Highway.

Thunderbird Park

This is a small but interesting strip of grass beside the Provincial Museum. It holds a collection of both plain wooden and recently painted totem poles. Some of them are labelled.

Butchard Gardens

If you're coming from the east you probably noticed the signs for this attraction beginning in Banff. They are without a doubt the most publicised of all Victoria's sights. No doubt the gardens are beautiful and extensive, but it's $7 a ticket, making it the costliest admission in town. Whether it's worth it I can't say – depends on you and your budget.

Parts of the gardens are sectioned into specialties like the English Rose Garden and the Japanese Garden. There are hundreds of species of trees, bushes and flowers. You can walk through in about 1½ hours, but linger as long as you wish.

In the evenings, from mid-July through September, the gardens are illuminated, giving a very different effect from daylight. There are also concerts and puppet shows given around dusk. On Saturday night there is a spectacular French fireworks display set to music – no extra charge.

Open 9 am to 10 pm daily, the gardens (tel 656-2066) are about 15 km north-west of downtown on Saanich Inlet, at the foot of Keating Cross Rd. City buses go within one km weekdays, three km on Sundays.

Classic Car Museum
This museum (tel 382-7118) has 40 beauties on display for auto lovers, ranging from the 1904 Olds to the 1967 Lincoln Limo. The address is 813 Douglas St.

Miniature World
Here you'll find numerous layouts depicting in exacting detail different themes, for example, the world of Dickens. The highlight is a large model train representing the development of the Canadian Pacific Railway from 1885 to 1915. The model is very realistic. Open daily. The address is 635 Humboldt, beside the Empress Hotel.

English Village
This is a gimmicky but well-done re-creation of some English Tudor-style buildings. Highlights are the replica of Shakespeare's birthplace and the thatched cottage of his wife, Anne Hathaway. The village (tel 388-4353) is authentically furnished in 16th-century antiques. It's at 429 Lampson, across the harbour from the Empress Hotel, and is open daily all year.

Crystal Gardens
This seems to be one of the popular commercial attractions but it's not real cheap. Designed by (who else?) Francis Rattenbury it was fashioned after London's Crystal Palace and built in 1925. Once a focal point for the social elite, it was restored in 1977 as a visitor attraction as well as remaining a venue for splashy events. The principal draw is the indoor tearoom overlooking a tropical-like garden complete with wildlife.

Helmcken House
Right beside the Provincial Museum, this is the oldest house in British Columbia that has remained unchanged. The rooms are shown much the way they would have appeared in the early 1850s.

John Helmcken, a doctor and politician, was very active in the local community. The house contains much period furniture and examples of decorations and implements. The staff is friendly and helpful, and a visit is free. Open Tuesday to Sunday 10 am to 5 pm.

Point Ellice House
This beautifully kept house of 1861 was sold in 1868 for $2500. The buyer, Peter O'Reilly, was a member of government and a successful businessman. Many of the house's immaculate furnishings belonged to him and his wife. Admission is free; same hours as Helmcken House. It's at 2616 Pleasant St, off Bay St at Point Ellice Bridge.

Craigflower Manor
This is the third house in the historical set. The manor house was built by Kenneth McKenzie in 1856. It was the central home in the first farming community on Vancouver Island, beginning the change from a fur-trading settlement to a

permanent one. Built to remind McKenzie of Scotland, the house was decorated with the many furnishings he brought over from his homeland. It became a social centre for Fort Victoria and the Esquimalt Naval Base, as the family entertained frequently. Admission is free; open weekdays. It's at 110 Island Highway (tel 383-7876), a little way out from town, toward Highway 1.

Regents Park House

At 1501 Fort St is a large award-winning restored Victoria Italianate house from 1855. It has a collection of antiques and Victorian furnishings as well as eight sizeable fireplaces. You'll notice the smell of age as soon as you enter. Admission is $2, and it's open from 1 to 6 pm daily. It's really a bit too far to walk, but it's a short bus ride.

Fort Rodd Historic Park

This scenic 18-hectare park overlooking Esquimalt Harbour contains some historical points of interest. There are the remnants of three turn-of-the-century gun batteries. These artillery installations were built to protect the naval base in the bay. Until 1956 these facilities were regularly updated, but then such a defence system was deemed obsolete.

Also in the park is Fisgard Lighthouse, which still works and has been in continuous use since 1860. Too bad all machinery doesn't do so well. It was the first lighthouse to shine its beam across the water in western Canada. There are informative signs around the park, as well as guides. Open daily 9 am to sunset. Free.

The park is about 12 km north-west from downtown Victoria, off Ocean Boulevard on the far side of Esquimalt Harbour.

Government House

This is the official residence of the province's lieutenant-governor. The impressive grounds are open to the public. The building is not far from the art gallery, away from downtown, on Rockland Avenue.

Craigdarroch Castle

Near the Government House, but off Fort St on Craigdarroch, this rather impressive home was built in the mid-1880s by Robert Dunsmuir, a coal millionaire, for himself and his wife. The interior remains decorated in the manner of that time. Free admission.

Sealand

Sealand (tel 598-3373) is at 1327 Beach Drive at Oak Bay Marina. This is Canada's largest oceanarium and includes octopi, seals, sea lions, sharks and many other creatures. The feature is a show put on by a 5000-kg killer whale. Tickets are $5. From the Inner Harbour double-decker buses run to Sealand every 15 minutes.

Fisherman's Wharf

This is on Victoria Harbour around the bay from the Inner Harbour. It's at the end of Dallas Rd and is worth a look. You can walk from downtown around Laurel Point. It's a busy spot with fishing boats and pleasure craft coming and going. Try the fish & chips at *Barb's*, or you can sometimes buy fresh seafood from the boats or the little shed. At one end of the dock check out the moored houseboats – there are a few that wouldn't be bad to call home.

Scenic Marine Drive

Starting either from Fisherman's Wharf or Beacon Hill Park, the Marine Drive skirts the coast on Dallas Rd and then Beach Drive. There are views over the sea. At Marine Park there is an underwater sanctuary at the breakwater on which you can walk out. There's also a waterfront walk along here. The road continues past some of Victoria's wealthiest neighbourhoods and Oak Bay, a retirement community. You'll see many parks and a beach or two along the way. The double-decker buses include Marine Drive in their tours. The drive also makes a good bike trip.

Lookouts

At the end of Shelbourne St, the Mount Douglas Park Lookout provides views over the Saanich Peninsula, the strait, islands and over to Washington. Good views are also to be had at Mount Tolmie Park Lookout off Richmond Avenue.

Dominion Astrophysical Observatory

Here you can peer out to space through a 72-inch telescope. There is also equipment used to record earthquakes. This is also out of the centre but further at 5071 West Saanich Rd on Little Saanich Mountain.

Events

The Victoria Day's Festival during the fourth week of May features a parade, performances by the town's ethnic groups, stage shows and many sporting events. Many of the townspeople dress in Victorian-style clothes, and some shopkeepers dress their windows in period manner.

The Swiftsure, a major sailing race, ends the event. The last weekend can get pretty wild – a real street party.

The start of the annual Victoria-to-Maui Yacht Race is another cause for celebration.

Activities

Diving & Fishing The waters around Victoria are renowned for both diving and deep-sea fishing, the latter with salmon being the top prize. There are numerous shops and charters catering to these activities. There are lakes and streams within an hour or two of Victoria as well as up-island, good for freshwater fishing for trout and/or salmon. Campbell River is good salmon water. The Tourist Office can supply you with more information on fishing.

For deep-sea fishing there are scores of charter companies offering trips of varying lengths. I would think the minimum cost is around $20 to $25. Most supply all equipment, bait and even coffee.

Aside from excellent fishing (a friend and I caught a delicious dinner of rock and ling cod not far from Oak Bay last trip out here) the waters of Georgia Strait are renowned for world-class diving. The undersea life is tremendously varied and has been featured in National Geographic. Although cool, of course, visibility is best in late winter and early spring, when the plankton has decreased. There are diving charters and equipment shops around the island. There's an underwater park right at Ogden Point by the pier, with kelp 'forests' and quite a bit of sea life.

Swimming One of the best swimming places is known as the Sooke potholes, about an hour's drive from town, by the town of Sooke on the south shore. Watch for signs at Milne's Landing. You can find your own swimming hole but the water ain't balmy. Good picnicking, some walking trails. Don't get caught drinking: the fines are heavy.

Another popular spot is Thetis Lake Municipal Park not too far from town (20 mins), off Highway 1 up-island. It's very busy at the main beach but if you hike around the lake you'll find a quiet spot where bathing suits can be discarded.

Other Windsurfing is also popular, and both rentals and lessons are available. One company to try is Ocean Wind on Cadboro Bay near the University. Willow Beach is the local hangout; there's windsurfing here too.

A few people offer horseback trips – overnight camping in the nearby highlands is two hours away.

The Crystal Pool Recreation Centre at Quadra and Wark – an easy walk from downtown – has a pool, sauna, whirlpool and locker rooms, $1.75.

Places to Stay

Hostels There's a good, central *Youth*

Hostel (tel 385-5313) at 516 Yates. It has room for 100, and a kitchen, good noticeboard and adjacent camping shop. Memberships are available. The cost is $8, $10 for non-members. Linen $1. The door's locked at midnight. Find out here about the good mini-hostels around the island, many of them in convenient or relatively remote places.

The *Cool Aid Hostel* (tel 384-3634), is actually a half-way-type place for out-patients or for those on the skids or out of work. It takes in travellers, too. The place is not great and is a ways from town at 1900 Fernwood, at Gladstone; take a No 10 bus from Woolworth's downtown. The rate is $8.

The *YM-YWCA* (tel 386-7511) are both in the same building at 800 Courtney St. The residence is for women only; they have 31 beds in single and double rooms. Cost is about $18.50 for singles, $29 for doubles. There's a cafeteria that anyone can use, and a swimming pool. Closed Sundays.

The *University of Victoria* rents rooms from 1 May to the end of August. The rate is $17.50 for a single but only twice that for three people in a room. Breakfast is included. There are several cafeterias on campus and facilities to make use of. Contact the Co-Ordinator of Residence Services (tel 721-8395). The No 14 bus on Douglas goes to the campus. It's about 20 minutes from downtown.

Bed & Breakfasts This form of accommodation is very big in town and makes a real alternative to standard hotels. There are several B&B associations that approve members, list them and make reservations at one central office. Prices run to about $30 for singles, $45 to $50 doubles.

Some associations to try are VIP (tel 477-5604) at 1786 Teakwood Rd, Victoria Bed & Breakfast (tel 385-2332) at 1054 Summit Avenue, and Bed & Breakfast in Heritage Homes (tel 384-4014) at 809 Fort St. This latter has only turn-of-the-century homes within three km of downtown. Good prices, too. They'd be my first choice. Old Victoria Registry (tel 592-5038) uses mansions only.

Many other places advertise independently; see the pamphlets at the Tourist Office. Here are a few.

The Battery St Guest House (tel 385-4632) is central at 670 Battery St. It's an old house from 1898 run by a Dutch woman. Singles cost from $25 to $30, doubles from $40 to $50.

Craigmyle Guest House (tel 595-5411), 1037 Craigdarroch Rd, about 1½ km from downtown, is next to Craigdarroch Castle. Singles/doubles are $32/47, including breakfast.

Laird House (tel 384-3177), at 134 St Andrews St, is a 15-minute walk to downtown. The building dates from 1912. They will pick up from ferries or bus station, and offer free coffee and tea all day. Non-smokers only.

Bryn Wyn Guest House the blue house at 809 Burnett is as close to the centre as any house in town.

Hotels – bottom end There are a good many reasonable places right in the downtown area. Many are cheaper after 1 October. I'm listing a lot of accommodation because the city really fills up in summer.

First opened in 1897, the *Cherry Bank Hotel* (tel 385-5380), 825 Burdett Avenue, is up the hill a few blocks from downtown, opposite the law courts – close to Beacon Hill Park. It's simple but good value at $30/32 for singles/doubles, including breakfast. Rooms don't have TV or phone but there are a bar and restaurant on the premises.

At the *Sussex Apartment Hotel* (tel 386-3441), 1001 Douglas, all rooms come with private bath and shower. Singles/doubles cost $36/47. Apartment units with kitchen and dinettes are available too: singles/doubles $45/54. They are clean and good, suitable for families.

Hotel Douglas (tel 383-4157), centrally located at the corner of Douglas and

Pandora, offers rooms at $38/42 for singles/doubles. There is a restaurant and bar downstairs. The *Strathcona* (tel 383-7137), 919 Douglas St, is better but still moderately priced, with singles/doubles for $45/53. The good, modern rooms come with bath and TV. There is free parking, and several bars and a restaurant.

The *Fairfield* (tel 386-1621) is more basic and not really geared to visitors, but it's cheap and perfectly located on the corner of Douglas and Cormorant. It's an old place; many of the rooms have cooking facilities. Rates are about $20/25 for singles/doubles, or $100 a week.

A similar place is the *Ritz* (tel 383-1021) at 710 Fort. It's mainly rented long-term to local people but visitors are taken.

Better but good value is the *James Bay Inn* (tel 384-7151). It's the big, old place with bay windows at 270 Government St, a few blocks from downtown in a residential area of small, attractive houses. Prices vary a lot: singles are $23 to $45, doubles $33 to $95. Triples are also available; in fact, some rooms sleep as many as six – a good bargain. Others have kitchens. There's a TV room, and a bar, restaurant and food machines downstairs.

Hotels – middle *Helm's Inn* (tel 385-5767), 668 Superior St, offers kitchen units at singles/doubles $55.

Best Western Olympic Hotel (tel 388-5513), 642 Johnson St, has kitchenettes at $60/65 for singles/doubles.

Dominion Hotel (tel 384-4136), 756 Yates St, has singles/doubles for $60/65.

Hotels – top end The *Empress Hotel* (tel 348-8111), 721 Government St, charges $100/145 for singles/doubles.

Oak Bay Beach Hotel (tel 598-4556), 1175 Beach Drive, has rooms ranging from $60 to $260.

Courtyard Inn (tel 385-6787), 850 Blanchard St, charges $79/89 for singles/doubles.

Laurel Point Inn, generally considered the best of all, is also the most expensive.

Motels *Doric Motel* (tel 386-2481), 3025 Douglas St, is a five-minute drive from downtown. It offers TV, laundromat and free coffee. Singles/doubles for $36/46. Kitchen $5 extra.

Crystal Court Motel (tel 384-0551) is at 701 Belleville, downtown beside the bus station and the Provincial Museum. Available for sleeping or housekeeping. Singles/doubles are $38/41, and a kitchen costs just $2 more. There's TV, radio and phones. It's white, blue and gold.

A good area for motels is along Gorge Rd, also called Highway 1A, not far north-west from downtown. A little further and the road becomes Island Highway 1A.

Budget Host Maple Leaf Inn (tel 388-9901), 120 Gorge Rd East, has a sauna, heated pool and laundromat. Singles range from $32 to $44, doubles from $34 to $44.

Capri Motel (tel 384-0521) is at 21 Gorge Rd East. Singles range from $30 to $38, doubles $34 to $42. It's a five-minute drive to town.

Gorge Motel (tel 384-6675) is at 7 Gorge Rd West. Singles are from $30 to $37, doubles $37 to $47.

The *Royal Victoria*, at 230 Gorge Rd East, charges $32 to $42 for singles and $36 to $46 for doubles. There's a heated pool and laundromat, and some rooms come with a kitchen.

Cheaper is the *Casa Linda* at 364 Goldstream Avenue (Highway 1A).

Camping Closest to town is *Fort Victoria Park* (tel 479-8112), at 340 Island Highway 1A, 6½ km from the city centre. They have 150 camping spots. There's a bus stop at the gate. The site has full facilities. The charges for two people are $10 to $14.

Oak Park Trailer Court (tel 478-1823), 616 Goldstream Avenue (Highway 1A), has grassed campsites. Two people $10 to $12.

Thetis Lake Campground (tel 478-3845) is at 1938 Trans-Canada, Rural Route 6. It's about a 15-minute drive from the city centre. All facilities are available, including those for laundry. There's a store and lake swimming close by. Two people $10. Open all year.

The Tourist Office can tell you of other campsites not too far from town.

Places to Eat

Though a small city, Victoria has a varied array of restaurants, partially due to all the visitors who must be fed. Prices are generally good, and the fish & chips are the best I've had anywhere – including England. In the list below are restaurants for full meals, then places for lighter lunches and sandwiches, and finally cafés and snack places.

We might as well start at the *Empress Hotel*. They have a very good lunch buffet – soups, salads, meats and then an array of desserts – all you can eat for $10.95. It's offered every day but Sunday in the Empress Room.

The *Bengal Lounge*, also in the hotel, is a real treat. Every day they serve a different curry for $7.75 (other daily specials are less). The service and the style make it well worth the price. There is a tiger skin on the wall; it's all very colonially British. Downstairs in the *Beaver Pub*, they serve a cheaper lunch.

For dinners the *Spare Rib House* in the Cherry Bank Hotel is good. They serve rib dinners – the specialty at $8 – and steaks as well. There's a children's menu too. The restaurant features live entertainment.

Pescado's, 314 Government, is a seafood restaurant with a good selection of local sealife offered at very reasonable prices. This is probably the cheapest place to have a salmon dinner and it's simply but attractively decorated to boot.

Other dining rooms offer good lunch specials but are fairly pricey in the evenings. *Pagliacci's* on Broad St between Fort and Broughton is mainly Italian. It's $6 for lunch, a little more than twice that for dinner. It's one of the 'in' spots in town and the food is good.

Taj Mahal is an Indian restaurant at 679 Herald St, near Chinatown. They have a good selection, including vegetarian, and food is spiced as hot as you like. It's not cheap. Open every day. Another is the *Tandoor* for dinner only, at 1010 Fort St.

For a splurge try *La Petite Colombe Café* on Broughton near Government. They have crepes but the main fare is seafood in French style. With appetiser, lunch is about $10, dinner $20. It's small, quiet and has a good reputation. Or try *Ports* in Inner Harbour Square Mall. They offer fresh seafood, steaks and a view. You can get a good meal at the *French Connection*, 281 Menzies, a couple of blocks from the Parliament Building. Full table d'hôte costs $14.95.

The best seafood house in town is *Chauney's*, 614 Humboldt.

Much more modest and casual is the *Day & Night* at 620 Yates. It's good for any meal, with good value plain food, including the cheapest breakfast in town. Full meals, soup to dessert, cost from $5 to $6. Or try the *Maple Leaf* on Douglas, with old photos of BC.

Smitty's, at 850 Douglas is an old standby, best for cheap pancake breakfasts.

Sunshines at 1219 Wharf is a good, inexpensive health food/vegetarian spot serving soups and veggie burgers. *Studio Cafe* is a small, arty café serving felafels and pitta pizzas. Sandwiches $3. It's on Johnson near Broad. The café has a noticeboard listing counterculture and other events. Open to 8 pm, closed Sundays.

The fish & chips are excellent in Victoria and there are several outlets for them. Try *Old Victoria English Fish 'n' Chips* at 1316 Broad St. Small, medium and large orders all come with chowder and bread. Beer from around the world is offered. Open every day.

Burrito Express, 1315 Blanchard, has quick Mexican items such as tacos for under $5. It's a pleasant little place and is licenced. *Los Flores*, 536 Yates, is another inexpensive Mexican place but with an outdoor courtyard. Canadian breakfast is served too, and the hostel is nearby. Another cheap but good place is busy *Eugene's* at 1218 Broad. Simple, basic Greek foods. Closed Sunday. For hamburgers, the *Cultured Cow*, corner of Blanchard and Fort, specialises in them. Unfortunately, I found them expensive and nothing special.

Market Square has several places to munch at; try *Annabel's* for sandwiches, and the *Bavarian Bakery* for good bread.

Chinatown, marked by the Gate of Harmonious Interest over Fisgard, has its usual share of eating spots. The *Don Mee*, serving Cantonese food at 538 Fisgard, is the poshest. Combination plates are good value at lunch. The *Foo Hong* is very small and very basic yet has good, simple Cantonese food.

Cafés As befits a tourist town, especially one with British roots, there are numerous cafés and tea shops around town. *Sam's Deli* under the maroon awnings at Wharf and Government, diagonally opposite the main Tourist Office, is a perfect spot for an espresso and writing a postcard. There are about 10 tables outside on the sidewalk and more inside, where the walls are covered in 1920s and 1930s posters. This is a popular place with a European flavour. They serve soups, salads and sandwiches.

Demitasse, corner of Blanchard and Johnson, is a tiny café serving various coffees and sandwiches. Espresso is 85c, and they also serve café au lait. You can get a continental breakfast or croissant with camembert, fruit and a coffee any time of day.

The Old Town Cafe at 535 has expanded and moved across the street from last visit but is still a low-key, inexpensive light food cafe. The *Herald St Caffe*, 546 Herald is busy after 10 pm.

For afternoon tea, the tradition is upheld in the lobby of the *Empress Hotel*. Just don't take one of the regulars' seats – you may get a smack with a cane. A good alternative is *Murchie's Tea Room* on Government St in the new Eaton Centre. Murchie's is a west coast tea merchant with, I think, the best teas available, and a decadent assortment of pastries. Scones with strawberry jam and Devon cream cost $2.25. *The Victorian Tea Room* at 919

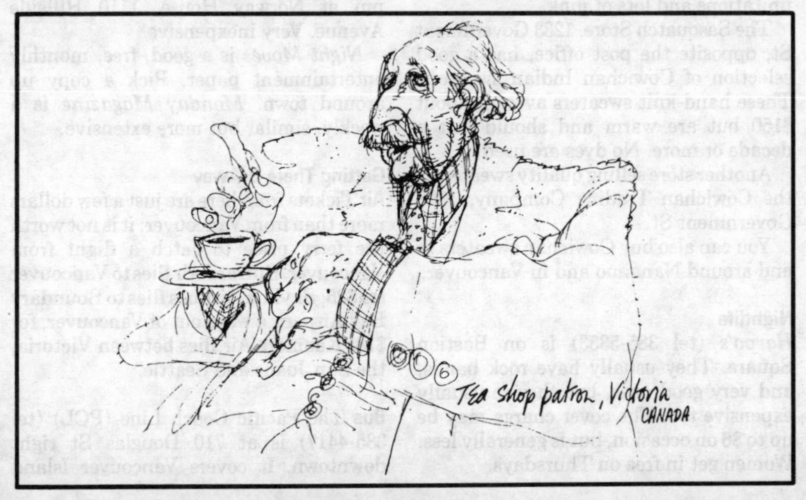

Fort, away from the crowds somewhat is more formal in style and decor. The most popular place with the locals is away from the centre at 2250 Oak Bay Avenue, the *Blethering Place*.

The Causeway Cafe, right on the harbour, below the Tourist Office, with a few tables outside is a nice spot for an afternoon brew. And, lastly, *Roger's Chocolate* dating from 1855 is a treat to both nose and tongue. It's at 913 Government. Try one (or more) of the Victoria creams, chocolate-covered discs in 15 flavours at $1.25. Everything is made on the premises.

Things to Buy

For the best in native Indian arts or crafts, go to Arts of the Raven on Douglas St.

Canadian Impressions, a store on Douglas near the Tourist Office, specialises in Indian crafts and has some quality items. Check the Indian prints upstairs, $25 to $150. The greeting cards – replicas of the prints, but signed by the artist – make good presents or souvenirs at $3.

There are a number of craft shops along Douglas selling sweaters, moccasins, carvings and prints. Be careful; the good stuff is expensive. There are lots of imitations and lots of junk.

The Sasquatch Store, 1233 Government St, opposite the post office, has a good selection of Cowichan Indian sweaters. These hand-knit sweaters average about $150 but are warm and should last a decade or more. No dyes are used.

Another store selling quality sweaters is the Cowichan Trading Company, 1328 Government St.

You can also buy Cowichan sweaters in and around Nanaimo and in Vancouver.

Nightlife

Harpo's (tel 385-5333) is on Bastion Square. They usually have rock bands, and very good ones, but they're usually expensive too. The cover charge may be up to $6 on occasion, but is generally less. Women get in free on Thursdays.

Merlin's Nightclub (tel 388-6021) at 1208 Wharf St, features rock music. It's on the Inner Harbour, down the stone staircase, opposite Bastion Square. Cover charge is $2 to $3. Amateur comedy nights are held on Thursdays. Merlin's opens at 8 pm; for a younger, raunchier crowd.

The *Alhambra Club* is the rhythm & blues club, with ventures into blues or jazz. Somewhat dressy. It's in the hotel of the same name, Government St. Free before 9.30 pm.

In the same building as the *Strathcona Hotel*, 919 Douglas, there are at least four or five bars – most of them discos charging $3 admission. *Old Forge, Ivy's* and *The Sting* are open until 2 am.

Open Space Gallery, 510 Fort, presents young poets, dancers and musicians.

A pub worth getting to is *Spinnaker's*, 308 Catherine St, right on the water of Victoria Harbour off Esquimalt Rd west of downtown. The attraction is the variety of excellent beer made in-house. In fact, this was Canada's first brew pub.

At 514 Fort is *Yuk Yuk's*, one of a chain of comedy houses, featuring stand-up comics.

The *Victoria Music Society* has a coffee house with live music every Sunday at 8 pm at Norway House, 1110 Hillside Avenue. Very inexpensive.

Night Moves is a good, free, monthly entertainment paper. Pick a copy up around town. *Monday Magazine* is a weekly, similar but more extensive.

Getting There & Away

Air Tickets from here are just a few dollars more than from Vancouver; it is not worth the ferry price to catch a flight from Vancouver. Burrard Air flies to Vancouver for $25; Skylink Airlines flies to Boundary Bay Airport, a ways out of Vancouver, for $18; Kenmore Air flies between Victoria, the San Juans and Seattle.

Bus The Pacific Coach Line (PCL) (tel 385-4417) is at 710 Douglas St right downtown. It covers Vancouver Island

and some of the south BC mainland. There's a bus to Vancouver every hour or two, between 6 am and 9 pm; cost is $15.25 including ferry. Same price to Vancouver Airport.

Island Coach Lines covers Vancouver Island. To Nanaimo and north Island points, there are about 10 buses a day including to Port Alberni, Courtenay, Gold River. Fares: to Nanaimo $9.80, Port Alberni $19.60.

You can get a bus for Seattle once daily for $29, which includes the ferry. It takes seven hours.

Train The VIA Rail Station is close to town right at the blue bridge on Esquimalt Rd, near the corner of Johnson St and Wharf St. The Island's train runs between Victoria and Courtenay. There is one train in each direction a day – northbound from Victoria at 8.15 am, southbound from Nanaimo at 3 pm.

Fares, one-way: to Nanaimo $11, to Courtenay $20.

One-day or one-week return fares are much cheaper than two one-ways.

Good one-day return trips can be made up-island; get a copy of the Malahat Railiner pamphlet from VIA. Reservations are often required.

Ferry BC Ferries run frequent trips from Swartz Bay to Tsawwassen, on the mainland. The 38-km crossing takes about one hour 40 minutes. There are between 10 and 15 sailings per day; the schedule varies according to the season. Walk-on fare is $4.50, driver and car $20.50. Taking the bus to the ferry terminal, then buying your own ferry ticket is the same price as buying the package bus deal downtown, so don't bother doing it yourself. One reader has written to say you can take city buses all the way, for about $2.10 plus ferry.

For Washington State, there are several alternatives. Firstly, there is either the *Princess Marguerite* or the *Vancouver Island Princess* which ply between Seattle and Victoria's Inner Harbour, for $25, with car $48. Each boat goes once daily and takes 4½ hours. There are slot machines on board. Much quicker at 2½ hours is the *Victoria Clipper* which sails between Seattle and Ogden Point, not far from downtown Victoria. The Clipper is a water jet-propelled catamaran and costs $35. No cars.

Much cheaper is the American *Blackball Ferry*, sailing between Port Angeles and the Inner Harbour. Port Angeles is just across the Strait of Juan de Fuca. It costs US$5.50, with car US$22. It's a 1½-hour trip, and there are four a day in each direction during the summer months. The office is at 430 Belleville St in Victoria.

Lastly, there's a ferry from Sidney through the San Juan Islands to Anacortes on the Washington mainland, costing US$5.50, with car US$25.30. See San Juan Islands for more details. There are stops on the Islands and it's a very scenic trip.

The Tourist Office has information on all these possible trips.

From Swartz Bay, BC Ferries (tel 386-3431) runs trips to the larger Southern Gulf Islands such as Galiano, Saltspring and the Penders. Service is pretty frequent, about one or two a day. Walk-on fares are low, no more than $3.50, usually less. Cars and bicycles are taken. Note that buses run from town to Swartz Bay.

BC Ferries also links other more northerly islands in the Georgia Strait to towns along the coast up island. For ferries north to Prince Rupert see Port Hardy at the end of the Vancouver Island section.

Getting Around

Bus For local transit information call 382-6161. The city buses cover a wide area and run quite frequently. The normal fare is 85c, but you can get a day pass for $2.50 for as many rides as you want. Bus drivers sell them. In the Information Centre at Wharf St is a Victoria Transit map showing all the routes. A city bus route goes to the airport – slowly. Also, the circular Explorer Shuttle Route takes you around the central core and out to Ogden Point.

Hustle Buses (tel 388-9916) run to and from the airport to meet all scheduled flights. Departures are from the Courtyard Inn, 850 Blanchard, and the fare is $9. The 25 km or so takes a while.

For BC ferries at the Swartz Bay Terminal, take Route No 70, there or back.

Bicycle Oak Bay Bicycle (tel 598-4111) is at 1968 Oak Bay. Gray Line (tel 381-2453) bicycle rentals is at 434 Kingston St, and they include a suggested tour map. They have a good selection of bikes. City Scene Rentals (tel 384-1433), 1007 Langley St, offers mopeds, scooters and bicycles.

Car Rentals ADA (tel 388-6230) is at 752 Caledonia (across from Memorial Arena). Used cars cost $8.95 plus 3.5c per km. A week's rental is discounted 10%.

You can also try Rent-A-Wreck (cheap), and Budget. All the major companies and more are represented in and around the central area.

Tours Ask about walking tours at the information office.

There are several companies offering a range of tours, from downtown Victoria to quick trips around the Island. It's best to decide what you want and then shop around a little. A couple of companies operate on the street right in front of the Empress Hotel.

Marguerite Tours Ltd (tel 388-9383) is in front of the Empress. They have six different tours; the basic sightseeing trip around Victoria takes 1½ hours and costs $10. You go in a British double-decker bus.

Gray Line Buses (tel 388-5248), 710 Douglas St, offer a variety of tours here, as they do in so many North American cities. Their city tour is $15 for 2½ hours, and takes in the major historical and scenic sights. Many of the tours include admission to attractions like Sealand.

There are many other tours by other companies, including harbour boat trips, day and evening. You can choose from tours by horse-drawn carriage, self-drive tours using recorded tapes and tours up-island to view wildlife.

Heritage Tours offer more personalised tours in London-style taxis.

AROUND VICTORIA

Western Shore

From Metchosin the road runs along the coast to Port Renfrew at one end of the West Coast Trail. There are numerous parks along the way for walking, beach combing, picnicking, etc. At Port Renfrew, often the destination for a day trip from town, there's a hotel with a pub, a bed & breakfast and not a heck of a lot else. The main attraction is Botanical Beach, a sandstone shelf, which at low tide is dotted with tidal pools containing all manner of small marine life: starfish, anemones, etc. To continue back to Victoria without retracing your tracks, there are logging roads across the island which will take you to Lake Cowichan and from there better roads connect to Duncan.

San Juan Islands (US)

Lying north-west off the coast of Victoria are the San Juan Islands just beyond the US border, making them a part of Washington State. The big three of the grouping, San Juan Island, Orcas Island and Lopez Island, form a rough circle about halfway between Vancouver Island and the American mainland. Washington State Ferries connect Sidney with Anacortes on the Washington mainland via the islands, making it a very scenic route between these ports. Stops are made at Orcas, Shaw, Lopez and San Juan Islands. Cars, bicycles and kayaks are taken. Buses connect from Sidney to Victoria and/or Anacortes to Seattle. In Seattle, contact Evergreen Trailways.

The islands are very good for cycling and are accustomed to accommodating this form of travel. The ferries sell a very good road map with the topography indicated, and there are numerous campgrounds and guest houses on the principal islands. Note that you must pass through Customs. Also, foot passengers may travel free between the main islands in either direction.

Gulf Islands (Southern)

Lying north-east of Victoria, off Sidney really, at the top of the Saanich Peninsula, this string of nearly 200 islands is squeezed between the mainland and southern Vancouver Island. The ferry from Tsawwassen edges between a handful of them on its route into Sidney.

With a few important exceptions most are very small and nearly all of them virtually uninhabited, but this island-littered channel is a boater's dream. Vessels of all descriptions cruise in and out of bays, harbours and marinas much of the year. The fishing is varied and excellent and seasonally includes the prized salmon in several species. BC Ferries connects with some of the larger islands, so having your own boat is not required to visit a few of them.

Due to the mild climate, abundant vegetation and fauna, relative isolation and natural beauty, the islands are one of Canada's escapist-dream destinations. Indeed, many of the inhabitants are retired people, artists, or counterculture types of one sort or another.

Salt Spring Island

Salt Spring is both the largest in size and population, with about 5500 residents. The island has a long, interesting Indian history followed by settlement not by the white people but pioneering American blacks. Seeking escape from prejudice and social tensions, a small group of settlers formed a community at Vesuvius Bay. Unfortunately the Indians didn't care for them any more than they did the British in the area. Still, they stuck it out, farms were begun and schools set up. Later immigrants came from Ireland, Scotland and England.

There are three ferry terminals: Long Harbour serving US mainland ferries; Fulford and Vesuvius are for ferries plying back and forth to Vancouver Island.

Ganges, not far from the Long Harbour landing, is the principal village and has a summer arts & crafts fair, a few tourist oriented shops and a Saturday morning market. Artists welcome visitors to their studios – the information office in Ganges has a list.

Mt Maxwell offers excellent views. There is camping and walking at Ruckle Provincial Park. There is no public transportation on the island other than taxi. Bicycles are good but this is a fair sized island. For accommodation there are quite a few bed & breakfast places. Some will pick you up at the ferry terminal.

Scattered around the island are resorts which really means (usually) cottages for rent, maybe with some camping too, a beach, boat rentals, etc. These cottages range from $50 a night for doubles to much more for those with fireplaces, hot tubs and other creature comforts. There are also a few motels around the ferry terminals and these tend to fall into the medium price range.

North & South Pender Islands

Together these two islands have a little over 1000 people. Again there are craft and art studios to visit and the ever-present golf course. Accommodation is mainly bed & breakfast and cottages, but for splurging there is also a heritage farmhouse, *Corbett House* near the ferry terminal, which has singles/doubles for $40/60.

For beaches, try Hamilton on North Pender and Mortimer Spit on South Pender (just after crossing the bridge). You might well see some of the more-or-less tame deer around the islands. You can camp at Prior Centennial Provincial Park.

Mayne Island

You squeeze right by Mayne Island and Galiano going through Active Pass on the ferry to Victoria from the Canadian mainland. Village Bay on the southern side is the ferry terminal although there are docking facilities for boaters at other points. There are some 100-year-old buildings at Miners Bay, including the museum, formerly the jail. There are only a few inns to stay at, so it's best to book ahead.

Saturna Island

At Saturna Point by the ferry terminal there's a store and pub. A good sandy beach is at Winter Cove Marine Park. At the top of Mount Warburton Pike is a wildlife reserve with wild goats and fine views. There are also good views to the Washington Mountains along the road on the island's leeward side.

Boot Cove Lodge, less than two km from the ferry landing, has rooms for $25/30 for singles/doubles. They offer boat and bicycle rentals, and meals are available.

Galiano Island

Despite its relatively large size, Galiano has only 700 residents stretched along its long, narrow land mass. About 75% of the island is forest and bush. Again, local artists and craftsmen invite visitors to their studios. It is a good island to visit for several reasons. There are bed & breakfasts, several places with cottage rentals, and camping at Montague Harbour Provincial Park. The *Hummingbird Inn* on Sturdies Bay Rd not far from the ferry (but they'll pick you up), has some rooms with shared bath at $30/40 for singles/doubles, breakfast included. There's a pub on the premises.

Sutil Lodge dates from the 1930s and is on the beach at Montague Harbour. They have a two-night special with a sailing picnic for $50 per person. There are several other places to bed down as well – check in Victoria.

There are a couple of restaurants. At the *Trincomali Bakery* you can get a cappuccino and pastry.

There's a place which rents canoes and mountain bikes and they also offer evening, one and two-day kayak trips along the coastal waters.

You can hike almost the length of the east coast, climb either Mt Sutil (323 metres) or Mt Galiano (342 metres) for views of the Olympic Mountains about 90 km away. Good cycling, too, but lots of hills. Porlia and Active Passes are good for diving and fishing, and you can fish into Active Pass at points from the shoreline. Canoeing along the western shoreline is possible in the calmer waters here. The coast is lined by cliffs and small bays.

From the mainland there are two ferries daily, tying in at Sturdies Bay. From Swartz Bay, Vancouver Island there are two or three a day arriving at Montague Harbour.

DUNCAN & AREA

About 60 km from Victoria along Highway 1 is the small town of Duncan. It marks the beginning of the Cowichan Valley running westward and containing the large Cowichan Lake. This is the land of the Cowichan Indian, BC's largest Indian group, here before the white man and, though with problems, still maintaining aspects of their unique culture.

Since 1986, Duncan has developed a project with the Cowichan Indian Band which has totem poles carved and displayed in the town area. There are now more than 20 examples of this west coast art form. The train station houses a locally oriented museum. At the Old Stone Church near the Cowichan Native Arts & Craft Shop, the excellent, locally-made, hand-knitted sweaters are available.

There really isn't much in town but the Valley and area are good for camping, hiking, swimming, fishing and canoeing.

Sawmill Tours

The valley is a logging centre, worked by several companies. Some of them offer free tours of their mills. They are: MacMillan Bloedel, Chemainus Mill (tel 246-3221); Doman Industries (tel 748-3711); and BCFP Crofton (tel 246-3241). The tours run Monday to Friday in summer.

Forest Museum

This is about three km north of Duncan, offering on its 40 hectares both indoor and outdoor features. The museum is open daily in summer from 10 am to 5.30 pm. Admission is $3.50. There's a stand of original forest of Douglas firs, 55 metres tall, that were present before Captain Cook arrived in 1778. A small train, included in the price, takes you around the site. You can visit a bird sanctuary or view a replica of an old logging camp and logging equipment. There are also indoor displays and movies of logging that took place years ago.

Places to Stay

There are motels but camping is best and there is a wide variety offered. The Provincial Government operates a few campgrounds. The biggest is at *Gordon Bay*, with 131 sites on the south shore of Cowichan Lake. Four km south of Mill Bay Village is the *Bamberton* site on Saanich Inlet. There are others, smaller and with fewer facilities.

For more off-the-track camping, some of the forestry companies have set up unsupervised sites mainly between Cowichan Lake and the west coast of Vancouver Island. The Tourist Office or the logging companies have more information on these.

If you can get a ride, the *Tent Island Provincial Park* is a good spot. It's on an island a few km offshore from Crofton and has beautiful beaches and minimal facilities.

Getting There & Away

Buses go to Duncan from Victoria, as does E & N Railway (VIA Rail). The 70-minute train trip costs $6.50. There is one a day in each direction.

Getting Around

Hitching here and all over the Island is common and accepted. The area around Cowichan Lake is full of logging roads, some of which you can use, though they're often rough. For some advice and rules ask at the Tourist Office. The well-used logging road from Lake Cowichan to Port Renfrew is in good shape and with a basic map, you shouldn't have any difficulty. The detailed maps showing all the logging roads look like a dog's breakfast so are more difficult to follow.

There are ferries from Crofton to Saltspring Island, which is made up of farming and fishing communities. The population swells from 6000 in winter to three times that in summer. There are several campgrounds on the island, some with sandy beaches.

Activities

There are many hiking trails around Cowichan River and Lake. One is the Cowichan River Footpath. It's about 18 km long with a good variety of scenery along the way. You can do it in a day or camp on the way. The path goes to Skutz Falls; from here you can head back to Duncan or keep going up the river. Maps of the trail are available at sporting stores. The lake gets warm enough to swim in. There really isn't anything in the town of Lake Cowichan but it does have a travel information centre with guides to the area. At Youbou there's a working sawmill. A good day trip from Victoria is to head up to Chemainus, then over to Lake Cowichan to Port Renfrew and down the coast back to town. It's a lot of driving but if you're in no hurry and can stop a lot it makes an interesting, full day.

Chemainus

About 20 km north of Duncan is this small town with a novel and interesting way to put itself on the tourist map. In 1983 the town sawmill shut down, and to counter the inevitable slow death, a unique and tremendously successful saviour concept was nursed to fruition. Art. An artist was commissioned to paint a large outdoor mural relating to the town's history. People took notice and another mural was painted. Now with 20 murals and more being added, a bustling and prosperous community has developed, and now the sawmill has re-opened. Craft shops have sprung up as well as several new restaurants, all making a short visit into town a worthwhile proposition. Two murals I like are Company Store and Chemainus Tugboat.

Off Chemainus are Thetis and Kuper Islands. The former is primarily geared to boaters; it has two marinas. There is a pub, however, and one place to eat, although it's part of a rather pricey resort. At Pilkey Point there are sandstone formations along the beach. For day-trippers, the ferry takes about 30 minutes. Kuper Island is an Indian Reserve.

Ladysmith

This is a small town on Highway 1 with the Black Nugget Museum, originally a hotel built in 1896. Many of the turn-of-the-century buildings have been or are being restored. Also in town at Transfer Beach Park, the warmest sea waters north of San Francisco are said to flow.

Ladysmith sits on the 49th Parallel which on the mainland divides Canada from the US of A. Just north of town off the highway at Yellow Point Rd, pub aficionados will find the oldest English-style brew dispensary in the province.

NANAIMO

Nanaimo is the island's second city and over the past several years, has grown rather dramatically. Though primarily a pulp & paper centre and terminal for the BC Ferries, its small town character is growing to that of a modern city. It makes a convenient stop-off point for trips around or off the island.

Seven Indian bands once shared the area, leading to its name of Sne-Ny-Mos. That all changed when coal was discovered. For the next 100 years, coal mining was the main industry and building block of the town. Coal has faded in importance, but the city is now the centre of a forest products industry as well as a major deep-sea fishing port.

There are a few points of interest in town as well as some in the immediate vicinity.

Orientation

The city is about 120 km north of Victoria. Just off Nanaimo Harbour are a number of islands. Behind the harbour is the central core. Cameron St, running to the harbour area, has the museum. At the foot of Cameron, near the water, is the bus depot. Running parallel to the docks, a few blocks west, are Commercial and Terminal Sts, where the restaurants and shops are. Nicol St to the south leads to the Trans-Canada Highway. Terminal St to the north leads to the Island Highway for Comox.

The BC Ferry Terminal is north from the downtown shopping area in Departure Bay. It's not far, but you can get a bus if you want.

Information

The Tourist Office (tel 754-8474) is at 266 Bryden St.

Nanaimo Centennial Museum

This small museum (tel 753-1821) at 100 Cameron St displays things of significance in the growth of Nanaimo. Included are Indian, Hudson Bay and coal mining artefacts. Open daily in summer, Monday to Friday in winter; admission is inexpensive. Down the steps is Fisherman's Wharf.

The Tourist Office has a walking guide

of the town's historic area around the harbour. Many of the original buildings have been destroyed and are now marked only with plaques. The highlight is the Bastion, built by the Hudson's Bay Company and believed to be the only one in existence. Built in 1853 for protection from Indians, it was never used, but remains standing on Front St at the corner of Bastion, near Wharf St.

Georgia Park

Here there is a display of Indian canoes, including a large war canoe, a few totem poles and a fine view of Nanaimo Harbour. The Promenade, beginning at the seaplane base, leads to Georgia Park and beyond to Swy-A-Lana Lagoon (good for children to splash in), then on to Maffeo-Sutton Park. Near the beginning there's a pub and restaurant.

Petroglyph Park

About three km south of Nanaimo on Highway 1, this park features some ancient Indian carvings in sandstone.

You can tour a pulp mill and a local cannery in summer. Ask the Tourist Office for details. These tours are interesting and free.

Other Parks

For hiking or canoeing three nearby spots are Nanaimo Lakes, Nanaimo River and Green Mountain. There are many parks in the area. Hikes from Colliery Dam Park lead to Harewood and Overton Lakes. Buttertubs Bird Sanctuary isn't far from the centre of town.

Newcastle Island Provincial Park

Just offshore from downtown, a short ferry ride away, the island offers cycling, walking, beaches. Good for a picnic or overnight camping. Further out into the strait is Gabriola island.

Events

The best known event is the Nanaimo Bathtub Race to Vancouver, held annually in mid-July. Hundreds of fibreglass tubs start out, about 100 sinking in the first five minutes.

Through July and August the Shakespeare Plus theatre festival presents both classic and modern plays.

Places to Stay

Mini-Hostel Nanaimo has a mini-hostel seven km south of town toward Victoria: *Verdun Thomson's* (tel 722-2251) at 1600 Cedar Highway. The local bus stops right at the place. It offers use of the kitchen and canoes.

Bed & Breakfasts There are a few of these in town now; ask at the Tourist Office. Rates drop by about $5 per person outside of June-September; otherwise they're roughly $40 for doubles.

Motels Back on the mainland, four blocks south of the city centre, is the *Diplomat Motel* (tel 753-3261) at 333 Nicol St. Singles/doubles cost from $26/28.

Two blocks further south is *Big 7 Motel* (tel 754-2328), 736 Nicol St (Island Highway), which offers singles/doubles for $25/34. There is a restaurant. In North Nanaimo at 950 Terminal Avenue is the *Colonial Motel* (tel 754-4415). It's near the ferry terminal and has free coffee. Singles/doubles cost $28/31, with a kitchen an extra $4.

Camping The best places to stay are not in Nanaimo itself but on the islands just off the coast. Not far from the mainland is Newcastle Island, a provincial park. There are beaches, walking trails, picnic areas and camping. No cars allowed. The island was once dotted with mine shafts and sandstone quarries but later became a quiet resort. In summer a small ferry travels between the island and the mainland every hour.

Further out is the much larger Gabriola Island. This island ferry takes cars for $4.75 but only charges $1 if you're walking. After 2 pm you're stuck on the island until the next morning when the ferry returns, but there is a campsite. The ferry trip takes about 20 minutes.

Another campground is situated eight km south of town. Tents and trailers.

At Malaspina Galleries on the island are some unusual sandstone caves carved out by the wind and tides.

Getting There & Away

The BC Ferry to Horseshoe Bay (Vancouver) takes about 1½ hours for the 50-km trip. There are about 12 in each direction daily, depending on the season. Tickets are $4.50, $16 for a vehicle. Try the clam chowder on board; it's very good.

PARKSVILLE & QUALICUM BEACH

These towns and the coast toward Comox are known for long stretches of sandy beach. You can stop by the road, tone up the tan and have a quick swim in the nippy water. At Parksville you'll find the road to Port Alberni and the west coast.

Between Parksville and Port Alberni are several other good parks.

Cathedral Grove

Right by the road is a grove of virgin forest with huge Douglas firs and red cedars dating back hundreds of years. This half-hour stop is a must.

Englishman River Falls Park

This provincial site has falls, hiking, swimming and camping.

Little Qualicum Falls Park

This is another good provincial park, also with hiking and camping. Both areas are forested and scenic.

PORT ALBERNI

Half-way across the island is this town built on forestry and fishing. Over 300 fishing boats work out of the area. At dockside there's an observation tower with views. Visitors can tour both the paper mill and the sawmill.

Hikers can reach Dalla Falls (see Strathcona Park) by an alternate route: canoeing the length of Great Central Lake from Port Alberni and taking the trail up from there.

Perhaps the most noteworthy feature of Port Alberni is the MV *Lady Rose*, which sails out of the town's Argyle St dock to the west coast of the island. The freighter, which takes mail and cargo as well as passengers, plies between Kildonan on the Alberni Inlet, Bamfield at the end of the West Coast Trail, the Broken Islands and Ucluelet. For those planning on canoeing or kayaking around the Broken Islands, you can take your boat on board. The ferry company is one place that rents canoes and kayaks. Fares to Bamfield are $13 one-way, $15 to Ucluelet or $30 return. One-day return trips allow passengers some free time at Bamfield and Ucluelet for exploring. On summer Sundays a longer stay in Bamfield is possible.

The basic schedule from Port Alberni is Tuesday, Thursday and Saturday all year to Bamfield, and from June 1 to Sept 30 Monday, Wednesday and Friday to Ucluelet and the Broken Islands. In midsummer, Sunday cruises to Bamfield only. Regardless of the weather, take a sweater and/or rain jacket.

PACIFIC RIM NATIONAL PARK

Of the many parks in the area, this is the granddaddy! A rough, rugged, inhospitable yet beautiful coastal area, the park is a long, thin strip of land divided into three distinct sections. Each is separated by land and water and is reached by a different route.

Long Beach

The most northerly third of the park is Long Beach. It is the easiest to get to and the most developed. The scenic road from Port Alberni leads into this park section.

Long Beach is exactly that, 10 km of wide, log-strewn, sandy beach. At other parts, the waves pound into a craggy, rocky shoreline. At each end of Long

Beach is a small fishing and tourist village.

There are two campsites – one serviced, the other primitive – and both are often full in summer. Arrive in the morning to get a place. Entry to the park is free but camping costs about $5. Around the villages are private campgrounds and some motels.

In summer there are interpretive programmes and guided walks.

There are several short hiking trails in the park; the office will have a description of them. The South Beach trail leads to an area good for watching and hearing the huge waves roar in. Half Moon Bay Trail leads to a calm, sandy bay. Radar Hill is good for views and has trails leading down to some small, secluded beaches.

Another activity is looking for and maybe watching some of the local sea life. Seals, sea-lions and porpoises are common, killer and grey whales a possibility. The best time to see the greys is during their migration period from mid-February to June. Peak time to catch them heading north is mid-April. Good viewing spots are Schooner Cove, Quistis Point, Radar Hill with its telescope, and Combers Beach near Sea Lion Rocks.

Hundreds of thousands of geese and ducks fly overhead in spring and fall.

Also, the pools left behind by the tides are often filled with interesting life forms: starfish, anemones, sponges, fish, snails and many other small creatures.

Note that the weather is generally poor here. Cold, windy and rainy are the weather conditions on a normal day. A warm, sunny day about a km or so from the coast can disappear into mist and fog at Long Beach. The water, too, is cold – those doing any water sports should use wet or dry suits.

Tofino

At the north end of Long Beach, just outside the park boundary, is the picturesque fishing village of Tofino, population 700 in winter, about 1000 in summer.

There are several places to eat, and *The Common Loaf Bake Shop* is recommended. It has just a few tables but a large selection of excellent, delicious home-made muffins, cookies, breads and cakes. In the morning try the bran muffins or the still-warm cinnamon buns. The latter are ready at about 11.30 am.

There are charters of several types in town. For fishing, check at the MV *Sea Joy* on the Lower Government Dock (Whiskey Dock). It'll cost $30. For sightseeing charters, try Sea Forth Charter at the Mackenzie Beach Resort (tel 725-3439). The tours last between two and five hours. Ocean Pacific runs three-hour boat trips to see grey whales which in spring and summer frequent the area. Take your own meals.

At the dock near the Company-op stores you can find out about the seaplane tours. They cost $40 to $50, so for a group it's not too costly. A good trip is to get the plane to take you to Hot Springs Cove where a 20-minute hike will lead you to Hot Springs overlooking the ocean.

There are several pools, progressively cooler down the hillside to the sea. You can also get a boat to the cove. Overnight camping is possible.

Highly recommended is a trip to Meares Island, a 15-minute cruise by the Harbour Islands from Tofino. This is a magical place of virgin rainforest with trees of boggling age and stature. One granddaddy is over 1000 years old and 19 metres in diameter. Many are large enough that you could cut a car tunnel through them. Species include the spruces, yew and cedar. You can arrange trips out to the island at Weigh West Motel for $11. One dollar of that goes toward fighting logging plans for Meares. There are several rugged but well-marked trails on the island; the basic loop takes about 2½ hours.

For accommodation, aside from camping around Tofino, there are several places offering housekeeping cottages for rent and four or five motels. Prices are about $40 and up for doubles. There is also a mini-hostel/guest house, *Tinwis*, on the main road within easy walking distance of everything. Cheap, but no meals or cooking facilities.

Ucluelet

This town, population 1600, is more tourist oriented than Tofino and not as attractive. Whale-watching trips can be a highlight of a west coast trip. In April, Pacific grey whales migrate up the coast from Mexico to the Arctic Ocean and in late fall head back south. At these times your chances of seeing one are not bad at all.

Subtidal Adventures in Ucluelet is an outfit offering whale-watching trips, at $24 for three hours, in March and April only. They also run tours around the Broken islands and will drop off those wishing to camp on an island. A full day trip to Bamfield, and scuba cruises are also offered.

A couple of walks around Ucluelet are to Amphitrite Point with the lighthouse and the trails at Terrace Beach.

For accommodation, Ucluelet offers camping, several motels and a couple of simple cheaper hotels. The *Ucluelet Lodge* on Main St costs about $25 for a double; *Burley's* on Helen Rd is about $10 more. It has shared baths.

Broken Group Islands

The middle section of Pacific Rim National Park is called the Broken Group Islands, made up of about 100 islands at the entrance to Barkley Sound. The only way to reach this section is by boat, either from Ucluelet or Port Alberni. There are some primitive campsites on the islands.

This is a good area for wildlife and offers some of the best scuba diving in Canada. You can view wrecks in shallow waters and the abundant sea life found around all the islands. The waters off Vancouver Island are home to the world's largest octopi, as well as thousands of other species.

West Coast Trail

The third section of the park is called the West Coast Trail. It's a 72-km stretch between Port Renfrew and Bamfield. Either end can be reached by road, but to reach one from the other you've got to walk – and that's a challenge along this rugged, often rain-soaked path. The trail is clogged with trees, and the camping areas are wherever you can find one. Passing cliffs, beaches and rainforests, the trail takes between five and eight days to travel. You must take all your own food. The southernmost part is the most rough and difficult. For your trouble you get some spectacular scenery and a test of stamina. The trail has historically been used as a life-saving route for shipwreck survivors.

Boats linking Port Alberni and Ucluelet go down the coast, past the Broken Group Islands and along the inlet. The cost is $15 one-way. For hikers, there are trips to Bamfield.

Bamfield, the village at the northern head of the west coast trail, can be reached by boat or by 100 km of gravel road from Port Alberni. A bus service connects the two towns, the Pachena Bay Express. There are only two places to stay and they're expensive so most north-bound hikers should try to get to town in time for a boat to Ucluelet or Port Alberni. There is a campground but it's 20 km north of the town. Bamfield has a Marine Biological Station, a lifesaving station and not much else.

At the other end of the trail is Port Renfrew which itself is reached by dirt road from Lake Cowichan or a mainly paved road along the coast from Victoria. There is a trail information booth and to begin, you must get one of the locals to boat you across the narrow San Juan River. Getting out of the bay here is, well, let's say, one of the less enjoyable segments of the trail northbound. You can camp along the beach or there is a hotel with pub and one bed & breakfast. There is also a small store but supplies are very limited. Botanical Beach, not far from town, is pleasant to pick over at low tide, peering in tidal pools and watching the waves.

NORTH UP THE EAST COAST

Not far beyond Qualicum off Highway 19 are the Horne Lake Caves situated in a provincial park. Tours of the caves, of varying length and difficulty, are given by knowledgeable guides. Admission is charged; bring a sweater. There is camping in the park as well.

Further up the coast are two lesser known Gulf Islands, Denman and Hornby, a short ferry ride away. Each has a provincial park, hiking and camping, also beaches. There's good bird-watching on Hornby. There are a few guest houses and bed & breakfasts.

Comox & Courtenay

Basically commercial centres for the local farming, logging and fishing industries, these two towns are also important as supply hubs for Mt Washington and Forbidden Plateau, two major summer and winter recreation areas. Courtnay is the larger of these two essentially adjacent towns. It has an Information Centre at 2040 Cliffe Avenue.

In town there is a small museum and not far out is the Pantledge River Salmon Hatchery. Miracle Beach, north of Comox, has a campground and a long, sandy beach.

There is very good hiking in the area, from afternoon walks to overnight climbs. Comox Glacier is a good two-day hike as is Mt Albert Edward, which offers an excellent view. Ask at the Tourist Office for more information. You must register if you're going on an overnighter. At Forbidden Plateau the ski lift runs in summer and there's a restaurant at the top. There are lots of trails and trout fishing in the lakes on the plateau. In winter it's a major ski area.

At the Canadian Air Force Base in Comox an annual air show takes place each August.

Six km out of Courtenay at 4787 Lake Trail Rd is the *North Comox Lake Mini-Hostel* (tel 338-1914), which charges $10. Meals are available and they can pick you up at the bus or train station. It's open all year and in summer there is extra sleeping space in an Indian style teepee. In both towns you'll find numerous motels, and near Comox are several places renting cottages by the beach. The *Economy Inn*, 2605 Cliffe Avenue (Island Highway) is the cheapest of the lot but still has a pool.

A good circular tour is to take the ferry at Tsawwassen to Victoria on Vancouver Island, travel up the island to Courtenay, go back across to the mainland by ferry to Powell River and then down to Vancouver along the Sunshine Coast.

Valley of a Thousand Faces

Near Saywood, north of Campbell River, is this trail through the woods. As you walk along, faces, figures and animals peer out at you from the trees. There are over 1400 figures painted on slabs of cedar, using the natural wood grain as a base for the image. The slabs are then nailed onto trees. They are the work of a Dutch-born artist, Hetty Frederickson. The trail is open between April and September; a dollar is asked to help maintain the place. It's worth a visit. Facial portraits, with their wide variety, are best.

Telegraph Cove

Off the main road back on the strait side of the island, this small community is one of the best of the west coast's so-called boardwalk villages. Most of the buildings are built over the water on pilings. Another attraction is killer whale boat tours out into Johnson Strait, offered from June to October.

Port McNeill

Three major logging companies have

regional offices in this town of 3000. There isn't much to do but there are several camping areas nearby and hotels, etc. A ferry runs to Alert Bay on nearby Cormorant Island where a museum and cultural centre show examples of Kwakiutl Indian art. There are also a few minor historical sites and a huge totem pole within a park.

Port Hardy
This small town at the northern end of the island is best known as the departure point for ferries through the famed Inside Passage to Prince Rupert. BC Ferries run the 15-hour, 440 km trip along the coast, around islands past some of the province's best scenery. There's a stop at Bella Bella about a third of the way up. The fare is $56, jumping to $174 with a car. Please note that to take a vehicle in summer you should reserve months in advance. Binoculars may be useful as you're often close to land, and wildlife viewing is good as well. Possibilities include porpoises, seals, whales and bald eagles.

Once in Rupert you can continue on Alaskan ferries further north; catch BC Ferries to the Queen Charlotte Islands, or go by land into the BC interior or up to Alaska.

There's not much in Port Hardy itself but nearby Cape Scott Provincial Park is good, with some long hiking trails. There are also shorter ones and beaches around San Josef. The area has good salmon fishing. There are motels and campgrounds in and around town. Note that the west coast of this northern tip of the island is known for strong winds, strong tides and heavy rain. Be equipped if you're going on camping trips.

STRATHCONA PROVINCIAL PARK
This is the largest park on the island and basically a wilderness area with a few unfortunate exceptions. Campbell River is the main access point. Mt Washington, just out of the park, and Forbidden Plateau, however, are reached from Courtenay. The highway between Campbell River and Gold River cuts across the park and provides access to campgrounds and some developed trails.

Two well known trails are the Elk River hike and the Flower Ridge hike. Both lead to very fine alpine scenery. Like other developed trails, these two are suitable for all age groups. Other less developed trails demand more preparation and lead to remote areas.

There are many excellent back-country hiking trails within the park. The Dalla Falls hike, for example, is a tough two or three day walk but is great for scenery and ends at the highest falls in North America. You need a good map. Other good walks are crossing the Big Interior Massif up to Nine Peaks and the Beauty Lake area. Camel Ridge apparently has some still unknown species of lichen and alpine plants.

The highest peaks, such as Golden Hinde and Colonel Foster and others in the 650 metre range, make it possible to see both the ocean to the west and Georgia Strait to the east. One thing you won't have to look at is a grizzly bear: there aren't any on Vancouver Island.

Strathcona Park Lodge is at the edge of the park, near Campbell River. Accommodation ranges from a *Youth Hostel* to cottages to deluxe apartments. Rates range from $10 to $95. Camping is also available, as is camping equipment. Meals are offered but are not cheap. You can rent canoes, kayaks and bicycles, or go hiking and swimming. Or you can take organised day trips if you wish. Courses are offered in various outdoor activities. To phone, call the operator and ask for Campbell River Radio, Strathcona One, H688568.

There is a campground near Campbell River and numerous motels around town. Campbell River marks the beginning of the north island, a less populated, less visited, rugged area with lots of opportunities for outdoor activities. Island Coachlines run a couple of buses north and south from town each day.

You can also catch a ferry to Quadra Island, then another ferry to Cortes Island, which has plenty of deserted beaches and lots of wildlife. There's a store near Mensen's Landing and fresh produce can be bought at the *Linnaea Farm Hostel*, which is on the shores of Cunflint Lake. The hostel rents canoes and bikes for exploring this scenic area. Accommodation in dorm rooms is $10 per bed and there's a kitchen, laundry and attractive balcony with a view of the lake.

GOLD RIVER

In the centre of the island, west of Strathcona Island, Gold River is the last stop on surfaced roads. The little town is a caving capital and is the headquarters of BC's Speleological Association. Visitors can join in on spelunking trips to Upana Caves and also to the deepest vertical cave in North America, but I'm not sure how regular these opportunities are. Summer cruises go to Friendly Cove, where Captain Cook first met the west coast Indians in 1778. A smaller freighter makes year-round trips to villages in the area.

Southern British Columbia

HOPE

At this smallish town the road from Vancouver splits. The famous 'Hope slide' once wiped out the town and you can still see the rock pile. Highway 1, the Trans-Canada, goes north up the Fraser River Valley toward Kamloops. This was the route the old wagon trail took up to the Cariboo gold rush. The road follows the river, which winds and twists through the canyon it has made. As the river is just off the edge of the road, there are many points of interest and viewing areas.

About 50 km from Hope is the Hell's Gate Airtram, a widely advertised cable-car system that goes down to the rushing Fraser River. You need more money than brains to bother. Highway 3 from Hope leads first southward and then into the Okanagan Valley, the dry, beautiful fruit-growing region of the province. The newly opened Coquihalla Highway also leads from Hope; it's a wider, straighter, quicker express route to Kamloops going in a north-easterly direction. However, it is a toll road and will cost you a few bucks. Services are few, so leave with a full tank. Good scenery and frequent stop areas along the way.

North

The further north you go, the drier the land

becomes and the fewer the trees, until at the Cache Creek area the landscape resembles cowboy-movie topography.

A number of companies offer raft trips down the Fraser River. Hell's Gate Enterprises (tel 863-2336) in Yale have one-day to one-week river trips, on which they supply food. River Rogues (tel 458-2353) in Spences Bridge do roughly the same thing. Both trips include rapids and lots of white water. This is a popular activity in BC and there are other companies working in the area using a number of different rivers. Tourist offices will have up-to-date information.

East

The green hills of the Hope area fade as the road heads toward Osoyoos. Highway 3 goes to the Okanagan and beyond.

West

The road flattens past Chilliwack and is uninteresting straight into Vancouver. From Chilliwack to Vancouver there's no use hitching; it's illegal for cars to stop for you. It's more or less expressway right into the city.

KAMLOOPS

Sitting at the point where the North Thompson River meets the Thompson River, Kamloops has always been a service-communication crossroads. Today, the Trans-Canada cuts through town, Highway 5 heads north to the Yellowhead Highway, 97 cuts east-west and the Coquihalla leads down to Vancouver. Both CNR and CPR have rail lines running through Kamloops. With this strategic location the city has grown rapidly since the late 1960s and is the major service and industrial centre for the district.

The city is not all business, though, and is surrounded by some 200 lakes, making it a good fishing area. The dry, rolling hills make interesting scenery and excellent ranching territory. This can be a very hot spot in the summer.

Kamloops, with a population of just 75,000, is spread over a very wide area. Many motels, restaurants and other services stretch both ways along the Trans-Canada. The core itself is quiet, clean and pleasant.

Vancouver lies 422 km to the south-west, Calgary 627 km to the east.

Orientation

Train tracks separate the Thompson River's edge from downtown. Next to the tracks, running east-west, is Lansdowne, one of the main streets. The other principal streets are Victoria, then Seymour, both parallel to and south of Lansdowne. The Trans-Canada is a few blocks further south. At the north-western corner of the city along Lorne St is Riverside Park, a pleasant spot for picnicking and swimming. The North Thompson meets the Thompson across from the park's shoreline. There are some great sunsets to watch over the Overlander Bridge from this point.

Information

The Tourist Office (tel 374-3377) is at 10-10th Avenue.

City Museum & Art Gallery

These are in the same building, on Seymour St, near 2nd Avenue. On display are pioneer implements and Salish Indian tools and ornaments. Admission is free.

Kamloops Wildlife Park

This park (tel 573-3242) is 18 km east on the Trans-Canada. Open year round, they have many animals found in Canada's west as well as camels, jaguars, monkeys and other animals from foreign lands. Admission $3.

Activities

You can fish for salmon, trout and steelhead. As a general rule, the bigger the lake, the bigger the trout. The Adams River is said to have very large sockeye salmon. There is even a Kamloops trout.

There's skiing in the area, both downhill and cross-country. Tod Mountain is the best spot with long, powder-snow runs.

Places to Stay

Hostels The *Men's Hostel* on West Victoria, not far from 1st Avenue, offers free accommodation. While not great, it's suitable for a night or two. It is essentially a community service.

There is also a *Women's Hostel* about a block away on West Seymour, but here it's $8.

The *YMCA* has no rooms.

Motels The *Bambi Motel* (tel 372-7626) is at 1084 Battle St, which runs east-west just south of downtown. Single/doubles cost $30/34.

There are two motels on the highway east of Kamloops. The *Monte Vista* (tel 372-3033), 2349 Trans-Canada, is an old motel with singles/doubles for $30/32. They serve free coffee and ice. The other is *Thrift Inn* (tel 374-2488), 2459 Trans-Canada. Singles/doubles are $26/27. Rooms are air-conditioned and have colour TV. There's also a heated swimming pool.

The central *Plaza Motor Hotel* (tel 372-7121), 405 Victoria St, has singles/doubles for $22/24. There's a restaurant and bar downstairs.

Camping *Knutsford Tent & Trailer Park* (tel 372-5380) is south of town on Highway 5. It's about six km from the Trans-Canada. All facilities are available, including laundromat. Two people $8.

Kamloops View Tent & Trailer Park (tel 573-3255) is about 10 km east of town on the Trans-Canada. It has all facilities and a pool. Information on fishing is available. Two people with tent $8.

Places to Eat

Victoria St has several restaurants, including a pizza place and a couple of Chinese ones.

The *Silver Grill*, serving Canadian and Chinese food, makes the standard fare well and has changing lunch bargains every day.

Getting There & Away

Bus The Greyhound Station (tel 374-1212) is at 235 Lansdowne. It's open 5.45 am to 9.30 pm and then 10.40 pm to 12.45 am.

Prince George: 11.45 am and 9.15 pm – $34

Jasper & Edmonton: 7.05 am, 7.50 pm, 11.55 pm – Jasper $29, Edmonton $46

Okanagan points: 9 am, 5.45 pm, 10.45 pm.

There are five buses daily to Vancouver and four daily to Calgary.

Train The train station is at Lansdowne and 3rd Avenue, beside the shopping mall with the Tourist Office. Train No 1, westbound, leaves at 10.45 pm daily. Train No 2, eastbound, leaves at 6.25 am daily.

One-way fares: Vancouver $30, Jasper $35.

Okanagan Valley

The Okanagan, a beautiful and unique area of Canada, is a series of valleys running about 180 km north-south in south-central BC. To the east are the Monashee Mountains, to the west the Cascades. The valleys were carved out by glaciers and are linked by a series of lakes, the largest of which is Okanagan Lake. The varied and interesting landscape makes the entire region very scenic.

The north end is gentle green farmland which climbs to woods of evergreens. The further south you get, the drier the terrain becomes. Near Osoyoos, cacti grow on desert slopes which get only 25 cm of rain a year. And everywhere are the rolling, scrubby hills, narrow blue lakes and clear skies.

The hot, dry summers attract many visitors, but in combination with the fertile soil have made the region the country's top fruit-growing area as well.

Through April and May the entire valley is enlivened with blossoms from thousands of fruit trees. In late summer and fall the orchards drip with delicious fresh fruit. Stands dotting the roads sell the best and cheapest produce in Canada. Twelve hundred hectares of vineyards hold grapes, the last fruit of the summer to ripen.

Okanagan Lake is said to contain a monster similar to that of Loch Ness, known as Ogopogo. The Indians first reported it and would offer the creature sacrificial animals before venturing on the lake. Though sightings occur occasionally, no one has yet photographed it.

If backpacking along some of the old, historic trails in the Okanagan interests you, pick up the booklet 'Old Park Trails' put out by the Historical Society. Look in bookstores in Penticton, Osoyoos, Oliver or Hope.

VERNON

Vernon, the most northerly of the Okanagan's 'Big Three', lies in a scenic valley encircled by three lakes – the Okanagan, Kalamalka and Swan. The town developed because of its location. First there were the fur traders, then the gold seekers streaming up the valley to the Cariboo district. Later, cattle were brought in, and in 1891 the railway made it. But it was in 1908, with large-scale irrigation, that the town took on an importance that was more than transitory. Soon the area was covered in the orchards and farms present today.

Vernon's population of 21,000 is surprisingly cosmopolitan with good numbers of Germans, Chinese and the original Indians, who have a reservation to the west of town.

Orientation

Surrounded by nearly bare hills, downtown Vernon is a clean, neat, quiet place. Main St, also called 30th Avenue, is lined with trees and benches. Above it, 32nd Avenue is most important; below it's 25th Avenue. The major north-south streets are 27th St, which is actually Highway 97, and 32nd St, a few blocks west.

There are an amazing number of Jehovah's Witnesses in town. You'll see them standing in pairs throughout the downtown area, clutching their magazines, *Watch Tower* and *Awake*.

At 27th St is the Courthouse, the city's most impressive structure.

All the downtown sights are within easy walking distance of each other.

Information

There are three Tourist Offices. The biggest one, with lots of maps, pamphlets and information, is in the Chamber of Commerce (tel 545-0771), which is downtown at 3700 33rd St. Another is south from downtown on Highway 97 toward Kelowna, near the army camp. Either one will be able to give you details on any local events. There's also an office at City Hall, 3400 30th St.

Jobs Fruit-picking work is available. It's hard work and the pay isn't great, but you don't always need a work permit and you'll meet lots of young people. Arrive early and shop around if you can. In the northern portion of the valley, times are:

25 June-25 July: cherries
20 August-1 September: pears
28 August-30 September: tomatoes
9 September-18 October: apples, grapes.

Remember there are overlaps and other produce to fill in the gaps. The season starts first around Osoyoos where the weather is warmer.

Polson Park

This is in town and very pleasant, with lots of flowers and shade. If it's hot this is a good rest spot, especially if you're hitching or cycling. The Japanese influence is obvious (as is the Chinese) in the open, cabana-like structures dotting the park. At the end of the park is a floral clock.

Provincial Courthouse
Built entirely of local granite, the courthouse sits majestically at the east end of town. In front is a rather bizarre garden and waterfalls made up mainly of concrete sculptures.

Vernon Museum
This is in the Civic Centre, corner of 32nd Avenue and 31st St, behind the glockenspiel-like clock tower. On display are historical artefacts from the area, including old carriages and clothes. There's a good antique telephone collection and lots of photographs of the area and of the local people. Open daily except Sunday, admission free.

O'Keefe Historic Ranch
This ranch, 12 km north of Vernon, was founded and lived on by the O'Keefe family from 1867 to 1977. Most of the buildings and artefacts were the property of this family. See the original log cabin, a general store and the oldest Roman Catholic church in the province. Open spring to fall, 9 am to 5 pm, seven days a week. Admission is charged.

Beaches
Kalamalka Beach is on blue-green Kalamalka Lake east of town, with campgrounds nearby. There's also Kin Beach on Okanagan Lake, west from town on Okanagan Landing Rd. There's a campground here, too.

Activities
Silver Star Provincial Park is 22 km east of Vernon. It offers good walking in summer, with views possible all the way to the Coastal Mountains.

Places to Stay
Hostels On my last trip, there were two mini-hostels, one open in summer, one in winter for skiers. Get the updated list from the hostel association. The summer one is *Hyrcan's* (tel 542-9349). Meals are available.

Hotels The *National Hotel* (tel 545-0731) at the corner of 30th Avenue and 30th St, is a reasonably kept downtown hotel with the usual working-class bar downstairs. Singles/doubles are $24/26. Sauna available. Rooms include bath and colour TV.

Motels *Polson Park Motel* (tel 542-9010) is opposite the park at 24th Avenue. Good value, it offers a heated pool, bath and TV movies. Singles or doubles are $28 to $38, kitchen $2 extra.

Schell Motel (tel 545-1351) at the corner of 35th St and 30th Avenue has a heated pool, sauna, TV and air-conditioning. Singles/doubles are $30/35.

There are many, many other motels in Vernon.

Camping By far the best campground is *Ellison Provincial Park*, 25 km south-west of Vernon on Okanagan Lake. The trouble is that it's often full; call ahead. There are only 54 campsites.

There are lots of privately owned campgrounds, some close to town at Okanagan and Kalamalka Lakes. These, too, get crowded. About $8 for two people tenting.

Places to Eat
For a small town, Vernon has lots of restaurants, particularly little coffee shops and sandwich places. It seems to keep the quality up and the prices reasonable.

Vernon's Schnitzel Haus is near 30th Avenue and 30th St. This is an excellent spot, highly recommended – you never know where you'll find them, do you? It's run by friendly German-speaking people serving mainly German food at very good prices. There are about a dozen tables covered with yellow & blue flowered tablecloths. With the brown chairs and decorations, it looks quite like a European café. The borscht is great and only $1.60. Choose from five different kinds of schnitzel at $5.50, including salad and fries. Fresh bean salad daily, 90c, other salads about $1. Everything is home-made.

Sweet Bloomers, 3210 30th Avenue, is an unusual spot, selling fresh flowers and plants and wicker furniture as well as café items. Teas and coffees, home-made pastries, good blueberry-bran muffins for 75c and ice creams are served at the four small tables.

Little Hobo Restaurant at 30th Avenue and 31st St is a neat, popular place with wooden tables and chairs and large windows out to the sidewalk. They have all kinds of sandwiches from $1.75 to $4 as well as home-made pastries and brownies. You'll see a few of these restaurants around the Okanagan; it's a small chain.

On 30th Avenue at 34th St is *Jackie's Coffee Shop*, popular with the locals. The food is the usual, the prices normal and the decor plain, so who can tell why. They do have lunch specials. Open 7.30 am to 5.30 pm.

The many Asian people here not only worked on the gardens in the park but have also set up several Chinese restaurants. There are four restaurants together on 33rd St, near 30th Avenue. *Goon Hong*, the most expensive one, has a good smorgasbord at dinnertime. The other three are a toss-up.

The Incredible Smorgasbord, 2700 32nd St, is good. Open at lunch and dinner only, it closes at 9 pm. They have an all-you-can-eat lunch for $5; dinner is $9. The smorgasbord includes hot and cold dishes and a salad bar.

5th Court Health Bar is across from the Greyhound bus station in the Vernon Racquet Centre. Eat in or at the one outside table. The selection is limited but nutritious – smoothies ($1), juices, salad bar. A roast beef sandwich is just $2.50.

RJ's at 2900 31st Avenue has chicken and ribs.

Nightlife

OK Corral is at the corner of 30th Avenue and 29th St, near the Courthouse. They feature live country or country rock nightly. On Fridays and Saturdays there's a $2.50 cover. Music from 10 pm to 2 am; opens at 7 pm.

Getting There & Away

Bus The Greyhound bus depot is at the corner of 31st Avenue and 30th St, and it could be the cleanest bus station in Canada. Wipe your feet.

Kelowna-Penticton-Vancouver: 7 am, 3.10 pm, 8.55 pm

Kamloops: 9.35 am, 5.45 pm

Revelstoke-Golden-Calgary: 8.55 am, 3.45 pm, 8.35 pm.

Fares, one-way: Kelowna $4.50, Banff $31.

Train The closest train station is in Kamloops where the VIA Rail goes east and west.

NORTH FROM VERNON

At Sicamous there's a major highway junction. Highway 1 heads east and west to Kamloops or Revelstoke; Highway 97 heads south through the Okanagan. Both routes can be used to get to Vancouver, and both are about 600 km.

The district around Mara Lake and Skuswap River is picturesque with its green, wooded hills and farms. The grazing cattle and lush, cultivated land make a nice change of scenery no matter where you're coming from.

Of the many campgrounds, Mara Provincial Park is the best, though probably not the least busy.

KELOWNA

I'd say Kelowna is one of the most pleasant small cities in the country. It sits halfway down Okanagan Lake, midway between Vernon and Penticton. All around are the rounded, scrubby hills typical of the valley. Closer to town they become greener, with terraced orchards lining their slopes and, unusually, the greenest area is the town itself with its many parks and gardens. Under almost-always clear skies, sandy beaches rim the dark blue water of the lake.

There are nearly 2000 hours of sunshine here each year. Summer days are usually hot but the nights are pleasantly cool. Winters are not harsh either. The combination of excellent weather and a good water supply makes Kelowna an ideal fruit and wine-producing area as well as a popular tourist destination. The dry, mild climate attracts both young and retired people.

Kelowna is the largest city in the Okanagan, with about 60,000 people. As the hub of the fruit-growing area, and with an important lumbering and wine industry, it is a valuable economic centre. Nevertheless, the town has a distinct resort feel.

The name is an Indian word meaning 'grizzly bear'. A number of Oblate missionaries, including Father Pandosy, arrived in 1859. He established a mission and planted the area's first apple trees. He has become Canada's lesser-known equivalent of America's Johnny Appleseed. With his successful work as an example, the first full-scale planting of apples was done in 1890. In 1892 the townsite of Kelowna was drawn up and today it is in the centre of Canada's largest fruit-growing district. There are about 10,000 hectares of orchards now growing in the Okanagan.

For some reason it seems popular among Kelowna young people, male and female, to be tattooed on the shoulder blade.

Orientation

The best place to start is in the large City Park on the lake's edge, serving as the western boundary of town.

Bernard St running out of the park is the city's main drag. It starts at the park by the big, white, modern sculpture. Other important streets are Water, Pandosy and Ellis. Highway 97, called Harvey in town, is the southern edge of downtown. It heads westward over the bridge for Penticton.

At the north end of Pandosy at Queensway is the town clock tower standing in a fountain that marks the new Civic Centre. Beside the fountain, surrounded by flowers, is the museum and art gallery contained within the National Exhibition Centre.

There are 31 parks in the city area, including seven along the lakeshore. Several of them are south of town on the other side of the bridge. The beach continues a long way in this direction.

On the east side of town for about 15 km on Highway 97 is a commercial strip. The road is lined with gas stations, junk food spots and motels.

Information

The Tourist Information Office (tel 769-4140) is at the far end of Floating Bridge on Highway 97. It's an easy walk from the downtown beach in the city park. There's a Tourist Office at 544 Harvey Avenue (tel 763-2451).

The secondary office is also on Highway 97 but north out of town about 10 km on the way to Vernon.

The Information Centre for Transients & Fruit Pickers (tel 762-4242) is at 578 Leon Avenue. Its hours are Monday to Saturday 8.30 am to 4 pm. The centre offers a referral service for work, and social services for travelling youth.

The Employment Centre at 471 Queensway also has information on job opportunities.

The post office is at the corner of Pandosy and Queensway, near the clock.

On Leon St one block up from the park

is *Paperback Shack*, a used-book store that will trade.

City Park

Time stands still here. In the two trips I've made, 10 years apart, nothing had changed. Frisbees still fill the air, boys toss girls in the lake, some people strut, some work overtime on the tan and the odd waterskier flies by in a foamy wake. It's an excellent park with sandy beaches, lots of trees for shade, snack bars and water just slightly cooler than the summer air at 23°C. There are flower gardens, tennis courts, and with the view across the lake, it's no wonder would-be fruit pickers are sitting around picking only guitars.

This is the best site with its beach running from the Yacht Club to the bridge. The bridge to the left of City Park is the only structure of its kind in Canada – it floats. It's supported by 12 pontoons and has a lift span in the middle so boats up to 18 metres can pass through.

Fintry Queen

At the foot of Bernard St, behind the model of Ogopogo and the Regatta sign, the old ferry boat *Fintry Queen* is moored in the lake. Now converted into a restaurant, it also provides lake cruises. Open every day at 5 pm for dinner. If you just want the evening cruise – no food – it's $9 on Friday and $14 on Saturday. The cruise includes a dance orchestra.

National Exhibition Centre

Housing the museum and art gallery, this centre is part of the Civic Complex at Pandosy and Queensway. There are numerous Indian artefacts; note especially the basketwork of BC Indians. The old stagecoach is good, too. Other exhibits include models of some of the town's first buildings and stores, stocked with goods and relics. The museum is open 10 am to 5 pm Monday to Saturday, 2 to 5 pm on Sundays. Free.

Father Pandosy Settlement

This is the major historical site in the area. On the spot where this Oblate priest set up his mission in 1859 are some of the original buildings. The church and school from that time have been restored, as have a couple of other buildings: the barn, one furnished house and a few sheds from what was the first white settlement in the Okanagan. The site is small, and there's not a lot to see, but it's free. To get there, go south along Pandosy St and Lakeshore Rd, then east up Casoro Rd to Benvoulin St. Open from 8 am to sundown.

Beaches

As well as the beach in town, there are several south of Floating Bridge along Pandosy St, which becomes Lakeshore Rd. You could walk this far. Some of the campgrounds along the lake also have beaches.

Wine Tours

This is one attraction you might not want to miss. There are seven wineries in BC and five of them are in the Okanagan. From Kelowna southwards, there are 1200 hectares of vineyards. Several companies are located near Kelowna. They offer tours and free samples. Calona Wines, right in Kelowna, is BC's largest producer and was the first in the Okanagan: it started in 1932. The address is 1125 Richter St.

South of Kelowna about 13 km in Westbank is Golden Valley Wines Ltd, Rural Route 1, Mission Hill Rd, which has tours, tastings and sales. Another 12 km or so south is Claremont Wines (tel 767-2992) on Trepannier Bench Rd in Peachland. There's a good view from the tasting room.

Brenda Mine Ltd

This company gives free tours during the summer only, 9.30 am Monday, Thursday and Friday. It's west of Peachland. For reservations call 763-3220. Wear pants and flat shoes.

Events
The biggest event of the year is the Kelowna Regatta, usually held around the end of July. The week-long festival includes all manner of activities but of course focuses on the many boat races. There are competitions for canoes, yachts and hydroplanes as well as boat displays. The Armed Forces put on shows with their Voodoo jets and parachutes. Activities include water-skiing, windsurfing, folk music concerts, beer gardens, parades and fireworks. Needless to say, the town is pretty busy for the week.

Every Sunday afternoon during the summer there are free music concerts in City Park.

Places to Stay
Hotels By far the best place is the *Willow Inn Hotel* (tel 762-2122), 235 Queensway at the corner of Abbot. It's right by City Park and the lake, with a restaurant and bar on the premises. Singles and doubles are priced from $32/40. There aren't many hotels, and with no hostel, staying right in the city is a problem if the Willow is full.

Motels There are two good choices north of town, not far past the Highway 3 junction. Book early in the day as places fill up fast here in summer.

Town & Country Motel (tel 860-7121) is at 2620 Highway 97 North. Singles/doubles are $38/41. It has air-conditioning, TV, pool and sauna.

Western Budget Motel (tel 860-4990), 2679 Highway 97 North, is the cheapest of the lot with singles/doubles at $23/28.

Harvey St north of town has numerous motels. At 1864 the *Ponderosa* (tel 860-2218) is reasonable at $35/38 for singles/doubles. Some rooms have kitchens.

Camping This is the cheapest way to stay in the area, though you'll be a way from town. The best parks are the *Provincial Park* south of Vernon or *Okanagan Mountain Provincial Park* south of Kelowna, 24 km north of Penticton. Both are relatively small and very popular. The Tourist Office might know if they're full or not.

There are numerous privately owned places around the city. The grounds are usually crowded, the campsites close together. South of the city about eight km at 4576 Fuller Rd is the *Shady Lane Campground* (tel 764-4032). It's on the beach. Open 15 May to 15 September. Two people $9. There are several campgrounds in this area.

The other campground area is north from town, along the lake. Here there are many spots for about $8 to $10 for two people with a tent. To get here, head north up Highway 97 and then turn off at Boucherie Rd. Follow this for quite a while and you'll hit the so-called resort area. This area is quite far from town – you'll need a car.

Places to Eat
Many of the eateries are on Bernard, the main street. *Savoy Restaurant* on Bernard near Water St is the basic Canadian restaurant, with reasonably priced breakfasts. Two eggs and toast is $2.35. A lunch of soup, cheese, a chicken or ham sandwich and coffee costs $2.85. Other things are a bit on the expensive side.

The *Pancake & Omelette House* on Bernard opposite Woolworth's is also good for breakfast. Two eggs, toast and hash browns also cost $2.35. All types of pancakes and omelettes are available, priced between $2 to $4. Open seven days a week.

The *Old Spaghetti Factory* at the corner of Bernard and Bertram, like others in the chain offers good food at good prices in an interesting atmosphere that makes you feel you're spending more than you are. The decor includes hanging lamps and lots of wood. A complete meal is about $6.50.

Mr Jake's, also at Bernard and Bertram, serves cheap steak dinners. A dinner of 140 grams of ground beef including salad, bread and potato is $2.79. Other meals range from $5 to $9. Open 11 am to 8 pm daily, from noon on Sunday.

Woolworth's on Bernard has the standard very cheap cafeteria.

Little Hobo Sandwich Shop is at 438 Lawrence; there's another on Pandosy at Queensway. Closed on Sundays and after 4.30 pm daily. The place specialises in sandwiches of all kinds and is very popular with office workers.

Hansel & Gretel Schnitzel House on Water St near Bernard is a little bit of a splurge but not much at lunch hour. Open 11.30 am to 2 pm, Monday to Friday. The daily special is $5.95; Bavarian meat and dumplings is $5.95; home-made meat loaf with vegetable and potato is $6.25; German bratwurst, sauerkraut and potato is $6. Omelettes are $5.25. Dinner prices go up to $9 to $14.

Nightlife

The *Royal Anne Hotel*, right downtown on Bernard St, is an expensive place to stay but contains a very popular bar downstairs. It's frequented by all types, mainly young, and has cheap beer, pool tables and pinball. The bar is busy during the day, too. Groups of French people from Quebec meet here as well as visitors, workers and locals.

Dusty's Cabaret, corner of Bernard and Abbot, has live rock music nightly. No cover during the week.

Kelowna Cave Cabaret (tel 762-2208), 425 Leon Avenue, has new wave rock nightly, 7 pm to 2 am. There's a small cover charge.

Brock & Friends Coffee House has folk music each night, usually with local musicians.

Getting There & Away

Air The airport is 12 km north of Highway 97. There are daily flights to and from Vancouver, Calgary and Edmonton by Pacific Western.

Bus The Greyhound terminal is east out of downtown on Cooper St. To get there, take the Highway 110 city bus from Bernard and Ellis. It goes back and forth roughly every half hour from 6.30 am to 9.30 pm. The bus goes to The Bay department store in the shopping centre across from the bus terminal. The station is open 7.30 am to 10.30 pm daily.

Penticton and Vancouver: 8 am, 12.35 pm, 4.10 pm, 9.55 pm

Vernon, Banff, Calgary and east: 7.45 am, 2.35 pm, 7.25 pm

Vernon, Kamloops, Prince George: 8.20 am, 4.20 pm.

Fares, one-way: Vancouver $26, Calgary $37.

Other For hitching south walk over the bridge and start. Northbound, take Highway 110 until it turns off Highway 97.

There is no train in Kelowna.

Getting Around

For local transit information call 860-8121.

Car Rentals Rent-A-Wreck (tel 763-6632) is at 380 Harvey at Pandosy. Open 8 am to 6 pm. Their cheapest car is $8.95 plus $2.95 insurance plus 8c per km.

The Tourist Office sometimes has promotional coupons worth $5 on a rental car from Thrifty Rent-A-Car (tel 763-1265). They have free pick-up and drop-offs.

PENTICTON

Penticton, the southernmost of the three Okanagan sister cities, sits at the south end of Okanagan Lake. The sun shines for an average of 600 hours in July and August about 10 hours a day, and that's more than Honolulu. It's not surprising, then, that the number-one industry is tourism.

To the Salish Indians, Pen-Tak-Tin means 'place to stay forever', an idea that more and more white people are taking to heart. The population has risen from 13,000 to 25,000 in 10 years. Penticton became a townsite in 1892 with several nearby mine claims being developed. The Canadian Pacific Railway made it a freight terminal and fruit companies started buying up land in early 1900. The industries grew and by the 1930s Penticton's location and climate was gaining a reputation. It soon became a vacation destination.

There is not a lot to do, but this land of peaches and beaches makes a good spot to cool your heels for a day or two.

Orientation

The downtown area lies just south of Okanagan Lake. Most of the land around the lake is park. Lakeshore Drive runs west through this land from downtown to the highway for Kelowna. The main street is Main St, running north-south. At the far south end it becomes Skaha Lake Rd and then turns into Highway 97 to Vancouver. The downtown area is about 10 blocks southward from the lake. Martin St to the west is also important. Running west-east, Westminster, Nanaimo and Wade are the principal streets. Most of the restaurants and bars are in this area, as are the bus station and the Chamber of Commerce. This central area is small and easy to get around.

Information

Tourist Information (tel 492-4103) is in the Jubilee Pavilion of the Chamber of Commerce, 185 Lakeshore Drive. The South Information Centre is south of town on Highway 97. The North Information Centre is on Westminster at Eckhardt Avenue.

The Farm Labourers Pool has an office on Main St for fruit-picking information.

Beaches

Okanagan Beach, close to downtown, is about 1300 metres long. It's sandy and the water temperature is about 22°C. Near the Tourist Office you can rent windsurfers. Lessons are available as well.

You can be pulled around the bay 50 metres in the air with a parachute. You start on the beach and a speedboat pulls you up. People say the feeling and the view are worth the money.

Skaha Beach at the southern end of town is about 1½ km long and has sand, trees and picnic areas.

Casabello Wines

This winery (tel 492-0621) at 2210 Main St offers free tours with taste samples. It's near the turn-off for Skaha Lake Rd. Closed Sunday.

Dominion Radio Astrophysical Observatory

Seen many of these lately? The observatory contains radio telescopes that receive radio waves from the solar system. The waves are then amplified and analysed to provide information that conventional equipment cannot. Tours are given on Sundays between 2 and 5 pm in July and August. At other times you can see the equipment and hear a recorded explanation. It's on White Lake Rd 9; the first turn south of Kaledan Junction on Highway 97.

Agricultural Research Station

This centre was designed to study fruit trees, their growth, diseases, and production. There is an ornamental garden displaying a variety of plants and trees, as well as picnic grounds. It's 11 km north of town on Highway 97.

Summerland Trout Hatchery

You can tour the hatchery 8.30 to 11.30 am, 1.30 to 4.30 pm all year, for free. Summerland (tel 494-3346) is one of three BC hatcheries used to stock lakes. Here they concentrate on rainbow, eastern brook and kokanee trout. It's at 13405 Lakeshore Drive.

Okanagan Game Farm

On 240 hectares of semi-desert overlooking Skaha Lake, this game farm has about 650 animals of 130 species, including Canadian and more exotic animals. It's eight km south of Penticton on Highway 97. Open all year, 8 am to dusk. Admission $5, students $3.50.

Edible Dried Goods

At 667 Eckhardt Avenue West is this store and company selling fruit leather, which is a blend of fruit purees dried into thin sheets and pressed together. It's great for backpacking and hiking. They have tours at 10 am and 2 pm and offer free samples to taste. The store is open 8 am to 5 pm, closed Sundays.

White-Water Slide

Adults' and children's slides are at 282 Waterford Avenue. Full-day tickets cost $8. Open in summer 10 am to 10 pm daily.

Events

The city's premier event is the Peach Festival, a week-long event that has taken place around the beginning of August since 1948. There are sports activities, novelty events, music and dance, nightly entertainment and a major parade held on Saturday.

The week following the festival is the Annual British Columbia Square Dance Jamboree. It goes on for six nights 8 to 11 pm, and about 3500 dancers take part. There's an enormous dance floor in Kings Park. There are also street dances, dances held at both lakes – in the water! – pancake breakfasts and other activities.

Places to Stay

The beach closes at midnight and stays that way until 6 am. If you try to sleep on it you'll probably be rudely awakened by the police. There is no hostel or YMCA so you're stuck with the usual alternatives.

Hotels *Three Gables Hotel* (tel 492-3933), 353 Main St, is the only reasonable hotel. It's right in the centre of town, three blocks from the beach and there's a good pub downstairs. Singles/doubles $32/35.

Motels The area is chock full of them. On Riverside Drive in town is *Coral Beach Motel* (tel 493-0651), 40 Lakeshore Drive. It's simple but close to the beach. Singles or doubles are $32 to $38.

Majestic Flag Inn (tel 493-6616), 152 Riverside Drive, has all conveniences and extras. Singles or doubles are $32 to $48.

The cheapest motels are south of town along Skaha Rd. *Holiday House Motel* (tel 492-8422), 3355 Skaha Rd, is near the beach. Singles/doubles $36/42.

Paradise Valley Motel (tel 492-2756) is at 3118 Skaha Lake Rd, also near the beach. It has refrigerators. Singles/doubles $34/35, kitchen $8 more.

Camping There are many tent & trailer parks, especially south of town around Lake Skaha. Many are just off Highway 97. Most are about $8 for two people in a tent. This is in no way wilderness camping, but is a cheap place to stay. The Tourist Office has complete listings.

Places to Eat

Nearly all the restaurants are on Main St, but there isn't a lot of choice here, either. The *Sands* and *Elite* restaurants with the Las Vegas-type signs both serve ordinary food in a plastic environment at too high a price. But the 1950s-style signs are good.

Taco Granden at 452 Main St is maybe the best place to eat. They serve Mexican food – tacos, burritos, enchiladas – all under $3 for one. Also taco burgers, Mexican-style beans and salads.

Also on Main is *Boston Pizza*, part of the chain you see a lot in BC. Pizzas from $4 to $12. They have a lunch for $3.50, consisting of soup, salad and garlic bread, that's worth the money.

Nightlife

Tiffany's at 535 Main is the rock place in town, bringing in bands from Vancouver. There's usually a cover charge.

A quieter spot at night or during the day is the *Gables Public House*, a large pub-like bar open from 10.30 am. It's part of the Three Gables Hotel on Main St and is white with dark brown exposed wooden beams.

Getting There & Away

There is no train station. The Greyhound Station is at Nanaimo and Ellis, one block from Main St.

Vancouver: 9.45 am, 2.15 pm, 5.45 pm, 11.15 pm – $23

Vernon: 6.30 am, 1.20 pm, 3 pm, 6 pm – $8

Prince George: 7 am, 3 pm – $52.

Getting Around

For local bus information call 492-5602. City buses go from town to both beaches. The No 202 from Wade and Martin goes to Skaha Lake down South Main St. There are no buses on Sundays or holidays.

OSOYOOS

Osoyoos, a small town at the southern end of the Okanagan Valley, is unique in several ways. In an area of stark, dry, rolling hills, it sits at the edge of dark-blue Osoyoos Lake, Canada's warmest. Across the lake lies the country's only desert. This true desert runs about 50 km north to Skaha Lake and is about 20 km across at the widest point. Because of the small size, it's known as a 'pocket desert'. Averaging less than 200 mm of rain a year, the area has much specialised fauna and flora, including the calliope hummingbird (the smallest bird in Canada), rattlesnakes, painted turtles, numerous species of mice, and coyotes. In the plant world are various cacti, desert brushes and grasses.

The area is actually an extension of the northern Mexican desert and the life found is remarkably similar to that at the 600 metres level in the Mexican portion.

In 1975, in co-operation with the provincial government, the locals decided to adopt a theme to beautify the town. Because of the climate, topography and agriculture, a Spanish motif was chosen. Today many businesses and houses have taken on a Spanish look. With the desert background it's quite effective and some of the new-look buildings are beautiful.

With the warm, dry weather Osoyoos produces the earliest and most varied fruit and vegetable crops in Canada. Look for roadside stands selling cherries, apricots, peaches, apples and other fruit. Aside from the orchards there are many vineyards growing grapes for wine.

Osoyoos is at the crossroads of Highway 97 north and Highway 3 running east-west. The US border cutting through Osoyoos Lake is just five km to the south.

Information

The tourist booth (tel 495-6052) is on the corner, where Highway 3 branches off westward from Highway 97, slightly north-west of town. There's another information office (tel 495-7142) in the Lakeview Plaza.

Museum

There is a small museum (tel 495-6723) on Main St.

Vinitera Winery

This gives free tours and includes a tasting room. It's on Highway 11 West.

Anarchist Mountain Lookout

At 700 metres, just east of town on Highway 3, the lookout offers a superb view of the town, valley, desert, lake and the US border. You need a car or a ride to get here.

Dutch Windmill

Less than a km east of town is this windmill (tel 495-7318), a replica of one built in Holland in 1816. You can tour the windmill and see grain being ground. Don't ask why it's here; I've no idea.

Lake

The warm water and sandy beaches make the lake good for swimming. In fact, I've been told this is the warmest lake in the country.

Places to Stay
Boundary Motel is on Rural Route 2 close to the US border. Singles/doubles are $22/24. *La Posada Rialto* is downtown near the beach. It has colour TV and air-conditioning. Singles/doubles $28/34. Good value.

The area is chock full of campgrounds. Though often crowded and not very natural, they are the most economical places to stay. *Cabana Beach Campground* (tel 495-7705), East Lakeshore Drive, Rural Route 1, has small cabanas for rent at $15 to $30 for doubles, as well as tent and trailer space. Two people tenting, $12. *Brook Vale Campsite* (tel 495-7514) along the same road offers the same thing for the same price.

PACIFIC CREST HIKING TRAIL
Between Osoyoos and Chilliwack near the town of Copper Mountain, close to the border, this mega hiking trail begins. You can follow it south all the way to Mexico. See you, good luck.

Northern British Columbia

PRINCE GEORGE
Prince George, 'The Gateway to the North', is not an interesting town but does serve as a useful crossroads point. Highway 97 from Cache Creek cuts through the centre of town on its way north to Dawson Creek and the Alaska Highway. The Yellowhead Highway (16) runs east-west through town. Westward is the long, winding route to Prince Rupert on the coast. East, the Yellowhead goes through Jasper and on to Edmonton.

The town of 69,000 sprawls over a large area. To serve the through traffic there are dozens of motels and several hotels. Pulp & paper is an important industry. The prices are high in this area – you'll notice it most in the restaurants.

Orientation
The downtown area is small and remarkably new-looking, with little character. The main roads running east-west are 2nd, 3rd and 4th Avenues, parallel to the train tracks. The main north-south street is Victoria. Patricia, which is actually Highway 16, is also a main street.

Information
The Tourist Office (tel 563-5493) is at the corner of Highway 97 and the Yellowhead or No 16, south of downtown. There is another office (tel 562-3700) at 1198 Victoria St.

Museum
This is the only sight in town. There are a number of stuffed animals, some Indian artefacts and a few pioneer leftovers. It's in Fort George Park, south-east of town at 20th and Queensway. It's open daily 1 to 4 pm and charges $2.

Places to Stay
Hotels The *National Hotel* is all right for a low-budget place. Accommodation is about $15. It's on 1st Avenue at Dominion, one block north of the train station. On the ground floor is a popular restaurant and a bar with live music at night. The bar also serves food during the day.

Prince George Hotel (tel 564-7211), 487 George St, is the second choice and better. Singles/doubles cost $28/30, with TV. The cheaper ones are bathless. There's music in the bar at night.

MacDonald Hotel at the corner of 3rd Avenue and George St has singles/doubles for $23/28. The bar presents rock bands.

Motels The better places to stay are all motels. There are many, most a bit expensive. A best bet close to town is the *Bel Air Motel* (tel 562-1191) at 1811 Victoria St. Singles/doubles are $32/38. There's colour TV and free coffee.

Slumber Lodge (tel 563-1267) at 910

Victoria St has all the features for $36/40 singles/doubles.

Camping The *Prince George Municipal Campground* (tel 563-8131) on 18th Avenue, is opposite Exhibition Park and close to town. Open 15 May to 5 September. There are hot showers. Two people $9.

Places to Eat

The older hotel bars usually serve a decent cheap meal that goes well with a draught beer.

Getting There & Away

Jasper is 377 km away, Prince Rupert 734 km, Vancouver 781 km.

Bus The Greyhound Bus Station (tel 564-5454) is at 1566 12th Avenue, near the corner of Victoria and Patricia. Open 5.30 am to midnight, until 10.15 pm on Sunday. There's a restaurant.

Vancouver: 12.01 am, 8.30 am, 6 pm
Okanagan: 8.30 am, midnight
Jasper, Edmonton: 8.30 am.

Fares, one-way: Kamloops $34, Prince Rupert $46, Jasper $26.

Train The station is on 1st Avenue at the top of Victoria St. For information and fares call 112-800-665-8630 at no charge. The westbound train leaves daily at 11.15 pm. The eastbound leaves daily at 6.10 am.

The Rupert train only goes three times a week and the days vary, so check. The Vancouver train goes to Jasper first, so be prepared for a long ride. The small local train to Vancouver is an historic route following the Caribou Trail which led to Quesnel, an old mining town. The train goes by numerous very small towns.

Fares, one-way: Jasper $31, Vancouver $68, Prince Rupert $41.

AROUND PRINCE GEORGE

There are dozens of lakes with good fishing around Prince George. Some have camping spots; most have boats for hire. Ask at the Tourist Office for more information.

Barkerville Historic Provincial Park

South of Prince George, 88 km east of Quesnel, is this restored town in the northern reaches of the gold rush district known as Cariboo Country. Between 1858 and 1861 the Cariboo Trail, now Highway 97, was pushed north from Kamloops to Quesnel. It was lined with hastily-built towns and gold seekers from around the world. In 1862, a Cornishman, Billy Barker, hit the jackpot, making $1000 in the first two days of his claim. Soon Barkerville sprang up to become the largest city west of Chicago and north of San Francisco. The big boom was instrumental in British Columbia becoming a Crown Colony in 1858.

The town quickly faded but today you can see how it was, with its general store, hotel, trade-shops and, of course, saloon. In the Theatre Royal, dancing shows are staged in the manner the miners once whistled at. There is also a museum which gives some of the background story and displays artefacts. Open 9 am to 4 pm daily. You can try your luck panning for gold at the site, too. Maybe you'll have a town named after you.

There's no bus to Barkerville so you'll have to hitch if you don't have a car. There are campsites in the park and hotels in the nearby towns. Admission to the park is $5.

Bowron Lake Provincial Park

There is an excellent circular canoe route near Barkerville in Bowron Lake Provincial Park. A number of lakes, separated by rapids and portages, form a connecting route around the perimeter of the park. Canoe rentals are available: a two-person canoe is $10 per day for seven days or more. Rentals for less than a week cost a couple of dollars more per day. The 116-km route takes an average of seven days to complete. Mountains in and around the park are about 2000 metres high.

Alexander Mackenzie Trail
Not far from Quesnel, this recently rediscovered and refurbished route follows ancient trails from the Fraser River west to Bella Coola on the Pacific Ocean. Mackenzie made the first recorded crossing of continental North America on this same route in 1793. His graffiti can still be seen carved in a rock near Bella Coola. The trail goes over Indian lands, ranches, private property and archaeological sites as it winds its way through forest and mountains. It's about 250 km long and is a tough 16-day walk. At least one food drop is required but you can do some of the more accessible segments for a few days: for example, in Tweedsmuir Park, which the trail cuts through. A detailed map book and guide is available, produced by the Nature Conservancy of Canada. It's available by mail and perhaps in some of the better outdoor stores.

TOWARDS PRINCE RUPERT

At Kitimat there are tours of the Alcan Aluminium Plant, free. Just outside Hazelton is K'san, a restored Indian village. The local Tsimshian tribes are known for their craftworks in gold, silver and hardwood. There are long-houses, totem poles and examples of their tools. You'll also see several mines and mills along the route which offer free tours.

There are plenty of places to camp at along the way. Hitching is not good due to little traffic and unpredictable weather, although a traveller has written saying the hitching was good when he was there and that the campgrounds close after Labour Day (early September).

Pacific Northwest

PRINCE RUPERT

Other than Vancouver, Rupert, as it's called, is the largest city on the BC coast. It's the fishing centre of the Pacific Northwest, although it can no longer lay claim to being the world's halibut capital. That the sign indicating this title remains on the highway into town tells you something about the pace here. Despite being one of the rainiest spots in Canada, the town can look magnificent. If it's not misty, foggy or under heavy cloud you'll appreciate the setting. Surrounded by mountains, sitting at the mouth of the Skeena River, looking out at the fiord-like coastline, the area is ruggedly beautiful.

Prince Rupert is a good starting point for trips to Alaska and the Queen Charlotte Islands. Recently too many people, mainly young, have arrived here in summer looking for work. The town of 18,000 fills its needs quickly. Remember, too, that with the influx of tourists, accommodation in July and August can be scarce.

Information
The Prince Rupert Visitors Information Bureau (tel 624-5637) is at 1st Avenue and McBridge.

All West run tours in and around town, nearby islands and the Skeena Valley.

Things to See
The Museum of Northern British Columbia (tel 624-3207), has a good collection of Indian art and craftwork including masks, carvings and beadwork. Outside the museum are some fine totem pole examples. Note that the Indians are called 'Natives' in this neck of the woods.

The gondola up Mount Hayes will take you to some scenic viewpoints. There's skiing here and around the area in winter.

Tours of the fish canneries in Rupert are free. They do much of their own processing. Try not to say 'something smells fishy around here'.

Not far from town are some Indian petroglyphs. Ask at the information office.

The Salmon Festival is actually a

north coast Indian festival, drawing people from the district.

Places to Stay

There is a hostel-type place, though not a CYHA, on Hays Cove Circle. Those looking for work often put up here.

The *Campground*, with the best views in town, lies right at the centre of things, by the hospital.

Cheapest of the motels is the *Aleeda* (tel 627-1367) at 900 3rd Avenue West. Singles/doubles are $35/45. Car storage is available.

Places to Eat

The *Smiles Seafood Café* on the waterfront, next door to the Yacht Club, serves very good food. The neighbourhood pub, *Solly's*, at the north end of town, is where people drink.

Getting There & Away

Ferries Prince Rupert is the terminal for the ferry to Alaska. Numerous ferries ply the Alaskan Panhandle; you can sleep on them without getting a room. First stop is Ketchikan, but you can go north past Juneau to Skagway where the Klondike Highway to Whitehorse comes down from the Yukon. Ask at the Alaskan State Ferries office. Various commercial cruise lines do the route as well. An example is Princess Cruises, with trips to Vancouver or San Francisco. Other cruise lines such as Admiral, Cunard, Exploration and Royal Cruise ply the west coast. Each offers a variety of lengths and stopovers. They have good private rooms and good meals; some offer nightly entertainment and all are costly. The ferry systems are much, much cheaper.

BC Ferries (tel 624-9627) runs ships southward and to the Queen Charlotte Islands. The route from Washington State to the Alaskan Panhandle is known as the Inside Passage. It's a long, expensive trip but offers beautiful scenery past many bays, inlets, islands and small Indian settlements. It's not uncommon to see seals, herds of sea lions or pods of killer whales. You can take just part of the trip rather than the whole voyage. The *Queen of the North* from Rupert stops only at Bella Bella and Ocean Falls, both without roads, so for this part of the trip you must go all the way to Port Hardy on Vancouver Island. The straight one-way fare for a walk-on is $56, car and driver $174. Rooms are extra. The trip takes about 15 hours. Reservations are a good idea and if you want to take a vehicle book well in advance.

QUEEN CHARLOTTE ISLANDS

The Queen Charlottes, sometimes known as the Canadian Galapagos, are an archipelago of some 154 islands lying 80 km off the BC coast and about 50 km from the southern tip of Alaska. As the only part of Canada which escaped the last ice age, the islands are rich in flora and fauna as well as native history. Essentially still a wilderness area, the Charlottes are warmed by a Japanese current and hit with 50 inches of rain annually. All these factors combine to create a landscape of 1000-year-old spruce and cedar rainforests, abundant animals and waters teeming with marine life.

The islands have been inhabited continuously for 10,000 years and are the traditional homeland of the Haida Nation, generally acknowledged as the el primo Indian culture in the country upon the white man's arrival. Their arts, notably the totems and carvings in argillate (a black, glass-like stone) are world renowned. They were also fearsome warriors and dominated the west coast. Today they are still a proud, defiant people who led the internationally publicised fight to preserve the islands from further logging. This environment-versus-economy debate raged bitterly until recently, when the federal government decided to save South Moresby and create a National Park. Chalk up one for Mother Nature.

Graham Island contains 80% of the

population and has the only real road system. Skidegate at the south end and Masset at the north, both on the eastern shore, are the principal towns. The north-eastern part of the island is taken up by Naikoon National Park; most of the full 60 km of the east coast is sandy beach. Near Skidegate is a good museum on the area's history including an excellent collection of native works. Skidegate and Masset both have a couple of motels and there is camping in the north.

Most of the region is very inaccessible. Tiny Anthony Island, at the southern end of the chain, is a provincial park and United Nations World Heritage Site. It protects an old Haida village, Ninstints, called the most impressive coastal Indian site in the Pacific North-west. There are 32 totem poles and remains of 10 longhouses. The only trouble is you can't get there!

Getting There & Away

The ferry from Rupert, MV *Queen of Prince Rupert*, makes five trips a week, each taking 6½ hours and costing $12.75 walk-on, $60.75 for car and driver. Some crossings are day trips and some over-nighters. The terminal is at Skidegate.

At Sandspit on Moresby Island, south of Skidegate, is an airport with service from Rupert and Vancouver.

Eastern British Columbia

The eastern part of the province is dominated by the major mountain chains of the Rockies, the Selkirks, the Purcells and the Columbias. This is an area for outdoor activities – camping, hiking, climbing in summer and some of North America's best skiing in winter. The south-east corner of the province is a series of populated valleys nestled between the parallel mountain chains. There are national and provincial parks throughout the area. Summers are short in the Rockies; it's not unusual to have snow in the mountains at the end of August.

Wells Gray Provincial Park

About halfway between Kamloops and Jasper is this huge, undeveloped and relatively little-visited wilderness park. There's hiking, canoeing and camping here. Access is by gravel road.

REVELSTOKE & AREA

This small town of 8000 looks big on the map because it's on the Trans-Canada. The town is pleasant, with quiet residential streets lined with neat wooden houses and tidy gardens. It's surrounded by mountains at the edge of Mt Revelstoke National Park and is about halfway between the Okanagan and the Rockies.

For a small place, Revelstoke is busy as a railway centre and now as home to workers on the nearby dam construction site. There are a fair number of bikers in the area.

The main street is 1st St. Tourist Information is in the Chamber of Commerce at 109 Connaught Avenue.

Most of the things to see are not in the town itself but around the Revelstoke area. You'll need transport.

Museum & Art Gallery

On 1st St at the corner of Boyle, this is open Monday to Saturday, free. It holds changing exhibits and a permanent collection of furniture and odds and ends from local history. There are also mining, logging and railway artefacts. It's worth a few minutes. The gallery is open daily in the afternoons.

Canyon Hot Springs

These are a great spot for a quick visit, 35 km along the highway. The site consists of a hot pool (40°C) and a larger, cooler swimming pool. Admission is only $3.50 and that includes a locker and shower. If you go to the Tourist Office and pick up a pamphlet on the place, you'll get a pass good for one free admission if one adult ticket is bought. The site opens at 8 am, and early in the morning you can have the place to yourself – stay as long as you want.

Mount Revelstoke National Park

This is a relatively small national park, just east of Revelstoke in the Selkirk Mountains. The Selkirks have jagged, rugged peaks and steep valleys. The view of these from Mount Revelstoke is excellent. A 26-km road leads to the peak through cedars, alpine meadows and near-tundra at the top. There are some good hiking trails from the summit, with back-country camping permitted. Other than this there is no camping in the park. There's good skiing in the very long winters. Much of the summer is rainy.

Three Valley Gap

On the Trans-Canada 20 km west of Revelstoke is this re-creation of a pioneer community. It's still under construction and about 20 buildings have been put up. Nearby is the site of Three Valley, a mining town which blossomed and died in the late 1880s. There's a saloon, an old hotel, a barber shop and a blacksmith's, amongst other buildings.

Dams

BC Hydro runs two free tours of the new Mica Dam daily. One of the world's highest dams, it's 136 km north of Revelstoke in a bend of the Columbia River. The Revelstoke Dam, five km north of town, is now being constructed. Tours can be arranged here, too, but are less frequent.

Places to Stay

King Edward Hotel (tel 837-5104), corner of 2nd and Orton, is a good, low-budget place. Singles/doubles $22/26.

Revelstoke Motor Inn is one block down from King Eddie on 1st and Orton. There's a bar and small restaurant where the locals gather for breakfast and coffee. Singles/doubles $22/28. The bath is shared. *The Peaks Motel* (tel 837-2176), five km west of town on Highway 1, charges $28, with TV.

There's a campground at *Canyon Springs*.

There are many other places – nearly all motels – which are better, newer and more expensive.

Getting There & Away

Greyhound Bus Lines makes four trips east and west daily. VIA Rail passes through town daily, once in each direction.

GOLDEN

As you come from Alberta along the Trans-Canada, this town of 3600 people is the first of any size in British Columbia. Golden is the town to which workers in the area come for something to eat and a booze-up. *The Mad Trapper* on 9th St beside the railway is a pretty good pub-like bar. There's also a bakery and a laundromat in town.

The Tourist Office (tel 344-7125) is in the Chamber of Commerce caboose.

GLACIER NATIONAL PARK

This 1350-square-km park lies about halfway between Golden and Revelstoke. There are more than 400 glaciers here and it snows nearly every day in winter. The annual snowfall can be as much as 23 metres. Because of the sheer mountain slopes, this is one of the world's most active avalanche areas. Around Rogers Pass you'll notice the many snowsheds protecting the highway. With the narrow road twisting at up to 1327 metres, this is a dangerous area, sometimes called Death Strip; an unexpected avalanche can wipe a car right off the road. Still, the area is controlled; often snows are brought tumbling down with artillery before they fall by themselves.

YOHO NATIONAL PARK

Yoho Park is in the BC Rockies, adjacent to the border and Alberta's Banff Park. The name is a Cree word expressing wonder. It's a park offering peaks and valleys, glacial lakes, beautiful meadows – a bit of everything. It's more accessible and the weather is better than at Glacier.

The town of Field, lying in the middle of the park, is the first town in BC along the highway. There's a grocery store – closed on Sundays – which is good for supplies if you're going to stay in the park. It's cheaper than the store near the falls. There is a Tourist Office 12 km from the Alberta border.

Near Field is the turn-off for Takakkaw Falls, the highest in Canada at 380 metres. There is a campground nearby and a good *Youth Hostel* across the street.

Also near Field are the famous spiral tunnels, the feats of engineering that enable the Canadian Pacific Railway trains to navigate the challenging Kicking Horse Pass.

The trail from Takakkaw Falls to Twin Falls makes a good day hike. The trail is mostly flat with lots of rapids and waterfalls. There's camping on the way. The *Tea Chalet* at the top has a $2 minimum.

Emerald Lake is a beautiful green lake with a walking trail around it. It's small and warm enough for a quick swim in late summer. O'Hara Lake is another beauty spot with excellent hiking. You can hike the 13 km in, or take a bus for a couple of dollars. It's a busy spot, though.

The rushing Kicking Horse River flows through the park and has a natural stone bridge near Emerald Lake.

KOOTENAY NATIONAL PARK

Kootenay Park is solely in BC but is adjacent to Banff Park and runs south from Yoho. It has a more moderate climate than the other Rocky Mountain parks. In the southern regions especially, summers can be hot without much rain. Highway 93 runs down the centre and is really the only road in the park. From the top to Radium there are campgrounds, points of interest, hiking trails and views of the valley along the Kootenay River.

Bighorn sheep

There is a short, easy trail into what are called 'paint pots', which are ochre beds. For years, first Indians and then white people collected this oddly coloured earth as a colouring agent. Now artificial dyes are used.

Stop at Marble Canyon for the walk here – it is a real adrenalin-maker. The trail follows a rushing river from side to side, crossing frequently on small wooden bridges with longer and longer drops below. Nearby, across the road, the campground is good. It's a basic one with no electricity. We saw a moose right by the tent.

Along the highway you may see a park warden by the side of the road with pelts from the many types of animals that have been hit by cars.

Radium, at the end of the park, is a rather ugly or, let's say, plain little town but the hot springs here are always worth a visit.

MOUNT ASSINIBOINE PARK

Adjacent to Kootenay is this less-talked-about, less-visited provincial park. Though there's no campground, there's camping and hiking – walk-in only. Access is from the 93.

KIMBERLEY

This is the highest city in Canada. Before 1973, the town of 8000 people looked like what it is – a small mountain mining town. But as one of the province's 'theme' towns, it has been made to look like a Bavarian alpine village. Most of the downtown section has been transformed with enough detail to make it interesting. The skiing is excellent in winter. The July festival is a weekend of dancing, parades and lots of beer.

CASTLEGAR

This is an area where many members of a Russian Christian pacifist sect – the Doukhabors – settled at the beginning of the century. There is a reconstructed Doukhabor village to visit and a cultural centre including a restaurant which serves their specialities.

NAKUSP

This is the main town in the valley south of Revelstoke, east of the Okanagan. The dry, picturesque valley follows a chain of lakes between the Monashee and Selkirk Mountain Ranges. There is a major road to Vernon, south of Nakusp, going over the Monashee Pass. Near Vernon, the road goes through beautiful country scenery of small farms and wooded hills. There are campgrounds and a few small provincial parks along this route.

In Nakusp itself is a pleasant hot springs site with a campground.

Yukon & Northwest Territories

Area	Yukon:	483 450 square km
	NWT:	3 246 000 square km
Population	Yukon:	23 150
	NWT:	45 740

Canada's northern territories make up a vast tract of land stretching from the northern provincial boundaries to within 800 km of the North Pole and from the Atlantic Ocean to the Pacific. A third ocean, the Arctic, links Alaska and Greenland across the many islands of the far north.

For the most part, this land of the midnight sun is as reputation has it: a barren, treeless tundra that's nearly always frozen. But it is definitely not all this way. There are mountains and forests, abundant wildlife and warm summer days with 20 hours of light.

In general, the development of the far north occurred where conditions were most hospitable and the land most varied and scenic. Fortunately, these places are still the most accessible; tourism increases each year.

The designation of the Yukon and Northwest as territories rather than provinces is a political one. With relatively few people, full status in parliament has been withheld, something the locals have been moving to change in recent years.

Yukon Territory

The Yukon is a triangular slice of northern Canada wedged between the Northwest Territories and Alaska. To the south is British Columbia; the north is bounded by the Beaufort Sea in the Arctic Ocean. It's a sub-arctic region about one-third the size of Alaska.

Mountain ranges, including some that continue from the Rockies, almost entirely cover the Yukon. In the Saint Elias Range, Mt Logan at 5950 metres is Canada's highest. Forests, wooded hills, lakes and streams flow and grow amidst the mountains.

There are only about 25,000 people in the area of 480,000 square km, and most of them live in towns. Over half are in the Whitehorse region. The bulk of the rest live in and around mining camps. By far the majority of the people are white. Indians number under 3000. The Yukon Indian people, the Denes or Athapaskans, are thought to have inhabited the region for 50,000 years, which would make them the oldest residents of North America.

In the 1840s, Robert Campbell, a Hudson's Bay Company explorer, was the first white man to travel the district. In 1870 the area became part of the region known as the Northwest Territories. But it was in 1896 that the biggest changes began. Gold was found in a tributary of the Klondike River, all hell broke loose and the ensuing gold rush attracted hopefuls from around the world. The population boomed to over 35,000, quite a bit higher than today's. Towns grew up overnight to support the rough-and-ready wealth-seekers. Suppliers and entertainers rather than prospectors were the ones raking in the money.

In 1898, the Yukon became a separate territory with Dawson City the capital. In 1951 Whitehorse became the capital, for it had the railway and now acts as the main distribution centre. The people of Whitehorse are condescendingly known

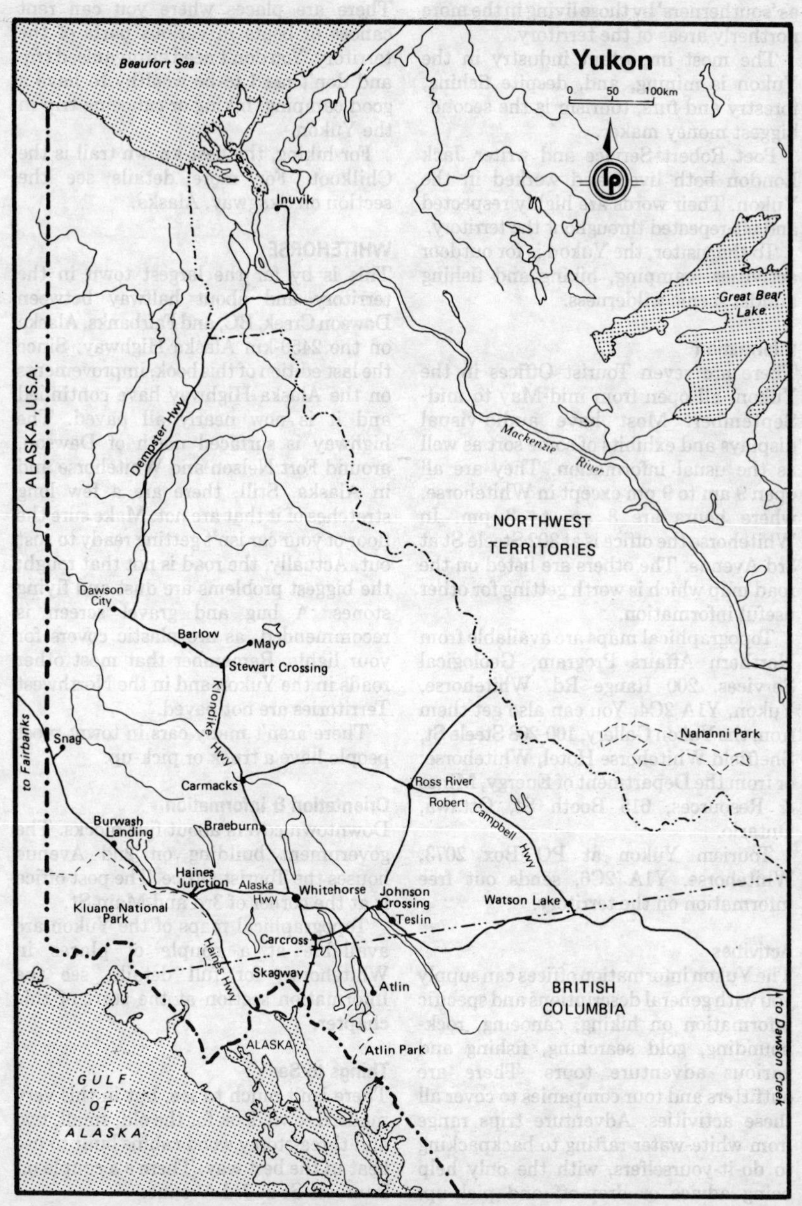
Beaufort Sea
Yukon
0 50 100km
Inuvik
Great Bear Lake
Dempster Hwy
ALASKA, U.S.A.
Mackenzie River
NORTHWEST TERRITORIES
Dawson City
Barlow
Mayo
Stewart Crossing
Klondike Hwy
to Fairbanks
Snag
Nahanni Park
Carmacks
Ross River
Robert Campbell Hwy
Burwash Landing
Braeburn
Haines Junction
Alaska Hwy
Whitehorse
Johnson Crossing
Teslin
Watson Lake
Kluane National Park
Haines Hwy
Carcross
Skagway
Atlin
BRITISH COLUMBIA
to Dawson Creek
ALASKA
Atlin Park
GULF OF ALASKA

as 'southerners' by those living in the more northerly areas of the territory.

The most important industry in the Yukon is mining, and, despite fishing, forestry and furs, tourism is the second-biggest money maker.

Poet Robert Service and writer Jack London both lived and worked in the Yukon. Their words are highly respected and oft-repeated throughout the territory.

To the visitor, the Yukon is for outdoor activities: camping, hiking and fishing amidst scenic wilderness.

Information

There are seven Tourist Offices in the Yukon, all open from mid-May to mid-September. Most have audio-visual displays and exhibits of some sort as well as the usual information. They are all open 9 am to 9 pm except in Whitehorse, where hours are 8 am to 8 pm. In Whitehorse the office is at 302 Steele St at 3rd Avenue. The others are listed on the road map which is worth getting for other useful information.

Topographical maps are available from Northern Affairs Program, Geological Services, 200 Range Rd, Whitehorse, Yukon, Y1A 2C4. You can also get them from the Yukon Gallery, 100-208 Steele St, Sheffield Whitehorse Hotel, Whitehorse; or from the Department of Energy, Mines & Resources, 615 Booth St, Ottawa, Ontario.

Tourism Yukon at PO Box 2073, Whitehorse, Y1A 2C6, sends out free information on the territory.

Activities

The Yukon information offices can supply you with general descriptions and specific information on hiking, canoeing, rock-hounding, gold searching, fishing and various adventure tours. There are outfitters and tour companies to cover all these activities. Adventure trips range from white-water rafting to backpacking to do-it-yourselfers, with the only help being advice or drop-off and pick-up. There are places where you can rent canoes or boats in various parts of the territory. You don't need an organised trip and don't need to be wealthy to have a good camping, hiking or canoeing trip in the Yukon.

For hiking, the best-known trail is the Chilkoot. For more details see the section on Skagway, Alaska.

WHITEHORSE

This is by far the largest town in the territory and about halfway between Dawson Creek, BC, and Fairbanks, Alaska on the 2450-km Alaska Highway. Since the last edition of this book, improvements on the Alaska Highway have continued and it is now nearly all paved. The highway is surfaced north of Dawson, around Fort Nelson and Whitehorse and in Alaska. Still, there are a few long stretches of it that are not. Make sure the floor of your car isn't getting ready to rust out. Actually, the road is not that rough; the biggest problems are dust and flying stones. A bug and gravel screen is recommended, as are plastic covers for your lights. Remember that most other roads in the Yukon and in the Northwest Territories are not paved.

There aren't many cars in town: most people have a truck or pick-up.

Orientation & Information

Downtown covers about five blocks. The government building on 2nd Avenue houses the Tourist Office. The post office is at the corner of 3rd and Main St.

Topographical maps of the Yukon are available at a couple of places in Whitehorse; for full details, see the Information section at the start of this chapter.

Things to See

There isn't much to see, but in this very modern town, look for the old, small, two and three-storey wood cabins built to use heat in the best way. There's a couple on Lambert St at 3rd Avenue.

SS Klondike
The *SS Klondike* was one of the last sternwheel riverboats used on the Yukon River. It is now restored and moored. Open daily, free.

MacBride Museum
This is in a log cabin on 1st Avenue at Steele St. It contains a collection of materials from the gold rush days and displays of Yukon wildlife. Open until 9 pm, $1.50 admission.

Old Log Church
This was built by the town's first priest in 1900. Known as the only wooden cathedral in the world, it is also the oldest building in town. Inside are artefacts from early churches around the territory. Services are held on Sunday evening. At other times, admission is $1. The church is on Elliot St at 3rd Avenue.

Takhini Hot Springs
These hot springs are 27.4 km from town on the Klondike Highway. Bathing suits can be rented. Open all year, from 8 am to 10 pm daily.

Black Mike's Gold Mine
About 30 km south from town at Black Mike's Gold Mine there is a museum where a mine tour is available. You can also try panning for gold. Open daily.

Places to Stay
For a smallish town, Whitehorse has plenty of hotels and motels but they are not cheap. About $60 to $65 a single is average. Generally speaking, the smaller places cost less.

The Whitehorse Bed & Breakfast Agency (tel 633-4609) is worth trying at 102-302 Steele St, open all year. They have homes in town and in other parts of the Yukon, including Dawson City.

The *Youth Hostel* (tel 668-4582) up here seems to change a lot but there usually is one. At last check it was at 15 Chalet Crescent. It's open all year. Members pay $10, non-members $15, but it's small, with just six beds.

Alternately, there's the *Yukon Youth Centre* north of town which takes in travellers. It's at Mile 20 (32 km) on the Klondike Highway toward Dawson City, about a 35-minute drive from town.

The *Lake Lebarge Campground* (tel 633-5265) is across the highway. The centre is a non-profit organisation geared to helping young people, but travellers are also welcome. There are various projects to take part in for a week or longer, such as farming, etc.

Back in town, at *St Joseph's Hostel*, not far from the Super Valu supermarket, men can stay for free. Apparently, there is also a women's hostel and it will take in men as well. Cost is reported to be about $20. The Tourist Office should have the address and other information on the ebb and flow of these hostels.

Places to Eat
Food is also more costly here than further south but not greatly so. There are several fast-food outlets and Chinese restaurants, which should do. Most of the hotels have restaurants or dining rooms. *The Deli* at 203 Hanson is reasonably priced for light meals. Pizza is available at *G & P* in the Kopper King Complex. In the Qwanlin Mall at 4th Avenue and Ogilvie, *Woolworth's* has cheap meals. The *Keg & Cleaver*, on 3rd and Jarvis, has steaks.

Whitehorse is the last town going north (at least in Canada) where the food is not too pricey. At Inuvik, for example, costs are nearly three times higher, so take supplies with you. Alaska, however, is cheaper than anywhere in the Yukon. One letter I received noted the only things cheaper on the Canadian side were canned salmon, canned raspberries, grapes and tea!

Nightlife
Back in town, the Frantic Follies is a 1890s-style review with comedy skits and dancing girls. The show is held nightly in

the Sheffield Whitehorse Hotel through the summer.

Tours

The Yukon Historical & Museums Association conducts free guided walking tours of the downtown area. The Association is at Donnenworth House, 3126 3rd Avenue, and opens daily.

The Yukon Conservation Society (tel 668-5678) offers free nature walks in the area on weekdays.

Close to town there are also organised two-hour boat trips down through Miles Canyon from Schwatka Lake in early June to mid-September. Various other local tours are available.

KLUANE NATIONAL PARK

Kluane (pronounced klu-ah-nee), a rugged wilderness area, sits in the extreme south-western corner of the Yukon adjacent to Alaska. The park is very mountainous. Mt Logan, part of the St Elias chain, is, at 5950 metres, Canada's highest mountain. The world's largest non-polar ice fields are also here. Valleys, lakes and tundra make for excellent scenery and hiking. There are several good trails, some following old mining roads, others, traditional Indian paths. There's a hiking trail leading to Kaskawulsh glacier – one of the few that can be reached by foot. Fishing is good and wildlife abounds, including moose and Dall sheep which can be seen on Sheep Mountain even from the road. There's also a small herd of caribou and grizzly bears, as well as 150 varieties of birds, among them the rare peregrine falcon and eagles. Temperatures are comfortable from mid-June to August.

There is only one campground within the park which costs $6 for an unserviced site, and it is at Kathleen Lake. There are several others just outside the park. Of course, you can try back country tenting along overnight trails. At Haines Junction there is a Park Reception Centre with information. There's another at Sheep Mountain.

NORTHERN YUKON NATIONAL PARK

Northern Yukon is a new national park of 6,000 square km which has been created along the Beaufort Sea adjoining Alaska. It's on a caribou migration route and is also a major waterfowl habitat. Its facilities are apparently minimal and, though there's no road access, there are probably flights on one of the regional airlines that will get you there.

ATLIN

South of Whitehorse in BC is the small town of Atlin and its provincial park and lake. The scenery is good: forest and snow-capped mountains around the lake.

SKAGWAY, ALASKA

Skagway is on the Klondike Highway, which goes north through Whitehorse to Dawson City. The drive from Whitehorse takes about three hours, passing lakes, mountains and meadows. A narrow-gauge train service between Whitehorse and Skagway, completed in 1900 over White Pass, was, until 1982, the last one operating in the Yukon. (For more information on the train, see the Getting There & Away section in this chapter.)

Skagway is the northern terminal for many Alaskan and BC ferry trips down the Panhandle; you can go all the way to Vancouver along the scenic Inside Passage. (See the section on Prince Rupert, BC, for more information.)

Skagway was the landing point for many in the gold rush days. From here began the long, slow, sometimes deadly haul to the Klondike gold area near Dawson City. The old route, the Chilkoot Trail over the pass, is used today by hikers. You can see dumped hardware, tools and supplies along the trail. At several places there are wooden shacks where you can put up for the night. Take a few layers of clothes and be prepared to constantly peel them off and then pile them back on. The pass trail takes three to four days and is 52 km long. At the end, you can catch a boat to Carcross at Lake

Bennet or head to the highway and a bus to Whitehorse.

STEWART CROSSING

This town is a supply centre between Dawson and Whitehorse. A branch of the main road heading north-east goes to three old, small mining and fur-trading towns. Mayo is the starting point for a popular canoe trip to Dawson via the Mayo and Yukon Rivers. Keno Hill offers good views, with its signposts and distances to cities all over the world.

DAWSON CITY

The Klondike Highway from Skagway, Alaska, through British Columbia and Whitehorse, Yukon, to Dawson City, more or less traces the trail some 40,000 gold seekers took in 1898. Dawson City became the heart of the gold rush. Today, it is the most interesting of the Yukon towns with many attractions remaining from its fleeting but vibrant fling with world fame and infamy.

Once known as 'the Paris of the north' with deluxe hotels and restaurants, plush river steamers and stores stocking luxury items cherished by the world's wealthy, Dawson is now a small town of about 1500 people. It lies just 240 km south of the Arctic Circle.

Many of the original buildings are still standing. Parks Canada has restored or preserved quite a few, giving the town an odd mix of authentic gold rush architecture and new modern.

Diamond Tooth Gerite's Gambling Hall

This is a re-creation of an 1898 saloon, complete with gambling, honky-tonk piano and dancing girls.

Palace Grand Theatre

This large, flamboyant opera house/ dance hall was built in 1899 by 'Arizona Charlie' Meadows. Like other restored buildings in town, it has a western movie-type false front. The Gaslight Follies present stage shows nightly – musicals or melodramas with villains in black and Mounties to the rescue.

Dawson Museum

This museum houses a collection of 25,000 gold rush artefacts and displays on the district's people. Admission is $2.

Gold

You can try panning for gold in nearby creeks. There are tours, or you can go by car, to one of the historic mining sites. Many other claims in the area are private, so pick your spot carefully. People have been killed for less.

Klondike-era films on mining, the gold rush and other subjects are shown daily in summer at 9 am and 5 pm in St Paul's Church, which opens from 1 June to 1 September. They're worth a look. Admission is by donation.

Readings

Of literary interest are professional recitals of poems by Robert Service in the log cabin where he lived from 1909 to 1912. His poems are concerned with the hardships associated with life in the developing wilderness. Parts of 'Songs of a Rolling Stone' were written here. In 1898, Jack London lived in the Yukon and wrote many of his popular animal stories. He's best known for his *Call of the Wild*. In his re-located cabin, you can hear recitals from and about his works.

Riverboat

The SS *Keno*, one of the area's last riverboats, is on display as a National Historic Site in the Yukon River. Free.

Midnight Dome

Outside town is the Midnight Dome at 880 metres above sea level. It offers good views of the Klondike Valley and Yukon River. On 21 June the midnight sun barely sinks below the Ogilvie Mountains to the north before rising again.

Events
Events to look for include the Midnight Dome Race in July and the three-day music festival in late July. In August there's Discovery Days, a three-day event commemorating the discovery of gold in the Klondike in 1896. Featured are parades, music and dances. In early September – are you ready for this – is the 'outhouse on wheels' race through town.

Places to Stay
For accommodation, there isn't a great selection – a few hotels, a couple of motels and two campgrounds, one government and one private. You can also call the Bed & Breakfast Association (tel 668-2999).

Getting There & Away
The Klondike Highway is an all-weather gravel road to Skagway via Stewart Crossing and Whitehorse. There is an airport 19 km from town, with regular flights to Inuvik, Whitehorse and the Northwest Territories.

TOWARDS INUVIK, NWT
The Dempster Highway, also called the No 5, leads from Dawson City north over the Ogilvie and Richardson Mountains beyond the Arctic Circle and down to the ocean in the Northwest Territories. Inuvik is the town at the end of the line. The road opened in 1978 and makes road travel along the full length of North America possible. Inuvik is a long way from Dawson – 721 km of gravel road – but the scenery is good: hills, valleys, vast open space. See 'Inuvik' in the Northwest Territories section for more details.

GETTING THERE & AWAY
Air
Canadian Airlines (tel 668-3535) has daily services to Whitehorse from Edmonton and Vancouver. Air North connects Whitehorse to Alaskan towns such as Fairbanks and Juneau.

Within the Yukon a number of small airlines and charters feed the smaller towns and settlements. Alkan Air has scheduled flights to Inuvik, NWT, Dawson City, etc.

Bus
Alaska Yukon Motorcoaches has runs between Haines, Skagway, Fairbanks and Anchorage, with connections for Alaska ferries, Coachways buses and the train. Coachways buses offer services between Edmonton, northern BC, Whitehorse, Dawson City and Alaska. Norline coaches connect the Yukon with Alaskan points and services a number of towns in the Yukon such as Tok and Beaver Creek. Others connect smaller towns to bigger centres.

Train
There was one short train line called the White Pass & Yukon Route (WP & YR), which connected Skagway, Alaska and Whitehorse over 177 km of narrow gauge. The train relied more heavily on fees raised from transporting ore from mines than on people. Unfortunately, since 1982, when several mines closed, the train has not run and the Skagway station is evidently now a giftshop. The re-opening of the line depends on the world's metal markets, so check at an information office. The trip is an interesting one over rough terrain with a good historical angle, too. The line opened in 1900 to feed the gold rush.

Ferry
Skagway is the northern terminal for ferries and cruise ships plying up and down the continental west coast. Beginning in San Francisco, Seattle, Vancouver, Vancouver Island and Prince Rupert, these ships edge along the coastline to Skagway. From there, buses connect to Whitehorse. The American ferries, known as the Alaska Marine Highway System, run south to Prince Rupert and have an office in Juneau, Alaska. They also have one trip per week that goes further south, all the way to Seattle or vice versa. BC

Ferries handles most traffic south of Rupert. See the section on Prince Rupert, BC for details.

GETTING AROUND

Road

The road system in the Yukon is fairly extensive, if rough. Most roads are gravel.

The main highways in the Yukon are the Klondike, the Dempster and the Alaska. The Tourist Office has information on all the highways and what there is to see from them.

The Alaska Highway, the main road in the Yukon, is 2,450 km long and starts in Dawson Creek, British Columbia. It enters the Yukon in the south-east and passes through Whitehorse en route to Fairbanks, Alaska. It was built in just nine months in 1942 as part of the war effort. Now, each summer, the Alaskan is very busy (some even say clogged) with visitors mainly driving recreational vehicles, RVs. At times there are ten of these homes-on-wheels for every car or truck.

There are roads connecting most southern towns. North of Dawson City, the Dempster Highway, which ends at Inuvik, NWT, is the only choice.

A good circular trip is to travel from Whitehorse to Dawson City to Fairbanks. Coming back, take the Alaska Highway past Kluane Park to Whitehorse.

There are campgrounds along most of the highway routes.

Driving Gasoline prices along these highways are pretty outrageous any way you look at it, but you're stuck with them unless you take advantage of cheaper places and fill up even if you don't need to. Generally, along the main routes, there's a station every 50 km, but in some areas there may be no competition for 150 km. Prices are less in the main towns than out on the stretches, but can really vary for no apparent reason. Three places where the petrol is not so expensive are Dawson Creek, BC, where the Alaskan Highway begins, Whitehorse and Dawson City. Petrol is very expensive in Inuvik; expect to pay, pay, pay. The good news is that prices all over Alaska are much cheaper than in Canada.

Rentals

Because most of the roads are gravel, your own vehicle is the best way to get around.

There are car rentals in Whitehorse, including Hertz, Tilden and Avis outlets.

Recreational vehicles or RVs are mobile homes which range from moderate campers, basically a small apartment on a pick-up truck, to full-size motor homes. The majority you'll see are from the US, but many RVs are also rented in Canada – at rental outlets in places like Whitehorse, Vancouver and Edmonton – by non-Canadians to use as their mobile vacation hotels. If you're surprised by the size and features of some of these suckers you should be: they come with price tags of up to half a million dollars.

You can also rent other means of getting around such as boats and motors, canoes or kayaks.

Bus

Bus is a good alternative; see the Getting There & Away section for more information. The major towns are connected.

Places to Stay

If you rent or buy a recreational vehicle, you've not only got a means of transport, but a place to stay as well. The Yukon government's series of campgrounds is good, with many along the highways. There are also numerous private grounds, some geared strictly to the RV market.

Northwest Territories

The Northwest Territories cover an enormous area – nearly a third of Canada. Stretching from the Yukon to Greenland, the region includes many islands in the Arctic Ocean. About half of the land area is north of the Arctic Circle.

With an area of over three million square km and a population of just 50,000, the territories have a density of about one person per 100 square km. That's a lot of breathing room. The inhabitants include about 13,000 Inuit and 7000 Indians; the rest are mainly whites recently arrived.

Around the Mackenzie River and Great Slave Lake the people call themselves the Denes, or Athapaskans, and, together with the Inuit, are the original northern peoples. The word 'Inuit' refers in general to an Eskimo in Canada, as opposed to the Eskimos of Asia or the Aleutian Islands (Alaska). The term 'Eskimo' is not appreciated by the Inuits, and has been used less and less.

Until the 1950s, the entire area was one of the world's last undeveloped frontiers. The search for oil, gas and minerals changed some areas rapidly. Other resource-based products include fish, fur and handicrafts. But with the ever-fluctuating fortunes in natural resources, the territory is relying more each year on tourism as a money-earner. A variety of outdoor, adventure and cultural possibilities are being offered and promoted.

The territories are divided into three districts: Mackenzie, Keewatin and Franklin.

The district of Mackenzie is the most accessible area, being the only district with any roads, and is where most visitors go. It borders on the Yukon, north of Alberta. This is the only area of the territories with a forestry business and has most of the fishing as well.

The Mackenzie Mountains lie along the Yukon boundary with peaks of 2700 metres. The Mackenzie River, the longest waterway in Canada, runs north along the Mackenzie Valley to the Arctic Ocean. Yellowknife, the capital, sits on Great Slave Lake. Most of the population lives on this lake or around Great Bear Lake with its many mines. The two national parks in the Mackenzie district are Nahanni in the south-west, and Wood Buffalo, which spreads across the Alberta border.

Mackenzie has fairly warm summers with an average temperature of 13°C. All of the Northwest Territories are dry and ice-cold in winter.

Keewatin is a vast, rocky, barren plateau of the Canadian Shield with only 4000 people. Very little vegetation grows here. Most of the Inuit population lives in this district.

The district of Franklin is the most northerly and has many islands, including Baffin, one of the world's largest. The island contains Auyuittuq National Park. A new National Park, Ellesmere, consists of the northern section of Ellesmere Island way up at the peak of the Canadian Arctic, not far from Greenland's north-western edge. Not one tree grows in the entire Franklin district but many flowers bloom during the short summer. The northern regions are almost completely uninhabited. There is the odd weather station, military installation or biological research centre.

The Vikings were the first Europeans to see the Northwest Territories in about 1000 AD. Later the search began for the legendary Northwest Passage – a sea passage from the Atlantic to the Pacific Ocean and the shortest route to China and its riches. Canada was thought of as merely a stop-off point for carrying on to the Far East. From 1524, British, French and Dutch adventurers all joined the search for a waterway through the continent. Many died but the north was mapped out in the process. The first successful navigation was made in 1906 by Roald Amundsen. Since then, several others have done it, mostly in military vessels. In 1960, the US submarine *Seadragon* was the first to do it under water. Today the route is used little except as a supply line during the very short summer thaw.

Canada and the US are currently

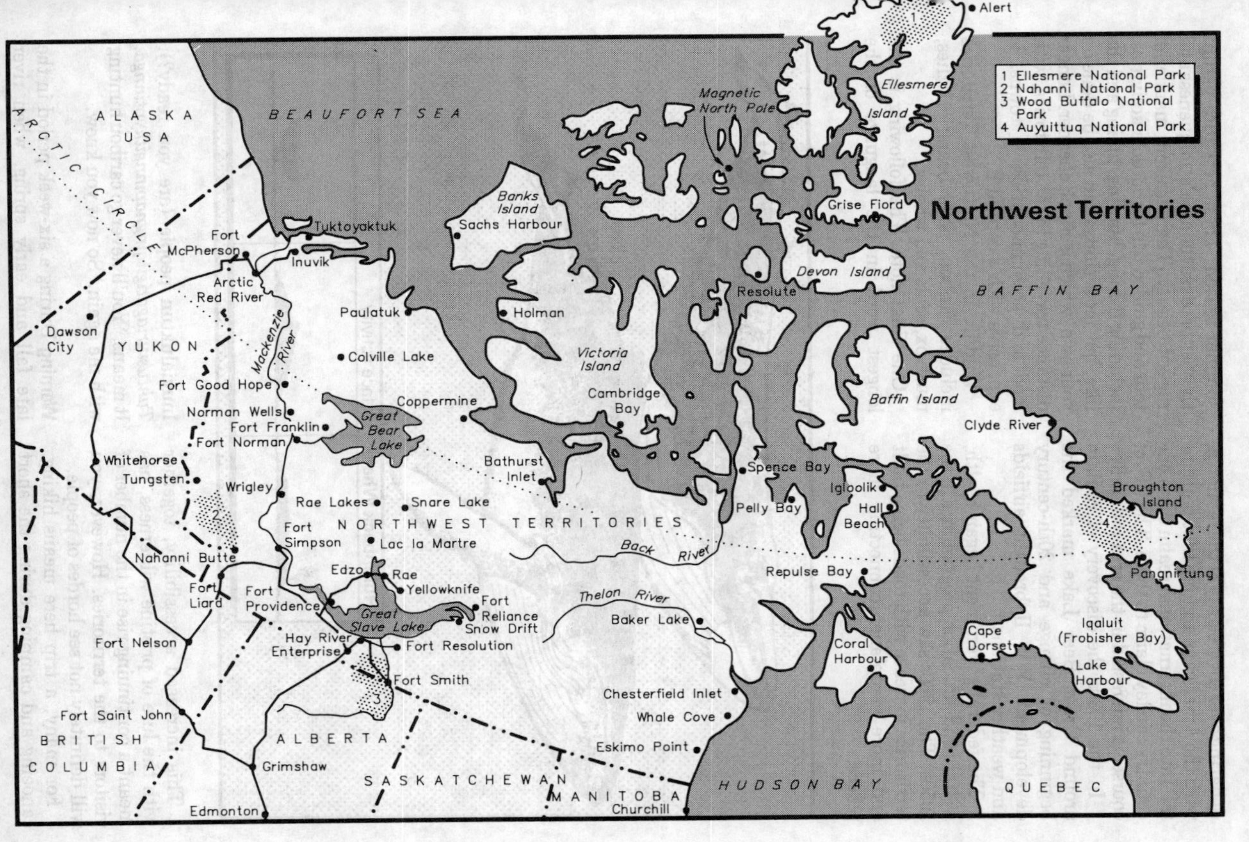

Northwest Territories
1 Ellesmere National Park
2 Nahanni National Park
3 Wood Buffalo National Park
4 Auyuittuq National Park
Alert
Ellesmere Island
Magnetic North Pole
Grise Fiord
Devon Island
Resolute
BAFFIN BAY
Baffin Island
Clyde River
Broughton Island
Pangnirtung
Iqaluit (Frobisher Bay)
Lake Harbour
Cape Dorset
QUEBEC
Igloolik
Hall Beach
Spence Bay
Pelly Bay
Repulse Bay
Coral Harbour
HUDSON BAY
Banks Island
Sachs Harbour
Holman
Victoria Island
Cambridge Bay
Bathurst Inlet
Coppermine
BEAUFORT SEA
Tuktoyaktuk
Inuvik
Paulatuk
Colville Lake
Great Bear Lake
Fort Franklin
ALASKA
USA
ARCTIC CIRCLE
Fort McPherson
Arctic Red River
Mackenzie River
Dawson City
YUKON
Fort Good Hope
Norman Wells
Fort Norman
Whitehorse
Tungsten
Wrigley
Rae Lakes
Snare Lake
NORTHWEST TERRITORIES
Fort Simpson
Lac la Martre
Back River
Nahanni Butte
Edzo
Rae
Yellowknife
Fort Liard
Fort Providence
Great Slave Lake
Fort Reliance
Snow Drift
Thelon River
Baker Lake
Fort Nelson
Hay River
Enterprise
Fort Resolution
Fort Smith
Chesterfield Inlet
Whale Cove
Fort Saint John
BRITISH COLUMBIA
ALBERTA
Eskimo Point
Grimshaw
SASKATCHEWAN
MANITOBA
Edmonton
Churchill

debating over sovereignty of the far north, with the Americans arguing that portions fall into the international realm so no one country can lay claim to them. The US, of course, is interested in the area militarily.

In the 1930s the discovery of radium around Great Bear Lake marked the beginning of change and 20th-century development. WW II brought airfields and weather stations.

The federal government began health, welfare and education programmes in the 1950s. The 1960s saw accessibility to the territories increase with roads being built and more aeroplanes connecting more places.

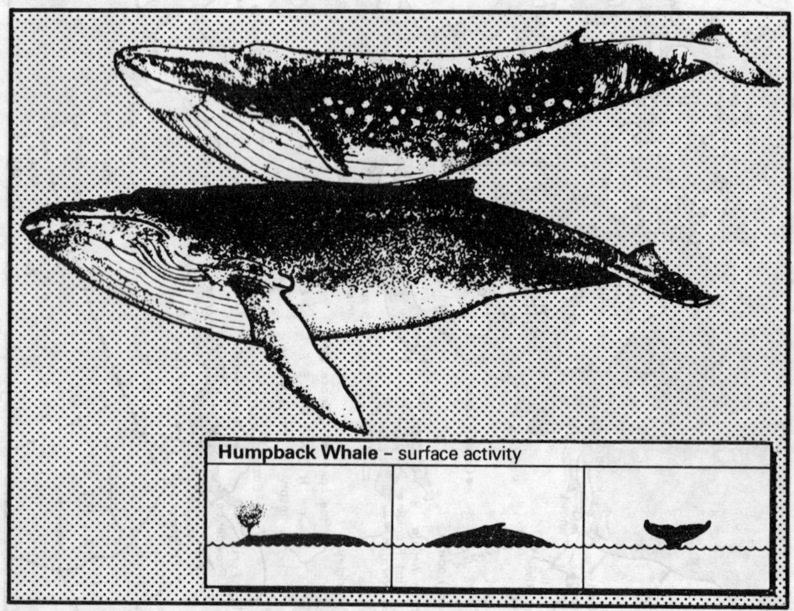

This increased accessibility, together with the lure of pristine wilderness, has meant a continuing rise in the number of visitors to the territories. However, you will definitely not see hordes of people.

For many, a trip here means hiking, canoeing and camping during the short summer season. These activities permit the visitor to see the area's uniqueness and rugged beauty. There is every manner of tour and guided trip for outdoor activities, including fishing, hunting, hiking and the like; but most things can also be done on your own, which is much cheaper. Longer distance travelling in the territories, with food and accommodation in towns, is expensive with a capital E.

Wildlife in the Northwest Territories includes caribou, polar bears, grizzlies, musk ox, seals and whales.

One final note. The following is the longest word in the language of the Inuvialuktun people (are you ready?): *Tuktusiuriagatigitqingnapinngitkyptinnga*. It means, 'You'll never go caribou hunting with me again.' So now you know.

Warning During a six-week period in the late fall and early spring, when river freeze-ups and ice break-ups occur, ferries cannot run over the rivers on highways north of the Mackenzie River. Therefore there is no road access or bus service for this period. This includes Yellowknife.

Information

Travel Arctic, the government tourist office, is in Yellowknife on 50th St, mailing code X1A 2L9. They have maps, canoe routes and a guide to settlements across the territory, and also special fishing, canoeing and motoring guides.

In Yellowknife, detailed maps are available from the Mining Recorder's Office (tel 873-4221) in the Bellanca Building. Another spot to try for topographic maps is Charts Unlimited (tel 874-2516) at Box 1038, Hay River, NWT X0E 1G0.

The Canada Map Office has all types of detailed maps of the territories including small-scale topographicals, good for hikers. Write to them at 615 Booth St, Ottawa, Ontario K1A 0E9. They'll send you an index and you'll have to pick the map numbers you need from that. Maps in Yellowknife are in short supply, so getting one beforehand is not a bad idea.

There are Chambers of Commerce with visitor information in Yellowknife, Fort Smith, Hay River and Fort Simpson. Lastly, there's a Visitor Information Centre on Highway 1 at the Alberta border, open from May to September.

Activities

Both camping and canoeing are possible along the Northwest Territories highway system. Several communities rent boats or canoes. From roadside campgrounds, trips can be taken around the lakes, and away from the roads you can pick your own camping spot. It is not hard to have a lake to yourself; enquire at the Tourist Office for more information. Remember that the water is cold enough to kill you in 15 minutes, so keep close to shore in a canoe.

Places to Stay

There are campgrounds all along the territorial highway system. Permits are required; get them from park or information offices. Campgrounds have firewood and are open 15 May to 15 September. Camping or sleeping in a van is really the only way to see this part of the country at a reasonable price.

DISTRICT OF MACKENZIE

YELLOWKNIFE

With a population of 11,000, this is by far the largest town in the territories and is also the capital. It's a modern, fast-growing town on the north shore of Great Slave Lake.

Yellowknife is essentially a government town but also acts as the regional commercial centre. You'll meet people from all over Canada now living and working here. You may also note the armed guards at stores and banks; don't be put off, things aren't really that wild.

Gold first attracted Europeans here in 1834; in 1984 the town celebrated its official 150th anniversary. Today, visitors use the town as a base for camping and fishing trips and for exploring the rocky landscape and nearby lakes. It is 341 km from Fort Smith by road (Highway 3). For information, visit the Northern Frontier Visitors' Association (tel 873-3131).

Gold Mines

Cominco and Great Yellowknife are gold mines which offer tours in summer.

Prince of Wales Northern Heritage Centre

This is a good museum with diorama displays on northern lifestyles and natural sciences. Admission is free.

Eskimo Dog Research Foundation

Here, at Bowspringer Kennels, you can see a project under way which is attempting to preserve the 'kingmit', a rare Eskimo dog. There are 100 at the kennel on Kam Lake Rd at the south-east end of town.

Detah

This is a small Dogrib Dene Indian village across the bay (21 km by car). There are no tourist facilities.

Crafts

Yellowknife is the distribution centre and major retailer of craft items from around the territories. Of course, prices are cheaper in more remote areas but also more expensive in southern Canada. Whether artistic or purely functional, the goods are not cheap but are authentic and usually well made. Northern Images has various Indian and Inuit works. The Langlois Gallery also displays and sells arts and crafts.

Inuit ivory object

Activities

For a good view of the town, walk up to the Bush Pilot's Monument in Old Town. You can see over the lake and the town's odd assortment of housing.

There are several hiking trails around the town, some easy, some harder. Prelude Lake, 30 km east, is a pretty spot with good fishing. If you have a vehicle, the Ingraham Trail leads to areas good for fishing, hiking and camping.

Sportsman on 50th St rents canoes by the day.

Events

During the summer months, there's an open-air theatre programme in Petitot Park with plays related to life in the region.

There are various other festivals and events held periodically through the year. The information office will have an up-to-date list of activities planned.

The Caribou Carnival is an annual festival held in late March each year, with parades, concerts, skits and contests like igloo building. Or try the Canadian Championship Dog Derby, a three-day dogsled race about 240 km long.

Places to Stay & Eat

As in the Yukon, accommodation is costly if you're not camping. Best is the *YWCA* (tel (403) 873-4767), on Franklin Avenue at 54th St. They take in both sexes and offer a range of rooms priced by the night, week or month. Private kitchenette apartments are $38, shared rooms and kitchens are $28 a night. Shared rooms with no cooking facilities are $18. Couples are allowed and there are 70 rooms. The *YWCA* is at the corner of 50th St and 54th Avenue. Open only during the summer.

There are also several bed & breakfast places which have only recently opened. Prices seem pretty standardised at $45/50 for singles/doubles. Try *Barb Bromley* (tel 873-4786) at 31 Morrison Drive; *Sharon Robinson* (tel 873-5574) at 36 Bromley Drive; *Yetta Turner* (tel 873-5219) at 43 Otto Drive, or *Bernard Straker* (tel 873-2893) at 46 Otto Drive. None of these places have a lot of space, so phone before going. There are probably other bed & breakfasts, too.

In the hotel category, the *Gold Range Hotel* is reasonable with rooms from $35 for singles, $42 for a double. Others are priced considerably higher. For example, the *Twin Pine Motor Inn*, halfway between the old town and the centre of town, is $75/80 for singles/doubles. There are other hotels around.

There is camping at Long Lake Park, which is within the city limits.

Restaurants are a bit pricey. Look for the fast-food places in the basement of the mall complex. The *Miner's Mess* in the Yellowknife Hotel is said to be interesting and is where many northern workers drink.

Tours

A couple of companies offer local area tours. Frontier Tours (tel 873-4892) has two-hour bus tours of the city and nearby gold mines for $12 or $10 if the van is full. They also arrange half-day trips along the Ingraham Trail. Raven Tours is similar. Yellowknife Traders offer cruises on Great Slave Lake: one to Detah, a Dene village, $22; and another to an island for walking and fishing.

AROUND YELLOWKNIFE

East of town, Highway 4 – called the Ingraham Trail – extends for 72 km before petering out. Along the way are picnic sites, campgrounds, canoe routes and the start of various hiking trails – some very short, good for an hour or so. The Yellowknife River is used for both short and long canoe trips. At Madaline Lake there is a 3.2-km trail. Not far from Yellowknife (about 30 km), at Prelude Lake, there is camping for $5.

At Cameron River there is a trail to a small waterfall where the local people swim, though these waters ain't Miami Beach. Sixty km along from Yellowknife is another $5 campground at Reid Lake. You can canoe or hike back to Yellowknife from here. Not much further along, the road ends at Tibbet Lake, which is said to be excellent for fishing and is also the start of some charted canoe routes – ask the Tourist Office for more details.

FORT PROVIDENCE

At this town of 600 the road connecting Yellowknife crosses the Mackenzie Highway, which runs east-west. There are a couple of places to stay, including the *Big River Motel* (tel (403) 699-4301), which is $40/50 for singles/doubles. By the Mackenzie River is a campground, about four km from town.

FORT SMITH & WOOD BUFFALO NATIONAL PARK

Fort Smith, a town of 2500, is on the Alberta border at Mile 0 of the Northwest Territories Highway system. It was once a fur-trading post in the north-western system of depots. Nearby is the entrance to Wood Buffalo National Park, for which the town acts as supply depot. Get your food in town; there is nowhere to buy it in the park. For details on the park, see the Alberta chapter. The main attraction is the free-roaming herd of 6000 bison. Also out of Fort Smith are the Slave River rapids where white pelicans nest. There is a campground at Queen Elizabeth Park.

In town, the *Pinecrest Hotel* (tel (403) 872-2104) is quite reasonable with bathless rooms at $30/35 for single/doubles.

HAY RIVER

With a population of 3400, this is a fairly large town. Sitting where the Mackenzie River joins Great Slave Lake on the southern shore, it is a major distribution centre where barges load up for trips to settlements on connecting waterways. Fish packing is done here too. Alexander Falls, 32 metres high, is a short distance south.

There are several hotels here but they're not inexpensive. *Mackenzie Place* (tel (403) 874-2535), the highest building in the Northwest Territories, has furnished apartments with all cooking needs for $55 a day. The *Migrator Motel* is about the same price; others are more. There is a campground in town on Vale Island.

Aside from the road, two airlines service Hay River: Canadian Airlines, which flies to points south and Ptarmigan, to Yellowknife.

NAHANNI NATIONAL PARK

A wilderness park east of Great Slave Lake, Nahanni is close to the Yukon border. UNESCO has named this preserve a world heritage site because of its spectacular and beautiful pristine nature.

It is visited mainly by canoeists wishing to challenge the white waters of the South Nahanni River. Canoeists should know that runs rushing through the three huge canyons are only for the experienced.

The park has plenty of wildlife, with good hiking and photography opportunities.

Also in the park are waterfalls such as Virginia Falls, which at 90 metres are twice the height of Niagara Falls, and sulphur hot springs. For camping, there are seven primitive sites with tables and fireplaces.

The park is not easy – or cheap – to get to. Fort Simpson, on the road up from Yellowknife, is the park access point. From here or from Watson Lake in the Yukon, you can fly in by charter. The opening of the Liard Highway which connects Fort Liard to Fort Simpson may have made Nahanni more accessible. The road runs along the opposite side of the river and as yet I don't think a bridge has been constructed. When this is done, getting to the park will be a lot less hassle and considerably cheaper as well.

Tours

At Fort Simpson, about 360 km from Yellowknife, there are camping facilities, park information services and river boat trips to the park. A five-day trip costs several hundred dollars. The park superintendent can also supply details of other tours. A couple of other outfits that offer tours are: Nahanni National Park Tours (tel 703-4421) in Fort Liard; Trail Head, based in Toronto, for canoe and hiking trips; and White-Water Adventures, based in Vancouver, for rafting tours.

NORMAN WELLS

Halfway between Nahanni and Inuvik, this town of 800 has long been (and remains) an oil town. Of more interest is the Canol Heritage Trail, a hiking trail designated a National Historic Site which leads 372 km to the Yukon border. From there, a road leads to Ross River and the Yukon Highway System. Along the trail is much evidence of WW II army camps and abandoned oil exploration equipment, as well as peaks, canyons, barrens and lots of wildlife. There's a campground in town and a couple of hotels. Air service is available from Edmonton, Yellowknife and Inuvik.

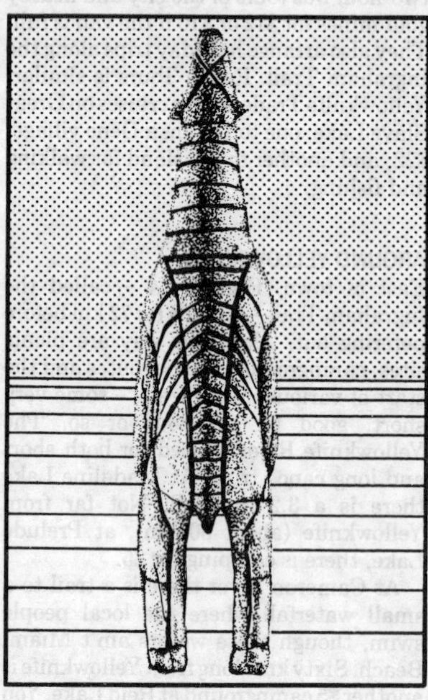

Ivory bear carving, found near Igloolik

INUVIK

Inuvik, with a population of just over 3000, is one of the territories' largest towns, although it was founded as late as 1955 as a supply centre. The population is roughly one-third Inuit, one-third Indian and one-third white. It's a modern town. Walking, bus and boat tours are available; crafts, including parkas, are for sale.

Note that the first snow flies sometime around the end of August.

Tuktoyaktuk

A couple of local airlines take tourists to

Tuktoyaktuk, a town 100 km north-east on the coast of the Arctic Ocean. It seems a popular trip. Antler Aviation, which caters exclusively to visitors, charges $85 and that includes a one-hour buzz around 'Tuk' by car. Aklak also does the trip but gives you a full day there, although no car ride. Beluga whales can sometimes be seen. The town is a land base for some of the Beaufort Sea oil explorations. Both airlines also offer other day and longer trips to villages in the area and along the Arctic seashore.

Events

The Arctic Northern Games, the biggest northern games of their kind, are often held in Inuvik in July, but the location and dates change, so ask where and when somewhere further south. The games feature traditional Indian and Inuit sports, contests, dancing, music, crafts and the 'Good Woman' contest, during which women display various household skills.

Delta Daze is a smaller celebration held on Thanksgiving weekend (October) before the long winter sets in.

Places to Stay

Four hotels in Inuvik all charge about $110 a double, slightly less for singles. Cheapest is the *Finto Motel Inn* (tel 979-2647). They all have dining rooms.

There are a couple of campgrounds. *Chuk Campground* is three km before town – a bit of a walk or a $10 taxi fare. It's open from June to October, has hot showers, wood is supplied, and the office is open 24 hours a day for the duration. This campground is operated by the Dene band; the charge is $5 and various activities are put on. It's got a good view and the breeze keeps the mosquitos down a bit. In town, *Happy Valley Campground* is the same price but without showers and hasn't been so well recommended.

Places to Eat

As for food, a typical restaurant meal is not cheap at all. *The Roost*, a take-out sandwich and burger place has the lowest prices in town. The back bacon sandwich is worth a go. Over at the *MacKenzie Hotel*, try the tasty Musk Ox stew, another something you won't see down south. If you're driving, consider bringing in your food (especially from Alaska) and you'll save a few bucks.

Tours

Gray Line (tel 979-2941) offers two-hour bus tours of town for $10.

Getting There & Away

Gray Line (tel 979-2941) run Inuvik to Whitehorse buses along the Dempster Highway through Dawson City for $449 one-way or return.

Mackenzie River Outfitters run an eight-day river boat/camping trip up the Mackenzie River to Fort Simpson. You can go either way. All food and gear is supplied. The 1300-km trip includes stops at villages, old trading posts and abandoned trappers' cabins.

DISTRICT OF FRANKLIN

IQALUIT

This town, formerly called Frobisher Bay, is on the east coast of Baffin Island in the eastern section of the territories. It was established in 1942 as a US Air Force base and is now a fairly large settlement of 2500. It's the first stop on the fly-in trip to Auyuittuq National Park. There is not much to see or do here but a variety of side trips are possible. Most people coming here stop off as part of a package en route to somewhere else. Hotels are expensive: cheapest is the *Discovery Lodge* at $75/85 for singles/doubles, and three meals at $40. See what I mean? There is a campground as well. In late 1984 the town voted to change the name back to Iqaluit, its original native name.

AUYUITTUQ NATIONAL PARK

Auyuittuq is one of the world's few national parks north of the Arctic Circle and is beautiful pristine wilderness. Pronounced 'ah-you-ee-tuk', the word means 'the land that never melts'. Actually, most of the park consists of mountains, valleys, fiords and meadows excellent for hiking. In June and July, the park is covered in bright flowers.

Most visitors go for the hiking, between late June and early September. From May through July, the park has 24 hours of daylight each day, being north of the Arctic Circle.

The problem with the place is getting there. It's expensive. First you must fly from one of the major cities to Iqaluit. From there, you've got to catch another flight to Pangnirtung near the southern edge of the park or to Broughton Island, at the eastern edge. There is a lodge at Pangnirtung and a campground at Overlord in the park. There are also seven emergency shelters along the Pangnirtung Pass. For more info on the park, write to the Superintendent, Auyuittuq National Park, Pangnirtung, NWT, X0A 0R0.

Getting There & Around

Nordair operates between Toronto, Ottawa, Montreal and Iqaluit, which is nearly 300 km from the park. From there, flights go to Pangnirtung or to Broughton Island. From either point you can walk to the pass.

Many tour companies offer trips in the park.

PANGNIRTUNG

This town of 1000 is beautifully set amidst mountains at the entrance to Auyuittuq National Park. It lies at the end of one of the main passes and is the jumping-off point for park visitors. Available here are boat tours, craft sales, accommodation and meals. No alcohol is permitted in the town; several northern communities have voted themselves 'dry'.

Getting There & Around

Nordair flies from Montreal to Iqaluit. There are several small companies which run flights and charters around this portion of the Territories.

ELLESMERE NATIONAL PARK

This new national park, way up at the northern tip of Ellesmere Island at the top of the world, is for wealthy wilderness seekers. It features Cape Columbia, the northernmost point of North America, Mount Barbeau, one of the highest peaks on the east side of the continent, and Lake Hazen, which is surrounded by a thermal oasis.

GETTING THERE & AWAY

Air

Canadian flies from Edmonton, Winnipeg and Whitehorse to Yellowknife, Inuvik, Fort Simpson and other places.

Northward Airlines, with offices in Yellowknife, covers the western area of the territories.

About 10 small companies have scheduled flights between points within the territories. Many more operate on a charter basis, landing on lakes in summer, skis in winter. Charter fares can sometimes be figured by finding out the price per distance rate, say $1 per km as a rough guide.

Bus

Canadian Coachways at the bus station in Edmonton, Alberta has a daily service to Hay River. Connections for points further north are available three times a week by NWT Coachlines (tel 874-2216) in Hay River. Fares and schedules are available through Greyhound Lines.

The NWT Coachline runs between Hay River and Yellowknife three times a week and has daily service between Hay River and Fort Resolution. This bus line is part of the 'Ameripass' system. If you're coming from Edmonton you can change buses in Enterprise and continue via Fort Providence and Edzo to Yellowknife.

Train

There is no train service in the territories.

Road
Only the District of Mackenzie in the west, north of Alberta, is accessible by car. The highway north from Edmonton is paved to the Alberta-NWT border. Unpaved roads connect Hay River, Wood Buffalo National Park, Yellowknife and Fort Simpson. The Mackenzie Highway is the name for the section linking Alberta to Fort Simpson and Fort Smith.

The Liard Highway, also gravel, opened in 1983 and links northern British Columbia to Fort Liard in the NWT and continues on to Fort Simpson, connecting with the Mackenzie Highway.

The road segment from Fort Providence north to Yellowknife runs along the edge of a bison sanctuary and it's not uncommon to see bison on the road. Sandhill cranes and ptarmigans from the bird world are also fairly common. The ponds you'll notice by the side of the road are due to holes dug for sand and gravel needed for the road's construction.

In the northern part of the district of Mackenzie, the Dempster Highway connects the Yukon with Inuvik. This route passes through excellent mountain scenery much of the way to the Mackenzie River Delta, nipping into a portion of the huge Reindeer Grazing Reserve before ending up at Inuvik.

Precautions There can be long distances between gas and service stations, so travellers should have some gear and food with them. Also, don't forget to bring insect repellent.

Some people protect gas tanks and lights with coverings.

GETTING AROUND

Road
Northwest Territories highways are all gravel roads. For information on conditions call Zenith 2018. For information on either Liard or the Dempster Highway the number is Zenith 2022. Both numbers can be called at no charge.

Car Rentals
There are vehicle rental outlets in. Hay River and Yellowknife, including Tilden and Avis companies.

Tours
Apart from the tour companies mentioned in the Yellowknife section, other outfitting and wilderness businesses offer longer-term, much more expensive specialised trips in the Yellowknife area. Qaivvik has a five-day caribou-watching trip to a camp on Courageous Lake. Great Slave Sledging Company has dog-team expeditions for one week to two months. These would be great trips, travelling some traditional routes and seeing wildlife, but they're very, very costly. The Tourist Office has lists of companies, their addresses and tours.

This past year, a New York-based cruise ship became the first tourist vessel to navigate the legendary Northwest Passage, from Newfoundland to Alaska. The 40-day history-making trip cost each passenger a tidy $20,000. Sign here.

Index

Abbreviations

Alb	Alberta
BC	British Columbia
Man	Manitoba
Nf	Newfoundland
NB	New Brunswick
NS	Nova Scotia
NWT	Northwest Territories
PEI	Prince Edward Island
Ont	Ontario
Que	Quebec
Sas	Saskatchewan
Y	Yukon

Map references in **bold** type.

MAPS

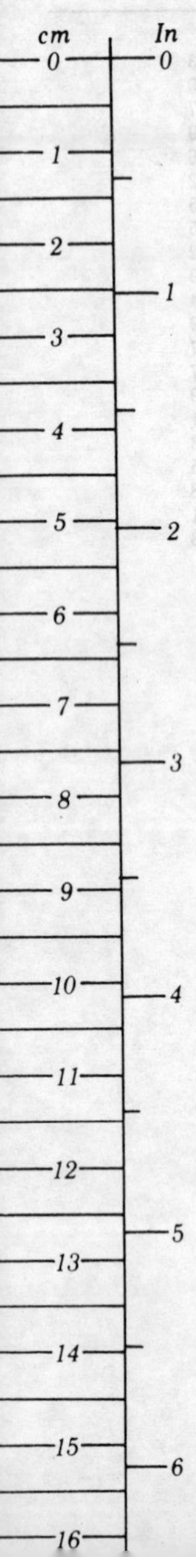

Temperature

To convert °C to °F multiply by 1.8 and add 32

To convert °F to °C subtract 32 and multiply by ·55

°C	°F
50	122
45	113
40	104
35	95
30	86
25	75
20	68
15	59
10	50
5	41
0	32

Length, Distance & Area

	multiply by
inches to centimetres	2.54
centimetres to inches	0.39
feet to metres	0.30
metres to feet	3.28
yards to metres	0.91
metres to yards	1.09
miles to kilometres	1.61
kilometres to miles	0.62
acres to hectares	0.40
hectares to acres	2.47

Weight

	multiply by
ounces to grams	28.35
grams to ounces	0.035
pounds to kilograms	0.45
kilograms to pounds	2.21
British tons to kilograms	1016
US tons to kilograms	907

A British ton is 2240 lbs, a US ton is 2000 lbs

Volume

	multiply by
Imperial gallons to litres	4.55
litres to imperial gallons	0.22
US gallons to litres	3.79
litres to US gallons	0.26

5 imperial gallons equals 6 US gallons
a litre is slightly more than a US quart, slightly less than a British one

311 Marten St — Earliest Noon
762 3648

45 | 35
share tax

½ - Pr roo —

BI M Lodge — away from bus. 65 inc br.

Hol Lodge — line busy
nr bus.

30th Sept & 1st Oct.

$55
Room with

central ✓

✓ conf.

✓ conf.

IN96PI

683 7111 - U/A @ AIRPORT.
3RD OCT. - TO SFO @ 11.35am 3.29pm
1011 - Arr.
1643 1.30pm - 3.29

1-800-661-1676 - Banff Res.

AIR N.Z. - 701 West Georgia
1200 suite

604 - 689 3331

Corner Georgia / Howe St,
2 blocks

EVENINGS 3RD & 4TH OCT

Hotel Californian $69 } Page 80
Carlton $70

File No. IC2SIG

TRY [illegible]

Guides to the Americas

Alaska – a travel survival kit

A definitive guide to one of the world's most spectacular regions – including detailed information on hiking and canoeing.

Chile & Easter Island – a travel survival kit

Chile has one of the most varied geographies in the world, including deserts, tranquil lakes, snow-covered volcanoes and windswept fjords. Easter Island is covered, in detail.

Ecuador & the Galapagos Islands – a travel survival kit

Ecuador is the smallest of the Andean countries, and in many ways it is the easiest and most pleasant to travel in. The Galapagos Islands and their amazing inhabitants continue to cast a spell over every visitor.

Mexico – a travel survival kit

Mexico has a unique blend of Indian and Spanish culture and a fascinating historical legacy. The hospitality of the people makes Mexico a paradise for travellers.

Peru – a travel survival kit

The famed city of Machu Picchu, the Andean altiplano and the Amazon rainforests are just some of Peru's attractions. All the facts you need can be found in this comprehensive guide.

Argentina – a travel survival kit

Argentina has been likened to a mixture of southern Europe and outback Australia. This guide shows you the whole country.

Guides to the Americas

South America on a shoestring

An up-dated edition of a budget travellers bible that covers Central and South America from the USA-Mexico border to Tierra del Fuego. Written by the author the *New York Times* called "the patron saint of travellers in the third world".

Baja California – a travel survival kit

Mexico's Baja peninsula offers a great escape, right at California's back door. This comprehensive guide follows the long road south from raucous border towns like Tijuana, to resorts, untouched villages and deserted villages.

Colombia – a travel survival kit

Colombia is the land of emeralds, orchids and El Dorado. You may not find the mythical city of gold, but you will find an exotic, wild and beautiful country.

Bolivia – a travel survival kit

Bolivia offers safe and intriguing travel options – from isolated villages in the Andes and ancient ruins to the incredible city of La Paz.

Brazil – a travel survival kit

One of the largest countries in the world, Brazil offers excitingly diverse travel options

Lonely Planet Guidebooks

Lonely Planet guidebooks cover virtually every accessible part of Asia as well as Australia, the Pacific, Central and South America, Africa, the Middle East and parts of North America. There are four main series: 'travel survival kits', covering a single country for a range of budgets; 'shoestring' guides with compact information for low-budget travel in a major region; trekking guides; and 'phrasebooks'.

Australia & the Pacific
Australia
Bushwalking in Australia
Papua New Guinea
Papua New Guinea phrasebook
New Zealand
Tramping in New Zealand
Rarotonga & the Cook Islands
Solomon Islands
Tahiti & French Polynesia
Fiji
Micronesia

South-East Asia
South-East Asia on a shoestring
Malaysia, Singapore & Brunei
Indonesia
Bali & Lombok
Indonesia phrasebook
Burma
Burmese phrasebook
Thailand
Thai phrasebook
Philippines
Pilipino phrasebook

North-East Asia
North-East Asia on a shoestring
China
China phrasebook
Tibet
Tibet phrasebook
Japan
Korea
Korean phrasebook
Hong Kong, Macau & Canton
Taiwan

West Asia
West Asia on a shoestring
Trekking in Turkey
Turkey

Mail Order

Lonely Planet guidebooks are distributed worldwide and are sold by good bookshops everywhere. They are also available by mail order from Lonely Planet, so if you have difficulty finding a title please write to us. US and Canadian residents should write to Embarcadero West, 112 Linden St, Oakland CA 94607, USA and residents of other countries to PO Box 617, Hawthorn, Victoria 3122, Australia.

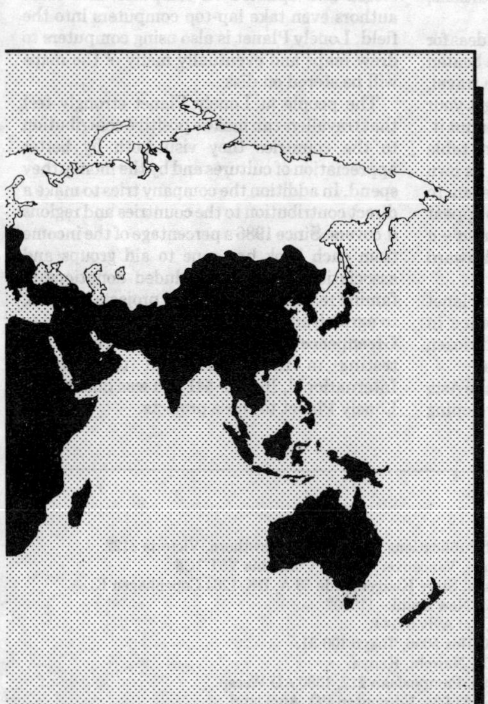

Eastern Europe
Eastern Europe

Indian Subcontinent
India
Hindi/Urdu phrasebook
Kashmir, Ladakh & Zanskar
Trekking in the Indian Himalaya
Pakistan
Kathmandu & the Kingdom of Nepal
Trekking in the Nepal Himalaya
Nepal phrasebook
Sri Lanka
Sri Lanka phrasebook
Bangladesh
Karakoram Highway

Africa
Africa on a shoestring
East Africa
Swahili phrasebook
West Africa
Central Africa
Morocco, Algeria & Tunisia

Middle East
Israel
Egypt & the Sudan
Jordan & Syria
Yemen

North America
Canada
Alaska

Mexico
Mexico
Baja California

South America
South America on a shoestring
Ecuador & the Galapagos Islands
Colombia
Chile & Easter Island
Bolivia
Brazil
Peru
Argentina

Lonely Planet

Lonely Planet published its first book in 1973. Tony and Maureen Wheeler had made a lengthy overland trip from England to Australia and, in response to numerous 'how do you do it?' questions, Tony wrote and they published *Across Asia on the Cheap*. It became an instant local best-seller and inspired thoughts of a second travel guide. A year and a half in South-East Asia resulted in their second book, *South-East Asia on a Shoestring*, which they put together in a backstreet Chinese hotel in Singapore in 1975. The 'yellow book', as it quickly became known, soon became *the* guide to the region and has gone through five editions, always with its familiar yellow cover.

Soon other writers came to them with ideas for similar books – books that went off the beaten track with an adventurous approach to travel, books that 'assumed you knew how to get your luggage off the carousel,' as one reviewer put it. Lonely Planet grew from a kitchen table operation to a spare room and then to its own office. Its international reputation began to grow as the Lonely Planet logo began to appear in more and more countries. In 1982 *India – a travel survival kit* won the Thomas Cook award for the best guidebook of the year.

These days there are over 70 Lonely Planet titles. Over 40 people work at our office in Melbourne, Australia and another half dozen at our US office in Oakland, California.

At first Lonely Planet specialised in the Asia region but these days we are also developing major ranges of guidebooks to the Pacific region, to South America and to Africa. The list of walking guides is growing and Lonely Planet now has a unique series of phrasebooks to 'unusual' languages. The emphasis continues to be on travel for travellers and Tony and Maureen still manage to fit in a number of trips each year and play a very active part in the writing and updating of Lonely Planet's guides.

Keeping guidebooks up to date is a constant battle which requires an ear to the ground and lots of walking, but technology also plays its part. All Lonely Planet guidebooks are now stored and updated on computer, and some authors even take lap-top computers into the field. Lonely Planet is also using computers to draw maps and eventually many of the maps will be stored on disk.

The people at Lonely Planet strongly feel that travellers can make a positive contribution to the countries they visit both by better appreciation of cultures and by the money they spend. In addition the company tries to make a direct contribution to the countries and regions it covers. Since 1986 a percentage of the income from each book has gone to aid groups and associations. This has included donations to famine relief in Africa, to aid projects in India, to agricultural projects in Central America, to Greenpeace's efforts to halt French nuclear testing in the Pacific and to Amnesty International. In 1989 $41,000 was donated by Lonely Planet to these projects.

Lonely Planet Distributors

Australia & Papua New Guinea Lonely Planet Publications, PO Box 617, Hawthorn, Victoria 3122.
Canada Raincoast Books, 112 East 3rd Avenue, Vancouver, British Columbia V5T 1C8.
Denmark, Finland & Norway Scanvik Books aps, Store Kongensgade 59 A, DK-1264 Copenhagen K.
India & Nepal UBS Distributors, 5 Ansari Rd, New Delhi – 110002
Israel Geographical Tours Ltd, 8 Tverya St, Tel Aviv 63144.
Japan Intercontinental Marketing Corp, IPO Box 5056, Tokyo 100-31.
Kenya Westland Sundries Ltd, PO Box 14107, Nairobi, Kenya.
Netherlands Nilsson & Lamm bv, Postbus 195, Pampuslaan 212, 1380 AD Weesp.
New Zealand Transworld Publishers, PO Box 83-094, Edmonton PO, Auckland.
Singapore & Malaysia MPH Distributors, 601 Sims Drive, #03-21, Singapore 1438.
Spain Altair, Balmes 69, 08007 Barcelona.
Sweden Esselte Kartcentrum AB, Vasagatan 16, S-111 20 Stockholm.
Thailand Chalermnit, 108 Sukhumvit 53, Bangkok 10110.
Turkey Yab-Yay Dagitim, Alay Koshu Caddesi 12/A, Kat 4 no. 11-12, Cagaloglu, Istanbul.
UK Roger Lascelles, 47 York Rd, Brentford, Middlesex, TW8 0QP
USA Lonely Planet Publications, PO Box 2001A, Berkeley, CA 94702.
West Germany Buchvertrieb Gerda Schettler, Postfach 64, D3415 Hattorf a H.
All Other Countries refer to Australia address.